D1032448

The Letters of
JOSIAH ROYCE

Robbins Library of Philosophy, Harvard University

Josiah Royce at Meadville, Pennsylvania, 1902

The Letters of JOSIAH ROYCE

Edited with an Introduction by

John Clendenning

The University of Chicago Press *Chicago & London*

Standard Book Number: 226–73066–2

Library of Congress Catalog Card Number: 74–89514

THE UNIVERSITY OF CHICAGO PRESS, CHICAGO 60637
THE UNIVERSITY OF CHICAGO PRESS, LTD., LONDON

Published 1970

Printed in the United States of America

Contents

Illustrations

Preface

As the first comprehensive edition of Josiah Royce's letters, this work has two main objectives: first, to present a documentary biography of Royce; and second, to offer a reference tool for future research in American thought. Arranged in chronological order, the letters have been selected for the light they shed on Royce's life, his character, his intellectual development, and on the period in which he lived. Certain categories of epistolary matter—telegrams, memoranda, inscriptions, calling cards, and marginalia—have been regularly and silently excluded. Letters written for publication are also excluded on the grounds that these are actually essays in epistolary form. Otherwise, all of Royce's letters which I have seen are either printed in this edition or listed and summarized in Appendix C. Those letters which are included are printed in their entirety according to the principles described in the textual note of Appendix B.

This project, though not formally undertaken until 1963, had its beginnings during my graduate studies ten years ago in the American Civilization Program at the University of Iowa. My professors during those days—principally, John C. Gerber, Stow Persons, and Richard H. Popkin—first awakened my interests and shaped my scholarly habits. I grow more conscious yearly of the fact that whatever value my work may have is due largely to them. More recently I have learned a great deal from my friends and colleagues, Professors James L. Woodress of the University of California at Davis, Philip P. Hallie of Wesleyan University, and Harry Finestone and Richard C. Blakeslee of San Fernando Valley State College. My most specific debts are to my fellow Royceans, the Reverend Frank M. Oppenheim, S. J., of Xavier University, Ignas Skrupskelis of the University of South Carolina, and John McDermott of Queens College.

This work could not have been completed without the generous assistance that I have received from several sources. In 1964–65, I received a study fellowship from the American Council of Learned Societies. At the same time, in cooperation with Wesleyan University, I was made a junior fellow of the Center for Advanced Studies. Special thanks are due to the Center's former Director, Paul Horgan, whose wisdom and skill created the finest atmosphere for study. During the present year, 1968–69, I am again a fellow of the American Council of Learned Societies. Assistance was also provided through a travel grant from the San Fernando Valley State College Foundation in 1967 and a special leave for research from the California State Colleges in 1968. To all these persons and agencies, I am deeply grateful.

It would impossible for me to name the hundreds of scholars and librarians who have offered help of various sorts. While categorically thanking them all, I wish to express special thanks to Kimball C. Elkins and the entire staff of the Harvard University Archives, Miss Frieda Thies and Mrs. E. C. Goodall of the Johns Hopkins University Library, J. R. K. Kantor of the University of California Archives, Estelle Rebec of the Bancroft Library, Rodney G. Dennis III and Joe McCarthy of the Houghton Library, Robert E. Brownell, Associate Registrar of the University of California, Grant T. Skelley of the University of California Library, Hannah D. French of the Wellesley College Library, C. Lynn Donovan of the Radcliffe College Library, Hugh Macdonald of the Columbia University Library, James de T. Abajian of the California Historical Society, Kathleen Jacklin of the Cornell University Archives, Mrs. Margaret Griffin, Secretary to the Harvard University Department of Philosophy, and Charlotte Oyer of the San Fernando Valley State College Library. I wish also to acknowledge the valuable help of scholars whose work in allied fields has contributed greatly to my work—especially Gay Wilson Allen, Alfred R. Ferguson, Nathan G. Hale, Jr., Dorothy Ross, Hugh Hawkins, and Max H. Fisch. My thanks also go to Ester Lanman Cushman, who shared her memories of Norton's Woods, and to Cynthia Goodenough, who let me live there.

For permission to publish the letters of Josiah Royce, I warmly acknowledge authorizations from David Royce, James Royce, Josiah Royce, Mrs. Charles Royce Cogswell, Sidney Westerman, Guardian for Randolph Royce, and Theodore M. Rossi, Conservator for Katharine Royce. Acknowledgment is also due to the following libraries and depositories for permission to publish materials from their collections: Boston Public Library, Bryn Mawr College, Bancroft Library of the University of California, University of California Archives, Regents of the University of California, California State Library, Columbia University Libraries, Cornell University Archives, Harvard University Archives, Houghton Library of Harvard University, Harvard Medical Library in the Francis A. Countway Library of Medicine, Henry E. Huntington Library and Art Gallery, University of Illinois Archives, Johns Hopkins University Library, Library of Congress, National Library of Australia, Public Library of Newark, New Jersey, New York Public Library, Pierpont Morgan Library, Arthur and Elisabeth Schlesinger Library on the History of Women in America of Radcliffe College, Smith College Archives, Stanford University Libraries, Hoose Library of Philosophy of the University of Southern California, Markham Archives of Wagner College, Wellesley College Library, and Yale University Libraries. I wish to thank the following persons for permission to publish letters from their private collections: Max H. Fisch, Richard Hocking, Bertrand Russell, and W. E. Schlaretzki. For permission to publish Royce's letters to Richard C. Cabot, I thank Richard Hocking and Dr. Sidney Cabot, trustees u/w Richard C. Cabot, Clause III. My thanks are also due to Charlotte Whiting Reed for permission to publish Royce's letter to Paul Henry Hanus and to Bertrand Perry for permission to publish Royce's letters to Ralph Barton Perry.

Cambridge, Massachusetts

J.C.

Abbreviations and Short Titles

AL	Autograph Letter
ALC	Autograph Letter Copy
ALI	Autograph Letter Incomplete
ALS	Autograph Letter Signed
APS	Autograph Postcard Signed
BPL	Boston Public Library
California	*California from the Conquest in 1846 to the Second Vigilance Committee in San Francisco: A Study of American Character* (Boston: Houghton Mifflin Co., 1886). Edition used for this work: New York: Alfred A. Knopf, 1948.
CG (1895)	*The Conception of God* (Berkeley: Philosophical Union 1895).
CG (1897)	*The Conception of God* (New York: Macmillan Co., 1897). Rev. ed., contains Royce's supplementary essay, "The Absolute and the Individual."
CI	*The Conception of Immortality* (Boston: Houghton Mifflin Co., 1900).
CPP	*Collected Papers of Charles Sanders Peirce*, ed. Charles Hartshorne, Paul Weiss, and Arthur W. Burks, 8 vols. (Cambridge: Harvard University Press, 1931–58).
CSL	California State Library, Sacramento
CUA	Cornell University Archives
CUB	Columbia University, Butler Library
FE	*Fugitive Essays*, ed. J. Loewenberg (Cambridge: Harvard University, 1920).

Feud	*The Feud of Oakfield Creek: A Novel of California Life* (Boston: Houghton Mifflin Co., 1887).
HGC	*The Hope of the Great Community* (New York: Macmillan Co., 1916).
HHL	Henry E. Huntington Library, San Marino, California
HL	Harvard University, Houghton Library
HUA	Harvard University Archives
JHU	Johns Hopkins University, Milton S. Eisenhower Library
LC	Library of Congress
NLA	The National Library of Australia, Canberra
NYPL	New York Public Library
OP	*Outlines of Psychology* (New York: Macmillan Co., 1903).
PC	*The Problem of Christianity*, 2 vols. (New York: Macmillan Co., 1913). Edition used for this work: Chicago: University of Chicago Press, 1968.
PL	*The Philosophy of Loyalty* (New York: Macmillan Co., 1908).
PML	Pierpont Morgan Library, New York
RAP	*The Religious Aspect of Philosophy* (Boston: Houghton Mifflin Co., 1885).
RLE	*Royce's Logical Essays*, ed. Daniel S. Robinson (Dubuque, Iowa: Wm. C. Brown Co., 1951).
RQP	*Race Questions, Provincialism, and Other American Problems* (New York: Macmillan Co., 1908).
SCA	Smith College Archives
SGE	*Studies of Good and Evil* (New York: D. Appleton and Co., 1898).
SMP	*The Spirit of Modern Philosophy: An Essay in the Form of Lectures* (Boston: Houghton Mifflin Co., 1892). Edition used in this work: New York: George Braziller, Inc., 1955.

SRI	*The Sources of Religious Insight* (New York: Charles Scribner's Sons, 1912).
SUA	Stanford University Archives
TCWJ	Ralph Barton Perry, *The Thought and Character of William James*, 2 vols. (Boston: Little, Brown and Co., 1935).
TLC	Typed Letter Copy
TLI	Typed Letter Incomplete
TLS	Typed Letter Signed
UCA	University of California Archives, Berkeley
UCB	University of California, Bancroft Library, Berkeley
USC	University of Southern California, Hoose Library of Philosophy
WCL	Wellesley College Library
WI	*The World and the Individual*, 2 vols. (New York: Macmillan Co., 1899–1901).
WJ	*William James and Other Essays on the Philosophy of Life* (New York: Macmillan Co., 1911).
YUB	Yale University, Beinecke Library
YUS	Yale University, Sterling Library

Introduction

When Josiah Royce died on September 14, 1916, America was absorbed in news of trench warfare, U-boat atrocities, and a presidential election. Few took note of his passing; after the usual obituaries and memoirs, Royce was gradually forgotten as one by one his books dropped out of print. To many of the young men returning from the war and to still younger men who came of age in the twenties and thirties, the characteristic terms of Royce's philosophy—"Loyalty," the "Beloved Community," the "Absolute"— seemed quaint and unintelligible. He was one of the last men in America who could write a book so comprehensive as *The World and the Individual.*

William James once said that Royce was "the Rubens of philosophy"—rich, abundant, bold, colorful, imperfect. He was a system-builder, America's only international representative of post-Kantian idealism. He was moreover a philosopher with a deep sense of mission: he felt obliged, as a man of the late nineteenth century, to correct an imbalance left by the Revolutionary and Romantic eras, to seek a theoretical and practical bond between individual men and the social order.[1] This idea is present throughout his works, but in the later ones it comes with gathering force. As a child he had seen its urgency revealed in the new communities of California and in the war fought to preserve the United States. A few months before his death he saw it written in blood at Verdun. The war, he insisted, was not a conflict between nations, but between the community of mankind and the individual interests of nations.

Royce's life was thus framed by conflict between the social order and its members. He studied the conflict and sought to learn its meaning. His philosophy, his literary and historical writings, even his last efforts in logic show how deeply he was concerned

[1] "The Outlook in Ethics," *International Journal of Ethics* 2 (1891): 106–11.

and tormented by the conflict. Finding his ties to the community and practicing loyalty to its highest ideals were for him personal obsessions as well as theoretical problems. He did not find theory and experience to be fundamentally different, for he believed philosophy to be essentially a criticism of life. "You philosophize," he said at the opening of *The Spirit of Modern Philosophy*, "when you reflect critically upon what you are actually doing in your world. What you are doing is of course, in the first place, living. And life involves passions, faiths, doubts, and courage. The critical inquiry into what all these things mean and imply is philosophy." By studying Royce's life we may gain a clearer understanding of the personal sources of his philosophy.

Grass Valley, California, where Royce was born on November 20, 1855, was at that time, by most generous estimate, a bit more than six years old. Situated in the foothills of the Sierra Nevada near the trail connecting Sacramento with the Truckee Pass, the grassy land on the banks of Wolf Creek was first visited by Forty-Niners as they came looking for their strays. By September 1850, a man named Morey opened a store in Grass Valley, although, with confidence characteristic of the pioneer, he momentarily called the place Centreville. In October, a man named McKnight found a ledge, two feet thick, that yielded $500 in gold per ton. Miners began to pour in, a hotel was built, and in November, an election was held and a few laws were adopted. It is said that ballots were collected in a cigar box, and that on the following day four persons were arrested—two men for fighting, one for riding too fast, and a woman for parading in the street wearing male attire. By the end of 1851, Grass Valley had a post office, a church, and a school; by the end of 1855, it was incorporated and was developing a water system.[2]

Undoubtedly, Grass Valley, like other mining camps, had its share of outlaws and exotics. Newspapers were filled with stories of knifings, shootings, bad cards, and the rest. The notorious Lola Montez arrived in the early 1850s. Famous for her "Spider Dance," Lola had followed the gold hunters to California after some theatrical success in America and Europe. She had been a mistress to Louis I of Bavaria who had made her a countess. In Grass Valley she lived for several years with her husband and a pet bear. Accord-

[2] *Nevada County Mining Review* [a special issue of the *Grass Valley Daily Morning Union* (1895)], pp. 3–19.

ing to legend, she publicly whipped a newspaperman who had written an unflattering editorial, and she shot her husband after he killed her bear. Lola is also given credit for having discovered Lotta Crabtree, who grew up in Grass Valley and who later became one of the most popular actresses of the American stage.

Katharine Royce, the philosopher's wife, once said that "Grass Valley was a place that was nothing in a situation that was nowhere."[3] Her view was not entirely fair. Most of Nevada County's twenty thousand residents lived in Grass Valley, and by the time the Royces arrived in the spring of 1854, there were three churches with growing memberships. Quite clearly, the "camp" had become a "community." By the time of Royce's birth, the earth beneath Grass Valley had yielded $3.5 million in gold, and the wealth was to last as long as mining for gold remained profitable. This fact made Grass Valley different from the mining camps of the Mother Lode. There the gold was taken from placer deposits close to the surface; when the mines were panned out, the miners moved on. But the gold of Grass Valley was in quartz deposits deep in the earth, and getting it out required finance, technology, organization. The first ten years of Royce's life were spent in the midst of such agitation and development. His elders often told him that this was a "new community." To a small boy, that expression seemed very odd. "I wondered," he said much later, "and came to feel that part of my life's business was to find out what all this wonder meant."[4]

The father of this boy, Josiah Royce, Sr., had been born in Rutlandshire, England, in 1812, and had been brought by his parents to America at the age of four. He had grown up in the town of Dundas, Canada, on Lake Ontario, very near the border of New York. The Royces were pious Baptists who liked to remember that an ancestor had stood guard at the execution of Charles I. Such Protestant zeal led the elder Royce into Bible study, and according to his obituary, he could quote "passage after passage on the same subject, beginning often with the earliest prophesied, and adding one quotation after another bearing upon the same points until he ended with the Book of Revelation."[5] Evidently, he was,

[3] Katharine Royce to Ralph Barton Perry, January 13, 1933. Perry Papers. HUA.

[4] "Words of Professor Royce at the Walton Hotel at Philadelphia, December 29, 1915," *Philosophical Review* 25 (1916): 507.

[5] "Tribute to Josiah Royce," *Los Gatos News*, August 24, 1888.

like his son, relentless in conversation. In 1857, he joined the Disciples of Christ and seems never to have failed the high standards of his religion. Temperance, devotion, and discipline sustained him in the presence of irreverence and recklessness. At home he always conducted the family devotions; when living far from churches he spent his Sundays reading the Bible.

He was a good man, without doubt, and yet a dream of success made him hopelessly quixotic. Married in 1845, he took his young wife and infant daughter, Mary Eleanor, to Iowa in 1848; in the spring of the following year, they pushed on to California, blindly finding their way, luckily crossing the Sierra Nevada just before the autumn snow. In California, they moved restlessly from Sacramento to San Francisco, then to an unnamed town in the Bay Area, then back to Sacramento and on to the mining camps, finally settling down for twelve years in Grass Valley.[6] In the meantime, they had two more daughters, Harriette and Ruth, and a son, John Samuel, who died in infancy. What drove them on is not entirely clear. If they hoped to find gold, they were utterly disappointed. At times Josiah Royce spoke of getting a homestead, but in fact he moved from job to job, unable to rise from poverty. He was a farmer, a storekeeper, a traveling salesman, and a mailman. San Franciscans knew him as an eccentric fruit peddler who was too garrulous to make a success of his business.[7]

Like her husband, Sarah Bayliss Royce served her God with unbending loyalty. Born in Stratford-on-Avon, in 1819, she grew up in Rochester, New York, where she met Josiah and married him. Her narrative of their journey to California and their early life there reveals a woman of gentle endurance and courageous faith. Ruth described her as a "mystic," but she seems to have escaped her husband's eccentricities.[8] With a certain independence, Sarah Royce preferred the less evangelical Congregational Church to the Disciples of Christ; yet it must be emphasized that she was a devoted wife in all respects. The children, however, sensing her intellectual superiority and stability, seemed always to regard her as the head of the household, and when her son described the devel-

[6] Sarah Royce, *A Frontier Lady: Recollections of the Gold Rush and Early California*, ed. Ralph Henry Gabriel (New Haven: Yale University Press, 1932).

[7] Guy C. Earl, "Memorabilia," MS in Rowell Papers, UCB.

[8] Ruth Royce to Ralph Barton Perry, February 26, 1928, Josiah Royce Memorial Collection. University of California, Los Angeles.

opment of communal life in California, he repeatedly emphasized the crucial role played by women. Women, he observed, brought permanence to social relationships: their children needed churches, schools, and the other institutions that help to create lasting communities.[9]

Sarah Royce was undoubtedly the most important person in the life of the young Josiah—or Josie, as he was called by the family. His mother kept a school in Grass Valley, and until the family moved back to San Francisco in 1866, she was his only teacher. Concerned about the roughness of the neighborhood boys, she prevented Josie from making friends, and since the father was often absent on business trips, the boy had no companions except his mother and three older sisters. Loneliness, shyness, a sense of being excluded from life were among the first passions that he felt. But being a precocious boy, he turned his attention to reading. With the Bible as a favorite, he soon became an avid reader of history, memorizing battles, heroes, dates with enthusiasm. Ruth, only three years older than her brother, gave him his earliest lessons in dialectics. She remembered him later as a born talker. When their arguments grew too fierce, his mother would punish Josie by making him be silent for an hour. A certain intellectual stubbornness and marked independence began to develop during these years. Among his earliest memories was a dissatisfaction with the strict religious training at home. "In my home," he said, "I heard the Bible very frequently read, and very greatly enjoyed my mother's reading of Bible stories, although, so far as I remember, I was very generally dissatisfied with the requirements of observance of Sundays, which stand out somewhat prominently in my memory."[10]

In the spring of 1866 the Royces left Grass Valley and soon afterwards opened a fruit store, which was also their home, at 1032 Folsom Street, San Francisco. In June, Josie was enrolled in Lincoln Grammar School. The experience of being moved from the country to the city, from a small and highly protective family to a large and competitive school, was a shock and a source of childhood grief. The school, exclusively for boys, had an enrollment of 906, and was run with military orderliness. At the beginning of each day the boys assembled in the school yard, lining up by classes behind a captain and a lieutenant; following commands, they marched into

[9] *California*, p. 295.
[10] "Words of Professor Royce," p. 507.

classrooms and took their places.[11] It is conceivable that Royce's lifelong hatred of bullies, particularly military bullies, had its beginnings on the yard of Lincoln Grammar School. Totally unathletic, a born non-conformist, obtrusively homely, Royce was constantly besieged and tormented by the other boys. In Grass Valley he had acquired an air of superiority; the boys of San Francisco made him pay for such impertinence. He later recalled his years at Lincoln with a nostalgia very near to bitterness. There, he said with more than a touch of irony, the boys taught him the "majesty of the community."[12]

If Royce had failed to win the boys of Lincoln, he must have made a favorable impression on his teachers, for in July 1869, at the age of thirteen, he was admitted to San Francisco Boys' High School. Here, under the leadership of Principal Theodore Bradley, a mathematics instructor, Royce found an atmosphere quite favorable to scholarship. Well equipped science programs, particularly in physics and geology, complemented the traditional liberal arts study of language and literature. The school has had many distinguished alumni, including, during the late 1860s, Albert A. Michelson, the physicist and first American scientist to win the Nobel prize. Though Royce spent only one year in high school, he made significant advances. There he began his lifelong study of German thought with a reading of Goethe's *Faust*. Ruth remembered this as a major event in her brother's life.[13] In mathematics Royce was so far advanced that he completed a whole term's work in a few days and went on to solid geometry and trigonometry, devising his own system of logarithms.[14] At the end of the year it was decided that Royce should finish his high-school education at the new University of California in Oakland.

Accordingly, in August 1870, Josiah Royce, Sr. abandoned the fruit business, took a job as a traveling salesman, and moved his family to Brooklyn (now East Oakland). During the next academic year Royce was a member of the Preparatory Class at the Univer-

[11] "A Day at Lincoln School in 1866," Bulletin No. 31, Lincoln Grammar School Association; reprinted from the *Mining and Scientific Press,* March 17, 1866.

[12] "Words of Professor Royce," pp. 508–9. An intriguing contrast to the youthful Royce is provided by the fact David Belasco was also a student in Lincoln Grammar School at this time.

[13] Ruth Royce to Ralph Barton Perry, February 26, 1928.

[14] Earl, "Memorabilia."

sity, taking courses in English, French, and mathematics. He did particularly well in English, scoring a perfect grade of 100, and in mathematics, 93.9, though in French his 79.5 was just slightly above average. On September 23, 1871, he was officially registered as a freshman in the College of Civil Engineering, the 115th to register at the University of California. His original plans to become a mining engineer were soon changed. According to University records for 1872–73, Royce had become a student "at Large"—that is, a full-time student but not enrolled in a specific degree program. In his junior and senior years, however, when the University moved to its permanent home in Berkeley, he committed himself to the Classical Course in the College of Letters, and on June 9, 1875, at the age of nineteen, was awarded the degree of Bachelor of Arts.

The records of Royce's official college coursework, as preserved in the University Archives, indicate that he pursued a well-balanced, traditional curriculum.[15] He took a course in mathematics during each semester of his freshman, sophomore, and junior years—completing algebra, analytical geometry, differential and integral calculus; his final scores in these courses were consistently in the nineties. He took English, ancient history, and "belles-lettres" only in the freshman year, but continued his study of language and literature throughout each semester until graduation.[16] By that time Royce had taken ten courses in French, seven in Latin, six in Greek, five in Hebrew, three in linguistics, and one in Italian. In each of these courses, except in French and Italian, he scored in the high eighties and nineties. Royce began his science study in the sophomore year, taking physics and chemistry in the first term of 1872–73, going on with physics and adding geology, with Joseph LeConte, in the second term. He continued with these sciences, plus astronomy, until graduation. In all, he had eight courses in

[15] For information regarding Royce's undergraduate education, I am indebted to Robert E. Brownell, Associate Registrar, University of California, and to J. R. K. Kantor, University Archivist.

[16] These records raise two problems. First, Royce appears not to have studied German at the University of California, though it is hardly conceivable that he could have entered the German universities in 1875–76 without formal training in the language. Second, though Royce stated definitely, in 1916, that he had been a student of Edward Rowland Sill during his final two years of undergraduate life, the records indicate that Sill did not join the Berkeley faculty until Royce's senior year and that Royce was not a student in any of Sill's classes.

physics, two in chemistry, six in geology (all with LeConte), and four in astronomy. It is surprising, perhaps important, that among the sciences, Royce excelled only in geology; his scores in the other courses ranged from the low fifties to the high eighties.

Aside from his few bad grades, Royce's achievement at the University of California was exceptional, as the faculty, students, and leaders of the East Bay community were quick to recognize. Twice, in 1873–74 and again in 1874–75, he was given an honorable mention for scholarship and during these same years successively won the first prize in rhetorical contests for "The Modern Novel" (1874) and "Truth in Art" (1875). Students repeatedly chose Royce as their representative. Now, if not for the first time, he had intimate and permanent friends. The childish nickname "Josie" was dropped in favor of the more manly "Josh," and though his manners and appearance still invited satire, his companions' amusement, ceasing to be merely cruel, had become an expression of friendship. During his senior year he became an editor of and frequent contributor to *The Berkeleyan*, the student newspaper and literary review.[17] At his commencement exercises these achievements were appropriately emphasized: he was cited for exceptional scholarship, chosen Class Essayist, and appointed to deliver the Classical Oration. At the urging of President Gilman, a group of concerned townsmen set up a fund to support Royce's postgraduate study in Germany.

Wasting no time after graduation, he left California before the end of June and was sailing to Hamburg before the middle of July. As planned, he went temporarily to Heidelberg, where he evidently took some instruction in the German language and made plans for future study. His decisions, in retrospect, seem very wise. On October 19, he registered at the University of Leipzig and enrolled in five courses: logic with Wilhelm Wundt, anthropology also with Wundt, history of philosophy with Wilhelm Windelband, German philosophy since Leibnitz with Ludwig Strümpell, and Sanskrit with Heinrich Hübschmann. His progress in these courses can be traced through his notebooks. At first the notes are sparse and fragmentary; everything is written in English. Gradually as the months pass, the notes expand and grow more coherent, and the last third

[17] During the spring of 1875, *The Berkeleyan,* in its regular columns, "Lies of the Month," and "Collegiana," frequently aimed good-natured assaults at "Josh's" foibles—his appearance, timidity, capacity for work, etc.

of each notebook is written in German. Royce especially enjoyed Wundt's course in logic and, because of him, thought of staying for a second term. But he was more attracted by the opportunity to study with Europe's foremost metaphysician, Rudolf Hermann Lotze, and accordingly on April 10, 1876, he left the University of Leipzig, proceeded directly to Göttingen, where he was registered at Georgia Augusta University on April 19. From Lotze he took two courses, metaphysics and practical philosophy. He continued the history of philosophy with Julius Baumann, attended Karl Ueberhorst's lectures on Kant's *Critique of Pure Reason*, and rounded out his program with courses in mathematics, sociology, and Sanskrit. Royce's increased course load at Göttingen and his very full notebooks are indications of his growing facility with both the language and subject matter. In all, he succeeded in packing a great deal of learning into twelve months. When he told Gilman, anticipating his return to America, that he planned to bring his "*akademische Hefte*, and so shall be 'armed'," he was not exaggerating.[18]

Though Royce had considered the possibility of staying in Germany through two winters, he decided to return to America when Gilman, who had ascended to the presidency of the new Johns Hopkins University, offered him a fellowship. His two years in Baltimore were among the happiest and most stimulating times of his life. Hopkins was, as he reflected later, "a dawn wherein ' 'twas bliss to be alive'." There had been nothing like it in American education. Gilman envisioned the new university as a graduate-research institute. The permanent faculty was to be, at least at the start, relatively small, and the Fellows were urged to be both students and teachers. Royce needed no prodding. Later recalling his youthful fervor, he said: "One longed to be a doer of the word and not a hearer only, a creator of his own infinitesimal fraction of a product, bound in God's name to produce it when the time came."[19] Never one to hang back, Royce taught a course in Schopenhauer during the second term, 1876–77, from January through May, and delivered a series of five lectures on the "Return to Kant" during March and April. On March 1 of the following year, he

[18] "Records of Student Days," Royce Papers, vol. 53. HUA. See Royce to Gilman, July 17, 1876.

[19] "Present Ideals of American University Life," *Scribner's Magazine* 10 (1891): 383–84.

lectured on "Spinoza's Theory of Religious Liberty in the State," and during April and May, he offered a series of lectures on German Romanticism. Thus he taught his subject to himself by teaching it to others. To a great extent this independence was unavoidable, for once again Royce was a student of philosophy in a university without a philosopher. Courses in Aristotle and Plato were offered by Charles D. Morris and John M. Cross, but they were classicists. Only twice in his two years at Hopkins did Royce have opportunities to hear lectures in his chosen field: in January 1878, George Sylvester Morris gave twenty lectures on the history of philosophy; he was followed in February by William James who gave ten lectures on psychology.

In addition to its peculiarly academic attractions, Royce's Baltimore was a warm, sophisticated, and altogether attractive community. Years later, while confessing to his lack of artistic taste, he blamed the crudities of his California upbringing. In most respects, Baltimore was the cultural antithesis of San Francisco, and through Johns Hopkins University Royce found friends with whom he could experience its civilized life. He was a frequent guest in President Gilman's home and was admitted into lasting friendships with the professors and fellows. Indeed during his two years at Hopkins he formed three of the deepest and most loyal relationships of his life. William James, who was by all accounts his closest lifelong friend, came to know Royce quite well during the summer of 1877. Royce, with a year at Hopkins behind him, was spending a few months in Cambridge and called on James to ask if there might be a future for a philosopher in America. James quickly encouraged his young friend and, as Royce remembered it, "used his influence from that time on, not to win me as a follower, but to give me my chance."[20] Together, they lived through some of the best years of American thought. Another Hopkins friend who was to become a Harvard colleague and a Cambridge neighbor was Charles Rockwell Lanman. A Fellow in Sanskrit, Lanman became Royce's "Dearest Guru," guiding the young philosopher through the Bhagavad Gita and the Vedas. In turn, Lanman took Royce's course in Schopenhauer and carefully attended all of his public lectures. During their two years at Hopkins, Royce and Lanman were constantly in one another's company, and in 1876, they, with

[20] "A Word of Greeting to William James," *Harvard Graduates' Magazine* 18 (1910): 630–33.

several others, organized a German Club which met weekly for beer and conversation.[21] A third, an older and rather different Baltimore friend was George Buchanan Coale to whom Royce later dedicated *The Religious Aspect of Philosophy*. Coale, with a Maryland heritage that he traced to the seventeenth century and two ancestors who had signed the Declaration of Independence, was a prominent businessman and cultural leader. He was the President of the Merchants' Mutual Marine Insurance Company and founder of the insurance firm, George B. Coale and Son. Inclined toward the arts, he and his daughter Mary were active in the Wednesday Club, an amateur theatrical group, and in 1870, he founded and became the director of the Maryland Academy of Fine Arts. As Royce fell into friendship with this tasteful and brilliant family, his experiences must have seemed altogether new, and as he was drawn into a filial relationship with Coale, he must have sensed that here was a man who possessed those qualities which his own father so pitifully lacked.

Understandably, Royce regretted leaving Baltimore. In June 1878, though about to receive his Ph.D., he still planned to remain at Hopkins. In July, however, he was offered an instructorship in English at the University of California, where he was to teach elementary courses in composition and literature under the direction of Edward Rowland Sill, for an annual salary of $1,200. Dissatisfied with the prospects of returning to California and being diverted from philosophy, Royce waited for two weeks while he sought advice and explored other possibilities. Gilman was decidedly in favor of the California offer, and though he promised to make inquiries with Noah Porter, president of Yale, he did not encourage Royce to remain in Baltimore. On the Fourth of July, Royce took his problem to Lanman in New Haven, and together they called on Porter. It became clear, however, as the days passed that there were no alternatives to the California proposal. He accepted the offer in mid-July and within a month was on his way to Berkeley. On September 4, Sill wrote to Gilman with the air of a man who had just purchased a product through a mailorder catalog: "Royce has been duly rec^{d}, & found to answer the description."

Royce's fears of isolation in California proved to be well founded. Though surrounded by old friends and relatives, he felt detached, and though he plunged immediately into the university's activities,

[21] Diary, Lanman Papers. HUA.

his efforts seemed ineffective. The students, he found, were ill-prepared and undisciplined; faculty members, though superficially cordial, were wholly indifferent to philosophical inquiry; Californians in general were barbarians—a "blind and stupid and homeless generation of wanderers."[22] Sill, who was Royce's only intimate friend on the faculty and who was deeply sympathetic to his need to get out of California, looked upon the experience as a sort of forty days of temptation in the desert, while Royce himself described it as being exposed to intellectual tuberculosis.[23]

His characteristic solution to such dangers was work. Besides attending to his own classes, he gave ten lectures on philosophy to the senior class during November and December, 1878, and during the following spring, offered revisions of his Hopkins lectures on German Romanticism to the juniors. At the same time he put his freshmen through an introductory course in logic and spent the summer vacation writing a *Primer of Logical Analysis*. He also accepted in October 1878 the extra task of running the Circulating Library, and in 1880 organized and became permanent secretary of the Psychology Club. In addition to his work with students, Royce found time to participate in the Berkeley Club which he joined in September 1878 and served as secretary during the academic year 1879–80. During that year also he joined with Bernard Moses and others in forming the Fortnightly Club for Social Science and assisted in publication of the *Berkeley Quarterly*. In his four years on the Berkeley faculty he published more than a dozen major literary and philosophical essays.

If Royce learned that work helped him escape loneliness, he found further help through his marriage to Katharine Head. Kitty, as she was always known to the family, was the daughter of Edward Francis Head, a prominent San Francisco lawyer and later a Superior Court Judge of San Mateo County. She had been to preparatory school in Boston and was, when she met Josiah in 1878, a special student at the University of California, concentrating in modern language and literature. The Heads, a family of marked intelligence, were old friends of Edward Sill, who described Katharine as "a talented, refined, & handsome young lady,"[24] and they

[22] Royce to Coale, September 23, 1880.

[23] Sill to Gilman, September 4, 1878; April 26, 1880. Sill Papers. UCB. Royce to James, July 16, 1878.

[24] Sill to Gilman, April 26, 1880.

seem to have possessed those qualities of talent and good taste that Royce had previously recognized in the Coales. Katharine's sister, Anna, later established the Anna Head School in Berkeley, which is still one of the most respected schools in the East Bay. Nothing is known of the courtship between Josiah and Katharine except that they were engaged by January 1880 and married on October 2 of that year. They lived at Judge Head's home in Berkeley, where on April 11, 1882, Katharine Royce gave birth to her first son, Christopher.

Concerning Royce's thirty-six years of married life, little is known. If rumor is to be believed, Mrs. Royce's waspish manners proved too clamorous for her unworldly husband. This view, however, is probably more folklore than fact, as it should be emphasized that there is no documentary evidence to imply that they felt any serious incompatibility. The evidence does, on the contrary, suggest that while the marriage was not an affair of passion, it developed into a bond of mutual affection, animated perhaps by a certain amount of intellectual stubbornness. Gifted, as Rollo Walter Brown remembered her, "with picturesque speech which she did not hesitate to employ," Katharine Royce brought a good balance of unaffected vivacity and lethal irony into her husband's life. Intelligent as well as domestic, she was able to assist directly in several of his projects and as translator to carry out her own plans. If indeed, to gentler souls, her style seemed inelegant, it is not unreasonable to suppose that her candor and asperity contributed to his growth. Certainly he could not have failed to appreciate her triumphant parody of his argumentative tactics. Metaphysics, she liked to tell guests, is like a game of hide-and-seek. First, you hide a doll in an old trunk in the attic. Then, getting family and friends together, you ask, I wonder where that doll could be? You look all over the house, turning everything inside out. Finally you say, I wonder if the doll might be in the old trunk in the attic, and to your great delight and feigned astonishment there you find it.[25]

Regardless of the settling effect of having a growing family, Royce relentlessly sought a position in the East. He seems never to have considered the post at Berkeley a permanent one, though there is reason to suppose that he could have expected an early

[25] Rollo Walter Brown, *Harvard Yard in the Golden Age* (New York: Current Books, Inc., 1948), pp. 46–47. Mrs. Royce's parody is aimed particularly at the style of *RAP* and *WI*, 1.

promotion to the chair of English literature. Gilman apparently sympathized with Royce's ambitions, but for reasons not wholly clear, he resisted the urgings of both Sill and James that Royce be appointed at Johns Hopkins. Sill was particularly candid: "About Royce," he wrote to Gilman on April 26, 1880, "is there not some opening for him with you, or failing that, do you not know of some one of the reputable colleges where he could be Prof. of Logic, or Rhetoric, or Eng. Literature—or all of them together? As I have said to you before, I don't believe this is a good place for him."[26] At the same time, James was working for Royce quite as urgently and somewhat more fruitfully. In the spring of 1880, he recommended Royce for a position at the University of Minnesota, and in 1881 nearly landed him an assistant professorship at Harvard. Though neither of these efforts succeeded, James did find a way to bring Royce to Harvard for the following year. James had arranged to take a sabbatical leave, and was required, under the existing rules, to find a qualified temporary replacement for half of his pay, $1,250. Though it had to be understood that the appointment was for one year only, James felt that Royce would gain, if he took the job, an inside track on any future developments at Harvard. Royce acted suddenly and boldly. James's letter had been sent on April 23; on May 1, Royce wired his acceptance. After an anxious wait of more than three weeks, Royce received his letter of appointment, and on June 2, he presented his resignation to President Reid. Determined to sever all ties to California, Royce ignored James's advice that he leave his wife and child with her parents and spend his "first experimental year" in Cambridge alone.[27] Instead, on September 4, the three Royces boarded a train for Cambridge, and on September 10, Charles Lanman, who had himself recently joined the Harvard faculty, recorded in his diary: "Went to Boston to meet Royce, & his wife & babe in arms. They arrived from San Francisco well."

Royce moved to Harvard with slight hope of making Cambridge his permanent home. As a temporary replacement for James during the first year and for Palmer during the second, he was able to remain at Harvard for a third year only by accepting part-time work in the English Department. The spontaneity of these arrangements caused Royce to make considerable adjustments in his teaching. During the first year he taught an elementary course in logic

[26] Sill to Gilman, April 26, 1880.
[27] James to Royce, June 13, 1882. James Papers. HL.

and psychology, an advanced course in British empiricism, and another advanced course in psychology; during his second year he repeated the introductory course and added Palmer's advanced courses in ethics and metaphysics; in his third year he taught a half-course in philosophical theism during the first term, a half-course in oral discussion during the second term, and supervised advanced composition for juniors and seniors. A degree of permanence was guaranteed, however, when Royce received in April 1885 an appointment for five years as assistant professor, effective September 1.

The Religious Aspect of Philosophy certainly helped to resolve the problem of Royce's temporary status. He had been growing in the direction of this treatise since his first year's study of philosophy in Germany, but before 1880 his philosophic studies had been largely assimilative and only sporadically constructive. He had been fascinated with Clifford's "mind-stuff" theory, had struggled with Hodgson's *Philosophy of Reflection*, and otherwise had drawn ideas from a vast and various expanse of sources. Though he always tended to conceive of philosophy in Kantian terms, he was no longer willing, after the autumn of 1880 to follow Clifford on the quest for "things-in-themselves," but instead had come to see that the more significant problem left by Kant lay in determining the structure, not the limits, of knowledge. This line of analysis led naturally to "The Possibility of Error." Royce first signaled this direction in "On Purpose in Thought," a paper sent to the Johns Hopkins Metaphysical Club and read there in late autumn 1880. At about the same time he gave a lecture in Berkeley on "The Ethical Aspect of Modern Thought," which, as the title suggests, may have been an early version of *The Religious Aspect of Philosophy*. The book itself was, as Royce explained his methods, "founded on old lectures and essays of mine rewritten and joined with whatever new things come into my head."[28] He began its actual composition shortly after joining the Harvard faculty, and in March 1883 presented a series of four lectures entitled "The Religious Aspect of Philosophy." Lanman described the first of these lectures as a "splendid success" and loyally attended the entire series.[29] By all reports Royce was a huge success. In addition to his winning the respect of the Harvard community, he received the encouragement

[28] Royce to Coale, January 14, 1884.

[29] Diary, March 1, 8, 15, 29, 1883. Lanman Papers. HUA.

of Horace Scudder, an editor with Houghton Mifflin. After another year or so of rewriting, the book was sent to press in the fall of 1884; it was published in January. In February, James, filled with enthusiasm, described it as "one of the very freshest, profoundest, solidest, most human bits of philosophical work I've seen in a long time."[30]

A full discussion of the continuity of Royce's philosophy cannot be undertaken here, but it might be well to note briefly some traces of coherence between *The Religious Aspect of Philosophy* and *The Problem of Christianity*. At issue is whether the "Community of Interpretation" in the later work is inconsistent with the "Absolute Thought" of the earlier work; in other words, did Royce finally abandon his absolutism in favor of a merely social idealism?[31] In his own responses to the question, Royce repeatedly and firmly maintained that his various constructions were different paths to the same doctrine, that his latest work revealed additions and reinterpretations, but not inconsistencies. On two separate occasions he described the progression of his thought in terms of a genetic metaphor: the later philosophy was, he said, "a new growth"; the "germ" of his theory of interpretation, he insisted, was in "The Possibility of Error" in *The Religious Aspect of Philosophy*.[32] Retrospectively he felt that his "deepest motives and problems . . . [had] centered about the Idea of the Community," but that he had only gradually become conscious of the idea.[33] In short, Royce dissuades us from seeking inconsistency through a comparison of his earlier with his later theories, and suggests instead that we may, in studying the early works, find the "germ" from which "grew" the principle of "interpretation" and the idea of the "community." Recognizing the difficulties in this line of inquiry, one might tentatively suggest that this "germ" in "The Possibility of Error" is Royce's implicit attention to the triadic structure of knowledge. As he develops his

[30] *TCWJ*, 1: 772.

[31] Discussions of this problem may be found in John E. Smith, *Royce's Social Infinite* (New York: Liberal Arts Press, 1950); James Harry Cotton, *Royce on the Human Self* (Cambridge: Harvard University Press, 1954); and Peter Fuss, *The Moral Philosophy of Josiah Royce* (Cambridge: Harvard University Press, 1965).

[32] Royce to Mary Whiton Calkins, March 20, 1916; Royce to Reginald Chauncey Robbins, November 8, 1914; see also *PC*, p. 350.

[33] "Words of Professor Royce," p. 510.

argument, he shows that knowledge as a dyadic relationship—either perception or conception—is always subject to skepticism: John has an idea of Thomas, Thomas has an idea of John, but the real John and the real Thomas are never present in one another's experience. To have real knowledge, to bring the real John and the real Thomas together, there must be a mediator, a third intelligence which contains both John and Thomas. Acknowledging, of course, that the elements can be only roughly equivalent, we may say that the Universal "Thought" of *The Religious Aspect of Philosophy* corresponds to the "interpreter" (the "mediator," the "spirit of this universal community") of *The Problem of Christianity*.[34] The differences are not merely linguistic: in the earlier work, Royce has no clear ideas of time or of individuality, and his conception of the triadic structure of knowledge remains too loosely metaphorical. But he was undoubtedly right in describing his philosophical development as a "growth"; it was mainly a growth toward clarity.[35]

Before correcting proofs for this first major book, Royce was already deep into research for his second. Scudder, as editor of the historical series, American Commonwealths, had previously assigned the California volume to Royce's friend and fellow member of the Berkeley Club, William Watson Crane, Jr. But when Crane died suddenly in August 1883 Scudder turned to Royce, who, because he needed the money and expected to find the task amusing, accepted. He spent the entire summer of 1884 in San Francisco working at Hubert Howe Bancroft's library of Western Americana. There he worked closely with Bancroft's librarian, Henry Lebbeus Oak, who led Royce to the documents in the Larkin Papers which suggested that Captain Frémont's methods in seizing California had been wholly in opposition to U. S. policy and contrary to his orders. After Royce spent another year and a half of difficult research and writing, *California from the Conquest in 1846 to the Second Vigilance Committee in San Francisco (1856): A Study of American Character* was published in February 1886.

Clearly this was no light task. Though the work began as an entertainment for idle hours, it involved, as it grew, Royce's deepest personal and philosophic concerns. It was, in the first place, his

[34] *PC*, p. 362.

[35] See James Harry Cotton, *Royce on the Human Self* (Cambridge: Harvard University Press, 1954), p. 265.

attempt to understand the ambivalence he felt toward California—"this sad State wherein I had the odd fortune to be born."[36] More broadly significant, however, *California* was Royce's first careful treatment of the relationship between the individual and the community, and of the moral issues that bind them together. Believing that philosophy is inquiry into the meaning of life, that the eternal is constantly encountered in the temporal, Royce saw the upheavals of early California history as parables that might teach philosophic truth. Indeed the most original sections of *California*—the history of the conquest, the Downieville lynching, the Vigilance Committees, and the squatter revolts—are precisely those which dramatize the issues which Royce would later raise in *The Philosophy of Loyalty* and *The Problem of Christianity*. His treatment of John Charles Frémont is his clearest and most ambitious illustration of these issues. Those who admire Frémont and seek to justify his acts see him as a bold adventurer possessing an intuitive sense of his moment in history and a will to act when action was required.[37] Rejecting these views and refusing to celebrate the fantasy, Royce methodically proves that Frémont's Bear Flag War and subsequent seizure of California had been an act of open disobedience, irreconcilable with his official instructions. Royce was not, however, merely debunking a popular hero; he was offering an illustration of his ethical absolutism, setting himself firmly against the policies of expedience, greed, mendacity, and self-deception, showing the practical consequences of a man's decision to serve the personal interests of the moment, of his failure to be loyal to the higher values of the social order.

The same problem is the crucial theme of Royce's next book, *The Feud of Oakfield Creek*, a novel which he wrote during the summer of 1886. Like most "first" novels, *The Feud* is artistically imperfect: it is somewhat too long; its style is frequently awkward and declamatory; the characters are stereotypic; the action is slow to unfold and insufficiently dramatized. And yet it is well worth reading, if only for the further light it sheds on Royce's thought. A social-problem novel, *The Feud* concerns the relations among several men as they are involved in a struggle for the land. Revealing their greed, Royce exposes the inadequacies of rugged individual-

[36] Royce to Coale, September 23, 1880.

[37] See Allen Nevins, *Frémont, Pathmaker of the West* (New York: Appleton-Century, 1939).

ism and anticipates his theoretical treatment of "loyalty" and the "community." Unlike Royce's triumphant metaphysics, the progression of his novel is tragic, but without a hero or a villain. Indeed, though Escott is the immediate victim, his death is less significant than the catastrophe that comes to the entire community, a catastrophe brought about not by any one character's acts or motives, but in the collective failures of men to subordinate their private interests to the welfare of humanity and human institutions.

Royce's achievements during his first five years at Harvard testified to his great capacity for work, to the depth and range of his abilities. Much had been accomplished. He was beginning to gain national and even international recognition; his second son, Edward, had been born on Christmas, 1886; his professional future was secure. Yet Royce was to pay a dear price for his achievements. The work had left him physically and psychologically depleted, while the critical reception of all three books was disappointing. *California* was vigorously attacked; *The Feud* was quietly ignored; and though *The Religious Aspect of Philosophy* received some worthy attention, mainly from James and Renouvier, its most striking feature—the argument for idealism based on the possibility of error—was largely overlooked. These professional disappointments were compounded by a number of personal vexations. His tiny salary caused him to fall deeper into debt; members of his family were often dangerously ill; and early in 1887, two very close friends, Edward Rowland Sill and George Buchanan Coale, suddenly died. By summer, signs of an imminent breakdown had appeared. Depression, insomnia, and a general deadening of passion continued to vex him during the first term of 1887–88, and shortly after the mid-year it became clear that he could not continue. Receiving a leave of absence for the spring term, Royce left his family in Cambridge and, on February 25, sailed to Australia.

During his three months sailing voyage around the Cape of Good Hope and into the antipodes, Royce felt his strength gradually returning. At first there had been a long period of dejection—"an absolute negation of all active predicates of the emotional sort. . . ."[38] But near the end of May, as his bark was approaching Melbourne, Royce began to look toward future work with a good deal of anticipation. His stay in Australia was splendidly recuperative. There, through his friend, Richard Hodgson, he made the

[38] Royce to James, May 21, 1888.

acquaintance of Alfred Deakin, one of Australia's greatest statesmen. Possibly because of their vast personal and cultural differences, Royce and Deakin became lifelong friends. As traveling companions for two or three weeks they delighted in exchanging views on philosophy and politics, each finding inspiration by sharing in the other's experience. Leaving Australia, Royce sailed to New Zealand, then traveled by steamer to San Francisco, finding new strength at each stage of his journey. Arriving in Cambridge in early September, after an absence of more than five months, he wrote to President Gilman, announcing his return to health: "I feel like a bent bow, all ready to twang."[39]

The breakdown taught Royce the dangers of overwork. As a consequence the tempo of his life, if not the vigor of his activities, settled down considerably for several years after 1888. With the birth of a third son, Stephen, in May 1889, the Royces made a permanent move to a new and roomy house at 103 Irving Street in the freshly subdivided estate of Charles Eliot Norton. Here in the shade of huge elms, two doors from William James, around the corner from Charles Lanman, a short walk from the Yard, Royce spent the remaining twenty-seven years of his life. The tensions of his earlier life at Harvard gradually relaxed as the external signs of his emerging stature became evident. In the spring of 1891, with the formation of Stanford University, the new president, David Starr Jordan, urged Royce to accept the chair of philosophy. Convinced of his importance to Harvard and informally promised an early promotion, Royce decided to remain in Cambridge. In fulfillment of the promise, Royce became Professor of the History of Philosophy in the fall of 1892.

During these years, seemingly uncertain of his scholarly future, Royce undertook the lighter tasks of his profession. At different times, he proposed writing a book on Theodore Parker, a biography of Goethe, a study of Hegel, and an edition of the *Phänomenologie*. None of these plans was actually carried out. Yet when, in the fall of 1889, Mrs. Charles Dorr encouraged Royce to present a series of public lectures on some prominent modern thinkers, he flew to the task with enthusiasm. The result was *The Spirit of Modern Philosophy* (1892) which contains Royce's most important advance of the early 1890s, his distinction between "the world of appreciation" and "the world of description." This "double aspect" theory of

[39] Royce to Gilman, September 6, 1888.

reality enabled Royce to deepen his idealism and relate it to cosmology. The "world of description" is the physical world, the world of science—public and permanent; the "world of appreciation" is the ideal world, the world of feelings—private and spontaneous. But it is the appreciative self who lives in the "true Self" and who makes science and the entire world of description possible. The "double aspect" theory, therefore, gives a wider range of experience to the "Absolute Thought" than Royce had previously suggested and makes his idealism something more than "an idle comment upon the general connectedness of things."[40] It was probably this speculation that Royce had implied in his letter to James while en route to Australia; it had made, as he said, "the dry bones of my 'Universal Thought' live."[41]

Royce, in the meantime, had begun editorial work for two periodicals, work that led him into the most famous controversies of his career. Robert Underwood Johnson of *Century Magazine* decided to launch a series of articles on California history and asked Royce to assist as an editor and occasional contributor. This venture, which occupied Royce during 1890 and 1891, rekindled the fires of his conflict with John Charles Frémont and led to a skirmish with the daughter of General William T. Sherman. A more notorious incident, however, resulted from the establishment, in 1890, of the *International Journal of Ethics* for which Royce was one of the founding editors. In the first issue of the *Journal* he printed a lengthy review of Francis Ellingwood Abbot's *The Way Out of Agnosticism.* The result has been appropriately called "the Abbot affair."

After a fairly distinguished career as an independent clergyman and polemicist for the Free Religious Association, Abbot turned to philosophy. In 1881 he received the second Ph.D. in philosophy granted at Harvard; at the same time, he founded and became preceptor of the Home School for Boys in Cambridge. During the following year a piece from his dissertation was published in *Mind*, which Royce, though probably he had not yet met its author, found a "sad spectacle." When Abbot revised and expanded the article into a book, *Scientific Theism* (1885), Royce wrote a satirical review, in *Science*, treating Abbot as a harmless incompetent, one

[40] *SMP*, p. 381; the "double aspect" theory is developed throughout lecture 12, "Physical Law and Freedom," pp. 381–434.

[41] Royce to James, May 21, 1888.

who reveals "a not uncommon but highly amusing state of mind."[42] By this time Royce and Abbot were seeing one another occasionally at philosophical and psychical-research meetings, and though their disagreements were understood by all, their acquaintance was cordial if not intimate. Indeed when it became necessary, in the spring of 1888, to find a substitute lecturer for Royce's Philosophy 13—The Philosophy of Nature—it was Royce himself who urged Abbot to take the job. Fawning and self-effacing in his acceptance, Abbot's view of Royce soon turned hostile; in November, 1889, he wrote to a former student: "It was no fault of my class in Phil. 13, if they could not take in the tremendous meaning and strength of the argument I outlined; they had their heads stuffed beforehand with too much philosophical nonsense."[43]

Among the ironies that developed during "the Abbot affair" is the fact that *The Way Out of Agnosticism* had its origin in these lectures. Rewritten and published serially in the *New Ideal*, the book was typeset at Abbot's expense and given, without a royalty on the first thousand copies, to Little, Brown and Company. Abbot even offered to write and pay for his own advertisements. His anxiety and overconfidence seem to have reached a point of frenzy:

> If I can get a *fair hearing* from the *cultivated classes* at home and abroad, I know that there is a great future for this thought. I labor under the great disadvantage of not holding an *academic position*, and of being a mere *private American*. . . . No friend is at my back— I am only a lonely thinker tabooed in my own country; but I *know* the transcendent value of my thought, its coherency, power, and adaptation to the age.[44]

Obviously, Royce's blow, as all were soon to realize, struck Abbot when he was psychologically if not intellectually defenseless.

Royce's motives for dealing so sternly with Abbot remain unclear, but there is little doubt that he had set out to annihilate Abbot's reputation. Three points in his review gave particular offense: first, he characterized Abbot as a blunderer who had unconsciously borrowed from Hegel, but without the subtlety of the original; then, he gave a "professional warning" against Abbot's

[42] "Abbot's Scientific Theism," *Science* 7 (1886): 335–38.

[43] Abbot to Charles T. Sempers, November 16, 1889. Letter-Book 10. Abbot Papers. HUA.

[44] Abbot to George Iles, December 29, 1889. Letter-Book 10. Abbot Papers. HUA.

"philosophical pretensions"; and finally, he seemed to set the tone for future contests by asserting that he neither asked for mercy nor intended to be merciful. Deeply wounded, Abbot wrote a reply, entitled "Dr. Royce's 'Professional Warning'," which he submitted to the *International Journal of Ethics* on January 21, 1891.[45] Though the reply proved to be more abusive than the review, Felix Adler and S. Burns Weston agreed to publish it if Abbot agreed to remove the offensive language and if Royce were allowed to print a rejoinder in the same issue. Abbot agreed to the first condition, but was wholly opposed to the second. In April, a compromise was offered: Abbot's reply and Royce's rejoinder were to appear in the same issue, but Abbot was to be given a final opportunity to restate his case and close the dispute in a subsequent issue, providing that his final remarks were found to be impersonal and parliamentary. Unwilling to accept these conditions, Abbot withdrew his article, and the controversy broke out into the open. During the summer, both Abbot and Royce sought legal advice; there were threats and rumors of possible litigation. In November, Charles Peirce wrote a letter to the *Nation* charging that Royce had libeled Abbot in the original review and subsequently had used unfair means to stifle Abbot's reply. This brought answering letters from William James and Joseph B. Warner, and these in turn were countered in the *Nation* by Abbot. Royce in the meantime tried to remain publicly silent, while making it clear, through correspondence, that he was willing to apologize for seeming to attack Abbot's character but would not retract the substance of his remarks concerning Abbot's borrowing from Hegel. Abbot, however, seeking total vindication and taking Royce's "professional warning" to be equivalent to "professorial warning," printed two pamphlets–first an *Appeal* and then a *Remonstrance*–addressed to the Harvard Corporation and Overseers, accusing Royce of violating his academic trust. In October and again in January, the Corporation refused to hear the grievance, and the controversy faded quietly away.[46]

[45] See Abbot's letters to S. Burns Weston, January 21, February 3, 10, 13, 1891. Letter-Book 10. Abbot Papers. HUA.

[46] *A Public Appeal for Redress to the Corporation and Overseers of Harvard University: Professor Royce's Libel* (Boston, 1891); *A Public Remonstrance Addressed to the Board of Overseers of Harvard University: Is Not Harvard Responsible for the Conduct of Her Professors as well as of Her Students?* (Boston, 1892). See document signed by E. W. Hooper, Secretary of the Corporation, January 25, 1892. Abbot Papers. HUA.

Less notoriously but certainly more fruitfully, Royce devoted his major efforts during the 1890s to the development of philosophy and the American university system. When he had joined the Harvard faculty in 1882, the philosophy program consisted of four instructors and ten courses; George Santayana was a freshman, and Benjamin Rand was the only graduate student. Before the end of the 1880s major changes had begun, and by the turn of the century the number of courses and instructors had doubled. But the most dramatic change took place in the graduate program. Before 1890 Harvard had granted only four Ph.D.'s in philosophy, but during the following decade twenty were awarded. The new generation of philosophers included Charles M. Bakewell, Mary Whiton Calkins, William Pepperell Montague, John Elof Boodin, A. O. Lovejoy, and Ralph Barton Perry. The "golden age" of American philosophy had begun, and nowhere was it better represented than at Harvard with its brilliant quintet–Palmer, James, Royce, Münsterberg, and Santayana. From 1894 to 1898, in the midst of this extraordinary development, Royce served ably as departmental chairman.

The same years mark an important period in Royce's philosophical growth. In September 1894, he received from George Holmes Howison an invitation to lecture at the University of California during the summer of 1895. The proposed lecture was not to be a perfunctory appearance, but a major event for both speaker and audience. Howison's plan, as first proposed and subsequently developed was for the University's Philosophical Union to study *The Religious Aspect of Philosophy* throughout the academic year, 1894–95, and for Royce to appear in August to discuss some feature of philosophical theism, together with three others–Howison, Sidney E. Mezes, and Joseph LeConte–who would use Royce's paper as their point of departure. The prospect of returning in such a capacity to his Alma Mater keenly appealed to Royce, and he wasted little time in planning how he might approach the task. *The Religious Aspect of Philosophy* was nearly ten years old, and though Royce's reputation as a philosopher was faring rather well on the merits of that book, he was not at all satisfied with its form. He saw that the ethical theory dominating the first half of the book might be pushed aside so that the metaphysical argument for idealism might be given proper emphasis; thus, without altering the "kernel" of the earlier work, a new paper with a wholly new development could be offered, a paper on "The Conception of God," including both a definition of His essence and an argument for His existence. With more than passing interest, therefore, Royce did what he could to fit the California trip into his summer schedule, and even when his wife went into convalescence with a broken leg, he did not think of altering his plans. Accordingly, he arrived in Berkeley on August 28, delivered "The Conception of God" to a huge audience two days later, and spent the next two weeks lecturing and visiting friends in Berkeley and at Stanford.

Aside from merely reorganizing his earlier theory, Royce originally conceived of this new presentation as more explicitly teleological than *The Religious Aspect of Philosophy* had seemed to be. He felt that the Absolute as "Thought" in the earlier book, the passionless insight which explains the possibility of error, had obscured the voluntaristic aspects of his theory. The distinction between "description" and "appreciation" introduced in *The Spirit of Modern Philosophy* had significantly modified this earlier view by arguing that reality is two-fold, not only *idea* but also *will*. In "The Conception of God" Royce prefers "Experience" to "Thought," and the concept of "fulfilment" becomes central. Thus, "Absolute Experience is . . . an experience which finds fulfilled all that the completest thought can rationally conceive as genuinely possible."[47] Individual experiences are fragments of this organic whole.

In bringing his paper to Howison, Royce was submitting his theory to the criticism of a thoroughgoing Pluralist. According to Howison's "personal idealism," individual minds and the items of their experience constitute the whole of existence; these individuals are members of the "Eternal Republic," and God is simply "the impersonated Ideal of every mind." Predictably, Howison attacked Royce's theory on grounds of its inadequate account of individuality. It was, of course, a common criticism; Davidson had advanced it, and Royce's notorious "Battle of the Absolute" with James was, by the mid-1890s, in full swing. Without admitting the fault, Royce soon took steps to develop this aspect of his system, and by March 1896 he had written a paper on "The Principle of Individuation." Here maintaining that all purely theoretical definitions of an individual are inadequate, Royce argued that the concept of individuality is essentially ethical and teleological: "Objects are individuals in so far as they are unique expressions of essentially exclusive ideals,

[47] *CG* (1897), p. 44.

ends, Divine decrees."[48] In *The Spirit of Modern Philosophy* he maintained, as we have seen, that philosophy answers the question, "What am I doing?" According to Royce's philosophy of the mid-1890s the human self attains individuality through its effort to know and to fulfill its purpose.

During the following summer, Howison arranged with Macmillan Co. for a new edition of *The Conception of God* and invited Royce to submit a supplementary essay. Seeing the relevance of his newly formulated concept of individuality to the earlier discussion, he wrote "The Absolute and the Individual," making his paper on "The Principle of Individuation" the third part of the larger essay. Before the publication of this essay, however, Royce was presented with his greatest challenge: he had been invited, after James had declined, to deliver the Gifford Lectures at Aberdeen in 1899 and 1900. Recognizing that this would be "the effort of my life,"[49] he gave his fullest attention during the next four years, from the summer of 1897 through the summer of 1901, to the writing, delivering, rewriting, and publication of these lectures.

The result was *The World and the Individual*, Royce's most comprehensive statement of his philosophical system. In keeping with the purposes of the Gifford Lectures and in line with his previous efforts, Royce examined the philosophical bases of religious belief and attacked the problems of ontology through a study of the structure of knowledge. There are, he discovered, three historical conceptions of being: mysticism with its idea of immediate being, realism with its idea of independent being, and critical rationalism with its idea of valid being. Finding these inadequate and self-contradictory, Royce proposed in his seventh lecture, "The Internal and External Meaning of Ideas," a fourth Conception of Being. Here he offered a further development and metaphysical enlargement of "The Principle of Individuation": "*What is, or what is real, is as such the complete embodiment, in individual form and in final fulfillment, of the internal meaning of finite ideas.*"[50] This doctrine is what Royce called his Absolute Voluntarism. He was the first and perhaps the only American philosopher to attempt a systematic and comprehensive statement of the nature of reality.

[48] *CG* (1897), p. 267.
[49] Royce to Mrs. Dorr, August 7, 1898.
[50] *WI*, 1: 339.

With *The World and the Individual,* Royce had, quite indisputably, earned a permanent place in the history of philosophy.

Royce emerged from the Gifford Lectures thoroughly, if not dangerously, exhausted, and consequently for several succeeding years he attempted only less taxing activities. Even before finishing the second series of *The World and the Individual,* he escaped for a brief vacation at sea, and after both volumes were safely published he deliberately avoided the clash of intellectual contests. In the summer of 1902 he taught at Berkeley under circumstances that assured his serenity, and in the spring of 1903 he took a sabbatical leave which he spent with his son Stephen traveling, visiting, and otherwise relaxing in California. Here his only tasks were the correction of proofs for *Outlines of Psychology* and a little private study of logic.

When indeed he felt fit for more rigorous work, it was logic that attracted him. His teaching during the preceding years signalled this shift in interest: in 1898 and afterwards, his seminar—Philosophy 20c—directed its attention to problems in logic; and in 1900, he began to teach, on a routine basis, a course first known as Philosophy 15, Theory of Knowledge, and later as Philosophy 8, Advanced Logic. When, in 1903, he was invited to deliver a series of lectures on metaphysics at Columbia, Royce proposed that the series be devoted to the relations between logic and metaphysics. The resulting lectures, given in February 1904, were on "The Comparative Study of Scientific Concepts," a topic closely related to the activities of his seminar. By 1905 his logical researches had advanced to the stage that allowed Royce to outline his System Σ in "The Relation of the Principles of Logic to the Foundations of Geometry."[51]

Despite the attractions of logic, Royce did not abandon his earlier philosophy; indeed his final period of growth was about to begin. During the summer of 1906 Royce taught a course in ethics for teachers in the Harvard Summer School. At that time his moral philosophy fell into a newly coherent shape, and after working on the plan a bit more he was again ready to offer a major book. He planned this one as a series of lectures for the Lowell Institute, delivered in November and December 1907; Macmillan published

[51] *Transactions of the American Mathematical Society* 24 (July 1905): 353–415.

it as *The Philosophy of Loyalty* in April 1908. Here Royce offered his most sustained ethical theory, arguing that loyalty is the ground of moral activity. But this was no new departure. Indeed Royce himself said that he had been teaching this doctrine to his students for years, and when he summarized it for his future daughter-in-law, he insisted that he had raised his children on it.[52] Readers of Royce's correspondence might note that he repeatedly uses the words, *loyal*, *loyally*, and *loyalty* in the most cherished and even consecrated contexts. Loyalty is in fact Royce's principle of individuation examined from the ethical viewpoint. His message is simply that to achieve moral individuality one must find his cause and be loyal to it. At a crucial point of "The Principle of Individuation" Royce says: "Be loyal, indeed, to the universe, for therein God's individuality is expressed. . . ."[53] Royce gave a clearer hint of this close bond between his metaphysics of the 1890s and his later ethics in responding to a criticism made by Frank Thilly. Thilly had been unable to understand why Royce thought that "loyalty to loyalty" was the summum bonum. Royce's answer was that loyalty is intimately related to "the very essence of self-consciousness. . . . It is only when loyalty takes on the 'reflective' form, as an essentially self-sustaining process, that it becomes at once truly universal and truly individual."[54]

Though *The Philosophy of Loyalty* testifies to Royce's continuing strength and originality, he confessed privately that he felt himself "passing into an early but a well earned obscurity of professorial old age."[55] This feeling of depletion may have been related to a family crisis that was developing: his eldest son, Christopher, was suffering from a serious psychological disorder. Christopher had always been regarded as a strange and friendless boy who often embarrassed his parents by giving Cambridge subjects for gossip. Definite signs of illness had appeared before 1907, and in January 1908, Christopher was placed in Danvers State Hospital where he was to spend the remaining two and one-half years of his life. He died of typhoid fever on September 21, 1910, only a few weeks after the death of William James.

Despite the pain of losing both his son and his best friend, Royce

[52] Royce to Elizabeth Randolph, November 16, 1910.
[53] *CG* (1897), p. 268.
[54] Royce to Thilly, November 17, 1908.
[55] Royce to Deakin, April 18, 1908.

could not let himself be diverted from serving his cause. He had once remarked to James that he loved life for "its general meaning."[56] Merely living, for Royce, was not sufficient, striving to understand life was his special vocation. By the summer of 1911, he was busy again, assembling a collection of essays, *William James and Other Essays on the Philosophy of Life*, writing the Bross Lectures, *The Sources of Religious Insight*, and planning three other books–a treatise on logic, a volume on the "Art of Loyalty," and a new religious philosophy.[57] He had been given the Walter Cabot Fellowship for three years and so could look ahead to a period of sustained effort. By January 1912 he had decided to take a sabbatical leave during the next academic year and to give a series of Lowell Lectures on the "Vital Features of Christianity." Though his active life was momentarily called into question in February when he suffered an apoplectic stroke, the hemorrhage proved to be fairly slight and the resulting convalescence actually stepped up his schedule for publication. By June, the writing was well under way, and arrangements had been made to give the first eight lectures to the Lowell Institute and the entire series to the Hibbert Foundation, at Manchester College, Oxford. Incredible though it may seem, Royce–fifty-seven years old and recovering from apoplexy–produced *The Problem of Christianity* in less than a year.

If *The World and the Individual* was Royce's most comprehensive metaphysical treatise, *The Problem of Christianity* was the climax and coalescence of his life–personal, social, and intellectual. Once he described his book as a record of experience and reflection.[58] Certainly, his delving into the meaning of the Community and the Spirit had their beginnings in his childish wondering about his first home in California and in his earliest resistance to his parents' Protestant zeal. Ralph Barton Perry, who remembered him as painfully lonely, anxious and awkward in human relationships, suspected that Royce's celebration of the Beloved Community was a theoretical adjustment to a deeply personal problem.[59] It is possible also that Royce's reinterpretation of Pauline Christianity in terms of social ideals was, to some extent, a response to

[56] Royce to James, September 12, 1900.

[57] Royce to Brett, [August, 1911?].

[58] Royce to Miss Calkins, March 20, 1916.

[59] *TCWJ*, 2: 266; see also Perry's *In The Spirit of William James* (New Haven: Yale University Press, 1938), pp. 32–38.

America's Progressive Era. Some critics had assigned to him the unflattering reputation for being an academic snob who persistently remained aloof from social and political questions.[60] It is true that, before 1907, Royce tended to view contemporaneous events and movements with either irony or dread, but beginning with *The Philosophy of Loyalty* and thereafter he explicitly recognized and insisted that systematic thought must respond to social issues, must contribute to the social order. Finally, the stimulus of Charles Peirce had its culmination in *The Problem of Christianity*. Royce and Peirce had been friends and sometimes antagonists in various enterprises since the late 1870s. A severe critic of *The World and the Individual*, Peirce found Royce's logic "most execrable" and charged that the Absolute was "only God in a Pickwickian sense, that is, in a sense that has no effect."[61] Royce, in response, reread Peirce's early essays, and finding the logical theory of interpretation, saw how it might be enlarged and adapted to his metaphysical system. This theory gave Royce his "new growth"; set forth in Lectures XI–XIV of *The Problem of Christianity*, interpretation not only joins the individual to the world, but unifies all men in the Beloved Community.

By September 1913, with *The Problem of Christianity* published, Royce was prepared to give his full attention to the long-delayed treatise on logic—a plan that was again postponed and finally abandoned after the events of the summer of 1914. He had gone to Berkeley in July to teach in the summer school and participate in the twenty-fifth anniversary of the Philosophical Union. Planning his series as a further development of *The Problem of Christianity*, he gave six lectures on "Communities of Interpretation" preparatory to his Union Address, scheduled for August 27, on "The Spirit of the Community." After August 4, however, when the German army crossed into Belgium, spreading war throughout Europe, Royce set his prepared lecture aside and wrote *War and Insurance*. The earliest events of the war seemed to illustrate the inherent dangers in dyadic relationships. Royce saw that so long as peace depends on harmonious relations between individual states the security of the world will always be in danger; only when individuals are joined with communities in triadic relationships can peace be

[60] John Jay Chapman, "Portrait of Josiah Royce, the Philosopher," *Outlook*, 120 (July 2, 1919): 377.

[61] Peirce to James, June 12, 1902, *TCWJ*, 2: 425; see also *PC*, pp. 276–77.

preserved. Fascinated by the peculiar triads of the insurance business—relationships involving insurer, insured, and beneficiary—Royce proposed a scheme of international insurance. Though the specific plan has always been regarded as extravagantly impractical, the foresight of Royce's general principles is recognized implicitly in the charter of the United Nations.

From the first, Royce's view of the war had been emphatically philosophical and nonpolitical, an attitude that he maintained throughout most of the next academic year. Despite a cooling in his friendship with Münsterberg, who, suspected of being a German agent, had become a superpatriot, they remained cordial toward one another.[62] After May 7, 1915, however, when a German U-boat sank the *Lusitania*, Royce, no longer nonpartisan, told his classes and insisted publicly that the war was not a struggle between the Allies and the Central Powers, but between Germany and humanity. From this time until his death sixteen months later the conflict became his daily obsession. His physical deterioration was rapid, and his early death was supposed by many to have been hastened by the torment that the war caused him. Those who had known him in earlier years were stunned during the following spring to see him weakly and distractedly making his way across the Yard.[63] By summer he required close attention, and before the end of August he could not leave his bed. The final period of illness lasted only three weeks; he died at home on September 14, 1916.

He had been born at a time when America and the world were about to experience great changes. In 1855, when Walt Whitman published the first edition of his *Leaves of Grass*, Karl Marx was studying economics at the British Museum, Otto von Bismarck was proving his abilities in his first diplomatic post at Frankfurt, and Abraham Lincoln was emerging as the leader of the antislavery elements in America. In the following year Lotze began the publication of *Microcosmus*, and three years later Darwin turned the world around with the *Origin of Species*. Royce grew up at a time of turmoil and novelty, when the men who owned the railroads ruled America, when other men built universities and made philosophy. Like his biblical namesake, Josiah Royce taught the old ideals

[62] See Daniel S. Robinson, *Royce and Hocking—American Idealists* (Boston: Christopher Publishing House, 1968), p. 152.

[63] Horace M. Kallen, "Remarks on Royce's Philosophy," *Journal of Philosophy* 53 (1956): 132–33.

to a generation of idolaters and died in battle with a foreign enemy. Shortly afterwards a young Austrian soldier named Wittgenstein imprisoned near Monte Cassino wrote a book he later published as *Tractatus Logico-philosophicus*. The war had closed one era of thought and opened another.

Yet despite the changes of philosophical fashions, Royce remains a profoundly engaging thinker. To be sure, his appeal no longer issues from his construction of grand metaphysical systems or his lavish, exhortative style of writing. Each generation must redefine the significance of the past. Royce's significance today, I believe, lies primarily in his demonstration of the fast bond that holds individual men to the common body of humanity. His doctrine is the old, familiar, but sometimes forgotten one that no man is an island. Whoever we are, whatever we may hope to be, Royce teaches, our being derives from the community of which we are members. The institutions that give us selfhood are not mere aggregates of individuals, not impersonal machines, but organic beings; quite literally they are persons, and through interpretation they form the unity which St. Paul called the Body of Christ and which Royce calls the Beloved Community. Crucial to this central feature of Royce's thought are the processes by which the human self is given life, interprets its meaning, practices loyalty, and struggles to fulfill its purpose in the whole of humanity. In this sense Royce was fundamentally a humanist whose dying hope was that "humanity might be awakened, unified, strengthened in spirit, brought together in brotherhood."[64] His hope is still unfulfilled; but if he spoke the truth, there is no other salvation.

[64] Royce to Cabot, April 21, 1916.

The Letters

Part I

1875-1882

Part I

1875-1882

This section of Royce's correspondence begins with his graduation from the University of California, covers his periods of study in Germany and at Johns Hopkins, and follows him on his return to Berkeley as an instructor in English. It ends as Royce is preparing to take up his first appointment at Harvard.

He is nearly twenty when we first meet him and not quite twenty-seven at the end, but the qualities that he reveals in these early letters persisted throughout his life. Ambition, fear of loneliness, devotion to ideas, and hatred of materialism are the moods that Royce repeatedly expresses in his letters to Gilman, Coale, James, and Lanman.

Perhaps the most notable feature in this group of letters is the intellectual growth that it records. Two main subjects competed for Royce's attention: romanticism and the theory of knowledge. They were his past and his future, his youthful attraction to literature and his abeyant commitment to logic. Seeking to understand the former, he became gradually reconciled to its influence. But through the latter, he made his way out of scepticism, beyond critical philosophy, and toward a new form of idealism. What is the structure of knowledge? How is experience possible? What are the logical conditions of error? These are the questions that Royce begins to ask in these letters, questions that form the background of *The Religious Aspect of Philosophy*.

To Daniel Coit Gilman, June 14, 1875[1]

Oakland, June 14, 1875

President Gilman

Dear Sir

I have now $500 promised me for my European expedition and expect $500 more without much difficulty. I will leave here, if nothing prevents on Wednesday June 30. I will take the German Line of steamers to Hamburg, and thence to Heidelberg, where I shall stay till I have decided upon my University. I suppose of course you will have left for Europe before I come East. If you have any word to leave me, I can of course get it there, at your New York address. I am in good health, hopeful, and a graduate of the University. Your influence in getting me this assistance[2] is

[1] ALS. Gilman Papers. JHU.

[2] The identity of Royce's sponsors and the arrangements for the assistance—whether a grant or a loan—are not precisely known. It has been suggested that Royce's year of study in Germany was facilitated through the receipt of a fellowship, but this term does not, in a strict sense, seem to apply. Apparently Gilman appealed to certain San Francisco or Oakland businessmen from whom Royce received the money. It appears also that Royce arranged with *Overland Monthly* to obtain additional resources through the sale of articles.

going to be the making of my whole life. You have all the thanks I can give for it, you may be sure.

I remain very respectfully

Yours truly
J. Royce.

To Daniel Coit Gilman, July 11, 1875[3]

Brooklyn N.Y. July 11, 1875

Pres't Gilman

Dear Sir

Your note has been received. I am at present stopping here, having arrived in New York during the past week. I am well and quite as far advanced in every way as I expected. I expect to set sail for Europe by the steamer *Klopstock*, of the Hamburg Line, next Thursday. I will thence proceed directly to Heidelberg, and will remain there some time. I will write you again as soon as I reach there, and give you my exact address.

I left a second article in the hands of Mr. Fisher[4] when I left home. He expected to have it published in the *Overland Monthly* for August. He has given me encouragement to hope that I may get an article into that magazine as often as once in two or three months. Personally however he will probably not remain much longer on the staff of that paper, as he intends going to Europe soon.

With respects and sincere thanks for your interest and aid I am

Yours truly
J. Royce.

[3] ALS. Gilman Papers. JHU.

[4] Walt M. Fisher, ed. *Overland Monthly* (1874–75). Royce published two articles in *Overland Monthly* in 1875: "The Aim of Poetry," 14: 542–49; "The Life Harmony," 15: 157–64.

To Daniel Coit Gilman, December 11, 1875[5]

Leipzig, Dec. 11, 1875

Pres. Gilman:

Dear Sir

As you asked me to do, I write you a word as to how I am now getting on. The principal thing to say is that German, still retaining of course plenty of difficulties, has lost most of its terrors, and I now feel somewhat at home. I am taking some eighteen hours a week of lectures in the University, am a member of a "*Philosophischer Verein*," understand the most of what I hear in both places, have plenty to read, all I have time to see and hear, and am withal very comfortably housed during the winter.

The weather has been quite cold, snow having set in earlier, I am told, than is usual, and frost having been constant for some time past. My own health has been quite good until during the past week I was troubled with cold. That is now past, and I feel as well as ever. The chief trouble before me is the immense amount of work to be done.

I have learned from California that the succession of commercial misfortunes there keeps money at such high demand that it is just now impossible to send me any more from there. I have received no remittances therefore as yet from any quarter, and am now nearly out of money. Even my last article in the *Overland* remained unpaid, though I have received word that they will send me when they can.[6]

So far I have attempted no writing here. I cannot tell when I shall try, and am perfectly willing to wait for time to show me. As for further movements, I think it quite possible that I may go to Göttingen in the Summer, to hear Lotze in Philosophy. If I stay another winter in Europe, I hope to spend it in Berlin.[7]

If there is any sort of service I can do for you in Leipzig with the

[5] ALS. Gilman Papers. JHU.

[6] Royce had apparently not yet heard that *Overland Monthly* had ceased publication with the December issue; the eclipse lasted until 1883.

[7] Royce abandoned this plan in favor of entering Johns Hopkins University in the fall of 1876.

facilities here offered, I shall be very glad indeed to do it. At all events you may know that I am studying under as advantageous and as comfortable circumstances as possible, and am disposed to keep on as long as I can.

I am, With Respect
Yours Very Truly
J. Royce.

To Daniel Coit Gilman, February 2, 1876[8]

Leipzig, Feb. 2, 1876

Pres. Gilman;

Dear Sir,

I have to apologise for not writing immediately on receipt of yours enclosing the draft. The reason was that at the same time I also received news from home of serious sickness there, that of my sister. I feared that I might hear even worse news from there, and still further feared that, if the result were fatal, the fact that my mother would be left nearly alone might require me to alter some of my plans. In view of this it seemed best to wait before writing to you.

I have however received further and more hopeful news, so that in all probability no immediate change in my circumstances is apt to follow from anything in that quarter. So I write in more certainty than I would have done some time since.

I was very much obliged for the remittance, and hope to be in position to make it all good before more than a few years are past. I find all the advantage you had predicted in being able to think and study without the immediate pressure of work for my living upon my hands. But still I think that no great length of time can elapse before I will find the inclination to publish coming again, and then I shall certainly try. It is nevertheless a great task to be struggling with the thought of a foreign nation which has done so much work in so many departments as has this. It takes time, and it keeps one from thinking so much for himself. To be sure, what thinking he

[8] ALS. Gilman Papers. JHU.

does is better than it could otherwise be, but it is done much more slowly.

You ask me still as to my plans. I told you in the note I wrote some time since that I shall probably leave this University for perhaps Göttingen in March. The precise line of study which I shall follow in the next Semester is a little undetermined as yet, and will no doubt depend on the lectures which are advertised. The matter stands about thus.

Finding the language very soon no longer a serious obstacle to understanding lectures on philosophy, I dropped the special exercise work on that sooner than I had intended, and have been passing my time in hearing lectures, in reading the German and English magazines at the *Lesehalle*, and in the further reading of Spinoza and Fichte, in their originals. Thus I have begun to make headway in the History of German Philosophy, and also to get the first shadowy outline of that immense mass of learning and discussion, *contemporary* German Thought on philosophic subjects. In my lectures I have taken most especial interest in *Wundt*, the new member of the philosophic Faculty, formerly Professor at Heidelberg, the author of a prominent work on *Physiological Psychology*, and perhaps the first of the psychologists of Empirical tendencies in Germany at the present time.[9] I am hearing a course from him in Logic. In this more specially philosophic branch he has not yet written much, but he is understood to be a "man with a system," in Metaphysics as well as in Psychology.[10] So in him I have a thoroughly live man, and one who will quite possibly make a powerful impression on the thought of the next decade or so, for he is still in his younger prime.

I would gladly then hear him for another Semester. But I have a strong desire to hear *Lotze* at Göttingen, a professor who seems generally acknowledged as the first in constructive philosophy now living in Germany. He also has done much in Psychology, but his school is more traditionally German than Wundt's, and certainly with more of the Idealistic tendency in it. Now this next summer will be a very excellent time to hear him, especially as Göttingen is a place at which I ought to pass at least one semester while I am in

[9] Wilhelm Wundt, *Grundzüge der physiologischen Psychologie* (Leipzig: W. Englemann, 1874).

[10] Wundt's major philosophical works appeared in the decade following: *Logik* (1880), *Ethik* (1886), and *System der Philosophie* (1889).

Germany. So, in case he advertises promising courses, it seems very probable that I shall go there.

But there is still another chance which may take me away from here, and that is my desire to hear *Kuno Fischer*. If he advertises one or two first rate courses, and Lotze does not, I may quite possibly return to Heidelberg, instead of going to Göttingen. And it is still further possible that if no promising courses are offered in either place, and *Wundt* is again very prominent on the Catalogue, I may remain still here. Much therefore you see, depends on the University Calendar, especially as my courses must influence my reading considerably.

So much then for the present. I have much more that I could say, but I am afraid of wearying you. I shall at least keep you informed of my whereabouts—

With obligation I am

Yours Respectfully
J. Royce.

To Daniel Coit Gilman, July 17, 1876[11]

Göttingen, July 17, 1876

Pres. Gilman

Dear Sir:

I shall endeavor to be in Baltimore by the middle of September. Exactly when is rather more than I can determine. I think it quite possible that I may take the steamer from Bremen to Baltimore. I may also go over [to] England, and I may take the French line. I shall aim however not to be later than at least a week or ten days before the first of October.

I shall bring my little collection of books with me, order two or three German periodicals to be sent to me, take care not to lose my *akademische Hefte*, and so shall be "armed," I hope for what I am to do during the coming year.

With many thanks for the Circulars, I remain

Very Respectfully
Yours Very Truly
J. Royce.

[11] ALS. Gilman Papers. JHU.

To William Torrey Harris, January 4, 1878[12]

Johns Hopkins University,
Baltimore, Md.
Jan. 4, 1877. [1878]

Mr. W. T. Harris,

Dear Sir;

I send by express to your address this day a transcript of an essay of my own "The Ethical Studies of Schiller."[13] The essay was read a short time since before the Johns Hopkins Philological Association; and at Pres. Gilman's advice I take the liberty of asking you if you can make any use of the manuscript for the *Journal of Speculative Philosophy*. The subject is of course no new one; yet so far as I know there is no very extensive literature in English treating of it. In any case, Kant's influence on German Literature is a topic, it seems to me, that would bear much discussion.–If you would encourage the idea, I should like also at some future time, to offer an essay on the philosophic studies of Novalis, in which I should seek to discuss Kant's influence on the early Romanticists.[14]

I hope I do not trespass upon your time too much in thus addressing myself to you without having had the pleasure of a previous introduction. After all it may not be unwelcome to you to hear a word of the philosophic studies that a few at the Johns Hopkins University are engaged in; even though you may not find worth in what I herewith send.

Believe me Sir,

Very Respectfully
Yours Truly
Josiah Royce,
Fellow in Philosophy,
J. H. U.

[12] ALS. Harris Papers. USC. Printed in facsimile in *RLE*, pp. vii–ix; printed also in edited form in "Josiah Royce's Letters to William Torrey Harris," *Philosophical Forum* 13 (1955): 80; reprinted in Daniel S. Robinson, *Royce and Hocking–American Idealists* (Boston: Christopher Publishing House, 1968, pp. 128–29. The date, 1877, is emended to 1878 on the MS in another hand; the contents of the letter are consistent with the emendation.

[13] "Schiller's Ethical Studies," *Journal of Speculative Philosophy* 12 (1878): 373–92; reprinted in *FE*, pp. 41–65.

[14] Apparently this essay was never written, though Royce did discuss Novalis briefly in *SMP*, pp. 177–80.

To Charles Rockwell Lanman, June 6, 1878[15]

June 6, 1878

Dearest Guru[16]

I am so sorry that at the moment I cannot answer your two charming and benevolent and jolly letters as they deserve. I write this to let you know why—I am *nämlich* just off to Wash. for a day, leaving early tomorrow. Examinations all done, I think passably well done.—I shall hear more soon. I shall write you in some two or three days a *long* letter. Ever so much thanks to you & the Professor for kind words & thoughts & offers. More as to my plans in my letter.

Yours Ever
Josiah

To Charles Rockwell Lanman, June 11, 1878[17]

Baltimore, June 11, 1878

Dearest Guru

As I promised you in the postal card of last week, I am taking an early opportunity to express myself at length to you on many subjects. What I say is of great importance, and I hope you will pay attention. First as to the world. My system of the foundations of all things is now prospering.[18] It is highly approved by Porter, and, in another form, by Morris.[19] The latter sends me a letter stating that

[15] APS. Lanman Papers. HUA.

[16] The Sanskrit word for *spiritual teacher*, somewhat playfully applied since Royce studied Sanskrit under Lanman at Johns Hopkins, beginning in October, 1876. See Hugh Hawkins, *Pioneer: A History of the Johns Hopkins University, 1874–1889* (Ithaca: Cornell University Press, 1960), p. 88.

[17] ALS. Lanman Papers. HUA.

[18] Reference to Royce's dissertation, "Interdependence of the Principles of Human Knowledge" (Ph.D., 1878).

[19] Noah Porter, president of Yale, and George Sylvester Morris, professor of modern languages and literature at the University of Michigan. In absence of a regular teacher of philosophy at Johns Hopkins, Porter and Morris, who served also (after January, 1878) as lecturer on the history of philosophy and ethics, were Royce's doctoral examiners.

he has read my examination-paper with more interest than he would feel in reading a novel, and that it only depends on the efforts of such to make great things happen in American Philosophy. So my degree is about settled.—I am not at all vain. I do not say this to glorify myself, Oh no. I only want to prove to a Sanskritist such as you that there are more things in heaven and earth than are dreamed of in Böhtlingk's Crestomathy,[20] or in the noun-system of all the Rig Vedas this side of the infernal regions.—The degrees will be formally announced, in all probability, sometime this week. So finishes my work in this city for the present. For the rest I am going to stay during part if not all of next week, and then leave, I know not whither.—Next then as to my money–affairs. I am very much vexed that I am not rich. But in fact I am as poor as one wants to be. The present result is this. On the receipt of your letter, I was struck by a very wicked thought. As known I have $30.41 of yours in my possession. I had engaged to put this sum in the hands of your banker or Mrs. Egerton for you.[21] Now however your letter offered me a loan. And I found myself after paying pressing bills very short. If I had put the money into Mrs. Egerton's hands I should have not a cent myself left. So I thought thus: I will keep my Guru's money for that he is a hard master, always sowing his doctrine and his cash where there is not the faintest possibility that he should ever reap, I will keep his money for a few days, till my arrangements for the Summer are made. Then I will restore him his own, and beg his forgiveness. This wicked thought having seized me, I did as I was moved by the Devil, and have kept it till now. Meanwhile however I went to Gilman and stated the case of my needs for the summer. He has promised to do something for me, and I yet await the result. Now, though this is all wrong and contrary to my engagement, I hope you will forgive me for a few days, since I do not intend to trespass on the kindness you have shown at all, after I have once been assured of means to get through the summer, and shall return, I still hope, your loan before leaving Baltimore. Nor do I want, if that can be helped, to borrow anything of James. He is very kind, but I must not trespass, as I am always so apt to do, on people's good will.—This is all now important as

[20] Otto von Böhtlingk, *Sanskrit-chrestomathie* (St. Petersburg: Eggers & Co., 1877).

[21] Mrs. DuBois Egerton kept a frequently celebrated boardinghouse for Hopkins students, bachelor faculty, and Baltimore townspeople.

to this matter. I should like to know one thing from you still: How much is summer-board in New Haven?—I come now to still another point, viz. your kind suggestion to Prof. James,—and his and your kind suggestion to me, as to publication in the *Atlantic Monthly*. There are one or two things to be considered. First, within two or three years that magazine has printed some able articles on the Romantic School from the pen of Boyesen. Maybe they would not like to double. Tieck and Novalis were treated at length and appreciatively. What have I to add that would interest the readers of the *Atlantic?*—One thing however could be done. Boyesen did not treat Heinr. v. Kleist. I might add to his my work on this, and perhaps also on the other *Spätromantiker*. If it is thought worthwhile I should be glad to work up my material anew for this end. Are you writing to James? I shall write a short letter to him immediately on finishing this to you, but I do not know that I care to mention the matter just now to him, since he has said nothing of it to me. I will wait, and see if he mentions it to me. Gilman was kind enough to mention my name to *Scribner's* a short time since, *a propos* of my *first* lecture on the Romantic School as a whole. He received a favorable reply such that he has advised me to work up the lecture into an article for presentation to them. As soon as business is over and he has time, he will no doubt be able to pay a little attention to the subject.[22] Thus much therefore for this.

You have spent so much time in your two notes on poor me, that most of my answer is taken up you see with discussing the same insignificant foam-crest among the world-waves. I crown my sins by mentioning one more topic bearing in the same direction, viz. my work for the summer. *Maybe* I shall go to California. Nothing certain as yet however. If not, I want to prepare an essay of length and ambitious plan, on the Teleology of Plato in the later history of Thought (i.e. in modern times). I must also break ground for Herder, who is to form the subject of my next year's lectures. Hence, you see, the Adirondacks would not be healthy for my ends, excellent a thing as James' company would be. I should like to meet him somewhere for a while however.

[22] The articles on the Romantic School proposed for the *Atlantic* and *Scribner's* never appeared, but Royce did publish rewritten portions of his lectures on romanticism in the *Californian* and in the *Berkeley Quarterly* (1880–81). Most of these were reprinted in *FE*.

Now to approach nearer to you. I know you do nothing whatever but sit up all night and read proofs. I know you torture the printers insufferably, and that you think that they have nothing else to do but just to get out your essay. But this has no bad consequences in itself. I do not regret this youthful enthusiasm. I would rather encourage it. But one thing I would recommend to you. I fear that in this mass of inflections you are forgetting the truly and substantially Uninflected of which divine philosophy treateth. In other words you are forgetting to *think*. You were once trained to *think* in a certain class of young students of Schopenhauer, who sat at the feet of a venerable and penurious instructor.[23] I fear you are forgetting. Spend some two hours a day in *thinking*. Stand on your head if you would be saved, or stand in any other philosophical position, and *think* of *das reine Sein* of *die vierfache Wurzel*, and of

Yours Ever
J. Royce.

To William James, June 11, 1878[24]

J. H. U., Balt., June 11, 1878

My Dear Professor James

I have left yours of May 22 sometime unanswered, chiefly because I wished to be able to state the results of my examination, which was just on hand when yours was received. This is now a thing of the past. There is so far no official announcement, only a semi-official statement to the effect that all is right. Prof. Morris of Ann Arbor, the examiner in the main topic, writes to express his general satisfaction with the answers. If he is satisfied no one else will object. The examination was fair, but lengthy—all full of such requirements as: Give some account of Spinoza's doctrine of God & World; or of Plato's Dialogues; or of Aristotle on time, space, matter, motion, & the infinite; &c. Now I am through I will not complain.

For yourself I have only congratulations and best wishes.[25] Might

[23] I.e., Royce himself who taught a course on Schopenhauer at Johns Hopkins in 1876–77.

[24] ALS. James Papers. HL.

[25] This evidently refers to James's engagement to Alice Howe Gibbens. They were married on July 10.

all who philosophize do as well. On the whole however philosophy is a cold business. The world despises the man who engages in it, and he has to do his best to try to return the compliment. This is impossible. So he has to try the other plan and idealize the world. This ends in over-coloring and resulting disappointment.–Such is the "eternal process" of speculation.

For the summer I have no definite plans as yet. I much regret the causes which prevent you from carrying out your original kind intention of inviting me for a visit. I still hope to be able to meet you for at least once during the vacation. I doubt however about the Adirondacks,[26] much as I should enjoy a stay there & especially in good company. I have some work to do that requires libraries more than mountains to help it out. And then since I should be almost sure to take a certain new *Erkenntnisstheoretische Logik* by one [Wilhelm] Schuppe, and the new book of Shadworth Hodgson's[27] with me in any case, it is quite obvious that I should be, under the circumstances simply insufferable company. When a youngster will talk metaphysics the best thing to do with him is to shut him up by himself, or find some place where the people are as mad as he. And you, this summer, so I judge, will be remarkably sane.–I shall write again before leaving Baltimore to let you know what becomes of me.–I am

Yours Very Truly
Josiah Royce

[26] I.e., where the Jameses were to spend their honeymoon. The illness of James's sister, Alice, forced him to cancel an invitation to Royce to visit the James family in Cambridge.

[27] *The Philosophy of Reflection*, 2 vols. (London: Longmans, Green and Co., 1878).

To Daniel Coit Gilman, July 1, 1878[28]

Brooklyn, July 1, 1878

Pres. Gilman,

Dear Sir,

I have but just received today a letter from H. Stebbins,[29] dated S. F. [San Francisco] June 19, and containing the information of a "vacancy in the department of English Literature," with the request that I should undertake to fill the same. The position is described as "very eligible," as "affording advantages for philosophic studies," and as giving a salary of $1200. "Earnest hope" is expressed that I may accept. If I do so I am expected to appear in August at the University of California.

I regret that there was delay in the receipt of the letter, as I now have less time for decision.

Shall I trespass upon your time too much by appealing thus directly to you for advice?

My address for the next few days will be "care A. D. Savage, 303 E. 17th St., New York."[30]

I am Sir
Very Respectfully
Yours Truly
J. Royce

[28] ALS. Gilman Papers. JHU.

[29] Dr. Horatio Stebbins (1821–1902), minister of the Unitarian Church of San Francisco, one of the founders of the University of California, and member of the Board of Regents. The Regents' Minutes of August 7, 1878 show approval on that date of the request of the Stebbins Advisory Committee that Royce be appointed Assistant under the Professor of English Language and Literature.

[30] Alexander Duncan Savage (1848–1935) was a Fellow in Greek at Johns Hopkins and a close friend of Royce. Although there is clear evidence of a correspondence between Royce and Savage, none of the letters has been located.

To Daniel Coit Gilman, July 16, 1878[31]

Baltimore, Jul. 16, 1878

Pres. Gilman

Dear Sir

I have sent my written acceptance of the offer of Dr. Stebbins, and am now in Baltimore packing up my books. I may remain here for some two weeks. When I leave I shall go by way of New York, stopping at Buffalo, where I have friends to visit, and at one or two places further west. I want to go through St. Louis, and in particular to meet Harris. I should be much obliged if you could find it convenient to give me a letter of introduction to him. I think some acquaintance with him might be of advantage to me.

In my letter of acceptance I asked for an advance, and hope what I receive will be sufficient to enable me to pay up all arrears before leaving.

I thank you for the offer of letters to New Haven. I have already made a visit there. I spent the 4th in company with Dr. Lanman, and had the privilege of seeing Pres. Porter for a few moments. I shall not be in New England again, I think, before I go.

I leave Baltimore and the University with many regrets. They have been busy and profitable years, these last two, and your encouragement and advice have been throughout of the greatest help to me. I shall never forget the interest you have shown in my not very wise efforts to make a career to suit myself, and shall always be conscious how little I should have made of it all without your direction and assistance. May I someday, by means however insignificant, be able in some slight measure to repay you.

My address remains, until the 1st of August, here at the University in Baltimore.

Very Truly Yours
J. Royce.

Pres D. C. Gilman.

[31] ALS. Gilman Papers. JHU.

TO WILLIAM JAMES, JULY 16, 1878[32]

Baltimore, July 16, 1878

My Dear Prof. James

I write you this short note in some haste to let you know that my plans, such as they were, for the immediate future, are somewhat changed. I have received a call ($1200) to the University of California, Dep't. of English Literature. They will no doubt let me teach a little philosophy if I want, yea, study some even, if I give word to nothing atheistic in the presence of Freshmen. So, after asking advice from Pres. Gilman, I have resolved to go, and am now in Baltimore, packing up.

I am sorry. I shall be still more isolated there, and shall have to part with many good friends on this side. I shall be especially sorry not to see you for a good while. Your interest has encouraged me a great deal. I hope you will not forget me, but will drop me a line or two now and then.—After all I doubt whether I can endure the (metaphysical) climate of California for more than some two years. I shall grow consumptive (spiritually) and shall come East for my health. May the shade of good father Kant grant that I come not too late for recovery.

My address until Aug. 1, will be here at the University in Baltimore. Thereafter I can be reached at the address "University of California, Berkeley, Alameda Co., Cal."

Yours Very Truly
J. Royce

TO DANIEL COIT GILMAN, AUGUST 11, 1878[33]

Sunday, Aug. 11, 1878

Dear Sir

I leave Baltimore tomorrow, going by way of New York, Buffalo, Chicago, St. Louis, &c. to California. I have been detained

[32] ALS. James Papers. HL.
[33] ALS. Gilman Papers. JHU.

some two weeks longer than I had wished; but that is not at all surprising under the circumstances, and I am quite content. Dr. Stebbins finally sent me an advance of $300, telegraphing the same to New York. This sum will not after all be too much in view of various purchases that I must make before leaving, and I hardly see how I can pay anything now on my debt to the University, although I had wished to pay at least a part immediately. Of course it is not safe to travel without some surplus in one's purse. I shall try to settle my account as soon as possible after reaching Cal.

Please remember me to Dr. Adams.[34] I regret that I cannot meet you and him before leaving. Please accept this as a farewell greeting.—Please remember me also to Mrs. Gilman. I should have enjoyed much an opportunity to bid a personal farewell to you all; but a visit to New England would be now out of the question.—Many thanks for the encouragement and advice of your last letter.

Believe me Sir

Yours Very Truly
J. Royce

To Daniel Coit Gilman, September 16 1878[35]

Berkeley, Alameda Co. Cal.
Monday, Sept. 16, 1878

Pres. Gilman,

Dear Sir

I make with this letter, as it were, my first report to you from my new station. For I feel that you are about the only person who has so far followed me enough to make it possible for me to report on new conditions in their relation to past endeavors.

My new work is not, so far, very uncongenial; but it is for all that not exactly what I should choose as other than a preparation for more special tasks. I instruct the 3d & 4th Classes in Rhetoric, Composition, & Literature. The classes are attentive, and at moments quite bright; but their wants are very elementary, and the supplying of the same more of a strain on the patience than on the intellect.

[34] Probably Herbert Baxter Adams, the historian, and not Henry Carter Adams, the economist, who was in Europe during the summer of 1878.

[35] ALS. Gilman Papers. JHU.

—I have arranged with Prof. Sill[36] (who has done everything to smooth the way for me at the first) for the giving of a dozen lectures, to the Senior Class, on Philosophy.[37] These lectures will strain all my resources in the directions of brevity, clearness, and original work, and I look forward to the undertaking with no little interest. If I succeed I shall do myself much more good than I shall the class. Even if I make no success of it, the students may yet carry off a trifle of logic, or at least a few bits of useful terminology; and the effort will at all events do me no harm.

I received a note from Harris the other day, promising me that my Schiller-article shall appear in his October number.—I met him in St. Louis as I passed through, and have to thank you for a very interesting interview obtained through your introduction.—I shall make further efforts towards publication soon.

I doubt if Philosophy is destined to succeed well in California, or Literary Criticism either. If I want to continue my worship at these two altars I must make a pilgrimage again someday.

I find affairs at my home quite satisfactory; with one exception, the permanent ill-health of my father, now quite advanced in years. He has long been in failing strength.

Hoping you will remember me to all my Baltimore friends as you may meet them I remain

Very Truly Yours
J. Royce

To George Buchanan Coale, September 16, 1878[38]

Berkeley, Alameda Co. Cal.
Monday, Sept. 16, 1878.

My Dear Mr. Coale:

I have been intending for some days to write to you, but the

[36] Edward Rowland Sill, poet and professor of English literature at the University of California. As instructor in the Department of English Literature, Royce worked under Sill's direct supervision. Despite some evidence of a Royce–Sill correspondence, none of the letters seems to have survived. For Royce's indebtedness to Sill, see the letter to J. B. McChesney, April 6, 1887, and also *SMP*, pp. 465–67.

[37] The lectures, later reduced to a series of ten, were given during October, November, and December.

[38] ALS. Redwood Collection. JHU.

right moment would not come. The new duties are not very light; and at first they leave one but few spare hours.

I have thought of you and your household often since I left Baltimore, as you may well believe. I come among old associations here, and near to my home; but I cannot replace you, nevertheless. Here in the University I am after all much alone. It is not what it used to be when I was a student. The classmates are scattered, of course; and to be an instructor is to look on old scenes through new glasses. My own students are plastic, sometimes bright, often amusing; but they are no companions. The members of the Faculty are cordial enough; but all old teachers are self-absorbed men, with plans of their own. And I have plans of mine too, of course; and so we live for the most part to ourselves, each as happy as he finds it convenient to be, and without much love for communion with the others.

Perhaps if my studies were of a more sober cast I should feel more at home. But these studies are you know fantastic in nature; and one wants a little encouragement sometimes in the cultivation of the right kind of fantasy. This one lacks in California. The aims of the Californian are like the Coast Range hills in the regions where, for the most part, our immense wheat-crops are raised. They are I mean not lofty, and, left to themselves, rather barren. Take sufficient care to cultivate them aright and you shall have as return bread and butter in plenty, but nothing beyond.—I feel a trifle pessimistic about it sometimes; not I hope through personal discontent, but only or mainly on account of our future as a State. Civilization sends us out here to solve a great problem: i.e., how two races and civilizations can be accommodated side by side. And we fall to stock-speculating and wheat-raising, and leave the problem to the political hack and the strong-lunged agitator.[39]

Social life is not very active in Berkeley. The town itself is very small. Oakland, three miles away, has a good deal of all sorts of life in it; it claims in fact to be the Athens of California. So it is, if the anxiety to see and to hear some new thing be a test. The Athens however lacks so far its Pericles, its Socrates, its Phidias, in fact all its list of great names from Solon on. It also lacks both wit and

[39] Among evidences of social unrest in California during the 1870s the so-called "Chinese question" was perhaps most serious. In mentioning politicians and agitators, Royce apparently refers to the head of the Workingman's Party, Denis Kearney, and his followers.

wisdom in the ranks of the common people. But there are very pleasant people in it nevertheless, if you know where to look for them. At best however we Californians make but poor figures in our daily walk and conversation. Foundation for higher growth we sadly lack. Ideals we have none. Philistines we are in soul most thoroughly. And when we do talk, our topics of discussion are so insufferably finite!

So especially while I am absent from home, I have much occasion to let my thoughts wander back to Baltimore and you. Perhaps I am somewhat impressible, being young; but I did find you all very inspiring. I hope you will not let me drop out of mind.—That you have not entirely as yet I judge from the *Nation*, which I already begin to receive, and which I attribute to you. Many thanks.

In conclusion a few words as to matters external. My journey was prosperous, and not devoid of some little adventure. The great sights I enjoyed better than before; and the fine air of the summit of the Rocky Mts., the grand cliffs of the Wasatch Range in Weber and Echo cañons, the overwhelming, breath-checking sublimity of "Cape Horn," are all now impressed on my memory as they were not previously.—Home I found peaceful and happy, my Mother unchanged and as well-pleased to meet me as mothers usually are under such circumstances, my Father in poor health, but full of welcome for me.—My sorrow it was that I had to leave almost immediately for my new work.

But I must close. Please write me as soon as you feel ready.

Yours Very Truly
J. Royce.

P. S. What I had no room to write at the end of my letter I add here; viz. that I wish earnestly to be remembered to all the family, and feel some little regret that in the present stage of Evolution it would be impossible that my remembrances should be conveyed to the kitten, whom, in her own playful little place, I do likewise look back upon with regrets.

J. R.

To Daniel Coit Gilman, November 27, 1878[40]

Nov. 27, 1878

My Dear Pres. Gilman

I have been intending to write you for some weeks. I have been waiting until I could report some progress in my work. Even now I have not much to tell. Such as it is I let you know of it.

My chief undertaking so far has been a course of lectures on philosophy (mentioned to you last time as already planned). I enclose a copy of my Program. The course was intended to comprise what seemed to me most important as an introduction to the problems of philosophy. The division of problems may seem a little whimsical; but it represents genuine opinion on my part, and could as I think be justified.[41]

With the lectures, so far as they have been given, I am not discontented. With their success I am discontented; for they have not had

[40] ALS. Gilman Papers. JHU.

[41] A printed program and fragments from this series, entitled "Introductory to Philosophy," are preserved in the Royce Papers, HUA, vol. 58. In a prefatory note Royce remarks: "In substance they were an extension of the conclusions of the degree-essay.—The course was dialectically a tolerable success & pedagogically a monstrous failure." The program reveals the following divisions of problems:

Analytic Philosophy
- 1st Series: Logical:—
  - a. The Logical Analysis of Trains of Thought.
  - b. The Logical Analysis of Judgments.
  - c. The Simple Forms of Proof.
  - d. The Methodical Operations of Reasoning.
- 2d Series: Epistemological:—
  - a. The Philosophic Definition of Nature.
  - b. The Conditions of a Possible Knowledge of Nature.
  - c. The Principles of Knowledge.
- 3d Series: Dynamical:—
  - a. Knowledge as a Subjective Product.
  - b. Knowledge and a Sceptical Analysis.
  - c. Knowledge as found in the Individual Judgment.

Synthetic Philosophy
- 4th Series:: Dynamical:—
  - a. The Nature and Forms of Synthetic Thought.
  - b. The Principles of Knowledge as Syntheses.
- 5th Series: Cosmological:—
  - a. The World in the Synthesis of the Individual.
  - b. The World in the Synthesis of the Universal.

much. At the utmost a half-dozen students have followed with any very lively interest. Of these two or three have been really helped. As to the others, I cannot hope that I have done them much good.

As for my work in general, though it is not absolutely useless, I constantly doubt whether it is very effective for good. I do not find it irksome; but the air is not very enlivening here for University work, especially in the line of philosophy. And philosophic study is still my best beloved pursuit. I regret all the hours that are not in some way devoted to it or to that kind of study of literature in which I made a beginning last year in Baltimore. And the Freshmen here will not endure much of such subjects; nor the Seniors either, for that matter.

Prof. Sill is the one man to whom I can talk about the University. Every other lives in another planet. I should perhaps except Putzker, whose wisdom is however revealed mainly in single disconnected flashes. Slate is away in Europe.[42] Everybody else is friendly; but no one of the number except the aforesaid can tolerate any metaphysics.

I am in short a trifle isolated, as you said I should be. I must move on to some other spot on the planet after a year or two. For it will not do for me to give up my studies.

As for publication, I am about to propose to Harris to furnish three or four connected articles to his *Journal*.[43] If he encourages me, I shall be able in the course of a year or so to have something of definite character in print.

I am very much obliged for your kindness in sending the various printed slips to me.—I must apologise for the fact that through an error for which I am responsible my German papers have continued to come to my old address in Balt. I hope this will now soon cease to be the case; as I have notified my bookseller in Leipzig of the change.

Hoping to be remembered among my old friends in Baltimore, and especially by you, the oldest one I have there, I remain

Yours Very Truly
J. Royce.

[42] Albin Putzker (1845–1923) taught German at the University of California; Frederick Slate (1852–1930) was professor of physics.

[43] These articles were never printed in *Journal of Speculative Philosophy*, nor does the Royce–Harris correspondence suggest that the proposal was actually made.

To William James, January 14, 1879[44]

University of California
Berkeley, Alameda Co., Cal.
Jan. 14, 1879

My Dear James:

That I have not written you for so long a time is quite inexcusable, but not quite inexplicable. I have not had much to say; and I was not anxious to waste breath or ink or time on telling "first impressions" about my new position out here. My first impressions have passed away now, and I have quite a settled opinion of the place and opportunities about me. My settled opinion is that the place might be worse, but is execrable as it is; and that for the sake of the study of philosophy I had better look elsewhere if possible.— But all that by the way. Now for an apology.

I received your last favor, dictated to an amanuensis whose acquaintance I felt much honored in making.[45]—As nearly as I can now recollect, I was then on the point of leaving Balt. I put off an answer (in which I had intended to send my best wishes for future prosperity and long life); but resolved to write within three days. But my preparations, and my journey, and then the many duties of one who comes home and takes a new position and teaches strange pupils &c. all at once, all these things have kept a barrier between me and my correspondence which has made me fail in many duties. —I hope to do better again. Accept then my long delayed thanks and good wishes, and bear with me while I discourse yet again on my present position.

There is no philosophy in California. From Siskiyou to Ft. Yuma, and from the Golden Gate to the summit of the Sierras there could not be found brains enough [to] accomplish the formation of a single respectable idea that was not a manifest plagiarism. Hence the atmosphere for the study of metaphysics is bad. And I wish I were out of it.

On the other hand I am at home, and so among good friends; and further, as to my work, I am entirely free to arrange my course as I please, and to put into it a little philosophy. Thus, during the

[44] ALS. James Papers. HL. Partly printed in *TCWJ*, 1: 780–81.
[45] I.e., Mrs. James, who frequently served as her husband's amanuensis.

term before Christmas, I gave a course of ten lectures on philosophy in general, to our Senior Class. This term I have a Freshman Class in elementary Logic, and propose one short course of lectures to the Seniors on Modern Thought, and one longer course (an enlargement and partial rewriting of one I gave in Baltimore) on Romanticism in German and English Literature during the present century. All this I try to work up as best I can, using the sources as much as time and circumstances allow, and cultivating a certain kind of originality to perhaps too great an extent. I trumped up a theory of Logical Concepts last term and preached it to the Seniors. It was a kind of hybrid of Hume and Schopenhauer, with an odor of Kant about it. It was somewhat monstrous, and in this wilderness with nobody to talk with about it, I have not the least idea whether it is true or not.—Meanwhile I am trying to write an article or two. But I don't know what will come of them.—Of Libraries I have access to one very tolerable one in S. F., and to the University Library, which is small but useful. And I buy what new books are necessary myself.—The disadvantages are therefore not without mitigation. But they are disadvantages; and could I control a fair living anywhere nearer the heart of the *Weltgeist*, I should certainly be ready to change my place of living.

Harris, as you may have noticed, was good enough to publish an article for me in his October number. Now he wants me to write a short review of Shadworth Hodgson. I am willing—the flesh is, I mean—but the spirit is weak. I think the public ought to "honor" Sh. H. "with silence" (as Kant in the *Prolegomena* thanks it for having done to him), until *The Philosophy of Reflection* has been better digested. For it is no book of a day, that work, I am sure.—

I read your "Brute and Human Intellect"[46] with very great interest. It had something the same effect upon me as had Lessing's *Laokoon* when I first read that work: the effect I mean of immediate conviction, in so far as the conclusions reached were definite. But I don't know how soon I may be ready to change the standpoint.

I heard from Balt. a while since to the effect that you were certainly coming there to lecture.[47] But again, quite lately, Prof.

[46] *The Journal of Speculative Philosophy* 12 (1878): 236–76.

[47] James was forced to decline an invitation to lecture at Johns Hopkins in the spring of 1879 when the Harvard Corporation refused to appoint a substitute for his courses in anatomy and physiology. See Jonathan I. Cope, "William James's Correspondence with Daniel Coit Gilman, 1877–1881," *Journal of the History of Ideas* 12 (1951): 620.

Morris[48] had to announce (in a letter to me), greatly to his own regret he said, the fact that he heard you were not coming after all. He knew no reason. How is it, if I may know?

There is nothing more to say now I believe, except to beg you to write soon, just to comfort me with a metaphysical word or two. Please remember me to Prof. Child.[49]

With best wishes for yourself and yours I remain

Yours Very Truly
J. Royce

To Daniel Coit Gilman, January 26, 1879[50]

Jan. 26, 1879

My Dear Pres. Gilman,

Since my last writing I have made progress in some few things, though I have, after all, not much to relate. For this term I have planned and am now delivering a brief course of lectures on the modern thinkers from Des Cartes to Kant. Prof. Sill has in addition kindly granted me some of his time in literature with the Junior Class, that I may read them later in the term a revision and partial reconstruction of the course on the Romantic School that I gave at Baltimore. The new course is planned at ten lectures. I shall leave away many of the details, and add at the beginning a sketch of the beginnings of Romanticism, of the influence of Herder, Goethe, and Schiller &c, and at the end a continuation on Romanticism in England, & on the effects of the Romantic school on Southey, Scott, Coleridge, Shelley, Byron &c. All must be very brief; but I shall try to make the whole matter as plain as possible, and shall go to the sources rather than to the critics in so far as I have time and the books.

48 George Sylvester Morris, the philosopher, or Charles D'Urban Morris, the classicist. Since both were members of the Johns Hopkins faculty, they are sometimes confused. Royce seems to have maintained close relations with both, but none of his correspondence with either seems to have survived. For Royce's comment on C. D. Morris, see his letter to Gilman, March 29, 1886.

49 Francis J. Child (1825–86), was the great Harvard medievalist and intimate friend of James, had lectured on Chaucer and Shakespeare at Johns Hopkins in 1877 and 1878.

50 ALS. Gilman Papers. JHU.

This term I am taking my two Freshman sections through a course in Logic (Thompson's Outlines).[51] The Freshmen complain that the matter is very dry; but they are already beginning to wake up to ask of their own moving such questions as: "Can we think without language?" So I have some hopes for them.

I need not say that I am still restless. I am writing some, and have a long article nearly finished on the "Principle of Philosophy"; though I begin now to have scant hope that even Harris will be long-suffering enough to print it.[52] But the climate here is a very bad one for philosophizing. I live comfortably indeed; though I have made few new acquaintances, and have by no means kept up the old ones in all cases. Prof. Sill has been the means (as I suppose) of introducing me into the Berkeley Club, in which I have already passed a number of delightful evenings.[53] Even the Berkeley Club however is suspicious when it comes to metaphysics. And everywhere else philosophy is regarded as a kind of harmless lunacy; and this goes far to make me no patriotic Californian.

I received a letter the other day from Mr. Meyer,[54] asking for payment of my note of Jun. 19 '78, with the interest up to the present date. I regret very much not having been able to remit before, and do not well see how, with present demands, I can well remit for two or three months to come. I suppose, since the note continues to bear interest until paid, that it will be possible to let the matter remain as it is for awhile. I write to Mr. Meyer to that effect at the same time that I send this. If it is very important, I

[51] Probably William Thomson, *Outline of the Laws of Thought* (1842). With second and subsequent editions, title changes to *An Outline of the Necessary Laws of Thought: A Treatise on Pure and Applied Logic* (1849).

[52] Retitled as "Of the Will as the Principle in Philosophy," this article was submitted to the *Princeton Review*, but never published. See letter to Gilman, March 26, 1879. MS in Royce Papers, HUA, vol. 79.

[53] The Berkeley Club was a lively town-gown organization founded by President Gilman in 1873. It had semi-monthly dinner meetings at which one of its twenty-five members would read a paper. Royce was elected to membership on September 26, 1878, and served as secretary during the academic year, 1879–80. His autograph notes on the meetings are in the Berkeley Club Papers, UCB. During his active membership, Royce read papers on "The Practical Significance of Pessimism" (April 24, 1879), "Some Illustrations of the Structure and Growth of Human Thought" (January 8, 1880), "George Eliot as a Religious Teacher" (February 10, 1881), and "Evolution in its Relations to Philosophy" (December 1, 1881). After moving to Harvard, he resigned on November 26, 1882, and was elected to an honorary membership.

[54] Charles J. Meyer, assistant treasurer at Johns Hopkins.

can no doubt raise the money immediately; but it would give me some trouble.

About our University affairs I have little to relate. We have, as you know, our new buildings before us, and see fewer blank spaces as we look about. In the University life there is little to bring us together, and every man pursues his solitary way, much as if he were the only instructor in Berkeley. Prof. Moses is trying to form a Social Science Club, with fair hopes of success.[55] Someday I shall undertake to form a metaphysical club,[56] and may in that case perhaps succeed in hiring the janitor to join in case he is not obliged to keep awake. Many other members I should not find.

With kind remembrances for all Baltimore friends I remain

Very Truly Yours
J. Royce.

To Charles Rockwell Lanman, January 26, 1879[57]

Jan. 26, 1879

My Dear Lanman

That you were once very angry with me I know; but all that has now passed away, and you have entirely forgotten me. Look in your copy of your Petersburg Lexicon however, taking proper care of the buffers; and you shall find, on page 12, 416, 319 (I believe that's the one) of vol. 10, a little finger-mark I once left there when I visited you. I did not touch the book. I never did that; but I believe I looked crosseyed at it from the other side of the room one

[55] Bernard Moses, professor of history, organized the Fortnightly Club which launched, in 1880, *Berkeley Quarterly: A Journal of Social Science*. The journal, which lasted for only two years, published four articles by Royce: "The Nature of Voluntary Progress," 1 (July 1880): 161–89; "Natural Rights and Spinoza's Essay on Liberty," 1 (October 1880): 312–16; "Before and Since Kant," 2 (April 1881): 134–50; and "Pessimism and Modern Thought," 2 (October 1881): 292–316.

[56] This was never done, but Royce did, with the cooperation of E. R. Sill, organize the Psychology Club in November, 1880. The Club accepted members from the University of California faculty, alumni, and advanced students. Royce served as secretary until his departure in 1882 and occasionally presented papers: "The Scope and Study of Psychology" (November 10, 1880), "Intellect and Intelligence" (March 4, 1881), and "Association of Ideas in the Light of Theory and Experience" (March 4, 1882).

[57] ALS. Lanman Papers. HUA.

day, when the mentioned page was open; the result was the aforesaid finger-mark. Look thereat and remember me.

I have not forgotten you however, nor that I am in debt to you for much good advice, and much care over the quantities of my vowels and some cash. The latter debt has been largely the cause of my delay in writing. I wanted to remit you the sum as soon as I could, and I have kept hoping to be able to do so. But small as the sum is I have been cramped so that even now there are some payments pressing, and I am afraid I cannot send you the money until near the end of the academic year, i.e. by the first of May. You said once you would not absolutely need it till you went abroad as you expected to at the end of the present year at Baltimore. I am very sorry for the delay.

Of myself I need not say much. I lecture Californians on metaphysics all I dare. But they are a bad audience. I would most as soon lecture an audience of Sanskritists on the same subject. I am among old friends; but I am lonely, and wish myself once more off. I study hard, and teach Freshmen. That is all; except that I write a good deal.

I heard through Brandt[58] the other day that you are all about as ever in B. That you yourself are working very hard and making a good name for yourself I should know in any case. I wish sometime you would write me a little; for I should be delighted to hear from you.—Tell Savage I have forgotten all about him, even his name; but I think him a fine fellow for all that, and wish he would write. I wrote him once; a very nice letter I think.

But I am very busy. I shall write more another time

Yours Affectionately
J. Royce.

To Daniel Coit Gilman, March 26, 1879[59]

March 26, 1879

My Dear Pres. Gilman

It is high time that I answered your last very kind letter. I find

[58] Herman C. G. Brandt, associate in German at Johns Hopkins, was a member of the *Kneipe* which included Royce and Lanman.

[59] ALS. Gilman Papers. JHU.

writing to friends in the world beyond the very best method of freeing oneself of the mental stiffness that constantly creeps over us inhabitants of Berkeley.

I am at the moment over the ears in preparation for my Literature course on the Romantic Movement. I shall, I find, have to reconstruct my old lectures almost entirely. My views have not much changed; but my purpose in this course is different from my purpose last year in Baltimore. I shall go over more ground, and put in less minute shading. I begin with Rousseau and his effects on his contemporaries, and end with Shelley and Byron. In doing this I have to take much at second hand, of course; but I try to do as thorough and conscientious work as I can.

Meanwhile philosophy is not left out of sight. My long article on the "Princ. of Philosophy" I sent, for a trial, to the *Princeton Review* instead of to Harris. To the latter I have not written for a good while; because I want to send him a good article, and have not been able to get it ready. From the *Princeton Rev.* I have as yet received no answer. As soon as my literary course is finished, I shall return, thirsty and half-sick of shadows, to good substantial metaphysics again. I hope I may accomplish something more during the spring.

My class-room work has been after my own heart this term, in so far as that was at all possible. Yet I think that my good Freshmen would gladly exchange me for any other instructor in the world, if so be [sic] they might rid themselves of Logic. So sad news it is to most people to learn that they have minds and ought to use them.—

One trouble I meet with here, as was natural. I am an object of disgust to certain people, especially because I persist in doing what is not required of me. I suppose that is taken as a sign that I am unable to do what is required of me. Then some people who knew me as a Freshman, are disgusted yet more to see that I am not a Freshman still. To grow is something of a crime in the eyes of the stocks and stones that have attained their growth. Nor are there lacking certain students who are displeased, not because they have less brains, but because I have less years. You see they are kind enough and sensible enough to be enraged at the more easily curable defect; and for this they ought to be praised.—I mention these things not because they are important, but merely for the sake of giving you a total impression of the state of my feelings as well as of my head. Sometimes, with the strongest enthusiasm, it waxes a little ill about the heart, and I would willingly throw everything overboard and run away into a corner for the rest of my days.—Yet the people who are kind are very kind. Witness Prof. Sill, who has done much more for me than I could well tell.—But you wonder mayhap that I speak only of myself, and say nothing of University affairs. But in fact one knows very little here about the affairs of anyone but himself, or of any department but his own. I attend Faculty meetings but seldom, and seldom find myself lifted nearer heaven when I do.

The State is in the heat of contest on the Constitution-question.[60] That the proposed Constitution is bad, seems certain enough. But that does not secure its defeat, in fact rather recommends it to a large class of voters. If I were to vote, I should certainly not hesitate as to my side; but I fear that between delay and want of interest in politics, I have lost my opportunity. It would be my first vote, and like enough my last—not that I am intending to die, but that I am unable to warm with any patriotic fire in these days of political masquerades.

—I thank you much for the little prospectus of the Summer School of Philosophy at Concord.[61] I know not how the plan will succeed, since I have of course no knowledge of the resources and organizing skill that may lie behind. This I know however, that if the plan succeeds in very truth, the result will be an Eden revived again for five weeks. I am overcome with envy when I think of it.—The names look well, certainly. Have they ever before tried just the same experiment?

Please remember me to all the friends, and believe me

Very Truly Yours
Josiah Royce.

[60] The California State Constitution was ratified by a slim majority of 10,000 votes in a popular referendum and went into effect on July 4, 1879.

[61] The Concord School of Philosophy (1879–88) was a curious assemblage of latter-day "transcendentalists" (e.g., Emerson, Bronson Alcott, F. B. Sanborn, T. W. Higginson), St. Louis Hegelians (e.g., W. T. Harris, Denton J. Snider, Samuel H. Emery, Edward McClure), and more distinguished intellectuals (e.g., Benjamin Peirce, Noah Porter, James McCosh, G. H. Howison, G. S. Morris, William James, etc.). Royce, it appears, never participated.

To Charles Rockwell Lanman, May 15, 1879[62]

Berkeley, Cal.
May 15, '79.

Dear Guru

I have been detained from writing to you. I send herewith an Order for the amount of my old debt. I beg a thousand pardons of you for my delay.

I think a good deal of Baltimore, and every now and then I think of you, and what a good fellow you are; and now and then also I think of Sanskrit. I wonder how much I know of it now.—

But my business bears me even at this moment away. I thought I must write, even if only a word, to let you know that I thank you for all your kindness to me, and that I don't forget you.

I hope this reaches you before you leave for Europe, and that you will have a pleasant time abroad.

I should like to talk with you ever so much.

Remember me to Dr. Adams and to Savage & the rest.

Yours
Josiah.—

To William James, January 8, 1880[63]

Berkeley, Cal. Jan. 8, 1880.
10 P. M.

My Dear Prof. James

I have just come home, after reading a terribly dry and long-winded discourse on the relation of experience to thought at a meeting of a literary club whereof I am a member.[64] The thought occurs to me that I have not written to you for nearly a year, and that you have doubtless almost forgotten me. Since I am much impressed at the moment with the fact of the uselessness of trying

[62] ALS. Lanman Papers, HUA.

[63] ALS. James Papers. HL. Partly printed in *TCWJ*, 1: 783–85.

[64] "Some Illustrations of the Structure and Growth of Human Thought," read to the Berkeley Club.

to find a market for philosophic speculation hereabouts, I am all the more in the mood to think longingly of all eastern friends who love metaphysics. You will not be surprised that I forthwith set about the letter you see before you.

I read with interest and not without general assent the paper you published in the July No. of *Mind*.[65] I think there can be no doubt that before very long there will be enough written in the way of investigation of the structure of scientific thinking after the fashion wherein you and some others investigate it, to justify the application of that rough and cruel but natural term "school" to the style of thinking involved. I know that if you ever saw the term employed, you would be righteously angry. But then one might do worse things than to adhere to a rational and far-sighted tendency of thinking. And the distinguished marks of this school would be, I fancy, not so much a body of dogmas, as a disposition to inquire into two matters of which most of our scientific philosophasters never hear; viz. (1) What is the inner structure, the nature of thinking as a process of understanding things, and (2) what is the use, the inner and hidden motive, of making such assumptions as we are accustomed to make about the world of experience? Certainly the thinkers who first make molecules and then fall down in mute and holy reverence before the awful mystery of how the molecules ever could make them, are far from knowing what it is to cross-question consciousness with any real spirit in their questionings. If I understand you, it is such cross-questioning of consciousness which you want to have done.—Your Space-article in the J. of S. Ph.[66] was interesting if only it could have appeared in better company. For if there be anything appalling in later philosophical literature, I think it will be in the end the goodly company of opinions about the nature of space which the aforesaid journal is collecting. Opinions of California politicians about the nature of money are harmonious and consistent in comparison. I verily believe that space will yet be declared in that journal to be absolutely everything abstract,—position, negation, correlation, conjugation, polarisation, concretion, repulsion, and whatever else ends in *tion*. I am a little sorry your "Spatial Quale" was added to the list, though I have some movings to believe in it.—But in fact I know no

[65] "The Sentiment of Rationality," *Mind* 4 (1879): 317–46.

[66] "The Spatial Quale," *Journal of Speculative Philosophy* 13 (1879): 64–87.

problem so puzzling as this space-problem. The causality-problem is easy as compared to it. If Shadworth Hodgson would be good enough to express his great thoughts in better language, I am sure his last article in *Mind*[67] would be quite simple and concise, and would give a fair account of the chief points of difficulty in the causality-problem. But the space-problem, who shall master it? What is needed is I think this:—Someone must master the whole science of Geometry in its latest forms as well as in its long history. Then this same man must have complete control over physiological psychology. Then he must master all the uses that have been made of space-science as an aid to other sciences either directly or not directly dependent on it, and so come to see the true connection of geometry and logic, that matter on which F. A. Lange spent some of his latter years (v. the *Logische Studien*). Then he must have control of the philosophic literature about space from Zeno of Elea to Kant and the present day. On the basis of all this he must write a special treatise, say on the "Properties of Space," which shall develope the principles of a new philosophic science, a synthesis of all the previous material, an elaborate account of what is empirical and what is not empirical in our knowledge and application of space-properties. Give me ten years and nothing to hinder, and I will undertake that work myself. But I have neither the time nor the material.

You may want to know what I am doing in philosophic study. I am working rather slowly to be sure, but yet a good deal. I undertook last summer vacation to do some work on a logic text-book for one of my classes.[68] I made not much progress, becoming snarled on the principles between Lotze and some others. I have been obliged to spend some time on English literature, and have so lost some work. Meanwhile, feeling incompetent to do him philosophical justice, I have let my Shadworth Hodgson article lie unwritten. Getting more and more puzzled about the ways of human thinking, I have extended my study to mathematics, reviewing parts of the calculus, and dabbling in Modern Geometry and Quaternions. Perhaps I have done some scattering, but I could not help it. These things must be understood if I am to master thought-methods. Boole's Logic and Venn's *Logic of Chance* have come in

[67] "On Causation," *Mind* 4 (1879): 500–519.

[68] *Primer of Logical Analysis for the Use of Composition Students* (San Francisco: A. L. Bancroft and Co., 1881).

for a share of attention. Balfour's *Defence of Philosophic Doubt* I delighted in hugely, excepting only that much did not seem quite novel enough. We can all of us write something like that too. But it is a good book.—Just lately I have been reading Dühring's *Geschichte der Grundprincipien d. Mechanik*. And now I am projecting a book on the "Nature of Axioms." I am afraid that the publisher, like the book, is yet unborn.

Nobody really studies philosophy here. Metaphysically I am lonely. Socially I am well off, and am, among other things, engaged to be married. Yet for all that I know nothing that would hinder me from removing myself and all my prospects East in case I could get money enough on the other side of the continent to support myself and a home. I see no prospect of that however for a long time.

If you think it worthwhile to give me good advice, I shall be thankful for it. Ought I to write on the "Nature of Axioms," or on "Sh. Hodgson," or on both, or on neither? And is it worthwhile to discuss at great length the nature of the relation between the knowledge of the present and the knowledge of past and future? That is, is this problem as fundamental as I persist in believing that it is? Or do you, having convinced yourself about it, hold it to be not very fundamental or important? Maybe I shall not take your advice if I get it, but it will be welcome all the same.

Any further talk about the universe which may strike you as worthy of being wasted in a note to me, would be very acceptable to one as thirsty for philosophy as I am, in case you found time and inclination to write me at all.

I am
Very Truly Yours,
Josiah Royce.

University of Cal.
Berkeley, Alameda Co.
California.

To William James, June 7, 1880[69]

Berkeley, June 7, 1880
Alameda Co.
Cal.

My Dear James:—

I have done very wrong in not sending the portrait before. I can only plead that other things have kept me from writing a long letter which I had planned in which I intended to talk much of many things. As I thought everyday that I should soon be able to find time, I let one day after another slip by. Your note has determined me to send this answer right away, although it will of course find that you have already gone to Europe.

After much hesitation and time taken up with writing other things I have set about such a study of Hodgson as shall I think soon bring me to an article about him. Lately, in fulfilment of an engagement into which I had entered with the Metaphysical Club at Baltimore, I sent them an article on "Purpose in Thought,"[70] in which I discussed among other matters the nature of the Axiom of Uniformity, and for that purpose entered into a criticism of Hodgson's discussion of the matter. Now I am reflecting on the account he gives of the nature of succession in the chapter on "Presentation & Representation," and am reading again his logical chapter, "Percept & Concept."[71] My ideas get gradually clearer, and I think I understand him better than before. If you make anything by seeing him and talking with him about matters of difficulty, I shall be pleased to hear from you as to your success.—My present feeling concerning the *Philosophy of Reflection* is this:—In the distinction of "Primary, Reflective and Direct Consciousness,"[72] and in the immediate consequences of this distinction, the book seems to me perfect and unanswerable. A better account of the analysis of the meaning of the word existence, of the origin and

[69] ALI. James Papers. HL.

[70] Unpublished during Royce's life; included in *FE*, pp. 219–60. Royce's discussion of Hodgson's "The Postulates and the Axiom of Uniformity" (*The Philosophy of Reflection*, 2: 122–70) commands a major part of the essay (pp. 235–46).

[71] Vol. 1, bk. 2, chaps. 4–5.

[72] Vol. 1, bk. 1, chap. 2.

worth of the various scientific notions about it, of the work of science as opposed to that of philosophy, I never read. But one great unanalyzed notion seems to prevent this philosophy from being ultimate. The method of reflection pauses at one place, and is used no farther. In his satisfaction with having discovered the formal time-element in all consciousness, Hodgson seems to be willing to leave unanalyzed the nature of our knowledge of Past and Future. I say this, knowing that Hodgson himself would not plead guilty to the charge I make, but feeling that his whole discussion of the nature of succession is full of difficulties and not satisfactory.—In his analysis of what he calls *minima* of consciousness, Hodgson notes that in these minima there is already the time-element, already the rudiment of memory, already an elementary past and future. This I should willingly admit. I should at the same time call each one of these *minima* an ideally present moment, that is, a portion of consciousness that is not of necessity recognized as a present moment when it takes place, but that is capable of being so recognized. There is a succession in this moment, and the succession is present as such in consciousness. But the succession, if it contains the rudiments of a past and future is nevertheless, not otherwise than present, immediately given, undistinguished into a "was" and a "will be," but given as a direct perception of succession. Whether then consciousness comes to us or does not come to us primarily in the form of a series of present moments we are able, whenever our attention is aroused to regard any passing portion of the succession or "time-stream" as a Present, and to oppose it forthwith to a past that was and is no more, or to a future that will be and is not yet. We can cut up what Hodgson calls the continuous stream into disjointed bits; and then we have the singular result that when we do so, we have only one bit given to us at once. The whole stream is then gone as a stream, is no longer a datum, dissolves and vanishes. We hold in our hands one little present moment, and the past and the future are simply non-existent. Now, when we thus regard consciousness, the present moment is the only datum, how do we or can we know that there was a past at all, or that there will be a future at all? If the present moment is the only datum, is it not a pure assumption that there is any time-stream? Does not all knowledge of past and future resolve itself into this pure assumption?

To make clearer by example:—If the present moment is the only datum, then one can imagine a being created for one moment and annihilated the next. This being may be conceived as endowed with a perfect intelligence, manifesting itself for this once with perfect clearness. His content of consciousness may be any you please, so long as it involves either what we call conscious memory, or what we call conscious anticipation, or both. This being would believe that he had a past behind him, a future before him. He would be wrong. His past and his future would be baseless fancies. Yet his consciousness of past and future would not differ in kind nor maybe in precise content from my consciousness of past or of future at the moment of most vivid memory or of most careful foresight. If I can thus conceive his knowledge of past and future as wholly illusory, why may not mine be so too? In other words, what necessity is there in my supposed knowledge of past and future; what self-contained surety in my persuasion as to past and future, or as to the time-stream, or as to the supposed data with which I set out?

It would not do to answer that the present moment itself contains an immediately given succession, an elementary past and future. That is admitted. But the immediately given succession is not an immediately given knowledge that *a* has ceased to be, while *b* is and *c* has not yet come. When in a present moment I make three quick taps with my knuckle I have given directly a succession, one, two, three. But in this moment I have not given immediately with the second tap the knowledge that the first has ceased to exist. All the taps are given, together with the immediately perceived relation among them which I call succession. The data are simultaneous in so far as concerns their entrance into knowledge. It is an afterthought to say that in order for the three to have been in succession the first must have already ceased to be when the second came. For even so I know abstractly that the fifty-second hundredth of every second comes after the fifty-first and before the fifty-third hundredth. But to my consciousness three successive hundredths of a second are not successive in the sense that one ceases to be before the following one comes. The succession of the present moment is then indeed given, but it is not as given such succession as I believe to exist among the moments of the time-stream. For in that ideal succession, one moment ceases to be before the next comes. And if each is given alone, and all the others are not given, are non-existent, how can the time-stream be said to be a datum?—In brief then, I admit with Hodgson that there is the time-form in every present moment, that there are constantly given us what we may call momentary successions. But I deny that in this fact there is contained any justification for saying that Time, as a series of states, each one of which ceases to be before any other comes, each one of which exists alone while it exists at all, that Time as a stream is given or directly known at all. For the elementary successions of immediate knowledge are different, not only in quantity or duration, but in kind from the supposed successions of the time-stream as such. In the one, succession does not mean separation, in the other it does mean separation of one member from another so that the existence of one means the non-existence of every other. Where then shall we look for an account of our knowledge of past and future as opposed to the immediately given present? Hodgson would say still, as I suppose, in the time-stream itself. For my objection is after all only Ward's objection restated, and over Ward Hodgson triumphs without much apparent trouble to himself. To Ward's supposition of an Intuition as necessary to our knowledge of past, Hodgson replies[73] that all this depends upon an unwarranted separation of past and present. The time-stream is the datum. It is we who bring in our separations, who cut up the stream into moments, and then fail to find a bridge from one moment to another. The stream is continuous. Don't cut it, and then you will not be troubled about past and future. Present moments are not data as present, but constructions of our own.— So, at least, I now understand Hodgson, although on first or second reading, I confess I did not well catch his drift. But I am in no wise satisfied. Whoever was responsible for the cutting, the question is who shall now weave up the rope again? Nay, who shall create once more all the rope that has slipped away into nothing, leaving me this little present moment?—I admit that in our distinction of our present content of consciousness from an ideal past and an ideal future, both conceived as non-existent, we make the distinction with very varying degrees of clearness. But still we do in our thinking commonly distinguish & separate the two. How do we know about them? It is useless to say that distinguishing we ought not to have separated. This is only preaching on morals, not solving

[73] Vol. 1: p. 255. Hodgson regards the separation between past and present —and the whole notion of the 'present'—as "arbitrary and unphilosophical." He advanced this claim against William George Ward, "On Intuitions and on the Principles of Certitude," *On Nature and Grace* (London, 1860).

a problem. Now, at this moment, I do conceive, vaguely, confusedly, but really, of an indefinitely vast past time and future time, that are not data of immediate perception, that are not now existent, that seem not necessarily forced upon my knowledge as such and such in nature, but that must be conceived and validly conceived if I am to know a world, or to regard myself as in any definite place in life. Wherein the validity of these conceptions? Perhaps I ought not to have come to regard "now" as a datum separate from "then," but I actually have come to regard "now" as an immediate datum and so have separated it from "then." I ought not says Hodgson to have separated; for once I was happy in the possession of a time-stream not cut up into separates. I ought to return to it. So be it. But whatever I was, "now" I have come to separate present from past and to say, "what was is not now; what will be is not yet." "Well then," comes the critical query "how do you know that anything was, or that anything will be at all?" Hodgson does not, I claim, meet this query fairly or answer it with a proper appeal to "Reflection."—Yet the answer is near at hand. The past was and the future will be because what I mean by the past and what I mean by the future are in this moment, by an act of my own, by an act which I can experience but not describe, projected out of the present moment in that the present moment is declared to be present. Past and future are conceived for my consciousness here and now by an act occurring in consciousness, the same act by which the present content is declared to be present. Thinking a content of consciousness as present means setting it over against an ideal past and future, both themselves conceived as non-existent, but conceived also as standing in definite relation to this present. Our knowledge of past and future is the expression of an act wherein we postulate that an immediately given content of consciousness does not stand alone, but has definite relations to other contents not immediately given. Past and future are constructions of a present which becomes a present and not a mere content of consciousness in that it constructs them. They are projections of that whose nature it is to project them. They form the first and simplest case of an external world, postulated and given only in so far as it is postulated, not otherwise. And the validity of this knowledge of past and future lies in the fact that the postulate once made cannot be taken back. The postulating of past and future is the being certain of past and future. The purpose of thought in this postulate is to give significance to, or if you like to express the significance of the present moment. And the purpose in that it is made is accomplished. Belief in a past and future is the expression of a felt want. And the want is supplied by the expression.—But enough, I have been stating what may not be original, and what at any rate has been partly suggested by you and by Hodgson himself. I only carry out the principle of Reflection, and no doubt very badly. But, "it is a subject of which my heart" &c. This is my main objection to Hodgson's principles.—As to the Axiom of Uniformity, I think that a less important matter, but I think he is quite astray.—But it is a noble book, even if it is most unmercifully obscure in some places.—Of course I quite agree in the rejection of Ward's "Intuitions," &c.—

—But now for me. I am well, and pretty busy. I shall read during the larger half of my vacation.—Unless my salary is unexpectedly increased, I cannot well hope to marry for some time. Thanks for your kind wishes and interest.—Thanks also for the recommendation to the University of Minnesota. I doubt whether anything could come of it. I understand that positions there are very insecure, and that political influence is a very important aid in teaching the youth of that state. I dread political influence as I do dentists. I have heard however nothing definite, & I should surely jump at any good offer, especially if from nearer the world than California. —I think I mailed to you the other day a copy of an enormous diatribe of mine about the poet Shelley, which I wrote for a Club here, and printed in a young and sickly monthly called the *Californian*.[74] It was a weak essay enough, but the *Calif.* does not pay as yet for the manure that is put about its tender rootlets. One gives what one has; and I sent the journal to you to show you that I am not altogether lazy, even if results are not good, and to return in a very ill way your kindness in sending me your persuasive discussion about "Association."[75]—Better than the essay on Shelley will be, I think, a speculation about "Voluntary Progress"[76] which I shall have in the forthcoming number of the *Berkeley Quarterly* (a little journal printed by a Club of the Faculty here), and of

[74] "Shelley and the Revoluton," *California* 1 (1880): 543–53; reprinted in *FE*, pp. 66–95.

[75] "The Association of Ideas," *Popular Science Monthly* 16 (1880): 577–95.

[76] "The Nature of Voluntary Progress," *Berkeley Quarterly* 1 (1880): 161–89, reprinted in *FE*, pp. 96–132.

which I shall send you a copy. It has, this article, a little philosophic discussion in it.—

To Daniel Coit Gilman, September 5, 1880[77]

Berkeley, Sept. 5, 1880

My Dear Pres. Gilman

I do not write often, because I do not wish to talk too much of my numerous efforts and plans; and because I have little else than these to speak of. At Berkeley, as you doubtless know, we now live on in a very quiet way, without much to make us afraid, and also without much encouragement, kept alive by our own enthusiasm when we have it, and allowed to come as near death as we choose if we find enthusiasm irksome. The public says very little about us, and knows, I fear, even less. We do not very actively cöoperate, except in small bands. The Berkeley Club and our Fortnightly Club for Social Science, together with the "Chemical Association," and the Cal. "Academy of Sciences" seem to be the only organizations with which many members of the Faculty have much to do. The Fortnightly Club is just now reduced to an active membership of five or six, though we wish to have it larger.

It seems probable that I shall marry before very long. Waiting for a higher salary is monotonous, and not so far successful. The President informs me that I can without trouble be authorized to teach classes in philosophy, but that I should then have to add that work to my present work, and should get no more pay for the present. For the limit of our income is now nearly if not quite reached. Other things, a change of dwelling-place on the part of my Mother and Father, the fact that I shall in consequence be left alone, and that all things seem as favorable as possible, will tend to hasten my marriage. My father-in-law will be E. F. Head, at present Superior Judge of San Mateo Co. I do not know whether you ever met the family. They are old friends of Prof. Sill. I do not see that under the circumstances I should do well to wait, even if I marry with a debt on my shoulders. I shall hope to pay it nearly as soon as I otherwise could.

[77] ALS. Gilman Papers. JHU.

As for my studies, I understand philosophy better every day. At least I think I do, and am as enthusiastic as ever. Prof. Wm. James while in England this summer mentioned to Mr. Shadworth Hodgson some difficulties I had expressed in a letter to himself about certain obscure points in the *Philosophy of Reflection.* The result was that Hodgson wrote me a kind note, explaining my perplexities. I answered, asking for still more light, and yet await a reply. This very trifling matter pleased me much of course, for having nobody here with whom to discuss philosophy, I was delighted to have a chance of appealing by letter to a writer in whom I have long been interested. That I never wrote my intended essay on Hodgson, was the result largely of my failure to be sure at all points of his meaning.—I try in my philosophic reading not to neglect modern psychology altogether, though I am convinced that here one must specialize, and that he whose business is Theory of Knowledge, Metaphysics, and History of Thought will do well if he ever gets fair mastery of that department, and cannot hope to be a thorough master of experimental and of physiological psychology.—Next year, 1881, is the centenary of the appearance of Kant's *Kritik der reinen Vernunft.* I very much wish I had an audience here for a course of lectures and studies on Kant in his time and in ours.[78] I should greatly delight in going over the ground with that end. The years during which the critical philosophy grew, first in Kant's own mind, then in the minds of the public, are full of most suggestive problems and hints for our own age. And the coincidence seems odd that after just a century our philosophic thought is once more critical, and that Kant still means so much for us, while modern life with all its variety shows signs of being subject to many of the same problems that agitated that time. The discussion would need a much better hand than mine, but for my own sake I should like to attack it with that earnestness one never feels so much as when he is doing a piece of work for a particular audience. But though I may read about the matter, I have no hope of interesting any of my students in it.

You may be sure Sir that I remember Baltimore with delight,

[78] This opportunity materialized with the Kant Centennial held at Saratoga, N. Y., on July 6, 1881, to which Royce contributed his "Kant's Relation to Modern Philosophic Progress," subsequently published in *Journal of Speculative Philosophy* 15 (1881): 360–81.

and am greatly pleased with whatever news I receive of the doings at the University.

I am

Very Truly Yours
J. Royce.

To William James, September 19, 1880[79]

Sunday, September. 19, 1880.

My Dear James

I owe you a second letter for your kindness in giving me a sort of introduction to Shadworth Hodgson, from whom I received a very pleasant note. I answered him at great length as is my fashion when I once set about the business of writing.

For some time past I have been trying to get certain notions into shape so as to write them down for good. To be sure I have for a long time been working to the same end, only every new trial brings me against worse difficulties and into a bigger maze of puzzling questions. Yet I am as confident as ever, and think that before long I shall have done something worth doing. But I had better speak of my work in connection with what I have been reading of late; for I am still so plastic that the fashion and bent of my efforts must be affected with every new author, although my views such as they are, are stubborn enough.—To begin with, I have given up the work on Hodgson until I hear from him again, preferring rather to be set right by him than to compose a long criticism that might contain much misunderstanding. Devoting myself for awhile to psychological reading, I was gradually led back to old father Kant, whom I had neglected for a year or more. Him I now seem to understand much better than formerly, and I see much hope of a true advance in philosophy through a proper understanding and development of the critical thought. But I do not believe that people nowadays try the best way of developing the critical philosophy. At least I think that one way has been travelled long enough, until we have reached sufficient conclusions thereupon, and are in danger of being content with them; while in

[79] ALS. James Papers. HL. Partly printed *TCWJ*, 1: 787–89.

truth philosophy demands of us another and more difficult investigation in which as yet little progress has been made.

What I mean is this: Kant starts two great questions, one as to the objects (*Gegenstände*) and the limits of human knowledge, and one as to the structure of knowledge. The former question has been to my mind fairly settled in an idealistic sense. There are no "things in themselves," simply because the expression has no intelligible meaning. Consciousness knows consciousness. Thought is the elaborate restatement of experience. The world is the complex of the laws of succession of actual and possible experiences. Beyond consciousness there is nothing, just as beyond space there is no space, and just as there is no time out of the one true time. There may be untold forms of consciousness, but there is one *logical* condition of all existence, viz. consciousness. This is Hodgson's view,[80] and not his only. It is the outcome of the whole analysis of knowledge since Protagoras. The people who cannot understand it, and who quibble endlessly about "inner" and "outer," and the "double witness of consciousness to its own existence and to a world beyond it" and about the "veracity of consciousness" (as if that were in any wise in question) need not waste time in arguing about the matter; for they admit the whole point whenever they think. Every time one demands the "meaning" of a statement before judging of its truth he expresses his sense of the great fact that we conceive and assert only of what is in thought. So in that direction I think that we have very fairly exhausted the most important problems suggested by the *Kritik*. But another set of problems remains, suggested also by the *Kritik*, and still very far from solution. These problems are concerned with the structure of knowledge. The space and time problem is one of them. The whole question of the Kantian "Deduction of the Categories," and of the "Principles," especially of the "Analogies of Exper.," is here in-

[80] *The Philosophy of Reflection*, 1: 162–77. Hodgson concludes that the Thing-in-itself is a meaningless concept and attacks Clifford's mind-stuff theory. This discussion seems to have contributed towards Royce's " 'Mind-Stuff' and Reality," *Mind* 6 (1881): 365–77. Royce was clearly heading in this direction as early as October 1878 when he entered into his "Thought Diary" (Royce Papers) a proposal for an essay "*On the Problem of the Things in Themselves*": "An Introduction would start with Prof. Clifford's Article in *Mind*, and state the affinity of this with some other views, and its relation to the doctrines of Spencer, Lewes, & Hodgson, of whom the last-mentioned would be quoted as showing the nature of the problem most clearly in his treatment of it."

volved. Modern German Logic, Lotze, Sigwart, Wundt, Bergmann, & the others, and the efforts of such men as C. S. Peirce in his *Pop. Sc. Monthly* articles of two years ago, are labors in this field.[81] Your method of discussing psychological problems would make them a sort of propaedeutic to this deepest philosophic study. I say deepest; for to solve the problem of the structure of knowledge would be to gain an insight into everything in the range of philosophy.—Now here again I think that people are pursuing this study in too superficial a way. Everywhere one meets the question thus put: What relation in the structure of knowledge, does thought-work bear to the contributions of experience? This is a great problem, but it is not the deepest one. The deepest question is Kant's, how is experience possible? Only this question can now be understood better than Kant ever understood it. What is experience? A series of states of consciousness, known as a series. The definition has two parts. Experience is a series: that everyone admits. Experience is known as a series: that most writers regard as too simple a thing to mention. Yet just here is the kernel. How is a series of states to be known as a series? Tell us this and you have a philosophy. Leave this untold, and you stop half way. How is experience possible as a series of states known to be a series? So I put the case to myself, and here I make a beginning of all investigation.—My solution is in general something like this. For the series to be known as a series, each one of its states must know the others. But in each state only itself is given. Hence each state can know the others only by actively constructing or postulating them. Hence the series of states can be known as a series only through the conscious activity of each of its states or moments. Hence time as a series of states is never a datum, only a postulate or construction. Simple reception gives us no knowledge of anything beyond the present. Only spontaneity constructs the world in time.—Now this

[81] Lotze's *Logik* first appeared in 1843: it was revised in three volumes in 1874, a second edition of which was published in 1880. Christoph von Sigwart's *Logik* was published in 1878. Royce had heard Wundt lecture on logic in Leipzig in 1875–76; the first volume (*Erkenntnisslehre*) of his *Logik* was published in 1880. Julius Bergmann's *Allgemeine Logik* appeared in 1879. Peirce published six papers in *Popular Science Monthly* (1877–78) under the general title "Illustrations of the Logic of Science": "The Fixation of Belief," 12: 1–15; "How to Make Our Ideas Clear," 12: 286–302; "The Doctrine of Chances," 12: 604–15; "The Probability of Induction," 12: 705–18; "The Order of Nature," 13: 203–17; "Deduction, Induction, and Hypothesis," 13: 470–82.

looks very simple, but has in fact very far-reaching consequences. If experience is possible only through this constructive process, then what is the ultimate datum? Not matter, nor mind, not a series of experiences, not the distinction of object and subject, but just this: a moment of reception of some content, joined with a constructive act that postulates a world of other consciousness beyond the present data. Reception means a passive state of consciousness, construction an active state. An union of passion and action in one moment only, herein is contained all that we can think about the universe. Furthermore the world is not given as reflected in the minds of an indefinite number of conscious individuals; the ultimate units are not individual beings, but present moments, for each one of which the world may possibly be constructed in an entirely original way. And furthermore the business of philosophy is to find out first of all the forms of this constructing activity, the fashion in which each of these monad-moments builds up its world. These ways of constructing will be the highest principles of all thinking, whose truth is unquestionable, because they themselves produce all truth.

By analyzing these principles we should find, first the true categories; second the true difference between past and future, between presentation and representation, between space as an ultimate datum of feeling, and "figured space," as the mathematicians know it. For all these distinctions are not data, but constructions. Take away the activity of consciousness, and they all vanish. Alter this activity and they all change.—And finally, all these forms of activity appear as expressions of certain fundamental interests that we take in the world. In each moment we construct such a world because we are interested in doing so. The final basis of our thought is ethical, practical. These things are so because a given moment of activity must have them so. "Give me a world" is the cry of consciousness; and behold, a world is made even in the act of crying.—All this last which sounds so fantastical is not at all opposed to the work of science. Science expresses a particular kind of activity, especially distinguished by the ethical qualities of patience, self-possession, doubt, and universality of aim, coupled with much definiteness of construction. The difference between science and fanaticism is ethical. Else why prefer science?—Some of this you will, I think, agree with; some of it at all events I have learned from or through you; but I do not know whether you would approve of it when you saw it stated in full. I mean to state it.—One has hopes for modern thinking when one sees these many ingenious and incomplete efforts to escape from the dogmatism of science without dropping into the fashions of the orthodox. In the *Rev. Philos.* for Aug. I like the article of Tarde on "La Croyance et Le Désir,"[82] though I think the author does not understand the application of his subject to the calculus of probability.—Stirling's tirades about Kant in the *Journal of Spec. Phil.* please me somewhat,[83] though I think the author an offensive and quarrelsome old sinner, who after all does not know how to refute Kant, as who does but one who can understand more modern thought?—I have just read your article in the *Atlantic.*[84] Beware of *Grant Allen.* How he growls in the *Fortnightly*![85] How dare you be one of the flies to buzz around the great man's head as he sits at his vast task, and to seek to distract his mind. G. A. will come soon with a fly-driver in hand, and then away with you; while the master will sit absorbed as before in his vast task. Nevertheless you are meanwhile quite right of course, though that makes little odds to a Spencerian. There will come a reaction someday and that great man who has really done so much will be unjustly forgotten. And such is the result of having a school and of being worse injured by your disciples than by your enemies. Such an ill-natured storm of words as Allen's in the *Fortnightly* ("On the Ways of Orth. Critics") would ruin a man of less true importance than Spencer.

The fates will that I should marry quite soon, notwithstanding small salary. My future father-in-law is judge of the Superior Court of a county further south in this State, and having concluded to leave the old house in Berkeley vacant, invites the young people to take care of it for him, and to give him thus a good resting-place when his work permits him to rest. Therefore I am to be married by the early part of next month. Private lessons shall be given to increase my income a little, and on the whole I hope to be comfort-

[82] *Revue Philosophique* 10 (1880): 150–80; the article was continued in a later issue (pp. 264–83).

[83] J. Hutchison Stirling, "Schopenhauer in Relation to Kant," *Journal of Speculative Philosophy* 13 (1879): 1–50; "Professor Caird on Kant," *ibid.* 14 (1880): 49–109; "Criticism of Kant's Main Principles," *ibid.* 14 (1880): 257–85, 353–76.

[84] "Great Men, Great Thoughts, and the Environment," *Atlantic Monthly* 46 (1880): 441–59.

[85] "The Ways of Orthodox Critics," *Fortnightly Review* 28 (1880): 271–99. James attacks Spencer and Grant Allen for denying that individual men can be agents of social change; Allen's article is a slashing attack on Spencer's critics.

able. But there will be nothing to stand in the way of my leaving the state if I get enough salary to support housekeeping somewhere else. I am well content with the world and the future. My father-in-law is one E. F. Head, by birth, I think, a Bostonian. At all events he has relations there.

Your essay on the "Feeling of Effort" was duly received and greatly enjoyed.[86]

Many thanks.
—Yours Ever
Josiah Royce.

To George Buchanan Coale, September 23, 1880[87]

Berkeley, Sept. 23, 1880.

My Dear Coale

I was greatly delighted, you may be sure, when your letter came; and only the many other occupations of my time could have kept me from replying immediately. It does me good to hear of your life and fortunes, and I can assure you that my memory of your house and of your family and conversation remains yet vivid and pleasing. I sincerely hope I shall see you all again sometime, and renew some of the old talks. They were helpful to me in many ways. In the first place the men of your generation are now rare, and we young men meet you but seldom. By your generation I mean the men with the vivid sense and faith of and in the ideal value of life, as Carlyle and Emerson once taught that faith and sense, and as the whole generation of the Transcendentalists received it. We young men hear from our time no such doctrines preached. I know, as you used to say, that may be because there is no longer the need to preach and repeat what through Carlyle and Emerson has been made the common property of all; but I fear that we younger men have so much else to read and believe and puzzle over, that this heritage from the age of the Idealists comes to our minds in a very diluted, perhaps even polluted form. For my part I have needed the living man to help me in appreciating the meaning of this pure and

[86] *Anniversary Memoirs of the Boston Society of Natural History* (Boston, 1880).

[87] ALS. Redwood Collection. JHU.

hopeful spirit of faith, and in this way I owe you personally a good deal. Not that I am a disciple myself. The condition whose presence saves you, as you say, from Pessimism, is unfortunately lacking in my case; and though I am not properly a Pessimist, I am a dabbler in dangerous problems, and a very extensive doubter. But you emphasized, or at least greatly helped to emphasize for me one moment or element of the truth of which I sincerely hope never to lose sight. And for this I shall always thank you.

But of course beyond this I remember with gratitude the pleasant social entertainment of which I found so much at your house. And this too was helpful, and saved me from that plague of students, loneliness, and disgust with the world, and vague homesickness.

Your mention of books is interesting. I wish I had had time to read Mad. de Rem.'s *Memoirs of Nap.*;[88] but here are all the new periodicals to take up one's spare time, and there is old Kant, and there are the eternal philosophic puzzles and the strivings to get something completed that will do to print and be contented with, and there too is the work for my class-room, and finally there comes once and a while a club-paper, or something else of the sort: so that I may not read all that is interesting. By the way though, I did read quite lately a very interesting novel, viz. Blackmore's *Lorna Doone*, which I regret never having touched before. I suppose at your house they would regard me as benighted to have been so long ignorant of such a charming story; for doubtless you know all about it. But such am I that I let good novels unnumbered drift by while I pine away amid insufferably dry books, and never touch a new novel unless by accident, or upon being told to do so.—Thank you for your reading of my Shelley article.[89] I know but one or two other persons that have so far waded through it. Various things combined to make the poor thing more formless than by plan it should have been, and the whole was confused by declamation. The next thing I print shall be a model of simplicity, in diction and in whatever else was overdone and complicated in this article.

As for my fortunes here, I have been for some time past betrothed, and a fortunate turn of affairs has made my marriage possible sooner than I had expected to find it possible. The wedding-day

[88] Claire-Élisabeth Gravier de Vergennes, Comtesse de Rémusat, *Mémoires* (1879).

[89] "Shelley and the Revolution," *Californian* 1 (1880): 543–53; reprinted in *FE*, pp. 66–95.

is set for the second of October; so that not long after this reaches you I shall have ceased to be alone. My future father-in-law is a Judge of a County Court, is named Head, and is by birth and family connections a Bostonian.—As for the rest, my health and prospects seem good, and I know not that there lacks any cause wherefore I should not be for a while much happier than I deserve to be at all.

—You speak of this sad State wherein I had the odd fortune to be born. Alas, I know less of it than you do; for I have given up trying to follow its madness or to predict its behaviour. This I know, that this terrible Chinese question will be sooner settled by the street-cats of San Francisco, or by the sheep of the southern Sierras, or by the coyotes of our barren Coast hills, or by the wild asses of the Oriental deserts than by this blind and stupid and homeless generation of selfish wanderers who do the voting and talking for this part of America. To be sure our dangers are all remote. Of mobs and wars, or of any genuine Communism, or of anything but money-getting very actively pursued, have you just now no fear so far as California is concerned. The Californian is a businessman, and in business he is very shrewd. He will protect his property, and quell disturbances; and unsatisfactory laws will remain inoperative or be repealed. But meanwhile the evil gathers, and just what we need is lacking, viz., a man with the ability of a statesman and a public sentiment that will respect higher morality.

I hope I shall hear soon again from you. Of the prosperity of your son[90] I was very glad to hear. Everything that concerns your household is pleasing to me. I hope that you will give my kindest regards and best wishes to all at home, and believe me

Very Truly Yours,
Josiah Royce.

[90] Robert Dorsey Coale, Ph. D., Johns Hopkins, 1881; later professor of chemistry and toxicology, and still later dean of the combined medical colleges at the University of Maryland.

To Charles Rockwell Lanman, January 3, 1881[91]

Berkeley, Alameda Co.
Cal.
Jan. 3, 1881.

My Dear Lanman

I ought to have answered your kind letter before, just as I ought to have written to you long before the coming of that itself. But you have forgiven me often in our brief acquaintance, have forgiven me declensions unlearned (not to speak of conjugations), caramels eaten as bribes without any return rendered, letters unwritten, advice unheeded, in brief ingratitude without stint. Perhaps you are still as forgiving.

As for me I am married and happy. I wish I had my system of the universe more nearly completed. That is all that I lack. Here I am at the advanced age of twenty-five, at the extreme limits of civilization, and nothing finished to show for myself yet. Perhaps the coming year will bring more progress.–I teach logic and rhetoric, and correct compositions. Besides that I give private lessons. Some of these are Latin lessons. (Don't be too much frightened at that. When I *teach* Latin I *try* to be careful of my quantities, and to be as good as I can.) Such is the lofty nature of my life as a breadwinner. My contemplative existence I pursue over tea in the evenings, or on afternoon walks on the hills that look westward out of the Golden Gate into the sea. I still buy books, and my dear Stechert of N.Y., who now has the honor of supplying me, waits with more than Staufferian patience the slow moving remittances that from time to time bring up the rear of my modest processions of book-orders. Stechert charges well, but waits like a perfect angel. He writes beautiful English too: "The books you kindly ordered have been demanded, and shall I have the pleasure to forward the same in 5 to 6 weeks."–I shall send you another article of mine in the *Californian*.[92] I did not feel well satisfied with that Shelley article. It was too declamatory. There is the same fault in the one I send now. I must cure myself of the spouting tendency. But that is more easily said than done.

[91] ALS. Lanman Papers. HUA.

[92] Probably "The Decay of Earnestness," *Californian* 3 (1881): 18–25.

As for the use of doing any work here on this doomed planet of ours, I agree with you that one sometimes feels despondent about the future and about the worms that are to eat up the brain tissues that one is now so vigorously seeking to build up; but the whole solution lies here: we are alive now, and the worth our work now has is just the worth we choose now by our enthusiasm to give it. And present worth is all that concerns us. Damn the worms. We are alive now.

I hope you will write to me soon, and you may be sure that I remember you with real affection.—

Yours Truly
J. R.

To William James, April 3, 1881[93]

Berkeley, Apr. 3, 1881.

My Dear James:

Your letter of March 25 reached me yesterday.[94] Your kind suggestion has roused me to do forthwith what I can for myself, and I have spent most of today 'raking together' what I could find. This evening I have already mailed letters to Gilman & to G. S. Morris at Baltimore, and to Pres. Porter at New Haven (the latter two were my examiners when I took my Ph.D.), asking them to write direct to Harvard what they think about me. I suppose that plan is best in their case, to save time. Meanwhile I have also collected seven printed essays of mine, on "Schiller," "Shelley," "Voluntary Progress," Downfall of Transcendentalism (title sentimental: "The Decay of Earnestness"), "Doubting," "George Eliot," "Kant";[95] have added an old lecture-program, one or two printed

[93] ALS. James Papers. HL.

[94] James had prematurely announced an opening in the Harvard Philosophy Department; he wrote again on May 8, 1881, to say that "chances of a vacancy are for the present *nil*." See *TCWJ* 1: 790–91.

[95] The seven essays comprised all of Royce's postdoctoral articles to date: "Schiller's Ethical Studies," *Journal of Speculative Philosophy* 13 (1878): 373–92; "Shelley and the Revolution," *Californian* 1 (1880): 543–53; "The Nature of Voluntary Progress" *Berkeley Quarterly* 1 (1880): 161–89; "The Decay of Earnestness" *Californian* 3 (1881): 18–25; "Doubting and Working" *Californian* 3 (1881): 229–37; "George Eliot as a Religious Teacher" *Californian* 3 (1881): 300–310; "Before and Since Kant," *Berkeley Quarterly* 2 (1881): 134–50. All but the last are reprinted in *FE*.

notes, an abstract of an essay sent to the Metaphysical Club in Baltimore,[96] and two of Gilman's Annual Reports, with crows-feet in the margin at the places where I am mentioned; have collected at short notice three testimonials from men here, viz. from our Pres. Jno. LeConte, from his brother Joseph, whose book on Vision you reviewed the other day in the *Nation*,[97] from my dear friend and chief, the Prof. of Engl. Lit., E. R. Sill; and have supplemented with a letter to the Pres. and Fellows of H., telling of my past work and my wish to be considered a candidate. There is a pretty pudding as you see, and having cooked it I have mailed it in a registered package to the Harvard University authorities. I shall send on two or three more testimonials in a few days. So far that is about all I can do. I may therefore be regarded as swimming about with open mouth among the rest. But of course I am not sanguine of success in such an undertaking, and merely want to do what I can. For all your help, past and future, I am very grateful, and wish I could make fair return. My application being registered and having heavy stamps to carry on its back will doubtless loiter a trifle, and will be at least two or three days later than this letter in reaching Cambridge. I wish the "President and Fellows" joy of it.

Of course my best work is unprinted. I am full of plans and have a good deal of MS lying about useless. I want very much just now to print a volume of essays, but I know not what publisher could be prevailed upon to take my hodge-podge. But I have a fairly big volume of essays, printed and unprinted, ready with a little trimming for the honors of printer's-ink, were it not for the lack of a printer. I sent the other day a paper to *Mind* on "Mind-Stuff," which stuff I am now more and more coming to dislike.[98] The fate of the paper I shall maybe hear in a month or two. The fate of mind-stuff is I think pretty certain. A thoroughly uncritical hypothesis it is after all (viz. such stuff as dreams are made of), notwithstanding that Clifford and the rest, in making the hypothesis, are just trembling on the verge of genuine critical thought. Almost they are persuaded that all existence is for consciousness, when lo! off they shoot on a tangent and discover that consciousness itself

[96] "Purpose in Thought." See letter to William James, June 7, 1880.

[97] James's review of Joseph LeConte's *Sight: An Exposition of the Principles of Monocular and Binocular Vision* was published in *Nation* 32 (1881): 190–91.

[98] " 'Mind-Stuff' and Reality," *Mind* 6 (1881): 365–77.

is made up of a mass of elements that are not for consciousness at all. The man that stirred me up to write about Mind-Stuff just now was Frankland, in the Jan. *Mind*.[99] His mission seems to be to defend very ingeniously very ingenious doctrines to the end that through his consistent development of all absurd and contradictory elements in the views he defends, their faults may be made more manifest. Woe to the system that he adopts. He will reduce it to the absurd as soon as he has accepted it. But if Mind-Stuff fails us, critical philosophy does not, and for my part I feel nearer and nearer all the time to a consistent theory of certain fundamental matters. My essay on Hodgson, which is still unwritten, is delayed solely because I want to be quite clear on these points and on his relation to them.

I lately met Xenos Clark, our wandering *scholasticus*.[100] He has returned, as odd and earnest as ever. I can't make him out at all. He met you, I believe, several times. What do you make [of] him? I haven't seen him for some days, and he may be off to the north pole by this time in search of the ideal university. If ever he could find in the world what his soul needs he would be a great man, for I am convinced that his aims are of the highest. But will he ever find anything in this way?

With many thanks for favors,

Yours faithfully,
J. Royce.

To Daniel Coit Gilman, April 3, 1881[101]

Berkeley, Apr. 3, 1881.

My Dear Pres. Gilman:—

I received yesterday a letter from Prof. Wm. James, wherein he tells me that certain changes in the philosophical department at Harvard are about to take place, and that a vacancy will probably

99 F. W. Frankland, "The Doctrine of Mind-Stuff," *Mind* 6 (1881): 116–20.

100 Xenos Clark was an amateur philosopher, mystic, and occultist, who, like Benjamin Paul Blood, experimented with psychdelic drugs. He died in the 1880s. See *TCWJ*, 1: 727.

101 ALS. Gilman Papers. JHU.

occur in a $2000 assistant professorship. Prof. James kindly promises to support me in any application I may make.

As you know, I am anxious to find a good position East, and I therefore have resolved to make a trial of this, although I have no reason to be sanguine of success where good applicants are so many. I mail today, therefore, a registered package, addressed to the "President and Fellows" of Harvard, containing an application for any vacancy that may occur, copies of my printed papers, testimonials from a few here, and copies of the J. H. U. Reports of '78 and '79. Since my application must be prompt, I cannot wait to get any testimonials from the East to send with my application. And I therefore take the liberty of asking you to write to Harvard a word or two about my work as it is known to you. I shall be very thankful for the favor.

I write this in haste, and so cannot stop to give any special account of my life since my last letter. 'Tis enough I suppose that I am well, married, tolerably comfortable (in view of the high longitude of this place), with the same prospects here as ever (nothing changes in Berkeley, except the weather in the rainy season), and withal a little more given to printing than formerly. Enthusiasm for metaphysics no whit the less ardent. I sent you I believe a copy of my essay on George Eliot.[102] I send with this a number of the *Berkeley Quarterly*.

Very Respectfully
Yours Faithfully
Josiah Royce.

To William Torrey Harris, August 23, 1881[103]

Berkeley, Aug. 23, 1881.

Dr. Wm. T. Harris:—

Dear Sir:—

I am informed by Prof. Mears that you now have in your hands

[102] "George Eliot as a Religious Teacher," *Californian* 3 (1881): 300–310; reprinted in *FE*, pp. 261–89.

[103] ALS. Harris Papers. USC. Published in *Philosophical Forum* 13 (1955): 83; reprinted in Robinson, *Royce and Hocking*, pp. 133–34. See note 12 above.

the MS of an essay that I wrote for the "Kant Centennial."[104] I should be glad to know whether you can find a place for it in the *Journal*. I desire however as well to offer you an explanation and apology for my failure to fulfil my old promise of the summer of 1878 to write you a notice of Shadworth Hodgson. I have borne my promise in mind ever since, but have never felt sure of my ability to fulfil it. Hodgson seems to me an author difficult not so much in his own thought, though that is often obscure, as in view of his curious historical position. One feels a fair understanding of his doctrine before one feels able to judge of its importance; so numerous and subtle, not to say heterogeneous, seem his relations to other modern tendencies. My lack of historical comprehension of Hodgson has therefore stared me in the face whenever I have tried to begin my essay, which I have therefore constantly delayed until some one more book should be read or piece of work done. I can, now I think, undertake the work quite soon, and finish it. But perhaps you no longer desire such a contribution from me. A word of advice on the subject would be very welcome. I regret having been, or rather having seemed so neglectful.—One other matter I must mention. The extra Nos. you sent to me of the *Journal* for Oct. '78, containing my article on *Schiller*, were to be $3.75. I asked that they should be sent C.O.D. My express bill was $5.50, which I took to include the express charges and the original bill. If I was mistaken I am still owing you the old bill, and should be glad to know the fact if your books still show it. I have been constantly on the point of writing to you ever since, but have delayed, hoping to send the Hodgson article.—

Very Respectfully
Yours Truly,
Josiah Royce.

104 "Kant's Relation to Modern Philosophic Progress," *Journal of Speculative Philosophy* 15 (1881): 360–81. John W. Mears, professor of philosophy at Hamilton College, was the director of the Kant Centennial, held at Saratoga, N. Y., July 6, 1881.

To William James, August 28, 1881 [105]

Berkeley, Aug. 28, 1881.

My Dear James:—

Your very kind letter came the other day. Your comments on my article, or rather squib, concerning "Mind-Stuff"[106] encourage me a good deal. I am sorry to say that the supplementary article has not yet been sent.[107] Other work and a good deal of difficulty in certain important details have kept me from completing the work. I hope to send it in time for the Jan'y No. of *Mind*, should the Editor be as willing to print my contribution promptly as he was the last time. I may have a paper in Harris's journal some time this autumn—on Kant.[108] But as every other fool has a chance to appear in that journal and to air his notions on the incompressibility of time or on the metaphysical significance of Drake's address to the American flag, I may find myself low down in the list or crowded out altogether. Nobody can accuse Harris of intolerance towards imbecility. I myself have some reason to be grateful to him.

A wealthy California money-king has endowed a chair in the University for the teaching of "Moral and Intellectual Philosophy and Civil Polity."[109] The wording of the title sounds antiquated enough, but the purpose is a good one. I doubt if I should have any chance in a race for an appointment under this bequest. Some aged Methodist preacher will be more in demand than would be anybody under forty and suspicion of heterodoxy. Not that the University is sectarian, not that its professors are all orthodox. But for just that chair, you see, a man will be needed who can satisfy the minds of the vigilant orthodox foes of all State Universities. The newspapers have talked much about the endowment, and have shown no little wisdom. One of them, a lively little sheet (the *Bee*), took a high

105 ALS. James Papers. HL.

106 " 'Mind-Stuff' and Reality," *Mind* 6 (1881): 365–77.

107 "Mind and Reality," *Mind* 7 (1882): 30–54.

108 "Kant's Relation to Modern Philosophic Progress," *Journal of Speculative Philosophy* 15 (1881): 360–81.

109 D. O. Mills, a merchant and banker, who had also been a regent of the University of California, endowed this chair which George Holmes Howison later filled. Royce was eventually invited to assume the Mills Professorship in 1911 and 1916.

liberal stand and declared that: "There are but two men in Christendom who could properly fill this chair. They are Mr. Henry George and Mr. John Stuart Mill." The religious papers were more moderate in their demands. They desired only a safe man. No doubt they will get him. For the rest I should be glad of such a position just now, but merely as a stepping stone. Deliver me from Californian life and mind, and I shall be much nearer contentment.

My wife has been ill a good deal during the past spring and summer, and I have had, with her, considerable anxiety. But there is no reason to fear permanent weakness, and troubles are doubtless good discipline. I hope your peaceful summer with Mrs. James and your child will run on undisturbed to the end. Our vacation in California ends at the beginning of August. I am just now overwhelmed with horrible Freshmen.

I am reading Venn's book on *Symbolic Logic*. Venn is a writer for whom I have much respect, though I believe him philosophically very far at sea. But he seems to be on the whole a man.—That Kant-paper, of which I spoke above, was written for the "Kant-Centennial" at Saratoga, was sent by mail, and read for me there by some benevolent wretch, I know not by whom, though I pity him. The thing was an hour long.

I hope you will write me whenever you can, and will appreciate how welcome word from you is to me in this wilderness. If I am slow in replying the cause is not forgetfulness, but the fact that I feel the tameness of my lonely work and the difficulty of saying anything about it.

I hope somebody (besides Joseph Cook) will give our American public an account of Lotze and of his work.[110] Will Hall, do you think?

—Yours Truly
J. Royce.

[110] Rev. Joseph Cook was famous for his Boston Monday Lectures in which he often gave highly popularized accounts of modern German thought.

To Daniel Coit Gilman, August 28, 1881[111]

Berkeley, Aug. 28, 1881.

My Dear Pres. Gilman:—

I have not written you for a good while, lacking often the time, and sometimes the energy. I have to thank you especially for your kindness in writing on my behalf to Harvard, and to say that though nothing has yet come of my application I have reason to think that my general prospects have been improved by it and by the kind words that several of my friends were good enough to say for me on that occasion.

Of our affairs at the University here you are doubtless somewhat informed. Pres. Reid was inaugurated last Tuesday amid general good will.[112] The task before him is no easy one, but I think that the Faculty are anxious that he shall succeed, and that the students will cordially support him in most of his acts. Personally I like Mr. Reid very well, and hope that he will make an uncommon success.

My own anxiety to get away from California continues, and I am doing what little I can to finish work that shall be some evidence of qualification to teach philosophy. I communicated a paper to the "Kant Centennial" at Saratoga this summer, and have heard that the paper was read. I may be able to publish it. I also printed a paper in *Mind* for July.

Prof. Sill is now absent in Europe. My work is not much increased by his absence, since he took care to prevent that. Still I find my sixty odd Freshmen somewhat embarrassing, just as I find them every year.

With best regards to yourself and to Mrs. Gilman I remain,

Very Respectfully,
Yours Truly
Josiah Royce.

[111] ALS. Gilman Papers. JHU.

[112] William T. Reid was President of the University of California (1881–1885).

To George Buchanan Coale, December 5, 1881[113]

Berkeley, Dec. 5, 1881.

My Dear Mr. Coale:—

Your very kind and welcome letter reached me the other day. My work happens to be less pressing than usual—a little lull before the last agony of Christmas examinations—; and I hasten to write these lines while there is time. I am the more anxious to be prompt, since I owe you an ample apology for not replying to your very kind message on October 2d of last year. But a very busy little life has claimed me ever since. I should also say that my wife, to whom I have often spoken of your household, was only the other day urging me to make amends for my neglect, and was blaming me for my ingratitude to such kind friends.

Peace to all in your house! I am in a fashion peaceful, for though I have numerous Freshman compositions to correct, and a great desire to find a position nearer to civilization, and though my wife has been for some time past in rather poor health, still we are free from great troubles, and are hopeful for the future. I have been agitating for a position in some Eastern college, and have hope of success with time. I have been arranging for the publication of a few somewhat technical metaphysical articles, and have already published one such in *Mind*, a London Quarterly for Philosophy. I have been publishing nearer home a few more general discussions, one of which (on George Eliot) I sent you. These things may help to get one a position, but what or how soon I may not tell. My wife, who likes Eastern climate better than Californian, is as willing as myself to find another home. She has near relatives in the East. Her health will, we think, soon be completely restored.—I am glad to hear of the success of Mr. Dorsey as a chemist.[114] I have already noticed his name in the J. H. U. Bulletins and Circulars, and have no doubt that he has a good future before him.

I am no whit less metaphysical in my tastes. 'Tis the only sound and solid ground that my mind (as opposed to my heart) will ever find. In fact I am more and more inclined to connect philosophy

113 ALS. Redwood Collection. JHU.

114 I.e., Coale's son, Robert Dorsey Coale, who received his Ph.D. in chemistry from Johns Hopkins in 1881.

very closely with the heart itself. We students of today run through a certain circle of thought, well-known to our elders, but affected in character for us by the peculiar environment of modern ideas in which we move. We begin, like everyone, with some traditional faith, and then, when the doubting time comes, we make some day a resolution that feeling, emotion, personal desire, impulse, subjective faith, must no longer form or influence our beliefs. This resolution every young thinker ought sometime to make, and every earnest one does sometime make. We carry this out consistently, and for awhile belief seems to us to be a pure matter of external evidence that is collated and revised by us, but that is in its matter received or to be received with dumb passive acquiescence. If the belief is chilling or dreadful, so are north winds and death; and we submit, or think we ought to submit, unresistingly. But again with time it dawns upon us that even the most passive belief is action, and that even the coldest belief is to some extent emotional. And then our philosophy is once more driven back into the field of conduct, and we come to see that there is conduct even in steadfastly holding by the axioms of geometry. The deepest question after all then is, what is the purpose of our thinking; with what aim do we believe what we believe? Our necessary and heroic resolve of the purely sceptical time is seen to be after all an imperfect expression of the business of truth-seeking; for the truth is known to us rational mortals not as dead external reality, but as an inner harmony of our conscious being. Once having doubted, we can never quite go back to that early creed; but something of its spirit we regain when we come to see once more the worth of faith as faith, the moral and intellectual importance of a mind at peace with itself.—I remember the failing at heart when I first had to throw overboard my little old creed, and felt that I must for example accept the modern theory of evolution as the real truth of nature, against which a poor mortal with his blind hope of immortality might struggle in vain. The individual withered, and natural selection was more and more. Well, the act was an useful exercise of self-abnegation. But now, though I still accept (as a scientific hypothesis) evolution, and some of the rest of the modern creed, I regard such acceptance not in the light of something forced upon the human mind from without, but in the light of something built up from within. Evolution as a scientific doctrine is a convenient scheme in which to think phenomena, a beautiful little dream of the intellect, coherent and doubtless in the main destined to be permanent, but still a construction of our own, useful, and acceptable only as being useful. There is no necessary opposition between evolution as thus conceived and my other doctrine that we may for like uses accept. The business of thought is to think out coherent and significant schemes of reality, consistent with sense and yet agreeable to reason. The individual ought to wither, but not in favor of natural selection, but in favor of life as a whole. One ought not to consult his own personal desires in forming his creed; but one must consult the needs of thought as thought, of consciousness as consciousness, of man as man. And it is useless to talk of a creed that does not consult these interests. The highest maxim for the thinker is, according to many: "*Agree with external reality.*" I should prefer to state the highest maxim thus: "*Be perfectly unselfish in the desire that prompts thee to accept any given creed.*"

But I grow too talkative. I shall send you an article on this topic some time before long. I intended to send you a late article of mine on "Pessimism."[115] I sent away a number of copies, and I can no longer be sure that yours was among them. If not, please mention the fact when you write (which, as I hope, will be soon), and I will forward you a copy.—What you say about Carlyle seems to me just the right thing, especially where you mention your wish to tell him that you had been lifted by himself above caring for his snubbing of his admirers. I read and admired James's article; yet in some points I differed.—I wish very much that I could see you and talk with you. Once in a while I have a dream of your house, especially if my neglect as a correspondent happens to weigh on my conscience. I wander in my dream about Baltimore, live there maybe for some time, and fear to go near you lest you should have forgotten me. Then I go, clamber into the house by the front window or walk in without knocking, feel frightened and confused, cannot explain myself, am afraid to see anybody, hear you all perhaps in another room and cannot enter, or meet you and have nothing to say; but withal am very much delighted to have found the place once more, and to have actually succeeded in making a visit. I wake up highly amused, and resolve to write forthwith. You see the result. It is strange that I ever dream of you, for my dreams seldom go back more than a month or two in

115 "Pessimism and Modern Thought," *Berkeley Quarterly* 2 (1881): 292–316; reprinted in *FE*, pp. 155–86.

my experience for their material. But you were all uncommonly good to me, and I am not wholly ungrateful. I was an unspeakably raw little boy, in fact am so yet; and you did what you could for me.—Perchance I may be East in a year or two. If so, I promise to come, but not after the fashion of my dreams. So fear not. Please give my best regards to Mrs. Coale and to Miss Coale and to your sons.

I remain

Very Truly Yours
Josiah Royce.

To William James, December 28, 1881[116]

Berkeley, Ala. Co., Cal.
Dec. 28, 1881.

My Dear James:—

I have been prevented by heaps upon heaps of red- and purple- and black-ink essays, written by Freshmen on all subjects and on all kinds of paper, from answering your very kind letter. For since I finished this final agony of term-examinations, I have been too exhausted to write. But I shall have a little time to reflect during these holidays.

You were very good to find so much in the essay on Pessimism. For one thing it is not very original, since some of the best ideas in it were in great part suggested by you in some of our conversations during my summer at Cambridge. And my elaboration of the ideas is comparatively simple.—I have three articles on the point of appearing, one in *Mind*, one in the *Journal of Spec. Phil.*, one in our own *Californian*.[117] All three are efforts to state aspects of what I take to be the proper *Fortbildung* of Kant. The sum of them all is that ontology, whereby I mean any positive theory of an external reality as such, is of necessity myth-making; that, however, such ontology may have enough moral worth to make it a proper object of effort so long as people know what they mean by it; that phi-

[116] ALS. James Papers. HL. Partly printed in *TCWJ*, 1: 791–92.

[117] "Mind and Reality," *Mind* 7 (1882): 30–54; "Kant's Relation to Modern Philosophic Progress," *Journal of Speculative Philosophy* 15 (1881): 360–81; "How Beliefs Are Made," *Californian* 5 (1882): 122–29.

losophy is reduced to the business of formulating the purposes, the structure and the inner significance of human thought and feeling; that an attempted ontology is good only in so far as it expresses clearly and simply the purposes of thought just as popular mythology is good in so far as it expresses the consciousness of a people; that the ideal of the truth-seeker is not the attainment of any agreement with an external reality, but the attainment of perfect agreement among all truth-seeking beings; that ethical philosophy is the highest philosophy. In the *Mind*-article I have sketched a little ontology, partly my own, mostly very old; just to show what myths we can make if we choose. Then I tear up the myth and show how it was made. The lesson is of course much the same as was long ago taught by Prospero.[118] The *Speculative Philos.* article was read for me during the summer at Saratoga, whither I had sent it for the Kant-Centennial.

I received your "Reflex Action and Theism."[119] So did Prof. "Joe." as people familiarly (in his absence) call Jos. LeConte. "Joe" was very enthusiastic over it the other day when I chanced to meet him. And Joe is our great man here. As for me I accept most of it, and can only return your regret about the obscurity of the journal in which my article was published by the similar regret about the obscurity of your "medium." Your article however was in no sense obscure. I should like to talk with you over some of the matters, and especially about that subject of objective as opposed to subjective worth, whereof your letter had much to say. As I now understand you I substantially agree with you.

Delboeuf's criticism in the *Rev. Phil.* shows, I think, that your article on the "Sentiment of Effort" needed towards the end a little more definition of your concept of reality.[120] D. is puzzled at that point, and seems to me very halting. There is just the one doubt in much that you say about the general definition of reality: Do you or do you not recognize this reality of which you speak as in its known or unknown forms independent of the knowing con-

118 The allusion is to Shakespeare's *The Tempest*, act. 4, sc. 1, lines 156–58:

We are such stuff
As dreams are made on, and our little life
Is rounded with a sleep.

119 *Unitarian Review* 16 (1881): 389–416.

120 J. Delboeuf, "Le Sentiment de l'Effort," *Revue Philosophique* 12 (1881): 513–27, criticizes James's "The Feeling of Effort," *Anniversary Memoirs of the Boston Society of Natural History* (1880).

sciousness? Sometimes you speak as if the "Sentiment" were all, sometimes as if there were something above the "Sentiment" to which the latter conformed, or ought to conform. The same hesitation, if I am right in so calling it, appears in C. S. Peirce's papers on the "Logic of Science."[121] In one way he seems to regard reality as for us merely the representative of our determinations to act so or so and of our expectations that we shall succeed if we do act so. For such a view the determination and the expectation would be themselves everything. Instead of saying: there is this reality and I must conform to it, we should say: there is in me this determination to act so and so, and this expectation of success. That is all.—Yet Peirce is not content with this, but continually appeals to the transcendent reality as justifying our determination and our expectation. Now I want to be on this matter very explicit. I fear the ambiguity and the hesitation. For me the sentiment of reality, the determination to act thus and so, the expectation of certain results, all these facts of the active consciousness are together the whole truth. There is needed or known or conceivable above these facts of consciousness absolutely no transcendent reality. Not *Gefühl* but *Gedanke* and *Gefühl* are everything. I need not say that this *Gedanke* is not the Hegelian *Denken*. And yet I am no subjective idealist of the old-fashioned sort. Not *myself* is the ultimate truth, but Consciousness as such. Nor is this consciousness given as an ultimate continuous series of states, after Hodgson's fashion; but it is given as a single act of submission to a conceived other consciousness about it.

But I become lengthy. Thank you much for your kind interest.

Yours Truly
Josiah Royce.

A happy New Year to yourself and Mrs. James.

To William James, January 19, 1882[122]

Berkeley, Jan. 19, 1882.

My Dear James:—

Your inspiring letter put me the other day into a very good

[121] *Popular Science Monthly* 12–13 (1877–78); see fn. 81 above.
[122] ALS. James Papers. HL. Partly printed in *TCWJ*, 1: 793–94.

humour, which has survived even one of our dry unmerciful California northers.—As for your kind offer to write to some one of our trustees about me, I should of course be thankful for anything that you might say. I should be much better off if I had a position as teacher of philosophy even here. You might write to our President if you chose. I should be just a little tender about being called a luminary you know; red-haired men always are. You might use some other metaphor. But your judgment will decide that for you.

I have just been much delighted by an article in the current *Philos. Monatshefte*, by Johannes Volkelt, on the *Aufgabe der Erkenntnisstheorie*. As I have not read his Kant-book I do not know how he comes out in his further discussion of the subject, but this statement of the *Aufgabe* is one of the best and clearest that I have ever seen.[123] He sums up the main thought of what, as I fancy, is genuine philosophy, very prettily.—After asserting that we begin with the subjective, are driven to an effort to get out of it, and begin to search for objective *Erkenntnissprincipien*, he goes on:—"*Was ich auf Grund dieser Principien erkenne, beruht sonach allerdings auf einem objectiven Gelten gewisser Vorstellungen; allein dies objective Gelten wieder findet doch nur darum Statt, weil ich mich entschlossen habe, dem unwiderstehlichen, sich unmittellbar als sachlich bezeugenden Zwange, der mit gewissen Vorstellungen verknüpt ist, Glauben zu schenken.*" This brings one back to the thought you expressed in a late letter. We must have an objective sanction for our thoughts and for our acts, and so we resolve to regard such and such a conception as an objective authority. The last fact is our free surrender of ourselves to this authority, which for its own part, exists in and through our act of self-surrender. The consciousness of subjective and arbitrary independence is fatal to our thoughts and lives; therefore we freely render ourselves dependent, and put on our self-made harness. All thinking is putting on the harness, that we may gain in unity and fullness of life more than we shall lose by losing the lawless freedom of romanticism or of scepticism.—

Yours Truly,
J. Royce.

[123] *Immanuel Kant's Erkenntnisstheorie nach ihren Grundprincipien analysirt* (Leipzig: L. Voss, 1879).

To William James, February 1, 1882[124]

Berkeley, Feb. 1, 1882.

My Dear James:—

I hope that you may be not wholly wrong in your kind remarks about my *Mind* article,[125] but I have less interest in the poor thing now than I had a few months since. I acquiesce in the most of it when I read it over, but wish that it were not so sketchy and fragmentary. But I am still at work and hope to have better stuff in my bag pretty soon.

When is your psychology coming out?[126] I am quite anxious to see it. I understand that this rather garrulous fellow D. G. Thompson is about to print a psychology.[127] I haven't the least idea what the man believes, since his *Mind*-articles[128] trickled through my brain and were lost to me long since, but I have no confidence in him *a priori*. I was reading the other day a little of Bascom's *Science of Mind*,[129] and marvelling at the mixture of tedious Poloniusness and real wisdom there found. Really this talk about entities is becoming a common nuisance, and I have a sincere confidence that in your book I shall meet none of them. Let anybody be immortal as much as he pleases, but let his immortality be his own, not his "soul's." I judge then that we need a critical psychology written after the style of your essays on "Association" &c.[130]

Speaking of entities reminds me of Frankland's puzzle in his reply to me in *Mind*.[131] He wonders how, on my view an embryo ever comes by its consciousness. I must believe, he thinks, in special

[124] ALS. James Papers. HL.

[125] "Mind and Reality," *Mind* 7 (1882): 30–54.

[126] James's *The Principles of Psychology* was not published until 1890.

[127] Daniel Greenleaf Thompson, *A System of Psychology*, 2 vols. (London: Longmans, Green, and Co., 1884). Royce later vigorously attacked this work in "Thompson's Psychology," *Nation* 40 (April 23, 1885): 343–44.

[128] "Knowledge and Belief," *Mind* 2 (1877): 309–35; "Intuition and Inference," *Mind* 3 (1878): 339–49; 468–79.

[129] John Bascom, *The Science of Mind* (New York: G. P. Putnam's Sons, 1881).

[130] "The Association of Ideas," *Popular Science Monthly* 16 (1880): 577–93. On March 4, 1882, Royce read a paper to the Psychology Club on "Association of Ideas in the Light of Theory and Experience."

[131] "Dr. Royce on 'Mind-Stuff' and Reality," *Mind* 7 (1882): 110–14.

creation or metempsychosis. This is glorious fun indeed, this puzzle. Why does he not ask how on my theory I can explain the fact that time is a succession, or the reason why we are all of us living in the solar system instead of in the neighborhood of Sirius? These people that must needs have beings, entities, substances of some kind (unconscious things, or atoms, or what not), to explain whatever is in consciousness, seem wholly to forget that, given your Unconscious, or your mind-stuff, or whatever, the appearance of consciousness in this entity remains just as much a miracle as ever. One simply doubles his troubles for nothing. There is the whole conscious order to explain in the first place. To succeed in the explanation one adds little unconscious creatures behind the scenes, who shall contain the completion and rationalization of the conscious order. The laws of these entities must be fully explained before the gaps in the conscious series of facts can be filled up and explained. But when all this is done, what have we? Simply the miracle that out of the supposed unconscious order (the monads or atoms) there arises under given conditions consciousness, and this consciousness, strange to say, has just the order and just the facts of that consciousness from which we started. Thus to explain the facts A, B, C, I assume the invisible series *a, b, c;* and then after all my trouble find that out of *a, b, c,* there arises in a totally incomprehensible fashion, the series A, B, C, and that the latter series, in just the order in which we find it, is after all an ultimate and mysterious fact. I might have known that at the outset.—I suppose that old as all this stuff is it will be necessary to say it all again for the benefit of Frankland and T. Whittaker in some future number of *Mind.* T. Whittaker, you know, thinks that unconscious mental life must be assumed because it is "absurd" to suppose that a given nerve-tremor could be at one time associated, at another time not associated with a given mental state, whereas we know that consciousness is not thus always associated with given nerve-tremors.[132] That it is just as much and just as little absurd to suppose the latter as to admit the former of these two relations Whittaker does not notice. These fellows seem utterly ignorant of what constitutes an explanation. Lo the poor Indian, for example. But I must pause

Yours Truly
Josiah Royce.

[132] " 'Mind-Stuff' From the Historical Point of View," *Mind* 6 (1881): 498–513.

To Daniel Coit Gilman, February 1, 1882[133]

Berkeley, Feb. 1, 1882.

Dear Pres. Gilman:—

I have intended for some time to write to you to inquire whether your health is yet fully restored, and to express my regret for your illness of last summer. Business of all sorts has made me negligent. I hope soon to hear that you are quite well.

Our life here goes on nowadays with little visible disturbance. Discipline is sometimes a little troublesome, but our new President seems to have all desirable energy and firmness, and will undoubtedly control our students very well. Several changes in our program of studies are still but experiments whose result can only be hoped.

Personally I am as anxious as ever to get a good position East, and of late have been trying to get a little recognition as a student of philosophy by publishing a few essays. I intend to do yet more of the same sort. My studies follow still the old bent.

Your old friends here inquire after you of one another, and you may be sure that you are not forgotten, even amidst all these present and freshly remembered perplexities of the University.

Very Respectfully,
Yours Truly,
Josiah Royce.

To William James, May 2, 1882[134]

Berkeley, May 2, 1882.

My Dear James:—

In answer to your very kind letter, I telegraphed an affirmative last night, and now await hopefully something official. I am very willing to run risks and to make sacrifices to get a permanent foothold East. Even if they offered me something definite here, I should regard an egg in Cambridge as worth more than a brood of chickens here. I expect however nothing definite here, and consider that fact no judgment of my teaching ability. For I assure you that just now

133 ALS. Gilman Papers. JHU.
134 ALS. James Papers. HL.

nobody but the Professor of English Literature (Prof. Sill) knows or cares anything about my success or failure as a teacher. Our President, a very able man and an earnest worker, hardly comes into consideration as yet, for he has been in his place only a year, is beset by harassing cares and foes of all sorts, has large plans and limited means, and has no time to care much for individual tutors. Our Regents, a miscellaneous and comparatively ignorant body, are by fits and starts meddlesome, always stupid, not always friendly, and never competent or anxious to discover the nature of our work or of our ability. So what is said or not said by any one of them about one of us, proves nothing about our class-room work. I am in friendly ignorance about the teaching ability of most of my fellows, and they concern themselves as little about me. I have at least taught enough to discover a few of the blunders of my first efforts, and might hope slowly to improve.—For the rest I should not wonder to hear of no appointment to the new chair here for a good while. The Regents want to find a celebrated man, a man of forty or more, and an Eastern man. So at least I believe. I am a native, and that too is against me; for Californians generally, and on the whole with very good reason, regard one another with profound suspicion and contempt. The chair of English Literature is itself about to be vacated by Prof. Sill, and I might have some chance of getting that work, did I not fear such an appointment as a snare of the devil to tempt me from my real business. Thus I am very ready to go, and eager to accept your offer.

If the arrangement should really be made, I should have much to ask you about the practical questions that would suggest themselves. Just now I have only to thank you once more for your very kind interest in me and my work.—You were right in supposing my little sketch "recasting" &c. to be but a preliminary to an intended fuller statement.[135] For its obscurity—to the sated appetites of most of Harris's readers such very moderate obscurity must seem insupportably dull. For your sake I wish I had done better.

I have now a little son, three weeks old, who, with his mother, is doing wonderfully well. I shall be overjoyed at the thought of bringing him up in an Eastern atmosphere.

Yours Truly
Josiah Royce.

[135] See James to Royce, April 23, 1882, in *TCWJ*, 1: 794.

To William Thomas Reid, June 2, 1882[136]

Berkeley, June 2, 1882

Pres. W. T. Reid

Dear Sir

Having accepted an appointment in an Eastern Institution for the coming Academic year, I beg leave through you to tender to the Board of Regents my resignation of my position as Instructor in the English Language and Literature in the University of California, the resignation to take effect on the first of Sept. of the current year. As the teaching force of the English Department will probably undergo an entire change, and as some embarrassment might thus result in regard to the entrance examinations and the other work at the beginning of the next term, I venture to name the above somewhat irregular date for the conclusion of my work.

Very respectfully
Josiah Royce, Jr.

To Daniel Coit Gilman, July 12, 1882.[137]

Redwood City
July 12, 1882.

My Dear Pres. Gilman:—

Thanks to the kindness of my friends I have at last obtained a temporary appointment, with Instructor's rank, at Harvard. For one year, without any promise of future employment, I am asked to take the philosophy-classes of Prof. James, who has a year's leave of absence. The pay for the time is $1250. The position is surely a very modest one, but I feel very glad of it, for it means a chance, for a time at least, to live in a studious community and to do my own work. What becomes of me and my family after the end of a year does not appear, but I am very willing to take risks in a good cause.

136 ALC. Minutes of the Regents of the University of California.

137 ALS. Gilman Papers. JHU. Redwood City was the home of Royce's father-in-law, E. F. Head.

In intend to go to Cambridge about Sept. 1. I have a baby to carry with me, a healthy boy of three months. My wife and myself will live as may be in some cheap fashion for the year.—John Stillman,[138] as you may know, has already gone to Boston, to take a position there. His baby carriage is, thus far, larger than mine, and his health not so good as mine. But he doubtless goes to a much higher salary. With his going and Prof. Sill's the Faculty is once more thinned. Prof. Sill will probably stay at least a year in Berkeley, resting.

I hope to hear that your health is fully restored. I am glad to see by the Circulars how active and progressive the Baltimore Faculty still are. It is always a useful stimulus to the spirit of work in a man to read one of the circulars.—I hope you will remember me to Mrs. Gilman.

I am

Yours Very Truly
J. Royce.

To Charles Rockwell Lanman, August 14, 1882[139]

Berkeley, Aug. 14, 1882

My Dear Lanman:—

Yours of the 4th has reached me, and you surprise me indeed, after my long neglect, by pouring (or heaping, I forget which the Scripture saith) coals of fire on my unworthy red head. Your advice and your help will indeed be welcome to me, amid my many perplexities; but you must not spend time and trouble too carelessly on an ungrateful pupil that, out of laziness, has failed to answer letters, or otherwise to return your kindness to him in times past.

I go to Harvard with a mixture of trembling and impudence that will doubtless be charming to witness when I arrive. Doubtless I shall blunder through a year in some fashion, and I shall hope at all events to make no enemies, unless it be by my ugly face and my Californian barbarity.

I shall leave Berkeley (D. V., which is not swearing), Monday,

[138] John Maxon Stillman, A. B. from the University of California in 1874, was later professor of chemistry at Stanford University.

[139] ALS. Lanman Papers. HUA.

Sept. 4, and shall reach (B. & A. Station) about 7.30 Monday (Sept. 11). So it is now set down. D. V. means, however, if the baby does not get sick at some critical moment. He is well enough now, and weighs twenty-one pounds.

Yours Affectionately
Josiah Royce

The Letters

Part II

1882–1888

Part II

1882-1888

Royce's first six years at Harvard began with a trial and nearly ended in a tragedy: the first was a test of his professional abilities; the second was a struggle to escape permanent crippling from a nervous breakdown. With the assertiveness and resilience that friends often noted, he met both challenges. William James enjoyed saying that Royce was "ready for everything in this world or the next."

Royce regarded himself as essentially a worker. Unschooled in gentility, he introduced a raw, vigorous style at Harvard. Within a year after his arrival he had written a first draft of *The Religious Aspect of Philosophy* (1885) and while working on revisions had arranged for the publication of *California* (1886). After the treatise and the history were published, he turned to the novel, writing *The Feud of Oakfield Creek* (1887) during a summer vacation. To John Jay Chapman, then a student at Harvard, Royce "was a bumblebee—a benevolent monster of pure intelligence, zigzagging, ranging, and uncatchable."

One may see this vigorous style clearly revealed in the letters dealing with *California*. Those who think of Royce as primarily a philosopher may be surprised to note how sedulously he pursued his historical research. Angered yet amused by Frémont's seizure of California, he shaped his arguments carefully and pressed them with ruthless logic. As philosopher, historian, and novelist, Royce in the 1880s was tireless, loquacious, upright, and intellectually overwhelming.

To William James, October 31, 1882[1]

14 Sumner St. Oct. 31, 1882.

My Dear James:—

I have been trying to find time for some report to you about the state of my work. No doubt you by this time think me very neglectful that I have given you no account whatever. But in truth I have been very much absorbed. Harder and more delightful occupation I have never found. I am on the whole very happy and very hard driven. So much for the general condition.

My rolls have not yet assumed their permanent form, and I cannot tell you the exact numbers. The first of the month is, I believe, to bring printed lists and final statements of the classes. But as far as I now know, some 50 are taking the elementary course, and about 20 the advanced course (Locke &c.).

With the disposition of the majority of my students I am well pleased. They are manly and intelligent. They are not too industrious, but possibly that failing will wear off. Some of them can ask good questions. I hope to do a few of them a little good.—I am still however too far from my classes. I worry a trifle at not seeming as yet to be in any close relation to them. They do not talk enough. I question them, but am not altogether content with their answers. In

[1] ALS. James Papers. HL. Partly printed in *TCWJ*, 1: 391.

short, my true success as a teacher of philosophy is still not assured.

But what failures I make shall not be my fault. I am constantly planning and working over the classes. I am not inclined to be stubborn. I often long for some intelligent and merciless criticism, and wish that one could ever get students to express dispassionately and yet plainly what needs they actually feel.

Advanced Psychology I took. I determined to get out of it what I could. *Advanced* for me is not just what you would call advanced, and I was sure I should be doing my best if I contented myself with Senior students. I have two, Williams & Woodbury by name, who meet at my house. We shall have lectures, Ribot's sketch of German Psychol., and Theses.[2]

In the elementary Logic Course I took the liberty to add one text-book (Fowler's *Inductive Logic*) which I shall substitute for the last part of Jevons.[3]

Reading, you say, must be neglected for teaching in this my trial year. If I could only read as much as I need for my teaching I should be fortunate. As for writing, if I do any of that, it will be to help on my other work.

In fine, I know not at all if I am making any respectable success with the work. I only know that my heart & energies are in it.

My wife and myself spent, at the invitation of Mrs. James and her mother, our only evening out since we came here. That was last Thursday, and very pleasant indeed. We have had already many reasons to feel and remember the kind of thoughtfulness that both Mrs. James and her sisters have shown to us from the outset. We ourselves are healthy, and our baby grows vigorously.

Prof. Palmer is cordial and very genuinely friendly. I wonder how he can endure me with my slip-shod Western manners, and he so precise and *streng*. Nevertheless neither on our walks together nor in our little visits (both have been fewer than I wished) does he manifest any disgust for me. We have already been doctoring up the transcendental Ego in various ways, and giving our rival diagnoses of the poor fellow's case.

[2] Théodule Ribot, *La Psychologie allemande contemporaine* (*école expérimentale*) (Paris: G.-Baillière, 1879).

[3] Thomas Fowler, *The Elements of Inductive Logic* (Oxford: Clarendon Press 1866); William Stanley Jevons, *Elementary Lessons in Logic: Deductive and Inductive* (London: Macmillan and Co., 1870).

The new number of *Mind*[4] is a sad spectacle, with its three rival and self-sufficient absolute theories of ultimate truth, and its melancholy essay of Sidgwick's on the "Incoherency" &c.[5] I wonder if the editor did not regard that number with delight as a huge joke.

Please write me soon. I see after all but few people and am sometimes lonesome. A word from you will always cheer me.

Yours Truly
Josiah Royce.

To George Buchanan Coale, January 24, 1883[6]

14 Sumner St.
Cambridge, Mass.
Jan. 24, 1883.

My Dear Mr. Coale:

I know not whether any rumor ever reached you from my Baltimore friends that I am passing this winter in this place, instructor in my beloved philosophic hobbies at Harvard. I have meant, ever since I came, to let you know. But I have been very busy. My appointment here lasts but till July. I am filling Prof. James's place while he is absent. Whether there will be room for me next year I cannot tell; I do not want to go back to California, and took this place so as to get in the edge of a wedge somewhere on this side of the Continent.

[4] The "three rival . . . theories" in *Mind* 7 (October, 1882), were Francis Ellingwood Abbot, "Scientific Philosophy: A Theory of Human Knowledge," pp. 461–95; Thomas Davidson, "Perception," pp. 496–513; and Edmund Montgomery, "Causation and Its Organic Conditions," continued from previous issues and concluded pp. 514–32. This is Royce's first recorded response to Abbot's philosophy; as such, the remark presages Royce's notorious attack of 1890. Abbot's article, based upon his Harvard Ph.D. thesis of 1881 and later expanded into *Scientific Theism* (Boston: Little, Brown and Co., 1885), attacks idealism and defends a realistic theory of knowledge. Royce wrote a hostile review of *Scientific Theism* in *Science* 7 (1886): 335–38, but this attack is not nearly as stern as his review of *The Way Out of Agnosticism* in the *International Journal of Ethics* 1 (1890): 98–115. James shared Royce's disappointment with Davidson's article—see *TCWJ*, 1: 745.

[5] Henry Sidgwick, "Incoherence of Empirical Philosophy," *Mind* 7 (1882): 533–43.

[6] ALS. Redwood Collection. JHU.

My little family, viz., wife and son, the latter a very hearty boy of nine months, are with me. We are well and comfortable.—I am very desirous of hearing from you, and of knowing how your family have been since I last heard. Your letters are always of deep interest to me, and my memory of your household as bright as ever. I may possibly find time to run down to Baltimore at the Easter vacation on business. If I do so I shall find a chance to make you a call some evening. But I cannot tell how time will be ordered, and may after all be unable to leave Cambridge.

I hope to be remembered to all in your house.

Yours Very Truly
Josiah Royce.

To Daniel Coit Gilman, January 24, 1883[7]

14 Sumner St. Cambridge.
Jan. 24, 1883.

My Dear Pres. Gilman:—

I have intended for some time to write you a word, but my duties here have been very engrossing. I was sorry on reaching Cambridge last September to find myself too late to see you (for, as I believe, you had been in Boston not long before). I may possibly take the opportunity at the Easter vacation to run down to Baltimore, for I am anxious to see old friends and to note the great advances that have been made at the University since my day, advances of which I often read with delight in the Circulars and Reports.

My annual appointment here may possibly be renewed, but I still know nothing certainly about the matter. If Prof. Palmer takes a leave of absence next year, as he talks of doing, there will be room for me. Otherwise I shall have to seek other employment, though of course I have hopes of a more permanent position some time, whenever a vacancy occurs in the department. I have been treated very kindly by all here, have exceedingly enjoyed my classroom work, and hope that I have not given cause for serious dissatisfaction. But my future is still unsettled. I no doubt ran a serious risk in

[7] ALS. Gilman Papers. JHU.

weighing anchor and leaving Berkeley, but such seemed the only road to my special work, and I was determined to take it. I do not regret it, whatever the consequence.

I hope to hear that you and Mrs. Gilman are well. My little family prospers. Please remember me to all my friends when they may mention me.

Your Very Truly
Josiah Royce.

To George Buchanan Coale, May 7, 1883[8]

14 Sumner St.
Cambridge, May 7, 1883.

My Dear Mr. Coale:

After leaving Baltimore I found my way back, in chilly weather and snow showers, to Boston, and so to Cambridge, where the baby had prepared some new tricks to show me, and where all was otherwise well.

My little visit to Baltimore delighted me very much. I had not hoped to find so little change in your household, nor to be met so warmly as a familiar friend by you all; and I cannot conceive how, for this once only, every expectation and memory about a place not visited for five years should be either realized or a trifle exceeded, as mine were on my visits to your house.—I have little to say of my uneventful existence here, save that my arrangements for staying here next year are pretty well under way, and that I anticipate a great deal from my work in the way of solid pleasure.

Do you intend to spend any part of the summer in the north? I should be glad of a chance of meeting you, or of having any of your family who chance to journey in our direction come to us in Cambridge, so long as we are still in this house. Mrs. Royce would be delighted to make your acquaintance. Our own plans for the summer are uncertain, but we shall be in Cambridge until July 1 at least.

I hope that your health and your family's will continue, and that you will always manage among you to see as many aspects of the

[8] ALS. Redwood Collection. JHU.

universe as you did the evening I had the pleasure of dining with you.

Yours Faithfully
Josiah Royce.

To Horace Elisha Scudder, May 24, 1883[9]

14 Sumner St., Cambridge.
May 24, 1883.

My Dear Sir:

I am much obliged to you for your trouble and advice. The last plan that you mention, viz. that the publisher should assume the risks, but should make no payments until the expenses of the investment were recovered from the sale of the book, would be quite satisfactory to me if I should be able to get the book into a form that you would consider promising. I shall therefore try to reconstruct the lectures[10] in some such way as you suggest, and shall be glad to have the opportunity of submitting the result once more to your consideration. Please send me the MS by express, at my expense.

Yours Truly
Josiah Royce.

[9] ALS. Scudder Papers. UCB.

[10] The MS in question is undoubtedly an early version of *RAP*. Royce gave a series of four evening lectures on "The Religious Aspect of Philosophy" on March 1, 8, 15, and 29, 1883. Presumably it was this series that Royce submitted to Scudder. By May 11, 1884, he had submitted a revised and nearly complete MS, and by November 1, 1884, he had signed his contract. Note that these details concerning the origin and growth of *RAP* are incompatible with the frequently repeated story of G. H. Palmer, *The Development of Harvard University . . . 1869–1929,* ed. Samuel Eliot Morison (Cambridge: Harvard University Press, 1930), pp. 12–13. Palmer maintains that the lectures were constructed during Royce's third year at Harvard (i.e., 1884–85) and originally intended for the Lowell Institute, but that Royce withdrew when obliged to sign a statement of religious beliefs. It is clear, however, that Palmer's memory, at least so far as the dates are concerned, was imperfect.

To CHARLES W. BADGER, AUGUST 15, 1883[11]

14 Sumner St., Cambridge, Mass.
Aug. 15, 1883.

Mr. Chas. W. Badger;
Secretary, Berkeley Club:

Dear Sir:

I have just heard the very surprising and painful news of the death of Mr. W. W. Crane,[12] a man to whom I owed so much in many ways that his loss comes very near to me personally. During my very short stay in California a few weeks since I was unable by reason of other engagements to find time to visit him, a fact that I now very deeply regret.

And so, as I have no other way of expressing my feelings, I take this opportunity of expressing through you to the Berkeley Club, of which he was so faithful and honored a member, my sense of the great loss that the Club has sustained in his death, and my sympathy for them and for the whole community in my old home. Men of Mr. Crane's character are rare anywhere. He was a servant of the Truth.

I venture to add yet that I am very thankful for the Club notices which I have so regularly received from the Berkeley Club through you during the past year, and that I am also very grateful to the Club for its kindness in electing me to an honorary membership. Greet the brethren for me, and assure them that I shall never forget their cheerful circle, visited of late, alas too often, by death.

Yours Very Truly
Josiah Royce.

11 ALS. Berkeley Club Papers. UCB.

12 William Watson Crane, Jr., was a member of the Berkeley Club, a frequent contributor to local periodicals, such as *Berkeley Quarterly*, and author of *Communism: Its History and Aims* (San Francisco: A. L. Bancroft and Co., 1878).

To BERNARD MOSES, SEPTEMBER 7, 1883[13]

14 Sumner St., Cambridge
Sept. 7, 1883.

My dear Moses:—

I venture to trouble you about a matter that you may find of some little interest. The death of Mr. Crane, who had undertaken to write to Houghton Mifflin & Co. the "Commonwealth History" of California, leaves that firm without anyone whom they can at once look to for that volume of their proposed series. Mr. Horace Scudder, who represents them, has in this state of affairs asked me if I will undertake the work. Now I can truly say that I had never dreamed of such an undertaking, and was much surprised at the suggestion. But in view of the nature of the series, as a collection of essays not on the details but on the general tendency and lessons of the various historical periods that are to be treated, I now somewhat hesitate to reply in the negative, and have asked for time to consult others before I reply. I am offered what promises to be a fair price for the work if I do it, and can take at least a year, probably more if I need it, to get up the subject and write the book. I am, to be sure, much absorbed in other and very different work, but I am tempted, first by the money, then by the affection that I should feel for the task when once I had accepted it, and then by the good that would be done me if I undertook to examine the moral and general significance of just that set of concrete facts, to give my leisure hours to preparing such a book.

So much of my own feeling. What I wish to trouble you with is the question, whether you really think that I should do right to undertake that task as a mere accompaniment of other work, as a thing for leisure hours, and whether you would expect to find as the result of it all a respectable book that could be of any real use for the purpose of the proposed historical series.

You can estimate better than I can the difficulties of an historical study, and you know my faults as a worker in some respects better than I can know them. If considering all the drawbacks you still think it reasonable for me to try, I should be glad to know the fact.

[13] ALS. Moses Papers. UCB.

If you do not think that I have any business to assume such a responsibility, your opinion would have much weight with me in making up my mind. Please tell me plainly.

I hope that I do not trouble you too much. If there existed as yet any experts in California history outside the limits of the Bancroft workshop, I should not hesitate to say No to this offer. It is only because of the difficulty that the publishers have found in getting a man that I feel tempted by the above-stated motives.—I have to give an answer in about three weeks.

Yours Truly
Josiah Royce

To George Buchanan Coale, January 14, 1884[14]

14 Sumner St., Cambridge
Jan. 14, 1884

My Dear Mr. Coale:

I have been thus far passing very busily my second winter at Cambridge. I have several things on hand besides my regular College Courses, and altogether time passes very fast. My wife and baby are very well, and, as I think enjoy this winter much better than the last. Both of them are in perfect health.

I have been aiming to get a book on Religious Philosophy ready for the press very soon. I cannot tell whether I shall succeed, either in finishing it, or in getting it printed, but it gets shape more and more every day. It is founded on old lectures and essays of mine rewritten and joined with whatever new things come into my head. I hope it will not be either too dry or too dangerous. The former is most likely.

But meanwhile I have promised to have ready in a year or two a sketch of the history of my native State, California, and I am collecting facts as I have time. The book will be a side-work, an amusement of idle hours, not an attempt to do expert work; but then even such amusements are pretty serious things, and I do not want to do it ill. A study of the political life of a growing state is, I find, of great use to a man like me, whose airy studies take him often so far from concrete facts.

14 ALS. Redwood Collection. JHU.

I have been intending to take some time during the year to visit Baltimore, especially to see my friends and to do some of my work that I can, as it happens, best do at the Peabody Institute and at the University. I find, at last, after some hesitation and inquiry that the best time for me will be, after all, the little interval afforded by our "Mid-Year examinations," which begin next week, Jan. 24 and last more than two weeks. I have therefore, after some indecision, at last determined to leave my little family for a time, and to make a break in all my other work for the sake of this. I shall be in Baltimore some two weeks. I of course have no idea how you are, or even whether you are just now in town, but I shall hope that at least two or three times while I am staying in Baltimore I shall be able to see you and your family, and to have speech of things that we like to talk about.—I hope you all are well.

Yours Truly
J. Royce

To George Buchanan Coale, February 11, 1884[15]

14 Sumner St.
Feb. 11, 1884

My Dear Mr. Coale:

I write not only to you, but also to the whole family, for to all I owe very warm thanks for a delightful visit in your house.—My return homewards was not marked by any mishaps. I spent the next day and a half in N. Y., and came on in the afternoon train Thursday. On Friday I was busy with examinations, and since then I have been trying to get my regular work under way once more.

My wife and boy are in good health. The boy is every day more absorbed in his music. He knows how, in certain of his more familiar favorites, to turn the leaves at the right place. Sometimes he scolds with a long mournful Oh–h–h–h if a bad mistake is made in playing one of his favorite passages. He find several pieces by name, or when a little bit is played and he is then asked to find the place. Meanwhile he is a jolly fat boy, and can laugh very heartily and behave very wickedly, so that I find nothing unearthly about him, notwithstanding his music. But as he has no regular play-mate save

15 ALS. Redwood Collection. JHU.

his mother it is not surprising that he should regard her music as the most interesting of all games, and that I suppose is the meaning of his great application to the study of it. (I ought to say that the foregoing facts, although strictly scientific observations, are to be kept a profound secret from Mr. Dorsey, of whom I stand in great awe).—Saturday evening I went to the Boston concert, and heard your favorite Unfinished Symphony of Schubert very well played, although it was rather buried in a programme of poorer music—a trashy piano concerto of Raff's and a long Suite of Bizet's. This week we are to have a concert in Cambridge, with Mr. [Ernst] Perabo as soloist.

If Miss Mary is interested in Tourgénief after reading *Liza*, she may be interested in the translation of *Mumu* which has just been announced as published in New York. I have not seen it yet, but I suppose that it will soon be accessible at all the bookstores. It is published in some one of those cheap edition series. I know the story in German form, and think it one of the best of T.'s shorter sketches. I think that you would like it.

Please remember me to Mrs. Coale very particularly, and to all of the family, and let me hear from you soon and often. Mrs. Royce desires especially to be remembered to Mrs. Coale.

Your Very Truly
Josiah Royce.

To Daniel Coit Gilman, March 17, 1884[16]

14 Sumner St.
Cambridge, Mass.
March 17, 1884.

Dear Pres. Gilman:

I have just received from Pres. Eliot the following offer for next year:—Since there will be no vacancy in the regular force of the Philosophical Department, I cannot be employed in that work alone, but may have an opportunity to give one half-course in philosophy, with $500 as compensation therefore, and may piece out my income by taking charge of Forensic work in the English dep't, and of one other task in the same dep't, with a further compensation of $1500, making a total of $2000. I also receive a promise

[16] ALS. Gilman Papers. JHU.

of an appointment as Assistant Professor in Philosophy so soon as a vacancy shall occur.—The prospect of coming permanent employment is very attractive to me, but I dislike of course giving so much time to English next year. I shall probably be employed in the half-course in Philosophy for the first half year only. It occurs to me that I might possibly find some way to piece out my income for the year without leaving my philosophic work. Pres. Eliot consents to give me,—if I prefer that plan instead of the other, an appointment as Instructor for the year in Philosophy, with the understanding that I shall give only the half-course for $500, and shall live otherwise as I can. That plan pleases me better, if I can only carry it out. I venture therefore to ask you whether you know of any way in which I could teach or lecture anywhere in philosophy during the second half-year, between Feb. and June. If I see no opening, I shall of course accept the English work here; but I suppose that, under the circumstances it is my duty to ask first whether I can avoid the distraction of further English work.

I am sorry to trouble you for advice in such a matter after all the interest you have shown in me, and all the trouble you have taken in my behalf in the past; but until I have permanent employment in philosophy I shall be often puzzled about income, and perhaps the peculiar nature of the present offer will excuse me for bothering you again.

I ought to have written before to thank you for your kindness to me in Baltimore recently. Please accept my thanks now; and remember me to Mrs. and to Miss Gilman.

Your Very Truly
Josiah Royce.

To Daniel Coit Gilman, May 11, 1884[17]

14 Sumner St.
Cambridge.
May 11, '84.

My Dear Pres. Gilman:

I was much obliged for your kind letter and its excellent advice. I have accepted the Forensic work here, in addition to some philos-

[17] ALS. Gilman Papers. JHU.

ophy work; but I determined to relieve the monotony of the former by making myself responsible for a change in the plan of the course in Forensics. The change has met with a general approval, so far as I can judge, and the Corporation has given me an assistant to read the Forensics with me and so to relieve me of some of the work.

My book on *The Religious Aspect &c.* has been put in the hands of Mr. H. Scudder to examine for Houghton Mifflin & Co. I cannot tell whether he will recommend it for print, but you see that I have it pretty well finished. There remain but a few pages at the end of one chapter to be supplied hereafter.

Stanley Hall's appointment[18] causes great content among us all who feel the great importance of his services in the past, and the assurance that his methods and his mental power, as well as his wonderful power of work, are sure to make his department felt in the future all over the country. He will advance psychology as a science, and he will be of great practical worth, directly or indirectly, to teachers. I am sorry that his permanent residence in Baltimore will take him where I shall seldom see him in Cambridge. So long as he lives in Somerville, he is occasionally accessible for conversation and walks.

I am doing what I can with the Cal. work. I have now but a few weeks before me to prepare for my Summer's study of the history. I want to make a decently thorough examination of the most important facts, and I feel that there are a good many of them.

The completion of my philosophic study of the *Rel. Asp. &c.* reminds me quite clearly how much I have enjoyed in the past few years in the way of undisturbed opportunity for study, and how delightful the opportunity has been. I suppose that you are used to ingratitude from the young men you have helped, but I do not want you to think me so ungrateful as that I should forget, when I look back, how much of all this opportunity I owe directly to you, and how helpless I should have been without your interest in me. I assure you that I do remember it very gratefully.–

Your Very Truly
Josiah Royce.

[18] G. Stanley Hall was appointed professor of psychology and pedagogics at Johns Hopkins in 1884.

To William Carey Jones, September 23, 1884[19]

14 Sumner St., Cambridge, Mass.
Sept. 23, 1884.

My Dear Carey:—

Before leaving Berkeley[20] I found no time to write down for you my questions, the ones, I mean, that you so kindly offered to convey to General and Mrs. Frémont.[21] I now venture to trouble you with them.

[19] ALS. Jones Papers. UCB.

[20] Royce spent the summer of 1884 in San Francisco Bay Area doing research for his *California* at the Bancroft Library.

[21] William Carey Jones was a classmate of Royce at the University of California and a nephew of John Charles Frémont. This and several succeeding letters clarify Royce's research into the history of the American conquest of California in 1846. The outcome of this research was Royce's most ambitious and enduring contribution to California historiography, presented in Chap. II of *California:* "The American as Conqueror: The Secret Mission and the Bear Flag." Since, in these letters, Royce refers in abundant detail to the complicated and perhaps obscure events leading to and following the conquest, a resumé of pertinent facts may be useful.

During the winter of 1845/46, on the eve of the Mexican War, Captain Frémont of the U. S. Army Topographical Engineers moved a party of about sixty men across the Sierra Nevada and into the interior valleys of California. This was Frémont's third western exploration, and like the previous missions, his official purpose was to discover the best railway route to the Pacific Coast. Denying both political and military intents, he obtained permission from General José Castro to remain in California on the condition that he stay away from the coast. In March, 1846, however, while passing through the Salinas Valley, Frémont was met by a company of California troops under the command of Lieutenant José Chavez who delivered an order from Castro that the Americans move out immediately. Refusing to comply, Frémont retreated to a fortified position, raised the American flag, and prepared for an attack. When the attack did not come after a three days' wait, Frémont retired, as he said, "slowly and growlingly" to the San Joaquin Valley and proceeded northward toward the Oregon border. There, in May, he was overtaken by Lieutenant Archibald Gillespie who had recently arrived in California after an overland journey across Mexico. Gillespie had been sent by the government to deliver a secret message addressed to Thomas O. Larkin, the American Consul at Monterey, from Secretary of State James Buchanan. This crucial dispatch explains the latest official plans, as of October, 1845, to obtain California peacefully by encouraging the Californians to secede from Mexico and join the United States. To carry out these plans, Buchanan appointed Larkin "confidential agent," directed him to recruit sub-agents, and indicated that Gillespie would cooperate. Gillespie, as ordered by the government, repeated the contents of this dispatch to Frémont

If I had the right that a personal acquaintance would give me to address General Frémont directly, I should set forth to him the purpose of my little book, and should frankly ask him for help in certain matters of perplexity. I should explain my position by saying that in my little sketch, which is to be, you know, one of Houghton, Mifflin & Co.'s "Commonwealth Series," it will happen, as I believe, for the first time, that a native of California undertakes to write an outline of the story of his State. Naturally then, as I should point out to General Frémont, a native is deeply interested

---

and delivered a packet of letters from Frémont's father-in-law, Senator Thomas Hart Benton. Informed of these plans, but also considering Castro's hostility and the impending war with Mexico, Frémont decided that Larkin's secret mission was no longer practical, and feeling furthermore that there was an immediate danger that Great Britain would snatch California away from the United States, Frémont felt that he must act promptly, if discreetly, to seize the territory. Returning immediately to California and encamped on the Sacramento River, he was visited by American settlers who were buzzing with the rumor that Castro intended to drive them out. Without actually participating, Frémont offered the settlers strategic advice, and thus the so-called "Bear Flag War" was begun. On June 10, the settlers seized a band of horses from Lieutenant Francisco Arce; they then set off for Sonoma where, on the morning of June 14, they captured General Mariano Vallejo, his brother, Salvador, and two advisors. Here also they first raised the famous Bear Flag, proclaimed a new government, and sent their prisoners to Frémont. On June 25, Frémont arrived at Sonoma determined to intervene directly. Pursuing the California cavalry to Sauselito, he crossed the Bay and spiked the guns at Fort Point at San Francisco. In the meantime, Commodore John D. Sloat arrived in Monterey with the news of the Mexican War. Hearing of Frémont's activities and supposing that he had acted upon official orders from Washington, Sloat took Monterey, and within five days the American flag was flying also over San Francisco, Sonoma, and Sutter's Fort. From this point forward, if not before, Larkin's peaceful mission was at an end, and the conquest of California became a military operation. On July 15, Sloat was replaced by Commodore Robert F. Stockton. Frémont enlarged his force through the volunteer enlistment of the Bear Flag men, and placing himself under the command of Stockton, he took the war into the South. Los Angeles was taken on August 13, but lost soon afterward; finally on January 13, 1847, the last of the Californians surrendered to Frémont at Cahuenga, and the war in California was over. Stockton appointed Frémont governor of the new territory, but General Stephen W. Kearny, who had arrived during the last days of the conflict, insisted that he alone had the power to establish a government. Frémont sided with Stockton, but when news from Washington supported Kearny's command, Frémont was accused of mutiny, insubordination, and prejudicial conduct. A court martial found him guilty, but President Polk suspended the sentence of dismissal. Insisting on his innocence, however, Frémont refused clemency and resigned from the service.

in getting, in the true perspective, a view of the men and of the deeds that had most to do with the exciting times of the Conquest; and the native is also free from the memories and the interests that have colored all the published histories and other accounts of early California. The party strifes, the personal likes and dislikes of those days, are unknown to him save by hearsay. He only wants to get the heroes of his story into their proper relations to one another. When one of the most prominent of these is still living, he naturally desires to ask of this hero at least a few questions, the more so in view of the fact that this hero has always been the object of the most conflicting and prejudiced judgments, of extravagant praises and of malignant abuse. The native dislikes both of these kinds of judgment. General Frémont is to him for the first just one of the heroes of the Conquest of California.

Now in trying to estimate General Frémont's early work in California, there are some parts that fortune brought very early into the most serious and detailed investigation, viz., those parts which the well-known court-martial most especially considered. There is another part, again, still earlier in time, and of less historical moment for California of which General Frémont himself gave full account in his published report on the Expedition of '42–'44.[22] But there is one part remaining, intermediate in time between these two, viz., the connection of General Frémont with the opening of the Conquest in the Spring and early Summer of '46; and this part is, as General Frémont himself best knows, very imperfectly stated in most if not in all published accounts of the Conquest of California. Here it is that I, in common with so many others, desire more light. I am not aware how much General Frémont is even now able to tell about this period without violation of confidence, or how far he will feel it necessary to decline to give a full account of this time in advance of any intended publication of his own Memoirs. I only know that, if I had the right, I should be very anxious to ask General Frémont to give me further information. Of course I desire neither to glorify nor to condemn anything in the whole story of that period, until I know all that I can discover of the truth about it. But I have been taught from childhood, like many other natives of California, to respect and admire the career of General

[22] *Report of the Exploring Expedition to the Rocky Mountains in the Year 1842, and to Oregon and North California in the Years 1843–44* (Washington: Blair and Rives, 1845. House Doc. 166, 28th Cong., 2d sess).

Frémont as the explorer and conqueror, and when I come to study and to estimate his work for myself, I want to clear up such perplexities as I can, and above all to be just to all parties concerned. General Frémont will readily anticipate my particular perplexities; they are exactly those of all the books yet published upon this period; and yet I venture to restate them here in form as they now come to me. I set them down in the shape of numbered questions, with explanations of each. I venture to state them quite frankly.

1. When General Frémont appeared in the Sacramento Valley that year, and then went alone to Monterey to get permission to rest his company in the Sacramento or in the San Joaquin valley, had he then any knowledge that led him to expect a collision between the United States and Mexico soon enough to involve him and his expedition? Had he instructions as to what he ought to do in view of any probable collision? Is it possible that the Government had already given him to understand that he might do well to hasten a collision with the California authorities?—I ask these questions, because tradition, in some of its forms, as General Frémont knows, imputes to him already at this point a disposition to act so as rather to provoke than to avoid trouble with the Californian authorities. If he had such a disposition, it is to be presumed that he had instructions from Washington that would justify his action. But no such instructions have been made public. Is this tradition then wholly wrong?

2. Be this as it may, what was General Frémont's real reason for leaving the valley of the San Joaquin, after his scattered party had been reunited, and for coming through the hills so near to Monterey? This act led, as you know, to a quarrel with Castro. It is I believe not stated in the published accounts that General Frémont had any permission from Castro to come nearer than the San Joaquin valley. Why did he then go beyond what was permitted him? Does this not look like deliberate hostility?—I still ask this question, although it of course suggests a criticism on General Frémont's course at this time as Captain of the expedition, and I do so because I want to explain these matters in the fairest way in my book, and am still at a loss how to do so. I am sure that General Frémont, who knows so well how his acts have been discussed, interpreted and misinterpreted in the past, will not be surprised at my desire to get in an unprejudiced way at the truth about this and other matters that are still dark. I do not want to uphold this

criticism of General Frémont's course at that time, unless it is just to do so.

3. I now come to the great mystery, which General Frémont has never publicly discussed in full. I know not whether it is even now proper for him to do so. He knows well how much of mythology has naturally grown up, in the minds of interested but uninformed people, about his meeting with Gillespie in the north, and about the consequences of that meeting. General Frémont has long since given some account of the matter, first in letters to Mr. Benton, which seem to have formed the basis of some published accounts, and later in answers to the questions of a Congressional Committee.[23] But the most important part of the story is, according to tradition, the part which General Frémont was forced as a servant of the Government, to keep back. The same is supposed by tradition to be the case with regard to the answers made by Gillespie before the same Congressional Committee. "Still," says tradition, "we are ignorant of the secret instructions that Gillespie brought for Frémont from Washington. Still we are unaware of what was contained in the letters of Mr. Benton that Gillespie at the same time delivered." Now is tradition right just here? And can General Frémont at this late day, clear up the mystery, or any part of it? General Frémont knows how the Legend of the Conquest (for so we must call the popular accounts in so far as they deal with such mysteries as these) how this legend, I say, has interpreted Gillespie's secret instructions. Do they not in fact, these instructions, as they are commonly interpreted, somewhat compromise the honor of our own Government? Is it possible that the instructions ordered the chief of the exploring expedition to begin a half-secret warfare with the Californians before actual hostilities had begun between the two countries? How could our government justify this action? And yet, if the instructions were otherwise, how did they result in so sad a precipitation of bloodshed as the early part of the conquest would seem to anyone who did not think it a positive necessity?—Cannot General Frémont then throw any new light on this matter of Gillespie's instructions and their consequences? Were they intended for a state of war, or for a state of peace? Did they imply that the government wanted California

[23] This was the Congressional Claims Committee (Sen. Rept. 75, 30th Congr., 1st sess., 1848) to which Frémont applied for payment of expenses of his California battalion.

by means of a revolt of the American settlers, such as followed in the Bear Flag affair? Or did they counsel rather the use of peaceful influence to induce the natives of California to leave their Mexican allegiance, and go over to the United States?

4. And in the same connection, is it possible to ascertain or to use the contents of the letters from Mr. Benton to General Frémont as they were delivered at that time to the latter by Gillespie?

5. Finally, is General Frémont disposed to give any fuller account than now exists in print of his relation to the Bear Flag affair as it subsequently developed itself?

I see of course that to ask these quite elaborate questions might involve putting General Frémont to much trouble. I do not want to be the cause of trouble or of waste of valuable time for him. If there is now existent in MS any answer to these or to similar questions, I should esteem it the greatest favor to be allowed a look at the same. If possibly a conversation could at sometime be allowed to me, without putting General Frémont to any serious inconvenience, I should be deeply thankful for it. I repeat that my sole object is to find out the just and true way to answer these questions that I must speak of in my book, and that I do not want to treat so ignorantly and blindly as many popular writers have done. General Frémont will see no doubt, how I desire neither to praise nor to blame unduly, but solely to do justice to a prominent historical character. I hope that he will not think me under the circumstances too bold, or find my requests altogether too troublesome. Upon any one or more of the foregoing matters I shall be grateful for any possible help, even if on the whole my request cannot be granted in full.

I am sorry to trouble you with this long letter, which is, as I must add, written in considerable haste, notwithstanding its length. Our old acquaintance and friendship encourages me in daring to give you so much labor.

—Yours Very Truly
Josiah Royce.

To Henry Lebbeus Oak, September 23, 1884[24]

14 Sumner St.
Cambridge, Mass.
Sept. 23, 1884.

My Dear Mr. Oak:

I send herewith a letter to Mr. Bancroft, which I beg you to forward. The address in Salt Lake City I forgot, with my usual historical accuracy. I have had hardly time to turn round here so far, as the term's work is approaching, and there are multitudinous vexatious details awaiting one when he gets back to such business. Still I find it good to be at home, and Cambridge is greener than Bernal Heights.[25]

I shall be some time in getting my Cal. book much forward. You shall hear from it further as soon as any of it is ready. I shall miss your advice very often, and I am sure that I shall always hold your kind help in grateful remembrance. I know not whether any of my leads will turn out of value. If I pick up any scrap of any worth, you shall hear of it; but am not very confident of success.

I shall always be glad to hear from you. Believe me

Yours Very Truly
Josiah Royce.

To George Buchanan Coale, November 1, 1884[26]

14 Sumner St.
Cambridge, Mass.
Nov. 1, '84.

My Dear Coale:

I have long owed you a good letter, but you know my ways of

[24] ALS. Oak Papers. HHL. Typescripts of all Royce letters in this collection are in Oak Papers, UCB.

[25] A district of San Francisco. The library of Hubert Howe Bancroft, where Royce had spent the summer of 1884, was located on Valencia near Mission, just at the northern edge of Bernal Heights.

[26] ALS. Redwood Collection. JHU.

old. I shall write you more soon, but just now I want to ask of you a favor, which you must not grant unless you really desire to do so. It is this:—My book on *The Religious Aspect of Philosophy*, having passed all the dangers of much rewriting, of much weeding out and of much burning up, and having fought its little fight with a ferocious publisher, has at last peacefully entered that publisher's fold, and, contracts for its publication having been signed, is expected to appear in print during this winter, possibly about Feb. 1, and possibly a little sooner. I want to know if you will let me dedicate it to you, in grateful memory of many happy hours spent with you and your house, as well as in recognition of the many helpful suggestions and the valuable stimulus that you have given me in my work. Were you anyone else, almost, I should fear to ask you this knowing, as I do, that you will disagree with some of the doctrines of my book. But I feel sure that I may hope for some sympathy from you with much of the spirit of the book, and I do not believe that accepting so small a thing as my dedication will make such a man as you feel at all responsible for all that I choose to maintain, or uncomfortable in view of our differences. At all events, I know of no other man to whom I desire to dedicate my first book nearly as much as I desire to dedicate it to you, and I shall hope for a favorable answer.

Remember me very warmly to all of your delightful household. My wife and boy are in very good health and spirits. More soon

Yours Very Truly
Josiah Royce.

To Henry Lebbeus Oak, December 9, 1884[27]

14 Sumner St., Cambridge, Mass.
Dec. 9, 1884.

My Dear Mr. Oak:

Last Saturday I had a long interview with General Frémont at Staten Island. I take the first opportunity to tell you about it, because, while the most of it was rather unfruitful, there was one

[27] ALS. Oak Papers. HHL. Partly printed by Robert Glass Cleland in his "Introduction" to Royce, *California* (New York: Alfred A. Knopf, 1948), p. xviii.

development that still seems to me, in my ignorance, decidedly startling. The full notes of the interview shall be copied and sent to you as soon as Frémont himself has seen a copy, and has added any remarks that he may wish. He is very willing to let me give Mr. Bancroft anything that I can get from himself.

The General is well-preserved, a pleasing old gentleman, quiet, cool, self-possessed, patient, willing to bear with objections of all sorts, but of course not too communicative. Mrs. F. is, I grieve to say, none the better for old age—very enthusiastic, garrulous, naïvely boastful, grandly elevated above the level of the historical in most that she either remembers or tells of the past. Both were very cordial to me, and I owe them quite a debt for their good will and their patience. I spent practically all the time on the operations before Sloat's seizure of Monterey. I hastened as fast as possible over the "grand issues," and the "great policy of my Father," upon which Mrs. F. eloquently insisted. I cross-questioned concerning F's motives, the Gillespie dispatches, the Benton letters of that mysterious "packet," and even the De Haro brothers[28]—all miserable little detestable incidents that Mrs. F. plainly regarded as worthy only of the attention of a very small-minded historian. I could get no access to any documents. The outcome was, as I said, not very different from what you would expect, save in a few things. Frémont gladly assumes a good deal of responsibility. He took a risk in acting as he did. The government "might disavow" him; that he well knew when he seized Arce's horses. He makes no plea of self-defense, and no point of Castro's mythical "proclamation to the settlers." He does not remember even when or how he first heard of the McNamara business,[29] and does not try to plead that as a motive (and for obvious reasons). He acted because he "desired to serve the country" (i.e. the U.S.) in this way; he was sure that the government "wanted him to do all that was possible to get Cal.,"

[28] Among the several persons killed by the Bear Flag men, after their seizure of Sonoma, were the twin brothers, Ramón and Francisco de Haro.

[29] Eugene McNamara, an Irish priest, petitioned the California government for a grant of 3,000 square leagues to which he intended to bring 10,000 Irish colonists. The plans did not materialize because California fell to the Americans before arrangements were completed, but the scheme did increase American fears that McNamara was a British agent and that England intended to acquire California through massive colonialization. Although Frémont did not repeat these fears to Royce, he did later use the "McNamara business" to justify his part in the conquest: see John Charles Frémont, "The Conquest of California," *Century* 19 (April 1891): 927–98.

and he felt that, if no war with Mex. followed, he could say that he had in acting taken a "personal risk that the government knew him to be taking and wanted him to take." I give the substance of his words somewhat roughly.

All this you will have expected. All this, you will say, is a falsification of what we know from the real Gillespie dispatch ⟨of which I said nothing whatever to Frémont⟩. Frémont you will say chooses thus to falsify, not having any notion of the existence of the opposing evidence.—But now, the startling thing is behind, which makes me hesitate to accept this very simple explanation. I convinced myself as well as anyone could be convinced by such evidence that, now at least, *Frémont is wholly ignorant that Gillespie brought any dispatch to Larkin at all, or* ⟨wonderful!⟩ *that Larkin was a secret agent of the U.S. at any time*, or had any secret connection with any of the business of the acquisition of Cal.

Here of course the evidence of such a curious ignorance cannot be fully given, and is of course also indirect. Let me sum it up as I can.—I made, as I say, no mention of the Larkin dispatch. I asked Frémont the old questions about what Gillespie brought him. I received the old answers, somewhat revised and completed.—Then I said: "Larkin knew of all this of course?"—"Larkin?" answered F. with seemingly sincere surprise, "Larkin knew nothing." "Did not Gillespie bring him anything?" I said.—"Nothing, I am sure," said F.—"I could not have failed to know. I was the only person entrusted with anything."—I of course took the attitude of innocent inquirer and found a safe refuge in telling Frémont about J. S. Hittell's account of the business,[30] as sufficient basis or explanation for my conjecture. Thence I went on to probe the matter. I returned to it several times. I insisted and explained. I told how Larkin was supposed to be a Secret Agent, how he wrote, in the letter that Hittell publishes, expressing in a mild official way his disappointment at what Frémont had done, how everything indicated that there was something between the government and Larkin of special weight.—To all Frémont listened with every sign of genuine surprise and incredulity. He had not read Hittell, he had never heard of the report about Larkin, the thing was very improbable indeed. Larkin was not the sort of man for that business. Larkin and he had often talked things over; but never was there mention of this or of

[30] *A History of the City of San Francisco and Incidentally of the State of California* (San Francisco: A. L. Bancroft and Co., 1878).

anything like it. That Larkin may have been instructed to conciliate the natives in a general way was possible; but Secret Agent—never.

Mrs. F. could not restrain her indignation at Hittell's absurd notion. Larkin she knew very well in '49. She was at his house. He was very hospitable—Mrs. L. not so.—But he was an ignorant and utterly tactless man. He never could keep a secret. He was deaf—very deaf. He talked therefore incessantly, being unable to listen. He spilled over with everything. He was prodigiously vain. Had he ever been Secret Agent, he would have boasted of it endlessly.—Such a man for a delicate secret mission—Absurd! Impossible! All through this demonstration, you must know, I had the precious dispatch in copy in my pocket, as I had been reading it over that very morning. I thank you most heartily for one of the keenest delights of my life, in that, through your kindness and Mr. Bancroft's I was enabled to sit there and hear these two distinguished historical characters demonstrate that this dispatch, which so nearly affected them both, was yet nonexistent, impossible, absurd, a fantastic bit of nonsense. I kept my secret pretty well I hope. I appeared puzzled; and I was. I said nothing about what was in my pocket. I simply wrote them both down.—My admiration for Larkin, however, rose rapidly. Vain and garrulous,—unable to keep the smallest secret: give us all that man for a secret agent who manages to convey such an impression of himself—and to keep his secret still!

But to return.—Both the Frémonts seemed anxious to have me get at State Papers in Washington. I announced my intention to do so if possible. They offered to help me in this. They were above all anxious to prove that this story about Larkin, of Hittell's invention, is an utterly unfounded absurdity. They wanted me to see the papers to convince myself.—In short, in every possible way they showed sincere surprise and even indignation. Evidently my very reference to Larkin really took them by surprise. They gave every sign of never having dreamt of that side of the story.—I may be mistaken, and I beg for your advice about it; but at this moment I cannot but believe them sincere in that point. I do believe of course in Frémont's professions on all the other important points. But just there I seemed to strike a vein of genuine feeling. About Larkin he had not been prepared to hear. I therefore *do not believe that he knows about what Gillespie brought to Larkin, or knows that Gillespie brought anything to Larkin.* Gillespie then must have had a secret from Frémont.

The point is of fundamental importance. If Gillespie brought *two* sets of instructions, *and was instructed to keep that fact secret from Frémont* ⟨perhaps also from Larkin⟩, then may there not have been duplicity in Buchanan himself? Was it his plan to set two men working different ways? Absurd and detestable as this hypothesis seems, I am compelled to think twice of it.[31]

So there is still some mystery here, or am I wholly mistaken? How do you explain all this seemingly sincere surprise about Larkin? What motive can Frémont have to ignore Larkin maliciously. How could he venture to? What would be the worth of it all? Why kick against evidence if he knows the truth? Why hope to conceal what Hittell has published?

Out of these mysteries I see just now no way but to get at the State Dep't. papers. If I can do so, you shall have a copy of every one that I can get. Meanwhile I am delaying my whole undertaking till I get more light. Whenever the MS is advanced, you shall see it. Believe me

Yours Faithfully
Josiah Royce.

To Henry Lebbeus Oak, January 1, 1885[32]

14 Sumner St. Cambridge.
Jan. 1, 1885.

My Dear Mr. Oak:

I want to report a little progress, though not much. A copy of my notes on the Frémont interview, properly supplemented by my memory of what passed, has been sent to the Frémonts for their marginal notes and corrections, and is still in their hands. Meanwhile, in answer to my urgent request, Mrs. Frémont is trying to give me further evidence about the Larkin matters, or rather, about the impossibility that there should have been any Larkin matters of consequence at all; also, similarly excellent evi-

[31] Royce eventually rejected both hypotheses (i.e., that Frémont was ignorant of Larkin's mission and that Buchanan had issued two contradictory sets of instructions). Frémont ("Conquest of California," pp. 922 ff.) later admitted that Gillespie did tell him of Larkin's mission, but insisted that he had private, unwritten instructions to possess California by any means necessary.

[32] ALS. Oak Papers. UCB.

dence concerning the well-known "race" of Seymour with Sloat.[33] She has accordingly written me a letter declaring once more very positively that there is not any possibility of Larkin's agency, and that she never heard of such a thing before. Then she adds the accompanying formal preliminary statement of evidence, intended, as you will see, to show that she knew all about the Mexican War, and is an infallible person. I have thought that the document might amuse you, although in itself it is a trifle discouraging. As it contains nothing that can help me, I show no generosity in presenting it as a New Year's gift to the Bancroft Library, where it may take its place among the curiosities, and serve to instruct you all a little as to the true feminine way of writing history. Notice the beautiful *sequitur* in the whole discussion:—One Mrs. Greenough was drowned during the Civil War, while she was landing from a blockade-runner with a quantity of English gold on her sinful person. This gold, which so justly then and there drowned her, had been given to her by the base English government in payment for ancient services rendered by her as a spy during the Mexican War on our State Department. *Ergo*, the English must have intended Seymour to take California.—

The MS of the interview will follow soon, I hope.—I have still no assurance about the papers in Washington, but shall do my best.—When I write *my* book, I shall try to do what I can to respect your rights in regard to the Larkin dispatch.—I am putting on the screws a little with the Frémonts, but I have not yet revealed to them the existence of the dispatch. That will keep.—

Yours

J. Royce

Another bit of historical evidence to which I must especially call your attention, is the matter of T. H. Benton's Brussels carpet, mentioned in Mrs. F.'s statement. You have probably never considered what grand evidence an old carpet can furnish.—Talk of the *dusty* tomes of history!!

[33] Legend had it that Admiral George Seymour, commander of the British frigate *Collingwood*, had raced Sloat to Monterey, suggesting that if Seymour had arrived first he would have seized California for England. Seymour did follow Sloat from Mazatlán to Monterey, but having arrived after Sloat had raised the American flag, Seymour merely exchanged courtesies and left. Royce viewed the entire legend as fictitious.

To George Buchanan Coale, January 7, 1885[34]

14 Sumner St.
Cambridge.
Jan. 7, '85.

My Dear Coale:

I write in the midst of numerous little occupations to ask you what I ought to have asked before. I have just finished my proofs of the text of my book, and now proceed to the preface, table of contents and dedication. The latter I shall put in the common and simple form, but I suppose that I ought to print your *full* name. As for your middle name, however, I rack my weak brains in vain to bring it up again. A year since, when I was with you, I asked it of Miss Mary, with this dedication, as I confess, already in mind. She kindly told me, but now alas! it refuses to come. I want also to follow your preference as to the matter; perhaps you would prefer simply the "George B." form.

The book will hardly be later than the middle of February in appearing. I hope that it will be earlier.

Give my affectionate regards to all the family. I thank Mrs. Coale very heartily for her kindness in expressing a wish to see me again. It is faintly possible that I shall be obliged to go South this spring on some business connected with my work on California. I cannot say. I should be delighted at the chance of seeing you all in passing. My goal would be Washington.

My family is well. The boy is as hearty as ever, and he and I frequently talk philosophy together. The other day he found for the first time a picture of a centaur. It was in an Almanac. He was much concerned, and brought it to his mother. "O mamma," he said, "This man has broke his horse." I tried to introduce the suggestion that this horse had broke his man; but as Christopher resisted all efforts to introduce that aspect of the subject, I gave it up. Mrs. Royce sends best regards.—Hoping to hear at once as to the immediate occasion of this letter, I remain

Yours Truly
Josiah Royce.

[34] ALS. Redwood Collection. JHU.

To George Buchanan Coale, February 3, 1885[35]

14 Sumner St.
Cambridge.
Feb. 3, '85.

My Dear Coale:—

You must forgive a delay that was not of my choosing, but that I certainly ought to have explained, and that in fact I should have explained much sooner, had I realized how long it would last. This is the story thereof:—

A sudden decision of the publisher, influenced by some business consideration or other, ordered me, just as I was nearing the end of my proofs, to finish all my work in great haste and to let the book out at once, viz. Jan. 24.—I was willing, and the thing was pushed through forthwith. As soon as the sheets reached the binder, I went to him to order your copy specially bound in plain leather; for I was not minded to put you off with vile cloth. The binder responded that whereas cloth bindings could be run off in 24 hrs. at a press, leather needed *ten days*. So I was in the vexatious dilemma either of having to let the public see the book days before you, to whom it is dedicated, or else of having to give you your first look at it in the aforesaid vile cloth. I chose the former alternative, with the delay as you have experienced it; but I had expected after all to get the book two or three days at least before I did. I had also meant to write to you at once in explanation. But the moment of publication being a rather scatter-witted one, not to say busy, each day went by without my duty done.—I hope that you by this time have the sober little leather copy that I expressed the other day; it is at least flexibly sewed and tolerably durable. I put in a verse or two of Schiller's on the fly leaf—about the good things that flit away in this changing world; and felt the verses more or less appropriate in a book whose dedication will, with many other things, always associate its pages with the very happy student-days in Baltimore, and with the quickly past early youth that your friendship and that of your family helped to make delightful, and to me very valuable. To anything further in the way of a dedication-epistle I

[35] ALS. Redwood Collection. JHU.

could not bring myself, who am no writer of compliments, and can only assure you in private that I mean what my dedication says, and much more too.

The book had meanwhile to be marketed and sent abroad. A good many will have seen what was meant for your eye before you have seen it. Meanwhile I hope that you will forgive my delay, and the vexation that it caused you.

With best greetings from mine to yours I remain

Very Truly Yours
Josiah Royce.

To HENRY LEBBEUS OAK, FEBRUARY 11, 1885[36]

14 Sumner St., Cambridge.
Mass.
Feb. 11, '85

Dear Mr. Oak:

Do you want a copy of a MS statement received by me through Mrs. J. C. F., and purporting to be from the dictation (to his own amanuensis) of Rodman Price?[37] This statement is all that the accursed Frémont mill has further ground out for me as yet. The MS copy of my interview with J. C. F. stays with Mrs. J. C. [Frémont] still for notes & what not. The statement of Rodman Price details his part in urging Sloat to raise the flag, and adds the weight of his name, if that is anything, to the opinion that Admiral Seymour did in person confess that his mission was to seize Cal. The statement has quite recently been made, is freshly and earnestly written, and is prepared especially for Mrs. J. C. [Frémont] and me. Of course I know nothing about the trustworthiness of the man, and have no idea whether you have all the information that you want about him. The original of the statement Mrs. J. C. F. wants herself, and I cannot keep it. But you shall have the copy that I

[36] ALS. Oak Papers. HHL.

[37] Rodman Price, later governor of New Jersey, had been, in 1846, the naval purser aboard the *U. S. Cyane*. Price claimed that he had secret information on California affairs from President Polk; he further claimed that he related these secrets to Sloat, and emphasizing his fears of a British plot, he caused the Commodore to raise the flag at Monterey.

(not Mrs. J. C. [Frémont]) shall have made from the MS, if it will be of the slightest use to you.

The only chance at Washington is to wait until this miserable political pother is over,[38] with the 4th of March, and then to go down myself and make a nuisance of myself until I get some satisfaction. Satisfactory answer by mail I can get none.—Completion of my own MS is postponed until summer with my publisher's consent.

Please let me know your pleasure about the Price matter, and believe me

Yours Very Truly
Josiah Royce

To George Buchanan Coale, March 14, 1885[39]

14 Sumner St., Cambridge.
March 14, 1885.

My Dear Coale:

I think of going south during our "fast day" vacation. "Fast day" is proclaimed by the governor for Apr. 2. The vacation is to be a week long.

My special business, I am sorry to say, lies this time in Washington, albeit I seek not office, but a look at a few State Papers, which ought to be extant in the State Department at Washington, and which, if they are extant and accessible will solve for me a fascinating problem about the Secret History of the Conquest of California by our brave Administration in '46. If these papers are found at all, a short time will suffice to learn from them what I want to know.

How long the search may last, I cannot say, nor how my time will be arranged. But if the wish that you so kindly expressed in a recent letter should find reinforcement just then in your convenience, I should indeed be delighted to see something again of you and your household, either in passing, or even during a part of my search, which may occupy only a little time each day.

Please give your family the best wishes of all mine. We prosper here very well. My book meets a reasonable and for the most part

38 Royce here refers to the patronage crisis caused by the election of Grover Cleveland, the first Democratic president since James Buchanan.

39 ALS. Redwood Collection. JHU.

kindly though of course very quiet reception, from the few critics who have dealt with it thus far. To be sure, some of the more vigorous among them have been moved to friendly remonstrance, and of these one calls me an "atheist," another a "learned ass." I hardly venture therefore to hope for the approval of my more critical friends in future.

Believe me meanwhile, whatever else I may prove, to be

Yours Truly
Josiah Royce.

To Henry Lebbeus Oak, March 14, 1885[40]

Cambridge, Mass., March 14, '85

Dear Mr. Oak:

The accompanying MS, which will rather amuse than instruct you, is sent as an "original," so far as Mrs. Frémont's notes are concerned, and may find a place in the Bancroft Library.[41] I have copied the MS for my own use, but feel that the copy ought to remain with me, while the original properly belongs to you, as to the collectors of original material, rather than to myself, the professed dabbler. I consign to you therefore the precious autograph of Mrs. Frémont.

Let me state once more the source and growth of this MS. In December last I visited Mr. and Mrs. Frémont at Staten Island, and spent part of a day in an interview with them upon the matters herein set forth. Mr. Frémont led the conversation, and Mrs. Frémont took charge of the episodes. I do not write short-hand, but took the best notes that I could in long-hand, asking for careful dictation of whatever assertions seemed to me most important, and summarizing other matters as nearly as possible in the order of their presentation. On returning, I wrote to you my impressions of the interview, and also wrote out my own notes, and sent the latter to Mrs. Frémont in the form in which you now see them. Half of each page I left blank, to invite her to write a little history in her own hand. The

40 ALS. CSL.

41 Royce's autograph notes on his interview with the Frémonts, with marginalia by Jessie Benton Frémont, are in the Oak Papers, UCB.

result has been this not voluminous, but somewhat characteristic collection of notes in her writing.

For the accuracy of *my* summary, the fullness of my notes, and the freshness of my memory in supplementing them, must be my chief guarantee, since the fact that Mrs. F. accepts them is chiefly of use in proving that they did not for the most part offend her. In carrying on the conversation I used my own judgment in the order of topics discussed. I mentioned Mr. J. S. Hittell, as you see, and also read to Mr. Frémont a MS statement that I have from Bidwell, which criticises Mr. Frémont very sharply.[42] These matters I introduced under the plea that such and such criticisms are publicly made, and that I desired, as a student of the history of the affair, to estimate the same justly. Of your Larkin dispatch I said nothing; and the Frémonts are still in profound ignorance, or forgetfulness (or by whatever other name you will call it), of that same paper.

In case you want to refer in a note to this statement, I may as well add that I have full permission both to print, and (meanwhile) to hand over to you this whole statement; saving only that the portion which Mrs. Frémont has with rare tact and discrimination stricken out, as being too true to be kind, ought not, as I suppose, to be publicly quoted, although I feel quite free to save from the flames so characteristic a specimen of Mrs. F.'s historical method, and one that does such honor to her insight and generosity.

In conclusion I ought to acknowledge the great kindness and courtesy that Mr. and Mrs. Frémont so generously showed me, as well as their obviously disinterested efforts to help on the cause of eternal historical truth. There is a certain passionless serenity in the statement, and in Mrs. Frémont's notes, which indicates a curious loftiness of mind, far above little passions. Especially in the mention of the De Haro incident, in the crushing reflections on the little brief authority wherewith Larkin was insolently puffed up, in the determination to insist on the vastness of the plans that led to the acquisition of California, and finally in the sublime alteration of the word "admitted" to the word "said" in one part of my MS ⟨showing that Mr. Frémont is far above the littleness of having

[42] John Bidwell, an early settler at Sutter's Fort, had been a lieutenant and quartermaster in Frémont's battalion. Royce found the Bidwell MS in the Bancroft Library and used it as a primary source in his *California*, pp. 78–81. In a rewritten version and with some editorial assistance from Royce, Bidwell's account was published in "Frémont in the Conquest of California," *Century* 19 (February 1891): 518–25.

to "admit" anything⟩: in all these matters the statement impresses me with the simple sublimity of the confessions of the great. It is because you are, as I know, used to the sublime in the writings of the early conquerors, trappers, governors, generals, horse-thieves, priests, miners, politicians and smugglers of California history, that I venture to anticipate for you some amusement in reading what arouses in me only reverence.

Yours Truly
Josiah Royce.

To Horace Elisha Scudder, April 14, 1885[43]

14 Sumner St., Cambridge.
April 14, 1885

My Dear Mr. Scudder:—

I have returned from Washington with excellent success. All important papers bearing on the matter have, I am fairly sure, been included in what I asked for. And all that I asked for, the department very courteously showed, not, to be sure, without some rather amusing show of delay and mystery, intended only to satisfy the demands of official custom and propriety.

The result looks bad indeed for the Frémonts; and I have given them a chance to explain, a last chance, and for them, I fancy, a chance of some trifling importance. They have never before been directly threatened with the official documents.—My probable result, I am bound to say, will be, so far as my present foresight can tell me, simply a confirmation of H. H. Bancroft's view, reached on the basis of his secret documents. The archives at Washington seem to show that he has in his possession all the essential facts. Yet that result, if for me somewhat negative, is important in itself, since now I can for the first time speak with a confidence that Washington holds nothing of importance not known to us in this matter; so that the Larkin papers in Bancroft's library tell not only the truth, but practically the whole truth.

When I hand in my MS in the last of the summer sometime, I shall doubtless want to ask the firm to consider whether it will estimate the lump value of my MS, deduct therefrom the balance

[43] ALS. Scudder Papers. UCB.

due on my Religious Philosophy plates, and pay me the remainder in cash. If the firm consents to that arrangement, I shall get possibly a less payment than I should otherwise have, if I waited for sales, but I shall doubtless need any cash I can get, as this year has been a little expensive to me, and I have fallen a trifle behind. I shall be glad to know, in case you happen to have heard, how my Religious Philosophy is selling, if at all. I have not asked before, and have heard absolutely nothing about the matter, since the first day or so of the book's life. I am tired of the few reviews I have got, and my soul is actually set upon nothing but gain, as you well know, else why do I publish?

My regards to Mrs. Scudder; and if my wife knew of my writing, I am sure she would join me.

Yours Very Truly
Josiah Royce.

To Henry Lebbeus Oak, April 14, 1885[44]

14 Sumner St., Cambridge, Mass.
April 14, 1885.

My Dear Mr. Oak:

I have just returned from Washington, whither I went on the great quest, viz., not office, but the Frémont documents. I come back almost wholly a convert to your point of view. To sum it all up in the briefest form: Neither in State nor in War Departments, so I am officially informed, does there exist any secret instruction in 1845–6 to any officer in California relating to acts before the war itself, saving alone the instruction that Gillespie carried to Larkin. That indeed exists, as large as life, and the State Dep't still regards it as a pretty little secret, and hesitates a good while over it, but is willing at last to show it all but one paragraph, viz. the one telling Larkin how he "should not fail on all proper occasions prudently to warn the government and people of California &c."—I suppose that those prudent warnings, intended to make rebels of Mexico's faithful Californian subjects, seem just a little unfair, so that the Department is not proud of them. So the dispatch is, with much show of mystery, displayed at last by the "Keeper of Indexes

44 ALS. Oak Papers. HHL.

and Archives," with a sheet of paper pinned over that page. I had the pleasure of reading that covered paragraph to the keeper from my note-book, and of asking him if the Department had any serious objection to letting me know whether my surmises were correct. Thereupon the Department consulted with itself a little more in private, and solemnly informed me that my surmises were "substantially correct." So the science of conjectural emendation advances a step, and meanwhile, by my visit, the authenticity as well as the importance of your Larkin dispatch receives a chance of official confirmation that no thousand of Williams's can call in to doubt. There the dispatch is, safe in the books of the Department; and the books of the department contain, save the originals of Larkin's Consular correspondence, nothing else of importance bearing on the matter. In short all that Washington is at all apt to yield is now in your possession! !

Yet my visit was in no wise fruitless for me. It has given me the means of applying the thumb-screw to the Frémonts as I never could do or tried to do while I had only seen your papers. The Frémonts would throw up dust, deny the authenticity, decline to notice, insist that the only true information must be in Washington archives, and I know not what else they might do by way of evasion if I had spoken only of your papers. Now however I look for fun. I want to do them justice, and shall give them a very fair chance; but it will be best for them to use that chance. What means I have taken, I however want you to know; so I shall send you a fair draught of the letter to Mrs. F. which I am now preparing, a draught prepared by my wife and written in shape to keep as a document, if you so desire, in this investigation. For with my letter before you, you can better judge of Mrs. F.'s letter when it comes; for of course you shall have it so soon as it comes. Perhaps she will take to the woods, and refuse to answer.

With the draught I shall enclose a reply that I received from the Secretary of War to my humble petition for information in his archives. Also you will find a copy of two curious letters from the consular books, found by me in the State Department, mere straws indeed, but of a little interest, as tending on the whole in the same direction as the other evidence. They bear on the history of the mysterious "packet" that Gillespie brought from Benton to Frémont.–Oct. 17, Gillespie's mission was determined upon, and the dispatch to Larkin dated. Gillespie, according to his own testimony before the claims committee, set out in the early part of November. His letter of introduction to Frémont is dated Nov. 3.—What had detained him does not appear. But meanwhile, Oct. 27, there has appeared in the State Department a "packet" for Frémont. It is undoubtedly the Benton packet. Buchanan has consented to forward it. He is disposed to trust it across Mexico, and so determines to send it to Black[45] & Larkin by an ordinary post. Second thoughts arise, the little letters to Black and Larkin are, as you see, cancelled, and the packet entrusted to Gillespie. This little piece of evidence goes to show that the Benton packet itself & consequently that the content of the Benton packet *was not in Buchanan's mind* when he wrote the dispatch of Oct. 17, and that, when this packet, Oct. 27, was put into the hands of the Department, it had *no necessary connection in Buchanan's mind with Gillespie's mission*, and was thought of possibly as some ordinary private thing of Benton's, to be sent across Mexico by post, care of Consul Black. Only the *after-reflection* that Gillespie would serve for the purpose made him then the bearer of the packet which Frémont would have us think almost his whole business. How does that combination seem to you?

As for the use of my Frémont interview by you in your forthcoming volume, you are welcome to any use that the present unfinished state of my work with the Frémonts makes fair, not to me (for I am very glad of *any* possible use that you can make of what I may send), but to the Frémonts themselves, who of course want their position fully understood before they are criticised for their statements. You will understand from the accompanying letter to Mrs. F. the peculiar delicacy of my present relations to them both, and will appreciate my anxiety to have them feel that whether I bless or curse them I yet keep my historical obligations intact towards them, by awaiting patiently their fullest explanation of my difficulties, and by fully and fairly stating their side. If you bear me in mind in this sense in what use you make of their statement, I am sure that you will use the interview rightly, and you are abundantly welcome to it in every sense.

With regards to Mr. Bancroft I remain

Yours Very Truly
Josiah Royce.

I hope that my free revelation of the Larkin dispatch to the innocent and maltreated Frémont will not seem to you indiscreet. Of

[45] John Black was the U. S. Consul to Mexico.

course it must be quite new to him, poor fellow, and he might at once print it, in advance of us all, out of a pure love of truth! But my opinion is that the screws must be well applied, and I know no better way than this.

To Jessie Benton Frémont, April 14, 1885[46]

14 Sumner St. Cambridge.
April 14, 1885.

Dear Mrs. Frémont:

I am sorry to have once more to weary you with a long letter; but the knowledge that you and General Frémont will naturally take a personal interest in the present state of my investigation of the problems of the Conquest of California, encourages me to undertake a letter that is no less an act of common justice to you than an effort to help on my own study. As I have several times assured you, I am as historical student concerned only with the truth about this matter, and have no desire either to vindicate or to attack anybody, save in case I must. When I present objections and difficulties to you, I do so because I should prefer to get them solved before I go to print, rather than to let them stand unjustly in my book. In this letter I accordingly have to state certain difficulties that appear to me when I compare, as I have just had the opportunity to do, General Frémont's interpretation of his position and conduct in the Spring of '46 with the official documents on file in the State Department. I have just been in Washington, have had very good opportunities there, have been very courteously treated at the State and War Departments, and have seen, as I fancy, very nearly all that the government of that time has left on record of its California policy. I find it hard to reconcile what I find with General Frémont's understanding of his own position, save on the hypothesis that the Cabinet and Gillespie were not frank in their dealings with him. It is therefore but just both to you and to General

[46] ALC. Oak Papers. UCB. This letter is a copy in Mrs. Royce's hand prepared for The Bancroft Library; it is marked in Royce's hand, "Copy of my letter of inquiry to Mrs. Frémont," and was undoubtedly sent as an enclosure with Royce's letter to Oak, April 14, 1885. Presumably it was to this letter that Royce referred in *California*, p. 116. The original has not been located.

Frémont that I should state somewhat explicitly what I have found. The papers at Washington are doubtless as open to you as they were to me, and you can easily discover whether I am right in my interpretation of them.

In the first place then, you and General Frémont are mistaken in supposing that Larkin had no secret instructions or confidential mission from the government. This is no longer a matter of opinion, but of simple fact. In the archives of the State Department I have seen a letter, addressed to him by Secretary Buchanan, appointing him Secret Agent, and instructing him as such. The mission in question is regarded by the government as important. Larkin receives special pay for it. It is a mission of the sort that Hittell mentions, a peaceful mission, whose object is the acquirement of California by means of an intrigue leading to the free transfer of the department to the U.S. by the will of its own inhabitants.

I will not leave this interpretation dependent on my own judgment, but will give you quotations from the document, sufficient to show you the purpose of the instructions. I underline some more important passages: all underlinings are my own.

"The future destiny of that country is a subject of anxious solicitude for the government and people of the United States. The interests of our commerce and our whale fisheries . . . demand that you ⟨Larkin⟩ should exert the greatest vigilance in discovering and defeating any attempts which may be made by Foreign Governments to acquire a control over that country. *In the contest between Mexico and California we can take no part, unless the former should commence hostilities against the United States; but should California assert and maintain her independence, we shall render her all the kind offices in our power as a Sister Republic.* This government has no ambitious aspirations to gratify, and no desire to extend our Federal System over more Territory than we already possess, unless by the free and spontaneous wish of the independent people of adjoining Territories. *The exercise of compulsion or improper influence to accomplish such a result, would be repugnant* both to the policy and principles of this government. But whilst these are the sentiments of the President, he could not view with indifference the transfer of California to Great Britain or any other European Power. The system of colonization by foreign Monarchies on the North American continent must and will be resisted by the United States." ⟨Then follow one or two sentences in the same vein, ending thus—⟩ "Even Great Britain by the acquisition of California would sow the seeds of future War and disaster for herself."

So much for the long preamble. Now for the particular instructions. In view of these dangers and of the above-mentioned wish of the Government to get California "without compulsion or improper influence," in case such can be done before the war with Mexico opens, Larkin is instructed as to means as follows:—"On all proper occasions you should not fail *prudently to warn the Government and people of California* of the danger of such an interference to their peace and prosperity,—⟨i.e. foreign interference⟩ *to inspire them with a jealousy of European dominion, and to arouse in their bosoms that love of liberty and independence so natural to the American Continent.* Whilst I repeat that this government does not, under existing circumstances, intend to interfere between Mexico and California, they would vigorously interpose to prevent the latter from becoming a British or French Colony. *In this they might surely expect the aid of the Californians themselves*" ⟨The italicizing is mine⟩.

"Whilst the President will make no effect and use no influence to induce California to become one of the free and independent States of this Union, *yet if the people should desire to unite their destiny with ours, they would be received as brethren whenever this can be done*, without affording Mexico just cause of complaint. *Their true policy, for the present, in regard to this question is to let events take their course*, unless an attempt should be made to transfer them, without their consent, either to Great Britain or France. *This they ought to resist by all the means in their power.*" —The dispatch then instructs Larkin to collect all possible information about the province, and to employ, if necessary, other persons to help him. It ends by announcing to Larkin his appointment as Secret Agent. Pay *$6.00 per diem* and his expenses.

Now my interpretation of the foregoing dispatch must be made in the light of Larkin's previous letters to the Department, which I have also seen. He had long been trying to effect a growth of American influence in the territory, and had been letting the State Dep't know of his efforts. In approving of his work, as Buchanan expressly does, and in appointing him, as is done at the end of this dispatch, Secret Agent, the Dep't makes tolerably clear its policy, at least for the moment. Translated into unofficial language this dispatch means very plainly: "Prepare the Californians to cöoperate with us in getting the province from Mexico before the war begins. Prepare them at all events to accept willingly the transfer to our flag when the war has begun. We know from your correspondence what coldness exists between California and Mexico; take advantage thereof. Make the Californians regard us as brothers, *prudently inspire them with a hatred alike of England and of Mexico*, assure them of our good will. In a word *intrigue for us*, and get California, or help to get it, peacefully."—Meanwhile, of course, the Cabinet was ready with its known instructions to the Naval Commanders to take Cal. whenever the news of war should come to them. But until that time, Larkin's intrigues are evidently intended to prepare the way, so that, when the navy appears, there may remain no resistance to overcome on the part of the already only very feebly loyal Mexican Californians. Larkin is by his friendly overtures to make the Californians rebels against Mexico and friends to us.

This, I say, is the plain meaning of the dispatch to Larkin on its face. If that was not the Cabinet policy, the Cabinet at least deliberately chose to make Larkin believe so, and to pay him $6.00 a day for acting on such belief, and for carrying out this scheme.

Otherwise the Cabinet had no sort of reason for troubling Consul Larkin, garrulous and deaf as he was, with their plans at all. Surely then they wanted his services in the manner above described.

You proved to me so clearly the impossibility of this dispatch to Larkin, that I feel very deeply how incredible its existence, and the existence of the policy outlined in it would be, if the dispatch were not in black and white, both among Mr. Larkin's own papers, and in the archives at Washington. As it is, I have to deal with this fact as I am—and the most plausible theory would be, apart from the date of the dispatch, that the Cabinet, after thus instructing Larkin, came once more to its better, or at least to its more warlike senses, and resolved to instruct Colonel Frémont in the sense mentioned in his interview with me, viz: in his words, so as to "include such means as were actually used under the circumstances," and so as to get "California if there should be the least chance opened and by force if necessary." For so General Frémont understood the Government's position. He is sure that *there is no chance that one knowing his instructions could accuse him of disobeying them.* Yet how could his acts, and consequently his instructions, be reconciled with the policy of the Larkin dispatch? This one policy says: "Intrigue peacefully with the Spanish Californians." The other says, "Take possession of the province forcibly if the least chance offers." The only policy runs: "Assure the inhabitants that they are our brethren, that we shall cordially welcome them as such if they will cut loose from Mexico, that they ought so to cut loose, that they may expect in such case 'kind offices' from us, that their prosperity lies with us, and that we will fight at their sides against the English should the English come." The other policy determines deliberately upon beginning war against these very people, in order to conquer their territory from them. It offers them no 'kind offices as a Sister Republic,' seeks not to induce them to separate peaceably from Mexico, undertakes no intrigues with their chief men, but, on the contrary, seizes their government's horses when a band of these pass near, takes possession of Sonoma, and after seizing prominent men as prisoners, prepares for war to the end. No one could recognize the policy of the Larkin dispatch in the gallant and vigorous "disregard of red tape,"[47] with which General Frémont courageously assaulted the authorities whom Larkin was "prudently to warn."—The antithesis is perfect.

In yet one other way however, I venture to insist upon a contrast that is in itself extremely obvious. The importance of the matter must excuse my prolixity.—*If* Larkin, acting on his instructions, *had* gone on to take part in a plan for the independence of California under United States protection, *if* this plan had been nearly ripe, and *if* in the midst of it had come the taking of Sonoma &c., with all the hostility, and *if* both Larkin's intrigue and General Frémont's gallant onset had been equally the result of instructions from our Government, in what position would our Cabinet be placed? Plainly in a very unbearable position, which would justly have seemed to the Californians, and to us Americans also, whenever we came to know it, not such a position as we are usually proud to believe our Government willing to assume. To intrigue for a friendly delivery of the department on one hand, with assurances of brotherly love, of "kind offices" &c.; and, on the other hand, even while we were so attracting the attention and lulling the suspicions of prominent men, to instruct an able and vigorous

[47] Here Royce is quoting William Barrows, *Oregon: The Struggle for Possession* (Boston: Houghton, Mifflin and Co., 1883), p. 273.

young officer to do what he could in the way of force *whenever the least opportunity offered:*—what treacherous Cabinet would be so rash as this? Surely not an American one, surely not the patriotic cabinet whose policy you have so well and enthusiastically described to me. Surely such double dealing would seem too reckless and too false for any cabinet.

There would seem, then, nothing for it but to assume that the Larkin dispatch expresses an earlier, less developed, less intelligent plan of the cabinet, a plan that, under the wise influence of your father, was changed to the vigorous and gallant policy for which General Frémont has received so much credit, and which resulted in the seizing of Arce's horses, with all that therefrom followed.

This hypothesis, however, necessary as it would seem, I am still not at liberty to adopt. The date of the Secret Instructions to Larkin is Oct. 17, 1845. A messenger was instructed to bring them to Larkin. *This messenger was Lieut. Gillespie.* He was, in the dispatch itself mentioned as a person instructed to "cöoperate" with Larkin in carrying out the plan of the dispatch. And all this is no matter of opinion on my part. It is the plain record in black and white in the archives.

Furthermore, I am assured, by the official word of the Keeper of Indexes and Archives of the State Department, that there is *no record* in that Department of *any other* instruction to any Government agent in California in 1845–46 before the outbreak of the war, saving only this dispatch that Gillespie carried, and the ordinary consular instructions to Larkin. There is no record of any, even the most formal instruction to General Frémont, nor is there in the War Department any trace of any instruction to General Frémont between 1842 and 1847. The whole documentary evidence, then, taken by itself, goes to show (1) that the Government had secret plans in California, (2) that Gillespie went to carry them out ⟨So far we all of course agree⟩; but that (3) these plans were the plans of the *Larkin dispatch*, and *not* the plans that constituted General Frémont's understanding of the situation.—

If now, without first communicating with you, I were simply to publish, as I had promised to do, an accurate summary of General Frémont's statement to me, together with the official documents, or an accurate summary of them, I should, as I am sure, in view of the present state of my information, do him (and you too) a serious unkindness, such as after all your courtesy to me I should be sorry to do. And until I get further information from you, I should very much fear that such publication would be a serious injustice. For, up to this time, the nature of this dispatch that Gillespie brought to Larkin has been wholly unknown to the public. Its very existence seems to have remained unknown to you, although Gillespie mentioned it once in his testimony before the Claims Committee, in the 31st Congress, 1st Session.—It has generally been identified in people's minds (wrongly I suppose) with the dispatch that Gillespie brought to General Frémont, a dispatch of which as you see no record exists. Now, when the nature and contents of the Gillespie-Larkin dispatch become known, the State Department having seen fit thus to reveal it, *the inference that the responsibility for General Frémont's aggressive action remains with himself, and not with the cabinet*, will seem to many readers almost irresistible. Hittell's ill-humored attack will seem irrefutable, at least to hostile critics of General Frémont, and I shall, without further help from you, find great difficulty in defending you. That General Frémont understood his instructions otherwise, and that you yourself, who were personally so closely in the confidence of the Government, should have understood the matter as you do, is indeed important. But you will readily see the difficulty of maintaining the validity of a personal impression over against documents. And I very much regret that, of necessity, *one* defect in your acquaintance with the Government's plans will appear on the face of the matter, viz. your ignorance of the existence of the secret instructions to Larkin, and your very strenuous insistence upon the opinion that your own confidential acquaintance with the government's plans made the existence of such instructions, without your knowledge utterly impossible. If *this* mistake has been made from your side, a critic will say, what confidence can he have, as mere critical stranger, in the validity of your further impressions, in case the documents are against them. I do not wish to seem captious, but in my present ignorance I should be quite unable satisfactorily to answer such a critic, confidently as I expect that you can give me further light, and enable me to answer him. As things at present stand, either General Frémont did not correctly appreciate the position of the Cabinet, as expressed in the instructions to him, or the cabinet very wrongly concealed important information from General Frémont while inducing him to believe himself in their confidence. Either supposition is very disagreeable to me. The captious critic might add the assertion that, but for the unofficial hints, whatever they were, in the letters of Senator Benton, General Frémont could have had no instructions from the government *save the instructions that Gillespie may have repeated to him from the Larkin dispatch.* These however would have *directly discountenanced* the aggressive action that was immediately undertaken. The captious critic would appeal to the documents in support of his views. In answer I could only show him General Frémont's and your own words, with the unfortunate mistake that they involve concerning the Larkin instructions. This would not convince him. My book would do harm and not good to General Frémont's renown. Your courtesy in helping me would have resulted in injury to yourselves. This I do not desire.

This result is, without further help from you, simply inevitable, even apart from my publication. I am not the only person in possession of the facts of which I speak, and I am at present at liberty to assure you who else knows them. The Larkin dispatch although never yet published, has been known for some time to Mr. H. H. Bancroft, with whom, as I told you, I am in correspondence. To him by your permission I have given knowledge of your statement. Through Mr. Bancroft I have, however, learned this:—The papers of Consul Larkin, containing his whole correspondence with the Department, including copies of his own letters sent to the Secretary of State have since Larkin's death fallen into the hands of Mr. Bancroft. Among these documents there are *two* copies of the instructions that Gillespie brought to Larkin. One of these copies was sent *as a duplicate* by one of the war vessels bound for the Pacific, and reached Larkin some time after Gillespie's visit. The other copy is, I believe, in Gillespie's handwriting. At all events it is a copy *made from memory by Gillespie* when he reached Monterey in April '46, *the original of the dispatch having been destroyed as Gillespie crossed Mexico.* This dispatch has always been regarded by the public as an unattainable secret, or as lost. But the copies in Mr. Bancroft's possession are, as I am now able to assure you, *identical with the dispatch that I saw the other day in the State Department*, and *that I have above described to you.* When Mr. Bancroft reaches the conquest history, he will therefore be accurately informed on the matter, even if I were to say nothing. He will freely draw his own inferences, and should they be unfavorable to your view of the matter, I have shown you with what reason and force they might be urged, in the absence of the further light that you can throw, as I doubt not, on the whole matter.

It seems to me then quite important for the credit that Mr. Frémont no doubt so justly and reasonably claims, but that the unlucky documents do momentarily so surprisingly and ill-naturedly cloud,—it seems very important, I say, for these your interests, that whatever further evidence you may have on this matter should be placed within my reach, or be published in some form before my book appears, as it must soon appear. Let my long letter be evidence of my anxiety to treat you and General Frémont with real fairness in my book. If I had wished to do you an unkindness, I could have used your statement, which you have already permitted me to use, and the documents, which at first sight seem so unpleasantly to contradict the statement, just as they all stand. But this would be unjust. I prefer to lay the whole case before you, assuring you of my sincere desire to get at the truth, and of my honest opinion that the time has come when you *will serve your own interests by making public in some shape any further evidence, and above all any original documents of that period, which you may be able to discover*, which will support General Frémont's now *almost wholly unsupported* view of the situation. The government reveals its secrets, why not you yours in this matter?

Begging your pardon for the length of this,

I am
Yours Very Truly
J. Royce.

To Henry Lebbeus Oak, April 20, 1885[48]

14 Sumner St.
Cambridge, Mass.
Apr. 20, '85.

My Dear Mr. Oak:

The Frémonts reply very promptly and good-humoredly to my indictment, thanking me for my trouble on their behalf, and promising a full and careful answer as soon as the General shall be

[48] ALS. Oak Papers. HHL.

free from an *immediate and pressing piece of business.*—So far then good. You may be sure that I shall press the matter very vigorously, now that they are fairly cornered. If they can vindicate themselves, I shall be only too glad; but they must look sharp.

The State Department has just sent me an official copy of the Larkin dispatch, and of certain among the later of L.'s letters to the Dep't. The copy of the dispatch is in full this time, save for the business details at the end.

Please rest assured that I still regard the dispatch as your property (by your I of course mean Mr. Bancroft's), now, just as much as ever, and shall make no public use of it unless you approve. We are equally interested, I fancy, in the outcome of the Frémont correspondence. I hope for more soon, & shall let you know promptly

Yours Truly
J. Royce.

To Henry Lebbeus Oak, May 4, 1885[49]

14 Sumner St.
Cambridge, Mass.
May 4, '85

Dear Mr. Oak:

I have yours of the 26th April. No more yet from the F's since the note of which I informed you by mine of a week or so since.—The letter of introduction, dated Nov. 3, 1845, which Gillespie was to present to Frémont, is a document of no special moment, but I am surprised that you have not seen it. I found it in the Claims Debate, quoted once by a Senator, and I think yet again by another. At all events you will find it in Mr. Clarke's speech in the Senate, printed in the *Appendix to the Congressional Globe* for 1847–48, under date of April 27, '48, on page 570 of said *Appendix*, 2d col.—Clarke's whole speech is well worth reading.

More, I hope, soon

Yours Very Truly
Josiah Royce.

[49] ALS. Oak Papers. HHL.

To George Buchanan Coale, May 31, 1885[50]

14 Sumner St.
Cambridge, Mass.

My Dear Coale:

I am not only guilty of great impropriety, but also of serious want of a proper show of gratitude, that I have not sooner written to you to thank you and all the family for my pleasure in my Baltimore visit, and for the trouble that you all took in my behalf. I have been meaning ever since to express my gratitude somehow, but my forensics and my California-work, and my frequently wearisome business correspondence, have kept me from doing any proper duty at any proper time for the last two months. Yet I have very often and very warmly remembered you all; and I have no stories that more delight little Christopher than those that I tell him about my experiences in Baltimore, which seems to him the most wonderful place on earth, next possibly to California. His favorite tales of Baltimore are those about "doggie Scamp," and how he gazes into the street and barks, and how he shuts the door, dies for his country, &c.; and also the one about "the lion and George Washington"—how George stands on the very high tower, and how the lion all made of bronze sits beneath and says, "Don't you venture to come down, George Washington," and how they will both stay right there till the "crack o' doom." "Pussy Lynx" also is a much beloved subject of a story, and so I have no lack of material. My wife, however, hears yet pleasanter things of you all. —I have been meaning, whenever I should write, to ask you if you have yet seen Austin Dobson's beautiful new volume *At the Sign of the Lyre*, and to say that, if you have not seen it, I have a copy that I want to send to the family, with my compliments, because I know that you all like the genial Dobson. And this volume, as I think, outdoes his former one. Please let me know whether you have seen one. Nearly ended is now my term's work. One great pile of blue-books containing examination forensics lies on my table to be read and marked. And then I shall be about free for my California-book. The Frémont business is still pending; but the matter looks no better for Frémont than it did when I last saw you.

[50] ALS. Redwood Collection. JHU. The date here is that of the postmark.

Otherwise I am getting on well enough with the work. The little family are all well, and desire to be remembered to you.

This part of the country produces, so far as I know, no such displays of art-embroidery as the one that Miss Mary kindly took me to see. In fact, for the moment, art hereabouts has nearly disappeared from our lives in our enjoyment of the brief New England spring. The winter concerts have ceased, and we think mainly of how we may most easily and quickly get rid of work and enjoy sitting out of doors. Naturally, however, it is the busiest time of all. Christopher still loves his music, but he does not devote so much time just now to that as to playing horse-car conductor out of doors in our large lot of land.—No doubt you intend to take plenty of rest and enjoyment this summer. I shall do a good deal of work myself on my book. My family will go to Newbury port, and I shall spend time vibrating back and forth between that place and this, reading up Cal. matters, and enjoying myself, as I hope, very fairly.

As for my philosophy book, I know not yet, and do not expect to know before the publisher's return comes into my hands on the first of August how the thing is selling. It ought to be doing reasonably well however; for it has received not a few good reviews. The one in the *Nation*, and that in the *Atlantic*, you will have seen.[51] The latter is by my friend Wm. James. The *Nation* review is by someone to me unknown. In the *Overland Monthly* in Cal., my old teacher Prof. Jos. LeConte has reviewed the book in a very friendly way.[52] Curiosity ought to give the book a trifling sale, even in California. I expect the most sale, if there is any at all, immediately hereabouts, in Boston and vicinity.

But time presses. I must bid you farewell for the moment. Remember me to all most kindly, to Mrs. Coale and Miss Mary in particular for the trouble they took on my behalf and for the much pleasure that they caused me.

Yours Affectionately
Josiah Royce.

[51] *Nation* 40 (May 28, 1885): 447–48; *Atlantic* 55 (June 1885): 840–43.
[52] *Overland Monthly* 5 (May 1885): 542–44.

To GEORGE BUCHANAN COALE, JUNE 15, 1885[53]

14 Sumner St.
Cambridge, Mass.
June 15, 1885

My Dear Coale:

All the past week I have been preparing my examination reports, and have thus been too busy to write. The little book is a very great delight to Christopher, whose favorites so far are the "Cuckoo" and the tale of "Cicely and the bears." He insists that Cicely is giving the two bears in the picture "chocolate drops," and I have to read the text in that way, instead of reading "cherries."

I send by express today the book that I promised. I hope that it will reach you safely. Mrs. Royce has written a word of thanks to Mrs. Coale, to whom please remember me. We are still having very pleasant weather, although the heat is gradually increasing beyond the spring point. On the whole summer has been slow in coming. This week and the next are the closing ones of our college year. Hoping to hear good news of you all frequently, I remain, with best wishes for all the family,

Yours Truly
Josiah Royce.

To HORACE ELISHA SCUDDER, JULY 9, 1885[54]

20 Lowell St.
Cambridge, Mass.
July 9, '85.

My Dear Scudder:

My dwelling is changed, as you see, but I am spending the summer still in Cambridge, where I am hard at work on the *California*. It is every way important for me to get the book into your hands by Oct. 1, and that is what I expect to do. Of course I may be disappointed, but I am at all events anxious to be prompt.

[53] ALS. Redwood Collection. JHU.
[54] ALS. Scudder Papers. UCB.

My next academic year, the first that sees me in a permanent position, will be an especially exacting one, since I shall have to work out courses that will take a definite and settled place in the curriculum. It will therefore be advisable for me to clear my hands of this cloying and delicious California preserve before I go to the other work. I have had my fingers in it too long already for a good child of Pres. Eliot, and shall need a scolding soon if I am caught in the mischief.

Yours Truly
Josiah Royce.

I am near your neighborhood now, and shall hope for a chance to meet you a time or two if you are in town here ever during the summer.

To Henry Lebbeus Oak, August 8, 1885[55]

20 Lowell St.
Cambridge, Mass.
Aug. 8, '85.

Dear Mr. Oak:

In accordance with my promise, I have just mailed, as a registered letter, a somewhat portentous parcel, containing, for your inspection ere you return it, *my* symphonic poem, which I *might* have entitled, the "Pathfinder and the Settler" or "Frémont's League with the Devil."[56] And now I must send in this letter, which ought to reach you two days before the registered MS, an explanation thereof, and a report of the last appearance on any stage of the path-finder himself as a witness in this business. Unable to get an answer from him, of his own accord to my last great letter, I wrote him some weeks since that, as I was about to pass through N. Y., on college business, I should be pleased to get his final explanations. Mrs. F. responded with accustomed cordiality. I accordingly called one evening. As you very rightly say in your sketch of F's. life, whose proof you kindly sent me, they are now in N. Y. city, Staten Island having become uncomfortable by reason of new cuttings and

[55] ALS. Oak Papers. HHL.

[56] I.e., chap. 2 of *California:* "The American as Conqueror: The Secret Mission and the Bear Flag."

embankments near their old house. I still cherished, foolishly enough, as you will say, a hope that, now all his official secrets were out, and his road in that direction cut off, he might have some revelation to make, that would show Benton's plans more clearly, or implicate Gillespie, or that he might furnish documents to support his theory. But no; cordial he still was, dignified and charming as ever, and the good Jessie sat calm and sunny and benevolent in her easy chair; but alas, he lied, lied unmistakably, unmitigatedly, hopelessly. And that was his only defence.

Of course, if the now almost demonstrated personal guilt of his original act is genuine and thorough-going, just exactly this course was at this time his simplest. The plainest, least artful, most honest lie, if I may so speak, was obviously better now than any essentially new additional explanation. And accordingly what he said was what I have given at the end of my MS, now forwarded for your inspection. He could only repeat: Larkin's mission was a mystery to him, the Larkin dispatch was essentially different from the instructions that he received; the Larkin plan was in opposition to what he knew. He also said what I cared not to write down for my book, that Buchanan's dark and deceitful way, must have been to blame. Alas, it is too late for that explanation now. If his case had not been made to rest on Buchanan's submissive plasticity in Benton's hands, there might be some use in such a theory. But when we pretend to know all about the government's plans, and then thwart them, it is plainly useless to say later that the vile government deceived us.

I am deeply sorry to add two more facts. Mrs. F. this time had the absurd courage to assure me that, in case there had been opposition, "Polk and Buchanan were simply nonexistent for my Father when he had his own plan to carry out." I have neither the right nor the intolerable cruelty to use this speech in my book. I do not want to; but it is simply a desperate confession that the affair was a family plot, a confession all the worse for the lying that accompanied it.—The other thing that I add with regret is that Frémont himself, after all this, had the face to return to the deliberate assertion that all his information then assured him of the imminent hostility of Castro. This defence I promptly checked by assuring him now, very good naturedly, that his information was all wrong.

To lighten my woe I have one cheerful thing to report. Seeing my drift as to the wrong done the natives, the venerable pair began themselves to dwell, with a melancholy regret, on these cruel wrongs. "Often have I said," explained Mrs. F., "I lament that we ever came and conquered these people, whom we have since so bitterly wronged and so cruelly robbed of their property." This was the effect of her words. While the lamp holds out to burn—

I need not add that, for myself, I carefully concealed my feelings, and our conversation was one of the most cheerful and harmonious interviews imaginable. They offered to give me all desired further help. I shall send them the proofs of the fatal chapter before it comes out. And so we parted, to meet no more, I suppose, in *this* world. Now as to my MS. I have of course left it to the reader to judge of the honesty of Frémont's revelations to me. Of course as I frankly admit, it is *conceivable* that his memory and not his design is *now* the deceiver. Of that doubt I have to give him the benefit, and I do, throughout the chapter. What my opinion is, notwithstanding all my formal and necessary disclaimers, every reader will see. Yet I feel that I have treated Frémont fairly, in fact much better than a man deserves after cheating a whole generation of his countrymen about his own wicked acts. Once or twice in the chapter I have shown my teeth and growled at the man, while the act is formally and seriously condemned from the start. But I hope that he, who has deliberately sought to outwit me, will have no cause of complaint. What do you think?

When I wrote you, after my first interview with him, that I felt confident of his having been deceived about Larkin, I had not clearly enough in mind Gillespie's testimony, and I had not yet been to Washington. Now I have utterly surrendered myself to the view that he alone is the deceiver about that matter. And this last interview confirms me.

Thus then I am in the main, by my original promise, at your mercy. Of essentially original evidence I have little to show. My whole chapter is, whatever I say or want it to be, an elaborate attack on Frémont's honor, and the success of the attack makes necessary the use of all that is essential about your Larkin dispatch. Of course, as I say in the MS, this dispatch is still your property, although I am even now, it would seem, the only outsider who has ever seen it in the Washington archives, and although I have a complete official copy of it from the State Department. But to the Bancroft Library is due the credit; and you, with Mr. Bancroft as final court of appeal, must decide how far it is right for me to use it. Both in this chapter and elsewhere, and most especially in my preface, I hope to make such acknowledgement of my indebtedness as will serve to give the reader a proper sense of the facts in the case, and will, I hope, whet his appetite to know what else your material has to show. Under these circumstances, and in view of Mr. Bancroft's own repeated assurance that I am welcome to all that I have been able to find, I hope that there will be no difficulty about my present use of your material, a use which, in accordance with my promise, I now submit for your approval, so far as this chapter goes.

Chap. I is not ready yet. Chap. III will be sent soon. Those chapters will contain my principal indebtedness to you. I enclose return postage for this MS, including charge for registration. Please register the parcel. As for the time of return of the present MS: I want to use the MS for the sake of reading a part of it, as a part of my forthcoming book, at a meeting of the American Historical Association at Saratoga, I think on Sept. 9. If there is no objection to my using the material for the book, surely there will be none to this reading. I shall not read the whole of course, nor shall I draw the conclusions at great length, but shall try to attract the attention of the Association to the research, and of course to the Bancroft Library as the source of it all, and shall then refer them to my book for further elucidation. I have even a slight hope that Mr. Bancroft himself may be there, as I presume he has been invited to attend. I hope that the aged Geo. Bancroft may be present also, to answer a question or two.—Therefore, if you will send back the MS as soon as convenient, I shall rejoice.

In telling my tale, I have no doubt made blunders, perhaps bad ones. I put on you no sort of responsibility of course, and in fact want to be responsible myself for my own deeds; but if you chance, in running through the MS to see any serious blunders, I should be glad to have a word of advice, in case that would not too much trouble you. Have I correctly summarized, in my few lines devoted thereto, the general character of the Californian political situation?—The use that I have made of the newspaper letter from Yerba Buena, June 10, '46, written by the man who has just talked with Gillespie, is my own, in as far as I accidentally found the letter in a newspaper here, and not at the Bancroft Library. I doubt not you have used the same letter. Do you know who wrote it? Leidesdorff?——No?[57] It is at any rate a curious and important proof.—My desire to avoid serious errors is of course in this chapter

[57] William A. Leidesdorff was U.S. Vice Consul at Yerba Buena. Royce used this letter in *California*, pp. 84–6, but the authorship remained uncertain.

especially strong, since the whole so much affects the honor of a living man, to whom I must do no injustice, liar as he is.–

I enclose herein my *last* document from Washington, written in reply to my last, quite hopeless inquiry. Its negative is of course not wholly unimportant–

Yours Truly
Josiah Royce.

I have written a letter to Mr. Bancroft himself, which goes with this one.

To Jessie Benton Frémont, August 20, 1885[58]

20 Lowell St., Cambridge, Mass.
Aug. 20, 1885.

Dear Mrs. Frémont:–

I have just been trying to put into final shape my chapter on the Bear Flag affair. I think it but fair, in view of your and the General's courtesy to me, to let you see hereafter, when the chapter has got into type, the proofs not only of your own statement, but of my whole discussion, as I foresee that you will not agree with a good deal that I shall say in criticism of the undertaking. In case you choose to add any brief note or comment upon what I say, I shall thereupon be glad to print the same in your name, worded just as you desire, in the book, as note or appendix. Of course you may not see fit to take advantage of such opportunity, and I shall only offer it to be used at your good pleasure. At all events I think it proper that you should be able to anticipate my own comments before they are published.–I ought to say that two or three months may pass before the proofs are ready, and that, in case of delay, you must not suppose that I have forgotten my promise, as I shall hold back the book till you have seen this portion of it.

Early next month, I shall read a paper, not more than 20 minutes long, on the "Secret History of the Acquisition of California," before the American Historical Association at Saratoga. In this public utterance I shall be disposed to confine myself, as far as

[58] ALC. Oak Papers. UCB. Partly printed by Robert Glass Cleland in his "Introduction" to Royce, *California*, pp. xix–xx. This letter is a copy prepared for the Bancroft Library; it is marked in Royce's hand: "Copy."

possible, to those facts about the Cabinet plans which are proved by the Larkin dispatch, and by similar evidences. I shall not there endeavor to examine at length your part in the matter. I shall be unable to state your side in so short a space, and shall accordingly refrain as far as possible from any criticism of General Frémont's action, merely saying in substance that "the reasons why this plan could not be carried into effect, and why Captain Frémont was induced to act in opposition thereto, cannot be discussed in the present paper, although it is proper and fair to add that General Frémont has recently expressed to me his surprise at the existence of such a plan, and has given me his assurance that he understood the purposes of the Government in a very different way, such as fully justified, in his own opinion, all that he did." I shall expand this statement a little; but it will cover fairly the substance of what I shall say at Saratoga about your side, leaving a detailed criticism of the evidence to be presented in my book. I shall present the other plan to the Historians at Saratoga, merely because its existence is, to the mass of historical students, just as it is to you, an entire novelty, and because it seems to me to throw light on the general purposes of the Cabinet before beginning the Mexican War.

Meanwhile, let me ask you one further question. Your present statement of the case, as I understand you, leaves the matter thus: The Larkin dispatch exists, and expresses a government purpose, without any doubt. But your understanding, and the General's memory, would make the true plan wholly inconsistent with the Larkin dispatch. To maintain your view, you leave the fact that, as General Frémont remembers, Gillespie brought him an oral communication from Buchanan that was quite inconsistent with this Larkin dispatch plan, and that gave General Frémont full warrant for his understanding of the private information contained in the stronger "family cipher" letter from Senator Benton.

Against the adequacy of this memory of the General's I am bound to tell you that there exist two very strong and early evidences. One is Gillespie's own testimony before the "Claims Committee" in '48. For Gillespie there distinctly says that he repeated to Captain Frémont the contents of the Larkin dispatch. And Gillespie was then testifying in General Frémont's own behalf. The other evidence is indeed negative, but it is peculiarly strong, because it is contained in a letter written by Capt. Frémont himself, on May 24, 1846, a *fortnight after* the meeting with Gillespie, and addressed to Senator Benton, and published by the latter in the Washington *Union*, of that time, in vindication of Capt. Frémont's course in California. This letter reads, as I find it in the *National Intelligencer*, of Nov. 12, 1846, which copied it from the *Union* immediately, thus: "Your letter" ⟨i.e. Senator Benton's private "cipher letter"⟩ "led me to expect some communication from Mr. Buchanan, but *I received nothing*." The italics, as indicated, are in the newspaper. Now since, by Gillespie's testimony, if that is correct, Capt. Frémont *did* hear the Larkin dispatch, and since, by his own testimony, in this letter to Senator Benton, he received *no* personal communication from Mr. Buchanan, I find it impossible to demonstrate that his present memory of the matter is correct, according to which he did *not* hear the Larkin dispatch, and *did* receive, through Gillespie, a message from Buchanan, addressed to himself personally. You see of course that such facts as this must appear in my account, although, now as always, I shall be glad of your authoritative explanations. My question then is: How shall I explain these facts consistently with General Frémont's present memory?

I hope that you and the General are both quite well. Believe me

Yours Very Truly
Josiah Royce.

To Henry Lebbeus Oak, August 29, 1885[59]

20 Lowell St.
Cambridge, Mass.
Aug. 29, 1885

Dear Mr. Oak:

Yours of the 29th has just come to hand. It is with shame I confess that my failure to use the Frémont letters of May 24 & the other, was due to the basest negligence. They were within my grasp, & though I knew not *just* where to find them, I knew where to look for them perfectly well. But I took, like a lazy novice that I am, the venerable Benton's word about them, & never ventured to suppose their contents so important. Yet even now I must assert myself enough to claim that I found them by accident, late, but

[59] ALS. Oak Papers. HHL.

independently, just after sending you the MS; and, about a week since, I made them the subject of a letter to Mrs. F. (in my usual affectionate tone), which *still remains unanswered.* I thank you all the same very much indeed for your hint. I had been intending for some days to write you, and claim the credit of my tardy industry. —I feared, when I found them, that you would point them out. I found them in the *National Intelligencer* for Nov. 12, '46, and shall use them in my final version.[60] I suppose that your source is *Nile's Register*, which is incomplete in Harvard Coll. Library; I have seen however in Von Holst's history a reference to *Nile's Reg.* for them, but cannot verify it here in Cambridge.—The letters are indeed amusing. We must however remember that they too were doubtless in "family cipher," and that when Frémont italicized the words "*received nothing*," such italicizing was family cipher for "received a long dispatch telling me to swallow the Californians alive." How is that for interpretation?—But I shall use the second of the two letters freely. I enclose my affectionate note to Mrs. F., offering to print her reply to me if she likes, which, if it remains unanswered, as it may, will be itself a documentary proof of their inability to answer it. If I get an answer, I will enclose it.—You observe my device for keeping still a hold on the Frémonts.

Mr. Bancroft writes begging me not to risk any more MS in the mails. I infer that he does not want the time of his assistants too much taken up with correcting my blunders, and as he is satisfied with my way of using his material I shall not send any more, unless you wish it.

I thank you much for your letter & comments.

How do you like my *Overland* Paper on the Squatter Riots of '50?[61]

Yours Truly
J. Royce.

I am delighted with the Second Vol. of your California.

[60] See *California*, pp. 82, 86, 104–5.

[61] "The Squatter Riot of '50 in Sacramento," *Overland Monthly* 6 (September 1885): 225–26; reprinted in *SGE*, pp. 302–48.

To Henry Lebbeus Oak, September 17, 1885[62]

20 Lowell St., Cambridge, Mass.
Sept. 17, 1885.

Dear Mr. Oak:

Your very pleasing letter of Sept. 9, with the enclosure, has come to hand. In looking over my MS of the Frémont affair, I am surprised to see how I was capable of saying that those early letters had never been published. Surely, when I wrote those words, I had already seen the reference to the text of them in Von Holst's history; but my lazy intention to regard them as unimportant, and as already known well enough through Benton's summary, must have put them out of my mind, until my accidental meeting with them revived the whole matter. It is fearfully hard to tell the truth in these things. Again and again I write what I think I have just learned from a document or book, and, looking again at my source, have to tear up my MS in disgust. If California history were only philosophy! For the Infinite, as philosophy deals with him, never talks back, leaves no documents on record, and always stands still to be counted. You need not interview him; he is entirely indifferent to all the lies you tell about him; and your reader is as well and as little up in the secret history of him as you are. That is the sort of thing to deal with, something submissive and plastic! !

I shall be delighted to accept at once your kind offer of your copy of vol. III, a little in advance of publication. Please express it at my expense as soon as convenient. My first chapter I shall write last of all. I will of course return your copy of Vol. III promptly, with many thanks.

I spoke my piece at Saratoga without opposition or mishap.[63] The Association would have amused you prodigiously. There was very little history present, and much fooling. Pres. White told funny stories from the chair, having possibly some intention to use his place to make himself a popular candidate for Governor of New

[62] ALS. Oak Papers. HHL. Partly printed by Robert Glass Cleland in his "Introduction" to Royce's *California*, pp. xxvii–xxviii.

[63] See Herbert B. Adams, "Report of the Proceedings, Second Annual Meeting, Saratoga, September 8–10, 1885," *Papers of the American Historical Association* 1, no. 6. Royce's paper on "The Secret History of the Acquisition of California" was delivered on September 10.

York in the coming canvass. He also read from the galley-proofs an immense paper, full of learned citations from French, German, Italian, ecclesiastical Latin, English, American (especially New England) writings, wherein he proved elaborately the wholly novel and wondrous historical truth that people, and especially divines, used to be—superstitious about comets.[64] This he called a contribution to the History of Civilization—just as the foam on a glass of beer is a contribution to the world's supply of nourishing food. Prof. Herbert Tuttle read a forty minute long contribution made up *entirely* of a list of *titles* of recent books and collections that bear on the History of Frederick the Great;[65] he is a handsome man, with a pleasing voice and manner, and there were numerous ladies present. Prof. Goldwin Smith, who was also present, discussed from time to time, in an eloquent and time-devouring way, "*tendencies*," viz. the tendency of Canada, or of the Protestant Reformation, or of anything else you please in history, to be, or to become something or other that only a clever man can understand.[66] The hours thus sped swiftly by, especially when some women appeared on the platform, and discussed the need for an education of womankind in history, and also the blessings of liberty, and the part that woman is hereafter to play in preserving liberty. Between sessions we college-instructors all sat about in the corridors of the hotel, drinking beer and punch, writing reams of letters to the press, and discussing with one another the functions of the State, the future of Colleges in America, the state of Greek archaeology, the definition of philosophy, the difference between the weight and the inertia of matter ⟨this I discussed with a fellow-metaphysician before dinner, and doubtless illustrated after dinner, although I don't remember doing so⟩ and in short absolutely everything that did not concern us, nor yet the business for which we had come there. Saratoga niggers swarmed, like big black flies, in the vast dining-hall of the hotel; but they waited on nobody in particular, save when they received unheard of fees. They grinned

[64] Andrew Dickson White, president of Cornell University, was also the president of the newly formed American Historical Association; he read a paper on "The Development of the Modern Cometary Theory."

[65] Herbert Tuttle, at that time an associate professor at Cornell, spent his life writing a *History of Prussia;* his paper at Saratoga was designed merely as a summary of current research.

[66] Goldwin Smith of Toronto delivered a paper on "The Political History of Canada."

and chattered, and we ate what we could find. There were two or three other such associations meeting in the town; and, on the whole, it was a perfect madhouse. My contribution was well attended to, for the rest, and I have no complaints to make, save that the newspapers *would* misreport my statement of my obligations to Mr. B.—I enclose two scraps from the *Boston Daily Advertiser*, which explain themselves. The false report gave me, you see, a good opportunity to say a word, of the sort that I can most easily and without any qualification say, about the Bancroft Library and its doings. I hope this will be satisfactory as far as it goes.

Let me say in closing that I have discovered, and shall correct, several minor slips in my Squatter Riot article. In that connection, however, as I must add, I have discovered a mine of useful comments on affairs in '50 and '51 in the letters of Cal. correspondents to the Eastern journals, especially the *N. Y. Tribune* (not Bayard Taylor's '49 letters, otherwise published). Other papers are also fruitful. Many of these letters have never seen the light in other shape, and are trustworthy contemporary evidence. Thus, in the *N. Y. Tribune* of '50, I have just found some most valuable letters from the Sacramento squatters themselves, stating their purposes and views very frankly, and confirming what I had otherwise gathered. Has your library ever searched out or collected from eastern journals such historical matter as this, to any great extent? If not, I suggest to Mr. B. the importance of these scattered sources, as I now begin to find them.—

Yours Truly
Josiah Royce.

To Henry Lebbeus Oak, November 12, 1885[67]

20 Lowell St.
Cambridge, Mass.
Nov. 12, 1885.

Dear Mr. Oak:

Your copy of your *Cal.* has been forwarded to the address of Mr. Edson Oak. I am much obliged for the use of it in advance.

[67] ALS. Oak Papers. HHL.

I have now time only to say that I have been seen by Mr. D. R. Sessions,[68] for whom I could do not very much of course, but to whom I gave whatever suggestions time and my great press of work let me; and that, further, I have been asked to review Vol. III of the *Cal.* for the *Nation*,[69] a job which I undertake with a mingled delight and sense of the delicacy of the task, both of which I fancy that you will understand. It will be of course some time before this review appears. I hope at all events that it will express something of my respect for thoroughness.

Yours Truly
Josiah Royce.

To George Buchanan Coale, December 30, 1885[70]

20 Lowell St.
Cambridge, Mass.
Dec. 30, 1885.

Dear Mr. Coale:

It is long since I wrote you, but the other day Christopher received a very pretty Christmas card, which I attribute to the kindness of Mrs. Coale or Miss Mary, or both. We have had for some months a picture of the little rogue on hand, which we ought to have sent before, and I think you must have got a copy by this time.—I want much to hear how you and the family all are. I wish that we could see some of you here this winter. Is there any chance of a journey northwards? One reason why I have not written for so long has been the fearful sloth wherewith my California work has been distinguishing itself. I have been ashamed to confess my inefficiency. Now at last, however, the book is off my hands, so far as MS writing goes, although I still have proofs to read. Whenever the thing is done, you shall have a copy early, in memory of the

68 David R. Sessions was one of H. H. Bancroft's assistants in the History Company. He worked primarily on biographical matters for *Chronicles of the Builders of the Commonwealth*.

69 Royce's unsigned "Two Recent Books Upon California History," *Nation* 42 (March 11, 1886): 220–22, is a review of T. H. Hittell's *History of California*, vol. 1, and Bancroft's *History of California*, vol. 2 (1801–24), and vol. 3 (1824–40).

70 ALS. Redwood Collection. JHU.

portion of the work that I so cruelly inflicted upon you and your kind household, nearly a year ago.

I hope that you will remember me kindly to all, and believe me

Yours Very Truly
Josiah Royce.

To Abigail Williams May, January 5, 1886.[71]

20 Lowell St.
Cambridge, Mass.
Jan. 5, 1886.

My Dear Madam:

I always think it a duty, and find it a pleasure, to accept such an invitation as I have received, through yourself and Mrs. Gilman, from the Mass. Society for the University Education of Women; and I shall be glad, accordingly to spend some ten or fifteen minutes at your Annual Meeting in saying a few words about the topic that you suggest.—Concerning the plans and work of the Annex, *in general*, I know, as I am forced to confess, only what the public generally knows through the printed circulars. I am employed there, I meet my classes there, and carry on my own lectures as I choose. But with the executive, or financial or general advisory work of the institution, I have had, of course, nothing to do. The Annex instructors have no Annex faculty meetings, and thus we remain, possibly, a little too isolated in our undertakings, each one being employed for himself and meeting his own students at his own hours. The general management is left to the "Executive Committee" of the "Society for the Collegiate Instruction of Women"; and anyone of that Committee could, of course, tell you far more about the general plans, purposes, and character of the whole body of students, and about the practical conduct of the whole under-

[71] ALS. The Arthur and Elizabeth Schlesinger Library on the History of Women in America (Radcliffe College). Partly printed in *Radcliffe Report on the Women's Archives, 1964*, p. 4. It is doubtful that the address mentioned in this letter was actually given. Neither the *Ninth Annual Report* (January 1886) nor the *Tenth Annual Report* (January 1887) of the Massachusetts Society for the University Education of Women mentions Royce, though the Reports do offer detailed records of speakers.

taking, than I possibly can.—I know my own students only, and in them, to be sure, I have taken much interest.—The topic, however, that you chiefly suggest, bears upon my work with them, and as to that I may be able to say something, if you think that worthwhile.

As I understand your view, then, it would be in accordance with the purposes of your Annual Meeting if I were to read a brief paper there on "The Study of Philosophy in the Higher Education of Women," in which I should frankly set forth both the advantages and the disadvantages that, according to my experience, the young women under my charge have seemed to me to possess in respect of this study. I think, to sum up my view in the briefest form, that the supposed difficulty that women are said to meet in forming abstract ideas, and so in grasping philosophical subtleties, does not exist, in case of young women who chance to be interested in philosophy. The true difficulty, however, which such young women do meet with in their study of philosophy, is rather a moral than an intellectual one: it is a certain fear of standing alone, of being eccentric, of seeming unduly obstinate in thought. This fear makes them, in the long run, too docile followers of a teacher or of an author, and so hinders their freedom of constructive thought. Now eccentricity of thought is, indeed, never the ultimate goal of philosophic study; but it is a necessary stage on the way to real success in thought. And this stage young women are less apt to reach. I wish therefore to suggest this lesson as possibly helpful to young women who may be studying such topics.—If such a statement, made at due length, would be helpful to your meeting, you are welcome to it.—Yr's Truly

Josiah Royce.

To Henry Lebbeus Oak, January 30, 1886[72]

20 Lowell St., Cambridge, Mass.
Jan. 30, 1886.

Dear Mr. Oak:

It is long since I wrote, but I have not forgotten you. I want to enclose some amusing little documents that I received the other day

[72] ALS. Oak Papers. HHL.

from Mr. Clements R. Markham, an English writer of travels, and a South American expert of some authority, whom I lately met when he was staying at a friend's house here in Cambridge.[73] He was you see, as a boy, on the terrible *Collingwood* at the fatal moment. His authority as to the Admiral's secret intentions is not great, but he thinks that nobody on the ship gave any sign of a purpose to seize forthwith upon Monterey, as the *Collingwood* approached that place. His copies of the documents posted on shore are interesting to me. They contain a variant of Ide's proclamation that I never before saw, although you must know it, I suppose. What M. copied must have been something that Ide wrote towards the end of his great vigil. One feels that he often nodded over that particular Proclamation. Markham's own frank and boyish diary is, however, the chief thing of interest in the little collection. I am sure that it is amusing enough, mistakes & all, to make the keeping of it worthwhile. For the reasons formerly mentioned, I think the Bancroft Library a better place than my desk for papers such as these. Please therefore file them as it best pleases you.

The book is far advanced in printing. The horrible delays that I had over the last of the MS are now done. I shall soon see the thing all in its full dress.

I hope to show you my opinions erelong in the expected *Nation* review,[74] which may be a trifle slow in coming out, but will be sure to come. You know, of course, that I in no wise connected you in my mind with the matters that I mentioned in my last & that you spoke of in your letter.—I hope to hear from you soon.

Yours Truly
Josiah Royce.

[73] Sir Clements Robert Markham, "Annexation of California" [Bancroft C-D 253]. This is an extract from a journal and copies of proclamations posted at Monterey, June/July 1846. The collection contains a covering letter to Royce, December 30, 1885.

[74] See fn. 69 above.

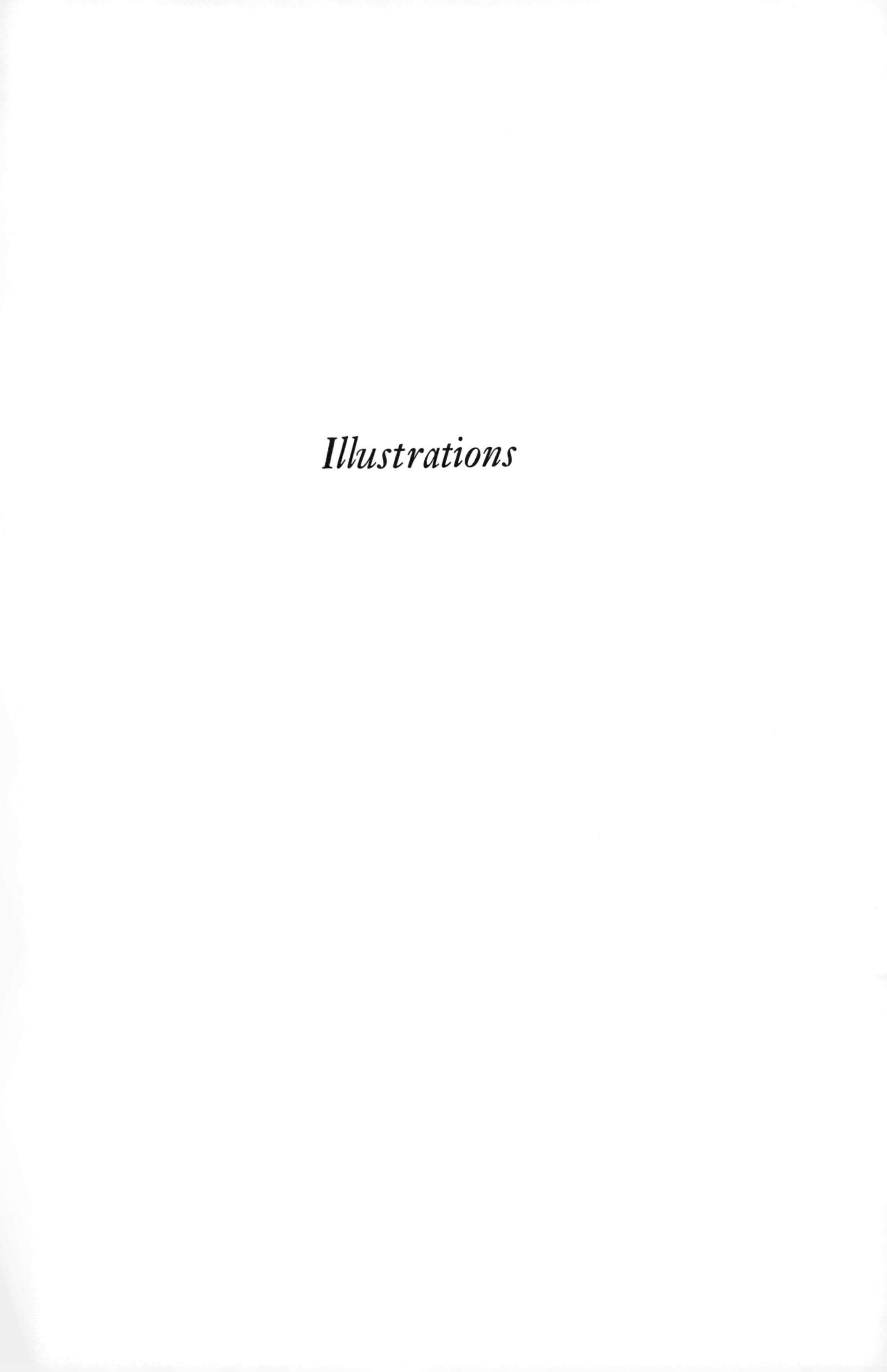

Illustrations

Josiah Royce
at different
periods of
his life

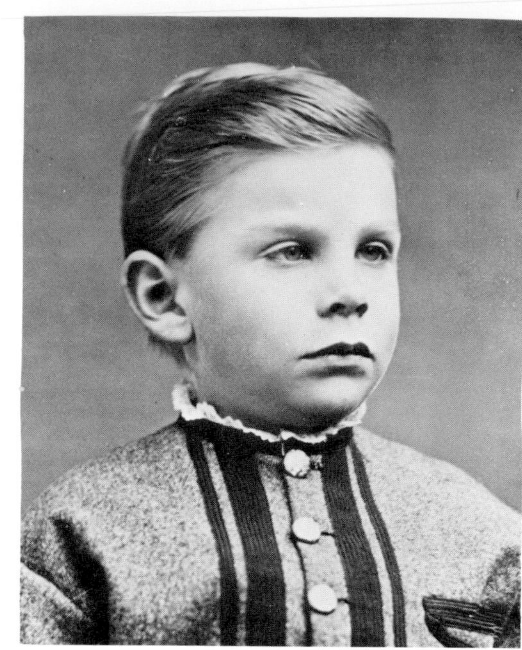

Harvard University Archives

circa 1860

University of California Archives, Bancroft Library

1875

Harvard University Archives

circa 1885

Eisenhower Library, Johns Hopkins University

1914

(2) [1907?]

no date

good will. I thank you very deeply for that, and for all that you have done. [I hope that my criticism, in answer to your question, did not seem austere or too blind, this afternoon. A man's personal tone is his own. Yours is a most effective one. I have no wish to urge any subjective attitude of mine regarding your

Four surviving sheets of a letter from Royce to William James (1907?). The notes made in another hand appear to be those of Ralph Barton Perry.

method in your Pragmatism book. And all that I have said in an appreciative tone about the book is sincere, — heartily so. As to the one criticism, — I can only say: Consider your own manner & method in the "Dilemma of Determinism" aswell as in the "Varieties of Rel. Exp." & the rest. It does seem to me that then there was no danger of having the people regard the discussion just as some of them now do regard the *Pragmatism*, — viz., as in large part a splendid joke, — a brilliant *reductio ad absurdum* of all attempts at serious grappling with any philosophical issue. This was in no sense your intent; but, as a fact, the externals, — the mere setting & style of the *Pragmatism*, tend to

produce on the man in the street this
impression, — an impression that those
earlier papers would not make, and that
you in no sense mean these to make.
Meanwhile, no criticism of
mine is hostile. — Life is a sad long road,
sometimes. Every friendly touch and word
must be preciously guarded. I prize everything
that you say or do, whether I criticize or not.
Yours Affectionately
Josiah Royce.

James Papers, The Houghton Library, Harvard University

Harvard University Archives

Royce with William James

Eisenhower Library, Johns Hopkins University

Royce with Charles William Eliot, 1911

To George Holmes Howison [1886?][75]

20 Lowell St.
Cambridge, Mass.

Dear Prof. Howison:

I want to acknowledge your kindness in sending me a copy of your Concord-Overland paper on "Is Modern Science Pantheistic?" I had already during last summer read with interest extracts from the paper which appeared in the *Boston Transcript* (or *Advertiser*, I forget which); and had also read the whole as it appeared in the *Overland*. You may know, if you have had time to glance at my book, how far I have the good fortune to jump with you as to the generalities. The immortality business I shall yet undertake to treat in another place.[76] I have my doubts about John Smith's rights in the matter, as you seem to state them. John Smith, if he has a conscience, must, according to you, say to God: "I am not willing to be damned for thy Glory; hence, in the name of my conscience, I demand of thee eternal life for my own person." Now, as I think, John Smith's conscience does both demand and promise for him, individual life *so long as he shall in his individual capacity, be of any value as an instrument for the moral law*. But how long that

[75] ALS. Howison Papers. UCB. The date, 1886, is written in another hand at the top of p. 1 in brackets. Since Howison's "Is Modern Science Pantheistic?" was published in *Overland Monthly* 6 (December 1885): 646–58, it seems probable that Royce's letter was written early in 1886. Howison's essay was read at the Concord School of Philosophy, July 31, 1885; it was later revised and reprinted under the title, "Modern Science and Pantheism" in Howison's *The Limits of Evolution and Other Essays* (New York: Macmillan Co., 1905), pp. 56–100.

[76] The question of immortality, seemingly remote from the question raised in Howison's title, is related to his objections to pantheism: if God is all, then the free individual personality is denied, and therefore immortality is denied. Royce here, as in his later discussions of immortality [see *CG* (1897), pp. 322–26; *CI*; *WI*, 2: 431–45; *WJ*, *pp.* 257–98], views the problem in relation to his teleology: an individual is such because he possesses a will and has certain purposes; the world-will is continuous with the individual will; if the purposes of the world-will were ever fulfilled in the finite life of an individual, that individual would be no longer needed; but since no individual's goals are finitely attained, his immortal life is necessary to the fulfillment of the infinite will.

shall be, is not John Smith's to know. He has indeed a right to demand that, as servant of God, he shall not be damned for God's glory. But annihilation is simply not damning; it is pointing out, so to speak, a limitation, and, beyond the limit, a necessary cessation of the further direct usefulness of John Smith. John Smith was *not* "damned" during the ages before he was born. He was simply *not yet needed*.

Why, to this *not yet needed*, there *may* not someday correspond a *no longer needed*, I cannot see; and I am sure that I do not know anything about how long a moral order requires John Smith. It *did not* require him once, viz., during all the past temporal life of the universe. Hence it *may* not need him ten minutes longer. God knows whether it actually does; but such knowledge is simply God's & not ours. This being so, I think John Smith's moral attitude is, in this respect, as in all others that concern his mere fortune, one of simple resignation. As the good citizen says, "The State, as a moral order, is bound to use me as its instrument so far as I can be of service, but is not bound to provide me three acres and a cow just because I am its subject." Even so, the good man says, "God, being good, will not suffer any of my powers that I freely devote to his service to be in any true sense lost; but God is not bound on that account to deal out my individual life to me century after century merely because I am once there; only is he bound to use me until I am no longer useful." When that time comes, *if* it ever does, then let heaven invert John Smith "like an empty cup." That seems to me a perfectly pious wish.

As for one other point, of detail this time:—You speak of the doctrine of the conservation of energy as implying or declaring that the "sum-total of movement is constant." Is this at all accurate? "Sum-total of movement" must mean the sum of all quantities mv, or the sum of all the products of mass and velocity in the world. But what *is* conserved anywhere in the universe in the transformation of motion is, in case of any body, not its mv at all, but a very different quantity, $\frac{mv^2}{2}$. If a moving body C, having mass m and velocity v, were somehow to transfer its whole *store of energy* (as determined by this mass and velocity), to a *previously resting body*, whose mass was say $100m$, instead of m, then the new body, *after* the energy were transferred, would have a velocity v', determined by the equation:—

$$\frac{mv^2}{2} = \frac{100mv'^2}{2}$$

$$\therefore v'^2 = \frac{v^2}{100} \therefore v' = \frac{v}{10}$$

But *if* the first body transferred simply the *quantity of its motion*, or mv to the new body, without regard to any conservation of energy, the resulting velocity of the previously resting second body would be determined by the equation $mv = 100mv'$, or $v' = \frac{v}{100}$—a very different result, as you see, and one that *does not* take place in the physical events of our world.

To take another well known example, to illustrate the difference between energy and quantity of motion, when a cannon ball is fired from a cannon, the *momenta* or quantities of motion given to ball and cannon *are*, in this case, *equal* and *opposite*, action and reaction being equal; *but the energy imparted to the light ball is vastly greater than that imparted to the heavy cannon*. For *mass of cannon* × *velocity imparted to cannon* = *mass of ball* × *velocity imparted to ball* after the powder is just burned. But the respective energies are measured by the ½ masses into the *squares* of these velocities. The greater velocity therefore here gives the greater energy.

—Yours Truly
Josiah Royce.

To Daniel Coit Gilman, March 29, 1886[77]

20 Lowell St.
Cambridge, Mass.
March 29, 1886.

Dear President Gilman:

I foresee that I shall be quite unable to go southwards this year, or to attend the anniversary exercises of the Johns Hopkins University. Both the conflict of the college duties, and my press of other engagements, forbid me to think of leaving this year. I much regret the fact, for a visit to Baltimore is always delightful, and this promised to be most of all delightful, in view of the occasion.

[77] ALS. Gilman Papers. JHU. Published in Fabian Franklin, *The Life of Daniel Coit Gilman* (New York: Dodd, Mead and Co., 1910), p. 372.

How deeply I felt the death of Prof. Morris,[78] it was not very needful for me to say. You know how my fortune with him was just that of so many other young men, viz., to find in him a fatherly friend, of the warmest, the freest, and the wisest sort. His place is one that you can never fill, if you wait a century. I feel sure that no other misfortune of equal seriousness has come upon the University during this its first decade. I hope that nothing so ill may soon again befall.

Permit me, while deeply sympathizing with you for this calamity, to congratulate you most earnestly that you have finished these ten years with such a generally happy and with such a wonderfully well ordered and successful progress to show to the world. These ten years are, after all, *my* first ten years also, in one sense, and a strong feeling of personal gratitude to you, to whom I owe so much good fortune, joins itself with my admiration of your great work in Baltimore.–

Yours Truly
Josiah Royce.

To Henry Lebbeus Oak, [May 31, 1886?][79]

20 Lowell St.
Cambridge, Mass.

Dear Oak:

The enclosed slip, from the *Boston Herald*, explains itself, and may amuse you. As for me, I burn to know how you regard my book, now it is there. I also sympathize deeply with the loss that the fire must have entailed to your interests also, as well as to the interests of the whole undertaking. I understand from the circular sent out that the loss, such as it is, is not regarded as a permanent or irrecoverable one, and that the work will go on in due time.–Gen. F. has been burnt out too, as you see from the enclosed.[80]

[78] Charles D'Urban Morris, professor of Greek at Johns Hopkins, died on February 7, 1886.

[79] ALS. Oak Papers. HHL. The date, "5/31/86," is written in another hand at the top of p. 1.

[80] On April 30, 1886, a fire destroyed the Market Street building of A. L. Bancroft and Company. Royce may also be referring to a fire of a few years earlier that destroyed Morell's warehouse in New York that contained many of the papers and personal property of John Charles Frémont.

I am charmed with the 1840–45 volume. I regret to hear of the loss that called you East, and I hope you will let me add my regret that while you were East I could not have seen you, although of course I understand the impossibility of such a thing under the circumstances.

I feel unutterably lazy, just now, but shall have to work all summer to keep body & soul together by more writing, of some sort or other. My works, such as they are, have more ink than money in them, and my College salary barely keeps me out of the poor-house, as in fact is commonly the case with men in my position.

I hope that my forthcoming review of Hittell's vol. II, and of your latest,[81] will not displease you, and that I may hear of you and from you often.

Yours Very Truly
Josiah Royce

To Henry Lebbeus Oak, June 20, 1886[82]

20 Lowell St.
Cambridge, Mass.
June 20, 1886.

My Dear Mr. Oak:

Your very friendly letter of the 9th has given me, of course, a great deal of pleasure. Of expert criticism my book will of course be apt to get very little for a good while. The literary critics are some of them wroth with the slightly eccentric style which I have chosen, or fallen into. But one's style is like one's person, and, however much or little it may be really chosen, it seems very natural to one's self, and very odd, sometimes to one's neighbors. People of course find the Frémont argument too long, and a number of them find it inconclusive. The reasoning faculty of many is, in fact, weak, and one man of some little note, George Parsons Lathrop, in a review in the N. Y. *Star*, says that it is odd how I cannot see that the

[81] Royce's unsigned review of T. H. Hittell, *History of California*, vol. 2, and of Bancroft's *History of California*, vol. 4, was printed in *Nation* 43 (July 29, 1886)): 99–101.

[82] ALS. Oak Papers. HHL.

government, in its oral advices to Frémont through Gillespie, must have confided to the captain "a much more confidential message" than was confided to Larkin. My whole talk rests, he thinks, on a "purely arbitrary assumption" or on something of the sort (I forget his exact words), the assumption namely that the government could not have confided one mission to Gillespie for Larkin, and another to the same for Frémont. You, who remember my scepticism on this very point, will see how far I was from arbitrarily assuming what I spent a long time in doubting and in proving. Several other of my critics have with equal solemnity assured me that intrigues are complex things, that the administration supported Frémont's action by its conduct in later days, and that Buchanan was a rascal. Reviewers, of course, always tell us novel things, that we overlooked ourselves.

I wish that you would let me know when your work is to be done with Bancroft. I have no present knowledge of any hog-ranch or other enterprise in which you would be likely to invest, but it is just possible that I might hear of something of the sort if I knew when you would be at liberty. A man of your services should not be altogether stranded too early, and I have no idea that you will be. But, at all events, please keep me informed as to your state. I am a person of no influence, but I might some day hear of what you might like to know.—

Yours Truly
Josiah Royce.

To Milicent Washburn Shinn, July 16, 1886[83]

20 Lowell St.
Cambridge, Mass.
July 16, 1886.

Dear Miss Shinn:

Please accept my hearty thanks for the trouble which, as is evident from yours of July 7 (Did you choose the great anniversary on purpose for your note?), you have taken on my behalf. I do not know how ferocious your wicked reviewers are going to make of me, of course; but be assured that all the ferocity shall be spent

[83] ALS. Shinn Papers. UCB.

upon them, in my soul, and that distracted editors, worried by unmanageable historians, shall come in for no share of my poor resentment.[84] For the rest, I really hope, despite my natural pin-headedness of soul that the reviewers will not make me so very wroth. One is so apt to forget that to denounce A. B. is *precisely equivalent* to being denounced by A. B.! Of course I am *ipso facto* condemned by that which I condemn. How could it be otherwise? Why then, when I condemn, with cheerfulness, should I growl if I hear in return my own condemnation, simply interpreted into the other's tongue? If my reviewer, or anybody else, thinks that good—e.g. the treatment of the Californians or the brutal freedom of the pioneers—which I have found vile, how can I complain if he says so? What I do hate, of course, are my own blunders, when they are pointed out, blunders, *viz.*, in matters of fact. I know that there are and must be many such in my book. I want them pointed out for history's sake, yet I lament them bitterly. To be sure, I have not found many yet, although there may be many more forth-coming.

—Th. Hittell is right. I reviewed his book. I put "Bancroft" above him, because that is the actual relation, "Bancroft" namely being understood to mean what in my review I called the resultant of the combination of H. H. Bancroft himself and his unrevealed collaborators. In fact, as I perfectly well know, and as I somewhat esoterically said, in my *Nation* review, "Mr. Bancroft and his collaborators" are here equal to *one* man, that man being (as I was not at liberty to say in public, and as I beg you not to repeat in public), Henry L. Oak, by far the first living specialist in early California History. This "Bancroft" is above Hittell, because he has more authoritative sources, and has worked much harder. I am sorry to have in form to attribute any part of this excellence to H. H. B. himself. I said that I was sorry in my review, using all the irony about H. H. B. that I dared, under the circumstances, and in view of my rights as a privately informed person. But I made plain that Hittell seemed to me poorer, not than H. H. B. in person, but poorer than H. H. B.'s book, a very different thing, as the public already knows, and will know more and more clearly as time goes on. As I have before said to you, it is impossible to take Bancroft to

[84] An unsigned, hostile review of *California* appeared in *Overland Monthly* 8 (August 1886): 222–23. Oak answered the review in *Overland Monthly* 8 (September 1886): 329–30.

task in public any more for his "methods," because he has frankly confessed what is in so many words true, viz., that other men supply him work in "various" states of preparation in "various parts" of his great work, and that he reads, and alters where he likes, and undertakes to be responsible himself for what is printed. All that is perfectly true, and the rest, if you will, is a matter of taste. Bancroft says to his reader, "I sell you this book with my name on it, and tell you that I use others' help, even in the writing of it, and that I will not reveal to you how much of the text is mine." This being so, no reader has a right to do more than enter his general protest against this plan. And one is bound to call the book by Bancroft's name in public, and to praise or blame it as Bancroft's. This I have done, in my *Nation* review, although I do happen to know, by private means what I deem it right to say to you rather confidentially, for the moment, that the part of the work which I criticized is simply Oak's, and nobody else's. This of course will in time be universally understood, though one cannot publicly say so yet.—Hence, of course, my disparagement of Hittell is not really an exaltation of H. H. B.'s person. I am sorry to have been the cause of vexation to Hittell. He has the best possible right to say whatever he pleases about me. Had I desired to have a soft thing of it, I should have praised him of course.—My book is full of kindling that I split and of matches that I collected to heat the water for myself. Let the water boil.—I ask one thing only, that *if* my reviewers need replying to, you will give me a proper place for reply.

Perhaps you do not especially long for more articles from me. But please let me know if you would print a brief article on the work of the "American Society for Psychical Research," which is so much misunderstood, and a sketch of the "Roe Lynching" in Sacramento in 1851.[85] These are two things that I should like to send soon.—Also, does the *Overland* now flourish?—Also, please let us know more of yourself personally. Katharine sends love. She is not in *perfect* health, but is fairly well to do. We stay in Cambridge all summer.—

Yours Truly
Josiah Royce.

[85] Neither of these articles appeared in *Overland Monthly*.

To Henry Lebbeus Oak, July 26, 1886[86]

20 Lowell St.
Cambridge, Mass.
July 26, 1886.

My Dear Oak:

I confess to a feeling of warm sympathy with the poor grandson of Sloat when I yesterday read his letter of the 19th. I replied at once, ignorant of course that he had deposited his copy with you, or had sent one to J. C. F. My reply was somewhat on this wise:—The unfortunate tone of his letter, I said, would have prevented me from offering any acknowledgement, if I had not desired one thing more from him, namely his kind permission to use his letter for public purposes. It came to me, I said, as a private letter. I could not deposit it in a library of historical reference (I meant in this case Harvard Library), or publish it, without knowing that he intended it ⟨as you know the Frémonts intended their letters to me⟩ for historical purposes. I begged him in reply to give me permission to make such use.

But, I said, there was one thing more. I wanted, namely, as a personal favor to him, to warn him of something. I admired his zeal, I said, even though his letter was one which a previous generation would have interpreted as intended to lead to "further complications." And because I admired his zeal, I wanted to warn him of the existence of Secretary Bancroft's letters of reprimand and recall (the letters of some later date in 1846, in the Claims Commission Pamphlet) addressed to Sloat on receiving his also *ibidem* published confession of vacillation of July 6, the day before he raised the flag. To have these dragged to light, discussed, and given their due weight, would, I said, be distressing. I had carefully avoided mentioning them in my book, and I didn't want to be the cause of dragging them out of the old Congr. Doc. volumes now. I would warn the good Lieut. Whittemore, for his dear grandfather's sake, not to be responsible for what I had carefully refrained from doing.

So much for him. I forgot to ask you for that list of my mistakes which you kindly offerred me for a new edition of my book. I may

86 ALS. Oak Papers. HHL.

need it before long. My regards to Mr. Bancroft. I hope that the new volume will get the success it deserves. I am glad if I have been of any service.

I shall hope to hear from you soon, and especially to learn of your own prospects. I have been looking about lately a little, but I hear of nothing new as yet. I also want to know if the library should run any immediate chance of being disposed of.

Yours Very Truly
Josiah Royce.

To Charles Rockwell Lanman, July 28, 1886[87]

20 Lowell St.
Cambridge, Mass.
July 28, 1886.

Dear Lanman:

In answer to your farewell, I must bid you a *very long* one. Ere you can reply to this, I shall, namely, be stretched, (or perhaps, as you will soon see, I should say scattered) upon the Field of Honor, weltering in my Blood. For there has just come to hand a letter, written by a California military man, a grandson of the Commodore Sloat who took California in 1846. I unluckily called Sloat, in my book, a "morally timid man," and added that he was "of a very vacillating temperament." The grandson, whose name is J. B. Whittemore, writes to say that he has "read with successive feelings of astonishment, scorn, resentment, indignation and contempt," my "ignorant, mendacious, and malicious *attempt* to asperse and belittle the character" of the aforesaid grand-daddy "Rear-Admiral John Drake Sloat, U. S. N." The grandson, you see, makes up for the grandsire's defects of temperament. He further calls me a coward, and takes occasion to insinuate that I am subsidized by the English Government.

Of course I shall have to give him satisfaction, you see. For this from a soldier, with his card accompanying the document, means a challenge soon to follow. But now you see also that the spectacle of this fellow (doubtless six-footed, straight as an arrow, a dead shot, a master with the sword) towering at one end of the Field of

87 ALS. Lanman Papers. HUA.

Honor, with sword or pistol, and poor me, with a weapon that is like "to kill me deader behind than him before," cowering and chattering my poor teeth in limitless misery at the other end—this spectacle, I insist, is not somehow just what it ought to be. Hence, after consulting with my friends, I have resolved, at the suggestion of one of them, when the challenge comes, and I have a choice of weapons, to chose Dynamite. Bowen consents to be my second, having for obvious reasons no fear of being blown up, since the all-pervasive wind, whistling between his shanks and about his venerable head, has never yet found how to catch on anywhere,—and no more can the Dynamite. The expense of the surgeons will be saved. There will only be needed what Portia wanted Shylock to get:—

"Have by some basket, Shylock, to pick him up, that nothing may be lost."

—My will is just in process of making. To you I bequeath my gift of carrying weight aloft *without* walking home by way of Brattle Street. Nobody will need it, (viz. the gift) more than you in future. I also bequeath to you any MS relics, that may be found among my papers, of those happy days of youth when we studied in Sanskrit together. Think of me occasionally when you wonder what has become of some book in your library, or why your bank-account is so plethoric. Forget not to drop a tear.

My poor family, all unconscious of their swift-coming fate, are absorbed in the frivolities of pianoes, clocks, nonsense-stories, and huckleberry pie. There is nobody as yet who realizes the truth but myself. Farewell! A last farewell! ! If I had served my God as I have served my bank-account! ! !—But enough! ! ! !

Yours *im Todesangst*
Josiah Royce *aus* G. V. [Grass Valley]

To Henry Lebbeus Oak, July 29, 1886[88]

Cambridge, Mass.
July 29, '86.

My Dear Oak:

My confounded memory played me an unimportant trick, the

[88] ALS. Oak Papers. HHL.

other day, when I wrote to you and Whittemore. Geo Bancroft's reprimand and removal of Sloat were based, of course, on the Commodore's letter of *June* 6, not *July* 6, as I stupidly said. But of course the slip is not only unimportant against me, but is rather a fact in my favor. Sloat vacillated at Mazatlan already, while I had remembered only his vacillation at Monterey, after he had heard of Frémont's behaviour. I don't know how I should have got the thing twisted in this way. The fact is that the vacillation of Sloat is such a complex affair that, as I once for all refrained from tracing it out for my book, I had never got it well straightened in my mind at all, only assuring myself of its existence.

I suppose I did wrong to fool with Whittemore at all, and that I should not have put in his hands a letter that, as it contains a slip, he may somehow manage to use to my discredit. Therefore, in any case, I beg you to keep this on file as record of my discovery of my own blunder immediately after I wrote to him. Moreover I have written him again, today, admitting the mistake, but adding that of course the fact of this early and outrageous vacillation at Mazatlan is worse evidence against Sloat's character than could be the thing as it had somehow got fixed in my mind. My "warning" has therefore, I remind him, more force in its amended than in its original form. So much for that little thing. I have ventured in conclusion to refer Whittemore to your forthcoming volume for further information.

Please let me know in case there should be any noteworthy attack on my book from any respectable source.

Yours Truly
Josiah Royce.

What will be left of me, I wonder, when the next *Overland* comes out?[89] Doubtless it is already, and I am utterly crushed—and don't know it. But at least I have been warned in advance.

[89] See fn. 84 above.

To Milicent Washburn Shinn, August 7, 1886[90]

20 Lowell St.
Cambridge, Mass.
Aug. 7, 1886.

Dear Miss Shinn:—

Katharine and I read with much interest your long and lively letter. As for the review business, I am surprised to find that the writer was not Hittell, after your previous expressions, which led me to think so. But no matter—my letter of day before yesterday, written upon first seeing the review, holds good as far as it goes, whoever wrote the sketch. I have no complaint (in the serious sense) to make of any point but the one. That, viz., the accusation that I have used a private letter, whose contents I have wholly imagined, to base my charges upon against Frémont, is so false, and so dishonorable to myself, that I hope it is not oversensitiveness that leads me to demand its withdrawal.

—About the book itself I may still say a word. Reviews founded on *a priori* notions of what readers had been led to expect from the prospectus of the Commonwealth Series, I can afford to ignore, because once for all that prospectus, which I didn't write, was very vague, and in so far as it promised anything, promised such an outline sketch of certain commonwealths as would show the distinctive and at the same time nationally important elements of their life. Now of the mere annals of a commonwealth only a small portion can ever be said to have this quality of distinctiveness and national importance. One had to select. I selected, after much labor and consideration, the conquest, one of the most significant events of our national history at the period in question; the formation of the state, one of the most remarkable undertakings of its sort; the gold period; and the vigilance-committees. What would one have me do? Select more? I could have done that but at the expense of conscientious work. And for conscientious labor upon what I did undertake, I certainly can claim reasonable recognition. As for the soundness of my views, I am willing to leave them to the reviewer who chances to have time to discuss them, or even by chance to read them.

90 ALS. Shinn Papers. UCB.

That is my justification as against the purely *a priori* reviewers. Most of my reviewers have been *a priori.* If my book ever comes to be read by anybody for what it distinctly offers, on its title page and elsewhere, I don't fear the result. Hatred it was my duty to arouse in a number of cases. Of course I lament the hatred, but I couldn't help arousing it. I was not to blame.

For your position, of course, I have entire respect. It seems to me just conceivable of course that, directly or indirectly, the *Overland* might some day do me the justice of a single more cordial word; since, as I know, there are some aspects of the matter, and some views of my book, that are not perfectly expressed by this man, who accuses me of a dishonorable act that my text took the greatest pains to avoid even seeming to commit. Since you were forced to give this sort of reviewer an official position, I should indeed take very kindly any possible, say very casual and informal, and not undignified word of recognition that my book is not altogether a piece of convict labor. But, as I say, your judgment has to govern all that, and I don't doubt your kindness and good will at all. Whatever you do, I have no present fear that I shall be at all put out with your part of the business, and I certainly thank you for your trouble so far.—And now, as for my further work for the *Overland*, I am quite clear about that. *If* you desire me, then it is a matter of duty to go on. I shall not feel "uncomfortable" in your pages at all. In so far as your reviewer was simply plain-spoken, I may differ, but I don't feel called upon to decline further intercourse in the same columns with him. Why should I? Plain speech is as much his duty as mine. In so far however as what he said was, in that one respect, objectionable, doubtless he will withdraw his words. And meanwhile I have some things to say that must be said if there is a place for them. Odd as it may seem to you, this piece of "contract-labor" has actually put upon me a responsibility, as a child of the State, to say something more in her service (how the reviewers would laugh at the word *service*!), and in the course of a few years I mean to do so. The *Overland* is a good place to let things simmer in. If I delay at all, the reason will not be, then, my discomfort at the thought of appearing in your columns, but the fact that I am struggling very hard nowadays to earn a decent living in an expensive town, on a very insufficient salary, and have to work all summer at what I hope may bring me a dollar or two now and then. Other work has to wait therefore but I will be as prompt as possible.

I shall never get through these selfish personalities, I fear, but there is still one thing that I want to mention. My old and still highly esteemed friend and classmate, W. C. Jones—you know how he is connected with this thing. I told him, two years since, how Frémont's case needed a defense from Frémont himself, because the thing looked bad. J. accordingly introduced me to the F's, and Frémont himself, in the two interviews, then treated me to the charming and courteous mendacity already known to you. I was in an amusing but delicate position. How I dealt with it, you know. My sense was that the thing was a public duty, that I had no possible choice, and that my only obligation to the F's was to do precisely as I had promised them, viz., to state their case, and to do them the fullest justice, and then to tell the truth. I am sure, however they may represent things hereafter, that and that only was what I represented to them as my intention when I went to them. "Tell me your side," I said, "and I will state it, and then give my judgment upon it as I have to do." That was all. But now, how in consequence does W. C. J. feel? Do you know? And is his feeling any cause of Moses's bitterness? You see how I lament the personal aspect of the thing. Yet I feel absolutely free from guile myself. I was only over-conscientious, and hence prolix. But if you know how W. C. J. stands, and how his friends regard things, I may better be able to judge how I may proceed further.—

I hope that ends, or nearly ends what I have to say on my side of this business. Peace to the ashes of the book! Katharine is very quiet this summer.[91] She and I take a few outings on the Charles River together, for I can bring the rowboat up very near to the house for her to get in. Otherwise she seldom goes out. We are doing a good deal of work together this summer, of a light sort, but such as makes my pen swing a trifle. I think that we learn the arts of Cambridge life slowly but surely, and with all the meagreness of the salary, and the expensiveness of the town, it is the most delightful of all places to live in in all the world. I never am discontented with it. The boy is as bright as ever. He loves his music, and developes his ear, more and more. But nobody has yet tried to worry him by systematic teaching in that or any other branch. He was four in April, you may remember. His mind is still as free as a bird's.

[91] Mrs. Royce was ill throughout most of her second pregnancy; see the letter to Coale, December 30, 1886.

I still hope the best for you and your *Overland*. Please write us often, and believe me always your warm friend.

Very Cordially Yrs.
Josiah Royce.

To Henry Lebbeus Oak, September 1, 1886[92]

20 Lowell St.
Cambridge, Mass.
Sept. 1, 1886.

Dear Mr. Oak:

I am much obliged for the list of corrections. I shall have occasion to use it, I hope, erelong. My good friend J. B. Whittemore has written to apologise for his "tone." He still of course is unconvinced; but he "regrets" &c. So much for him.

I write, as it chances, in great haste, but I want especially to beg you, for your own sake, to cultivate Winsor,[93] who, as I feel, is decidedly interested in your work, and in yourself, as he ought to be. He has spoken of you frequently in a very pleasant way. He is a good hearty fellow, if you approach him for any end that he can appreciate; and he does appreciate history. Moreover, while I don't know anything definite, as yet, that he can help you towards undertaking, I do feel sure that there is no man in the country who is more apt to appreciate you, or to show his appreciation, sooner or later, in more practical ways. I have not failed, of course, to say my say to him about you; if I understand your wishes for the future, I hope, very vaguely of course as yet, that an acquaintance with Winsor may help to get you on the right track.

However, if all else goes well, but nothing turns up for you soon, why can't you come East, after November, and spend some of the time that you say you can pass in idleness, getting a casual acquaintance, in some natural and easy way, with a few of the scholars hereabouts, in Boston, or New York, or even Cambridge? They are an honest crowd enough, in *this* town. They like a good fellow;

[92] ALS. Oak Papers. HHL.

[93] Justin Winsor (1831–1897), author of many historical works, was librarian of Harvard University, a founder of the American Library Association and vice president of the American Historical Association.

they are discreet; they'll easily understand your past relations to Mr. Bancroft without the need of any lengthy explanations; they appreciate solid work, even if they don't all of 'em do it; and some of 'em, like Winsor himself, for instance, not only appreciate, but perform. For a scholar, they are also very accessible people. As for this Cambridge itself, I never passed four years of my life before where personal jealousies and the like were such rare and insignificant birds as they are here. Nobody quarrels, and nobody gives a damn for his neighbor's opinions, unless he chooses to share them. It's a perfect republic of letters. You'd be amused to see it.

If then, I say, you are loafing, after November or December, a little loafing in this longitude *might*, nobody knows of course, put you into congenial company for further work. And, as I've often said, your services to scholarship, so far, will insure you the regard of good men, anywhere quite apart from any delicate controversies about who wrote certain volumes. I assure you, men of sense will ask no questions, and will comprehend perfectly.—But here, at this point, just as I write, enters from the post your beautiful volume. I was just going to say that the *Nation* sent me the volume for review only two or three days ago.[94] I have had time to look at it, to read a few pages, and to find the note about myself. But I thank you most deeply for yours, with the unique title, and the full binding. I shall prize it very highly. The review, as soon as I have time to read for it, and write it, will doubtless be what the harmony of our souls will naturally dictate, marred, if at all, only by certain jarring notes for which the "History Company" and certain manifestoes which it inflicts upon reviewers, will bear the sole responsibility. The book is sure to have a very high place in literary work.

Well, for a fearfully occupied man, this letter must suffice from me now. I wish I could invite you to be my own guest when you come East. If my house is too small and crowded for that, I at least promise you my humble best in the way of introductions to the good fellows in history when you come, as I hope you will.

[94] Royce's unsigned review of Bancroft's *History of California*, vol. 5, was printed in *Nation* 44 (January 13, 1887): 39–40. In each of his *Nation* reviews, Royce raised the question of authorship with respect to Bancroft's *Works*. Although he knew that Oak had actually written most of the *California* volumes, his debt to Bancroft and his loyalty to Oak made declaration of this fact a matter of some delicacy, The copy presented by Oak to Royce, now in HL, bears the title, *Conquest of California;* Royce added in his hand, "By Henry L. Oak."

You may ask me why I'm so occupied in summer vacation. I wish I knew. I think it has something to do with earning my living.

Yours Truly
Josiah Royce.

To Horace Elisha Scudder, September 25, 1886[95]

20 Lowell St., Cambridge
Sept. 25, 1886

Dear Mr. Scudder:

Enclosed in the accompanying package, please find the promised novel, whose title is "Just Before Nightfall."[96]

I want to excuse in advance its portentous length by the fact that the plot is somewhat elaborate. The length, that is to say, isn't wholly made up by means of reflections and analyses. There are two bloody fights, three heroes, two heroines, several villains, and almost no morals in the book.

So much for prospectus. The rest is before you.

Yours Truly
Josiah Royce.

To George Buchanan Coale, December 30, 1886[97]

20 Lowell St.
Dec. 30, 1886.

Dear Mr. Coale:

I have been atrociously neglectful, although, I assure you, not forgetful. To begin with, we have had a long time of considerable anxiety about the rather disturbing condition of my wife's health. She was at no time seriously ill, but she has been confined to the house very closely for many months, and has had more than one

[95] ALS. Scudder Papers. UCB.

[96] Published as *The Feud of Oakfield Creek: A Novel of California Life* (Boston: Houghton Mifflin and Co., 1887). For the evolution of the title, see succeeding letters.

[97] ALS. Redwood Collection. JHU.

reason to be very cautious. But for the time, at least, our anxiety is lightened, and our comfort vastly increased, by the coming of a new boy, born on Christmas day!! My wife is now doing so well that I hope she will soon be stronger than she has been for years.—All this kept us here during last summer, and added to the cares of this world a good deal. As for me, meanwhile, I was at first very tired upon completion of my *California.* Then I was deeply in arrears with my College work, and had to struggle through the year as best I could. With vacation, however, I plucked up a stout heart, and fell to work, in all the time I could find for it, to write a novel. I kept hoping to finish the thing in short order. But it was a spider-web of a job, to use a metaphor stolen from a friend of mine; and it stuck onto my fingers more and more as I tried to get it off them. I reached the end of summer vacation half-dead, but the autumn air forthwith made me feel as jolly as ever, and I am now perfectly well. I had been planning all along to write and tell you about the novel, of which I sometimes felt very vain, although the thing is poor enough stuff now it is all done. I kept waiting, first until I should be through with the novel, and then until I could get a publisher's verdict upon it. All this dragged along, until now at last, just as I am able to announce the new baby. I can also announce that the novel is pretty sure to appear during the spring. So you see, if I wait long, I have something to prattle about when I do write.

The baby is, of course, the real treasure, although it behaves so far only like a small mouse and sleeps as well as it ought. My boy Christopher thinks this an age of miracles. He attributes the baby to Santa Claus, of course, but after accepting this suggestion, he has thought out all by himself a theory of the sequence of events. Santa Claus came, namely, to the house, to fetch Christopher's presents, and chancing to look up stairs, saw some baby clothes, in good number and order, in some drawers. "Ah," said the good Santa Claus, "these people must be wanting a little baby." Whereupon the old fellow trudged back whence he came, found a baby, and brought it to the house for mama.—Among the other presents, Christopher failed not to notice the card you sent. He often speaks of you with fond regard, for he has reason to remember your household very well, for all that he has never seen you.

All this about myself!—Your health I have not yet mentioned. I hope sincerely that all is well with you. As for the family, I owe them all hearty apologies for my so long neglect. It has been a very kind household to me so often. Mrs. Coale wrote me one very pleasant note last year, which I fear I never answered. Please remember me to her most cordially. And Miss Mary, who has so often and so generously exerted herself on my behalf when I was with you—please give her my warmest New Year's greetings. My wife, who has been much impressed by your goodness to me, joins me in all this. She is very proud of the baby, and I hope will be henceforth very happy after her long and tedious imprisonment.

I wish that we could see you. I want to fly southwards sometime in spring. If I have a day in Baltimore, I will make you a call. Tell me if any of you come northwards. Write soon, please, and give me all the news you can about yourself and the family.

Yours Truly
Josiah Royce.

The novel—you see I run over with it still—is of course about California life. I hope you will like it when it is done. You shall have a copy sent you next spring, I hope.

To Horace Elisha Scudder, January 13, 1887[98]

Boston, Jan. 13, 1887.

Dear Mr. Scudder:

I should propose as title "Oakfield Creek." I don't quite like "Escott" as title, and I see the objections to my own title. Perhaps, however, the trouble over the land might be made prominent in the title somehow, as "The Affair at Oakfield Creek," or "The Eldon Land-Title," or "The Land War at Oakfield Creek," or "Escott's Land Claim." In any case it is the trouble with the land-title, or the geographical name associated therewith, that we shall do best to make prominent, I suppose, if the name is changed. Please write me any further suggestions.

Please arrange to have duplicate page proofs sent to me from the first, so that I may keep one set constantly before me as I correct.

Your Truly
Josiah Royce.

98 ALS. Houghton Mifflin Papers. HL.

To Houghton Mifflin Company, January 22, 1887[99]

20 Lowell St.
Jan. 22, 1887.

Houghton, Mifflin & Co.

I have of course every reason to accept the proposal of your letter of Jan. 21, so far as concerns the possible arrangement with M. de Varigny for the translation of my forthcoming novel, and for its publication in French newspapers, in case he likes it. Of course I understand the impossibility of making any terms save such as he thinks best to make, and therefore, since you have been so kind as to offer to send him proofs as the book goes through press, I shall very gladly leave the whole matter in your hands. Please therefore do as seems fairest to you, and as you judge most practicable, about the whole negotiation, and I shall accept whatever I get in consequence in the way of compensation. That is all that I need say, I suppose, in the way of signifying my entire acceptance of your kind proposal.

As to the *title* of the book, I now propose, after reading your proposal, the following revised title: "The Land Feud of Oakfield Creek." *Feud* seems both a more accurate and a more attractive word than *War*. "Land Feud," if it is not too awkward a compound for a title, is suggestive of the whole business, and will carry the reader more easily past the preliminary statements of the nature of the coming trouble, statements which may weary him unless he knows what is coming out of them all.

Yours Truly
Josiah Royce.

To Houghton Mifflin Company, January 28, 1887[100]

20 Lowell St.
Jan. 28, 1887.

Houghton, Mifflin & Co.

Please make note of the title which was provisionally and ver-

[99] ALS. Houghton Mifflin Papers. HL.
[100] ALS. Houghton Mifflin Papers. HL.

bally agreed upon at my last interview with you, and which I still like, unless you have since formed objections to it. I have asked the proofreader to correct accordingly. This revised title is

The Feud of Oakfield Creek.

I remain
Yours Truly
Josiah Royce.

To George Buchanan Coale, February 6, 1887[101]

20 Lowell St.
Cambridge.
Feb. 6, 1887.

My Dear Coale:

I ought to have written more promptly by far (and should have done so had not the distractions due to a new baby and an invalid mother prevented),—to express my warm interest and very hearty good wishes on the news of your daughter's engagement. I remember Mr. Redwood very well, having met him at your house, and I retain a very pleasing impression of him in every sense. I doubt if he will remember me as well, but I hope that you will express to him my good wishes and congratulations. To Miss Mary please express my earnest hopes for her happiness, and my confidence that fate means her to have the best. As for yourself, and Mrs. Coale, I trust that with your daughter near you, and prosperous, all will go well, notwithstanding the lonesomeness.

I am much pressed for time, and I have only chance to add that you must surely write me the date of your proposed visit northwards, and my little home will be only too glad to receive you. There will always be plently of room, and a warm welcome. My wife's health is now so much better that I feel sure she will pass the rest of the winter in almost perfect strength.

Affectionate greetings from our house to all of yours.—The novel is about half in type.—Of Shakespeare &c., I want to talk when we meet.

Yours Very Truly
Josiah Royce.

101 ALS. Redwood Collection. JHU.

To Caroline Dorsey Coale, March 13, 1887[102]

20 Lowell St.
Cambridge, Mass.
March 13, '87.

My Dear Mrs. Coale:

That I have not written since my telegraphic reply to your message, announcing Mr. Coale's death, is due chiefly to my feeling of the impossibility of saying what I ought at such a moment. I feel that I have been very neglectful indeed of late, and have been very wrong in not letting Mr. Coale know of my interest oftener, but now at least I want you to be reminded that I have lost a very, very great deal in him. My acquaintance was too much interrupted by fortune and by my profession to enable me to speak my mind to him often, but I have never known a completer specimen of American manhood, nor a person who attracted me in just his way. I shall bear my recollection of his words and of his spirit all my life, and I deeply wish that I could in any way live up to what he has suggested to me. All this, I feel, is but a poor expression for my true feeling, but it is the best I can do.

To you and to your daughter, at such a time, I can say nothing that you can find it worth while to hear, but you have all been so kind to me in the past, and I owe so much to your good will that I hope you will let me give you my heartiest sympathy in this great trouble. My wife joins with me in this. Let me say also that if ever I can serve in the least or in the greatest you or yours, you must think me wholly at your service. May I hope to hear from you erelong? I shall never forget any of you.

Please remember me warmly to Mr. Dorsey, & Mr. George, as well as to Miss Mary herself, and believe me always

Yours Very Truly
Josiah Royce.

[102] ALS. Redwood Collection. JHU.

To Joseph Burwell McChesney, April 6, 1887[103]

My Dear McChesney:

Nothing that I can say about dear Sill seems to me just now worth saying at all. It was my fortune to stand for some years very near to him in certain regards, and to gain an insight into his fearless, devoted, and generous heart that I may not hope to describe to anybody else. It was also my lot to owe to his friendship, counsel, and intercession, the attainment of some of the greatest prizes that I shall ever dream of finding in life. Meanwhile, so much about his nature remained in the midst of all this intimacy beyond my power to appreciate as I ought—in so many ways he was too wealthy a soul for me to respond to—that I am sure you could not find a worse person among his friends than myself if you want to get a fair account of his genuine character and quality. I know too little of him, after all. What most strikes me about him, at this moment, is the fact that he was, I might almost say, slain solely by his zeal for his ideals. With other men ideal aims are often matters of aspiration. With Sill they were his constant companions from moment to moment. With other men, too, such ideals are apt to be rather dreams than task-masters. Sill's ideals were as exacting as calls of the most prosaic and harassing business, even while they were the ideals of a born poet. You could never catch him at a moment when he was or could be false to them. He was full of humor, but he could never jest at his ideals. Once in sportive conversation I remember his chancing to say, in condemnation of some philosophic doctrine: "If that be wisdom, may I never be enlightened! But no," he added at once, and reverently, "I will not say that even in jest. Whatever comes, may we be some day enlightened." Sill loved his friends, and was the most loyal of men to them, but he could never hear from them an offence to these ideals; and at such a time he always spoke plainly.

In the service of these ideals he cared of course nothing for popularity, although by nature he was intensely sensitive to personal conflicts of all sorts. Once I found him very gloomy. His

[103] MS unknown. Printed in *A Memorial of Edward Rowland Sill* ([Oakland, Cal.?] 1887). McChesney was secretary of The Berkeley Club which authorized the publication of this volume.

work at Berkeley was wearing him out, and certain of his worst pupils, to whose interests he had been showing his usual unsparing devotion, had just been paining him by bitter speeches and cruel misunderstandings. I gossiped on about the affair to him, in an irresponsible way, of course, until among other things I said: "You see, Sill, all this comes from your determined fashion of casting pearls before swine. Why will you always do it?"—"Ah, Royce," he responded, with a perfectly simple and calm veracity in his gentle voice, "you never know in this world whether you were really casting pearls at all until you feel the tusks."

As for Sill's ideal itself, it was an ideal of the highest manhood, an ideal towards which he desired all his friends to strive. His ideal future man was the combination of the truth-seeker and the doer of good into the one person of the true poet. He never would admit any real opposition between the scientific and the poetical spirit, or between either and the capacity for simple practical devotion to one's daily tasks. We ourselves, he taught, make in our false one-sidedness the so-called oppositions of these ideals. In themselves they are one. Science is, or ought to be, poetry, and poetry is knowledge, and the humanity of the future will not divide life, but will unite it. To bring such manly unity into his own life was his constant effort, and he perpetually invited others to join in the truly humane task that he wanted to have proposed to the men of this so divided and unhappily specialized generation. Laboring in the service of such things, Sill sacrificed his health, and finally his life.

I beg your pardon for the inadequacy of these few pages.

Yours very truly,
Josiah Royce.

Cambridge, Mass., April 6, 1887.

To George Bucknam Dorr, August 12, 1887[104]

Cambridge
Aug. 12, 1887

Dear Dorr:

I have delayed writing because I wanted to take time to consult

104 ALS. Royce Papers. HUA.

a little with my wife the friendly offer that you and your father and mother so kindly made. We have given full consideration to the whole matter, and I assure you that we have found the notion a most attractive one. But there are a number of difficulties in the way, and my wife feels it necessary to say with much regret that it seems to her impossible to go. She loves the mountains and water even more than I do, and thanks you many times for the goodness of your plan. Perhaps in some other season such a thing might be just possible.—But the future is its own guardian. In any case don't imagine for a moment that we underrate your generous and considerate enthusiasm for our welfare, or the advantages of your offer.

As for your other offer—the bicycle—my wife wants me to try it. She fancies that if I could learn to use it, she would have more respect for me. My reputation for dexterity is not high. Perhaps I might do something, however, and I think I had better try, if you still want me to. If I succeed, we might arrange for a purchase some day. If I don't succeed, you must behave as a sewing machine man always promises to do, and take it back. Meanwhile, do you want to express it to me at my expense? If so, I shall regard you with more admiration than ever.

And now I want to thank you very warmly indeed, and, if possible, your father and your mother yet more warmly still, for a few charming days that I shall certainly never forget. They came most opportunely, and at a moment when I especially needed to get my mind off some harrassing temporary vexations. The result has done me much good. Your mother seems to me now a minister of comfort, pure and simple, and I only regret that in her house I was but a receiver of pleasure, and must have been, especially to her, but a poor amusement. In future I hope to see much more of you all, at times when I am more alive myself.

I hope you will remember me to Mr. and Mrs. Wolcott. I ought to say to them that in my better moments something in my heart will rise up and say that, after all, a mummy is *not* a mineral.[105] This may show I am not wholly hardened.

Hodgson must ere this have left you. If not, please say to him that

[105] A typed copy of this letter in the Royce Papers contains the following note: "This refers to a discussion raised by him at Oldfarm as to whether a mummy might not be termed a mineral, he taking the side, for argument's sake, that it could."

I have just found the best possible description of my beloved form of "memory-hallucination" in the current *Archiv für Psychiatrie*.[106] I am as triumphant as you please over it.

I hope soon to hear of your continued prosperity. Mrs. Royce desires to be remembered most warmly to you all.

Yours Very Truly
Josiah Royce.

To Daniel Coit Gilman, February 9, 1888[107]

20 Lowell St.
Cambridge Feb. 9. 1888

My dear Mr. Gilman,

I have joined the too great army of scholarly blunderers who break down when they ought to be at their best. The break-down is nervous of course and needs nothing, I am assured, but a long sea voyage all alone, to make me myself again. I don't know when I shall go, but we are now looking for the ship. The College has given me leave of absence for the rest of the year on half-pay. I feel nearly all the time very well and nobody meeting me on the street would call me ill, but the little devil in the brain is there all the same, and this kind goeth not out but by travelings and hard fare. As you are the principal cause of my existence in the academic life, I suppose that you will hear with vexation of my mishap, not to say carelessness. I think that there is no cause for apprehension, and the experience as such is peculiarly edifying, instructive, and even fascinating to one who loves to study his own mental states. I need hardly add that the expenses of this method of recovering from my troubles are not furnished from my own savings, but are freely given to me by a very dear friend to whom I shall always be deeply indebted. The same kindness insures for me the safety and comfort of my family during my absence, and in this entirely unexpected and undeserved way what would be a very dark path is rendered a very light one.—

[106] Emil Kraepelin, "Ueber Erinnerungsfälschugen," *Archiv für Psychiatrie* 18 (1887): 395 ff. Royce cited these findings in his "Hallucination of Memory and 'Telepathy'," *Mind* 13 (1888): 244–48.

[107] ALS. Gilman Papers. JHU. The letter is written in Mrs. Royce's hand.

All this will prevent my being present at the lunch February twenty-second. I send the heartiest greetings. Please remember me to Mrs. and Miss Gilman and believe me as ever—

Yours loyally
Josiah Royce.

To Francis Ellingwood Abbot, February 9, 1888[108]

20 Lowell St.
Cambridge Feb. 9. 1888.

My Dear Abbot:

You have heard of my mishaps, and of my consequent desertion of my post. I understand that you were asked to undertake my Phil 13 or advanced course, for the rest of the year; and that your horrid boys, whom you have to torment yourself over, do not permit you to accept the place.[109] I write to say that I am heartily sorry that you could not accept the work. I am glad that you were asked to do so. You know how we differ, and how freely we both have expressed the difference. Yet I am so sure of the value of the clash of minds, and I have so true and hearty a respect for your mind, that I deeply regret that, whatever happens, my class will miss the stimulus and the moral support which your presence and your enthusiasm would have given them. I must leave soon, and may not be able to see you. Hence I must say Goodby, & God (I mean of course *my* God) bless you.—

Yrs.
Josiah Royce.

[108] ALS. Abbot Papers. HUA.

[109] From 1881 to 1892, Abbot was preceptor of the Home School for Boys, in Cambridge. On February 12, Abbot replied to Royce, saying that he had been able to rearrange his schedule in order to teach Philosophy 13. Abbot continued: "The audacity of my daring to undertake such a task overwhelms me; I shall only rattle round in your shoes. . . . As to your class, they will barely tolerate me, even if they come at all. Too well I understand my own unfitness to carry on *your* work. . . . As to our 'differences' etc., I shall have nothing to say; *my* work is constructive and controversial only in the most general way." Letter-Book 10. Abbot Papers. HUA.

To Charles Rockwell Lanman, May 21, 1888[110]

500 miles out of Melbourne
Long. 130 E. Lat. 40 S
May 21, 1888.

Dear Lanman:

Don't expect a long letter. I'm too lazy. The story of this voyage is a very long one, and only to my wife have I tried to be anywhere nearly complete. For the rest, I am now enjoying myself like a sea-bird (except that they don't have to write letters). My head is no longer tired, I am anxious for work again, and I know no reason why I shouldn't return a very much cured man. At all events pray for me, and receive meanwhile immense thanks for the tobacco and the pipes. The solace that that tobacco has been you can hardly estimate even yourself. It is going to last me almost precisely and evenly to the voyage's end. Then I shall load up in Australia for the return passage. I shall probably go back by steamer.

How long I shall stay in Australia depends so much on causes beyond my present knowledge, e.g., news from home, reception by new friends, my own feelings, &c., that I may not now predict. I shall try to write you some of my impressions, but, if I don't, you must not fancy that I forget you.—Nor must I neglect to thank you for the lovely charts, whose elaborate and sound information has been a marvel to me all the way along.—The ship's company is a jolly one, on the whole, and I have had an excellently good time all the way, except for a long siege of dull spirits at the outset of the voyage, a siege which I well expected.—Much love to you from

Yours Truly
Josiah Royce.

[110] ALS. Lanman Papers. HUA.

To Horace Elisha Scudder, May 21, 1888[111]

Barque *Freeman*
Monday, May 21.
1888.

My Dear Scudder:

In the note that accompanied your kind introductions, you wanted to hear how I felt on reaching Melbourne. I can only say that now, in long 135°E, Lat. 40 S, two or three days sail from Melbourne, and after what seems to be a very jolly and prosperous passage, I feel full of enthusiasm, and want nothing so much as to get back to work, after a little more time spent in seeing the world. I hope that you may be able to reserve that Theodore Parker for me, as, in my present humor, I want nothing better than some such engagement.[112] I named *two years*, not because I could not at least *hope* to be able to do the job earlier, but because I don't want to make any more false promises, nor to endanger my health by overwork again.

I find the sea a perfectly satisfactory cure for my head-weariness, and can only recommend any over-tasked man of my type to go and do likewise, in case, to be sure, his digestion is still intact, and his vegetative organism in general is free, like mine, from disturbances. An invalid in any general sense might find the sea bad, but for overtasked nerves as such, uncomplicated by any organic or other deep trouble, the sea is a "balm and a soother." The worst evils are salt codfish, and ditto beef, and the other natural inconveniences of even the most modern sea-diet.—The experience has been in many ways highly educating (and not only so for my stomach).—Please remember me very cordially to Mrs. Scudder. I thank you for the letters, and shall use them if I am able to stop at the Sandwich Islands.—

Yours Truly
Josiah Royce.

[111] ALS. Scudder Papers. UCB.

[112] The Houghton Mifflin Company was then engaged in publishing a series on American Men of Letters. Royce had evidently been asked to write a volume on Theodore Parker.

To William James, May 21, 1888[113]

Southern Ocean
Lat. circa 40°S.) circa 600 mi.
Long. ″ 135°E.) out of Melbourne.
May 21, '88.

Dear James:

It ought to be a long letter, if it were to undertake to tell the whole story of my life since I last saw Boston Light; but it must be a short one, since I have so many others to write. My wife will have the whole of the longer story in a MS whose mailing costs I so far hardly dare compute.

I don't know of course how I shall feel on land, but here in my place of safety I seem to myself to be entirely cured. There was indeed a long period of depression—not exactly the sort of discontent that was to be feared, i.e. not exactly a *longing* for anything good or evil, but simply the dullness that Tolstoi describes in his Confession, or the "grief without a pang, voiceless and drear," that Coleridge so well portrays. It was a diabolically interesting nervous state, although while it lasted I never could make out precisely why I ate my meals, or kept aboard at all. To call the thing misery would be a mistake. It was an absolute negation of all active predicates of the emotionl sort save a certain (not exactly "fearful") looking-for of judgment and fiery indignation.—But all this pathology is no longer in order. With the winds and the birds of the southern sea came a new life. My wits indeed had been working all along. In the deepest of my nothingness I read mechanics, and mathematics, and Martineau, and even Casanova, with an impartial insight into the essential nothingness of definite integrals, easily conquered maidens, and divine laws—one and all. But while I mused dispassionately upon the world of passion, my head was clear so far as the mere mechanics of thinking went. And now that passion has come again, and the good Lord seems to have some life in his world of "*Sonnen und Milchstrassen*,"[114] my wits grow more constructive, and I more and more look upon the voyage as a very highly educating experi-

[113] ALS. James Papers. HL. Partly printed in *TCWJ*, 1: 800–802.

[114] An allusion to the conclusion of Schopenhauer, *Die Welt als Wille und Vorstellung*, bk. 4.

ence. In fine, I have largely straightened out the big metaphysical tangle about continuity, freedom, and the world-formula, which, as you remember, I had aboard with me when I started, and I am ready to amuse you with a metaphysical speculation of a very simple, but, as now seems to me, of a very expansive nature, which does more to make the dry bones of my "Universal Thought" live than any prophesying that I have heretofore had the fortune to do.[115] The fields of speculation are very wide and romantic, after all, and great is the fun of bringing down new game. I must live to tell about this new specimen, at any rate. But I despair of describing it to you in this letter. I must wait until we meet. Suffice it that the old trouble about Continuity has come to seem to me very enlightening for the whole range of metaphysics, but particularly for our question about Freedom and the Ideals. I can't imagine why people will thrash the old straw in discussing this question. Dear good Martineau runs the same old treadmill for half his book. The thing has endlessly numerous novelties in it, just because it is a burning problem of life. Why not be somewhat vital and personal in thinking out what is after all an immediate vital issue of every moment?—But alas! perhaps my suggestions will seem to you as arid and old as any others. But wait till we meet, and we shall see.

My plans for a new story are also still active. I am holding myself back from any hard work, but by the time I get back I think that I shall be ready for an outburst of literary toil. I shall indeed "lean no more on superhuman aid" and shall dread fatigue more than I used to do; but so far as I can see, my strength is going to be once more excellent. As for my security against relapse, it lies rather in the fact, not that "a burnt child dreads the fire," but that, in the words of my favorite Buddhist homily, I feel "like a fire that returns not to the place once burnt over." *That* experience is done for and over forever. New lands and worlds call for me now, so at least I fancy, and though I shall never amount to much in any of them, I *can't* go back.

I feel much curiosity about Abbot, & Cambridge affairs in general, and about whether I ever can really get back into the saddle, and ride the old nag again. I hope for a letter from you at Mel-

[115] This speculation led to Royce's distinction between "appreciation" and "description," first presented in "Physical Law and Freedom: The World of Description and the World of Appreciation," *SMP*, pp. 381–434.

bourne, of course; but unless there is gravely important news, I shall not answer until I have moved about awhile on land, and have seen Hodgson's friends. I am not anxious to write very much until I reach California, and I have many to write to. I long now for a pedestrian tour on land.

My mineral water and figs were a great comfort, as also the French novels. My companionships aboard the ship have been highly agreeable. The Captain, as Yankee and Cape Cod man, who has read a good deal in the long sea hours of his life, is contemplative. Once in awhile I have to explain to him metaphysics, as thus: We sit on deck in the tropics, gazing into the heavens, and talking over Newcomb's Astronomy, which Captain has been reading. He grows now more and more meditative over the vast stellar distances, and the rest, and at last observes: "Well, sometimes it seems to me like nothing so much as a dream. Don't it ever occur to you that perhaps the whole thing above there, and our life too, is a dream of ours, and perhaps there ain't anything anyhow, that's real?"—I admit having had such thoughts.—"Well now, what do you teach your classes at Harvard about all this?"—Thus called upon to explain amid the trade-winds, and under the softly flapping canvas, the mysteries of absolute idealism, I put the thing thus: "There was once a country man," I say "from Cape Cod, who went to Boston to hear Mark Twain lecture, and to delight his soul with the most mirth-compelling of our humorists. But, as I have heard, when he was in Boston, he was misdirected, so that he heard not Mark Twain, but one of Joseph Cook's Monday Lectures. But he steadfastly believed that he was hearing Mark. So when he went home to Cape Cod, they asked him of Mark Twain's lecture. 'Was it *very* funny?' 'Oh, it was *funny*, yes,—it was *funny*,' replies the countryman cautiously, 'but then, you see, it wasn't so *damned* funny.'—Even so Captain," say I, "I teach at Harvard that the world and the heavens, and the stars are all *real*, but not so *damned* real, you see." The Captain has been a devout student of the *Religious Aspect* from time to time ever since, though in lucid intervals, he affirms that the whole is consarned nonsense, and thereupon he falls back upon Macaulay's essay on Bacon, which he reads to his wife as a fortification of his common-sense.—The rest of the ship's life is very amusing, on the whole. I escaped altogether seasickness, at the outset of the voyage, probably because of my abnormal nerves.—God be with thine house. Remember me to Mrs. James most warmly.—

Yours Very Truly
Josiah Royce.

Fair weather and quick passage all the way so far.

To Alfred Deakin, June 21, 1888[116]

Oram's Hotel.
Auckland, N. Z.
June 21, '88

My Dear Deakin:

Talks with Sir Saul Samuel, and with one or two other passengers on the *Zealandia*, moved me to the unexpected decision in favor of making this place the breaking place of my journey, instead of the Sandwich Islands. I am glad that I determined to do this, for I find that I shall by the aid of Sir Saul &c. get a good deal of franking through this land, shall see more than I should in the S. I., shall get more ideas on your political life in the colonies in general, by remaining within range of your newspapers, and shall see several noteworthy people. I am sorry of course that I did not see the matter in this light before I left Sydney, for I could have got important help from your advice; but we live in this world largely by changing our minds. Any note addressed to me at this hotel will reach me if it is delivered before July 16. On that day I am a passenger by the *Alameda*, which leaves Auckland for San Francisco then.

I shall always remember with more gratitude than you may imagine the delightfully cheering little journey that I owe to you. I had been needing for some time a kind of championship that you gave me in an underserved degree of fullness. I can't tell you how much you brightened me up.—I find the air and scenery here in N. Z. very jolly. I am going to have one trip to Wellington, and one to the Hot Lakes.—

Yours Very Truly
Josiah Royce.

116 ALS. Deakin Papers. NLA.

To William James, Auguet 10, 1888[117]

Los Gatos, Cal.
Aug. 10, '88.

Dear James:

I have meant to write you once or twice more, but my stay in the colonies, while it was a very healthy and curative one, gave me little time for writing. I spent some time with colonial magnates of various sorts, to whom Hodgson had introduced me, or whom I met by virtue of introductions in the colonies. I wandered a little in Victoria, in New South Wales, and in New Zealand. I found the climate of especially the latter region very tonic, and seem to have recovered my wits pretty completely. The colonies are charming studies in human nature and in politics, and I return feeling much older and wiser,—not to add, immensely happier. As to my original trouble, it is all gone. My letter to you mailed at the close of my voyage to Melbourne, confessed my sorrows on the sea, and told you how I felt just then. Since then I have found my will all sound, and my nerves too. The old affair was a tremendous experience, but it is over, and I fancy that to a fellow of my sort such a thing won't occur twice. I have many things to tell you about philosophy and the rest, but let that go till we meet.

Reaching California, I find my own family in not the best condition. My father is recently dead,[118] and one of my sisters is barely convalescent from a long and weary illness. I am in no state pecuniarily to be of help to the household, although so much trouble has put them in a place where, though they aren't at all suffering, help from a good son who had been careful of his health and of his means, wouldn't be a bad thing. So I once more have cause to feel that when we play with our strength, we hurt more people than one. But I won't let myself be discouraged. The devil has had his own in my past. Perhaps he won't have so much in my future. We shall see.

Very pleasing to me are the announcements for next year in the elective pamphlet, which I see now for the first time as I land. I like your plan for your course most immensely. Henceforth you

[117] ALS. James Papers. HL.

[118] Royce's father died on June 23, 1888.

too are amongst the prophets. Remember me to Mrs. James, & believe me always most affectionately

Yrs. Truly
Josiah Royce

To Charles Rockwell Lanman, August 20, 1888[119]

Los Gatos
Aug. 20, 1888

Dear Lanman:

Reaching these shores from the storm-tossed ocean, I learn that thou too hast been wafted into the happy harbor of home life during my absence.[120] For plenty of friendly greeting and intercourse I trust to the happy future that awaits us, I hope, in Cambridge. For now I send, hurriedly, and in the midst of much travelling to and fro, my heartiest blessing and warmest congratulations. More anon (which means pretty soon), when I see thee.

Thine Truly
Josiah Royce

[119] ALS. Lanman Papers. HUA.
[120] Reference to Lanman's marriage on July 18, 1888.

The Letters

Part III

1888-1900

Part III

1888-1900

Through the twelve years covered by this section of Royce's correspondence, one may trace his growth from local to national and finally to international eminence. At the beginning he could describe himself as "quite an unknown young college professor," but before the end of the nineteenth century he had become an ambassador of American thought.

After a few years of apparent aimlessness and debilitating quarrels with Frémont and Abbot, Royce gradually settled down to make this his most productive period. In addition to more than a hundred shorter pieces, his publications of the 1890s include *The Spirit of Modern Philosophy* (1892), *The Conception of God* (1895; rev. ed., 1897), *Studies of Good and Evil* (1898), *The World and the Individual* (1899, 1901), and *The Conception of Immortality* (1900).

Certainly the most significant development of this period was in Royce's metaphysical theory. The distinction between "description" and "appreciation" advanced the cosmological aspect of his philosophy, while his lecture before the University of California's Philosophical Union led to a revision of his idealism and gave his theory a more explicitly teleological character. The California experience also led him to formulate the principle of individuation. These various developments finally resulted in Royce's most comprehensive statement in metaphysics with the Gifford Lectures.

To Daniel Coit Gilman, September 6, 1888[1]

20 Lowell St.
Cambridge, Mass.
Sept. 6, '88.

Dear Pres. Gilman:—

I have returned from my quest for health—perfectly restored. My sleep is very sound and cheerful, my spirits are of the best, and, as to my strength, I feel like a bent bow, all ready to twang.—My journey was to Australia, round the Cape of Good Hope, with three weeks passed in very good company in Melbourne, Sydney and the Blue Mountains of New South Wales; thence by steamer *Zealandia* to Auckland; thence still in good company, to Wellington, and afterwards to the great volcanic regions of the North Island; thence back to Auckland, and by steamer *Alameda* to San Francisco; and finally, after three weeks of visiting in California, the homeward journey was made *via* the Mt. Shasta route and the Canadian Pacific. I think that I'm now good for about ten years more of solid work. At all events there is no question about my present soundness.

I see that I was elected President for the year of the Alumni Ass. of J. H. U. I suppose the office to be purely ornamental; but if

[1] ALS. Gilman Papers. JHU.

there is anything for me to do, I will most gladly do it. Who is the Secretary?

My news of home affairs has been very fragmentary all this time. I learn now with surprise and satisfaction of Stanley Hall's promotion.[2] His new work will be a very exacting one, and I have high hopes that he will make a great success of it. Still, it is a pity to lose him from psychology, as I fear we shall do.—I note also with great regret reports that the University in Baltimore is somewhat pinched by the misfortunes of the B. & O.[3] I hope that the reports are at least greatly exaggerated.

I have much to tell about the journey, and my impressions of the antipodes, but I have no time now to write more, and I doubt whether you have time to hear more. Please remember me very warmly to Mrs. Gilman and Miss Gilman, and believe me

Very Truly Yours
Josiah Royce

To Daniel Coit Gilman, January 2, 1889[4]

Baltimore, Jan. 2, 1889

My Dear Pres. Gilman:—

I have twice called today in the hope of finding you, but fortune is against me. I am just returning from a short trip as far west as Cleveland, whither I went as representative of the College at the annual dinner of the Harvard Club of that town. It was a pleasant

[2] Hall left Johns Hopkins in 1888 to become the first president of Clark University.

[3] The University's initial endowment was provided by the John Hopkins estate, valued at approximately $7 million, the bulk of which was invested in the Baltimore and Ohio Railroad Co. Since Hopkins's will directed the trustees to keep its B. & O. stock, the University's budget depended heavily on income from its 15,000 shares. Thus financial crises of the B. & O. during the 1880s indicated a disaster for the University. In November, 1887, a dividend was omitted, and the University's finance committee estimated a deficit of $98,000. By the fall of 1888, the trustees made a public appeal to save the University through an emergency fund of $100,000. This financial plight was alleviated after 1889 through additional endowments and through expansion of the undergraduate and medical programs. See Hugh Hawkins, *Pioneer: A History of the Johns Hopkins University, 1874–1889* (Ithaca: Cornell University Press, 1960), pp. 316–26.

[4] ALS. Gilman Papers. JHU.

outing. Returning *via* Baltimore, I have spent part of the day with Mrs. Coale, and have looked in at the J. H. U. I was sorry to be unable to attend the Historical Ass. meeting in Washington.—My health is of the best, and I hope to keep it so for awhile at least, although I haven't exactly my old reserves of strength, and have more than once felt a little weary when the term's work was at its full. But a brief holiday rest sets all well again.—I read with interest your last report, and I deeply regret the embarrassments to which the work here seems to be just now subject. Every lover of the good must sympathize heartily with the recent friendly editorial in the *Nation*,[5] and I am sure we all hope for speedy help in your troubles. Perhaps I ought to add that in a conversation I had with Eliot just before I left Cambridge, he expressed warm interest in the prosperity of the J. H. U., and a clear sense that everybody owes you a great deal for the results here. Doubtless, however, you know Eliot's sentiments already.

So much, then, as a passing greeting from a son of the University. I hope to be able to come to the Anniversary meeting this year, and shall see you then. Please remember me very kindly to Mrs. Gilman.

Yours Truly
Josiah Royce.

To Alfred Deakin, February 28, 1889[6]

20 Lowell St.
Cambridge, Mass.
Feb. 28, '89.

My Dear Deakin:

You pour many coals of fire upon me. When I returned I found myself in a mass of business, which continueth unto this day, and my frequent thoughts of you have not somehow found chance to take shape heretofore in anything but my tardy dispatch of my three books, which I accomplished once during a hastily arranged visit to my publisher. But having your letter, I must indeed delay no longer.

[5] "The Johns Hopkins University," *Nation* 47 (December 20, 1888): 493–94.

[6] ALS. Deakin Papers. NLA.

I regret extremely your repeated illnesses. You probably need another long journey, and I feel a certain hope that, although you may have no further acute troubles, you may be led on some quasi-diplomatic tour through these regions, and that before very long. My health is now in general excellent, and my sleep, with a trifling use, at long intervals, of bromides, keeps itself almost as sound as it was in my boyhood. My tasks are varied. I have written on Australia two rather lengthy magazine articles for the *Atlantic*.[7] They are to appear, I am informed, in the May and June nos. I wonder how you will find them. They make use of my reading much more than of my observation. Their title runs "Reflections after a Wandering in Australasia." After a brief opening I speak, in article one, of the conditions of the Australian life as determined by your general physical surroundings and your history. All this is very superficial, but it is addressed to the blind by a one-eyed man, and is to be judged accordingly. Our public know nothing of Australia. After sketching your early explorations and your eternal fight with the desert, I speak of your political state. As my authority for this I give your journalistic literature (having been a subscriber to the *Leader* since my return). I add the effects produced by conversations with several public men, none of whom, of course, I may name in that connection, as privacy is privacy. The men are chiefly yourself and the good Sir Saul, who was with me much of the time in N. Z., and on the steamer to S. F.—Of yourself I speak as a "prominent Victorian party-leader, who, being in ill-health, forsook politics, and betook himself to hospitality." I make several references to our talks in the Blue Mts., but not such, I hope, in view of my suppression of your name, as will seriously compromise your future, or lead to your execution for treason against the Empire. Elsewhere, in criticizing the State Socialism of the political tendencies in all Australasian life, I have occasion to quote your speech (which you so kindly sent—the speech on the Budget), and there of course I name you.

My second article is devoted to two things:—first, remarks on the social conditions, based upon various accidental observations.

[7] "Reflections after a Wandering Life in Australasia," *Atlantic Monthly* 63 (May 1889): 675–86; (June 1889), 813–28. See also "Impressions of Australia," *Scribner's Magazine* 9 (January 1891), 75–87, which contains Royce's sketch of Deakin and an account of their conversation on American and Australian politics.

Here I dish up our enthusiastic friends of the "Conference of the Society for the Federation &c.," whom we met at lunch in Sydney. I also sketch an amusing and excellent fellow, Welch by name, bushman, explorer, and newspaper man, whom I met on the *Alameda*. These and similar attenuated data suggest to me the usual omniscient observations which travellers make on a society that they have not had time to see.—Secondly, and lastly, I forecast with mathematical precision and marvelous, mill-stone penetrating insight, your future, showing just why Imperial Federation is a humbug, and wherefore you will separate from the Empire. The form of the demonstration is so novel that it may give points even to the *Bulletin*.—Such is the first fruit of my journey, and I expect nothing less for it than a vote of thanks from your Parliament. Of the N. S. W. parliament I can expect nothing, having alluded disrespectfully to their greatest statesman.

I have kept some track of your own doings this past session through the *Leader*. You must have been made very weary by your Opposition, which seemed to outrun itself in stupidities. I felt some doubt whether your insistence on the "Federation Principle" was not premature. The matter is one partly of necessity (and then it will take care of itself), and partly of education (and then I feel that tariff proposals are poor means of educating the people). In fact it is not possible to beat down jealousies. You can only increase the ties that bind. The more intercolonial business comes to exist in spite of tariffs, the more will the absurdity of intercolonial tariffs, and of all else that is founded on jealousies, dawn upon the people of both & of all colonies. And then the colonies will be sure to federate of themselves, to the exclusion of such taxes. Meanwhile, if you begin by talking of tariffs, the reply, "Why does N. S. W. not take the lead by protecting herself against foreign countries, and so making possible our commercial union?" is very easy, and, as I gather, was made. In short, the tariff between colonies is a festering wound indeed, but to try to remove it, or to reduce it, or even to prevent its growth, by direct measures, is, I fancy, only to cause pain by tampering with the bandages. The sore then grows worse. People rail more at the fellows across the border, and are not converted to Federalism. Healthy growth will cure the desire for an intercolonial tariff altogether. Nothing else will.

That is my conjecture, founded on vague impressions. Still, I heartily wish you success in all that tends towards unity, by whatever means you work. I have no doubt that you will come out well in the election.

Thanks for your criticisms of my work.[8] You are throughout too friendly, and all your blame is just. The books have none of them been startling successes. If you ask visiting Americans who I am, the wisest will meet you with a blank stare of surprise. I am quite an unknown young college professor, and you do far too kindly by me to speak of my books as specially related to the "literature" of the country. American literature is, I am persuaded, quite ignorant as it ought to be of having received any additions from me. Sales of the three books are approximately: *California* 2000 copies (a little less), *Rel. Asp. of Phil.* 1000 copies (a little less), & the novel ditto. The sale of the philosophy book is of course quite satisfactory under the circumstances. As for the others, I can only shrug my shoulders, and go on. I shall doubtless write more and fare worse, and in any case I care but little, since just to have written a book & got it off your hands does one so much solid intellectual good, that no harm results even if nobody reads it.

Sir Saul Samuel was very good fun. His puns are bad, and his ideas lack genius, but his temper was perfect, and he was a charming travelling companion. His thoughts in the volcanic region were exclusively devoted to his carriage springs and to brandy and soda (in their relations to gout), but still he never really grumbled after all. I liked him extremely.

Hodgson is well. I shall soon send you a long Psychical Research article for which he has furnished the facts and I have spun out the fictitious theories.[9] College lectures take up all the rest of my time.—

Yours Very Affectionately
Josiah Royce.

[8] Deakin to Royce, December 31, 1888. Deakin Papers. NLA. Deakin confesses that he has been unable to read *RAP*. He finds the *Feud* strong in plot and character, but slow to unfold. *California*, he feels, is more original than the novel and the exposé of Frémont is unanswerable. He concludes: "You have reason to be proud of both of your books and so has your literature."

[9] "Report of the Committee on Phantasms and Presentiments," *Proceedings of the American Society for Psychical Research* 1 (1889): 350–526, 565–67.

To William James, April 15, 1889[10]

20 Lowell St.
April 15, '89.

Dear James:

The Fox letter was meant to be satisfactory, and is so. I withdraw. I negate the negation, and reaffirm the *aufgehobene Bäume.* May the *höhere Einheit* follow, a result which the *Geist der stets verneint,* in my bosom, declares after all a little improbable. For haven't I after all somehow carried my point? I have thrown the ring into the sea, as an offering. Alas! it comes back to me at the first drag of the net! Without doubt I am doomed, and I am about making my will and preparing to pass over to the unknown future and the Loisette professorship forthwith!

I don't know how you in your house feel after this Apia disaster. Our fleet is comparatively dilapidated. Mrs. Royce would have written an olive branch letter, for she really felt great regret and sympathy for all the pain that our efforts to do righteousness caused to Mrs. James,—but alas, she too was somewhat tossed to and fro, is very weary, showed a momentary sign of light collapse once today, then recovered perfectly, as it is the wont of her temperament to do,—but had to go to bed early. She now sleeps in great comfort, and is quite well, but she could find no chance to write. She will write tomorrow, when, as I am sure, she will wake in perfect peace. I hope sincerely that Mrs. James will never give a further thought to a slight misfortune which she so nobly and generously overcame. I have no feeling but admiration for both her frankness in the first place and her devotion to our service afterwards. Nobody could

[10] ALS. James Papers. HL. The incident that motivated this "olive branch" letter remains obscure. It may have been related to the fact that the Jameses, the Foxes, and the Royces were then building neighboring houses on Irving Street. The allusions contribute to the mock-heroic tone of the letter. The "*Geist der stets verneint*" is Mephistopheles of Goethe's *Faust.* The "Loisette professorship" apparently refers to "Professor Alphonse Loisette," the pseudonym of Marcus Dwight Larrowe, a popular lecturer on memory improvement. On April 18, 1892, Loisette gave a lecture on "The Improvement of Memory" to the Harvard Philosophical Club. According to an undated letter from James to Royce, Loisette had once offered to endow a professorship in the Harvard Department of Philosophy and Psychology. The "Apia disaster" refers to James's home at 18 Appian Way, Cambridge.

have been more humane, or more magnanimous in a true sense.—I regret, of course (just because she must have regretted it), that she had to confess the harmless and even praiseworthy weakness of getting momentarily out of patience with poor me. Nobody deserves it more than I. I haven't been an odious little creature all these years without fully knowing the fact, and I think of none so highly as I do of those who share my appreciation of the odiousness in question. Please treasure up this fact to impart it to all who declare, as some will do, that I am not only odious, but vain-glorious. Doubtless I am, but not save as Satan dwells in me.

Well, as said, the hurricane subsides, the wind becomes a zephyr, and the trees still stand. Fox's glory is still untarnished, and his letter is a model. As for me, I have written no word on Loisette yet, nor could I put pen on paper once last evening. The only thing about me that is unsubdued is and shall be my appetite for food.

Yours Ever
Josiah Royce.

To Mary Gray Ward Dorr, June 21, 1889[11]

20 Lowell Street
Cambridge, Mass.
June 21st, 1889

Dear Mrs. Dorr,

I have delayed my answer to your very kind letter of Sunday in order to consult with my wife as to the possibility of her accepting your invitation to stay with you at Bar Harbor. She feels very grateful for it, and has been trying hard to plan so as to go; but after fullest consideration we have decided that so good a thing may not now be. The new house on Irving Street which is building for us [sic] unites with various complications suggested by the three children to exclude the possibility of her going, either with the baby, or without. As for me alone, however, I am free, or at least still may hope to be so, for as much as a month. You offer me "all of August." I hope I shall not be rating my poor presence for too much if I venture, in advance, to accept for that time, or a few days less, as fortune may determine. You are so kind in asking me

[11] TLC. Royce Papers. HUA.

for a whole month, that, were I not too greedy of a good rest to restrain myself, I no doubt ought to make the time shorter. But, as it is I shall hope, with your assent, to appear as near August 1st as proves to be possible, giving you due notice of the precise time as it approaches. You do not know how much good your kindness will do me.

With warmest regards to all, I remain

Yours very truly,
Josiah Royce.

To George Holmes Howison, July 13, 1889[12]

20 Lowell St.
Cambridge, Mass.
July 13, 1889.

Dear Mr. Howison:—

I am much pleased to hear of the Constitution of your Philosophical Union, and to be able to recognize amongst its members several of my former friends and students. I am deeply grateful for the honor conferred upon me by my election as a Corresponding Member. I have not yet received the Secretary's Letter, but of course I shall at once accept the offered position, and shall be very glad if at any time in future I can be of direct or indirect service to the Union. Please always count on me.

During the past academic year I have managed to keep very much my old health, and have had a fairly successful time. I have been especially gratified at the growth of the Graduate work amongst us. I have given a course on Kant's *Kritik*, read in the original, to seven graduates from both our own and other institutions, and have been delighted to deal at last with men who were fairly free in their German, and who would read an article on Kant in German without whining and without the dictionary. All my men were, as graduate students, aiming at the academic life, and at least three of them have already good prospects as academic teachers of philosophy. So, as you see, even *we* progress. During the coming year I am to give a graduate course on Hegel's *Phänomenologie*, once more of course using the original. In fact *das*

[12] ALS. Howison Papers. UCB.

versteht sich, since what *but* the original could one use? I am already aiming towards a book on Hegel, who will never be to me what he is to you, but whom I find a very interesting fellow, after all. I shall treat the *Phänomenologie* next year as a sort of philosophical Wilhelm Meister, as it is, and shall discuss its historical background at some length.

—Meanwhile various things are causing my views on general philosophy to concrete into more systematic shape. After a few years I hope, in case health permits, to finish a tentative book on the general topic. At the moment I am publishing a sort of pyrotechnic display, viz., an essay on "Evolution" in the *Unitarian Review*.[13] I wish I could send you a copy, but the *Review* gives me no extra copies, so how can I? If you chance to see the thing, take note that I was invited to lecture to a Yale Philosophical Club, on very short notice. So I dictated this essay to a shorthand reporter, corrected it hastily, and read it as it was. My chief esoteric aim and intent in it was, by way of intercollegiate courtesy, to confound the Yale intelligence. I unquestionably succeeded herein, and then, reflecting that anything was good enough for a New England Unitarian country parson, I persuaded my friend J. H. Allen to print it as aforesaid. Allen is a very good fellow, and is rather easily pleased, so he made no objections. The essay prepares the way for a more philosophical discussion, at some future day, of the relations between teleology and mechanism, a topic which forms the central core of my second college course, called at present "The Philosophy of Nature: Spinoza & Spencer," with a critical discussion of Evolution. I think I have some light on that whole topic, although, if you chance to see my *Unitarian Review* essay, doubtless you will declare that I keep my light pretty dark. Remember the circumstances, however. Someday I hope to do better.

I write this to let you know in general my status, since you have been so kind as to remember me in so friendly and hearty a fashion. As for the rest of our department, Palmer has been spending a year in Europe to break in his new wife, who will doubtless return to this land a philosopher and saint of the noblest order.[14] I shall be glad to see Palmer again, for I find him a great stimulus, not to say

[13] "Is There a Philosophy of Evolution?" *Unitarian Review* 32 (1889): 1–29, 97–113.

[14] After his marriage to Alice Freeman, formerly president of Wellesley College, Palmer was granted a sabbatical leave.

a shining example of the holiness to which I shall never attain. James has been building a house this past year, and so has gone over the water for a needed summer's rest. He will return in autumn.

Please remember me to Mrs. Howison, and, very filially, to Joseph LeConte, to whom I owe more than he knows. Please greet all my other friends for me also, in case they ask you about me. My formal response to the Union will follow as soon as I get the Secretary's letter. I shall be delighted to hear more of your work and to have you write soon.

Yrs Truly
Josiah Royce.

To Charles Royce Barney, August 24, 1889[15]

Bar Harbor, Me.
Aug. 24, 1889.

My Dear Roy:

Your letter gives me great pleasure, although it is not altogether a surprise to me to hear of your Harvard plans, for I had always believed you an enterprising young person, and was prepared at any time to find you ambitious for a college course in the East. Let me begin by assuring you, and, through you, your father and mother, of my most cordial sympathy with your plan, and of my desire to give you, now and hereafter, any advice or assistance in my power. Don't hesitate to appeal to me as often as you wish.

As you see, I am this time rather slow in answering your note. The delay comes from the fact that I am away from home on holidays, and that my mail has to be forwarded to me. Moreover, as I am visiting at a very charming country house by the sea, and as the place is full of company, it is hard to get time to write. I take my first chance.

You ask first about the requirements for admission. The full statement I have not by me, and it is very lengthy, because there are nowadays so many "electives" and "alternatives" in our scheme, so that you can enter by very various paths. I will send you the printed statement so soon as I am again in Cambridge, which will

[15] ALS. CSL. The Bar Harbor address was that of Mrs. Dorr's summer home; see Royce's letter to her of June 21, 1889.

be at the end of next week. I can assure you at once, however, that you can't enter without elementary preparation in *one* ancient (i.e., *either* Latin or Greek) *and* in one modern language (i.e., *either* French or German). These requirements, however, need not frighten you *if* you only get into a place where you are well taught.

As to what place you had better study in, however, I of course find it hard to advise you, and when you consider my advice in company with your father and mother, you must all remember that I can't pretend to know just what the advantages are for you at present and at the home schools, but only what the general aspect of the thing is as seen from Cambridge. To be at home is a great thing for one at your age, and I don't want to say a word to hasten the separation of a good boy from his father and mother, but you ask what my whole impression is from the point of view of a teacher in Harvard, and I can only answer that, if you want to learn to swim, you had better take to the water as soon as possible, and that, even so, *if* you want a college education in the East, you had better prepare in the East. You are no child now, and there is no reason why, with proper advice and counsel, you couldn't get on very fairly and safely in school in New England. Some of the best preparatory schools hereabouts are, of private schools, Andover Academy, in Andover, Mass., and Exeter Academy, in Exeter, N. H.; of public schools, the Cambridge, Brookline (Mass.) and Boston High Schools. There are many others, but these are of the first rank. Now California has excellent schools, and one or two of them (notably Mr. W. T. Reid's school at Belmont) make a special point of preparing boys for Harvard, but these school can't equal the Eastern ones in the number, experience, and strength of their teachers; and in the Eastern schools you would meet with more students who were aiming in the same direction as yourself. Not only this, but you would meet on the whole a higher grade of student, you would engage in a keener competition for rank and worth, you would have more stimulus for work, and, always supposing, as I do, that you retained a good moral fibre, and that you chose always the best companionships, you would grow much faster in wisdom and in capacity. In all this I say nothing against California boys; but remember that in the East there is a much larger population from which the school boys of higher attainments are, as it were, picked out, so that the naturally selected scholars who go [to] the greater schools have more chance to be first class fellows, whose companionship would be in the highest degree valuable to you.

There is another point of some importance. Harvard is unquestionably a decidedly trying place for a young man, as indeed it ought to be, and is proud of being. To be one of more than a thousand students, of all reasonably possible degrees of wealth and of poverty, of excellence and of indolence, of indifferent character and of noble character;—this is a great but also a very serious test and training of one's manhood, courage, ability and moral fibre. The first effect on one who, like yourself, comes from a distance and has not precisely known the great world before he comes, must needs be, let us say, a trifle bewildering, perhaps somewhat lonesome or even disheartening. I don't say this to frighten you,—quite the contrary is my meaning. I want to suggest that when you come you'll be on your mettle, and if you're the man I hope to find you, you'll be all the better a swimmer for plunging into deep water and losing breath for a moment when you begin. Only, remember (I speak as a California boy myself) the East, and, above all, a great college like Harvard, will and must seem to you at first very imposing, and a little overwhelming in its bigness and its dignity of new life. Now, if you are to come into such an atmosphere, I want you to be prepared to breathe it. And so, I feel sure, you would find it easier to begin by some schooling for awhile in the East first, so as to get used to the new life and its ways, and so as not to be obliged to take all your bewilderment at once when you first come to Harvard. My general advice is then, come East for schooling as soon as practicable.

Meanwhile, look about you in California for further advice. Your father might write to Mr. W. T. Reid at Belmont, and to one or two other California teachers for advice. Consider the ground well, and don't move hastily. But still, as the road you have chosen is once for all a hard and at the same time very delightful one, don't fear to act, after due consideration, boldly, heroically, and at considerable personal sacrifice. Don't consult mere feeling about it, above all don't yield to mere timidity about a change of schools and of methods of instruction. What you want is the *best* schooling, even if it loses you a year or even two of time. Unless you want the *best* preparation, it isn't worthwhile to think of Harvard. *If* you want the best, I'm with you, and will help you all I can.—I know that I should have been much aided in my own career by the course that I am now suggesting to you.

It is possible that you might want to enter school in the East this autumn. If so, decide as quickly as possible, and write me at once. It wouldn't be worthwhile to come east *much* later than October first, although to do so would be of course not impossible. The best thing would be a private school, one of those I mentioned. If you decided to study in Cambridge itself, I could help you to settle yourself in some school. There are several, public and private.

Much love to your household. Your mother and father know that I am a poor letter writer but I am always ready to serve them as I can.

—Yours Truly
Josiah Royce.

To Charles Royce Barney, September 15, 1889[16]

20 Lowell St.
Cambridge, Mass.
Sept. 15, '89.

Dear Roy:—

On looking over the field a little, I find that you could make a very good use of your time if you came East any time before Nov. 1 or even Nov. 15. I find that while most of the schools open for the winter about Oct. 1, there are some that open later. Moreover, there are so many families sending boys in from the country, or returning to town themselves, quite late, that it is always possible to get into studious work until November. After that everybody is engaged for the winter, and it is almost useless for any fresh person to appear on the scene. Therefore, if you can come during October, I'll engage to get you in somewhere under good care as a student. I knew that Oct. 1 was rather early for you to decide, and mentioned that date as the best one because I wanted to have you as promptly on the spot as possible. But, as I say, on further consideration I find that if you can come during October, or even during the first half of November, you can get started for the winter

[16] ALS. CSL.

very well. If you can't come by that time, then you had better go to Oakland or to some similar place, where you can begin French, which you ought not to delay much longer, and where you can get the most advanced instruction accessible in California.

As I have said however, and as I still think, *if* you fully intend to go through college here, you had better prepare East; and if you are to prepare for college in the East, then any further study, either at home or away from home in California, will prove in large part wasted. For when the change comes, you will find so much difference in your surroundings, that you will need all the time at your disposal to get used to the situation, and to take advantage of the new opportunities. At some sacrifice you will therefore do well to come East at once, rather than to wait a year.

As for what can be done for you here in case you come before the middle of November, (the sooner, of course, the better), the alternatives are these:—you can go to the public school, as Eleanor Ingraham did.[17] I don't advise this plan in your case. It was best for her, because she could afford nothing else, and because she meant to return to California in a short time to teach in public schools herself. You mean to go through college, and you can afford, I suppose, something better. Private instruction is better for two reasons: (1) The teachers are more expert, ambitious, and responsible; (2) There is more chance of getting in private instruction something adapted to your individual needs, whereas the public school deals with a mass of students all together and as a mass. The reason why, especially in this community, the private school teachers are more expert and ambitious, is that once for all the well-to-do, and also the professional people, send their children to private schools, so that the teachers are keenly competing for high reputations and a strong patronage, and have their careers to make; while public school teachers have much less chance to be well-known and highly esteemed in the community, and think less ambitiously of their own careers. I don't say that this *ought* to be so. I only say that it *is* so, in this community at least. As for instruction adapted to your personal needs, of course you can't get that so well in a public school.

This other alternative, private instruction, exists here in many forms. The chief choice lies between private "tutoring," given in

[17] Eleanor Ingraham (1868–1943) was Royce's niece—the daughter of his eldest sister, Mary, and O. P. Ingraham. She had lived with the Royces in Cambridge while attending school in the mid-1880s.

the family of the teacher himself, in whose house you then board along with two, three, or four other students; and the larger private schools, where you are one of a class, and meet many boys. Both plans have their special advantages. The household tutoring of the first class mentioned is the best, *if* you want the most rapid advance possible in your studies as such, and if you desire the constant personal advice of a teacher. The other plan, the large school (preferably the boarding school) is the best for acquiring a knowledge of the society about you, for getting the discipline of life, and for cultivating a healthy spirit of emulation in good things. The first of the two plans is of course the more expensive. The very best teachers are thus employed in receiving boys into their families in small groups, and devoting all their time to these few boys. But the best schools are also very good, though not quite equal as mere places of study, to the houses of private tutors.

If I were to advise you for the immediate future, I should say that, in case you can afford the expense, the first year, say this coming winter might very well be passed in receiving private instruction under an expert teacher in his own house, along with a few other boys. This *one* winter, I say, that plan comparatively expensive though it might prove, would be the very best, because thus you would most readily get over the first difficulties of your change of place and of studies, and would be sure of the best care of your health during your first Eastern winter. *Then* it would be well and easy to choose a good private school to finish your preparation in. I am sure that I could make a good arrangement of this sort for you. As I believe that I told you, my own family is now too large for me to take you as a lodger into my own house, but I should be glad to have you near me, and to give you whatever care I can.

Don't regard it as necessary, however, for you to adopt this plan as to the private teaching if you come. I can easily find you a good place to board and then have you go to the High School, which, as I told you, is a very good school of its kind, here in Cambridge. Whatever you decide, count on my readiness to advise and assist. Remember me affectionately to your father and mother, and believe me

Yours Always
Josiah Royce.

I have mentioned your health during the first winter. I have very little fear about that however. There is seldom any severe cold before Christmas in Boston. And there is in any case little to dread in cold weather.

To Mary Gray Ward Dorr, October 31, 1889[18]

Irving Street, Cambridge
October 31, 1889

My dear Mrs. Dorr,

I have seen Mrs. Whitman, and for the moment, as I understand the matter, the plan for the lectures appears in the following provisional form: the twelve lectures are to be given one per week, probably on Tuesday afternoons, beginning early in December, always providing, of course, that my kind clients desire to have them given at all. The subject proposed would be: "Some Noteworthy Persons and Doctrines in the History of Modern Thought." I should sketch the persons and characters of half a dozen thinkers, more or fewer, as say Spinoza, Leibnitz, Berkeley, Kant, Fichte, Hegel, Schopenhauer. I should give some idea, not of the technical details of their systems, but of their personal attitude towards the world, towards the ideals of life, and towards God. Then I should try to characterize some of the problems of modern life and philosophy, as determined, in a measure, by these very thinkers. In conclusion, I should try to suggest something of my own attitude. How would that do?

I hope you won't find me a failure. I am a very much beset man at present as to the uncomfortable tasks of cares of life, and am likely to be much overworked before winter is over. *This* task, however, would be to me both a delight and a rest, at any rate if you approved the outcome.

Yours very truly,
Josiah Royce.

[18] TLC. Royce Papers. HUA. This and the succeeding letter to Mrs. Dorr are concerned with Royce's series of lectures on "Some Prominent Men, Issues and Tendencies in the History of Modern Philosophy." The twelve lectures were given during the winter of 1889–90; later expanded and rewritten, they were read twice in 1890 and finally published as *SMP*.

To Mary Gray Dorr, December 19, 1889[19]

103 Irving St., Cambridge
December 19, 1889

My dear Mrs. Dorr,

I await, with some eagerness, such criticisms (the more negative the better, so long as they express the opinion of any note-worthy person) upon my first lecture as shall enable me to get nearer to my audience in future. At present we—my audience and I—are rather far apart in spirit; at least I feel so, and that in part by my own fault. I don't write in any spirit of discouragement, for it was a very kindly and delightful audience, and I am sure that I shall yet hit much nearer home, but just now my feeling is, from what I can gather, that the affair on Tuesday was indeed a reasonably innocent beginning, but that I didn't quite convey as much as I wanted to. I was too afraid of being dull, apologized too much for philosophy, made too long a preliminary, quoted too many poets, confused some hearers with excess of illustration, and others by lack of salient points, and in short did not do so well as I shall try to do hereafter. This I learn not from inner consciousness but from friendly criticism. I am now preparing number two. I shall try to be more simple, direct, organic in structure of lecture, &c. To this end I shall welcome criticism from you and George, and that with the frankest good will and gratitude. The whole affair is an experiment, which pleases me much, but which I shall have to modify much as I carry it out. Won't you aid me with a suggestion or two?

Yours truly
Josiah Royce.

I am in the best of spirits and health. I write as I do because I really want suggestions for practical use.

[19] TLC. Royce Papers. HUA.

To Robert Underwood Johnson, June 4, 1890[20]

103 Irving Street
Cambridge
June 4, 1890

Mr. R. U. Johnson:

Dear Sir—

I enclose notes on the interesting article by Mr. Fitch.[21] The often told story of the Congressional Debates over the Admission of California has suggested to me, in Mr. Fitch's version, no comments, although it is possible that in such time as I have given to the paper, I have overlooked minor errors. The controverted points in the earlier part of the paper have, on the contrary, led me to make, very possibly, fuller notes than you desired. I have even taken the risk of troubling you with a previously unpublished document, of recent date, but of good origin, bearing on the legendary "race" of Sloat and Seymour.[22] I hope, by the way, that the numerous legends of the conquest, about that race, about the Bear Flag, and the rest, will either be given you somewhat sparingly, or else will come in such shape as to admit of easy reduction to their foundation of fact (such as it is). For if you have to give attention to them all in such measure as they usually desire, I can only offer my sympathy for the vexation that they will cause you before they get through your hands. Beware, I should say to any fellow-student of those days, beware old Frémont's withered branch, beware the awful avalanche of yarns that the Sloat family,

[20] ALS. Johnson Papers. UCB. This and several succeeding letters to Johnson are concerned with a series of *Century* publications on California history. Royce assisted Johnson as contributor, editor, and general consultant.

[21] George Hamlin Fitch, "How California Came into the Union," *Century Magazine* 40 (September 1890): 775–92. Fitch's article is printed with notes, signed "Editor," but probably written by Royce.

[22] This document was presumably a letter to Royce from Sir Clements Robert Markham, who, remembering his service on the *Collingwood* in 1846, asserts that there was no race and that the English had no plans to seize California. Parts of this letter, together with parts of a letter to Markham from Admiral Lord Alcester (also on the *Collingwood*) were published in Royce's "Light on the Seizure of California," *Century Magazine* 40 (September 1890), 792–94. See fn. 73, Part II above.

the children of the settlers and the like, have in store.—But I don't desire to seem officious. You no doubt already know far more of the troubles than I have ever had occasion to know. I only venture my word of sympathy.

I don't know that my notes are what you wanted. As for cutting, perhaps no harm would be done if all the early part of Mr. Fitch's paper, before the gold discovery, were remorselessly reduced to half a dozen MS pages. His best work, I think, comes later.—

Yours Truly
Josiah Royce.

To Robert Underwood Johnson, June 6, 1890[23]

103 Irving Street
Cambridge
June 6, 1890

Dear Sir:—

I am sorry if my delay in responding concerning the MS on California caused you any anxiety. I put off acknowledgement until I should have time to devote to the notes on the article; and the MS, with comments, was forwarded to you by express yesterday, so that you will doubtless have received it before this letter. Perhaps I ought to have added the observation that, as Mr. Fitch's discussion of the work of the Constitutional Convention of '49 is founded, as he himself observed, upon my own account in the *California* volume, and only carries out more in detail at some points the views to which I was led by my former study, I can of course only agree with what he says in that part of the article. I shall of course, again, be pleased to have the occurrences put in their true historical light before your larger audience, because the Constitutional Convention of '49 seems to me a very interesting body.

Yours Truly
Josiah Royce.

[23] ALS. Johnson Papers. UCB.

To ROBERT UNDERWOOD JOHNSON, JUNE 12, 1890[24]

103 Irving Street
Cambridge
June 12, 1890

Dear Mr. Johnson:

Here is my note.[25] I am a little sorry not to refer in it to my previous use of its novel information in my *Nation* review, because I am a little squeamish about such matters of double use of the same stuff. I did so refer in my former notes, but I find my words stricken out in the MS which you returned. Of course you are a better judge than I am of such little points, as I am sure that you are the proper judge of the pecuniary value of my very modest offering. I once spent a long time over this thing, but of course I write such a note easily now.

Yours Truly
Josiah Royce.

To HENRY RUTGERS MARSHALL, JULY 12, 1890[26]

103 Irving Street
Cambridge
July 12, 1890

Mr. Rutgers Marshall,

Dear Sir:—

I have never published a book or pamphlet on "the subject of pleasure." I have referred to its ethical aspects somewhat incidentally in my *Religious Aspect of Philosophy* (pp. 176–200, *et passim*), but a reasonably good psychological discussion of it I have never been able to prepare. The topic has indeed much interested me, from the fact that the relation of pleasure and pain to the will is still so unpsychologically and persistently distorted, as I think, in

[24] ALS. Johnson Papers. UCB.
[25] Probably Royce, "Seizure of California," pp. 792–4.
[26] ALS. SCA.

much of our modern literature. My view in general is that pleasure and pain seem to be fragmentary and on the whole decidedly capricious representatives in consciousness of a portion only of the organic processes which accompany what we call Will; and that so far from their being primarily the *motives* of conduct, they are always, *in the first place*, the *results* of conduct, and can become motives of conduct only *secondarily*. When however they do become motives of conduct, as in maturer life they of course do, it is *not* universally the rule that the pleasurable is sought, the painful shunned. On the contrary we often find ourselves seeking pain, as the tongue seeks to lacerate itself on the newly formed point of a freshly broken tooth, or as the weary eye still sometimes feverishly turns to the dazzlingly bright light (e.g. to the electric lights at night on the street), or as the irritated man long dwells on the affront whose memory keeps him in the sulks, or as the mourner resists comfort, or as, finally, the morbid patient gloats with horror and tormenting fascination over his "fixed ideas" or "insistent impulses," which he regards with loathing, and yet hugs to his consciousness with a sort of gloomy frenzy (e.g. Bunyan, as he describes himself in his "Grace Abounding to the Chief of Sinners").—[27]

I quote such cases, all indeed more or less abnormal, to suggest the poverty and innocence of that psychology which supposes the experiences of a banquet or of any other healthy occasion when we are merely seeking comfort, to exemplify the sole fashion in which pleasure and pain act as motives.

On this line I have often lectured to my classes, but I have thus far published nothing of note but what I have just referred to. The subject surely needs careful study.

I regret the delay of my response. I have been long absent on a tour in the West, where my correspondence had to be altogether neglected, and my vacation unbroken. The foregoing suggestions, as you will see, aren't at all original. Yet they surely are, as I said, too much neglected in our modern literature.—

Yours Truly
Josiah Royce.

[27] See Royce's "The Case of John Bunyan," *Psychological Review* 1 (1894): 22–33, 134–51, 230–40; reprinted in *SGE*.

To Henry Rutgers Marshall, July 17, 1890[28]

103 Irving Street
Cambridge
July 17, 1890

My Dear Sir:—

I have not had time yet to look up your *Mind* article,[29] to which I am glad to have my attention attracted. At the moment, however, I am impelled by your note to ask a question of a purely psychological character. You say, "It appears to me that the Will act *per se* is necessarily pleasurable (although the pleasurable quality may be masked by coexistent pains not directly related to the Will act)." This view you suggest, not of course as giving the *motive* of the will act, but as explaining why hedonistic psychology has erroneously made pleasure the motive, whereas you make it the necessary accompaniment or outcome. Yet now, *even* in this view, aren't you laying too much stress on those simpler cases, where this is indeed true? Have you looked into the abnormal cases that I mentioned in my last? If so, don't they suggest will acts that are *per se* either painful, or at best essentially *mixed* in tone of feeling? Is the pleasure concomitant of will constant? To exemplify by some cases of the "fixed idea" or morbid impulse type:—A weary man is tormented by a fear lest he has misdirected his letters. The fear appears as a morbid impulse to tear them open so soon as he has sealed a number of them, that he may reexamine them. The impulse is painful. His better judgment corrects his fear. But the impulse persists. Where is the pleasure?—Even so, a nervous man looking from a height feels the well-known impulse "to jump down." Some men feel this impulse indeed with a thrill of reckless joy. Others, however, as I have noticed, feel nothing but horror, and refuse to look down, whenever they can avoid doing so. But if they by accident are where they *must* look down, the impulse comes. Where then is the pleasure in it? Biologically speaking, I take such

[28] ALS. SCA.

[29] "The Classification of Pleasure and Pain," *Mind* 14 (1889): 511–36. After publishing several subsequent articles on the same subject in *Mind*, Marshall published *Pain, Pleasure, and Aesthetics* (London: Macmillan and Co., 1894). Briefly reviewed by Royce in *International Journal of Ethics* 3 (1893): 276.

impulses to be the "overflow," as one has called them, of the wealth of a sensitive nervous system. They aren't "teleological" in the physiological sense of the word. We live in spite of such impulses, not by means of them. Yet abnormal as they are, they are real facts. —I have under my own observation a friend of mine, a professional man who has studied with me, and who is a prey to a whole system of morbid "fixed ideas," which he has confided to me as a psychological student in hope of relief. There are no delusions. The man is of more than average mental ability. His intellect is intact. His general sanity is regarded by a neurological specialist who has examined him as quite secure. Yet his morbid impulses which resemble those described by John Bunyan (in his autobiography, which I before mentioned) are insistent, agonizing,—his daily burden. They are impulses to doubt himself, to draw back from life, to wonder whether he isn't lost, helpless, a wretch, to wonder whether others don't think wrongly of him or misjudge him, &c., &c. *ad inf*. They affect his will deeply. Their results are agonizing. They themselves are *never* pleasure-giving. Have you looked into facts of this sort? If not, I can suggest to you something of their literature.—

Yrs. Truly
Josiah Royce.

To Horace Elisha Scudder, August 24, 1890[30]

Aug. 24, 1890

My Dear Scudder:—

You ordain a reduction of 350 lines of print.[31] I have taken out about 230 lines, if my own count is correct, and fail to see any chance of further reduction. My plan, as you see, involves two parts, first, a setting forth of the vague and romantic character of my hero, by means of an outline of the judgments passed upon him since his youth. Thus I bring the argument down to the central point, viz., that all depends upon his California achievement, which is the only "great" service of his life. To this assertion my Frenchman, Büchner, bears very curious witness, especially in view of the fact that (doubtless) Mrs. F. was his coach, and was the real author

[30] ALS. Scudder Papers. UCB.
[31] "Frémont," *Atlantic Monthly* 66 (1890), 548–57.

of all his nonsense. I can't well leave said Frenchy out without destroying the whole point. Then I proceed, as second division, to deal with the California affair itself. You asked a critical study of the General as a whole. The result is that I should have to rewrite the whole in order to justify the form of the California section if it stood alone. And I have now reduced the introductory half of the study, as I feel, to the lowest intelligible limits. The rest, of course, I must leave to your judgment. The article as a whole was written at the cost of considerable fresh research, but this research had to be carried out under such unfavorable circumstances that I must beg pardon for the carelessness of the MS as to one or two matters, personal and otherwise, which have been pointed out in the proof.

There is one thing more, which perhaps I should have mentioned earlier. In the Sept. *Century* I shall have a fine-print note on the "Seizure of California," devoted chiefly to the "English Plot." In the introduction to this note, which was written before F.'s death, I very summarily state the facts about the Cabinet plan, the Larkin dispatch, and the disobedience to instructions of F. This statement, by no means as full as the one in this article, is not made in such wise as to give F. prominence, as if he were the subject or hero of my note, as he is of this article. The principal bit of information in that note refers to the English, and not to F. at all. I say this to assure you that the two papers, despite a certain stereotyped manner of expression that must always be found in any summary of this Gillespie & F. business, will be in no danger of seeming concurrent articles. However, it may be better, for that very reason, to keep in this article the form that I chiefly had in mind when I wrote it, viz., not a mere summary of the California business, but a general analysis of the great myth of F.'s whole life.—

Yrs. Truly
Josiah Royce.

To Mary Gray Ward Dorr, [Summer, 1890?][32]

103 Irving Street
Cambridge

My dear Mrs. Dorr,

I have been too busy of late with the repetition of my lectures

[32] TLC. Royce Papers. HUA. Date provided on typescript.

to seem as mindful as I am of my friends. The holiday time this year is a welcome rest from work, but the work itself has of late been cheerful and healthy and, as I hope, progressive in a fashion that is due, I can hardly tell how much, to your sympathy and kindness in setting me on my present track, and in helping me to go on with it. It isn't easy to find any offering that will suggest to you my grateful recognition of your friendship. It occurs to me, however, that you may be interested to look a little at the latest Harvard contribution to the historical study of the origin and growth of spirituality in Religion—I mean the book of my valued friend, Professor Toy, on *Judaism and Christianity*.[33] A scholarly and analytical treatise like this, embodying the latest results of research, can't be light reading, but there are chapters in it profoundly suggestive of the way in which the spiritual, after hiding itself in all sorts of seemingly petty human disguises, triumphs through Evolution after all, because it owns the world. Perhaps you may find the "Introduction," the chapter on "The Doctrine of God," the chapter on "The Kingdom of God," and the final one on "The Relation of Jesus to Christianity," suggestive, and I fancy that one can pretty easily separate in Toy's text the general results and outlooks from the scholarly apparatus. In any case the volume is a good one for reference, and it suggests that at Harvard men are travelling by many roads to much the same goal.

Mrs. Royce joins with me in the kindest remembrances.

Yours very sincerely,
Josiah Royce.

To Charles William Eliot, August 25, 1890[34]

103 Irving St., Cambridge
Aug. 25, 1890

Dear Mr. Eliot:—

I have just received your letter of the 23d, notifying me of your

[33] Crawford Howell Toy, *Judaism and Christianity: A Sketch of the Progress of Thought from Old Testament to New Testament* (London and Cambridge, Mass.: Sampson Low and Co., 1890). Toy was Hancock Professor of Hebrew and other Oriental Languages at Harvard.

[34] ALS. Royce Papers. HUA.

intention to appoint me on a Faculty Committee of nine, to consider the plan for a course of paedagogical instruction.[35] I answer at once, in order to assure you of my willingness to be of any possible service in the matter; but I cannot undertake to suggest "what could be offered in the way of specific instruction in paedagogy," until I have given considerable thought to the subject, and, as I suppose, you would prefer that I should do so before writing more definitely. At the moment it occurs to me to say that the most valuable instruction that the University can offer in this direction must of necessity take the form of "object-lessons," joined with lectures by successful academic teachers who shall tell what they can about the way in which they have found it best to teach. I doubt meanwhile whether we can deal with the most specific problems of the high school teacher, unless we may have been ourselves high school teachers. I confess frankly that I have so far been learning the trade of University teacher, that I don't understand that trade any too well, and have much more to learn of it, and that I conceive the art in question to differ from the art of the high school teacher (who deals with younger minds) sufficiently to make my experience a somewhat imperfect guide for students who should want to learn from me the latter art. Still, I should always be glad to give whatever results I could derive from my experience as teacher, for the benefit of anybody who was trying to learn the art in any of its branches.

My first notion, then, in responding to your inquiry, is one that has been forming in my mind for a good while. It is that any course in Paedagogy in the University must needs be a rather fragmentary, tentative, and composite affair, consisting of a plain statement by various people of whatever they have observed about an art which can indeed be learned, but which, in its fullness, can never be taught. There is no such thing as a science of Paedagogy, just as there is no such thing as a science of business life, or of executive skill, or of marriage, or of domestic economy, or of life in general. There are many scientific inquiries, physiological, psychological, sociological, which bear upon the art of the teacher, and

[35] As chairman of the Faculty Committee on the Normal Course, Royce wrote the report which was formally presented to the Harvard faculty on November 11, 1890, and finally adopted in revised form on December 16. Instruction in pedagogy, within the Division of Philosophy, was started in 1891; after several administrative reorganizations the Harvard Graduate School of Education was founded in 1920.

which it is profitable for a teacher to know. But there is no systematic science which can tell us how to produce teachers.[36] I suppose, of course, that this is your own view. I am sure that it is a very obvious one, and I state it formally only that you may know forthwith where I stand. For the rest, I have no doubt that a composite course of lectures, supplemented perhaps by a Paedagogical "Seminary," and by object-lessons, would be a valuable thing, and would increase the serviceableness of the University for men aiming at the high-school master's profession. The work of the Department of Philosophy in this connection would, I apprehend, be mainly of a sort intended to stimulate interest in the liberal and loving study of the psychology of young minds. The teacher ought to be a naturalist, fond of mental life for its own sake, and delighting in the examination of its wealth, its mechanism, its dangers, its caprices, and its growth. To such a study, we might help to "introduce" a young teacher (in the German sense of that word,—"*einleiten*"). As for a "philososophy of education" in any other sense—the Lord deliver us therefrom.—Yrs. Truly

Josiah Royce

I shall take pleasure in thinking out a more precise plan of work, and in submitting to you as soon as possible any suggestions that may promise to be of any real service.

To Robert Underwood Johnson, August 29, 1890[37]

Aug. 29, 1890

Dear Mr. Johnson:—

The hearty and altogether charming paper of Mr. Swasey I have just read.[38] While it contains no really new "light," it is well worthy

[36] See "Is There a Science of Education?" *Educational Review* 1 (1891): 15–25, 121–32.

[37] ALS. Johnson Papers. UCB.

[38] William F. Swasey was a bookkeeper at Sutter's Fort. His narrative [see his *The Early Days and Men of California* (Oakland: Pacific Press Publishing Co., 1891)] never appeared in *Century*, nor did the magazine undertake the program of publication which Royce outlines in this letter. The dispatch from Buchanan to Larkin was, however, printed in "The Official Policy for the Acquisition of California," *Century Magazine* 41 (April 1891), 928–29. This document was probably supplied by Royce, and the headnote, signed "Editor," was quite possibly written by him.

of publication, if only the facts are published at the same time. In connection with the Frémont article, and a few notes, it would give a chance for a sort of Battle of Armageddon over the whole issue of the Conquest. I may as well specify a few points.

1. As to what Larkin read to Swasey, I can very easily prove, from L.'s own letters to the State Dep't. that it must have been the Gillespie dispatch itself, whose full text, in a copy furnished to me by the State Department, is in my hands, together with official copies of L.'s letters to the Department. S's memory about the "destruction" of this letter by L. is easily explicable, and is, I doubt not, perfectly sincere, although, as I shall show you hereafter, it is inaccurate. The whole incident, as reported by S., suggests such a beautiful study in psychology, that it would be a pity to lose the tale as he tells it.

2. As to Larkin's intrigues with the Californians the documentary evidence is equally clear and simple, and should be presented side by side with S.'s denial of the possibility of the intrigue.

3. The evidence as to the "Junta" of April at Monterey is now all in, and should be summarized in connection with S.'s account. What happened will never be fully clear in all its details, but there can be no doubt of the substantial falsity of Vallejo's story. At the time in question Vallejo put himself on record as opposed to American success in California, as has been pointed out by Th. Hittell.

4. As to Castro's "proclamation," I think that there can be no doubt as to what proclamation Mr. Swasey read. The text of it has several times been published. There is strong evidence that, on the basis of this genuine proclamation of Castro's, which was a sort of general warning to trespassers on the public lands, and which was a perfectly legal and harmless document, there were made various altered transcripts, or possibly even wholly forged imitations, and that these were circulated in the Sacramento Valley just before the outbreak. Swasey, I think, exaggerates the proclamation which he saw at Monterey very seriously. The evidence upon this whole topic is very considerable, but it can be summarized in a brief space, if you desire.—

—As you see, Swasey's paper seems to me rather poor history if left to stand by itself, but an excellent thing in case his memory, in all its picturesqueness, is confronted with the documents. I don't know how it would agree with your plans, or be related to your space, or be consistent with your agreements with your contributors,—but if I might be allowed to suggest a plan wholly from my own point of view, I should offer this:—Let the *Century* publish this and the coming Frémont paper together. Then, as a supplement, print, with the necessary annotations, (1) The text of the instructions to Larkin, which have been quoted and summarized by Bancroft and myself, but which have never been printed in full. These I have in my possession in a certified copy furnished me by the State Dep't. They would not fill much space. (2) Print from MS Larkin's account to the Department of what he did with and about the instructions when he received them. (3) Reprint from Congressional Doc.'s the proof (very brief and conclusive it is) that what Gillespie brought to Larkin he repeated to Frémont. This proof would occupy only a few lines of type. (4) Print from MS Larkin's comment to the Department on the whole affair, written a few months later. (5) Reprint Castro's actual proclamation, and summarize the indications that this proclamation was falsified to the settlers in the Sacramento Valley. (6) Summarize the evidence about that Junta.—All this, as supplement, could be got into a few columns of your fine print, I can't be sure how many, but can be sure that it would be no very great tax upon your space.

If I should prepare this supplement for you, I should try to avoid unnecessary comment or enlargement, and should confine my notes to a simple explanation of the relation of the documents, and to a summary of their meaning. The result would be an authoritative statement of the central truths whereby the whole growth of the story in the mouths of various people must be judged. Argument I could reduce to a minimum, because I have elsewhere argued out the whole case rather too elaborately. Nowhere, so far as I know, has the simple statement of the contents of the accessible documents been put together in one place with a minimum of comment; so that, even where the substance of the evidence is well known, *such* a presentation of it would be new. And as I say, a large portion of this evidence is yet unprinted.

And now, once more, as to that "letter" which was so dark a secret, which L. read to Swasey and then "destroyed," which H. H. Bancroft shall have presumed to ignore, which was not in L's archives, and which neither Gillespie nor Frémont ever read! This letter, I assure you, was nothing but the now well-known dispatch of Buchanan to Larkin. Gillespie *did* know its contents, and in fact brought them in his head. They were repeated later to Frémont. As for the "destruction," S. is remembering confusedly, as a man will, the fact that Gillespie had destroyed the original, after committing it to memory, and before crossing Mexico. For consider the story as Swasey gives it. We know, as a matter of fact, that Gillespie *did* bring a secret letter from Buchanan to Larkin, and that (so secret was the letter), G. destroyed it as above stated. For Larkin he wrote it out from memory when he reached Monterey. *This* has been known by Congressional Documents for forty years. *What* the letter contained we knew not until lately, but we now know, both from L's archives, which preserved a copy of it, and from the State Dep't, which gave me my copy. Now Swasey's memory, if it were accurate, would tell us of *another* letter, inconsistent with the known one, (mentioning Frémont as the known one does *not*, and giving instructions which the known one doesn't countenance). *This* second letter was *so* secret that Larkin had to destroy it at once. Yet Gillespie, who had feared losing his other and now known dispatch so much that he destroyed it in crossing Mexico, actually carried this second, and heretofore unknown dispatch in his pocket all through Mexico. And Larkin, who kept the known dispatch in his archives, found this other dispatch of such dangerous character that he *couldn't* keep it in his archives. In other words, the *more* dangerous dispatch was carried through hostile Mexico, but destroyed as soon as it reached a place of safety! The *less* dangerous dispatch was destroyed before G. crossed Mexico, but was reproduced for safe-keeping at the place where the other had to be destroyed! To this, you see, our good friend is ready to take his oath. Could there be a more beautiful study in the psychology of memory?—

Yrs Truly
Josiah Royce

I venture to keep Swasey's article until I get your reply to my proposal, since, in case you want my annotations, I shall need the article.—In a forthcoming *Atlantic* I am going to publish a general article on General Frémont. It will contain no documents or new material, but will probably make some people wroth. This I regret, but my duty was plain.

To Horace Elisha Scudder, September 18, 1890[39]

103 Irving St.
Sept. 18, 1890

Dear Scudder:—

The job of putting Schopenhauer to rights for you involves of course some serious reflection.[40] I have been too busy so far since my return to set about the new task. Now, as I approach it, I feel the need of advice. The actual lecture, as it lies in the rough before me, occupied some 75 minutes or more in rapid delivery, and would make the impossible length of 19 *Atlantic* pages, by careful and close count. Nor can I easily see where to divide it in twain. However, much of the matter at the outset is summary of previous lectures, and there are many intermediate passages that would be cut very naturally in dissecting out this discussion from its environment in the course. Only my puzzle is, on what principle to dissect? The principle will be needed to guide me as to where to cut. Two such principles occur to me. As I understand, you are willing to print two, or perhaps three papers made from my series. Now I have analyzed *both* Hegel and Schopenhauer with reference to their general scheme of life. There is a fine contrast and analogy between them, and it pervades and determines my sketch of the latter in a fashion hard to get rid of. Hence my *first* possible principle of dissection might run:—Make a brace of papers on Hegel & Sch. as students of life, discussing their common relations to the business of philosophy, and the contrast between them. To this end connect the two papers, but make the *first* one mainly on H., the *second* mainly on S. Write—(1) Introduction on attitude of papers, (2) place of H. & S. in developement of Idealism, (3) Characteristics, personal and reflective of H. This would be paper the first. Then write the sketch of S. as twin paper to the first. This could be done with the *least* derangement of present text.—My second possible principle might run:—Force Sch. willy-nilly into a paper all by himself. Cut off all but the most vital links that bind him

39 ALS. Scudder Papers. UCB.

40 See "Two Philosophers of the Paradoxical," *Atlantic Monthly* 67 (1891): 45–60, 161–73. These two articles were rewritten from Royce's lecture series of 1889–90 and included, in still another form, in *SMP*.

to the others, and trust the old heretic to interest alone. This however would much alter my text.

Which of these plans do you prefer? How much room can you give me? Do you want as many as three papers from my series? Do you want to try one first, and wait to see the effect before venturing on more? Or may I plan two, or all three at once? If I offered the brace as above, and you wanted a third, one of my concluding lectures would furnish the stuff. The quicker you can decide these many problems, the sooner will your readers bask in the true light.

Yrs. Truly
Josiah Royce.

I called at the office today and got a copy of the *October* no., with my Frémont in it. The article seemed to me, on hasty reading, the most cold-bloodedly cussed thing that ever I attempted. I hope that it will be received as it deserves.

To Robert Underwood Johnson, October 1, 1890[41]

103 Irving St.
Cambridge, Mass.
Oct. 1, 1890

Dear Mr. Johnson:—

In the very brief time at my disposal in these days, which happen to be the busiest of the year, viz., the opening of the term, I have given only a very cursory glance at the Bidwell article, which seems to me excellent.[42] I found so far nothing to alter. I had hoped to study details tomorrow, and should have given considerable time to them; but your telegram seems urgent, and I accordingly shall put them at once in the mail.

Yours Truly
Josiah Royce.

Of the other matters more soon.

[41] ALS. Johnson Papers. UCB.

[42] John Bidwell, one of Frémont's volunteers in 1846, published three articles in *Century Magazine* 41 (1890–91): "The First Emigrant Train to California," November 1890, pp. 106–30; "Life in California before the Gold Discovery," December 1890, pp. 163–83; and "Frémont in the Conquest of California," February 1891, pp. 518–25. Considering the dates of publication and the contents of the articles, it seems most likely that Royce is referring to the last of these titles.

To Robert Underwood Johnson, October 19, 1890[43]

103 Irving St., Cambridge, Mass.
Oct. 19, 1890

Dear Mr. Johnson:—

I am interested in your intention to get documents from the Navy Dep't. In 1885 I received official assurance that *that* Dep't had upon record no instruction to any secret agent *in* Cal. before the Conquest. I did not ask for the full text of all the instructions to Sloat, not already published, because I was already satisfied about the nature of Sloat's instructions by the reading of the published ones. However, it is possible that my feeling upon the subject was too clear. At present I see the value, in view of the Frémont appeal to the reputation of Geo. Bancroft,[44] to supplement what we already know of his words by the publication of whatever was then kept secret. It seems easy to show where these secret dispatches, in part, at least, are to be looked for; and it seems pretty easy to make out their general import. Here are the data:—

The published instructions to officers concerned with Cal. appear for the most part in U.S. Govt. Doc. 29th Cong. 2d Session, House Exec. Doc. No. 19, and in 31st Cong., 1st Sess., House Ex. Doc. 17. It is in the former place that the principal letters to Sloat are to be found. In the Claims' Committee Report, in 30th Cong., 1st Sess., Sen. Rep., No. 75, there is another letter of Bancroft to Sloat, written later than the Conquest, but referring to the previous instructions in a useful manner. ⟨This last reference of mine I make from memory without Doc. 75 beside me, and can't give the page.⟩ The instructions to Sloat, either published or referred to in these places are as follows:—

1. Instructions of June 24, 1845. They are apparently printed in full.

[43] ALS. Johnson Papers. UCB.

[44] George Bancroft, who had been Polk's secretary of the navy, took Frémont's side in his controversy with Royce. In a letter of September 3, 1886, Bancroft asserted that Frémont's military action had been authorized by verbal orders from the government. The Frémonts used this evidence in "The Origins of the Frémont Exploration," *Century Magazine* 41 (March 1891): 766–71; and "The Conquest of California," *Century Magazine* 41 (April 1891): 917–28.

2. Communications of Aug. 8 and Oct. 17, 1845. These are the *least* known, and complete copies, certified as such, would have the most value. Above all, the instructions of Oct. 17, 1845, are only once referred to in the published material, and only one quotation, a sentence long, seems, so far as I can find, to have been printed from them. *They are of the same date as the Larkin dispatch, as Buchanan wrote it*, and are undoubtedly written with the same plan in mind as inspired Buchanan. Of their nature we have evidence in a private and "strictly confidential" letter which Sloat wrote to Larkin from Mazatlan, on May 18th, 1846, when the Commodore was still vacillating about whether or no to leave for Cal. This letter is given in H. H. Bancroft's *California*, Vol. V, p. 203, and is in the Larkin papers. Sloat says to Larkin, "It is my intention to visit your place ⟨i.e. Monterey⟩ immediately, and from the instructions I have received from my government, I am led to hope that you will be prepared to put me in possession of the necessary information, and to consult and advise with me on the course of operations I may be disposed to make on the coast of California." At about the time of the Larkin dispatch, a copy of it was sent to Slidell, in Mexico, and he was instructed, just as Sloat seems to have been, to consult with Larkin ⟨in Slidell's case, of course, by means of correspondence⟩. The publication of the full instructions of Oct. 17, 1845, from Geo. Bancroft to Sloat, could not fail therefore to be interesting, and would pretty certainly serve to bring the Larkin Mission into clearer light than ever.

3. The later instructions to Sloat, of May 15th, May 18th, and June 8, 1846, are apparently published with substantial fullness. It is these, taken in connection with the dispatch of June 24, 1845, which have led me to feel and to say that the position of Geo. Bancroft in those days is clear. All these letters are to the same general effect: "Seize California as soon as the war begins, but keep the peace with the Californians if you can." I am not quoting words here, of course, but the substantial meaning of the whole.

Result: If the Navy Dep't. will give you access to further documents, ask above all for a chance to inspect the instructions of Geo. B. to Sloat on Oct. 17, 1845, and then ask for the August ones, and for any others that may fall near that time. That is the critical moment.

Do you want the text of the Larkin dispatch? I will send it to you at any time you desire. Do you still expect that summary paper from me, to be published with or after the revised Frémont paper? I will promise, as I said, to keep my temper in that place. I am glad you have appealed to Wm. Carey Jones. He at least is a man of the highest and most honorable character,—much moved to be sure by unhappily blind family prejudice, of the sort so common in men with historical grandfathers. But I can't conceive him asserting what he didn't believe in the fullest degree. Nothing in this business has vexed me more than the duty which the research has put upon me to oppose his feelings, and, as I judge has been the case, to wound him. He is an early friend and classmate of mine.—Such is fate! In any case you couldn't look to a better man to state the family case, and you can be sure, however much he may misjudge this or that, that he is "square" himself.—I shall return the book at once. I haven't opened the package, presuming that only the book was in it.

As to my work. Once more, I can't in the least estimate its market value. If I send you an article, I take my cheque when I get it, from you, as from any other editor, as an authoritative estimate of what, in my ignorance of the literary market, I learn to be the worth of my small service. Even so with this job. You contented me before. This is not the same job, and is, as to time spent, a rather large one, but doubtless what you send will be sure to content me again. I am the more hesitant about estimating the thing myself, because throughout I have been writing you more than you asked for, at the risk of seeming officious, and on the bare chance of being serviceable, just as if I sent you any other voluntary contribution, with which of course, I shouldn't enclose a bill.—

Yrs. Truly
Josiah Royce.

To Horace Elisha Scudder, November 2, 1890[45]

103 Irving St., Cambridge
Nov. 2, 1890

My Dear Scudder:—

I return the proofs, with some rather long notes on my use of capitals,—a topic which has aroused the concern of the red pencil.

[45] ALS. Scudder Papers. UCB.

Otherwise I have found a few things to change, but the proof is pretty clean,—for metaphysics.

May I ask two favors? The two lectures, Hegel & Schopenhauer, are to follow almost at once here in Cambridge, viz. on Nov. 12 & 19 respectively. I want to read them in their revised shape, and of that you have the only MS copies. May I have (1) during this week a second proof of "Hegel" struck off and sent me to keep? (2) May I at the end of next week get the Schopenhauer MS, if that isn't sooner in type, for temporary use? I hope these requests won't prove burdensome.

One thing more. By the third week in January I shall finish reading my lectures. You have already expressed, I believe, a favorable view as to the chances that the firm would print them. Will it be possible, in advance of my actually delivering the completed MS to get a positive answer from the firm as to whether they will print the book or no? My proposition would be to entitle them: "Studies in Modern Philosophy: A Series of Popular Lectures." I should trim down the lecture-form a bit, excise repetitions, &c., but should prefer not to attempt in the book the hopeless task of making popular discussions look like a treatise. Hence I prefer to keep the name: *Lectures* as a secondary title.—If the firm can give me an opinion on the general impression that you now have of the book (whose length would be about six-times that of the two *Atlantic* papers together)—then when ought I to get in the completed MS, if I intend to publish in the spring?

Yrs. Truly
Josiah Royce.

To Robert Underwood Johnson, December 11, 1890[46]

Dec. 11, 1890

My Dear Mr. Johnson:—

I will write the 2000 words, if you'll only give me a *little* time.[47] Until Dec. 20 every moment will be occupied. I have looked

[46] ALS. Johnson Papers. UCB.

[47] "Montgomery and Frémont: New Documents on the Bear Flag Affair," *Century Magazine* 41 (March 1891): 780–83.

through the interesting diary already, but hastily. It will not contain any startling novelties, but it will be worth saving, most decidedly. And I will keep my temper this time.

Am I to have my chance at the aforesaid summary article after or at the same time with that of the Frémonts? I can make it as matter of fact and cool as you wish. How about the new docs. at Washington. Have you got them yet? And what, may I ask, are the two sources of information about the British intrigue? And if they produce nothing, will they continue long to be sources? I shall be glad to know.

If then you can give me until Christmas day to mail the desired note, I will write it. Meanwhile I shall take good care of the Journal.

Yours Truly
Josiah Royce

To Horace Elisha Scudder, January 25, 1891[48]

Jan. 25, 1891

My Dear Scudder:—

I am going off for a few days, for a combination of rest and business. When I return I will send you the note on the Schopenhauer book,[49] which I am now almost ready to send, only that the Mid Year intermission gives me a chance that I musn't lose.

I have resolved on what for me is a decided renunciation, i.e., to hold back the lectures for publication in October. As I understand it, they will be in time for that if they get into the printer's hands by June. Is that not so? There are a number of revision matters that I can't venture on now, until I have laid work aside, so far as they are concerned, for two or three weeks. They are now a little too worn in interest for me to judge them fairly.

I am still in doubt as to my title. How would this do:—"Representative Modern Thinkers and Problems: A Series of Lectures Introductory to Philosophy"? Or would this be better:—"A Study in Modern Philosophy, Being a Series of Popular Lectures"? Or shall I appeal to humbug at once, and call it "The Way of Salvation,

[48] ALS. Scudder Papers. UCB.
[49] I.e., *SMP*.

Being Philosophy for the Fair in Face and Mind"?—You see, I am more or less in despair about the title.

Yours Truly
Josiah Royce

To Robert Underwood Johnson, January 17, 1891[50]

103 Irving St. Cambridge.
Jan. 17, '91

Dear Mr. Johnson:—

Upon *three* matters the Mervine correspondence,—either as I now have it, or as it would be completed by the letters to Mervine mentioned by Drury,—would throw valuable light.[51]

(1). On the relation of the Bear Flag to Mervine's and Sloat's opinions as to the right moment for raising the Flag at Monterey. This is an old topic of controversy.

(2). On the exact circumstances of Mervine's repulse at the time when he tried to reach Los Angeles during the revolt at the close of '46. His own report has never before been known, only Stockton's account of the affair, & the native story of the fight.

(3). The true history of the "Sanchez" affair, during the revolt, in the early part of '47. As letters in the book before me show, this affair has always been very imperfectly recorded. It will be possible now for the first time to give a history of it.

A note on topics (1) and (2) would, I should say, be possible in brief space, and would, especially after the publication of Frémont's article, be interesting in your Californiana. Topic (3) is more local in interest. I should like to write on that an article say for the *Overland*, if you will authorize such a use of the *docs*. I should like also your permission to correspond direct with Drury, & get the other *docs* from him, subject of course to your wish as to the publication of any results from them.—

Yrs. Truly
Josiah Royce.

[50] ALS. Johnson Papers. UCB.

[51] Captain William Mervine, one of the "heroes" in the seizure of California, is best remembered for having been defeated outside of Los Angeles, in October 1846 by a small band of California troops. None of the publications suggested in this letter appears to have been carried out in *Century* or elsewhere.

To Jacob Gould Schurman, January 18, 1891[52]

103 Irving St., Cambridge.
Jan. 18, 1891

My Dear Schurman:—

I have had no time before this to consider your request, about the article, as it ought to be considered.[53] There occur to me three alternative topics, all of course requiring a decidedly technical treatment, but still capable, within the range of such a treatment, of being profitably discussed in brief essay form. I propose them as alternatives only:—

1. "Recent Investigation Concerning Kant's Development," 1770–81.

2. "The Characteristics of a Philosophical Hypothesis." (My title is here poor, but what I mean is the study of the general Logic of such hypotheses as the Leibnizian Monads, &c., as the history of thought exemplifies the thing).

3. "The Place of Teleological Conceptions in Modern Cosmological Theory." (This is the topic which I have most been studying of late, and I have some rather fresh shadings of statement about it).

You know best your plans, and can judge, more or less in what direction you would like to have me work, these being the alternatives.—

Yours Truly
Josiah Royce

[52] ALS. Private collection of Professor Max H. Fisch, University of Illinois.

[53] For Royce's later plans for articles in *Philosophical Review*, see his letter to Schurman, July 16, 1892.

To Robert Underwood Johnson, January 25, 1891[54]

103 Irving St.,
Jan. 25, 1891

Dear Mr. Johnson:—

I have written to Drury. I am very anxious to get an actual copy of the letter of Bancroft to Sloat, Oct. 17, 1845. Your note of it, as you told me in our last interview, was that therein Bancroft ordered Sloat to "consult with the American Consul," as well as to "conciliate." The full letter, copied, will hereafter be of service, not only to me, but *possibly* for you, now that Bancroft is dead; for a word on his "part in the seizure of Cal." might, for all I know, find a very appropriate place amongst the Notes of your *Californiana*, before long. I don't want, as I have told you, to prolong controversies unduly, but now that B. has joined the rest of the heroes of the Conquest, a relatively uncontroversial note might find a place. The kernal of such a note might be furnished by the letter to Sloat of Oct. 17, as aforesaid. Isn't it worthwhile then to get a copy? Or would the expense be more than the worth?

Yours Truly
Josiah Royce.

To Mary Gray Ward Dorr, February 21, 1891[55]

103 Irving Street
Cambridge, Mass.
February 21, 1891.

Dear Mrs. Dorr,

What would you think of this title for my lectures, when they come out next autumn: *The Spirit of Modern Philosophy?* The sub-title would then be: "A Course of Lectures on Representative Thinkers and Problems." I should be glad of advice as to my title. I think that a great deal depends upon it. I shall do erelong a little

[54] ALS. Johnson Papers. UCB.
[55] TLC. Royce Papers, HUA.

further rewriting, to improve my MS at one or two points. I need not say that I want to see you when I can.

Yours truly
Josiah Royce.

To Richard Watson Gilder, March 6, 1891[56]

103 Irving Street
Cambridge
March 6, '91.

Dear Mr. Gilder:–

Without mentioning any plan or name but my own, and speaking in vaguely prospective terms, I have got an opinion from my friend Dr. Kuno Francke, (expert in German literature) and an opinion that is very favorable to my undertaking a Life of Goethe should I ever wish to do so. The material is plenty, and will soon be yet more abundant, the possibility of work of relatively original criticism, and of a comparative as well as biographical method of treatment, is very decided; the need meanwhile may be said to be real. What is your present view of the task? The literary method of a work by Schöll: *Goethe in den Hauptmomenten seines Lebens und Wirkens*,–"Principal Features of Goethe's Career and Influence," or better "Goethe in his Time and in the World's Literature," suggests itself as some sort of model for the task. This task would be no light one. It would require some years. It would involve one, or perhaps two vacation trips abroad. But it certainly would command my most serious effort and enthusiasm. Have you any new opinion on the topic? James, to whom you authorized a mention of the matter, approves. I have no further positive suggestion as to the other task.

Yours Truly
Josiah Royce.

[56] ALS. Century Collection. NYPL.

To Richard Watson Gilder, March 16, 1891[57]

103 Irving Street
Cambridge
March 16, '91.

Dear Mr. Gilder:—

As I have cited to you the opinion, orally given, of my friend Dr. Kuno Francke, as to the Goethe biography, I feel it my duty to send you at once his note, just received, in which he expresses, after more careful reflection, a decidedly modified opinion.[58] In communicating this, I am bound to say that the relation of Goethe to his time seems to me as fascinating a topic as ever, and I believe still that a work on the lines that I first suggested, although perhaps with a stronger emphasis laid on the general history of the life and literature of the time than I at first contemplated, is feasible and desirable.

Yours Truly
Josiah Royce.

To Horace Elisha Scudder, April 7, 1891[59]

103 Irving Street
Cambridge
April 7, 1891

Dear Mr. Scudder:—

I write for a word of advice, and without any very definite proposal, concerning the last words of the Frémonts in the current *Century*. A rather factitious weight is there given to their defense by statements which they got out of Geo. Bancroft in 1886, and which, although not essentially novel in any way, the F.'s have used as an authoritative vindication. Recent facts have meanwhile

[57] ALS. Century Collection. NYPL.

[58] Francke (ALS to Royce, March 15, 1891) advised Royce not to write a biography, but suggested that he might write a book limited to Goethe's "view of life and to his internal development."

[59] ALS. Scudder Papers. UCB.

shown my old indictment to be stronger than ever, and it only wants now a very brief statement to set the thing at rest for all future students. I hate all the more, then to see what the less-informed public will regard, in many cases, as a conclusive refutation, go unmentioned, at the very moment when my own view is so near its final confirmation for all who are well-informed. I asked Mr. Johnson of the *Century*, the other day, whether there would be [a] chance for a word more in his columns. He has been very cordial with me in opinion for some time, and says that he would be glad to let me have the matter out for the sake of the truth of history; but he adds that his public is restive, as well as his publisher with the length of the Cal. series, and that, as he has to give so much space to both sides in so many California controversies, and as he has already had to decline one paper from the Frémont side, he has felt obliged to undertake to print no more of the controversy—not that he isn't interested, but that he has all California history on his hands, and must be cautious.

Well, my request of advice is this: In view of the finality and explicitness of the present Frémont document as a statement of their desires as to their definitive entrance into history, in view of the importance which many will attach thereto, in view of the wholly illusory but still seemingly large value of Geo. Bancroft's approval, and finally, in view of my recent utterances on the topic,—is any further word from me justified or advisable?[60] If so, would a five-page article in the *Atlantic* be in order, or not? I have of course written nothing yet. I have promise of a copy of a dispatch of Geo. Bancroft to Sloat, dated Oct. 17, 1845 (—same date as Gillespie's letter to Larkin); and this would be a new and brief document to add to the already known material. In a very brief space I could show: (a) That F.'s final statement contradicts his earlier ones; (b) That he now admits that he had no warlike orders different from those sent to Sloat; (c) That Geo. Bancroft's version fully agrees with what we have all along known, and with the dispatches of Oct. 17, 1845; (d) That Bancroft's approval of Frémont's conduct in 1886 was no expression of the result of any historical study of the facts, but is simply founded on an acceptance of F's own story, without any scrutiny or criticism.—If such a state-

[60] Royce eventually answered Frémont's article in "The Frémont Legend," *Nation* 52 (May 21, 1891): 423–25.

ment were given the same form as the one that I used in my October paper, would it, or would it not, be superfluous? If it isn't advisable to put it into the *Atlantic*, where can one best look for the place to leave it on record?—

My book MSS can be ready for the printer by the end of June—the philosophy lectures, I mean. Will that be in time for autumn? My projected title now is—"The Spirit of Recent Philosophy: A Course of Lectures on Representative Modern Thinkers and Problems."—

Your Truly
Josiah Royce.

To David Starr Jordan, April 15, 1891[61]

103 Irving Street
Cambridge
Apr. 15, 1891

Dear President Jordan:—

I have already given much serious thought to your gratifying offer, and must thank you yet again for the supplementary letters of April 9, with their additional explanations. If I still hesitate as to giving a decisive answer, it is easy to explain to you the reasons, which I will frankly do, although I do not naturally like any indecision as to professional matters where definiteness and clear choice are possible, and am sorry to delay in any wise the maturing of your own plans.

My first cause of hesitation lies in the fact that I have been consulting my official seniors here (the President, and the older members of the Philosophical Department) and have had strong representations made to me of their desire that I should stay, and of their feeling that important interests that have been committed to my care by them and by fortune, would seriously suffer if I went. These representations have been at once unexpectedly strong in their friendliness (not that I expected unfriendliness of any sort, but that I had not known myself to be so kindly and warmly regarded in my professional work here); and have also been accom-

[61] ALS. Jordan Papers. SUA.

panied with promises, not of immediate, but of comparatively early and unexpectedly prompt promotion. In the matter of salary, Harvard cannot indeed, at the best, equal what you are in position to offer; but you will see that it is hard to decide against so kind an expression of confidence from the men that I have been trying to assist. I don't exaggerate the significance of the matter, and certainly don't think myself deserving of much approval for the work that I have done in so hospitable and kindly an environment; but I must consider yet a little longer before I can be sure how to decide between the two duties.

My other reason for hesitation is an uncertainty about the tenure of office contemplated by yourself and by Senator Stanford in this offer. Is the appointment for any definite term of years? If for an indefinite term, under what conditions could a Professor be removed? And with whom, in the last resort, is the contract made? With Senator Stanford personally, or with the Trustees? Are not both the present Trust and the Administration of the University alterable at the will of Senator Stanford, during his life? If so, might it not be difficult,—in view of the number of interests sure to be considered, and in view of the somewhat stormy life that young institutions often for awhile lead in California,—to be as sure of my tenure of office, in case I went, as I now am here? I ask as a matter of business, and still with every desire to give this call all the consideration that I can. In conclusion then, while, as I say, I regret the delay, am I asking too much if I beg for a fortnight more to consider so important a matter? At the end of that time I will answer you definitely. I have business obligations here, in addition to my academic obligations, as I live in a heavily mortgaged house whose title I own; and these business affairs I could not decide to leave without further inquiry.

I hope that my request will not seem dilatory.

Yours Truly
Josiah Royce.

To George Bucknam Dorr, May 2, 1891[62]

Cambridge.
May 2, '91.

Dear George:—

I am heartily glad that my plan meets your mother's approval, as well as your own. The lectures are so largely hers, that I but render dues. My only hesitation was as to whether the dedication could be as acceptable an offering as it was hearty, for my book, after all, will be but a halting and fragmentary thing. There is a possibility, of course, so long as the MS is not yet actually in the printer's hands, that I shall fail to get it through press this summer. Whenever it gets through, it shall be dedicated, and I *hope* to offer the gift, such as it is, promptly.

But the form of dedication is still a matter concerning which I should like advice. Dedications, like ecclesiastical forms of address, often use, without any titular address, simply the full Christian name of the person to whom the dedication is made. For this, I think, there is good authority. Yet of course the custom is not universal. Sometimes the socially formal titular address is used. All depends upon whether the dedication is regarded as an act of a relatively solemn or a relatively social character. My own preference is for the former device. My first book I dedicated to a dear friend in Baltimore, now deceased, a gentleman about seventy years of age, who had no official title. The dedication, with his approval ran "To/My honored friend/George Buchanan Coale/ of Baltimore/" &c, as you can see by reference. Do you think such a form the most fitting? If so the form would simply give your mother's full name, which I understand to be Mary Ward Dorr. Or would you prefer, with her, Mrs. Charles Dorr? I prefer, as said, the former form.

I write this question to you now, instead of to her, because I am replying to your kind note. I hadn't time to ask her the other day.

Yours Truly
Josiah Royce

I want to see you here some day before you leave town. When are you out in Cambridge nowadays? All days of the working week, or none, or certain ones, or uncertain ones?

62 ALS. Royce Papers. HUA.

To Richard Watson Gilder, June 14, 1891[63]

103 Irving St.
Cambridge, Mass.
June 14, 1891.

My Dear Gilder:—

The liberal terms offered by the Magazine, both as to the compensation, and as to time, make me very glad indeed to accept your offer, while I feel very decidedly the responsibility of the task.

I agree then, to furnish "within one or two years" (I fear two will be needed, with all my other engagements), "six separate articles on Goethe," with a view to basing upon these articles a Life of Goethe, to be ultimately submitted for publication to the *Century* Co.[64] The terms mentioned for the articles, $2000, or $333 a piece, are fully satisfactory.

Your Very Sincerely
Josiah Royce.

To Joseph Bangs Warner, July 14, 1891[65]

Colonial Club
Cambridge.
July 14, 1891

My Dear Warner:—

I write the following letter in answer to the communication of July 11, from Dr. Abbot, and beg you, in case you approve my desire, to forward to him a copy of these my present words.

I am sorry to find that Dr. Abbot, after having read my proposed reply to the article that he intended to print in the *Journal* (but that he later withdrew), has any doubt as to the position that I am prepared to take in case of further public controversy, or as to the

[63] ALS. The Century Collection. NYPL.

[64] Royce's proposed book on Goethe was never written, nor was any of these articles published in *Century*.

[65] ALS. Abbot Papers. HUA. For a summary of the major events in Royce's controversy with Abbot, see editor's introduction, p. 29–31.

spirit in which I have written concerning Dr. Abbot's own writings. I am sorry to have to recur so frequently to a matter of so definite a character. I repeat, however, that the substantial identity of Dr. Abbot's theory with a portion of the Hegelian theory of Universals is demonstrable as an historical fact; and that the account of the Hegelian theory given by Dr. Abbot in his reply, and repeated in his letter of July 11, is based upon words that, thus isolated from their context, and from the circumstances under which some of them were written, do not represent correctly Hegel's real doctrine. This opinion of my own I am prepared to substantiate by the evidence set forth in my proposed rejoinder to Dr. Abbot, as well as by a large mass of other evidence. From this position I therefore cannot recede. It is taken unwaveringly and conscientiously. I have not the least hesitation in staking my personal honor and professional reputation upon the sincerity and the substantial justice of this view. I have freely consulted with expert fellow-students upon the matter, and have found no dissenting voice, except Dr. Abbot's own. Nor will there ever be any difficulty in making the matter clear to any impartial body of experts.

So much as to my view of the matter of fact in question. Now as to my feeling concerning what was regrettable in my article. I repeat, once more—regrettable, in my eyes, was the manner of the article in so far as it actually gave unnecessary pain to Dr. Abbot. And I regard any pain as unnecessary that may have been due *not* to my objectively justified opinion of Dr. Abbot's work (an opinion which I cannot alter in the least), but to any severity of expression that may not have been absolutely needful to give form to this opinion itself. Dr. Abbot's reply has shown him to be not merely alive to the strong difference of opinion that separates us, but personally offended by an attack that was intended to be indeed severe, but directed wholly to matters of professional, but not of personal concern. This attitude of Dr. Abbot's I regret, and in so far as I am to blame for it, I am willing to express my regret publicly.

Dr. Abbot will, I hope, see the inadvisability of any effort to get from me through you, or otherwise, any statements incompatible with the foregoing extremely deliberate expression of my position.

Yours Truly
Josiah Royce.

I have in my possession no proof-sheets or other copies of

Dr. Abbot's article. I put into your hands the only copy that I had, and have left the whole matter of returning it to your judgment.

To Robert Underwood Johnson, September 21, 1891[66]

103 Irving St., Cambridge.
Sept. 21, '91.

My Dear Mr. Johnson:—

In the returned proof of Coleman's article I note two or three matters that seem to me to need attention.[67] I have cut down the Sherman material somewhat.[68] It is hard to keep his tale essentially intact and yet cut down any more than I have now done. I can't recommend correcting any of his English (except such slips as *then* for *their*, & the like), since letters are letters, and the hasty speech is characteristic of the man and the situation. I have omitted Wool's letter to Sherman. Letter II of Sherman contains some repetitions of Letter I, but II was to be printed, I believe, "entire or not at all"; and both I & II are on the whole highly important.

I don't know what this job is worth. It was a rather manifold one, but I leave its estimate to you. The beginning of autumn, however, finds me rather embarrassed, and though nothing is due I suppose, before publication, a cheque within a few days would now be a great, though possibly an undeserved accommodation, whatever you make its proper contents to be.

Yours Very Truly
Josiah Royce.

[66] ALS. Johnson Papers. UCB.

[67] William T. Coleman, "San Francisco Vigilance Committees," *Century Magazine* 43 (November 1891): 133–50. The footnotes signed "Editor" were probably written by Royce.

[68] See fn. 69 below.

To Robert Underwood Johnson, October 6, 1891[69]

103 Irving St. Cambridge, Mass.
Oct. 6, 1891.

My Dear Mr. Johnson:—

Five hours of lecturing and three hours faculty meeting and consulting today, have left me but little time to examine the papers in the Sherman case, which have come to hand at the busiest moment of the year. Had I not so carefully considered these admirable and important letters of General Sherman at the time when I made my notes, I should be hopelessly unable, at this my first moment of leisure, late in the evening, to make any answer at all today. As it is I hope you will pardon the delay. I have made notes on the proofs

[69] ALS. Century Collection. NYPL. The so-called Second Vigilance Committee of San Francisco (1856) particularly fascinated Royce who several times gave a popular lecture on the topic. Anticipating his more technically formulated theories of loyalty and the community, Royce viewed the history of the Vigilantes as singularly illustrative; in *California*, p. 366, he wrote: "What it teaches to us now, both in California and elsewhere, is the sacredness of a true public spirit, and the great law that the people who forget the divine order of things have to learn thereof anew some day, in anxiety and in pain."

The Vigilance Committee also affected the early career of William T. Sherman. As Royce here suggests, General Sherman's heirs offered a series of his letters of 1856 to *Century Magazine*. R. U. Johnson enlisted the editorial help of Royce. The proofs with Royce's notes were submitted for approval to Miss Sherman who objected to some of his remarks. (Her notes have been preserved in the Century Collection, NYPL.) The letters were finally published in "Sherman and the San Francisco Vigilantes: Unpublished Letters of General W. T. Sherman," *Century Magazine* 43 (December 1891): 296–309. These letters illustrate, but in some respects contradict, Sherman's earlier account in his *Memoirs* (Bloomington: Indiana University Press, 1957), pp. 118–32.

The Committee itself was called into session after the murder of James King of William by James Casey—editors of rival newspapers. Sherman was at that time associated with a banking firm in San Francisco, and as a personal friend of Governor Johnson, he was appointed major-general and commander of the state militia. Prominent citizens, having no faith in the city government, established their own court and organized their own police. Casey was seized at the sheriff's jail, found guilty by the Vigilantes and executed. It was Sherman's duty to break the power of the Vigilance Committee, but when he was refused arms by General J. E. Wool, commander of the U.S. Arsenal, he resigned his commission in disgust and returned to his business.

themselves, and on the margins of Miss Sherman's memoranda. The very brief time makes these notes seem curt in form. But if Miss Sherman is at all interested to glance at them, or at this letter, before deciding what to do, I hope that she will pardon the brevity and directness of my reply,—qualities which, under the circumstances, are my only resort if I am to reply at all.

As to the questions of fact in my printed notes, two have been raised. As to both, my present MS notes make sufficient reply. Surely if Sherman accepted, as he expressly says, the Governor's Commission on Monday, and King was shot on the following Wednesday, the acceptance of the commission preceded and did not follow the outbreak. Surely if the Committee said in substance "We are no mob, and want the law to be maintained, and agree to your proposition about receiving our guard into the jail, and agree also to give you 'reasonable notice' and withdraw our guard first *in case* we decide to move on the jail"—this agreement admits of positively no interpretation such as General Sherman in the *Overland Monthly* and in the *Memoirs* put upon it. These are simple matters of fact. I must be excused at so busy a moment from dwelling upon them. I mean no discourtesy by begging you to assure Miss Sherman that there can be no doubt as to these matters, in my own mind, henceforth.

—But it is not of these things that you wish me to speak at any length. As to the much more delicate question of the propriety of using my notes in connection with the publication of the letters, I have a suggestion to make which I beg the heirs of General Sherman to consider. I hold no brief for the Committee. I am personally, & not intimately acquainted with but one or two of its members. Nor, on the other hand, did I in any way counsel the admirable frankness and love of historical truth that has led the heirs of General Sherman to propose this publication. I have only tried to see things as they are. This last is a hard task, and I may be very much mistaken; but at all events, now that the matter has come before me, I must state the case afresh thus:—

In previous publications, General Sherman felt bound to oppose the committee. I honor his firmness in doing so, and have observed in my notes why, being what he was, it was his duty to do so. But he went further. He explicitly charged men of preeminence on the Committee with deliberate breach of their pledges. He made this charge conscientiously; he insisted upon it sincerely; he must have done so very deliberately; he was fully aware of the seriousness of the charge. This charge has caused a natural feeling of pain in persons for whose reputation I have no sort of individual and personal concern, but who, as I fancy, have probably much the same concern for their own honorable reputation as their fellows have for theirs. This charge, coming from a source of such significance, backed by an authority so dignified, and by a name so justly prized and honored, is no common matter. The persons most involved have undoubtedly felt with becoming keenness the force of so stern a reproach. This reproach was *not* one against their course as leaders of an illegal organization. It was an accusation that they had solemnly undertaken one thing, and had treacherously done the opposite.

Well, as I say, the accusation was made and repeated,—with absolute sincerity I am perfectly sure,—without malice, and purely from a sense of duty, no one can question. And now, after General Sherman's death, these authoritative letters come to light. They are placed in my hands. I have no desire but to do justice. On examining the letters I find what seems to me conclusive proof that the later accusation grew out of a perfectly comprehensible misunderstanding, such as easily occurs at an excited moment between strong and honorable men. What is my *own* course as a man of honor? My part is indeed a very small one. I don't in the least exaggerate its importance. But what am I to do? Is the honorable course towards General Sherman's memory to hide, to cover over the facts, which, if they could have been in his mind when he wrote the *Memoirs*, would have wholly held back his hand from writing the words that have wounded the reputation of honorable men, who opposed him, and whom he dutifully opposed, but whom he never meant to accuse with any shadow of injustice, or to assault with any weapons but the facts? Is it not rather my duty to help towards peace between them and his memory, by pointing out the perfectly natural discrepancy upon which I have dwelt? Does not the publication of such facts as these do his true dignity the most genuine honor? Was I not right in remembering, as I wrote, the honor of the accused, which he above all would have held sacred if he had recognized what I now take to be the truth?

I confess that when I read these letters I was struck with no little admiration for the fine sense of honor that has led the heirs of the General to offer them for publication. A less broad view of what they owe to historical accuracy and to the reputations of comparatively obscure but still respectable persons, might have led the possessors of these papers to hesitate, on viewing the discrepancies which my notes have in no wise created, and to choose rather to let the very natural errors of the *Memoirs* stand as they were, than to correct them by the author's own clear and memorable contemporary papers. I trust that no mistake of mine will lead to any modification of this magnanimous course of action.

I have, at your suggestion, "touched" here and there in my notes by way of hasty modification. "Bitterness" is perhaps (as I now see) a false, certainly an illchosen word. Let it stand as "warmth." I have omitted some passages that lay perhaps unncessary stress on the Committee's work. All the rest so far as I have not now modified I regard as comment that is possible service in bringing out the truth that I was asked to present to your readers. In the short time that I have for decision now I can go no further in modification; and very cheerfully submit the whole matter to your judgment, for final decision as to what of my notes shall be used.

Yours Very Truly
Josiah Royce.

To William Roscoe Thayer, October 22, 1891[70]

103 Irving St.
Oct. 22, '91.

My Dear Thayer:—

What I want is *more* of this.[71] A Journal of Ethics must and should give the facts. It should also give some hint of the way out, if there is any, where the facts are diabolical; or if the way out isn't clear, the unattainable right should still be preached. Your own idealism will suggest then some statement of the moral of your tale, which I should be glad to have added to this paper. The paper,

[70] ALS. Thayer Papers. HL.

[71] A reference to Thayer's article, "Machiavelli's Prince," *International Journal of Ethics* 2 (1892): 476–92, with echoes of Abbot's *The Way Out of Agnosticism* (Boston: Little, Brown, and Co., 1890).

with such additions will, I doubt not, be very welcome in the pages of the *Journal.*

Yours Truly
Josiah Royce.

To William Roscoe Thayer, November 15, 1891[72]

103 Irving St., Cambridge.
Nov. 15, 1891

My Dear Thayer:—

I have just turned in your article to the *Journal of Ethics.* It probably won't appear for some time yet, and I shall reserve the privilege of making some changes in proof, whenever its time comes.

Yours Truly
Josiah Royce.

Here is a bit of commercial speculation for you! ! Abbot, as you know, goes for me in November.—Chas. Peirce, a friend of mine, backs him up in the *Nation.* The controversy will now rage unchecked for a month. Jokes, squibs, objurgations, fury, spite, envy, malice, evil-speaking, back-biting, rage, "professional warnings," "libels," shouts of "imposter," appeals to Corporations, Courts, the Public, the Moral and the Divine and the Diabolical Law, will go on far into December.—Holy Christmas will bring a lull. But in January the *Journal of Ethics* will tear open the wounds of all half-recovered combatants, will pour in venom, and will arouse more moans, sobs, shrieks, and cries of "no mercy asked or shown!"— Thus January will pass. In February—lo! my *Book* will appear, *& sell like hotcakes.* Children will cry for it. Grocers will give it away with every ten bars of soap.—And then (speak softly! ! Don't give the secret out! !)—*Peirce, Abbot & I,* will divide the proceeds of the sales amongst us. Mind you—keep mum. But that's the contract. Libel me and I'll libel you, and the public will be green enough to buy.

[72] ALS. Thayer Papers. HL.

To Charles Sanders Peirce, November 18, 1891[73]

103 Irving St. Cambridge.
Nov. 18, 1891

My Dear Mr. Peirce:—

You know, I suppose, that I have been consulting freely with William James as to the current controversy. You may know also that he is my most intimate friend outside of my own family. You will not then be surprised that, in view of the closing words of your letter to him yesterday, viz., the words "*Will Royce say he did not mean this?*" James has felt free to show me your letter. James knows that I like candid criticism, and that I feel perfectly sure that your letter in the *Nation*,[74] plain-spoken as it was, was written with the motive of clearing up the case, and of doing justice. James also knows that I deeply respect your work, and your opinion of philosophical matters. Of this fact you surely have been a long time aware. Under the circumstances then you surely will not object to my writing to you a plain statement of my state of mind about Dr. Abbot. I must leave to you the judgment of what it is best for you to think and say of it all. In appealing thus privately to one who will be my critic in future, as in the past, I don't do so for the sake of staying your hand whenever your mind is made up. I have the defects of my qualities, and no doubt many other defects too. I don't lament the pointing out of such defects in public where they concern my professional work, or the spirit of it. I can only gain by such criticism, where it is made with a knowledge of the facts, and by a man of your strength. I may not agree with you,

[73] ALI. Peirce Papers. HL. Partly printed in James Harry Cotton, *Royce on the Human Self* (Cambridge: Harvard University Press, 1954), pp. 297–300.

[74] "Abbot Against Royce," *Nation* 53 (November 12, 1891): 372. Peirce's letter is addressed to Abbot's two charges: (1) that Royce libelled Abbot, and (2) that Royce used unfair means to stifle Abbot's reply in the *International Journal of Ethics*. In this letter to Peirce, Royce answers both charges in reverse order. James answered Peirce under the same heading in *Nation* 53 (November 19, 1891): 389–90. Joseph B. Warner answered the second charge in "The Suppression of Dr. Abbot's Reply," *Nation* 53 November 26, 1891): 408. Abbot responded to Warner in "Mr. Warner's 'Evidence in Full' Completed," *Nation* 53 (December 3, 1891): 426. This ended the controversy in *Nation*.

but I shall carefully consider the matter in the light of what you say, and shall, I doubt not, profit by the experience.

I write, then, only to tell you, with all the plainness of speech of the private letter, what the facts in question are, as I conceive them.

1. As to the editorial conduct of the *Review* [i.e., *International Journal of Ethics*] in the matter of Dr. Abbot's reply, a fuller statement will very likely appear next week, written by Jos. Warner. That is a matter of history. I may perhaps not improperly ask you to defer any public comment on James's letter to the *Nation*, until you have seen that of Warner. A deliberate attempt to suppress the fullest possible argumentative defence on Abbot's part, would have been, as he says, an act of "incredible cowardice and meanness." At my request, and after hesitation on the part of the Editors as to the propriety of printing the personal passages of the thirty page reply that Abbot sent us, we decided to print it all, strong of speech as, in the opinion of a number of very impartial judges (who sooner or later had occasion to see it), it undoubtedly was. We also offered Abbot the last word in the further controversy, his reviewer agreeing never to make more than one rejoinder in the *Jounal*. But we did feel impelled, by the very necessity of explaining our course to our readers, to have the reviewer try to show, in his one pretty brief rejoinder, to be printed with the reply, that he hadn't spoken in heat, or with personal motive, and that he had had in mind some pretty definite reasons for his severe judgment. I say "we," for we had no chief editor, and consulted as to all these matters, although my own judgment was, so far, largely considered, and I don't wish to minimize my full personal responsibility for what was done. As for the "last word" which we gave to Abbot, we also insisted that, since it was to be never replied to in the *Journal* by me, it should be free from violent personalities of a distinctly unparliamentary sort. We left it perfectly free to annihilate my whole case by arguments that were never to be answered in the *Journal*. We had given ample room for personalities before.

As you know, Dr. Abbot hereupon declined to accept our conditions. That in these negotiations the April number was passed, was not my fault. I was anxious to have the affair over. I had made no delays at any point, and had written my rejoinder so promptly as to cause very little loss of time indeed there. If I am right in my memory I wrote it within 24 hrs. of receiving his reply in final form. The notice of the short time for the "last word" of which Abbot complains, was sent from Philadelphia by the "Managing Editor" there. I knew nothing about it, and had no control over the office management of the *Journal*. I was only clear that I had done all I could to hasten things. I was sorry when the matter was thus delayed.

In repeating this now weary tale to you, I only want you to consider, before you write again, whether, in view of these facts, the expression "brutal life-and-death fight from the first," expresses justly the true situation. There was a contest. I have had more than one in my life. But it was a contest about a matter of scholarship, not about anybody's life or death as to any other matter than just *this* question of scholarship. On my side I tried to observe the rules of the game. Dr. Abbot was equally sincere. We differed as to the right of personal abuse in his "last word," to which I was not to reply. That was all.

After the withdrawal, came the threats of legal process, or at all events what seemed trustworthy information that there were such threats made. I went to Warner for advice. I asked him in as conciliator first of all, as defender only in case I was actually prosecuted. He is a member of the Overseers' Committee of Visitors to the Philosophical Department. You know his type. He is surely no man for cruel measures. I beg you to read what he wrote to Abbot, if the *Nation* prints his words, and to compare that with Abbot's charges, before you regard his conduct in the case, or mine under his advice, which I have ever since followed, as anything but conciliatory as to this matter.

I sum up so far here by saying that I thus did everything in my power to get Abbot the chance to answer me in the most effective argumentative way, and in our *Journal*, to give him full space, to treat him with editorial courtesy as to his reply, and to give him in every way fair play. I am ignorant how I could have done better for him, consistently with my duty to the *Journal*, or to the public, which I had no desire to trouble with any scandal of personalities, in our Journal's pages, or outside them.

2. Now as to the spirit and intent of my review. I will speak with the most complete frankness. You may then judge my spirit as you think best. I am not writing to please you. I have no doubt I tire you much. I only want you to get as near the facts as I can put you, before you finally decide what to think of me. Then you may think as you will, and say it as you please.

I said the words about *giving and asking no mercy*. I said them with explicit reference *not* to the treatment of any man's character, feelings, inner life, general reputation, means of livelihood, or the like, but to the public judgment of his method of treating questions of the most significant and objective truth. I referred in the same context to Aristotle's so often quoted word about truth as the "greater friend than Plato." I said that, esteem a man as we may,—and I did heartily esteem Abbot,—we have to show no mercy to his work when his undertaking is of the most significant, when the demands upon his skill are of the most marked, and when the workmanship seems to us of low grade. I supposed all this a commonplace maxim of scholarship. Had I ever dreamed of a personal interpretation of these words by men of your experience and insight, I should of course have used others. I should perhaps have said, "In judging matters of such importance, we may feel every esteem for the man, every wish for his personal happiness, every desire to have him live long, prosper, get a good livelihood, and the rest; but our good wishes will not make his bad work good, nor change it an atom; and the truth, in the long run, is absolutely merciless to us all, in just so far as we err; whilst the critical cannot possibly do otherwise, where the cause is of such vast importance, than to speak honestly the critical truth as he sees it." That was what my "no mercy," in its context, with the reference to the "greater friend" phrase, and to the questions of fundamental significance as the topics about which no mercy is to be shown—that I say, is what it meant. May the Lord do so to me and more likewise if ever I desire the truth to be anything but merciless to my errors in philosophy, or my critics to do less than to say of me what they believe to be the truth concerning my philosophic work.

But, as you well say, philosophy is no science. Is such mercilessness, in view of our common ignorance, our right? If such mercilessness leads to "professional warnings" about the "philosophical pretensions" of an opponent, is not that an abominable assumption?

My reply is that I did *not* "warn" merely because Abbot and I differ about whether some doctrine, say "Idealism," is right or not, but because of the following expressed reasons fully stated in my review:—Here are topics of deep significance—none deeper. Here is a history of philosophy, working at them for ages. Here is a man who, not only in this book but elsewhere, very sternly attacks certain methods and notions that seem to me of the greatest historic prominence and worth in this historical process. Well, *so far* he is in his right as a scholar and thinker. I may assail him. I must not merely on *this* account "warn." Only now, in the next place, come his "pretentions,"—perfectly honest and sincere, but sanguine to an extreme. He tells us that, these long and historically momentous processes having gone utterly astray, and ended in Agnosticism, he has found the right method. He gives it a special name to characterize its epoch-marking significance. It is the "American Theory of Universals." It is "wholly new." The "Greek" and the "German" theories are the other principal ones. His is the third. Not only in the book before me, but in other public utterances (e.g. in a Lecture printed in the *Unitarian Review*)[75] he announces the far-reaching importance of the new thought.

Still, however, he is in his rights as a thinker. Did I differ here only, viz. as to the importance of his work in this respect, I could speak very plainly my difference. "Warning" I should have no right to give.

But last of all comes the question of historical fact as to all this. My own opinion, now, is, that, *after* this indictment of a great part of the evolution of philosophy as utterly wrong, and *after* this announcement of so momentous a discovery, the new theory appears with entire obviousness to be "a maimed version of Hegel's theory," as you paraphrase my view—"Hegel with the subtlety left out," as I myself put it. Now Hegel stands at the culmination of the whole historical process which my author so strenuously condemns. And yet the connection in question seems to me absolutely demonstrable. Hegel's patent as to the theory of the Organic Universal ought to be recognized by everyone who deals with this branch of the subject. The English Hegelians (e.g. John Caird in his *Philos. of Religion*, p. 229 sqq.) have for years popularized the thing. John Caird, pp. 241 and 242 of *op. cit.* uses for the theory Abbot's own illustration of the "Family." (I could multiply citations at great length.)[76] To get out of puzzles by that device of the Organic Universal is what the Hegelians have been counseling us for years. Some of us have struggled long to escape from the

[75] "Scientific Theology the Ground of All Liberal Religion," *Unitarian Review* 32 (1889): 481–99.

[76] Royce did so in his unpublished "The 'American' and the Hegelian 'Theory of Universals'," a rejoinder to Abbot's unpublished reply, "Dr. Royce's 'Professional Warning'." Printer's proofs for both of these articles have been preserved in the Abbot Papers, HUA.

Organic Universal, and have got caught. *No* idea is more characteristically Hegelian.

Well now, combining all these facts with this: I myself am a lover and teacher of the history of philosophy. I believe most ardently that *only* this history can help us out, that its principal outcome has been the movement which my author condemns, and that its principal methods are those of which the theory of universals which he propounds forms a fragment. If I am right as to the facts, must I not under the whole combination of circumstances find this "unconscious borrowing" a very important blunder, yes, in view of the significance of the problem, in view of the magnitude of the aforesaid "pretensions," a blunder that throws a very deep shadow over all of this portion of Abbot's doctrine? *This* portion of the doctrine being about all of the system that the present book and the *Scientific Theism* propound, I judge accordingly. It seems to me that such work is doing serious harm to the cause of philosophy and of its historical study in this country. It seems to me that the man ought long since to have recognized his historical position. It seems to me that his failure to do so is in itself a disqualification for his task. It seems to me that I must put this plainly. I do so. I am accustomed myself to plain speaking about scholarly matters. I have always profitted by my severest reviewers. The man before me is an experienced and doughty controversialist, who as Editor of the *Index*, was always earnest, often unsparing, and, as I believe, constantly insistent on the transcendent value of truth as against any other interest.—Well, with this all together in mind, I sincerely supposed, as I wrote, that my intellectual warmth of onslaught was in itself a tribute to his highmindedness. I did not suppose it possible that he would confound person and doctrine. I struck home for the truth, and supposed that I was meeting an armed man. The result has proved that I was assailing a man of the most sensitive tenderness.

I had never quarrelled with him. Our relations had always been cordial. I held him in high personal esteem. I said so in my review. I meant it. I now very deeply regret having so touched his heart when I struck home at his work. I had no desire to "ruin his happiness" other than in so far as the desire to do a necessarily severe thing in what seems to us a great cause necessarily involves, like any other severe act of business or of active life, the knowledge that severity isn't pleasant. But that knowledge does not forbid plain speech, and constitutes no part of our motive in such cases.

You see then, I don't conceal that I am *willing to have the reputation of a man who fights hard with intellectual weapons, in a scholarly cause,...*[77]

To Horace Elisha Scudder, November 28, 1891[78]

103 Irving St.
Cambridge, Mass.
Nov. 28, 1891

My Dear Scudder:—

I enclose two notes from a friend of mine, a Catholic clergyman and teacher of some mark, and of a pretty strong litera-sense [*sic*]. He has written a number of good things (one book on the *Philosophy of Literature*)—, & I think that you'll recognize his name. He is, meanwhile, although a very good fellow, no man of the world, and his timidity in approaching the firm with his present plans is not remarkable, in view of the receptions that he has doubtless met with elsewhere. I have marked passages in his two notes to me. They will explain themselves. I have replied advising him to send his MS to you, care of the firm, and have assured him that you won't bite, whatever else you do. For the rest, I have only to say that I have a very pleasant impression of Brother Azarias.—[79]

Yrs. Truly
Josiah Royce

Please return the notes.

[77] The rest of the letter is missing.

[78] ALS. Scudder Papers. UCB.

[79] Brother Azarias or Patrick Francis Mullany (1847–93) was the author of several works, including *An Essay Contributing to a Philosophy of Literature* (New York: P. O'Shea, 1890). The MS in question was *Phases of Thought and Criticism* (Boston: Houghton Mifflin and Co., 1892), for which Royce wrote a highly favorable review in the *Atlantic* 71 (January 1893): 126–29. See John Talbot Smith, *Brother Azarias: The Life Story of an American Monk* (New York: W. H. Young and Co., 1897).

To Mary Gray Ward Dorr, March 17, 1892[80]

103 Irving St., Cambridge
March 17, 1892.

My dear Mrs. Dorr,

My little life has been much hurried of late. Please forgive me for not writing at the same time when I sent you my book. Two copies went, one in the cover that everybody sees, one in a poor little binding (though the best one I could plan) which I have meant only for you. The dedication says the rest. I put it as well as I could, and studied a good deal over the form, which I hope that you will not find in any serious way inapt. The substance of it, at all events, comes from the heart.

I have heard about your journey from time to time a little. The other day Barrett Wendell told me of his letter from you. I hope that Mr. Dorr and George are well, and as deeply interested in it all as I easily believe them to be. I send them my warm love. I hope to hear the tale of some of the journey when you return.

My friends here, under Mrs. Whitman's very kind auspices, were good enough to listen this winter to a course of nine lectures on Ethics from my mouth, the conditions of the course being similar to those of your original plan. I suppose that another book may result.[81]

This book starts off well. A second edition is to go to press at once, and I am just sending to the printer a few *errata* for it .

Please excuse my haste. Life flies so fast, and carries me to the next thing. Mrs. Royce, who is very well, joins me in loving greetings.

Yours very truly,
Josiah Royce.

[80] TLC. Royce Papers. HUA.

[81] These lectures were never published together as a series; for a listing of six of the original nine, see Royce's letter to Davidson, April 3, [1892?].

To Thomas Davidson, March 21, 1892[82]

103 Irving St. March 21st.
1892

My Dear Davidson:—

Your letter of the 20th is extremely kind. I suspect that I can do better if I let my nine lectures of the present course reduce themselves to six, by omitting the less effective. I shall send a syllabus a little later, when I have got my choice made from the nine. The general title would be: "Some Recent Tendencies of Ethical Inquiry, and their Outcome." Let my first day of lecturing be Wednesday, July 20th. Let my engagement end by Friday the 29th. Let the rest be as you will. Such is my suggestion, subject to your wish.

You say: "Why should a world which I, *as unconscious being* construct, enter into my consciousness, any more than if it had been constructed by another?" Your question misses in part my position. I don't mean that "I *as unconscious being*" construct anything, but only that I *in so far as I am not now conscious of myself* am the true possessor of the outer or objective truth of things; i.e. my other or fuller and complementary consciousness is such a world-possessor.

The two phrases, yours and mine as above, have a very different meaning. *I* am not conscious of *your* mind; i.e., I *as this finite moment of consciousness* don't extend over to your consciousness of yourself in so far as you are another finite bit of a self. But you are not "my unconscious self," nor are you myself "as an unconscious being" although you are a bit of a self of whom I am not conscious in my present finite state, even as you aren't aware of me. The True Self includes both of us in a higher consciousness.

So much for the meaning of my own view. The whole of it may be restated thus:—

Nothing is more commonplace than that I don't now know how much of a self I am, don't know my own boundaries, am unconscious, just now, of what goes to make up the whole of me. Were I, on the contrary, so conscious of my boundaries, and of what makes up the whole of me, I should *not* be philosophizing. The

[82] ALS. Davidson Papers. YUS.

question, *Who am I?* contains notoriously all the issues of philosophy.

Well then, since I am *not* now conscious of the whole of me, the question arises: Where is the rest of me, and how can this the rest of me be defined? The abstract answer, as I conceive is: The rest of me contains all the truth that *if* I should suddenly become conscious of it, would thereupon be reflectively perceived to have been all along mine. My reflectively enlarged self *would* then consciously see what the True Self eternally does see, and what my finite conscious moment now misses, namely the rest of me, and the relation of this finite moment to that the rest of me.

So far the thing is indeed commonplace. Now comes idealism and declares (on grounds suggested in my book on pages 368–380)[83] that what an absolute reflection would discover to be the rest of me, is identical with the whole outside world including the finite minds of my fellows in one spiritual organism. This the rest of me is conscious. You personally are a part of it. It is I who in this finite moment am unconscious of it, not it that is "myself as unconscious being."

Do I make myself any clearer?

—Yrs. Truly
J. Royce.

To Thomas Davidson, April 3 [1892?][84]

103 Irving St.
April 3

My Dear Davidson:—

My titles will run as follows:—

Lectures on "Some Recent Tendencies in Ethical Doctrine."

1. Introduction: Kant's "Categorical Imperative."
2. The "Law of Love" in Recent Ethics: Schopenhauer; the Utilitarians; the Philanthropic Spirit.
3. The "Law of the Healthy Social Order": Spencer, von Ihering, Wundt, Paulsen.

[83] *SMP*.
[84] ALS. Davidson Papers. YUS.

4. Tolstoi, and the "Invisible Moral Order" in Recent Ethics.[85]
5. The Evolution of the Moral Consciousness.
6. The Authority of Conscience.

The titles may seem to you too diffuse. If so, cut them down. I leave them thus for your guidance in judging of the content of my papers.

I shall be very glad indeed to see you when you come to Cambridge.

Yours Very Truly
Josiah Royce.

To THOMAS DAVIDSON, MAY 15, 1892[86]

103 Irving St.
May 15, 1892.

Dear Mr. Davidson:—

When I set your letter, with its assertion of the "super-self self-maker," "apprehended by some faculty higher than self-consciousness," side by side with the extremely interesting summary statements in your book on *Aristotle and Ancient Educational Ideals*, on pp. 164–5 (where you seem to indicate your own relations with Aristotle), and on pp. 234–5 (where you indicate your relation to Christianity), I feel as if the seeming differences between your view and that of "modern philosophy" can hardly be irreconcilable, any more than are the seeming differences between your own various statements of doctrine as here indicated. Nor should we war as to the "tragic" element, if Dante's *Commedia*, that has its own hell in it also, is to be the standard of interpretation. In fact I suspect that, despite endless differences of terminology, we cannot be far from agreement. For you "all selves have a unity." So for me. For you the higher consciousness reveals that unity; so for me too. You don't want to "sink individuality" in "universal ideas of thought." In the latter part of my book, and elsewhere, I have avoided and rejected such "sinking." For me too, man is a free and moral voluntary agent. Despite your apprehension "by some faculty higher

[85] "Tolstoi and the Unseen Moral Order," *The First Book of the Authors Club: Liber Scriptorum* . . . (New York: Authors Club, 1893), pp. 488–97.
[86] ALS. Davidson Papers. YUS.

than self-consciousness," you don't want mysticism "to dispense with thought to lose itself in vacancy," but you do want it to "pierce the clouds of sense," and there "to find itself in the presence of the most concrete Reality." Herein I fully agree. Furthermore, you have, it would seem, a Theodicy, which, like Dante's, doesn't ignore evil. Despite my "tragedy," I have a Theodicy too, and don't hesitate to call this the best of possible worlds, although not all *in* it is for the best.—Is either of us then far outside the other's heaven?

But I didn't mean controversy. Your kindly appreciation and your book are alike delightful to me. I look forward to very happy days in your mountains.

Yours Very Sincerely
Josiah Royce.

To Hugo Münsterberg, May 16, 1892[87]

103 Irving St., Cambridge.
May 16, 1892

My Dear Prof. Münsterberg:—

Since writing you my letter of yesterday, I have seen, by James's kindness, yours of April 30, wherein you speak at some length to him of the practical aspects of the matter which you have undertaken. Accordingly, after making a little inquiry, I am moved to write again.—I learn from one of my colleagues (whose official duties as so-called "Regent" of the University, entrusted with the general oversight of students' dwellings, bring him into pretty wide knowledge of all grades of lodging and boarding houses in Cambridge), that very good and independent lodgings, with or without board, and in quiet private houses, can doubtless be secured for you and your family, to the extent that you mention, if one tries pretty early to make arrangements. Of course you must be left the greatest possible freedom of choice. I can only offer to do anything that you may authorize during the summer to get information for you about what is to be had, and to help you to communicate, directly or through me, as you please, with people who will be likely to satisfy you as to accommodation and terms. Early arrangements are advisable, as this place fills up very fast in September.

[87] ALS. Münsterberg Papers. BPL.

I want also to reassure you as to the language. Very authoritative colleagues observed to me today, in conversation, that you could not but do our advanced students good if, in the laboratory, you used as much German as possible, and *forced* them to understand *you*, just as you would at home. The more they know that advanced students of psychology need German as a regular tool of trade, the better it will be for them. I believe myself that the opportunity to hear technical German from you would act of itself as an attraction, and help to fill your Laboratory with strong men. In any case you are sure to find Nichols and myself able to help you over the brief stage of language difficulty. I am sure that it will be very brief.—I can only renew my assurances of welcome, and of wish to make smooth your path in every conceivable way.—

Yours Very Truly
Josiah Royce.

It occurs to me to warn you that our American Custom House is a great nuisance, being a disgrace to the nation, and that although of course both "personal effects" and "professional instruments" are by law free from duty, there is a chance that you may meet with official hindrances of a formal character, so that you will do well to take every precaution about choosing and sending your goods. I believe that you should see an American Consul before sending your boxes, and get a certificate from him.

To Jacob Gould Schurman, July 16, 1892[88]

103 Irving Street
Cambridge
July 16, 1892

Dear President Schurman:—

One who has broken many promises dares make no more, in case he still keeps a bit of conscience about him.—Still, *if* not prevented by other tasks, I will send you an article by September 10.—My former intent was to send you one on Teleology. In front of that sleeping princess there has grown however so thick a forest of Causation, that I must first, I find, hew my way through that, after the fashion indicated, but not developed, in my chapter on the

[88] ALS. Philosophy Department Papers. CUA.

"World of Description & the World of Appreciation" in my recent book. A paper on Teleology would then follow, in some later number.[89] Is that acceptable?

Yours Very Truly
Josiah Royce.

Permit me to offer my congratulations on your entrance to the Presidency.[90] It is well when the philosophers become kings. To be sure, I can't envy you the tasks of kingship, for I regard executive business with a deep and shuddering horror. But I envy your energy, and the joy in life which one must have who can consent to become a President.

To Thomas Davidson, August 12, 1892[91]

Cambridge, Mass.
Aug. 12, 1892.

My Dear Davidson:—

I have been remiss about writing, but I have not forgotten you. Engagements have followed thick and fast since I saw you, and hot weather has added its own special reasons for inability to write.

I gained from the stay with you and your company far more than I confessed, or than you saw. In particular the talks with you, —your deeper familiarity, your so vastly wider and heartier experience, in the regions of the universe where, in my best moments I have wished and even tried to make myself more or less at home,— your opinions, which embodied a great many thoughts that I have wanted to think,—all these things were inspiring, and will always remain so. Your school is undoubtedly a blessing to all who come, and that too, whoever else besides yourself chances to speak in it, or to be silent.

I can't mention by name all my friends in your group, for there are too many. Give all my warm love and greeting. I prized Mr. Harris's good counsel much, although I felt constrained to question

[89] The two proposed articles were "The External World and the Social Consciousness," *Philosophical Review* 3 (1894): 513–45; and "Self-Consciousness, Social Consciousness, and Nature," *Philosophical Review* 4 (1895): 465–85, 577–602. The second of these was reprinted in *SGE*.

[90] Schurman became president of Cornell University in 1892.

[91] ALS. Davidson Papers. YUS.

a few things that were his, e.g. the readings of his aneroid barometer, but for this I hope to be forgiven. If he is still with you, greet him for me; also Drs. Léon and Margolis, and Prof. Murray.[92] Others, I repeat, I dare not begin to try to name. I thank them all for their common hospitality.

Yours Very Truly
Josiah Royce.

To Charles William Eliot, September 2, 1892[93]

103 Irving St.
Cambridge
Sept. 2, 1892.

Dear President Eliot:—

In reply to your letter of Aug. 31st, in reference to the title of my proposed professorship, I have for the first to reply that my own preference would be to have this title read "Professor of Philosophy," without addition or specification. In other departments of the University, both within and without the range of the departments of the Faculty of Arts and Sciences, there are numerous precedents for such a nomenclature, in cases where, as a matter course, there is ample room for specialization within the province covered by the simple title: e.g. "Professor of Law," "Professor of Geology," "Professor of English." On the other hand, some of the now established and more lengthy titles of professorships are well recognized as descriptions which are imperfect in proportion to their length, so that, were it possible, the present holders of these titles would doubtless be glad to simplify them. "Philosophy" is itself, to be sure, a hopelessly large province unless one chooses with some care his range, but from the nature of the case the choice itself here depends largely upon the nature of the philosophical opinions to which one has committed himself, and an adequate general characterization of one's choice of work would be at best merely a characterization of one's own doctrine. For if

[92] Albert J. Léon gave lessons in Arabic and lectured on Arabic philosophers. Max Leopold Margolis lectured on Jewish literature. John Clark Murray was professor of philosophy at McGill University in Montreal.

[93] ALS. Eliot Papers. HUA.

Smith is "Professor of Philosophy," the only adequate qualification of his title would in my opinion be this, that, if he has views at all, he is professor of Smith's Philosophy. And this qualification is at once superfluous and objectionable, not to say impossible. Nor does this seemingly too personal way of stating the case apply to philosophy alone. A "Professor of English" must choose, in the end, according to his own opinions and upon his own responsibility, whether he will make the literary or the grammatical and merely linguistic element prominent in his reading and teaching. So also a Professor of French or German. Here too then, the generalized title seems justified. In general, if absurdly broad titles, such as "Professor of Natural Science" are to be avoided, arbitrarily specialized titles, such as "Professor of Deductive Logic" would seem, in a department such as philosophy, where so much depends upon the personal attitude and creed of the individual teacher, especially out of place.

Usage and established phrases must justify the present titles of Professors Palmer and Peabody.[94] The importance of the modern psychological specialties justifies the titles of James and Münsterberg; but in my own case the title "Professor of Metaphysics" would be very painful to me, owing to the somewhat accidental and crabbed history of that word, while the title, "Professor of History of Philosophy" (the least objectionable alternative title yet suggested) seems to me not nearly so expressive of what I am about, and always shall be about, as the simple title "Professor of Philosophy" would be. For my one business in life is to find out what little I can about philosophical truth, using to that end any means (history, psychological study, constructive effort) that may come to hand.

"Philosophy" may indeed be said to include Ethics, a department otherwise provided for. But so does "Law" include much more, I suppose, than Professor Thayer undertakes alone to teach.

I write at some length, because, as I know, Professor Palmer is of opinion that some closer specification of my title would be proper, and he will of course, at his pleasure and yours, give his reasons for this view—reasons which I recognize as of importance, but which I do not quite agree with.

[94] Palmer was Alford Professor of Natural Religion, Moral Philosophy, and Civil Polity; Peabody was Plummer Professor of Christian Morals; James and Münsterberg both held the title, Professor of Psychology.

If, however, specification must go farther than the word "Philosophy," I am ready, upon your advice, to accept of course the title, "Prof. of the History of ⟨Mod.?⟩ Phil."

With many thanks for your letter, I remain

Very Truly Yours
Josiah Royce

Pres. C. W. Eliot.

To Charles William Eliot, September 11, 1892[95]

103 Irving St.
Cambridge.
Sept. 11, 1892.

Dear Pres. Eliot:—

It is pretty certainly best that I should be content with the title: Prof. of the History of Philosophy. As for the limitations which you mention, it is true that I had them in mind in expressing my personal preference before,—a preference which, as I have already said, I have decided to withdraw in view of more general considerations. I am not disposed, however, in any case, to make too much of these limitations. The limits of a topic are determined by the purpose with which it is studied. The history of philosophy is studied, and, in my opinion, is to be taught, with constant reference to its bearing upon the problems of the present and the future. That is the only reason for the existence of the study as a *prominent* part of the work of every student of the problems of philosophy. The peculiar interest of the history of philosophy lies in the fact that its bearings on the present and the future are far more important than is usually the case with other branches of historical knowledge—the history of religion, perhaps, being excepted.

Be that as it may, I have already signified to Prof. Palmer, in a letter written since my last one to you, my willingness to accept the title now proposed. My preferences in the matter ought not to stand against the more general considerations that he urges. I have accordingly deliberately withdrawn them. In any case the form of a title like this is the last thing to lie awake over. In our department we have always easily agreed as to the actual distribution of the

[95] ALS. Eliot Papers. HUA.

work, and we shall doubtless continue to do so. It would be a pity if my private fancy for the title of "Prof. of Philosophy,"—a title which I should be glad to have uniform for all the professors in the dep't.,—should stand against the general fashions now in use in the department. And so, if you assent, the matter may, I suppose, be regarded as settled.

I haven't made at all light of my duties to Prof. Münsterberg, but have given much time ever since last June to helping him. I am very much pleased to meet him, but of course the problem of making a foreign family comfortable is, for him and for me, a rather puzzling one. I should be glad to explain, if there were time, and you desired it, the steps that I have taken, and the changes of plan which proved to be necessary before we decided to try the Mulford house.[96] As for that house itself,—we had at length to decide in great haste in order to get release from a previous engagement which Münsterberg had decided to abandon. We examined in a two days' search all the furnished houses (they were but few) which remained on Ellis's list, and which seemed available in the least. The Mulford house proved to be the best of these that could be obtained before Oct. 1. I had intended to try Murray Howe in Boston, but Münsterberg was anxious to be resolved, time was pressing, and we took the house. It is in some respects a disappointment; but we shall do what we can to make M. comfortable, and to make the best of the situation. James wanted more for his house than M. was ready to pay. Perhaps, had he been here, he would have come down to M.'s terms under the circumstances, but M. was not willing to wait further advices, and we were not sure enough of James's whereabouts to cable.

I shall do my best about the lectures to teachers, following your advice as given in your last letter.—

Yours Very Truly
Josiah Royce.

[96] Royce was more or less officially responsible for getting the Münsterbergs settled into Cambridge. One letter (August 26, 1892—not included in this edition) describes in detail Royce's elaborate preparations for meeting the Münsterbergs and the rooms he had secured for them. The rooms proved unsatisfactory; of the landlady, Royce remarked, "*la donna e mobile.*"

To Hugo Münsterberg, September 14, 1892[97]

103 Irving St.
Sept. 14, 1892.

My Dear Colleague:—

I enclose a scrap of a newspaper which came to hand the other day, and which will give you a moment's cause for merriment. Our friend Scripture, having got his laboratory at Yale, needs students, and I am sorry to say that the item enclosed represents one way, that has of late come into vogue in this country, of advertising academic mysteries, and exciting general curiosity. You will observe the marvelous novelty and unheard of boldness of the speculations propounded! "That no singer exactly hits the tone he wishes to"—what fearful news to concert-goers! None of us ever noticed anything of the sort before! It is unheard of that singers ever sing off the note! The Yale laboratory must be suppressed. *Delenda est Carthago!*—Meanwhile, don't you want to do some advertising too, with the aid of a newspaper reporter? As Hamlet said, "it is as easy as"—But no, I think we must leave that to Yale!

To be more serious, I am about to leave town, to return Monday. I hope that Mrs. Mulford will not serve you with promises only. My warm regards to Mrs. Münsterberg.

Yours Very Truly
Josiah Royce

To Paul Henry Hanus, October 17, 1892[98]

103 Irving St.
Oct. 17, 1892.

My Dear Hanus:—

Can you write a review of Adler's new book on *The Moral Instruction of Children* for the January No. of the *Journal of Ethics?* You will be quite free to criticize negatively, of course,

[97] ALS. Münsterberg Papers. BPL.

[98] ALS. Hanus Papers. HUA. Hanus's review of Adler's book appeared in the *International Journal of Ethics* 3 (1893); 251–54.

even if he is the first named of our list of editors. Both Adler himself and Weston join in this request.

Yours Truly
Josiah Royce.

If you assent, I have a copy for you.—I lament to say that there is no money in the job.

To William James, October 17, 1892[99]

103 Irving St.
Oct. 17, '92.

Dear James:—

In the dead waste and middle of the night, at the end of a busy day, it occurs to me to write you a bit of a letter. The delay has been long, but I miss you now;—would write sonnets if I could, entitled "The Deserted House," "The Darkened Path," "He Comes Not," and "Tired of all These ⟨Faculty Meetings, Deans, &c⟩ for Restful Death I Cry,"—if I could, I say.—Meanwhile as I can't write the sonnets, I ought to produce the letter, premising that Cambridge without you is like toast unbuttered, like the heart without blood, and that, to be brief, the night hath a thousand eyes, and the day but One, but—

Sentiment aside, the summer passed very fairly. I travelled some 5000 miles, lectured at Davidson's School, sat up with him nights till we were both talked blind, and broke religiously all the rules of his sacred community at Glenmore. I grew very fond of him. I have later visited the Dorrs at Bar Harbor. Mrs. Dorr is very loving now, and very gracious, but has reached such a spiritual height since she saw Egypt that I can but grovel in her presence, and weakly babble a little about hypnotism to please her.

Münsterberg is an immense success. His English is charming. The students love it as a mother her babe's first prattle. He fears them not, and they revere his wisdom the more, the more his speech seems shattered. To me he is a great comfort,—although of course no *Ersatz* for the aforesaid condition of my heart.—I am sorry he couldn't take your house, but somehow the bargain seemed to

[99] ALS. James Papers. HL. Partly printed in *TCWJ*, 1: 803–4. James spent his sabbatical year, 1892–93, in Europe.

have been missed on the other side, and I couldn't interfere. Our earlier plans for him were unideal, and faded like streaks of the morning cloud when once he began to warm the sky with his presence. After a few insignificant incidents we got him settled—in that sad little house of the Mulfords, where the rats do congregate, and daily do take counsel on his stairways to devour his tender infants. At least such I understand to be the domestic situation. But he is very sweet about it, and the lovely Frau (of whom we are all fond) spends her time in devising ways to induce the rats to bite at her traps, and in trying to make up her mind to be fond of tomatoes, and to pronounce *th* without being overcome with chagrin at having to stick out her tongue in the act. On the whole they are an ornament to Cambridge, and *very* lovable.

The term opens as usual, only more so—"unexampled numbers," endless opportunities to do good. One or two sorrowful hearts that have formerly confided in you, now come to poor me for relief and consolation. For such is the scarcity of comforters hereabouts. Over these I brood and psychologize. It seems to be, so far, a good deal of a year of giving advice. A young poet, whom you don't know, has joined himself unto me, and having found me psychologically sympathetic, has deposited the entire entrails of his spirit, contents and all, in my library for expert investigation. And there they lie now, among other things of the spirit, waiting a quiet hour. There is moreover a Nihilist, escaped over the frontier after a half year's imprisonment and much policing. He came first to Lyon with a philosophical thesis on Spinoza.[100] He wants to pass his life in academic leisure, but has so far, since landing mostly made shirts and taught arithmetic to Russian mechanics. He is a very clever, aged 24, and we have taken him up. Lyon bleeds wealthy Jews for him. I lecture to him on Evolution. He has become a Special Student. He has read absolutely everything that is radical, and in Russian too, so that you can't refute him. He is already a terror of my life. After lectures he gathers round me, outstays all other questioners, and talks Darwin, Spencer, idealism, mathematics, socialism, —everything till I flee. Then he accompanies me homewards. My brain whirls, I groan inwardly, I long for a little deep interstellar silence,—but in vain. At last, as I hurry and hobble along, hastening

[100] Stoyan K. Vatralsky—poet, social idealist, and mystic—was later described as the "Tolstoy of Bulgaria." See class folder, HUA. David G. Lyon was Hollis Professor of Divinity.

to be free, he says kindly, "But I detain you." "No, No," I cry, and to prove it take to my heels. The last I hear, as the spectre pursues me past Memorial Hall is: "But I don't agree wid Spencer, bud yed I do dink dat Indegration. . . ."—At night, whenever the floors crack, I lie dreading the emissaries of the Russian police who, as I doubt not, are already spying on this ill-starred intimacy.

In short, it is a busy year. Palmer is majestic, despotic, tender and lusciously sweet by turns. The Overseers received last Wednesday my nomination, and under the rules, have laid it over one meeting, as they are said always to do. Now some of them are beginning to worry their wits to remember what that horrible crime was that I committed against a poor servant of God named Abbot! I don't think they care much to find out, and hardly expect further words.

Mrs. Royce has been asleep some hours, or she would send love to your household. We are well. And so always the tenderest affection and greetings from

Yours Fondly
Josiah Royce.

To Charles William Eliot, November 17, 1892[101]

103 Irving Street
Cambridge
Nov. 17, 1892

Dear Mr. Eliot:—

In thanking you, as I do, very warmly, for your kind note of this morning, I want to add a word that can better be said now than, perhaps, at any other time. I have now passed ten years at Harvard—years in which very great kindness has been shown me. I am not, in public, one who wishes to seem demonstrative. I am afraid that I have often seemed impassively ungrateful. At heart, however, I am, like so many other bookish people, a pretty sensitive person; and accordingly I feel all the more, whether I show it or not, the largemindedness that has seen beyond my shortcomings, the patience that has borne with my incompleteness, the personal strength that makes life for me, as for so many other young men in this place, confident, cheerful, inspiring. This largemindedness and patience

[101] ALS. Eliot Papers. HUA.

and strength,—it is needless, and may seem effusive, to say how much I have honored them and been grateful for them in you. But this is a moment when I have a right to speak, possibly, with the frankness that comes from genuine feeling. The life here is indeed inspiring; the work to which my new appointment calls me is the largest that I have any right to hope for. I am not using mere words when I say that I know myself to be unworthy of the call and of the opportunity. But I cannot leave unspoken my deep feeling of thankfulness to you, not merely for calling me to the work, but for doing so much as you have done and are constantly doing to make work in this place not only a high honor (for that is relatively a small thing after all) but something that, through noble example and manifold progress in all about us, constantly calls out a man's best and most sacred ambitions.

There is meant to be nothing official about these words. They come straight from the heart. It is no very noteworthy heart, to be sure, but it is a real one.—

Yours Very Truly
Josiah Royce.

To William Torrey Harris, December 4, 1892[102]

103 Irving Street
Cambridge
Dec. 4, 1892.

Dear Mr. Harris:—

I will try to do what I can for Humphreys.

My expected book is to be made up of translated extracts from the *Phänomenologie*, with introduction and notes.[103] I am an admirer of that book, and mean to do what I can to make others feel

[102] ALS. Harris Papers. USC. Printed in "Josiah Royce's Letters to William Torrey Harris," *Philosophical Forum* 13 (1955): 85; reprinted in Daniel S. Robinson, *Royce and Hocking—American Idealists* (Boston: The Christopher Publishing House, 1968), p. 135.

[103] Plans for this book, also mentioned to Howison (see letter July 13, 1889), were never carried out. Later he translated Hegel's "The Contrite Consciousness" from *The Phenomenology of Spirit* with a brief introductory footnote for Benjamin Rand, ed., *Classical Philosophers* (Boston: Houghton Mifflin Co., 1908), pp. 614–28.

the beauty of its analyses, whose value is by no means conditioned upon an acceptance of Hegel as a whole, or upon any theory as to his progress in his later works.

Yours Very Truly
Josiah Royce.

To Hugo Münsterberg, December 12, 1892[104]

103 Irving Street
Cambridge
Dec. 12, 1892.

My Dear Münsterberg:—

I write, lest I hereafter forget, at once, after my own meeting of the Conference, to say, as to my very slight supper tonight, that it was especially agreed by the Department, by the advice of Palmer, that the supper offered to the students after the Conferences shall consist *only* of sandwiches and cakes, with some light drinks (e.g. chocolate, beer, ginger ale, or some such thing); and further that Palmer has asked me to pass on this decree to you for your guidance when the Conference falls under your care. Of course a relative uniformity as to such things seems advisable, and Palmer is much afraid of injuring the simplicity of the Conferences (with their noble ideal of "plain living and high thinking!!"), in case ice cream, or salad, or any such pernicious luxury, should creep into our suppers. As to the very little bit of sherry that appeared on my table tonight, that is already no doubt abomination enough in the eyes of the abstemious Palmer. But I wanted only to display my dark red decanter.—Please excuse these low material *Betrachtungen.*

Your Ever
Josiah Royce

104 ALS. Münsterberg Papers. BPL.

To William James, December 22, 1892[105]

103 Irving St., Cambridge.
Dec. 22, '92.

Dear James:—

At the moment we are all writing to you about the future of Nichols.[106] I add my mite, not because I want to make too much of my personal views in the matter, but because the interests of the department demand a general understanding of the matter. I have watched Nichols's work since the year began as well as my very busy life has permitted. I feel now very clearly that, anxious as he is for definiteness and permanence of outlook, we should do him great injustice to keep him here longer than the present year unless we can offer him a very good assurance of a permanent place in the department. I feel also that his strong ambition, his intense sensitiveness, and his vigorous disposition to assert himself for all that he is worth, would make it wholly impossible to keep him content with a permanently subordinate place, such as an Assistantship in the Laboratory. If he is kept, he must before long be as independent of his colleagues and as free to chose his own methods of work, and to make his own plans, as you and I are. He is galled and hampered by subordinate and restricted tasks.

Well, all this I feel, and I add, after very careful consideration, that, so far as I can judge of the man and of his work, he is absolutely unfit for any such independent and responsible position in Cambridge. He is a hopelessly ill-balanced thinker, investigator, and man. He is brilliant, industrious, full of ingenuity and of ideas, learned in his way, and ambitious without limit. He has devotion, ideal enthusiasm, and a great deal of personal interest of character. What he lacks, and hopelessly lacks, is judgment, self-criticism, self-restraint as to his foibles of thought and feeling, and power to avoid blunders. He is an agonized and agonizing bundle of sensitivenesses, suspicions, wild and over-confident hopes, speculations, despairs, plans, self-assertions, apologies, and extravagant hypotheses.

105 ALS. James Papers. HL.

106 Herbert Nichols was the assistant in Harvard's Psychological Laboratory. He was not reappointed for the following year, but was later, in 1896, a lecturer in experimental psychology at Johns Hopkins.

With men like Delabarre within easy reach, why should we continue to bear the burden of such a spontaneous variation as Nichols? He is indeed, after all, beautifully devoted to science, and his latest breath will try to serve psychology; but pathetic as his case is, and admirable as are the personal qualities that he in these respects shows, we can't desire him in Cambridge merely because we want to be considerate of his feelings. I have carefully considered the pathetic aspect of the case, and that is very sad. But I fancy that it is only cruelty to encourage Nichols to continue to struggle here longer.

What he does best appears to be the teaching of elementary classes. There the devotion, the self-sacrificing lavishness of his nature, shows itself unhindered. His theories are in the background. He is reporting and not constructing. He is then endlessly patient and even affectionate in bearing to his class. But there also he has less responsibility. In any more advanced or complex relationship of his work, his featherheadedness makes itself once more manifest. And as a schemer and a speculator Nichols is in the long run simply impossible, as a colleague, and as a contributor to thought. He will throw out useful suggestions, and write some brilliant papers, like the one on Pleasure and Pain,[107] which I think so far his best. But he is always on the point, at least, of committing hopeless errors of judgment. And he is far too old to learn. In a college where there was nothing but essentially elementary work to do, he would be at his best.

Well, this sounds illnatured. I don't mean it so. On the personal side there is so much good to be said of Nichols's moral quality, that if I weren't forced to write at this moment to suggest what I can in aiding you to know how N. has seemed in his work since you left, I should only cheerily refer to him as a good fellow, & say no more. But the situation is now one involving a serious choice.

I am in a great hurry with the holidays. Love to your family from ours, & best holiday greetings. I mean to write soon a pleasanter letter.

Yours Very Truly
Josiah Royce.

I have my professorship all right.

[107] "The Origin of Pleasure and Pain," two papers reprinted from the *Philosophical Review* 1 (1892): 402–32, 518–34. Briefly and favorably reviewed by Royce in the *International Journal of Ethics* 3 (1893): 275–76.

To Hugo Münsterberg, February 6, 1893[108]

103 Irving Street
Cambridge
Feb. 6, 1893

My Dear Münsterberg:—

I had been on the point of writing to you to express our regret that other engagements have prevented our acceptance of your kind invitation of the other day, and to explain more fully this matter, of which Mrs. Royce's note had already given you notice. But yesterday I learned through Miss Gibbens that you had bad news from home, and that there was no further question of invitations at present.[109] I had resolved to call today to express my sympathy; but your note of yesterday, just received, gives me now the painful news of your great loss. I reply at once, to express, first the deep sympathy of Mrs. Royce and myself at the thought of this very moving and sorrowful news, and then to express my deep sense of the powerlessness of mere sympathy, however warm and friendly, to give aid to our friends at such moments. I know well how hard it must be for you, and still more for your so sorely wounded companion, to be at such a moment upon foreign soil, and so far from home. But I want you at least to feel that you will not find yourselves forgotten, or in the least coldly regarded by this our academic community; foreign though we are, at this moment of your grief. Our friendship is new, but sympathy is as old as human life. Both you and Mrs. Münsterberg have won the genuine and affectionate regard of very many hearts amongst us since you came. Your calamity is ours, and I am mistaken if you do not meet with many tokens the warmth of feeling with which your sorrow will be shared by many, many, amongst your colleagues and their families. We cannot be your home friends at this moment, but we are not cold, nor forgetful.

For myself, you well know that it is much more than mere regard with which I have learned to remember you at all times. If a grasp of the hand or an honest word of hearty kindness could give you in any measure the comfort that I want to convey, you

108 ALS. Münsterberg Papers. BPL.

109 Due to the death of Mrs. Münsterberg's father.

should indeed feel that comfort. As it is I cannot help you, and I feel deeply my powerlessness, warm as is my feeling. One fears of course to intrude at such times. We do not venture to try to see you; but if there is anything that Mrs. Royce or myself could do or say to lighten in the least Mrs. Münsterberg's sad burden, or yours, at this moment, please let us know, and we will come to you at once.

Yours Very Truly
Josiah Royce.

To Hugo Münsterberg, February 17, 1893[110]

103 Irving Street
Cambridge
Feb. 17, 1893.

Dear Münsterberg:—

I have felt very neglectful for the past few days, knowing you to be suffering, at my neglect in not calling to inquire. But my lecture for Thursday kept me very busy. Now comes your bad news of today.[111]

Well—I will simply not believe that in the end it is going to prove more than a light visitation, soon to pass and leave all as before. You are too valuable a man to be left even for a brief period in the grasp of the enemy. It must not be. The enemy is of course a subtle and perhaps a treacherous one, but you are not the man to be daunted, or long beset, by such ills. You have the ardent hopes and good wishes of your friends. We all see dark days, and it is wonderful how great shadows in the end pass. We will hope, and you will, despite all, be cheery.

I hope that you will soon have the aid of a trained nurse. Mrs. Münsterberg, heroic as she is, will need such help. Mrs. Royce would write this evening were she not troubled with a slight indisposition which has sent her early to bed. As it is, she sends her heartiest sympathy and greetings to Mrs. Münsterberg.

It is a pity to have to be content with words when one wants to come to you, and to be of true service. At all events, however,

[110] ALS. Münsterberg Papers. BPL.

[111] I.e., Münsterberg's attack of diphtheria.

feel no care as to the work to be attended to in your absence. Your spirit is in the laboratory, and things can for the moment go on in that spirit, even in the absence of your body, although it will indeed be with joy that the students will welcome you back. Meanwhile, Nichols and I will do our best.

Call on me for whatever I can do at any moment. For myself, I should care little for infection; but my children forbid any carelessness. Yet outside of your doors though I must be, I mean to do whatever is possible for you.

Yours Very Truly
Josiah Royce.

To Hugo Münsterberg, February 19, 1893[112]

103 Irving Street
Cambridge
Feb. 19, 1893

Dear Münsterberg:—

We all of us beset your Doctor with inquiries, and talk much of what we hear, pained not a little if the news is not the best, rejoiced when, as is this evening the case, we get decidedly good news.

Of all this you will not be surprised to hear. The freedom with which the laboratory men volunteered themselves for any possible service, such as sending one from their number to stay in your house and to act as your messenger in case you needed to send any sudden messages—all this too will not surprise you, for you know how we prize you. I hope now that it will not be long before we see you in full convalescence.

Mrs. Münsterberg's success in her splendid battle with your enemy, we hear of with great sympathy and admiration. We wish that you both had more help near you, but you certainly seem to be well able to cope with your emergency. The President, and all your colleagues with whom I have spoken, join in sending their warmest good wishes.

Yours Very Truly
Josiah Royce.

112 ALS. Münsterberg Papers. BPL.

To William James, March 4, 1893[113]

103 Irving St.
Cambridge, Mass.
March 4, 1893.

Dear James:—

The robins, our colds, which are plentiful, and other such signs, have for some time indicated that the hounds of spring are on winter's traces. I ought long since to have written you, but simply had no time. The lectures to teachers, which I hate, but have been writing out in full, have taken every spare moment. I am in arrears with every task, except that of paying my bills (a matter that has on the whole gone better than usual, although of course it is a wee bit behind too). My health, until my latest cold, has been very good. The cold however, now hangs on a little, and vexes me, so that I am fain, between jobs, to read worthless novels, and to neglect letters. Still, it has been a good year, despite the Nihilist, and the other professional (or professorial) responsibilities of the time.[114] It will give me great joy to see you back again, however, and letters are poor substitutes, in my mind, for casual talks.

As for news. The Dept. met the other day, I with heart on fire to kill Phil. 1, which I had this time grown to hate deeply, Palmer with the usual sacred desire to serve the eternal and to dish you and me, Münsterberg, convalescent, but full of curiosity, disposed to agree with everybody, and to make notes on department meetings in American Universities, for future generalizations. Peabody was there, timidly righteous, in his seeming, and with the air of trembling hope about him that he has worn ever since, last autumn, his insignificant Hasty Pudding frailties were drawn from their dread

[113] ALS. James Papers. HL. James's response to this letter was characteristic. To Royce he wrote a postcard from Geneva on April 21: "Next to living in the light of your dear eyes, living far eno' away to get such letters is the greatest boon life can bring me. I giggled so over it at my hotel bkfet. table this A.M. that they nearly put me out of the dining room.—But I am deeply sorry for this sinister intelligence it conveys, and have just written to Palmer to say that since the sacrednes of Phil 1 as the only portal has been violated by the erection of your new course he must count me out of it altogether."

[114] A private joke at the expense of Abbot who had argued that there was a relation between Royce's "professional" and his "professorial" behavior.

abode in the Safety Deposits' vault, and held up to the scorn of the jeering and faithless multitude.[115] Santayana, who has suddenly grown to seem indispensable, to all the future work of the dept., was also there. Nichols was not invited. As, in any case, this poor fellow innocently blabs any and everything that he can, and helplessly engages from time to time in the most complicated, deep planned, transparent, and harmlessly wily intrigues to better his academic situation, the omission to invite him was necessary, perhaps, or, in any case, natural. Nichols has been informed by Eliot & Palmer that he has no chance for next year.

Courses for next year were under consideration. Phil 1 was the chief topic. Santayana and I both condemned it. Palmer defended it, and declared that, this Dep't. being no monarchy, but a republic, he proposed to leave no stone unturned to get his own views to win as against ours. This was pretty much his way of stating the case. I grew wrathful, as far as I ever do on such occasions. But Palmer, being in his heart sure that, in case of a controversy transcending the limits of the Dep't., he would have the support of Eliot, who believes in Phil 1, and also of Dunbar,[116] who is in favor of all such courses,—Palmer insisted. Thereupon I assured him that if Phil. 1 continued, I should in any case decline to take part in it, and should advise you also to decline, as I now do.—This holding out of one against three of the instructors who had taken the course, I said, was unprecedented, and the one who thus held out, could take the consequences. Whereupon Palmer threatened a general row.—Long we sought for a compromise. I railed very gently. He domineered with saintly calm. Münsterberg took notes, and agreed in qualified terms, and in sweetly translucent, although not always quite transparent English, with both of us. Santayana looked down upon the bloody arena with the contemplative peace of a Roman spectator ⟨My figures of speech are a little confused, but you will make out the essentials of the scene if you try.⟩—In the end it was proposed that if I objected to Phil 1, I might forsake it, and set up an Elemen-

[115] Francis Greenwood Peabody, Plummer Professor of Christian Morals, having returned from a year's leave in Europe, gave a series of six public lectures on "The Ethics of Social Questions" during October and November of 1892. His course on this subject came to be known as "Peabo's drainage, drunkenness, and divorce."

[116] Charles Franklin Dunbar, professor of political economy and first dean of the faculty of Arts and Sciences.

tary of my own, to run opposition. To this I promptly agreed, and the battle ended. So next year the thing will stand:—

Phil 1a. Logic ⟨The Holy Man leading⟩; Psychology ⟨taught by ? ? the Assistant, *if* you refuse, as I hope you will⟩; Metaphysics ⟨taught by Santayana, unwillingly, but as one led to the slaughter⟩. Phil. 1b.—General Introduction to Philos.—Hist. of Phil. in Outline. Principal Problems of Phil.—Excursions into Logic, Psychol., and Ethics, at the wayward pleasure of J. R.—Look on this picture—and on this![117]

Both courses to be given at *same* hours. My plan, you see, is to lead to a breaking up of Phil 1, which I intend to bleed so badly that it will be glad, another year, to be put out of its misery. Better I couldn't do this year, as I had no doubt the President and Dunbar would be against me if the thing got out of the department. Even now I fancy that there may be trouble.

You, meanwhile, would, on my plan, be relieved of all elementary work for the year. You would have the Cosmology, your Seminary, and your work in the Advanced Psychology. How like you this? I shall offer a new full course of 2 hrs. weekly + extra library work (instead of third hour) on History of Psychology from Locke to Bain (including Herbart). The German Philosophy Course (12) is to become a course of reading at sight Kant and Schopenhauer, with Bierwrith (now in the German dept.), and with Münsterberg to lecture, in German, about ⅓ of the year.—A very attractive course, isn't it? I have had a share in getting up the scheme, but Münsterberg is the keystone of the arch, and a noble one.

The President will write urging you to engage in Phil 1. Be as firm as you can, and keep out of it. *Und wenn die Welt voll Palmers wär'—es soll uns doch gelingen.*

[117] From 1890 to 1893 the introductory course in philosophy was Philosophy 1, General Introduction to Philosophy, including logic, psychology, and the history of philosophy. Each section was taught by a different instructor and occupied a third of a year. Royce's compromise, carried out in 1893–94, created two introductory courses—Philosophy 1a and Philosophy 1b, both titled General Introduction to Philosophy, and either of which satisfied prerequisites for advanced work. Philosophy 1a was merely the former Philosophy 1; Philosophy 1b, taught by Royce, focused on the history and problems of philosophy, with introductions to elementary logic, psychology, and ethics. This double-course program was abandoned during the following year, but was reinstated in 1897–98.

I speak seemingly ill of P., but really we haven't quarrelled. His noble traits shine with a more glittering burnishment daily, and, as you know, I am only making the old fun, such as it is, afresh. On the whole, he and I agree splendidly, and this is our only fight this year.

As for the Cosmology. I am using as my third book this year (in addition to LeConte & Spencer) Karl Pearson's *Grammar of Science*, a book in which ingenuity, soundness, and utter crudity, are mingled in such proportions as may delight a teacher's heart. You would have plenty of negative work to do with him. Yet he is a fine set-off to Spencer.—You may have time to introduce him yet. It is never impossible, I hold, to introduce new, if inexpensive, books unannounced into a course, if the students, in a comparatively small class, gain enough by the change not to regret it.

But time is short, and my pile of letters high. We are trying to do what we can for Nichols. Nobody dislikes him. Nobody can permanently find a use for him. His unhappy ghost will squeak and gibber in our streets for ages. And yet he might have been so good a man for the work if he had started early enough.—Love to your family. You can't tell how I shall rejoice to see you. Don't count my silence as a token of forgetfulness.—The moon revolves silently, but faithfully, round her nobler planet. Or is not that well put, now?—

Yours Fondly
Josiah Royce.

Mrs. Royce sends much love to Mrs. James. Is the family coming back at once with you, or will they linger a bit?

To Thomas Davidson, May 31, 1893[118]

103 Irving St., Cambridge.
May 31, 1893.

Dear Davidson:—

You may put me down, if you like, for the week from the 15th to the 22d of July, with a chance that I may stay a day or two over.

Four lectures, or at most five is all that I ought to undertake, if so small an offering can be of possible service. The fact is that I come solely to see you in person, if you desire my company, and I thank

118 ALS. Davidson Papers. YUS.

you heartily for giving me the chance. I take interest in your people of course, and don't despise the chance to lecture, but it's you I'm mostly after.

Yours Very Truly
Josiah Royce.

I shall smoke, get up late, and break all other rules in the known manner,—only worse; for I have been in hard harness this winter, and want to be an absolute loafer. So you know what you're taking, *if* "you like that kind of a horse" at all.

To Thomas Davidson, July 1, 1893[119]

Cambridge, July 1, '93

Dear Davidson:—

I have just returned from Chicago and Denver. To Denver I carried the examinations for Harvard. At Chicago I saw the Fair.[120] I am now busy with several matters which may, for all that I know, prove more engrossing and time-consuming than I had expected. If therefore I cannot set out from here before Monday the 17th, please do not think of me as breaking the spirit of my promise. I shall be ready to lecture at your school by Tuesday evening, the 18th, or Wednesday morning at latest, and shall stay a full week. I shall write my day more exactly hereafter.

Meanwhile, I have a favor to ask on behalf of a young friend whom I want to bring with me, in case such action seems advisable. —You may remember a certain Sheffield,[121] a man whom you have once or twice met in philosophical company here. He is not a man whom I have ever mentioned to you, but he is a man who just now needs some help in beginning to find his way upon his own resources. He is a Harvard Graduate (of '91) and has since been studying Law. As Undergraduate he read philosophy a good deal,

[119] ALS. Davidson Papers. YUS.

[120] Royce was a prominent member of the Advisory Council for the Philosophical Congress of the Columbian Exposition held in Chicago, August 1893. His stay at Chicago in June probably also involved him in some of the advance arrangements for this meeting.

[121] Justus Pearl Sheffield received his A.B. from Harvard in 1891; he studied at the Harvard Law School from 1891–93 and from 1896–98 without receiving a degree. Later he practiced law in New York City. He died August 11, 1953.

and is not without power in that field, although he will never make philosophy his calling. He knows his elementary mathematics well enough to teach in that direction, and would make also a good tutor in Logic, as in other elementary philosophy. He has been, in former times, a man fairly supplied with means, somewhat luxurious in his habits, somewhat undetermined in his reactions, somewhat touched by that paralysis of reflection of which, in other cases, you and I have sometimes talked. In short, he has been a skillful witted man who, having no responsibilities, lacked something of moral strenuousness. He has watched life rather than lived. He is moreover of a rather sensitive and delicate physique,—constitutionally a bit of an invalid,—just the man who needs hardening and sharp discipline,—just the man who, until lately, never got it. His health, while in no wise undermined, is softened; he is somewhat hypochondriac; he is not ill; he needs work, ideals, objectivity, strenuous habits, a chance to do service, as well as to use his wits.

Under these circumstances, a double problem is just now presented to him. Family conditions have suddenly thrown him on his own resources, long before he has finished the Law School. He has no means, and must fight his way into his profession alone, if at all. On the other hand, he is also just engaged to be married to an excellent woman (a widow of some means). He very honorably sets aside the notion of marriage until he shall be established in his Profession, although I believe that she would willingly marry him at once. But if he is to do the right thing, he must now work, and work hard for his living, until he wins a position, and is ready honorably to marry.

Accordingly, this vacation, he finds himself for the first time in his life in the labor market, and in the real presence of a serious issue of life. He is puzzled and stimulated at once. He has moral enthusiasm, and headaches; he hopes, despairs, economizes and advertises, as befits a soul that has just become aware of a pearl of great price. He suffers a good deal, and needs the right sort of tonic treatment. Just now, despite the advertising, he and I can't find any work for him to do. His beloved, by his own very honorable request, has gone to Europe to let him fight alone for awhile. He lives in a garret on sixpence a day, but can't earn it; and I don't like to see him warring with a certain invalidism, and with a rather adverse fortune at once.

It occurs to me now, first that you at sight would see enough of this man's heart to be a better counselor for him than I am. Secondly, it occurs to me that you may have, at your school, room to give him a chance to earn his living this summer—tutoring, hewing wood, drawing water,—anything would do, provided it didn't exceed his strength. Thirdly, I imagine that, amongst your company, he might, if acquainted, find some chance to learn of possible future employment. The plan then occurs to me to bring him to you, and perhaps pay his board for him for a week or a fortnight (if, as I suppose, he can't pay it himself), and then see if he proves to be one who can earn his way. How does the plan strike you? If the experiment fails, the cost, of course, is mine. Do you encourage the notion? I am very frank about him. You, of course, will be very frank in return as to whether there is any chance of an opening in the direction I mention.—

Yrs Very Truly
J. Royce.

All that I have said in characterizing my friend is, of course, said in the strictest confidence. He doesn't know how I have stated his case, although he knows that I write, & gives me liberty to say what I choose.

To Thomas Davidson, August 27, 1893[122]

Hotel New Netherland
New York.
Sunday, Aug. 27, 1893

Dear Davidson:—

I hope that you will not have misunderstood my long delay in writing. Cause enough I had and have to thank you, but the paper was to be prepared for the Congress, and another paper also had to be written,[123] and the two consumed more time than I should have

122 ALS. Davidson Papers. YUS.

123 Royce gave a paper to the Philosophical Congress in August on "The Two-fold Nature of Knowledge, Imitative and Reflective." He had previously delivered, through W. T. Harris, an address to the International Congress of Education (July 25–28) on "Can Psychology Be Founded Upon the Study of Consciousness Alone, or Is Physiology Needed for the Purpose?"—printed in *Addresses and Proceedings of the International Congress of Education of the World's Columbian Exposition* (New York: N. E. A., 1894), 687–92.

expected.—I am now here on my return from the Congress, and shall spend a day or two before going home.

The Congress, thanks to Foster's really remarkable energy and tact, went off admirably.[124] Seventeen papers, I believe, were read. Your paper and Harris's it fell to me to read, and into both of them,—especially into yours, which surely called for all possible enthusiasm,—I put whatever energy and grace, as a mere declaimer, I could; but surely your paper could not in this respect be added to. I had to read it offhand, without previous preparation; so I fear that the energy and grace were rather lessened than revealed. But I did my best.—We were very sorry, all of us, to hear of your illness, and I trust soon to hear that things go better with you.

I stayed with Foster, & enjoyed the family immensely. The friendship with his household is one of the many things that I have to thank you for.

My stay with you at the school was, as before, full of instruction and of profit. Even when you complain of being physically somewhat below par, the noble mind of you remains still; and it is a liberal education to be near you. I don't flatter, in any case, as you well know; but it may be in order to suggest once in a while how your friends prize you. I wish that I had more time to spend at the school. Give my affection to all my kind hearers, and believe me, despite this my traveller's haste

Yours Lovingly
Josiah Royce

Please write soon to me at Cambridge to let me know how you are.

[124] R. M. Foster, M.D., was Chairman for the Committee of Arrangements, The World's Congress Auxiliary, World's Columbian Exposition. Royce's enthusiasm for the success of the Congress was not universal; for a contrasting, partly ironic report, see L. Hannum, "Notes," *Philosophical Review* 2 (1893): 752.

To Charles Sanders Peirce, December 27, 1893[125]

Hotel New Netherland
New York.
Dec. 27, 1893

My Dear Peirce:—

I have received your letter, enclosing the prospectus of your proposed philosophical publication.[126] As you know, I have long wished to see the task of whose first results you have already given some very important though still, as I know, but fragmentary indications, put into adequate and permanent form. What has so far appeared has been so novel, so stimulating, so profound in many of its general conceptions, so ingenious in its combinations, that I only express my natural appreciation of your genius when I say that I deeply desire to see the finished product, and I am sure that the enterprise deserves the support of every lover of philosophic progress in this country.

As you know, in saying this, I do not mean to express either in advance, or as to what has already appeared, any unqualified agreement. You know that you and I have more than once found ourselves in disagreement, and has always taken a certain natural delight in expressing our disagreements. Where I can I want to learn from you; and I have very much to learn in this as in all other ways. Where I don't agree, I shall always know that you want the clearest expression of disagreement. The cheerful conflicts of philosophical students will doubtless long endure, and will be enjoyed. I shall doubtless have my chance to share them with you. But disagreement, where it exists, is perfectly compatible with the admiration that I feel for you; and, meanwhile, I am also well aware of many points of agreement between us, which I much prize.

[125] ALS. Peirce Papers. HL.

[126] Peirce had circulated a prospectus for a proposed twelve-volume work, *The Principles of Philosophy; or, Logic, Physics, and Psychics, Considered as a Unity, in Light of the Nineteenth Century*. This work and an edition of Petrus Peregrinus' *On the Loadstone* were to be sold by subscription, but because of an insufficiency of subscribers, the enterprise failed and neither work was published. See Max H. Fisch and Jackson I. Cope, "Peirce at the Johns Hopkins University," *Studies in the Philosophy of Charles Sanders Peirce*, ed. Philip P. Wiener and Frederic H. Young (Cambridge: Harvard University Press, 1952), p. 310.

If my earnest expression of a wish that you should find ample subscribers for your enterprise can induce anybody to join your band, I shall be glad to have you use my letter, informal and hasty though it is, at your pleasure.

Please also count me amongst your subscribers for the whole series announced in your circular.—

Yours Very Truly
Josiah Royce.

To Thomas Davidson, March 19, 1894[127]

Cambridge, Mass.
March 19, 1894.

My Dear Davidson:—

I have enjoyed immensely your letter, one of the rare sort that one so seldom gets in the modern world. Comment or direct answer there can be none, unless, *per impossible*, I "had a mind" to write as good an one myself.

But what I now have to write is this. In a hasty moment, the other day, because I am fond of you, and because of past good times in the Mts., I gave a general promise to come up to Keene to talk this summer. But now really, when I look over all that I shall have to do in preparation for next year's work, and take into account my actual prior obligation for the summer, I see that it was a sin to make this promise. Every summer so far I have got tied up in promises, and have been obliged to neglect something. You have not made your Announcements yet. So it is not too late to withdraw for *this* season. Only, this I can promise:—In 1895 my new course of lectures on Metaphysics will be worked out, and then, not well before, I can present a selection to your school (*unless*, indeed, I were to go abroad that summer,—a possibility which I don't expect, but must reserve from the promise).

Please forgive me, and let me withdraw. It is really important. There is so much to do, and I had not time to count up at the moment that you asked.—

Yours Very Truly
Josiah Royce.

[127] ALS. Davidson Papers. YUS.

To William Torrey Harris, April 15, 1894[128]

103 Irving St.
Cambridge, Mass.
April 15, 1894.

Dear Dr. Harris:—

Your kind offer, in your letter of April 13, to assign to me a place for a report on the "Relation of Hypnotic Suggestion to the Process of Learning," at the meeting of the National Council of Education, July 9, is at hand, and I find myself much attracted by the proposed task.[129] But I confess that, if you will permit me to make a suggestion, the topic as proposed could be a little altered in such a manner as to make a discussion of it still more profitable, in case my opinion is not at fault. The analogy between hypnotic suggestion and the process of learning is doubtless, as I tried to point out in the lecture to which you refer, a real analogy. But I suspect that a discussion limited in form to this analogy, would be likely to prove to many rather vague. The real point of the analogy would be brought out better if one made the topic: "The Psychology of the Imitative Functions in Childhood as related to the Process of Learning." If this topic could be the one chosen, I should be willing to take part, and should then be able to call attention to certain lines of "child study" that, as I think, can be profitably pursued in this connection. I might refer to the matter of the hypnotic analogy; but I confess that I do not want to discuss any topic in public on such an occasion if the *name* hypnotism is made too prominent in the title. The thing is interesting; the name is a little sensational in seeming. Besides "Imitation" names the really interesting topic.—Do you assent to such a change?—

Yrs. Truly
J. Royce

[128] ALS. Harris Papers. USC. Printed in "Josiah Royce's Letters to William Torrey Harris," *Philosophical Forum* 13 (1955): 85–86; reprinted in Robinson, *Royce and Hocking*, pp. 135–36.

[129] Royce's interest in pedagogy ran particularly high in 1893 and 1894. He made his remarks on the function of imitation in learning to a round-table discussion of the N. C. E. as indicated. His paper was not published nor is it preserved in the Royce Papers, HUA.

To William Torrey Harris, April 20, 1894[130]

103 Irving St.
Cambridge, Mass.
April 20, 1894.

Dear Dr. Harris:—

I will consent to read a paper, in response to the report of the committee, on the Psychology of the Imitative Functions in its relation to the process of learning, on July 9, the day that you choose from amongst the days in question. Only I shall need, I presume, ample notice of the contents of the Committee's report, as I shall prefer to prepare and read a paper, and do not want to leave my remarks to the chances of *extempore* speech. I assume then that I shall get such notice in due time.

Yours Very Truly
Josiah Royce.

To William Torrey Harris, May 13, 1894[131]

103 Irving St.
Cambridge, Mass.
May 13, 1894.

Dear Dr. Harris:—

I thank you for your kind encouragement. I will read at the Nat'l Educational Assoc'n when and how you want. But just now it is *facts* that I need, and I beg that, so far as there is the least chance, I may have the advice of your Bureau as to where and how to collect such facts—facts on all possible forms of imitativeness & of its apparent opposites when these exist. Can you suggest any further way to drum up facts?[132] Wide range of comparison helps,

[130] ALS. Harris Papers. USC. Published in "Royce's Letters to Harris," p. 86; reprinted in Robinson, *Royce and Hocking*, p. 136.

[131] ALS. Harris Papers. USC. Published in "Royce's Letters to Harris," p. 86; reprinted in Robinson, *Royce and Hocking*, pp. 136–37.

[132] Royce solved this problem through "The Imitative Functions, and Their Place in Human Nature," *Century Magazine* 48 (1894): 137–44, in which he invited his readers to send him autobiographical examples. Several of these are preserved in the Royce Papers, HUA.

in such matters, to correct the necessary defects of nonexpert observation. It is but a preliminary comparative survey of the field that I am now busy with.

Yours Very Truly
Josiah Royce.

To Richard Watson Gilder, June 4, 1894[133]

103 Irving St.
Cambridge, Mass.
June 4, 1894.

Dear Mr. Gilder:—

The actual replies so far received to my Imitation inquiry,[134] in so far as they contain genuine information, number, up to date, thirty-six. In a number of cases replies have led to further correspondence, which promises to be fruitful. As to quality, the communications interest me much. They are all good gossip, some of them of decided psychological value, most of them such as would be dear to mothers' & to teachers' hearts, several of them rather novel in type of incident narrated.

Are you disposed to give room for further publication? If so, what form would my next move take? Ought I to make a provisional report on the returns?[135] If so, how much space could my anecdotes fill? Some of them are rather jolly.

Your Very Truly
Josiah Royce.

[133] ALS. Century Collection. NYPL.

[134] See fn. 132 above.

[135] *Century Magazine* did not publish this, but Royce continued his research with an experimental study, under Münsterberg's guidance, the findings of which were presented in "Preliminary Report on Imitation," an address to the American Psychological Association (December 1894), published in *Psychological Review* 2 (1895): 217–35.

To Mary Gray Ward Dorr, August 1, 1894[136]

Cambridge
August 1, 1894

Dear Mrs. Dorr,

I have received your last kind letter, and in reply have to say that I now expect to reach you by the fast train on Monday, the 6th, reaching Bar Harbor at 5.40.

I shall bring with me some of my Ethical Lectures, and *if* you wish them, or any part of them, you shall have your pick of what I am to read to you. I shall also bring with me, as an alternative, a paper (my latest) on Meister Eckhart,[137] the first in order of time of the German Mystics, whose personal pupil was the well known Johann Tauler. I have prepared a pretty careful study of Eckhart, and I am not sure but you would prefer hearing about him to listening to any of my own poor ethics; for I don't criticize Eckhart, only portray, narrate, and, in a few passages, translate him, and he is a striking personage. In any case, I don't come wanting to read any more of anything than you wish to hear, and you shall have whatever fragments of me you want while I am about. For alas! after all, I am but fragments, much as I wish that I were whole.

With love and best greetings,

Yours very truly,
Josiah Royce.

To Mary Gray Ward Dorr, August 11, 1894[138]

Cambridge
August 11, 1894

Dear Mrs. Door,

I reached home, after a very long and refreshing sleep, in good time this morning. I am in every way better for the few delightful days at Oldfarm, where beauty of so many sorts, outer and inner,

[136] TLC. Royce Papers. HUA.
[137] Printed in *SGE*, pp. 261–97.
[138] TLC. Royce Papers. HUA.

combines to make one meditative, happy and free of soul. You cannot tell how much good you have done me, and I am sorry that it is so poor a return that I can make. I plan now, under the inspiration of your counsel, to make my study of Eckhart fuller and deeper, and to enlarge as well as improve my paper before I publish it, when, as I warmly hope, you will find it worthier of your kind interest than it has been in its present hastily wrought form.

I write just before going on to Plymouth.[139] Thank you again many times for the profit and pleasure of this visit. Give my affectionate greetings to George, and my thanks for all his care of me, too, and believe me

Yours very truly,
Josiah Royce.

To Thomas Davidson, September 17, 1894[140]

103 Irving St., Cambridge.
Sept. 17, 1894

Dear Davidson:—

I was sorry not to be able to come; but it was as I expected; the summer was very full of engagements. Next summer I will try, although I do not now venture to promise.

I have been thinking over my range of possible introductions to see what I could give you on your journey. But really,—whom do I know? I have not travelled abroad since I was a young student (1875–6). I have no closer personal friends amongst Europeans. I have a *very* slight correspondence acquaintance with two or three German colleagues. But these know nothing of me personally, and next to nothing professionally. It would be presumptuous for me to give *you* letters to them, when surely, through your already strong position abroad, you are certain to find the way to anybody you please through some personal friend of his. It isn't that I wouldn't gladly give you a letter to anybody, in heaven, earth, or elsewhere *if* you desired and I knew the person; but I am an utterly obscure

[139] Royce read his "Meister Eckhart" to the Plymouth School of Ethics in August 1894.

[140] ALS. Davidson Papers. YUS.

person, who knows nobody,—really nobody—outside of my native land, & few enough inside it. Forgive me for my obscurity. It isn't the worst of my faults, nor in itself especially an ill. Only I regret it at such a moment. For you indeed have given me many delightful hours, and I wish that I could render to you for them more than the warm thanks and hearty Godspeed on your journey which I send herewith.—Mrs. Royce joins me in these sentiments very ardently. Also my son Neddy.—

Yours Very Truly
Josiah Royce.

To George Holmes Howison, September 23, 1894[141]

103 Irving St., Cambridge.
Sept. 23, 1894

Dear Professor Howison:—

On my return from a final vacation trip I find your letter of the 13th awaiting me, and answer as well as I can on the spur of the moment.

I thank you and the Philosophical Union very warmly for your invitation, as kind as it is honorable.[142] To accept it, if possible, would be a positive duty, as well as a great delight. Nevertheless, as the matter now stands, I am impelled to ask you whether there cannot be made some change in the time for which you invite me. Were such a change possible, an acceptance of the call would not involve so serious a conflict of duties as would seem inevitable in case the time were the one that you mention.

The Commencement Season, especially of 1895, in California, would involve many attractions for me. I wish that the time were not so occupied here just then. But the middle of May, with us, is the most manifold time of year (if I may be allowed the expression) —the time when one drives the most horses abreast. One's courses are at a critical point. If they do not close right, no good comes of them. The Faculty as well as its Administrative boards (of one of

141 ALS. Private collection of Professor W. E. Schlaretzki, University of Maryland.

142 This and several succeeding letters to Howison are concerned with the arrangements for Royce's address to the University of California's Philosophical Union: "The Conception of God" (August 30, 1895).

which I am a member) is full of unfinished tasks. The Committee on "Aids to Graduates," of which I am also a member, holds all of its meetings in May, and its work involves a financial trust that cannot easily be delegated, as well as a vexatious job that one cannot easily ask a colleague to take off one's hands. In brief—to ask for leave in May is to ask for relief from duty at the moment when the ship is nearing port.

On the other hand, there are two possible alternatives as to time that I can suggest. The one that is the easier from my point of view will, I fear, not suit your plans. You end in May; you begin August. In August or in the first half of September, 1895, I could arrange to come to Berkeley very easily, and should feel very free as to time. But this, of course, would throw my coming over into another academic year, and would not harmonize with your plans for the coming year.

The other alternative would be the plan that I should come during our Mid Year Exam.'n period, at the beginning of February, '95. The precise dates I should have to arrange later. Now, as it chances, I have already made arrangements, which I think not wholly unchangeable, as to the disposition of a portion of this time. If however, you thought that period acceptable to you (and more so than the following August), then, if early notified, I could and would try to change the aforesaid previous arrangements, and to come to you then, although it is as yet impossible to promise anything, until I have heard again your pleasure, and have made my attempt to rearrange things.

As to your kind undertaking to discuss in the Philosophical Union, my book, please accept my thanks for the honor that you do that poor first effort at construction. You will indeed find much in it to criticize. It has more crudities of method than I for my part any longer care to count up. For I spend little time reading my own essays. And the doctrine involved has grown on my hands a good deal, and, I need hardly say, has undergone some not unimportant modifications. Yet as to the central theory of the book, so far as it there got any expression at all, I am indeed of the same mind. The mentioned growth is a growth upon the same basis; the modifications, if important, would relate to consequences and to secondary, even if very momentous, matters of doctrine. The kernel of the book would remain unchanged as to its essence. But it is above all the method of the book that I should never repeat—a method that has led and will lead to many unnecessary misunderstandings. The metaphysical theory, and the critical argument, of Chap. XI, still remain to me the real insight of the whole thing. I dislike it when readers attribute to me, as my own expressed and final view of things the transition stages of theory expounded in the chapters immediately preceding that one. As to the argument of Chap. XI itself, the only more or less serious criticisms that I ever saw of it were that of Paulhan in the *Rev. Philos.* (very brief), that of Renouvier in the *Critique Philos.* (in 1885 or 6), and the recent one by my own pupil and colleague, D. S. Miller, in the *Philos. Review* (Schurman's). James sketched it very well in his notice of the book in the *Atlantic*, but he didn't criticize it.[143] On the whole I care more for the line of thought there indicated (i.e., in my Chap. XI), than for anything else that I have ever done, although I admit that unless very much developed, supplemented, and supported by the treatment of allied problems, this line of argument will never mean to others what it does to me. This fact the aforesaid criticisms plainly enough show.

In the ethical section of the book it is again the method that is misleading, and that I should never repeat. The ethical doctrine I now hold in decidedly modified and supplemented form.—In brief, then, I should, throughout the book, restate my case today in a wholly new way: and I should say very much that my book left unsaid. In the light of what I should add, many would find my doctrine looking very different. The Thought-category would be still emphasized; but I should also lay stress on another element of reality, viz. the element that Fichte called *Leben*. The "world of the powers" I should indeed respect no more than of old; but the interpretation of the Absolute would be more obviously teleological than, to many readers, it seemed then.—But enough, I will not weary you with my confession. I feel very free of the book. Why does one write except to free himself from the bondage of a given form? But you are very good to give my work attention, and I shall be glad to hear from you as you go on.—

Yours Very Truly
Josiah Royce.

[143] François Paulhan, *Revue Philosophique* 20 (1885): 283–96; Charles Renouvier, "Josiah Royce: le panthéism idéaliste," *La Critique Philosophique* 4 (1888): 4–24, 85–120; Dickinson Sergeant Miller, "The Meaning of Truth and Error," *Philosophical Review* 2 (1893): 408–25; William James, *Atlantic Monthly* 55 (1885): 840–43.

To [Nicholas Paine?] Gilman, October 1, 1894[144]

Cambridge.
Oct. 1, 94.

Dear Mr. Gilman:—

My position as to the Eckhart paper is embarrassing. I lent it to a friend,[145] who is innocently keeping it in some mystic recess, unconscious of my pain, while I fear to break the sacred stillness of my friend's devotions by an impatient word. Finite things go in, but they don't easily get out, in these mystic regions—very awkward you see, for me. I fear that I shall have to go over until a later number; but one reckons not by quarter years where that essay has gone to dwell. Editorial and eternal concerns ought by right to be kept strictly in separate universes, and not mixed up, in this confusing way, in one universe. But if I ever can, I will send in the paper.

Yours Very Truly
Josiah Royce.

To George Holmes Howison, October 10, 1894[146]

103 Irving St.
Cambridge, Mass.
Oct. 10, 1894.

Dear Professor Howison:—

I gave a good two days to the consideration of your highly attractive request, in its renewed presentation. The telegram sent this morning represented simply academic necessities. To go at the

144 ALS. Bryn Mawr College Library. Positive identification of the addressee has not been established, but since Nicholas Paine Gilman was an editor of both *New World* and *Literary World* and since Royce is known to have corresponded with him, it seems likely that the letter was written to him and that Royce had anticipated that this article on Eckhart would be printed in one of these periodicals.

145 Probably Mrs. Dorr.

146 ALS. Private collection of Professor W. E. Schlaretzki, University of Maryland.

time that you most wished would involve an abandonment of tasks here, in May of next year, that I simply ought not to abandon, and must not. Prof. Palmer regarded the plan of your letter with strong sympathy, and was anxious to have me accept if possible. But neither he nor I could devise the how. The President viewed the matter cordially, and would, I am sure, have done whatever is fairly possible to arrange the case had any plan been feasible. But work is work. I have accepted tasks for the year which cannot be passed over to others at that moment without both unfairness to colleagues, and interference with their obligations. Nor can *every* part of any teacher's tasks and obligations be by any possibility transferred at all. Enough—I should do mischief if I tried to escape in May, and that cannot be. The visit, as you see, could hardly consume less than three weeks; for once in California, I should be bound to many friendly and pleasant ties, and should have to see more persons than those who have kindly invited me. So then, to my great regret, the chance of a Commencement visit is past. Please thank all who have, as you suggest, so kindly planned a welcome for me which I do indeed very little deserve.

But now as to the August visit.—Time will then of course give me a decidedly loose rein. I can stay surely some days at Berkeley, and I may venture to say frankly that I want to be prepared to do whatever I can to earn my welcome. As for the address mentioned for Aug. 30, that, as I understand, is to be a public and so a popular sort of discussion relating to philosophical Theism. Now as you well know, comparatively meagre is the serious philosophizing that can occur in the course of one such public lecture, delivered as a mere fragment, to an audience only in part composed of prepared hearers. I shall be glad to try the address in question, but since once for all your Union is on the spot, and consists of hearers who *are* prepared,—why may I not serve you if I offer, in addition, from one to three rather more serious lectures or papers, or what not, to be read, as chance may permit, to the Union, or to any members of it who have leisure and pleasure to hear; and to be read more in private,—perhaps with discussions by your members? If my poor book has by that time proved of any real service, during your winter's dissection of it, surely those who have gone over it will be more or less ready (some of them) to find how *I* might now be ready to supplement, or to correct, the impressions that they have gained from it. This I could do, in a measure, in from one to three papers of a more technical sort, which the general public would hear (should I try such a style in the public address) only with great weariness, but which your members, after a winter spent so benevolently in learning my ways, might possibly tolerate. After all, I confess that I am fairly tired of being so little *but* a grinder out of lectures in popular form. I long to meet at closer quarters students who like serious business. The general public is good,—very good,—but alas one tires of the long distances that part lecturer and hearer on public occasions.

How would such an offer serve you? Mind, I don't insist. I only want to offer freely what I can. My plan would be to bring in my pocket one address for the public,—and the said papers also for your Union. But perhaps there will be no chance to meet your members for philosophical work except on the public occasion. If this be true I must then give up what I should probably think the pleasantest part of my task, in case it were a possible part.

At all events, please let me know as well as you can what sort of a public audience is likely to gather for the desired Address, and what aspect of the general topic, as well as what fashion of treatment seems most likely to be serviceable to your purpose.

With warm greetings to the Union, and to all my friends, I remain,

Very Truly Yours,
Josiah Royce.

To Horace Elisha Scudder, February 17, 1895[147]

103 Irving St.
Cambridge, Mass.
Feb. 17, 1895.

Dear Mr. Scudder:—

Knowing you as I do, I don't believe that I can do better than to enclose this very frank letter, written for my eye only, but containing nothing, I think, that you will not gain by seeing, and the writer by having it seen (excuse my English), in case you decide to consider the matter.

Miss Coolbrith, of California, whom you once met at my house,

[147] ALS. Houghton Mifflin Papers. HL.

years ago, now wants to print, or rather reprint, her poems.[148] She seems to have financial backing for the undertaking—an essential fact, as I suppose, in any consideration of the case. She is a very noble woman, with a good deal of the artist about her temperament,—but heavily burdened by a hard world, and an oversensitive conscience, which led her to undertake overwhelming practical cares when she ought to have been growing in a literary way. California always gave her a devoted band of literary admirers. I don't think her a great genius; but I wish that she could get a hearing in the East, as she wishes.

Please return the letter, sometime. Meanwhile, I have the volume referred to in my possession, and can let you see it if you choose to consider the matter further.

Yours Truly
Josiah Royce.

To George Bucknam Dorr, February 26, 1895[149]

Cambridge
February 26, 1895

My Dear Dorr:—

I cannot thank you enough for thinking so kindly of me, and for making the offer as to the course in brain embryology. Were there the least chance of my finding the time, I should jump with joy. But alas! nobody gives the poor professor in term time his five, or three, or even two free hours a day for a new enterprise; and, as for the short vacation, that is already set apart for four lectures to teachers in New York, and for the necessary time lost in coming and going.

I envy you then the leisure, as I thank you for the friendship of your offer; but it is a physical impossibility for me to undertake the attractive programme. Were it only the long vacation—but I forbear wishes. Were wishes wits, I should have acquired some wisdom by this time.

148 Ina Donna Coolbrith, *Songs from the Golden Gate* (Boston: Houghton Mifflin and Co., 1895).

149 ALS. Royce Papers. HUA.

Please give my love to your mother; and to me your forgiveness for my share in the football catastrophe!

Years Heartily,
Josiah Royce.

To Charles William Eliot, March 11, 1895[150]

Cambridge.
March 11, 1895.

Dear President Eliot:—

There will reach you, I suppose, with this letter, the statement by James of his views as to the advisability of asking Charles Peirce to give the course in "The Philosophy of Nature," or "Cosmology," next year. I want to express my concurrence in James's wish.

We are going to be heavily crippled next year, by Münsterberg's departure, and by Palmer's absence. Our present plans for next year's work involve the carrying, by James, Santayana, and myself (with the possible addition of one Laboratory man as an instructor in laboratory psychology), of all the present elementary and advanced undergraduate work, with the exception of Santayana's Aesthetics, which must fall out, and James's Cosmology (a fairly large and very important course). The Graduate work gives us some trouble, in view of the importance of Palmer's Ethical Seminary. But as to that we have still to get aid from the Corporation, and we have thought, with Palmer's cordial assent, of applying to the Corporation for leave to ask Ladd to come on once a week from Yale, to give that Graduate Seminary only. Ladd will do this if we are allowed to ask him. By Palmer's absence we save, I assume, $2250. Allowing, in case the Corporation consents to an arrangement with Ladd, $1000 for that, and say $500 for the necessary Laboratory man's expenses, we should still have $750 to spend on providing a substitute for the Cosmology course, without increasing the expenses of the Department. I speak of course in an entirely hypothetical way,—none of the foregoing plans having anything but some consultations of the Department behind them.

The Cosmology course is, as said, very important. It would be

150 ALS. Eliot Papers. HUA.

impossible for me to undertake it next year.[151] The Department wishes Santayana to take Palmer's Ethics. We need, then, outside aid for the Cosmology. Now Charles Peirce, of whose practical availability I to be sure have no complete judgment, is known to me as a man of extraordinary mark in just that line of learning and research. There is just now no person at all available in this country who could compare with him (after James) in freshness of views, and breadth of information, about just the questions studied in that particular course. This he has already shown by published work.

As against this, I learn, or have heard from time to time, that Peirce is a hard man to get on with, and that he is not a successful teacher of elementary students. I don't feel afraid as to the former point. As to the latter, I am disposed to think that in his most chosen field of work, and in one course of lectures, he might prove more successful than he could do as a general teacher. Besides, the importance of his present views would be worth some pedagogical sacrifices. I also understand that many who have known Peirce more closely and personally than I do, express various practical objections to his presence here which I cannot in the least judge, but which you doubtless have fully in mind. I can only judge what I know, which is what I have just said, viz., that Charles Peirce is a man of extraordinary power in the particular field of the Cosmology Course. Accordingly I cordially recommend that he be appointed as James recommends. As he is out of work just now, I fancy that he would not be hard to get for any moderate compensation, so far as concerns the one course. If there are any reasons why this can't be done, they are such as I have never had occasion to know in my dealings with Peirce.

I beg you to pardon my troubling your vacation with this matter. I feel rather seriously the responsibility ahead of us for next year's work. But I hope that you and Mrs. Eliot have had a delightful time. Mrs. Royce joins me in wishing you both a successful time, and a happy return.

Yours Very Truly
Josiah Royce.

[151] With Harvard's refusal to appoint Peirce, however, Royce did teach the "Cosmology" course (Philosophy 3, Philosophy of Nature) during the academic year, 1895–96.

To Thomas Davidson, July 7, 1895[152]

103 Irving St.
Cambridge, Mass.
July 7, '95

Dear Davidson:—

On the 18th of June Mrs. Royce fell from her bicycle, owing to the slipping of the wheel on smooth stones and soft earth as she rounded a curve that was as familiar to her as her own parlor. Such is the fashion of accidents. She had not fallen for more than a year of very assiduous bicycling in all sorts of places. This fall occurred hardly fifty yards from our property, in broad daylight,—inexplicably. But the fall broke her left leg. Since then she has been on her back,—cheerful in the main, full of jokes, very courageous, but weak, and often in keen physical suffering. Medically speaking she is doing admirably. But the household, under my inefficient leadership, is like a dismantled ship. However, such as I am, I am needed here; and shall be until after the middle of August, at the very least. At the close of August I am due in California, to lecture to Howison's Philosophical Union.—You see that there is no chance of my coming to you.—I was sorry not to see you on your return from Europe; and still sorrier to hear of your ill health. I hope that you are now better. I deeply regret that I cannot come to the school.—

Yours Very Truly
Josiah Royce.

Mrs. Royce promises to recover, in the end, without any crippling, and completely. She sends her affectionate regards.

[152] ALS. Davidson Papers. YUS.

To James Mark Baldwin, July 9, 1895[153]

103 Irving Street,
Cambridge, Mass.
July 9, '95.

Dear Prof. Baldwin,

You may indeed be thinking me a worthless being, and so perhaps I am. But I have had to contend with a long siege of illness in my household. On June 18, just as my college work was completed and I was free, as I hoped, to pass over to the long-needed undertakings which included the revision of the article on "Self-consciousness"[154] and the preparation of the book-reviews—Mrs. Royce met with a bad bicycle accident. She fell, namely, from the bicycle as it sloughed in rounding a curve, and her leg was broken some inches above the ankle—both bones. She was quite expert and was doing nothing out of the common when the unaccountable slip came. Since then, the house has been full of care, which has included some illness on the part of the children, much alteration of the domestic service and the constant call on my own very inefficient powers as manager and general steward. Nurses, doctors, and the rest of the crew have passed in procession through the house, and as for me, in view of the natural capriciousness of domestic service at such times, I have had to "keep a dog and do my own barking," wherever the details of the domestic service were concerned.

Now this is nothing for me to complain of, on my own account. My poor wife has to bear the real trouble, and she does so with admirable cheerfulness and courage, and is doing well. The accident was an absolutely unpreventable one, and athletic accidents are always honorable mishaps, flavored with a certain glory. Only—one can't lose sleep o'nights, and watch closely all day, and do one's psychological duties too. Moreover, there had been illness in the

[153] Printed letter, original unknown. James Mark Baldwin, *Between Two Wars, 1861–1921: Being Memories, Opinions and Letters Received* (Boston: Stratford Co., 1926), 2: 232–33.

[154] "Some Observations on the Anomalies of Self-Consciousness," *Psychological Review* 2 (1895): 433–57, 574–84. Reprinted in *SGE*, pp. 169–97.

house before this particular trouble, and the whole thing had proved pretty distracting. However, we now see light ahead and seem to be coming out very well.

At the moment then I can only send you my paper unrevised. If it is not *too* bad, print it at your pleasure. I shall be here till at least August 15. Send proofs accordingly.

I did not write to express my sympathy for your personal affliction when I heard of it. I always feel how vain are mere words. I felt for you; and now feeling as I do how hopelessly inefficient, for professional duties, my present cares are just now making me, I feel also a great reverence for the unflagging way in which you seem to do all your work, despite your often delicate health and your various personal troubles. You are a marvel of true energy. But I am—what I am—a very useless sort of dabbler.

Yours very truly,
Josiah Royce.

To George Holmes Howison, July 30, 1895[155]

103 Irving St.
Cambridge, Mass.
July 30, 1895.

Dear Prof. Howison:—

I ought to have acknowledge sooner the receipt of your letter enclosing the kind remittance of $\$250\frac{00}{100}$ for the expenses of my coming trip to California. But for the last six weeks I have been pretty busy looking out for my household. Mrs. Royce on June 18, fell from her bicycle and broke her leg,—a pretty severe fracture of both bones a few inches above the left ankle. She has been recovering slowly, is doing well now, and will doubtless be recovered enough to permit me to go by the middle of August. But the superintendence of my house and children, at such a time, has left me little leisure for correspondence.

The remittance will of course be likely to cover all ordinary expenses. Miss Head has asked me to stay at her school during my

[155] ALS. Private collection of Professor W. E. Schlaretzki, University of Maryland.

visit,[156] and unless you have some other arrangement of an imperative sort for me, I am likely to do so. I expect to reach Berkeley at latest by Thursday the 29th of August. On the 30th, as I understand, I am to address the Union. I shall entitle my paper "The Conception of God." I should prefer "The Idea of God" if Fiske had not already a mortgage on that title. The three promised supplementary talks would fall at your pleasure at any time before the end of the following week, i.e. on any dates up to Sept. 7, inclusive. I plan to read three papers:—

1. On the Conception of Will as applied to the Absolute.
2. On Some Aspects of the Empirical Psychology of Self-Consciousness.
3. Considerations on the Metaphysics of the Individual Self-Consciousness (with a few hints as to the possibility of immortality).[157]

The three papers would not form exactly any sort of series, other than an accidental one; but they would contain discussions supplementary to those in my book. The second paper—altogether an empirical study,—would be necessary, I fancy, as a preliminary to make comprehensible my position in the third paper,—the second paper containing the empirical material of which the third paper would suggest a reflectively philosophical study. I hope that these fragments,—more or less hot from the oven, would be better for your purpose than any pawing over of such bits of cold victuals as your Union will have left after devouring my book, would be. In brief, I am to try not so much to defend as to supplement my book. So the thing now lies in my mind; although I am not sure whether my present statement precisely fulfils what I before led you to expect. I hope that it does.

I need not say how much I thank you for this chance. It will prove my only vacation—the affair aforesaid having engaged all my sympathies and energies so far since the lectures closed. I anticipate a good time, and shall try to earn my board.

[156] Anna Head, Royce's sister-in-law.

[157] Royce addressed the Philosophical Union on these topics on September 2, 4, and 6, 1895. It appears that the first paper became Part II of the Supplementary Essay, *CG* (1897), and that the second and third papers were versions of "Some Observations on the Anomalies of Self-Consciousness," *Psychological Review* 2 (1895): 433–57, 574–84; and "Self-Consciousness, Social Consciousness, and Nature," *Philosophical Review* 4 (1895): 465–85, 577–602. Both were reprinted in *SGE*, pp. 169–97, 198–248.

I shall have to make my visit a little short, as it will be unwise to leave my family very long.

Yours Very Truly
Josiah Royce.

Address me here until Aug. 17, in case you need to telegraph me for any cause before I set out. I shall stop once or twice on the way out, taking some ten or twelve days for the trip.

To George Holmes Howison, August 13, [1895?][158]

Cambridge, Aug. 13.

Dear Howison:—

I shall try to come to hand all right, and *may* be able to reach you Wednesday the 28th. I will at all events telegraph a day in advance. I shall stay at Miss Head's, unless she should for any reason be unable to receive me. At last accounts she was as able as she was kindly willing; but I have nowadays a great respect for accidents. I thank you however for your very kind offer, as well as for the generous provision for my expenses. Please thank Mrs. Howison for her kind invitation, both to your house in case Miss Head could not take me in, and to the dinner, whose date, when I learn it, I shall reserve. My programme I leave wholly in your hands and in Miss Head's. I am much touched by your kind words, and by the friendship of your Union's members. I can only hope that I shall not prove too disappointing and unworthy of your goodness. The visit will be a great treat to me.

Yours Very Truly
Josiah Royce.

[158] ALS. Private collection of Professor W. E. Schlaretzki, University of Maryland.

To George Holmes Howison, October 2, 1895[159]

Cambridge, Mass.
Oct. 2, 1895.

Dear Professor Howison:—

My return here has meant, after the brief rest of my journey, an immediate plunge deep into very complicated tasks. Please forgive, therefore, my seeming neglect in failing to write to you at once on my return. I don't know how to thank you and the Union adequately for the hospitality and the undeserved honor of my so delightful visit to you, as you planned and so successfully carried out its various events. I brought you professional work, which it is mere business to produce; you gave me in return a hearty kindliness that nothing can buy, and that I can never repay. Please assure the Union that as I can never forget, so I shall never cease to prize its thoughtful care and unexampled generosity of welcome. For your own personal labors, so self-effacing and so manifold, on my behalf, I owe you a life-long gratitude. Please let me know, at any time, what I can do, if anything, for you and for the Union.

Mrs. Royce is progressing slowly, but on the whole satisfactorily, towards recovery of strength. Please remember me most cordially to Mrs. Howison.

Yours Very Truly
Josiah Royce.

To George Holmes Howison, December 1, 1895[160]

103 Irving St.
Cambridge.
Dec. 1, 1895.

Dear Howison:—

I ought to have acknowledged sooner the copies of the pamphlet so kindly sent.[161] I feel as if I ought to pay for them somehow.

[159] ALS. Private collection of Professor W. E. Schlaretzki, University of Maryland.

[160] ALS. Howison Papers. UCB.

[161] *CG* (1895).

They mean a new debt to the Union. Perhaps, unless you will send me a bill for my share of the expense, I shall be able, in some future movement, to do your Union some service by way of the much needed return. Otherwise I remain all too deeply indebted.

Your own paper is very interesting—tantalizing of course in so far as you break off just when the real point was about to be stated, and the real proof about to be advanced—tantalizing, but profoundly interesting. Why don't you put this multipersonalitarianism once for all into its final argumentative rights by a complete and technical statement? That would be one of the most fascinating books of the century, for us who love dialectics, as well as truth. I doubt not that that point of view ought to get its fullest hearing. Why do you forever put us off with fragments? Still, I am thankful even for the fragments.

I can't see far ahead or behind just now, in this whirl of daily business. So forgive me for my haste as for my delay. Remember me cordially to Mrs. Howison.

Yours Affectionately
Josiah Royce.

To Gertrude Stein, March 27, 1896[162]

103 Irving St.
March 27, '96

Dear Miss Stein:—

Tuesday is my Seminary evening, and I can therefore give no Tuesday evening before the Examination period. I shall be glad, however, to read to the Philosophy Club of Radcliffe any Thursday evening in May, at 8 o'clock. Please make your own choice, if Thursday is a possible evening. Some Fridays would also be possible, but I am not so clear about them.

As to the subject,—I read to the Boston Browning Club, the other day, a paper on "Browning's Theism."[163] I also am preparing a pa-

[162] ALS. Stein Papers. YUB. Printed in *The Flowers of Friendship: Letters Written to Gertrude Stein*, ed. Donald Gallup (New York: Alfred A. Knopf, 1953), pp. 6–7.

[163] "Browning's Theism," *The Boston Browning Society Papers, 1886–1897* (New York: Macmillan Co., 1897), pp. 7—34.

per, to be read soon at Princeton, on "The Principle of Individuation."[164] The latter is a more technical paper, but is still adapted to a pretty general, if philosophically studious, company, on the problem, "What do we mean when we call any object an Individual?" or "What constitutes Individuality?" This problem is a pretty one, and is of practical interest to people who desire to call their souls their own.

Which one of these papers would you like? I am half disposed to offer you both, in case, upon different evenings, or for different purposes, they could be of any service to your Club, in whose fortunes I always feel a strong interest.

Yours Very Truly
Josiah Royce.

To Mary Whiton Calkins, N. D. [Spring 1896?][165]

103 Irving St.
Cambridge, Mass.

Dear Miss Calkins:—

I am sorry that I have never printed anything on the general notion. But your notes of my lecture touched upon only the elements of the theory.[166] There is very much more to it than what you got.

You have got the notion of the theory so far as it concerns elementary "appreciative" general concepts. But most general concepts, and particularly the higher ones, are the correspondents of more or less "imitative" reactions, that is, of reactions which have to do with expressing how the object is made, or picked out by the observer, or related to others in the external world,—such expression involving the imitative remaking of the object's structure, or of the process of finding it, or of its observed relations. Such ideas are "descriptive" general ideas. Their nature is best indicated

[164] The substance of this paper became Part III of "The Absolute and the Individual," *CG* (1897).

[165] ALS. WCL. The date cannot be fixed precisely, but internal evidence (reference to Miss Calkins's monograph [1896] and Royce's course in Advanced Logic, begun in the fall of 1896) makes the spring of 1896 the most likely date.

[166] It is not clear to which lecture Royce is referring—perhaps "The Principle of Individuation." See fn. 164 above.

in the gesture-language, where contour and color are imitatively defined, I believe, by acts that sufficiently differentiate the two processes of seeing the spread out surface, and of following with the eyes the contour.

No two distinguished classes of objects have the same "value" for the attention. But this value need not be the value as agreeable or disagreeable. It may be value for knowledge. The objects of any class A are felt to differ from objects of another class B by having a different structure, constitution, behaviour, or system of relationships. This is always the case unless class A and class B are mere classes of simple "appreciation." But if class A and class B are distinguished by structure, behaviour, or relationships of their typical objects, then such facts can be represented in consciousness only by a more or less nascent or explicit, truncated or developed, process whereby such structure, behaviour or relationships are imitated (as, in making a diagram, statistical curve, or gesture of pointing, not the qualities but the relationships or constitution of certain objects are constructively imitated).

The ordinary theory supposes an image, apart from its "value," i.e. apart from its significance as a signal for appreciative or descriptive conscious processes, to be capable, by reason of its vague or composite character, of serving as a general idea. To this my own view, worked out independently of Münsterberg & of Baldwin, but in substantial agreement, I believe, with both, is a correction. Images are of course usually present in general ideas; but it is their value for the attention that counts, be they word-images or other pictures.

But, as you suggest, what common sense calls separate individuals as well as instances of classes may be responded to by just such reactions, whether descriptive or imitative on the one hand, or appreciative on the other. Of course. But as I suppose you to recognize already, we have no completed ideas of *mere* individuals as such. We have only more or less precise general ideas. Of a really complete individual we know only as the goal of scientific knowledge. The concept of an individual in the full sense is a limiting concept, not corresponding to any fact of our conscious experience. We begin with vague appreciative general ideas, "nice," "nasty," "pretty," "moo-cow," "papa" &c. We pass to more and more definite descriptive ideas of form, number, place, of processes, structures, &c. &c. Our goal is the envisagement of the one real individual, viz., the whole universe. The so-called "individual" of logical analysis, is an object corresponding to an extremely general idea, based upon an abstraction of the usually pretty conventional structure, relationships &c. (form, size, coherency of parts, endurance, mobility, &c), whereby what is called an individual of any given type chances to be distinguished from what is not an individual of that type. No such individual can be a first object of knowledge, upon which generalizations are later based, simply because, until one has got control over general ideas of an elaborate type, no such individual can be known as such. The first ideas are vaguely universal. The conventional individual is a later construction.

To be sure, there are numerous conscious ideas, of an appreciative, as well as of a descriptive type, which appear early in life, & to which there actually correspond, in the physical world as viewed by other men, the objects called by developed thought, in the ordinary and conventional sense, individuals. Of these we have, very early, intensely interesting ideas:—e.g. an infant's mother, any interesting person known to the infant, a beloved toy,—or later one's home, room, books, body, &c. &c. are such individuals. But my point is that of every such individual, and of its individual *haeccitas*, we have, and can have, only an essentially general idea, to which, to be sure, only one object in the world of common sense chances to correspond, but which nothing *in consciousness*, or in the conscious value of the idea itself, prevents from being separately exemplified by thousands of individuals.

The true concept of what one means by an individual comes in sight only when one observes that while such general ideas as *dog*, *man*, *watch* would be satisfied not only by the presence of any object to which the description or appreciation involved in the idea applied, but also by any one object in an indefinite possible presented *collection* of dogs, men, or watches,—the idea of *my* dog, *my* friend (viz. *this* friend), or *my* watch, is on the other hand such that if two objects *at once* laid claim to be possessors of this *haeccitas*, there would be serious conscious trouble, (perplexity, terror, wonder) no matter how perfectly each object appeared to correspond to the idea in question. The child's consciousness contains not a primary idea of this individual, its mother, as this, nor an idea of this toy as this. Nor do I myself primarily know how even I myself am one individual to myself. One's primary ideas are implicitly general appreciations or descriptions which correspond either to the *haeccitas* of a common sense individual, or to the *essentia* of an exemplar of a class. Both sorts of ideas are however so far alike. But where one's idea refers to what is later called an individual, instead of to a class, the idea happens to be such as, for some reason which is not clear to consciousness, involves, in case of the presentation of two objects, the selection of which one of these is the one meant by the appreciation or description in question. Examples without number in perplexing double consciousness, in stories about the confusions over twins, & in other puzzles of mistaken identity.

Thus however the individual proves to be that whose essentially general idea (as present in me), does, for some occult reason (instinctively felt, unconsciously presupposed, but not defined in consciousness), exclude the co-presentation of any other representative of the class to which the individual belongs. How this implied exclusion of another case of the same class gets its basis in unconscious instincts, is another question. It does get such a basis, and the basis if unconscious, is still psychological, and is exemplified in the implicit exclusiveness of love, (two being company & three a crowd), of the homing sense, &c. &c. But the individual as such is thus never primarily known, but is always known secondarily, by virtue of this mysterious *exclusive attitude towards the other case*, if such case is presented as a *rival* of this one. The rival is the *not-this*, by contrast with which the individual as such gets indirectly presented to consciousness. Thus Israel had one God only by virtue of the "no other," while primarily the conception "god" had been a general concept. Just as polytheism precedes monotheism, so the abstraction, which might apply to any one of an indefinite multitude, precedes the knowledge of the individual as such, in every form of knowledge. The "no other" of the individual's nature comes to mind by virtue of exclusive but unconscious instinctive bases of feeling whereby any other case, viewed as a rival, gets rejected as impossible. These bases later get in science more explicit. They never become absolutely clear to us mortals.

But just for this reason none of us ever quite knows what constitutes the individual as just this unique individual, because the exclusion of the "other" is negative, and a product of considerations of which we are not fully conscious. Hence, I say, a true and *positive* knowledge of the individual is the goal, not the beginning of knowledge; and we have positive knowledge, in any grade, only of the universal, of the type, the general structure, the definable law of our objects.

But do you say: "The universal is the *identical* element in many"? And do you argue "These many must be many primary individuals"? Then I reply thus:—The universal, as the object of the appreciative or descriptive general idea, is, primarily, presented in what the psychologist, not the person whose experience this is, knows as this particular experience. Later experiences, or series of similar experiences, may and often do set, determine, define, what general aspect shall at any moment be presented as the interesting one, and responded to by appreciation or by imitation. This is the significance of the "many similar cases," which the ordinary theory unwisely supposes to be first presented *as* individuals, and later, by abstraction, generalized. The law of habit is the psychological, but not the conscious basis of our general ideas. The occurence of many similar cases brings us, by habit (i.e. by repeated physical impressions on sensitive nerve centres), to a point where we are so sensitively responsive that, at what the psychologist knows as this individual moment of the life of one of us—the person studied,—and in presence of what common sense calls this individual physical object, there springs into the mind studied a reaction, appreciative or imitative, which (1) will be later repeated whenever a sufficiently similar object (called by common sense, not yet by the mind studied an individual object) is presented, and (2) will serve to help the mind studied to hunt for other common sense individuals of the same character (i.e. apt to arouse this idea).—This idea is now known to the mind studied, not yet as an "identical element in many," but merely as an interest shaded thus and thus, by contrast with other interests, whenever it is present, and as an interest satisfied by present objects that are known, not yet as individuals, but, only as satisfying the interest even while they otherwise remain indefinitely various and unknown objects. Here you have the stage of primary general ideas, such as lower animals have. These ideas are general, but they are not yet known as general to anybody but the psychologist.

When the needs of carefully exact imitation, and of communication, become prominent, these primary ideas get to be themselves objects of consciousness, by contrast with one another and with the cases to which they refer. As they come in time to be presented as referring equally well to many presented objects that are *together* present (as when one compares objects, or sees many men at once), and as they are used when one hunts for objects that will satisfy them, although they do not predetermine *all* the characters of the objects that shall satisfy them (as when one turns over the leaves of a picture-book hunting for "man," and sees each time a new but satisfactory case), one thus gradually gets presented the fact of the contrast between the relative simplicity of the idea and the multiplicity of its examples, the relative unity of the idea, and the indefinite variety of the contents which may be present in objects that all the while satisfy it. And thus it is that the generality of the idea gets presented as such, i.e. as a relative identity in the midst of variety. Were not many cases of an idea presented at once, and were not these cases multitudinous in their other characters, one could not come to know the universal as such, any more than the individual. Yet the universal has the start as against its rival.

Imitative effort gradually sets the power of separating the idea of the universal (as the "way to do that," to draw that, to find that, to play that &c.), from its setting, and one now explicitly opposes it to the "anything that would be thus produced or imitated or found." The identical "thus" of the universal is not merely a mysterious one in many. But it is still more the presented imitative or appreciative "way of doing," or feeling of interest, as contrasted with the anything, the indefinite and dimly imaged mass of data that if present would exemplify the "thus" of the universal idea. Later stages of universality, including the development of the consciousness of the individual, have now been sufficiently suggested.

Infandum regina jubes renovare dolorem,[167] I might say, in thus passing over to you the desired tale of the universals, even in this unintelligibly brief summary. It is a long story, and one that I have long rather kept in the background. I mean to offer, however, a course in advanced Logic next year. I write in the midst of confused business of all sorts. Please excuse haste. I shall return the syllabi before long. I haven't yet seen your monograph,[168] but shall be glad to do so.

Yours Very Truly
Josiah Royce.

[167] Virgil *Aeneid*, bk. 2, line 3. Aeneas says this to Dido introducing his story of the Trojan War.

[168] *Association: An Essay Analytic and Experimental* (New York: Macmillan Co., 1896). A monograph supplement, no. 2, *Psychological Review*, February 1896.

To Frank Thilly, May 6, 1896[169]

May 6, 1896.

Professor Frank Thilly,

My Dear Sir:—

I have had to delay response to yours of April 24th.

As to your first question, I think myself ill described as an Hegelian, just as I think myself ill described as a Kantian, or a Spinozist, or a follower of Socrates. I have learned much from Hegel, as from the others mentioned. I make no doubt, however, that Hegel would have despised me, and I don't know why the term Hegelian should be applied to all those who, although Idealists, would have been called anti-Hegelians in the early 30's. Michelet well defines the term Hegelian in the old sense when he says, in his Autobiography, that in his youth the Hegelian school were conscious of being the only group of thinkers who had "a complete system of Categories" ready for application (as he explains) to all possible topics (I quote from memory only). Now I make very little of the series of the Hegelian Categories, and so very little of the system as such. Nor have I any system of categories to apply to all topics. I hold in entire contempt the "Philos. of Nature," and care nothing for the Hegelian technical Psychology (as such), nor anything for the characteristic technicalities of either the *Religionsphilosophie* or the *Rechtsphilosophie*, or the *Aesthetik*, or,—but why particularize? I have fully explained what I regard as the *positive* value of Hegel in my *Spirit of Mod. Phil.* I did not there write down what I have in the way of bones to pick with Hegel. Why should I? But if you think best to classify me as Hegelian, at all events call me Hegelian with some prefix, such as "Neo-," or "Pseudo-," or "Semi-," or "Hemi-," or "Pleistocene-," or something of the sort. I should describe the sort of Idealism that I hold as a sort of "post-Kantian, empirically modified, Idealism, somewhat influenced by Hegelian, but also not uninfluenced by Schopenhauerian motives, with a dash of Fichte added." But enough of that. I really mind this sort of classification very little, so long as one doesn't say that I was moulded by Green! I never could

[169] ALS. Thilly Papers. CUA.

bear to read Green with any continuity, and came by what ideas I have wholly without his aid,—however much alike, to some people, the views may seem. But I don't care to be thought any more original than I am, and of course I have picked up my ideas wherever I could.

I hope to get out the book of selections from the *Phänomenologie* within a year.

Thanks for your kind interest

Yours Very Truly
Josiah Royce.

To George Holmes Howison, August 31, 1896[170]

103 Irving Street
Cambridge
Aug. 31, 1896.

Dear Howison:—

Thanks for your kind letter. I am a little sorry to see my poor paper get into permanent form. I care very little for the mere chance to "reply," in the dialectical spirit, for really the antinomy between your view and mine is the most instructive element of the whole affair, and may stimulate more when left just thus than when fought to the always untidy "finish" of a human argument. My concern however, if you desire this continuance, would be: (1) To restate my central argument (the "Possibility of Error" sort of dialectics) at some length in a *technical* form, such as my paper, as it was, forbade; (2) To expound, in answer to you (if I must answer) my present definition of individuality,—a definition which might, after all, reconcile us. I have, just now, a startlingly "original" (let us say "American") theory of individuality, which I regret to be unable to publish "in time to influence the fall elections" (as Mulford wanted his book to be published).[171] But

[170] ALS. Howison Papers. UCB.

[171] Elisha Mulford, *The Nation: The Foundations of Civil Order and Political Life in the United States* (New York: Hurd and Houghton, 1870). Mulford, a retired minister who died in Cambridge in 1885, wrote his highly apocalyptic treatise to explain the meaning of the Civil War and the divine order of the State; though he hoped it would influence the elections, it made little impact on American ideology or political life.

this theory—an extension, in an unexpected form, of my views as stated in the minor papers of last year, could only be expounded at some length. As I say, it *might* reconcile us. The question is, How much space would you or the publisher give me for the "reply," which, if worth writing at all, would be a new philosophical paper, standing alone. I can't get back into a mere *form*, once abandoned. *That* affair, so far as my poor scribble went, is, for me, over. I can no longer take the literary tone of that evening. The delightful memory of my friends, of their greeting, of their hospitality, of their kindness, lasts forever. But my words,—I can't make any continued story of them. I can found a new paper on the discussion of that evening, as further reflection lights the matter to my mind. That is the best I can do. So then, would such a new essay, founded on the discussion of that evening, but free in form, serve your purpose,—its scope to be as indicated above? If so I can help you.

With kindest regards to Mrs. Howison I remain

Yours Very Truly
Josiah Royce.

To Mary Gray Ward Dorr, November 5, 1896[172]

November 5, 1896

Dear Mrs. Dorr,

On reading your kind letter, and in answer to your question as to what can be done about our dear LeContes, I feel moved to say, quite at my own risk, and on my own moving, that I believe that you and both the LeContes would prove such good companions that at least a brief meeting almost *ought* to take place. Furthermore, I believe that if you asked them, who are both of them born and trained nature-lovers, to come to your home for two or three days, whatever the weather, the leaflessness of the trees, or the nearness of winter, it would be a great pleasure to them, and, I hope, to you. They are both unique people; LeConte 74, yet full of life, thought and insight, a geologist, and yet much more than a geologist; his daughter, slight, eccentric—a lonely, yet on the whole, despite moods, sensitiveness and imperfect constitution, a happy nature—a not uninstructed lover of art, a thoughtful dreamer of

[172] TLC. Royce Papers. HUA.

airy visions, without poses, and unlike, in some respects, the other dreamers whom we see. They—the LeContes—adapt themselves easily to environment, have Southern, unworldly, but not unpleasing, ways, and both of them "keen," though in various ways, "to track suggestion to her inmost cell." They would please you; and they would be *so* pleased *with* you.

Now next week, beginning with Tuesday, they are free for some days from present engagements. LeConte is strong enough to travel. I don't venture to urge anything of course, but if you found it quite easy to propose to have them, they are among the very few people in the world whom I consider really worthy to meet you, even in the most unplanned way.

I write in haste.

Yours affectionately,
Josiah Royce.

To Mary Gray Ward Dorr, November 14, 1896[173]

Cambridge
November 14, 1896

Dear Mrs. Dorr,

I have heard from Miss LeConte in a letter written from Bar Harbor of your proposals as to the artistic publication of her book,[174] and of your advice to her to consult Mrs. Whitman. I am glad indeed of this advice from you, and take the opportunity to add a word as to the course that the affair has so far taken in my hands.

As you know, I agree with you that many things in the work of Miss LeConte are open to criticism. My only doubt was as to whether the oddities of style, etc., could possibly be altered, except here and there, by the author. My view was that this was simply the inevitable oddity of this person in this particular aspect of her nature; and literature is full of cases, to which all of us get used (e.g. Walt Whitman, Emily Dickinson, William Blake, Browning) where an author, who may be of higher or of lower degree, fre-

[173] TLC. Royce Papers. HUA.

[174] Caroline Eaton LeConte, *The Statue in the Air* (New York: Macmillan Co., 1897).

quently and persistently offends us by oddities that *we* feel unnecessary, but that are to him, as he writes just this or that word, simply necessary so that he cannot do otherwise than thus, while we have to accept or reject the work, as a whole, as he made it. Now it was my strong impression that, as a psychological fact, this woman, in this work, was just so forced to this manner and that no literary critic, however sympathetic, could noteworthily alter her little book without destroying it altogether. You agreed with me that it was worth saving, and our only question was as to the how.

Before acting I appealed to Horace Scudder for a judgment of just this question. He is certainly a literary expert, of great liberality and keenness, and of the most extended experience in remodelling and editing of every sort and condition possible. He came to the task quite impartially, and reported that he believed the oddities of style intrinsic, and saw no way to excise them, while he agreed with you that the book was worth saving. As Miss LeConte herself felt indisposed to further alteration, I thus saw no way but to go on.[175]

As to the artistic production of the book, I agree with you that the Riverside Press needs assistance in such matters. But my difficulty was that I knew nobody but Mrs. Whitman who could directly help there, while for an appeal to her, such as you so kindly let me make to you, there was no time before the LeContes, who returned from Europe earlier than I expected, should go South. I determined therefore to get the contract arranged at once, but I warmly welcome your present intervention at just this stage, so long as a more extended delay of the whole affair seems out of the question.

This by way of explanation. I thank you for your reception of the LeContes. I hope that they managed to show themselves on their deeper side, and that you and LeConte himself got together over the deeper interests of life. If so, I hope that you saw in them something of the interests that I know they found so vital in you.

Yours truly,
Josiah Royce.

[175] Negotiations with Houghton Mifflin were evidently unsuccessful; on July 1, 1897, Royce wrote to George P. Brett (a letter not included in this edition) to arrange for the publication of Miss LeConte's book with Macmillan.

To George Holmes Howison, December 15, 1896[176]

103 Irving St., Cambr.
Dec. 15, 1896.

Dear Howison:—

To assign my copyright, before sending the MS, i.e., before delivering part of the assigned goods, has seemed to me objectionable. But today I sent, by registered letter, the entire MS of my supplementary paper; and herewith I enclose the assignment.

Why the delay? Alas, you came in upon me, with your kind demand, at what proved to be the most distracted moment of my year. How hastily I promised, how foolishly I hoped to be prompt, you now know. Fate intervened at once. My term's work opened, my house unexpectedly filled with guests (LeConte & his daughter were two of them for ten days; but there were others before them); and everything rushed at me pell-mell, saying "Do this, don't forget that." I liked the guests, but I didn't like the jobs. I struggled, squirmed, lost some sleep, got a cold and a swollen jaw, lectured, did administrative work,—in short did whatever we indolent fellows here are accustomed to do,—all *but* finish my essay. Now you have it at last. I am now quite well again,—guestless, but not exactly at leisure.—You won't like the essay; it is too long, too unequal, too hasty, too unsound. But one thing is sure; I won't improve it; and I shall thank you immensely for this chance to print it.

You have doubtless been thinking ill of me, of late, but now that all is over, so far as I am concerned, please forgive & forget.—If you want to add some last words, I shall *not* object, but shall be pleased, and I release you from your promise on that score.

[176] AL. Private collection of Professor W. E. Schlaretzki, University of Maryland. This letter was sent with an enclosed, signed and notarized contract for the publication of *CG* (1897), providing Royce with a 5% royalty.

To Hugo Münsterberg, N. D. [January or February 1897?][177]

103 Irving St.
Cambridge, Mass.

Dear Münsterberg:—

I have written not at all, but I have thought of you often, and very warmly. Just now a little bird of the air, far flying, but trustworthy, warns me that you are talked of for a place in Europe, recently left vacant by the death of a man of mark, and that there is a possibility that you may be called, and may accept. My little bird knows little of your own state of mind; but the message, such as it is, moves me to say, on my own behalf, as well as on that of my colleagues, that *if* other temptations move you, you must remember that, over here, there are those (and I am one of them) who want you to return to us, not only in the interests of science, but in the interests of our own warm friendship for you, of the affectionate memory that we keep of you, and want to renew, and of the hearty greeting that we have ready for you if you will come back to us. I say this all the more earnestly because, as you see, I am a poor writer of letters, and want you to feel that when I do write, I do so because I feel personally a strong longing to have you come back to us, and join us. This longing I have not been disposed to urge, until now, because I wanted you to be free to work out your own choice, unteased by manifold repetitions of what we told you when we parted from you. But now I want you to know that if seas part, they don't make us forget. So remember us once more before you decide.

I write in great haste. Lectures with me, 16 hrs a week, in Harvard, Radcliffe, & elsewhere. Work very full. Laboratory fairly

[177] ALS. Münsterberg Papers. BPL. The MS is marked "[1897?]" in another hand; this date is consistent with the contents of the letter. Münsterberg had been appointed on a temporary basis for three years, from 1892 to 1895; at the end of this period he was offered a permanent professorship, but was granted leave for two years to think it over. He returned to Freiburg, and during the winter of 1896/97 he was negotiating with both Harvard and the University of Zurich. The latter negotiations broke down, and Münsterberg accepted the call to Harvard. See Margaret Münsterberg, *Hugo Münsterberg: His Life and Work* (New York: D. Appleton and Co., 1922), pp. 56–60.

prosperous, but in need of you. My family well. Mrs. Royce as good a bicyclist as ever. James busy with a Seminary on Kant. Faculty in frequent session. Weather very bad this autumn.—

Many greetings from Mrs. Royce and myself to Mrs. Münsterberg.—

Yours Affectionately,
Josiah Royce.

To Charles William Eliot, February 19, 1897[178]

103 Irving St.
Feb. 19, 1897.

Dear Dr. Eliot:—

I hear with great regret of your illness, and have no wish to trouble for a moment the enforced rest that it involves. But I know that you desire me to be as prompt as possible in reporting to you our view, in the Philosophical Dep't., as to our problem; and I therefore venture to send this statement, which has already been somewhat delayed by causes herein explained. I leave to you the judgment as to when the right moment comes for taking the matter up again. Of all men you have the best right to the comforts of intervals of rest. It is a pity indeed to have to risk any intrusion at a moment when your rest may well not be comfortable. May this come to your eye only when your present enemy has entirely left you in peace!

Palmer, James, and I have carefully conferred. We are in substantial agreement as to all the main points. The proposal of our colleague Münsterberg is somewhat perplexing.[179] We prize him as much as ever; we want him to come. But the question now is:

[178] ALS. Eliot Papers. HUA.

[179] After provisionally accepting the call to Harvard, Münsterberg had proposed that he come for the fall term only, compressing the entire year's work into a semester, and return to Germany in the spring. After conferring with Royce and others, President Eliot wrote to Münsterberg on March 3, 1897: "We have come to the unanimous conclusion that it is not in the interest of the University to accede to the precise proposal which your letter contains . . . ." The entire text of Eliot's letter is printed in Margaret Münsterberg, *Hugo Münsterberg: His Life and Work* (New York: D. Appleton and Co., 1922), pp. 58–59.

Does he really want to come permanently to us at all? His proposal strongly suggests that he still feels undecided, and desires, for another year, to keep matters open. We agreed, I think, that it is a pity to have any further uncertainty. Palmer and I feel perhaps more strongly on this point than James. I myself feel disposed earnestly to urge that we must ask M. to decide now at length, once for all, to come to us with the same permanence of purpose that binds any man to a professorship once accepted, or else to ask us to keep our affairs no longer in suspense. Of course no professor is bound forever to one place. All are free to resign, under known limitations as to giving notice. But that freedom is one thing. It is another thing to accept a place while still keeping one's heart and one's purposes largely elsewhere. I fear that that is what M. still feels forced to do. I don't complain of him for that. But is it wise for us to agree to accept further doubt and suspense? I cannot think so. We have waited long. We have suffered for our patience. Our students need permanent guidance. Our Department needs a permanent outlook. We cannot well go on without pretty definite assurances, unless we are willing to resign our place in the academic race. Moreover, there is something essentially disappointing about the spirit of a co-worker who, after two years of waiting, must ask for one more large indulgence. Will one who thus asks be able to be content with us at all? Whether he gets what he now asks or not, must not his feeling towards the work here, and towards his own sacrifices in changing his abode, always be liable to regret and to dissatisfaction? I speak for myself, and, I think, for Palmer, in saying that these seem to me to be grave considerations. James is willing, I understand, to make less of these aspects of the matter; but I am sure that he does not ignore them, or fail to regret them.

Apart from these general matters, we three are quite agreed as to the special matters mentioned in my memorandum indorsed on M's letter to you. The wording of this memorandum is accepted by all. We cannot agree to M's proposal as in itself acceptable. For advanced students it is just the second half year's laboratory work that is most valuable, and it is just then that, knowing well their Director and his ideas, they can gain most from personal intercourse with him. We should have to advertise our work, in our announcements, as limited, so far as M. is concerned, to the first half year. The impression of a half-hearted intercourse with us on his part would be strongly given. We should lose many good students, who would not be attracted by so poor an offer, and who would not like the prospect of spending half the year under unknown guidance. The crowding of his courses (say three half courses) into one half year, would disarrange our other courses. In brief, we are of opinion that the proposed arrangement is impracticable.

Thus we want M. to come, but we cannot sacrifice everything to secure even him, although our personal fondness for the man, and our hearty belief in his value as a colleague and as an investigator, are unchanged, and have been too often and too freely expressed to need further insistence here. Nobody can ask so many interests, however, to be sacrificed to his convenience as M. still finds it necessary to ask. We hope that he will not insist on his demand.

But, in thus deciding, we have not been unmindful of the very doubtful position that we should occupy as a Department should the Corporation agree with the foregoing expression of our opinion, should you decide to act on our advice as thus asked for and given, and should M. thereupon *not* withdraw his request, but, instead, decline to return to us. You are aware that Baldwin, of Princeton, has occurred to us as a possible man in case the negotiations with M. should fail. On discussing the case, we agree that, since James and I both know Baldwin quite intimately, are sure of his discretion, and have various confidential personal relations with him, it would be right privately to sound him, in a frankly unauthorized and confidential way, as to whether, in case negotiations with M. failed, and in case the Corporation should hereafter view the matter favorably, he could be induced to consider an opportunity to join his friends here. Baldwin has for years known, both from M. and from us, our various personal views of the various stages of our relation with M. Baldwin has taken a sympathetic interest in many interprises of ours, and understands our situation excellently. We felt that no harm could result from asking him a wholly hypothetical question. Accordingly, at the urgent request of both Palmer and James, I wrote to Baldwin that "a hitch" had occurred in the negotiations with M., and that "a concession" was asked for which we did not like to see granted. I explained no further the nature of the "hitch." I said that we hoped still to agree with M., and that in that case we all strongly desired to have M. with us. I said also that, should the negotiations fail, we three, Palmer, James, and I, agreed that Baldwin was the "one man whom we should first think of" as the man to suggest to the Corporation in place of the lost colleague. I said that, in advance of suggesting to the Corporation any course which might risk breaking off the negotiations with M., we felt it right to know whether we had any chance of our "one man" himself. I asked for a "provisional" answer; fully explained the "unofficial and unauthorized" character of my letter; asked Baldwin to telegraph "No" if he felt unwilling to consider the matter at all, but to write promptly what provisional answer he could give if he felt favorably disposed; and insisted upon the personal and confidential nature of the whole proposition. In reply I received this morning the enclosed letter from Baldwin, which he would of course be willing to have you see.

I thus leave the matter in your hands, feeling only that it is hard to make quite clear, with my space, both how much we still want M. to abandon his request, and to return to us permanently, and how strongly we at the same time feel that his present proposal would, if accepted, be the source of serious harm to our Department interests. Two things we should hope to have made clear to M., in case you accept our position. First, we want him to know that if he comes next year at all, he comes, not tentatively, but for good, accepting a permanent appointment in the same sense and to the same degree as any of the rest of us. We consider this of great importance to our prospects as a Department,—James, as I said, seeming to make less of this aspect than Palmer and I do, but all agreeing that we want a reasonable degree of finality. Secondly, we want him to know that we are ready to give him up altogether rather than to accept his proposal of the half year's work. I suppose that these two points could not well be made in a cable message. But we hope that it may at least be possible to get M's definitive reply by cable.

With renewed regret that you are ill, and that I have to be an official nuisance in this way at a moment when, were it possible, I should so gladly be a personal help or comfort to you, I remain

Yours Very Truly
Josiah Royce.

To Edwin Markham, May 20, 1897[180]

103 Irving St.
Cambridge, Mass.
May 20, 1897.

My Dear Sir:—

Schopenhauer has been translated and is accessible in English in most large libraries. His *World as Will and Idea* will stimulate opposition, and set you thinking on serious issues, however little you agree with him. If you have time, and are very seriously concerned to go into all the problems that you mention, try Bradley's *Appearance and Reality*,—a hard book, but one of the first importance (published by Macmillan). Or try Watson's *Christianity and Idealism*, published by the same house.

Yours Very Truly
Josiah Royce.

Mr. Edwin Markham.

To Thomas Davidson, June 10, 1897[181]

103 Irving Street, Cambridge.
June 10th, 1897.

Dear Davidson,—

There is no chance of my being able to get up into the mountains this summer. I have two or three books on hand, and a new course of lectures for next year, and the appointment to a Gifford lectureship at the University of Aberdeen for the years '98–99 and '99–1900. I wish I could come, and I shall think of you often; but life grows more exacting rather than less. I hope that you are quite well nowadays and that the old troubles do not return.

Yours very truly,
Josiah Royce

Please excuse haste. It is near the year's end, & affairs are pressing.

180 ALS. Markham Papers. Wagner College Library.
181 TLS. Davidson Papers. YUS.

To James Mark Baldwin, June 20, 1897[182]

103 Irving Street,
Cambridge, Mass.
June 20, 1897.

Dear Baldwin:—

With many delays, due to the exigencies of the examination period, I have at length read your paper,—with pleasure and profit, as I need hardly say.[183] I agree, of course, very largely. Excuse the following hasty comments, written under much pressure of cares.

As to criticism, I may speak first of the minor matters of the exposition. Your terminology is, I think, sometimes a little puzzling. The term "self-thought-situation" despite the pretty full explanation that precedes the use of the compound, is of a type always questionable, I think, in English. As a matter of the logic of relatives, any compound of three members has to be, in form, ambiguous. Our rule in compounds, such as *warehouse*, or *washtub*, is that the first member involves a qualification of the second by setting the second member in relations which the first indicates. But if there are three members, what is the modifier, and what the modified? The combination *a-b-c* can be read either as *a-(b-c)* or as *(a-b)-c*, and the "relative multiplication" here involved is not of the "associative type." Or your term, in the present case, can mean either a "situation" somehow modified by a "self-thought," or a "thought-situation" somehow qualified by, or related to, a "self." I myself am not sure which you mean. And each alternative opens the door to several interpretations of its own precise implication. I dread the compounds, freshly manufactured in English, more and more as I grow older. They are nests of vagueness in case anybody but the first coiner of them gets to using them. The word

[182] Published letter, original unknown. All but the fourth paragraph is published in Baldwin's *Between Two Wars, 1861–1921: Being Memories, Opinions and Letters Received* (Boston: Stratford Co., 1926), 2: 233–34. The fourth paragraph is published in Baldwin's *Social and Ethical Interpretations in Mental Development: A Study in Social Psychology* (New York: Macmillan Co., 1897), 569–70.

[183] James Mark Baldwin, "The Psychology of Social Organization," *Psychological Review* 4 (1897): 482–515; reprinted in revised form in Baldwin, "Social Organization," pt. 6, *Social and Ethical Interpretations*.

"method," as used in the first part of the paper *suggests*, rather frequently, "method of social science," instead of what you of course mean, viz., the type of functioning peculiar to social activities. I say the word has the former of these as its first and customary suggestion whenever your context doesn't directly fix attention on what you mean. Couldn't "type of function" be, at least sometimes substituted?

The latter half of the paper is perhaps a little too condensed, and has to be read twice to get the force. But I suppose that this is a good fault.

The "master and slave" business is expressly presented as but a very brief and primitive stage in the genesis of the social consciousness, even in the *Phänomenologie*. In going over the ground again, in the *Encyclopädie*, Hegel explained in some of the lecture notes (presented as *Zusätze* in his *Werke*) that that was a barbarian affair, not to be regarded as related to the modern civilized consciousness, where the *Anerkennung*, which is everywhere the essence of individual self-consciousness, is founded not upon mastery, but upon the dignity of social office. The genesis of this higher sort of consciousness Hegel refers, in all his works, to the Family, to the State, and to much the same special principles of correlation between growing self-consciousness and social surroundings which you and I now insist upon. Hegel was not interested much in individual psychology, but he analyzed the motives of social institutions and process in a frequently quite genetic and psychological spirit, so far as his time permitted. The family tie, the relation of self and one's critics, the relation of free citizen to other freemen,—these are very fundamental and fruitful in Hegel's account. What I miss in him is an express recognition of the *imitative* factor as such. Hegel's genetic theory assumes that the private self fundamentally *wants to possess everything*, but finds itself limited, not merely by physical forces, but by its sensitiveness to criticism, to counter-assertion of all sorts, and by that whole sense of the complexity of things which is the very correlative of its longing for universal mastery. This manifold limitation leads, in ways which Hegel usually mentions without any so general explanation as yours, but for all that by much the same road as your theory follows, to ethical selfhood. But your theory insists that the self, even in its private desires, not only wants to possess everything, but, within its limits, *to imitate everybody*. This involves, of course, an explanation of the phenomena of social sensitiveness which does indeed go beyond Hegel's. For his principles are special, yours and Tarde's are very general.

The "lectures" are to be the *Gifford*—not the Hibbert lectures,—at Aberdeen, in the academic years 1898–9, and 1899–1900. The subjects are not yet more closely defined. Thanks for your interest. —Congratulations too upon your very brilliant success in the prize-contest. We shall all be very proud to see the completed volume.[184]

You see, I am not yet producing fast on the *Dictionary*.[185] But now vacation is fairly begun. From now on I pledge some working hours of each free time to your task, until something has been done. Only, at the instant, I feel *very* tired. I must wait until about July 4 or 5, before getting back from a short journey that I shall take for rest, and cannot work at all until then. Please bear with me a little. Our official tasks have been very complex and severe of late.

Yours very truly,
Josiah Royce.

To George Holmes Howison, October 5, 1897[186]

Cambridge, Mass.
Oct. 5, 1897

Dear Howison:—

Thank you very much for the extra copies of the book,[187] and for your courtesy about sending extra copies generally.

The outer appearance of the book does not displease me. I like your extremely judicial introduction very well. And now if you will only buckle down to the job of telling the whole story of that City of God of yours right out, so that one can really make out what sort of a place it is, I shall be glad indeed. I wish that you had

[184] Baldwin was awarded the gold medal by the Royal Academy of Arts and Sciences of Denmark for his "The Person Public and Private," *Social and Ethical Interpretations*.

[185] James Mark Baldwin, ed., *Dictionary of Philosophy and Psychology*, 3 vols. (New York: Macmillan Co., 1901–5). Royce contributed about a dozen articles to the first volume.

[186] ALS. Howison Papers. UCB.

[187] *CG* (1897).

done so in this book. I wish also that there had been room at the end for Mezes. But one can't get everything at once.

I may frankly add that what I least can yet make out about the "City of God," as you so far reveal its mysteries, is what God (viewed as in any sense an unique or Absolute Being), has to do with it. So far as I can see, your view appears to be a polytheism, where anybody is as much God as he is even Christian. Or else God is merely the collective name for your crowd of polytheistic monads. I know of course that you can't really mean either of these things, but I indicate the helplessness of my mind by suggesting the question; and my helplessness may help to show you what some other readers must most desire to have added, by way of explanation, to the account that you have so far given. But at all events, I await, with keen curiosity, your outcome.–As for my book, I cheerfully resign it now to its fate, & care little therefore.–I now go on to my Gifford Lectures,–my next task.–

Yours Truly
Josiah Royce.

To The Macmillan Company, December 12, 1897[188]

103 Irving St.
Cambridge, Mass.
Dec. 12, 1897.

The Macmillan Company,

Gentlemen:

Your account of September, for $\$15\frac{88}{100}$ is in my hands, and I have been asked, in a renewed presentation, to "remit." I do not wish to delay improperly the settlement of any account; but in this case I beg to submit the following facts:—

1. This account, which I acknowledge as correct, is wholly for copies of my own book on the *Conception of God*, together with postage &c.

2. By copyright agreement between the "Philosophical Union" of the U. of Cal., and myself, 5% (five percent) of all the retail

188 ALS. Macmillan Papers. NYPL.

receipts on copies sold is to accrue to me, in case of the volume in question. I believe that you are notified of this arrangement, if not parties thereto.

3. I have of course to wait, say half a year or a year, for my copyright returns. I don't expect them to be large. They might however reach as much as $\$15\frac{88}{100}$. I should hope that they would. If so, we should be quits, and you could so notify me.

4. As a mere matter of principle, is there any more reason why I should be urged monthly about "kindly remitting" to you on the account of this book than that you should be asked to make a monthly return to me on the copyright? I should never think of asking for the latter accommodation. You would be right in refusing if I did. But as a mere matter of principle, why is one side of this account more urgent than the other?

I repeat, in view of these facts, that I am willing to settle if you really deem the matter urgent. But as a small, but real, matter of principle as to copyright accounts is concerned, I beg you to excuse me if, in all courtesy, I ask you to make note of these facts, and tell me what is the right view.

I beg to add a warm acknowledgement of your repeated courtesy in sending me reviews of the book, as well as other valuable information.

Yours Very Truly
Josiah Royce.

To Mary Gray Ward Dorr, January 9, 1898[189]

103 Irving Street
Cambridge, Mass.
January 9, 1898

Dear Mrs. Dorr,

As to the work in question[190]—"symbolism" is symbolism; this is a purely symbolic story. The children are Love and Faith. The

[189] TLC. Royce Papers. HUA.

[190] Maurice Maeterlinck's marionette drama, *La Mort de Tintagiles*, which inspired Charles Martin Loeffler to compose a tone-poem of the same title—first performed by the Boston Symphony Orchestra, with the composer as soloist, on January 8, 1898.

Queen is what I have called, in my *Religious Aspect of Philosophy*, the "World of the Powers," the world of Might as might, of the life, that is supposed to be the expression of Fact and of Force. That world is the world that most religious teachers, and all men of the world, most superstitious people, all materialists, and most believers in what they call God, believe in. Now, that world is the world which our nineteenth century has seen to the very bottom. That world is the world that slays Faith, and Love—helpless—mourns in the darkness. That is the tale of this drama, and that is the whole of it.

So sure am I of the inevitable doom of the World of the Powers and of all who live therein that I am not surprised or shocked to have the drama of Faith slain by Fate, and of Love weeping in the darkness portrayed. To me the tragedy is an old one, and I cannot find it hopeless. The solution is: "Good-bye, proud world; I'm going home."[191] But so long as there are those who will not go home, the tragedy remains.

Since that tragedy is a fact to be portrayed, I think music better able than words to hint that such an end is not the real end. Hence I like Loeffler's work very well.

This is a poor letter, but you asked for a report, and being in a great hurry this is the best that I can write. I love always to see you and to talk with you.

Your always,
Josiah Royce.

To Charles William Eliot, January 21, 1898[192]

Cambridge.
103 Irving St.
Jan. 21, 1898

Dear Dr. Eliot:—

I have meant for some time to address you as to the case of Dr. Santayana. I have asked a number of times for the opinions of my colleagues about him. I find that while Professor Palmer expresses doubts which he will doubtless be glad to explain to you, Professor

191 Emerson's poem.

192 ALS. Eliot Papers. HUA.

James, Professor Münsterberg, and myself seem to be wholly agreed that, as things at present look, Dr. Santayana ought to be, if possible, not only retained, but advanced, next year, to an Assistant Professorship.[193] His book,[194] the extremely marked and cordial reception that it has won, from decidedly competent judges, his slow but now unquestionable growth as a scholar, his wholly unworldly, but very steadfast devotion to his work, his really distinctive position amongst us, as differing from us all, in a very wholesome way, in influence and in doctrine,—these considerations, weighed together, now seem to me and I believe to James & Münsterberg in their present force, to outweigh any of our former doubts.

Dr. Santayana would not longer stay, I feel sure, as an Instructor. But his length of service, in view of his merits, seems to me to warrant at this point his promotion, if that is financially permissible.

While I haven't asked for any formal authority to represent James & Münsterberg as to this matter, I believe myself to have gathered their views rightly. May we now know your decision soon? The plans for next year must erelong be made.

Yours Very Truly
Josiah Royce.

To Charles William Eliot, January 23, 1898[195]

103 Irving St.
January 23, 1898

Dear Dr. Eliot:—

The merits of Bakewell[196] have frequently been discussed, and

[193] An announcement of Santayana's promotion to assistant professor was printed in *Philosophical Review* 7 (May 1898): 336. According to his autobiography, *The Middle Span* (New York: Charles Scribner's Sons, 1945), pp. 157–58, Santayana had been an instructor for seven years and was determined to leave Harvard if not promoted.

[194] George Santayana, *The Sense of Beauty: Being the Outlines of Aesthetic Theory* (New York: Charles Scribner's Sons, 1896), favorably reviewed by J. D. Logan, *Philosophical Review* 6 (1897): 210–12; E. B. Tichener, *Mind* 6 (1897): 559–63; Alfred Hodder, *Psychological Review* 4 (1897): 439–41.

[195] ALS. Eliot Papers. HUA.

[196] Charles Montague Bakewell had been an instructor at Harvard during 1896–97, replacing Santayana who had a year's leave of absence to study in England.

I am sure that they are in the minds of all of us. If Santayana were not in question, I should view Bakewell's right to immediate consideration as very good. As it is, I do not myself prefer Bakewell to Santayana, nor do I think him a better investment for the University. I now believe that Santayana ought to be advanced, and I have no misgivings in imagining him a full professor, before or after fifty years of age. I do think also, that he has a strong right to consideration at present; and such doubts as I felt two years since have been removed by his advance in the proofs given of strength.

Meanwhile, I fully admit my fallibility as a judge. Nor do I regard the case as one where an official report of a Department action can be as useful to you as a simple report of our individual views. I have asked Palmer, James, and Münsterberg to express to you their own views in their own way.

Yours Very Truly
Josiah Royce

To JAMES MCKEEN CATTELL, FEBRUARY 13, 1898[197]

Cambridge.
Feb. 13, 1898.

Dear Cattell:—

I regret the hasty state in which my paper was prepared and sent in.[198] The typewriter did a good deal to make me talk nonsense. And I had no time to make right corrections before you called in the MS. I have now gone over the proof pretty carefully. I have had to add two or three footnotes, but I think them necessary, if the paper is to be understood at all. As it is, I think it a very unfinished piece of work, and only print it because you and Baldwin say so. For my part, I don't like my own crudeness, and yet seem fated to stay crude.

Yours Very Truly
Josiah Royce.

[197] ALS. Cattell Papers. LC.

[198] "The Psychology of Invention," *Psychological Review* 5 (1898): 113–44.

To Granville Stanley Hall, February 14, 1898[199]

103 Irving St.
Cambridge, Mass.
Feb. 14, 1898.

Dr. G. Stanley Hall, President,
Clark University;–

Dear Dr. Hall:–

Your friendly call of Feb. 8, for cooperation, is as kindly worded as, coming thus directly from your hand and heart, it is imperative. Since receiving your letter, I have had no time to give it a proper reply, and I have now no time, even if I had the power, to give it an adequate reply. These few words as to your questions about philosophy, are meant only to express goodwill, and a willingness to proceed to closer quarters with the subject if I had time.

1. "Why is this necessary?" you ask, viz., why is it necessary that "every normal young man" sooner or later, "finds himself face to face with the whole problem of reality?"

I am not quite sure, from personal observation, that "every normal young man" goes so far as this. I suppose that there are great variations. The frequency of universal problems in the thoughts of sensitive youth is no doubt like that frequency of deeper religious experiences which your *Journal* has so elaborately studied, in more than one paper.[200] I am uncertain, as you are, regarding the factors, viewed in their whole meaning and connection. But some of the factors I think that I see, and in an abstract way I can, I believe, safely name a few.

a. An individual man's view of himself, of his status, worth, ideals &c., is in large part a product of social suggestions, such as the social animal receives, and imitatively accepts, from infancy on. One's childish obstinacy, one's love of social contrast-effects (e.g. of attracting attention to one's self), one's vanity, one's desire to be loved, and one's playful fondness for the whole social game of self-consciousness,–all these factors early add to the foregoing, imitatively accepted suggestions, *other* tendencies, which make the

[199] ALS. Royce Papers. HUA.

[200] Hall was founder and editor of *American Journal of Psychology*.

child more or less "original," and more or less disposed to be *un*like his surroundings. This play of like and unlike is the basis of normal self-consciousness. Hereby, namely by accepting the ideals of our society, and then opposing to these ideals our own little obstinacies, originalities, and queernesses, we get in childhood our normal early self-consciousness as to what we are good for, as to our business, our powers, and our status.

But youth comes into this world of half formed plans, purposes, self-estimates, hopes, and selfhood generally. Youth means a flood of new sensations, of new emotions, of novel social stimulations, and of resulting vague ideals. The old self simply gets broken up. I myself used to have fancies, at that age, along the lines of the familiar metaphors about the "voyage of life." Childhood had been like the "shore,"—relatively known, stable, and sure. Now I was embarking on a very "stormy sea," the shore was in sight, but fatally "left behind." I should "never get back." Where was the "pilot"? I felt confident, and helpless, all at once. Especially was it clear that this was the "grandest" part of life, but also the most "dreadful." The "grandest" it was, because we young people evidently "felt," and were "full of life," and "appreciated life"; while the older people were generally "commonplace" and "dull," &c. &c. The "most dreadful" it was, because we felt our unsatisfied sentiments,—their "nobility" and their "hopelessness,"—all at once. I have heard, and read, as you have, great masses of this talk from other young people.

In brief, the situation is that by this time one has learned, from childhood's little world of pretty well-knit social relations, what self-consciousness is and means, namely plan, assurance, purpose, and social position; while, on the other hand, in the flood of new experiences, one in youth has lost hold of the concrete facts of the childhood self. One cares no more for the old plans,—no longer is content to be a hunter or trapper (as in boyhood I had once meant to be when I should grow up). But one has not yet learned what else to become instead. For instance, one might prove to be poet, saint, world-reformer, or what not? While, in one's worse youthful moments, one plans to be rebel, or fears to become an outcast,—or perhaps fools insincerely, but demurely, with the thought of suicide. But through all this one has the idea, the ideal, the abstract picture or ground plan, of what selfhood would be,—viz., power, courage, plan, and above all social status,—a place among the "men my brothers,—men the workers." For *that* ideal of selfhood one had acquired already as child. Hence you have all the materials for a fundamental problem:—Who am I? What am I good for?

To heighten the struggle, society itself steps in, with its demand that the youth shall soon prove himself "somebody," with its merciless criticism of his "calfishness," with its frequent scorn if he goes wrong, with its pretty cruel indifference when, in his ideality and sensitiveness, he becomes bashful, and nurses a lonely love for some impossible closeness of sympathy, with friends whom he sees not.

Now Reality is, to any man, simply what he conceives as fulfilling the aims of his most rational Self. If a man studies science, and learns to submit, in an intellectual self-abnegation, to the hard facts, that submission comes only because he learns to see therein his most rational self-fulfillment. If a man becomes cynic or pessimist, and pretends to abhor all reality, he learns even such abhorrence only as a sort of falsely supposed rational virtue wherein his rational aims get their best practicable fulfillment under assumed hopeless conditions. If he remains sceptic, that is because he has not yet found himself. In brief, to seek *your place in* the Universe, is to be interested in the Universe; and conversely, the interest in the "whole problem of reality," involves, and means, an interest in solving the problem of *who I am*, of *what I ideally ought to be*, and of *what my life means*.

Since these latter problems are forced upon youth by the situation, the youth, *if* sufficiently thoughtful to come upon the truth as to his problem, easily finds that to think about the true Self, implies thinking about the whole problem of Reality. And here you have a first factor in the youthful facing of the "problem of reality."

b. Another factor lies of course in the normal obstinacy of youth. If one has broken with one's childhood, one must of course wonder whether its ideals were well founded at all. One had a childish faith in Santa Claus, God, and the rest of the folklore of the tribe, as one then understood these ideas, which were *then* alike mere folklore. One has given up childhood. Must one not give up the folklore too? If one has embarked on the "stormy sea," and left the "shore" behind, one has become independent of one's mother also. "*Da ich ein Kind war*," says Prometheus,—and you know the rest. Hence independence becomes a duty. One has already at least the bare form of self-hood, despite the absence of content; and one has learned from childhood that self-hood means contrast with the social environment,—individuality. And so one holds that what they often called one's naughtiness, when one was a child, is now one's sacred right,—viz., the right to differ, to be independent, to run free of the folklore, and to form one's own opinions.

But the old folklore itself dealt with the "whole problem of reality," and undertook to reveal all the mysteries of the faith. Has not one the sacred right then to deal with these problems for one's self? So one now reasons. And here is a second motive.

This purely "free thinking" motive is notoriously very common, although surely not universal, with intelligent men in youth.

c. And finally, the "whole problem of reality" interests many young men merely because the most characteristic emotions of youth, viewed merely in their psychological content, are vaguely universal. Here the factor that makes some young men metaphysicians, is identical with the factor that makes others, despite all the foregoing motives, faithful converts to this or that religious faith. "Reality" is big and so far vague; and youthful emotions love big things and vague things.

So much for some of the factors that lead to this study of the "whole problem of reality" in youth. My catalogue is incomplete, and commonplace, since I have said only what you already know. But you question in such an answerable shape, that I have to reply as I can.

Your question: "Why is this necessary?" proceeds however to the further query,—"What is it meant to accomplish?" I reply, it is meant to accomplish the end of making this struggling youth a Self, with an aim and a place in life. It is meant to give him a chance to learn life's meaning in more ideal and therefore in more plastic forms, so as to be ready to express life's meaning in more direct contact with the stubborn facts of life later. It is related to the practical interests of later life as the youthful art interest is related to the more concrete later observation of the facts of life. It is meant to "purge the soul" of the "pity and fear," of one's own Selfhood and destiny, by giving these emotions, as art does, their larger, their more universal, and hence their more cleansing expression.

2. How should it be guided? Like every other problematic interest of youth, this interest in "Reality" ought to be guided by a strictly individual treatment (if that were possible) of each case.

Only a fraction of those thus temporarily interested in Reality at large, ought to study any technical philosophy. Of the remainder, religious faith saves some; practical life forces a sort of solution upon others; science clarifies a certain number. Philosophy itself, beyond its elementary stages, ought to be a fairly well guarded and limited elective. Those who need technical philosophy are not exactly few; but they are not a majority of the young men of the academic types. Those who do need philosophy, for a short or for a long time, need it, *while* they need it, very badly. It is then the breath of life to them. To fail to grasp their need is a grave educational and social mistake. Without philosophy they are wrecked. But those who do not need philosophy, or who are helped only by a brief elementary "culture" course of study therein, are numerous, and are properly to be kept away from the subject, except in its most elementary forms. Most of them are protected by their natural indifference in the presence of philosophical technicalities. Others are wisely guided, by instinctive suspicions, to avoid an attempt to get a self-hood which does not belong to them; and such win their souls, and settle their accounts with reality, by other devices—religious, scientific, practical.

But for the men who are born to take their youthful interest in reality in a technically serious form, as an interest in definite philosophical study, a decidedly "deep-going" course is indicated. They should be instructed that for those who are born with the truly metaphysical eyes, it is not only a right, but a duty, to see,—to see all,—problems, doubts, sorrows, hopes, truths, and salvation,—God and the world,—to see coolly, fearlessly, dispassionately, unsuspiciously; to confess what they see, and to honor God rather than man as they do this. The "topics" should be for such, the deepest ones,—Reality, Right, Freedom, God. No dogma should to them be taught as dogma. Their sole philosophical problem, *while* they study philosophy, should be, not: What ought I to believe? ⟨that is often a problem in the practical world of business, of friendship, and of faith, but *never* in the world of philosophy⟩ but rather: What can I clearly see as to the deepest issues of my life? No philosopher cares, as such, what you say that he merely believes. He cares only to be sure that what he teaches as insight he has seen, and hopes to get others to see. The true born student of philosophy, *while* he studies philosophy, should act only as philosopher,—freely, fearlessly, unsparingly,—questioning as Job or as Plato, as Hamlet or as Kant questioned,–and questioning solely for the sake of insight. The teacher will guide his properly chosen student in this spirit, and would scorn to tolerate in the philosophical lecture-room and seminary, any but this absolutely tolerant spirit itself.

There are "dangers" in this. Your question implies concern about them. There are dangers in all of life's great activities. As the National Cemeteries show, it is a dangerous thing, on occasion, to serve one's country. As the Catacombs remind us, it is often a dangerous thing to abide by the faith. As the deaths of young medical men show, it is dangerous to work in dissecting rooms and hospitals. Child-bearing is a dangerous occupation for even the soundest woman. In fact, life itself is the most dangerous of our enterprises, and moral seriousness has often been most keenly aware of the dangers, constantly present, of damnation. All good works are dangerous.

Our problem as to such dangers is always twofold: (a) We want to hinder those not duly called from being uselessly exposed to them; (b) we want, for the duly called, to minimize them.

In this case, as to hindering the uncalled: I should try to keep out of the serious and more advanced, philosophical courses certain, happily not so very frequent, although somewhat various types of young men (and, I might add, some types of women), who are attracted by philosophy, who are not frightened away by the mere show of its technicalities, who hang about lectures and libraries in pursuit of something that they hope to find wisdom [*sic*], and who are still prevented, by defect of wit or of virtue, from ever getting out of philosophical study anything but foolishness. I have observed some such types with concern, and on occasion, and not without some success, have done my part to drive the people in question away from what is indeed for them, uselessly dangerous ground. The types in question are not hard to define, or to recognize. I have printed a little about some of them.[201] I have warned individuals of such types in connection with my elementary courses. When fortune gave me the opportunity, I have cheerfully cast a few of them, neck and crop, out of higher philosophical courses. They are some of them defective in wit, but of very high moral quality. Some of them, on the other hand, are extremely astute, but decidedly dangerous beings, and very defective in moral

201 "The Student of Philosophy," *Harvard Monthly* 18 (1894): 87–99; "The Study of Philosophy," *Occident* 24 (1895): 50–53.

quality. To suspect philosophical study, or to abridge the freedom of academic philosophical study, upon the behalf of such uncalled persons, would be as wise as to suppress printing because bad books get printed, or universities because some people do waste their time at universities.

As to protecting the properly called from the perfectly real dangers of their calling (dangers of "brooding," of "abstraction," of "dryness" &c.), a word may be said. The philosophical student should never long devote himself *wholly* to philosophy. He needs a broad basis, and a good background constantly and freshly enriched. Science, history, politics, practical life, should furnish the studies that, in one case or another, are to form this basis and background. Therein lies, in recent times, one great value of the Psychological Laboratories,—viz., that they give philosophical students one more opportunity to deal with the concrete. I hope for even more help, in this respect, in future, from Anthropological Museums, and from philological, biological, and physical studies, pursued by technical students of philosophy.

Moreover, the serious philosophical student, if a professional man, should help himself out early by *doing* something, something concrete, and useful to the brethren,—something such as tutoring, conducting charity work, marrying and raising his family,—anything you please that is wholesome, and that is a deed. A "life of contemplation," except as in constant contrast with a life of struggle, of activity, is indeed a misnomer. There is no true "life" of the sort. Hence the young student of philosophy should also be early instructed that he must not long reflect upon life without beginning to live, and to live in earnest.

3. No one early course of more serious philosophical (or even of "epistemological") study can be at all exclusively recommended. The roads into philosophy are many. An elementary "culture" course can be planned (Logic, Elements of Psychology, General Hist. of Philos.). But the more serious work must be early individualized, according to the needs of various groups of students. Kant is *not* the final solution. Every philosopher must, however, sooner or later learn from Kant. But scientific students need one, classical students often quite another road in high philosophy. Courses should be multiplied accordingly.

4. It is best "to find the way out of agnosticism." But we grow by mutual aid. An "ingenuous soul," *if* of the type distinctively

philosophical, i.e. of the type mentioned above, had better be helped out by fearless philosophical research and criticism, and had better not be taught any secretiveness, or any shame, as to the one obvious fact that our souls are finite, and must struggle for the light.

Well, here are your answers. Their one virtue, I suppose, is, that they are written at a moment of very great stress of work and of preoccupation, and despite a very disagreeable cold, merely because, in asking for them, you have given the signal of mutual concern which our common loyalty to our profession makes it always imperative to obey.

With every wish for your personal good fortune, peace of soul, and success, I remain

Yours Very Truly
Josiah Royce.

To James Ripley Wellman Hitchcock, February 16, 1898[202]

Feb. 16, 1898.
103 Irving St.
Cambridge.

Dear Hitchcock:—

I enclose at last my *Introduction*.[203] Things hereabouts don't leave me much chance to use my time as I wish. I haven't been able to leave Cambridge once since I saw you, except to talk to a few Psychologists at Ithaca,[204] and to prate a little to a Woman's Club. —No fooling so far this winter.—But I now mean to go to N. Y. for that friendly visit in April,—vacation time,—if you will take me in then. I think that then surely I can be free. I kept hoping, during Mid Year time, that the let up would come; but it didn't.

Yours Truly
Josiah Royce.

202 ALS. Hitchcock Papers. CUB.

203 For *SGE*.

204 Royce read the paper on "The Psychology of Invention" to the annual meeting of the American Psychological Association, Ithaca, N. Y., December 28, 1897.

To James Ripley Wellman Hitchcock, April 10, 1898[205]

Cambridge, Mass.
103 Irving St.
April 10, 1898.

Dear Mr. Hitchcock:—

I shall be glad to know when the book appears.[206] I have as yet no word about it. I enclose a list of copies that I desire sent at my expense, and I shall be glad to get, and to pay in due season, a separate account of these copies, since I desire to keep the copyright account clear of these extras.

As to my New York visit, I shall be glad to see you when I go down, if you still want me to come to you. I shall probably reach New York by 6 o'clock, Wednesday afternoon, the 20th April, and I can stay until the Sunday following, if all goes well here at Cambridge, and if the war permits us to visit or to receive visits after it once gets under way.

I fear somewhat that the war may spoil the sale of my book—in Spain! But of course we all have to bear our share of the common burden. And at all events, I suppose that we shall all have to dispose of our "castles in Spain" to the lowest bidder, regardless of cost. I hope that you don't own many. Alas, all my worldly goods are much of that sort.

Yours Very Truly
Josiah Royce.

To Charles Eliot Norton, April 25, 1898[207]

Irving St.
April 25, '98.

Dear Professor Norton:—

Thanks for thanks are not always supposed to be needed; but in case of your very kind letter such an echo, which is also more than

[205] ALS. Hitchcock Papers. CUB.
[206] *SGE*.
[207] ALS. Norton Papers. HL.

an echo, is called for.[208] I work a good deal alone, and have a much keener, and perhaps juster sense of my incapacities than it is usually prudent, or worthwhile, as the world goes, to express, or than I am supposed to feel. But one can only try, and so I try to work out and to state what little thinking, and what little defence of my cause, I am allowed to undertake under the very strict limitations of my present poor "form of consciousness." To be obliged to undertake so much, and to perform so little, is the evil that I most constantly feel. It is a very great comfort to get, from a judge like you, so very kindly an expression of appreciation for one of my attempts. You are very good to read me at all, and still kinder to give me that best of gifts which a man of your power and training can give to a man of my efforts and defects,—namely the hours of appreciative and sympathetic willingness to see past the defects to the intent of which your letter is the expression. Hence your letter gives me a very happy hour.

Yours Very Truly
Josiah Royce.

To Anne Whitney?, May 29, 1898[209]

103 Irving St.
May 29, 1898.

My Dear Madam:—

I am not able to sign the petition.[210] I do not approve of many of

[208] This letter is evidently a reply to Norton's letter of thanks for a copy of *SGE*.

[209] ALS. WCL. The letter was addressed to either Miss Whitney or to Adeline Manning, her companion who often assisted in Miss Whitney's various projects. WCL owns a copy of a reply to Royce in Miss Manning's hand, but this proves nothing since she frequently served as Miss Whitney's amanuensis.

[210] The petition, prepared by the committee on ethics of the Women's Educational and Industrial Union, was motivated by an announcement that the government intended to serve its armed forces with bread in wrappers marked "Remember the Maine." See "Is This A War of Vengeance?" *Boston Evening Transcript*, May 23, 1898. The petition was worded as follows:

To the HONORABLE SECRETARY OF THE NAVY,
HON. JOHN D. LONG, Navy Department, Washington, D.C.

We the undersigned, citizens of the United States, considering that the ostensible and only justifiable motive for entering upon the war with Spain, the motives by which I find men actuated at every time of popular and passionate excitement. But what advice it is best to give to the public at such times is a matter, not of one's own views, but of regard for the good one can hope to do in bettering people's motives. I think that the agitation which your petition represents can lead, at this present moment, only to stirring up yet further confusion in the emotions of precisely the people whom you wish to enlighten. If I have to deal with a deaf mute, I do not advise him to cultivate a taste for music. If I find a wanderer struggling through miles of swamp and mire, I do not take that moment to lecture him on the advantages of neatness and of bathing. It is one of the evils of war that, however noble its true purpose may have been meant to be, the act of war involves the deafness of hatred, and a wandering through the mire of the excitements incident to bloodshed.

The virtues that war encourages,—these however remain possible, and worthy of being popularly emphasized at such times. These virtues are loyalty, sacrifice, patience, and self-restraint. These are the best means of serving humanity. The rest of the war passions had better be, not indeed encouraged, not countenanced,—but gently ignored. Do you teach the deaf to hear by protesting against deafness, or the wanderers to be neat by calling attention to the mire? There are cures for such ills, indeed; but the cure belongs to the time of peace. This is the time to serve our country otherwise than by arousing new hatreds, through protests that are as certain to be misunderstood by passion as they are to be justified, by and by, by the enlightenment that peace will bring.

Yours Very Truly
Josiah Royce.

---

was the deliverance of a neighboring people from oppression, and ourselves from relations to them that had become intolerable, wish to express our abhorrence of the spirit of vengeance manifested in such a war cry as "Remember the Maine"; and beg you to refuse to purchase goods of any kind bearing this motto; and in all ways to discountenance the use of this or any other motto calculated to foster the spirit of savagery against which we are contending.

To Joseph Cummings Rowell, July 23, 1898[211]

Cambridge.
July 23, '98.

Dear Rowell:—

I don't know anything about the value *in money* of the H. H. B. Library, and I suppose that to be a pretty arbitrary matter.[212] As to the intrinsic & scientific value of the collection as a basis for serious documentary study of Pacific Coast matters,—I should rate that decidedly high, supposing that the collection, as I saw it in 1884, is still intact, has been kept in fair condition, and has not been hopelessly disarranged or neglected. The judgment passed on it by Th. Hittell, in his *History*, is not only partisan, but unwarrantable. The collection is (or was) very thoroughgoing and scholarly as to its methods of construction, and (at that time) as to its arrangement. But I have not seen it since '84. Bancroft was then rather obtuse as to the care of his books, and I do not know, of course, what degeneration may not, by this time, have taken place.

Yours Very Truly
Josiah Royce.

To Mary Gray Ward Dorr, August 7, 1898[213]

August 7, 1898

Dear Mrs. Dorr,

Your so kind letter came to hand yesterday morning. I have been wondering ever since whether I could not somehow arrange my tasks so as to get away at once, as you so kindly urge. I prize the urgency, and love to be so kindly remembered—prize it so highly that I am ready to make any possible effort to break the chains that

[211] ALS. Rowell Papers. UCB.

[212] The University of California acquired the Bancroft Library in 1905. Anticipating this acquisition, Rowell was, in 1898, asked to make an appraisal of the collection, both in terms of its scholarly and its monetary value. See John Walton Coughey, *Hubert Howe Bancroft: Historian of the West* (Berkeley: University of California Press, 1946), pp. 350–65.

[213] TLC. Royce Papers. HUA.

bind me just now to my desk. Yet I hope that you will see how I am placed, when I say that powers over which I have no control simply forbid me, just now, to turn away from the task set me. The Gifford Lectures are rapidly approaching. They are, or ought to be, in a purely technical or academic sense the effort of my life. If I cannot do them rightly, I shall do much more than fail; I shall be a false servant of Harvard, whose honor in a way any lecturer to foreign audiences has in such a case to guard in his own way and range. If I do not do them rightly, I shall be false, also, to the friends who have obtained for me this high trust, and to the cause of serious thinking on Religion and to the public concerned. To say this is not to exaggerate my poor personal importance; it is only to say that this trust concerning a very sacred task has been put upon me; and now I must live up to it.

Well, of course, such a task viewed in general is indeed consistent enough with the duty and delight of friendly meetings, and the whole spirit that surrounds you, and your so dear Oldfarm, would be, if I could but visit you, an aid and inspiration as to all that concerns my interest in the problems of my lectures and all that leads to the inner preparation for such work. Believe me, the memory of you and of your home and spirit and sympathy are with me, and *do* help me, in preparation for the task. But nevertheless, such tasks have two sides. One side has to do with the spirit for the work. That I have partly won through you, and I could only intensify it if I came to you now again. But the other side has to do with the purely mechanical scholarly preparation of the technical part of the lectures. That needs just brute time, the mere succession of hours, with continuity of staying pretty much alone at one's desk, or in the College Library, or in lonely walks, poring over logical details, looking up suggestions, collecting notes and thoughts. And for *that* part of the job the summer, I find, with its other inevitable tasks, is all far, far too short already. But the work is now in full swing, and I feel that I am at a very critical place in massing my materials. If I leave now, for any place or purpose but to amass more materials, the whole external organization of my work will, I feel, tend to suffer.

Well, these are decidedly material aspects of the affair. But if one lectures about a better world, one has to write one's lectures in this world, subject to all the material difficulties of time and ignorance, and slowness in reading, in reflecting, and in writing.

None the less, duty binds one to do his material best with the stuff he has in him.

So here I must sit and work, now that at last the job has got under way. Earlier in the vacation I was away a bit, but on professional tasks that I could not rightly avoid. From now on, I must stay pretty much alone, except for my family, until I have something to show.

When I can see you again, I most of all want to hear the new things of which you speak, that you have to read to me. Now I hope that in September, some time, the material way *may* look a little clearer before me in this task of mine. And *then*, if I still may, and you are not weary of my long delay, I will come down over some Sunday, solely to see you and George and to hear something of your news. Even that I cannot promise. It all depends upon whether or no I can get my task in hand, on its material side, enough to earn a few hours of the privilege of being with you. Just now I must not go from here, although I deeply long to do so.

I write fully, frankly, lovingly.

Please remember me warmly to Mr. and Miss Mason, to Mrs. Whitman and above all to George.

Yours very truly,
Josiah Royce.

To George Bucknam Dorr, October 23, 1898[214]

Cambridge
Oct. 23, '98.

Dear Dorr:—

Whenever you can find any time to look into our Philosophy work, you are sure, so far as I am concerned, not only to be welcome, but to do good by your suggestions. I know nobody, other than yourself, whose sympathy and whose criticism I should equally value as I should yours. On the other hand, I know how busy you are, and what a call upon your time such work involves; and I do not wonder that you ask help. As to the "young graduates" of whom you speak, those who are at all seriously philosophical are in professional positions, mostly elsewhere,—either as cler-

[214] ALS. Royce Papers. HUA.

gymen, or as teachers of philosophy. Of accessible people who have not been tried in my time as visitors, I think first of Dr. Richard C. Cabot, who is nearby, then of Edwin D. Mead of Boston, Rev. Francis Tiffany of Cambridge (not a very profound, but a practical sort of man, with an interest in philosophy), & Frank Sanborn of Concord,—all men who would be at least interested in the subject. I cannot answer for the way in which my colleagues would welcome any such visitors. Palmer, who has just been reappointed Chairman of the Div'n of Philos. (my term of four years having been served), always makes very light of any visitors, and rather drives them off. James does not care a copper. Münsterberg is new to the business, and probably would care little. I myself should always feel in duty bound to explain my courses and methods so far as visitors might choose to want to know about them, and should both welcome visitation, and value a report to the Overseers, if ever I came to learn what it was. Apart from a rather time-consuming study of our work, I suppose that a committee would never be able to say much about us.

And so I can only suggest that you get in some of the men mentioned, but above all that, if you give me your own presence again for awhile this winter, I will try to give you material for a report.— R. C. Cabot is taking some work as a graduate here; but is all the more able to act as examiner, since he now knows the ropes. He is a young man of mark, and of a very cool head, although perhaps a little too close to me, whom he kindly follows a good deal of late, to be as critical as he ought to be.

It was a great pity to be unable to accept your kind wishes, and your Mother's, this summer, and come to see you. But duty demands me here, and even now I have no time to do more than breathe and work, and sleep between times. My warm love and greetings to your dear Mother.

Yours Very Truly
Josiah Royce.

To William James, January 12, 1899[215]

Jan. 12, '99

Dear James:—

There is little time just now to do more than send a word to say that the lectures are safely launched. I send the report of yesterday's first lecture, along with other reports of lectures, as given in the *Free Press* of this city. As you see, I am by no means the only public attraction. The reverse of the newspaper leaf that I send you contains a most bloodcurdling and blood curdled report of a local murder trial, in so much that I may be violating postal laws in mailing the slip, for its "shocking details" are indeed unreadable enough; but it has its public, of course.

I have been doing well as a traveller. Many thanks for the notes of introduction. I saw all the philosophers of London & Cambridge whom I had intended to see. Caird & Bradley were invisible at Oxford, owing to holidays. I saw Sully, Karl Pearson, Shadworth Hodgson, Ward, Sidgwick, & find of course Stout and Sorely here. Sir Wm Markby (Law Professor) showed me Oxford. Dr. Garnett, of British Museum was cordial, & helped me. I found no time to meet your brother. This I regret, but shall try to pay him my respects when next I go to London.

All the thinkers met send warm regards to you. You are unquestionably by far the best known of all American philos'rs here, & your lectures will be eagerly awaited, & glowingly received. I haven't yet seen the Seths, having had to pass Edinburgh by in my hurry. I shall try to see them before returning.

Health so far very good, although the misty & raw climate makes a cold always a possibility to be looked out for.—Social life here already manifold. Everybody cordial. Cares have all slipped out of mind for the time, & I am making a very good vacation of it. How the lectures, as such will turn out, I cannot yet tell.

Well,—New Year's greetings to you and all your house. Manifold blessings attend you.

With affection & gratitude.

Yours

Josiah Royce

[215] ALS. James Papers. HL. As the contents make clear, the letter was written from Aberdeen, Scotland, while Royce was delivering his first series of Gifford Lectures.

To William Angus Knight, February 3, 1899[216]

Liverpool.
Feb. 3, 1899.

Dear Professor Knight:—

During the whole of my stay at Aberdeen I felt it one of my strong wishes to accept your kind invitation, and visit St. Andrews. The Aberdonians, however, kept me too busy to the very end of my leave of absence, to permit me to make any detour. Only one day, at Edinburgh, on the direct road to Liverpool, and by express engagement with the Seths, was left me in Scotland outside of Aberdeen.

I intended to write to you promptly regarding the matter; but I also hoped, until near the end of my visit, to be able to make some other arrangements, of which I could inform you. At the end of my visit, however, the days were too full even for letters.

So now I must return. But next year I hope to have more leisure. All of the Scottish Universities interest me greatly. I want to know more of them. And I am especially sorry not to see you, to whom I had the greeting of James, and of several other of your American friends to carry. As it is I can only thank you heartily for your courtesy, and promise myself better luck in 1900, when I return for the second half of my course.

Yours Very Truly
Josiah Royce.

To William James, March, 1899[217]

March '99.

Dear James:—

Your objections begin with a provisional acceptance of the

[216] ALS. PML.

[217] ALS. James Papers. HL. Printed with James's memorandum, "Royce's Argument for the Absolute" in *TCWJ*, 2: 726–34. James's marginalia on Royce's letter are given in footnotes below. The letter is twenty-three pages long, but p. 22 is missing.

"idealistic criterion" that you state. I suppose that, while this "criterion" demands its own separate justification, such justification does not belong here, and that, for the purposes of the present analysis, the acceptance, provisional and tentative although it be for you, must be taken in its full meaning, and must be regarded as applying within the whole range of your later discussion. This being the case, I have no difficulty in pointing out that your hypothetical instances, cited to refute the idealistic theses as to the Absolute, involve far more "facts," and so far more "thought" or, as I should now prefer to word it, far more "knowledge" or "consciousness of facts," than you seem to observe as you go. I have at present time to bring out only this aspect of your discussion.

I.

"Let us," you say "assume any finite fact A, first without thinking of B, C, D. . . ." "Let us next think B, C, D, along with A. . . ." "We must suppose that we ourselves build up this universe as we successively think its facts and relations. . . ." "If we supposed no other thinker . . . our thoughts would be the vehicle of continuity of the Universe. And that universe would not be known all together or at once."

The "facts" that your hypothesis here assumes include explicitly more than A alone, or than A together with B, C, D.—Explicitly you assume three other types of facts:—

1. That the A which is first thought alone is identical with, or the same as, the A which is later thought along with B, C, D.[218]

2. That "we," who do this thinking, are in some sense or other, I care not in what sense, really the same thinkers, or that we constitute the same thinking process all through, since we are, by your hypothesis such that our thoughts constitute "the vehicle of continuity," and it is said by you to be "we" who "successively think its facts and relations."

3. That the moment when A is alone, in our thought, and the moment when A is with B, C, D, are objectively real events in one time series, or that the one moment really follows the other.[219]

Now I do not force these assumptions upon you. It is you who

[218] "To the thinker it so comes—he feels no discontinuity or difference except the time difference." (James)

[219] "In brief: I assume 'Memory' and the kind of consciousness of things which it involves, in the finite thinker." (James)

have chosen to make them. By hypothesis they are "facts." By the "criterion," also presupposed, they are known facts, or exist only as facts thought of. I need not say that these facts are not reducible to the contents of *either* one of the two moments (α) When A alone is thought of, or (β) When A is merely thought with B & C. On the contrary the three sorts of fact that I have just pointed out are all of them *facts about the relations of the contents and consciousnesses and events of your two moments only in so far as these two moments are together equally real and are to be viewed as parts of one whole fact.* This whole fact, with its three aspects, you assume, and by the "criterion" it is fact only in so far as it is known fact, or fact thought of.[220] If "we" do not think it, the whole fact is still thought. This whole fact is once more this, that in your two events (1) A is the same A, (2) We are the same "we," and (3) In the same real time process, event the second, in your hypothetical tale, objectively follows event the first.

There *is* then by hypothesis a "thought," or as I should prefer to say here a "knowledge," or a "consciousness," which *knows* (not merely believes), *thinks* (not merely guesses) this whole fact to be what it is in these three aspects. If you deny this result,[221] you deny the "criterion" that by hypothesis you were to accept, and refuse to play the game that you have just agreed to play. If you accept this result, however, your statement: "that universe would not be known all together or at once,"[222] is forthwith abandoned. You have indeed assumed that "we" never know that universe "at once,"[223] but you have assumed that said universe possesses two sorts of sameness, and one character of objectively real succession, all of which have meaning only for the whole fact, or for the fact of your universe in its wholeness, and of its processes in their entirety of succession.[224] If all reality is known, then here is an assumed reality that "we" indeed know not, but that is known & exists only as known.

220 "And thought of *it is*, by the finite consciousness supposed." (James)

221 "Why should I be tempted to deny it?" (James)

222 "An unfortunately sweeping statement on my part, since we *would* know such parts of it at once as we reminiscientially tho't of together. Other parts which we forgot, w'd, then not be known *cum aliis*, and their relation being unknown would by the idealistic criterion be no 'fact'." (James)

223 "I am sorry for my slip of language. I meant '*need* not know it *all* at once'." (James)

224 "They have meaning all along so far as the finite thinker feels them, feels *no dis*continuity in his object, or in himself, as he feels time flow.—*Sonst nicht*." (James)

If you hereupon reply by simply denying that you meant A to be the same A in the two events, or "we" to be the same "we," or the succession to constitute one process in the one time, I shall only ask you to try again, and to state your case as you mean it.[225] If you reply that you long ago disposed of sameness, Ego, &c., in your psychology,[226] I shall answer that you did so there only provisionally, upon an explicitly realistic hypothesis, made, also provisionally, at the outset of that discussion. But here you are for the time playing quite another game,[227] namely, that determined by the hypothesis of the "criterion," to which we are now to adhere. If you reply by asking me whether *I* then believe in a transcendentally permanent "we," or in a "same thing" in successive moments of time, I respond that what I hold has been elsewhere told, but that the problem here is not what I think, but is merely what you have here chosen to assume. If the "vehicle" isn't any one vehicle at all, but only the one horse shay as it was after the crash came; if the *A alone* isn't the *A* later *found with B and C*,[228] but if the two are different *A*'s; if the succession in one time process wherein the one event really follows the other, is not real at all,—then indeed your whole hypothesis is so far a total incoherence. But if in *any* sense the sameness of the "vehicle," and of the A, and if in any sense the real succession of your two supposed events in one time is indeed real, and if by the "criterion" whatever is real is known, then there is, in your universe a knowledge of these three aspects. And these three aspects are knowable as such only if "that universe is known all together or at once," whereby of course I do not mean that it is known "all together" *in* either one of your temporally successive moments, or at any other temporal moment, or that "we" as you have defined us, ever know it at all.[229]

[225] "I certainly did mean them to be the same, for the finite thinker supposed (so long as he thinks them at all) so thinks them. To him they appear not different; and that is what the 'sameness' signifies or is known as." (James)

[226] "I disposed of it in no hostile sense. 'Sameness' in anything means the sameness felt there, and this time felt by the finite thinker." (James)

[227] "I can't see it!" (James)

[228] "It is that A, so far as the finite thinker may not have forgotten it when he thinks B & C. If he has forgotten it then *nobody* thinks the first A with the later facts, and its 'sameness' can't be said to exist." (James)

[229] "You ought to prove the impossibility of Memory, then. Why should the finite consciousness slide along, acquiring new objects, keeping these awhile with no sense that they are other, then letting them fade out?" (James)

II.

Let A change into F, as you desire, and "let A be an egg and F a chicken." The "realization in successive stages," the "surprise to the learner," the former finite "ignorance of chicken," the later "knowledge of chicken," the real relation of later chicken to that same egg whereof before there was knowledge when there was no knowledge in the "learner's" mind of the coming chicken, the sameness of the surprised learner to whom the new light comes (his sameness, I mean, all through the process)—these are now the elements of your more specifically defined universe, as you later assume it to be constituted.

Well these assumptions are yours, not mine. You tell the story. You give to its parts supposed real relations, some of which by your hypothesis, the "learner" himself never faces.[230] You accept the "criterion"; and yet you do not observe what the criterion demands of you as you go. The case is just as before. The foregoing argument afresh applies. The scene is more complex. The whole universe defined is assumed in its real succession, sameness, progress, and stages as real. This reality either is real as whole, or is not. If it is not real as whole, then the chicken comes not from the same egg that before existed.[231] The learner who is surprised is not the learner who was ignorant;[232] the one event does not really succeed the other in any one time at all; the "vehicle" crumbles, like the one horse shay, again, into the dust of mere separate facts, and your whole story remains a tale signifying nothing.

But if the whole succession, as a real time process, is real, if the vehicle is the same, and the egg of the first part of the tale is the same as the egg whence comes the chicken, then these real facts, by the hypothesis of the criterion,—yes, this whole real fact, by the same hypothesis, is known "at once";[233] for only when known "at once" (though not at any one temporal instant of the series in question), could its assumed relations be known, viz, the sameness, the connectedness of the parts in one time process, & the sameness of the learner. Once more, I am asserting, not my theories, but the content of your assumptions.

[230] "Alas for my lapus pennae which has given you all this trouble." (James)

[231] "The 'learner' never apprehends it as a different egg, does he?" (James)

[232] "He is conscious of no duality." (James)

[233] "Of course, when it *is* known, i.e., reminiscently by the learner, not before." (James)

III.

Something of a sense of this consequence must beset you when you seem to try to avoid a part of it by insisting, as to the mere time aspects of your world, that "It is an error to say that any proposition about the chicken is either true or false in advance of his actual presence."[234]

Do you mean this only because the chicken is so uncertain and insignificant a thing? But let us pass from chickens to other cases. Do you mean to assert any of the following propositions?

1. An astronomer's present assertion about eclipses of the year 1900 is neither true nor false until those eclipses occur.

2. It is neither true nor false today that I shall sometime die. (How then about life insurance policies? Do they relate to no reality?)

3. A promise made today about the future is neither a true nor a false promise. (How about false lovers, & swindlers, & true souls, and honest pledges? Do they then all alike relate to nothing true or false?)

4. It is neither true nor false that you are to be absent from Harvard during the next year. (What then were we talking about lately? Neither truth nor falsity? Nothing real?)

5. The announcements of next year's courses, when made, are neither true nor false. (I wish Palmer could see that. Then he wouldn't ask me for mine.)

6. If I today say: "The Mississippi River will flow into the Arctic Ocean next year," "The sun will then also rise in the west," "President Eliot will write Shakespeare's plays tomorrow," and "Tomorrow two and two will make four":—if I say these things, each one of my sayings, being about the future, is equally *neither* truc nor false.[235]

—If you mean to make any one of these assertions, you are welcome. *I* know however, in that case, that it is *now* true that you *will*, in substance, deny them the very next time that you make the

[234] "Truth, as I hold, being a perfectly definite external relation between a thought & s'thing in which it 'terminates.' Until the terminus exist, the truth is not constructed. The terminus *makes* the thought 'true'." (James)

[235] "*Neither true nor false*, in the strict sense! For the facts that could make these hypotheses either true or false are nonexistent as yet. Of course we practically treat them as true or false for ourselves, since we compare them as hypotheses with expectations of fulfillment or nonfulfilment that our minds supply, and denominate them accordingly. But this is only a case of *potential* truth, etc." (James)

least prediction about the future, or promise or attempt anything whatever.

But a world where future reality is even now an object of assertion,[236] true or false, is a world where the future reality, by the "criterion," is somehow known "at once" with the assertions about it.[237] "We" do not so know the future. But it is, by the "criterion" only as a known somewhat. If not so envisaged by "us," what follows?

IV.

I haven't at present time to go further into your objections. The foregoing attacks the main points. If you had taken note of them as I do, I fancy that you would not have written the latter part. On the whole the "odd conclusions" about the privative and negative aspects of reality with which you credit me are not altogether unlike what I should state as my own.[238] Only they are not even "odd," just as they very certainly aren't especially Hegelian. They are the mere commonplaces of Logic. The concept of *zero*, or of *nothing*, in its countless forms, is familiar both to common sense, and in the sciences. It is *always*, in some of its aspects, or in some wise a positive concept. To say that is simply to report the empirical facts about how men think. Read Teichmüller's pretty little chapter on the *Nichts* in his *Metaphysik*, if you want a very non-Hegelian expression of the same view. Consider Peirce's logical [page missing] It isn't I who say that. Any reflection can show it to you for yourself.

In the same way, it is not only true, but obvious to the least glance at countless types of fact, that objects are constantly qualified by their negations, that for me merely to mention A, and to mention A explicitly as in any sense alone, or as *alone by itself*, may mean for me very different ways of taking A. As to what follows herefrom, I have shown elsewhere. These things aren't disposed of by talking of "superfetations," but by observing what one means.—

J.R.

236 "Supposed true or false by us finites—I see no other truth in the field." (James)

237 "—all by us, namely, proleptically. Otherwise it is not known at all, & has as yet no truth save what we give it." (James)

238 "I never doubted this: But it does seem to me odd enough to drop in an absolute because foresooth there must be someone to think all this rubbish that we may forget to think ourselves." (James)

To David Starr Jordan, May 1, 1899[239]

103 Irving St.
Cambridge, Mass.
May 1, '99.

Dear Dr. Jordan:—

A. O. Lovejoy is an admirable man,—growing, learned, resolute, ingenious, and sensible. He has the one defect of professional inexperience as a teacher. Otherwise we all agree as to his powers and his promise. He certainly has a good presence, and a good power of exposition in presence of a company of men. I am myself not sure how far he has ever taught classes at all, but of course he has not yet been tested as a professor. He is a man of admirable moral fibre. I think that you could trust him early to make his way. That he has a future, I feel assured. I recommend him heartily for a place with you.

I am glad to hear that you are so much better off financially than of old, in your University; and I trust that no clouds will ever obscure the sun of prosperity. I rejoice to see what stand you take as to the Philippine business, and I wish that I could see how to take part in the fight effectively myself,—the fight I mean against militarism.

Yours Truly
Josiah Royce.

To Thomas Davidson, May 13, 1899[240]

103 Irving St. Cambridge.
May 13, 1899.

My Dear Davidson:—

I shall be busy all summer writing the second Course of my Gifford Lectures. My nose will be in the neighborhood of the grindstone, if not flat against it, until the task of grinding is done. And so, for still another season I dare not try to come to you.

[239] ALS. Jordan Papers. SUA.
[240] ALS. Davidson Papers. YUS.

Aberdeen proved to be a delightful place to visit, and although I found nobody there like you, I was often and pleasantly reminded of happy hours passed in your company when I met some of the heartiest and most keen-witted of your fellows in those regions. I would like to talk over the place with you, if only, in this world of distractions, there were ever time to meet and talk. I have heard with deep regret of your long and trying illnesses. I hope that luck will treat you this season better.

Greet my old friends, and believe me, spite of my inability to write frequent letters, always, affectionately,

Yours Very Truly
Josiah Royce.

To George Platt Brett, August 22, 1899[241]

103 Irving St.
Cambridge, Mass.
Aug. 22, 1899.

My Dear Mr. Brett:—

I enclose in a package that is today expressed to you by the American Express Co., the MS of my first series of *Gifford Lectures*, delivered in January of this year at Aberdeen, and now revised for print.[242] In accordance with the agreement already made, I offer this for publication by the Macmillan Co.

The MS as submitted contains about 130,000 words. I should like to have it printed in a form not very different from that of other Gifford Lectures, and shall be easy to suit, I presume, as to the appearance of the page, so long as that general plan is followed.

The MS as presented is in itself a complete whole, except for its promises of the second series to follow. Should I by chance fail to complete the second course, through any unavoidable mishap, this first course can perfectly well stand upon its own legs, as a treatise on general Metaphysics. So you need not hesitate about proceeding to print.

One further question, however, I wish to submit to your judgment at once, although it is a question that need not delay your

241 ALS. Macmillan Papers. NYPL.

242 *WI*, 1, copyrighted 1899, but actually published in January, 1900.

printing of what is here. I propose, with your approval, to send in a "Supplementary Essay," which will discuss the important problem (for me) of my relations to Bradley's *Appearance and Reality*,—a book to which I owe much, and which, despite some differences of opinion, I prize highly. The importance of Bradley's book, and its place amongst your philosophical publications, seems to justify an addition to the present volume,—an addition relevant to these lectures in every way, but not required in order to make them merely readable by themselves,—an addition devoted to a study of B's views in their relation to mine. As this supplementary essay would appeal mostly to technical metaphysical readers, I should be glad to have it follow in some finer print, say with 400 or 425 words to the page. It would then cover about 100 pages, at the close of my volume.

Now as to this supplement, I cannot of course ask you, under your agreement, to print it unless you think best. If printed, it would, in my opinion, increase the value of my book enough to make the addition objectively worthwhile. But if you decline to undertake the additional expense, I can try some other plan about the disposition of the MS. In no case will the decision as to this matter involve any necessary delay as to proceeding to print with the lectures themselves. The supplementary essay now lies on my desk, very nearly completed. If you decline it, or if, when accepted, it is not delivered in time, the lectures can be issued without it, and nobody will know of its absence. If you accept it, I will send it on within a very short time.

The lectures themselves have received much revision. Hence the delay. Now that they are finished, the sooner I can get them printed, the better. I want to use them, if possible, as a class text-book here in the second half of the coming academic year (say 25 or 30 copies by Feb. 15, 1900). If even I could have a copy or two to take abroad about Christmas, when I go for the second course, I should also be glad of that. But perhaps that is hoping for too much. In any case I will read proofs promptly when I receive them, and there shall be no cause of delay from my side.

I may have to be away from home during the coming week, but shall answer letters promptly after that time.

Yours Very Truly
Josiah Royce.

To George Platt Brett, September 1, 1899[243]

103 Irving St.
Cambridge, Mass.
Sept. 1, 1899.

My Dear Mr. Brett:—

I enclose in finished form, the proposed supplementary essay to the First Series of the Gifford Lectures. This would constitute all of what I hope to have printed in the volume. The Preface will be but a page or two.

In favor of printing this paper is its close relation to the most fundamental theses of my lectures, and its importance as defending my general doctrine against Bradley, and as introducing very central ideas that I cannot pause to explain at length in my Second Series, but that I must use therein. The main problem, that of the Infinite, has recently assumed new phases, which I have here discussed in the light of the most recent literature. In brief, the paper is one of the most serious and important things that ever I shall be able to write, or that ever I have written. Yet of necessity (unless I largely rewrote it) I could hardly print it apart from these lectures, so full is it of reference to them. It contains in the neighborhood of 48,000 words. It is technical, but, for students, will greatly increase the value of my book. It could be put into finer print. It need not now delay long the publication, as it is wholly finished.

I don't know why the practise as to former Gifford Lectures need be decisive as to this point. Supplementary essays, where relevant to the main point as this one is, never seem to me out of place in a philosophical book.

Yours Truly
Josiah Royce.

[243] ALS. Macmillan Papers, NYPL.

To Charles William Eliot, October 15, 1899[244]

103 Irving St.
Oct. 15, 1899

Dear Dr. Eliot:—

After thinking over your request of yesterday, I have decided to attempt to do what I can to meet your very kind wish. As I have already been asked to read a paper at Oxford, during my coming visit abroad, I must prepare something for that occasion; but I need not publish that paper as one prepared for that company. If I may read, as my proposed Ingersoll Lecture, a revised paper on "The Conception of Immortality" which I now have in one form, but which I shall adapt for the new case, and if I may then later use that paper, in advance of its publication, for the Oxford audience, I can make the proposed new engagement consistent with my present, very engrossing, engagements. Therefore, if this seems to you a proper plan, I am willing to undertake to meet your wish, as expressed to me in the conversation yesterday at Professor Shaler's.

In this connection, I have, however, one request still to make. In order to meet the proposed engagement at Oxford, I shall have to ask for a few days extension of my leave of absence. The Corporation has already voted me leave to Feb. 15 from Dec. 23. I cannot well visit Oxford before the conclusion of the Gifford Lectures, i.e., until after Feb. 1. This will lose me the steamer of Feb. 3. I may be unable to get any steamer sooner than Saturday Feb. 10, although I shall hope to get away by Wednesday the 7th. May I extend my leave accordingly in view of the Oxford call?—

Yours Very Truly
Josiah Royce.

[244] ALS. Eliot Papers. HUA.

To Horace Elisha Scudder, November 13, 1899[245]

Nov. 13, 1899.

Dear Mr. Scudder:—

I thank you for your kind letter. The University Publication Office, as I believe, has the authority to decide for the author as to how the Ingersoll Lecture shall be printed, under the terms of the Will. I understand from the President, and from Mr. Williams the Publication Superintendent, that the University wishes this volume printed in your Series, but that this time the title page should show, as I believe previous titles have not so clearly shown, that this is an Ingersoll Lecture, and is, in a sense, a University publication. I shall accordingly turn over the MS, when it has been revised, to Mr. Williams, who will take charge of the rest of the affair.

Yours Very Truly
Josiah Royce.

To William James, December 3, 1899[246]

103 Irving St.
Dec. 3, 1899.

Dear James:—

Getting one book through the press while writing another, isn't, in my case, conducive to much ability to do extra writing; and my letters pile up unanswered in a vast array. I have long meant to write to you; but the feeling that I soon shall see you, and that I shall hope for a good time in your company, has been an added factor in keeping me from launching out upon the letter that I owe.

I have grieved more than I can tell over the troubles that beset your health, and especially over their stubbornness in continuing to vex.[247] Dr. Driver and Dr. Putnam have both spoken, however, so *very* cheerfully and hopefully concerning what they have known

[245] ALS. Scudder Papers. UCB.

[246] ALS. James Papers. HL.

[247] James had gone abroad during the summer of 1899 to write his Gifford Lectures, but a very serious heart attack imposed a state of total invalidism for several months.

of your case in the past, that I heartily look forward to a return to vigor, in your case, before long, while I am thoroughly glad that you are getting a solid rest.

As for us,—you have surely heard of the College,—of Barrett Wendell's article on Radcliffe,[248] which, mild a matter though it is, and amusing in its own way, is perhaps our most contentious event, in a year which seems so far singularly free from academic contests. You know too how Marsh forsook the service of the Lord, to accept a fat place amongst the flesh pots of Egypt,[249] and how Davenport went to Chicago.[250]—And as to the city of Cambridge, you may also know that we are having an extraordinarly brisk muncipal contest over the Mayoralty. Champlin's reelection is opposed by Dickinson (a Harv. grad. of '88, & a man who has already been in the Legislature). The fight is extremely lively. Fox sides with Champlin. Dr. Cogswell is for Dickinson. I gossip with one party or another on the street, when I meet anybody who can advise me, and am much puzzled as to my own vote. On the whole I shall probably vote for Champlin, as the principal explicit objection to him is that he seems to people rather stiff-necked and cussed, and that he gets through his office business too early in the day for the convenience of the bores who want to find him. Cogswell knows other and profounder, mysterious reasons, but can't articulate precisely what they are. And in general Champlin has aroused antipathy, rather than definable objections. I suppose that such a record is, on the whole, creditable to an executive, as cussedness and dispatch are probably the most useful qualities for a Mayor; so unless I learn something new, I shall side with neighbor Fox.—As to the neighborhood,—your tenants are very welcome substitutes so long as any substitution at all is necessary. I am glad not to have your house vacant, as it was when last you left us; for it used to make me feel very lonesome to see it so. The other new neighbors are the Warrens,[251] Warren being our new Classical man, as of

[248] "The Relations of Radcliffe College with Harvard," *Harvard Monthly* 29 (October 1899): 1–10.

[249] Arthur Richmond Marsh, professor of comparative literature, resigned his academic post in September 1899, to accept a position with Planters' Compress Company, in the cotton business.

[250] Charles B. Davenport, an instructor in the Zoology Department, accepted a professorship at the University of Chicago.

[251] Minton Warren came to Harvard as professor of Latin after twenty years at Johns Hopkins.

course you know. Mrs. Warren is a great ornament to the neighborhood—a most picturesque and winning little personality; and her boy is a pretty constant companion of the rest of our neighborhood boys, amongst whom he takes an active place.—I see your boys from time to time, especially the youngest, who flourishes finely. It is a very interesting view that Harry gives of his life as Editor of the *Crimson*, in his paper in the current *Harv. Grad.'s Mag.*[252] I read it with much interest last night.

December comes, but winter lingers. "Nor ever falls one least small star of snow." Today was bright and warm, with the air of a September day. Only light rains have come for weeks, and Hassett is at his wits ends to keep his bills up to their proper height,—jobs being so few. The squirrels are numerous and very merry, and visit our windows for their daily meal of nuts in great numbers. The Warrens have imported a very clever cat, who excites the fury of the squirrels, and who hopelessly climbs the trees after them, while I, who love both cats and squirrels, in vain endeavor to persuade them all to take a monistic view of the situation. Like you, they persist in pluralism, and will listen to no reconciliation of the One & the Many.

As you see, thrilling incidents are in this locality few—in the visible world, at least; and I tell you only what I can find to tell. As to events on the higher plane, I do what little I can to report the same in preparing my second course of Giffords; the lectures aren't done yet, but are nearly so; and I think that I shall finish before starting. The former course is to be published in January, and I shall bring a copy when I come. The book contains a long Supplementary Essay on Bradley and the Concept of the Infinite, which I wrote last summer, and which stuffs out the whole to some 600 pp. —I am not very tired, but shall be glad of the little vacation.—All your friends ask often about you, and send greetings. Mrs. Royce joins me in warmest good wishes to you and Mrs. James.

Yours Always,
Josiah Royce

I now intend to leave by the *Etruria*, Dec. 23.—I shall appear in London about the first of Jan. I shall look for you, if you are there; but of course I see that your plans are liable to change, and that you may by then have found the country a better place.

[252] Henry James, 2d, "The Crimson," *Harvard Graduates' Magazine* 8 (December 1899), 181–85.

To Charles William Eliot, December 5, 1899[253]

103 Irving St.
Dec. 5, 1899.

Dear Dr. Eliot:—

There was not time for me to say, today, what I ought to have said before, namely, that I wish to thank you, and the Corporation, most heartily, for the appointment to the Ingersoll Lectureship. I may add that I took the task much more seriously than I had at first supposed it possible to do. When you first mentioned the matter, I had on hand a MS, which I agreed, in lack of a better, to use for the purpose. I felt at liberty to revise it for the new undertaking. The revision quickly became a rewriting. As a fact, the Ingersoll lecture, as delivered, contained only a very few pages,—not more than one eighth,—of the MS of the former lecture. The entire plan of procedure was altered. The new essay is a presentation such as I have never tried before. In its revised shape, my statement has been received with a kindness that, in its original form, it could never have called out, and that, inadequate as it still is, it would even very far less have deserved. It may interest you to know that, despite the Gifford engagement, I felt strictly bound to give my best efforts to this one, and that I really wrote a substantially new lecture.

I may add that I shall leave a copy with Mr. Williams when I go abroad, so that, in case of accident to me, or to the copy that I take with me to Oxford, there may be no failure of publication.

With renewed thanks, I remain,
Yours Very Truly
Josiah Royce.

[253] ALS. Eliot Papers. HUA.

To William James, December 11, 1899[254]

Cambridge.
Dec. 11, 1899.

Dear James:—

In my letter to you, mailed some days since, I said, I believe, that I should go over by the *Etruria*, leaving the 23d. Some pressing jobs to be done here have since made it necessary for me to wait until the 27th, when I shall leave by the *Teutonic*. If there is no delay, I shall reach Liverpool by Wednesday the 3d, or by Thursday the 4th. There will then be time to go on to London. Whether you will be then in London, I gather from conversations with your son Harry to be a little uncertain; and so I don't know exactly how to find you. But if you will address me, at about the mentioned date, at the American Express Company, 3 Waterloo Place (Pall Mall), London, I shall get the letter at once upon arrival, and can then know where to look you up, if you are near enough. I hope that you prosper, and that I can see you. I am to begin at Aberdeen on the 10th, and shall go on thither Monday the 8th. I have no engagements before then, after my arrival. But an hour with you would be a delight if I can get it.

Winter still holds off. After some days of dry cold, tonight is warm, and promises a rain of spring-like mildness. The mayoralty contest ends with a flood of circulars and signatures,—Richard Dana, Thorpe, Archy Howe, Norton, Eliot, Jabez Fox, Dr. Cogswell, and the devil, all in it together, exhorting voters, some on one side and some on the other. The academic world serene. Health good at home except a little asthma on the part of Stephen.—

Yours Always,
Josiah Royce.

254 ALS. James Papers. HL.

To William Angus Knight, December 22, 1899[255]

103 Irving St.
Cambridge, Mass.
Dec. 22, 1899.

My Dear Professor Knight:—

I have received your kind letter, and shall certainly try to arrange, this time, for a visit to St. Andrews. I have a paper on the "Conception of Immortality," which I have read here, as a public lecture, and which I am also to read, as a public lecture, Feb. 6, at Oxford. If your Philosophical Society meets privately, or semi-privately, so that the lecture, if read to you in January, would be sure not to be summarized in any newspaper report, I do not see that the Oxford people could object to its having been read at St. Andrews before I reach them. Of course, I ought not to make too much public duplication of papers formally presented.

As to dates, I am to be in Aberdeen, lecturing, thrice weekly, on Mond., Wed., Fri., at 3 or 4 P.M. from Jan. 10 to Jan. 31st. I could perhaps meet you, at St. Andrews, some Saturday, reading either in the afternoon or in the evening, and returning Monday morning. If you will write me at the "Westbourne House, 438 Union St.," Aberdeen, by Jan. 10, I think that we can arrange a date. I lecture in Glasgow Feb. 2, and at Oxford Feb. 6.

I thank you for the invitation. I am very sorry about dear James. I hope for the best in his case.

Yours Very Truly
Josiah Royce.

To William Angus Knight, January 10, 1900[256]

Jan. 10, 1900.

Dear Professor Knight:—

I have entered on my programme a visit to you, and to St. Andrews, on Saturday, Jan. 27, in accordance with your kind invita-

[255] ALS. PML.
[256] ALS. PML.

tion. My only condition is that I shall be able to return in time for my lecture here on the Monday following the 29th, at 3 o'clock. I assume that there will be no trouble about that.

I ought to confess that my lecture, on Immortality, which was an evening lecture at Cambridge, is precisely one hour and twenty minutes long, and that, owing to the crowded mass of materials discussed, it could be shortened only with great difficulty. Is such a length feasible with your company under the circumstances?—With many thanks for your invitation I remain,

Yours Very Truly
Josiah Royce.

To William Angus Knight, February 7, 1900[257]

R. M. S. "OCEANIC"
Feb. 7, 1900.

Dear Professor Knight:—

If time had permitted, I should have answered sooner your letter enclosing the cheque for expenses. I thank you for it, and shall deliver the contents of its proposals, so far as concerns Harvard, at once, to my colleagues upon my arrival. I am wholly unaware how plans for next year have developed in my absence, and can therefore make no forecast as to what reply I shall get when I arrive; but I have already written to Palmer in general about the possibilities that you suggest, and I feel sure that unless they are already excluded by some arrangement already decided upon and unknown to me, they will receive serious consideration.[258] You shall hear as soon as possible how I find matters upon my arrival.

Glasgow followed St. Andrews in my wanderings outside of Aberdeen. I have dined & discussed and wandered very busily. I concluded my visit with a stay in Oxford from Saturday last until yesterday. I am very full now of good things of the spirit; but I shall not forget my delightful visit to you. With warm regards to Mrs. Knight & Miss Knight, I remain

Yours Very Truly
Josiah Royce.

[257] ALS. PML.

[258] In an undated letter to President Eliot (not included in this edition) Royce recommends that Knight be invited to lecture at Harvard.

I am glad indeed to learn that my paper set any students to discussing its problem. Please give your students once more my most cordial greetings.

To William James, February 7, 1900[259]

R. M. S. "OCEANIC"
Feb. 7, 1900

Dear James:—

Your letter was a great joy to me. Best of all was the news of your improvement. Very grateful was your goodness in speaking so kindly of my book, which, to me, as I hope, will soon have faded like streaks, &c., into the infinite azure, &c., although I am still pretty near to it, & still more or less concerned in its fate. Your approval, in just the sense in which you give it, is worth more to me than that of anybody else.

My Catalogue of engagements has been: Aberdeen regular lectures; Lecture to Philos. Soc. at Edinburgh Jan. 20; ditto, St. Andrews, Jan. 27; Lecture as Honor'y Pres't of Philos. Soc. at Glasgow, Feb. 2; two extra lectures (one prepared *ad hoc*) at Aberdeen; dinners; teas; letters; good behaviour (so far as I was capable) as guest in people's houses during my visits away from Aberdeen; and finally, a visit from last Saturday until yesterday, with Dr. Carpenter in Oxford (where I met Caird, Stout, Dons that I do and Dons that I don't know, &c); a lecture at Oxford; and last this steamer homeward bound. All went well enough. Everywhere they ask about you, & regard me only as the advance agent of the true American Theory. *That* they await from you. I received endless kindness; but they have still far more, I am sure, in store for you if only fate would permit them to get at you.

This by way of mere report & for the instant, farewell. My warmest greeting to Mrs. James,—affectionately,

Yours Always
Josiah Royce.

[259] ALS. James Papers. HL. Printed in *TCWJ*, 1: 814.

The Letters

Part IV

1900-1913

Part IV

1900-1913

Royce's two greatest works, *The World and the Individual* and *The Problem of Christianity*, establish the boundaries of this fourth section of his correspondence. Remarkably different, however, were the circumstances that led to the two books. The first resulted from a lineal development of thought, climaxing a decade of intense concentration. The second was the product of a sudden, almost unexpected spurt of energy that concluded a chaotic and often tragic period of his life.

With the Gifford Lectures completed, Royce had attained a definite peak in his intellectual growth; the "aboulic" mood that he noted afterwards lingered for several years. During this period he published *Outlines of Psychology* (1903) and *Herbert Spencer* (1904), two of his least ambitious works. At the same time he agreed to act as consultant for the Macmillan Company. His best work, at least for the first five years of the twentieth century, was done in logic.

By 1908, though scarcely more than fifty years old, Royce appears prematurely aged. *The Philosophy of Loyalty* gave him some sense of renewed strength, but this was followed shortly by the tragic illness and death of Christopher Royce, and by the death of William James. Many feared that the cerebral hemorrhage which struck Royce in 1912 would end his productive years. But resilience served him well again. Cheerfully he set to work, and within a year he had written *The Problem of Christianity*.

To William James, September 12, 1900[1]

Cambridge, Mass.
103 Irving St.
Sept. 12, 1900.

Dear James:—

I suppose that I have seemed hopelessly unfaithful, but the fact is that the second half year's work, on my return, proved very exacting, giving me, towards the end, not indeed any serious physical tire, but a sense of being driven, a discomfort with the sight and presence of classes and responsibilities, that left me, at the close, morally tired,—mildly aboulic, so to speak. When my boy was graduated,[2] and my last importunate student disposed of, I found myself averse to any occupation but trolley riding with my wife, reading quasi-mathematical speculative literature, collecting my wits, and avoiding responsibilities. For writing I have had, all vacation, a strong aversion, due simply to writing so much and so long before. My unanswered letters are numerous. My little tire, such as it was, has mostly passed off. I have collected my thoughts, and am full of plans for the year. But it will be some time before I get my correspondence straightened out.

[1] ALS. James Papers. HL. Partly printed in *TCWJ*, 1: 815–16.
[2] Christopher Royce received his A. B. from Harvard in June, 1900.

Of you I have heard frequently, now from this and now from that source, and I have thought, I assure you, despite my silence, a great deal. The year to come will be very lonesome without you, and my own interest in Harvard is more bound up with my associations with you than it is with any one other interest. Philosophy I love for itself, and life for its general meaning. But Harvard originally meant to me *you*, and the old association remains still the deepest. I shall go on, and lecture; but the Department can have its real meaning to me personally only when you are here. And I ought the more plainly to say that, because I am so poor a letter writer, and so silent, that you must think me less bound up in you than I always am. My defect as a letter writer is simply a result of my writing so much otherwise. The writing centres rebel at anything but lectures and books. But the heart has its own life too, and I miss you deeply.

Well, as for news, Münsterberg will have seen you, and others too will have seen you, and they will have told you all last year's events. I can only say that I came back and lectured here until all was blue, and that even the Cubans[3] this summer (for whom, to be sure, I prepared two lectures which Mrs. Minton Warren translated into Spanish) I have little news to tell, while other official business did not much interest me. The Cubans themselves gave a very weird seeming to Harvard Square. Brock Brothers put up signs to the effect that Spanish was spoken there; Amee Brothers heaped up guides and other such attractions on their counters, and were always crowded with Cuban customers; all Harvard Square joined in inducing the visitors to trade away their little all; and "against the fence" leaned not only the mucker and the jobless workingman, but also the wide-trousered little squat swarthy Cuban, destroying cigarettes, and gesticulating, while his loud conversational voice, harsh and shrill, often made the square seem like a bird store when the parrots are lively. The Cuban women were far more picturesque. They sat in rows in the evenings, after supper, beneath the tablets of Memorial Hall. Their chaperones, and their visitors, male and female, clustered about them. We met more closely a very few of them, and liked them well.—From a human point of view the whole affair was, despite its amusing trivialities, in its essential features a great success—an object lesson in kindli-

[3] A group of Cuban school-teachers attended the Harvard Summer School in 1900.

ness of enterprise, and in the possibilities of international courtesy. It was well worth what it cost.

In the neighborhood, here in the Norton estate, a new street is cut through from the north end of the present Irving St, at a point immediately north of Mark's house, to the west.[4] Jabez Fox is become Superior Judge. He lives at the Colonial Club. He called on us the other evening, and seems well to enjoy his honors, but to be lonely for his family. His tenants during the absence of his family are the Eatons, who are excellent people; but their eldest daughter practises singing, without regard to the heat of the summer. Her purposes are professional, her conscientious devotion to them is absolute, and her voice is that of Brynhilde on a charger. I view her with profound, but somewhat timid respect, and am not altogether comforted for the loss of our admirable Foxes. Cummings, as you know, has joined the company of the saints, and is to be Edw. Ev. Hale's successor as a pastor. He will however still live amongst us, and the neighborhood gains in sanctity daily. Lanman, as I learn, has so impressed some of his Ceylonese friends with his work as editor of Buddhist Scriptures, that a shrine has been erected in his honor somewhere out there, and he is in the way to be worshipped with special rites! He himself, when I asked him about the matter the other day, denied all knowledge of the shrine, but was forced, when I pressed the point, to admit its possibility, in view of the Ceylonese habits. At all events, the story came to me from a source quite as authentic as that of most Oriental stories of our current news.

I visited Norton at Ashfield, and spoke at the Ashfield dinner this August.[5] Stanley Hall was there, took me driving, was almost

[4] Subdivision of "Norton's Woods" began in 1889. In 1900 there were six houses on the west side of Irving Street. From south to north: No. 95, William James; No. 99, Judge Jabez Fox; No. 103, Royce; No. 105, Minton Warren; No. 107, Mrs. Eliza P. Gibbens and Mrs. Margaret Gregor (Mrs. James's mother and sister); No. 109, E. L. Mark. There were two homes on the east side of Irving Street: No. 104, Edward Cummings (father of the poet, E. E. Cummings); No. 110, Robert H. Davis. Charles R. Lanman lived at No. 9 Farrar Street.

[5] Ashfield was the location of Charles Eliot Norton's summer home. In 1879 he inaugurated an annual "Academy Dinner"—a benefit for the local school. Prominent men each year were invited to speak to the townspeople on topics of national interest. See Kermit Vanderbilt, *Charles Eliot Norton: Apostle of Culture in a Democracy* (Cambridge: Harvard University Press, 1959), pp. 196–97.

affectionate in his friendliness, and stroked my fur down till it gleamed in the sunlight. Norton himself was the perfect host that he is bound to be, and I came away quite overcome with the dignity of Ashfield.—And now when you consider once more your neighbors, as these familiar names recall them to you, doesn't it make you feel almost ready to get back to Irving St? Where else are to be found such judges, clergymen, apotheosized Orientalists? But I forbear. At all events, I assure you, Irving St. needs you, and will miss you until you come.

We have all been rejoiced by Mrs. Gregor's safe weathering of the storm. The baby has been admired whenever it could be seen. I am sorry that at first its health was so delicate. But now, as I hope, all will go safely.

As you see, my news is not startling. In politics we are just now asked to choose whom (or which) we prefer, the devil or the deep sea. I shall vote for neither. A special private ticket hereabouts has nominated Archie Howe for Vice Pres., and I forget whom for Pres. I expect to vote for that, or for some other wild ticket.—I came rather near deciding, the other day, upon closing vacation by a coasting voyage by steamer as far as Galveston. I almost decided upon taking the Mallory Line boat of Sept. 1.—Considerations of economy, rather than anything else, finally led me to take a shorter trip, by the Clyde Line to Charleston and directly back. Had I followed out the first plan, I should have reached Galveston, if at all, along with the hurricane. Thus we see that no man can escape destiny.

Well, this gossip must close now. Much affection goes with it. I wish that real cheer could go also. But that I suppose, depends upon your luck. I hope that you do well as possible, and that the Gifford Lectures prosper.—My best regards to Mrs. James. Mrs. Royce greets you both heartily and with best wishes.

Yours Lovingly
Josiah Royce.

To James McKeen Cattell, October 14, 1900[6]

Cambridge, Mass.
Irving St.
Oct. 14, 1900

Dear Professor Cattell:—

Some time last summer, when I was too devoted to resting to follow closely public prints and gossip, and when I read *Science* to be sure, but only for its serious articles,—a rumor got abroad that I had been called to deliver a Course of Lectures at Dublin University. I missed the original publication of the rumor. But now it keeps coming back to trouble me. I can trace it, now that I try to do so, only as far as the notes in a number of *Science* in June or July. Do you know anything of the source of the rumor? I do not. I know nobody at Dublin University, and never received any communication from that institution, or from any of its officers. The whole thing must be a mere chance echo of the Aberdeen engagement (now quite finished). But the rumor vexes and pursues me. Can you help me to trace it? I don't want anything published further about it at this late day, but I should like to find the cause of the story.

Yours Very Truly
Josiah Royce

Science interests me constantly, and seems to be a beautifully edited journal. I like also the new *Pop. Sci. Mon.*

To Charles Eliot Norton, January 27, 1901[7]

103 Irving Street
Cambridge
Jan. 27, 1901

Dear Professor Norton:—

I have been away from home the greater part of yesterday and today, using the free time, that relief from lectures makes possible,

[6] ALS. Cattell Papers. LC.
[7] ALS. Norton Papers. HL.

for two or three little outings, one in company with Mrs. Royce, and also one alone, as well as one with a young student friend of mine. Hence not until this evening have I had time to sit down over the Cudworth, and make its acquaintance in this very interesting dress.[8]

I thank you very deeply for the gift. This Latin edition of Mosheim contains, I find, more than appears on the first glance,—the discourse on Immutable Morality, and the Dissertations of Mosheim, as well as other things. I had never examined this edition, having used the treatises only in the English; and I see now how much Mosheim added in the way of solid editorship, and how beautiful a piece of work he made of the whole. It will find a very valued place on my shelves.

I prize the gift for itself very highly,—and for your kind thought of me still more. There are many things that I have to thank you for, and many happy and wisely spent hours that I owe to your presence and to your hospitality. I thank you heartily for them all, and now especially for this new reminder of your friendship.—

Yours Very Truly
Josiah Royce.

To John Maxon Stillman, February 27, 1901[9]

103 Irving Street
Cambridge
Feb. 27, 1901

My Dear Stillman:—

More than once, during the painful discussions about your Uni-

[8] This was apparently a gift copy (now in the Robbins Library, Harvard University) of J. L. Mosheim's Latin edition of Ralph Cudworth, *Systema Intellectuale Huius Universi*, 2 tom. (Jena, 1733)—given to Royce probably for his participation in the Ashfield Academy Dinner of 1900. See fn. 5 above.

[9] ALS. Stillman Papers. SUA. This and the succeeding letter to Stillman concerns a case of academic freedom which erupted at Stanford University in the fall of 1900. Edward Alsworth Ross (1866–1951), a distinguished sociologist, resigned following a disagreement with President David Starr Jordan and Mrs. Leland Stanford over his right to free expression of political views. A supporter of William Jennings Bryan, Ross had written *Honest Dollars* (Chicago: C. H. Kerr and Co., 1896). He is best remembered for *Social Control* (New York: Macmillan Co., 1901) and a number of pioneer works in social psychology.

versity during recent times, I have wanted to write to you, to express my sorrow that the incidents in question should have come to pass, to give you the trouble that, as I know, they must have given. I have heard of course of the position that you have taken in the controversy, and have felt that position of yours to be, for me, one the strongest possible assurances that a closer knowledge of the facts must give a better ground than an outsider could see for the justification of Jordan's acts. As to the principle of academic liberty, you know my views of old. But I have of course always felt that no form of desirable or tolerable academic freedom justifies the retention of an unfit man; and I fully agree that the professor has a peculiar duty to be discreet in his public utterances. For me, as for others, however, the difficulty of forming an opinion about *this* affair has lain just here:—If we could feel sure that President Jordan, acting in the light of his judgment, *freely* decided Ross to be an unfit man for the place, then indeed the affair (so we felt) was nobody's business but that of those immediately concerned. On the other hand, if the dismissal of Ross was really due, not to Jordan's free judgment, but to an arbitrary decision of Mrs. Stanford, then, in view of the publicity that the affair has obtained, it would necessarily become, and remain (as we felt) an affair of general academic concern. And so we have had to wait for light.

Now only three days ago I was prepared, on the evidence then known to me, to regard it as pretty certain (1) that Ross had actually been dismissed for a cause probably quite sufficient, while (2) Mrs. Stanford had indeed had *more* to do with the dismissal than, in my opinion, any benefactor of education, has (as a benefactor) a right to have. I was disposed, therefore, to drop the subject as (to be sure) an incident of an unfortunate character (in view of Mrs. Stanford's having *any* decisive voice whatever in such an official act), but as a matter where probably the official act in question got rid of an officer who was "not the man for the place."

But on Monday I read the report of the Economists' Committee; and for the first time I learned the new facts upon which that report is based. The whole affair changes its aspect to me at once. And I write mainly to urge upon you, as your warm friend, my sense that academic opinion on this side will very justly regard the new facts as deeply affecting our whole confidence in Jordan, not only as a President but as a man, unless the new facts can be wholly explained. I doubt not that they will be as new to you as to me. I earnestly hope that some explanation will be forthcoming.

But I urgently must represent that Jordan's personal honor is involved in the issue now made, as it has been involved at no time before.

In May 1900, as it seems, he wrote, on his official responsibility, a letter containing a most unqualified commendation of Ross, not only as man, but as officer, and as occupant of this particular chair. The praise given is of the highest. Then later Jordan dismissed him, and then, while Ross's personal and professional reputation are at stake before the whole country, he now writes that Ross was dismissed because of his unfitness for the place. Now if all this series of events took place as now represented, Jordan's position as a President and as a man is affected, in the eyes of the entire academic public, in a way that I, who have always had a warmly friendly feeling for Jordan, find it extremely painful to contemplate. And the general public judgment of all that followed,–viz., of Howard's wild revolt, & the rest,–is profoundly altered also by this evidence that acts on the part of Howard and the rest which seemed mere madness, may have been due to a knowledge of what now appears as Jordan's actual conduct.

Now, my dear fellow, I don't want for an instant to believe this of Jordan, or to imagine that the reputation of one of his officers is in his eyes, a thing to be betrayed in the way indicated by the present evidence. I know perfectly well how you would view such an act as is now reported of him. I hope, therefore, most ardently, that you or someone can show me how the thing can be explained. Only pray urge, if you can, upon Jordan, that if he values the good repute of his University or of himself, he may not make light of the new evidence. I say this in the most friendly spirit, and not as any partisan.

Well, it is a pity to have so little space left for personal words. We both remember you (Mrs. Royce and myself) affectionately. I wish that I could see you again. Remember me cordially to all yours and believe me

Yours Very Truly
Josiah Royce.

You can show this letter to anybody you please, of course.

To John Maxon Stillman, March 17, 1901[10]

Cambridge, Mass.
103 Irving St.
March 17, 1901

Dear Stillman:—

Many thanks indeed for your long and very interesting letter. I have shown it to no one but Mrs. Royce and Mrs. Head (who is now with us), but I have read it carefully, and I feel both the frankness of its admirable temper, and my own indebtedness to you for the trouble that you have taken on my behalf.

Your own personal position I fully understand. You have no share in the origin of these misfortunes, and now you are doing your best for the good of your University in a serious difficulty. I have no doubt that you are acting, for your own part, upon sound principles. I am very sorry that you should be forced to take so much trouble for a cause that ought never to have been forced upon your attention at all by any official acts of your chief.

You ask whether your statement modifies my views of the affair. In some ways, certainly. It makes clearer the complexities, it gives me a clearer insight into the human problem as to how Jordan came to get into such a position, and it confirms the doubts that before I had as to the actual solidity of Ross's academic reputation.

Nevertheless, to my mind, the aspect of this matter which most interests, and most concerns, the academic public of America, now appears clearly in a light in which a substantial justification of your President's policy, in the case in question, seems, henceforth, impossible. As I told you, I have no sort of prejudice against Jordan, and every sort of good will for Stanford University (apart from this misadventure), and no shred of personal interest in Ross (whom I never saw, and of whose written or spoken words upon any subject I never saw more than the publications immediately connected with this controversy have forced upon my attention). I have no personal interest in defending Ross. His economic views, so far as I have heard of them, arouse in me no curiosity to know more about him or them. He is to me merely an unknown col-

[10] ALS. Stillman Papers. SUA.

league. That, I suppose, is what he is to most college officers who have talked over the case.

But our interest, in a professional sense, lies here:—This is a time of great academic expansion. Our common responsibilities to the public are increasing. A great deal of fresh endowment is constantly coming to us. Our public (and by that I mean the public about any American University), is depending upon our profession for very serious tasks, and is paying largely to get a great service. But now arises a natural and wide spread suspicion,—viz., that the teaching in our Universities regarding controversial matters, is, (just because of all these gifts), unduly influenced by subserviency to the good will of large donors. The charge is repeated and general. I find evidence that very many silently regard us all as at the mercy of influential benefactors. A certain number openly say that we are so. Our youth wonder how far our mouths are shut (or opened) by influences with which the love of truth and a just discretion have nothing to do. In brief, the substantial honesty of our profession is called in question.

Now for such general charges there is no better reply than honest work. That we all feel. But we are rightly sensitive at such a time about whatever definite act reflects upon the honor of our profession. Suspicions of a general sort we can take care of. But a case that means a public attack upon the standing of the profession, we all naturally regard with keen interest. It concerns us all.

But when such a case arises, we of course first look to the responsible man, to the head, to see what he has to say. If he says plainly: "The fact is that this man was dismissed because [he was] unworthy of his place," we are not likely to go behind the returns, unless we are forced to do so. But for that very reason, the head to whom we appeal must not trifle with us or with the public. We are disposed to trust him until we find his judgment untrustworthy. When we do find that, we have to feel that he ought to remember that he trifles with the honor of the profession when he is guilty of malpractice in a case of this kind. For this sort of affair affects not merely an institution, but the relation of our whole calling as teachers to our public. If the *principles* upon which the responsible presiding officer has acted in settling such a matter are sound, then indeed we have no concern with the inevitably complex personal details. But so soon as the principles involved are manifestly wrong, then it is inevitable that the profession should very generally be led to feel that we have to repudiate, privately or openly, as the case may require, all such principles, whatever we happen to think, or not to think, about the merits of a man like Ross.

Now as to just the principles involved, Jordan stands, to my mind, in a hopeless position. He may have shown Quixotic generosity in letting Ross have a copy of the letter to Mrs. Stanford. The generosity may have been, as a fact, unmerited. But in any case, just that free communication of that letter to Ross made the opinions expressed all the more surely something to which the President of the University was definitely pledged. He could not properly speak with one voice as advocate, and with another as judge. The matter was too serious for any such equivocation. For it involved the principle whether a University is bound to retain its officers for their value, and to support them against irresponsible interference. If Jordan was compelled by "major force" to give up that principle, he owed it to the public to say so, without doubleness of speech. But if Ross wasn't worthy of the protection of the principle, Jordan equally offended against that principle in appealing to it, in his letter to Mrs. Stanford, as a shield to defend Ross. As a result, it seems to me impossible to feel any further confidence in his ability to apply this principle in future. I myself shall never be able to tell hereafter, when he speaks about any serious academic issue, whether he is doing so as advocate or as judge, or what it is that he says in private letters to offset his public statements.

This is why I myself lay such stress upon the pamphlet of the Economists. The most important sentences in that pamphlet are written by Jordan, not by anybody else. The great variety of the signatures attached to that report gives it no little weight,—but not, I repeat, as a vindication of Ross,—rather only as a sign that the evidence before the signers showed how lightly Jordan had treated the principle that was really at stake.

Of course, as you say, Mrs. Stanford has interfered no more than Trustees have often done, and still often do. But the question isn't whether such interference occurs, but only in what spirit our profession is to meet it *when* it occurs. The question, again, isn't whether the irresponsible forces have the power to do this sort of mischief, but whether they get the moral support of the President in doing so. Now Jordan *didn't* say: "Zeus, you may sink me if you will, you may save me if you will; but whatever you do, I will keep the rudder true." Hence these sorrows.

Ross may be, for all that I know, poor stuff. Or he may be a great man. I care not. I know that, whatever he be, his dismissal has done more harm to you and to our profession than his presence could have done in years,—& that not because of his merits or demerits, but because of Jordan's policy as now made clear.—On the whole, then, I am inclined to doubt whether any good can now be done by further public discussion, say by any reply from you or Jordan. More drawing of fire would only tend to fix public attention on the main point, which is now no longer Ross's value as an officer, but the matter that I have made prominent in this and in my last letter.

Of course I am not at all concerned to defend the methods that the Seligman Committee took in their investigation. I knew nothing of their doings until their work was all done: I hoped that their main evidence, namely that regarding Jordan's position, could be better explained by further facts. As that cannot be, I suppose that the public discussion of the details had better be dropped.

How sorry I am, personally, to have such a matter causing *you* extra trouble! I know how foreign to you is the spirit against which I am contending. And I haven't the least wish to say in any public way anything that would seem to oppose any position of yours. I hope that when we meet again, hereabouts, or in California, or in the House Boat on the Styx, or elsewhere, we shall have only the old reminiscences, many of which are so dear to me, to go over together, and that then not a wave of academic or of other trouble will roll across your peaceful breast.

With kindest regards to Mrs. Stillman,

Yours Always,
Josiah Royce.

Like the last letter, this one may be shown to anyone you please.

To William James, June 21, 1901[11]

June 21, 1901

Hotel Millbrae
Frank P. Mills, Manager
Palenville, Greene Co., New York

Dear James:—

During the whirl of the closing events of the year's work I hoped to find time to write to you, but have been obliged to wait until the leisure of this first vacation time. Let me above all say how delighted I have been by the so encouraging news from you of late.[12] Your reception at Edinburgh must have been a beautiful experience, even though you felt yourself excluded by your regimen from the more various and intimate hospitalities that the good Scotchmen would surely have showered upon you if they had found you as robust as themselves. I understand that you kept yourself pretty quiet. They are indeed very dear people. I shall always remember them with ardent affection. And I know that where they were good to me, they would both desire and by rights be required to be, if possible, ten times as good to you. The report of the first lecture made me very curious as to what was to follow; and you may be sure that the book when it comes out will be almost (it cannot be quite) as welcome as you will be in Irving St. on your return, which now seems so near.

As for us at home, my family had a somewhat careworn winter, owing to the last illness and death in our house of our mother, Mrs. Head, who came on from California last October, to spend the winter with her daughter, and with the numerous old friends of her youth still surviving in the region about Boston. This plan meant at first a good deal of running about, on visits and excursions, on the part of Mrs. Head, who after a long period of invalidism in recent years in California, seemed to herself at the moment to have fully recovered, and who was, in the autumn, in the most happy and

[11] ALS. James Papers. HL. Palenville, N. Y., is in the Catskill Mountains near the Hudson River.

[12] A response to James's postcard from Edinburgh, May 17, announcing the beginning of his Gifford Lectures; see *TCWJ* 1: 818.

enterprising of moods. But the keen eyes of her daughter from the first detected ominous changes in her condition when compared with what it normally used to be; and we soon had decided reason for anxiety. After Christmas mother, who was seventy two years old, began rapidly to fail. Medical examination revealed a complication of disorders, wherein senile nephritis appeared to be prominent. By March 1 the patient had taken pretty completely to her bed. She was free from suffering and from any conscious insight into the seriousness of her troubles until about a fortnight before the end. Then indeed death showed his teeth, and the close was pathetic enough. She died May 6. Mrs. Royce had of course the burden of care and responsibility all through. But she is now doing very well again, and will, as I hope, with a quiet summer, return to a very good condition by autumn. The boys have had reasonably good health.

As for me,—you will first wonder what I am up to at this place.—I left home for a short vacation trip Wednesday morning. I am just here, as it happens, only for the day. Tonight I take steamer for New York, and tomorrow I have engaged passage on the Cromwell Line steamer *Proteus*, for New Orleans, where I am due the 29th. Then I shall return swiftly by rail, and by the first of July expect to be in Cambridge, ready for the summer's campaign. I have still the finishing touches to put on the second volume of Gifford Lectures, and must have them in the printer's hands sometime in August. I need of course a little relaxation before setting to work upon the summer job; I still don't know of any better relaxation than a sea voyage; I fear not the South, since it will always be cool at sea; and the New Orleans voyage is sure to be a quiet one at this season. As for expenses,—it costs $35, stateroom and meals included, to go to sea for five full days from New York to New Orleans; and the boat is a good new one of 5000 tons. That compares well with the European voyage as to expense, doesn't it? And if one wants a quiet journey, I don't know any better rule than to go in whatever direction the crowd is not going. Hence my present choice.—My general condition is very good. The year was a pretty tangled one as you see; but I seem not to have suffered so much as Münsterberg just now does. He, poor fellow, with the destinies of two different social orders on his hands, has been doing nobly, and is growing in breath and strength beautifully, as I think; but at the close of the year he gets fussy, just as Palmer gets especially saintly, with the burdens of the work, and this time Palmer disappeared to Boxford and Münsterberg to Clifton, contemporaneously, the one gently severe towards the sinful world in general as he departed, and especially sweet and tender in his bearing towards me,—the other cheerful and enthusiastic until the moment before he went, but then of a sudden much distressed with a sense of fatigue and a good deal frightened about himself. Now I was not especially out of sorts, once our season of winter cares had passed away into the gray quiet of mood that death leaves behind it when the aged die; but seeing that Münsterberg and Palmer had both fled, I bethought me that Commencement week is full of bores, and that I alone should be there to represent the Department if I stayed. So I fled too.—As a fact, I do not believe that Münsterberg is more than a very little fatigued, and no doubt he will write another book before October, or a tragedy, or a collection of essays on womankind.[13] Palmer has really been lovely of late; and if we ever get our Philosophy building made *with* hands (as it is now *not* made with hands, but eternal &c.), Palmer's bust must take its place therein as the saintly man. Of the prospects, by the way, of that Philosophy building, I know nothing; but Münsterberg says that we may hear something at Commencement.

The neighborhood thrives. Mrs. Gregor's most adorable child was the principal visitor as I left, and long may she prosper. Taussig is to be away next year.[14] Cummings has grown in importance immensely. All sorts of carriages with distinguished people stop at his door to consult him. Estlin has almost reached the fighting age.[15] The Foxes are to return in September, about when you do. It will be so good to be all together again with you and them.

I am sorry that I forgot to tell you about that report as to Dublin lectures. There was absolutely nothing in it. Newspaper rumor—whole cloth. I thought so little of it that I always forgot it when I was writing to you.

[13] An allusion to the fact that Münsterberg was notoriously prolific and versatile in his writings. As to the state of Münsterberg's health, however, Royce may well have been mistaken; a few months later Münsterberg fell ill with diphtheria, and a year later suffered a complete nervous breakdown. See Margaret Münsterberg, *Hugo Münsterberg: His Life and Work* (New York: D. Appleton and Co., 1922), p. 88.

[14] Frank W. Taussig of Harvard's Economics Department lived at 2 Scott Street.

[15] Edward Estlin Cummings (1894–1962), the poet and son of Edward Cummings.

As for thoughts, of late, I seem to myself to be on the track of a great number of interesting topics in Logic. Those lectures of poor C. S. Peirce that you devised will always remain quite epoch marking for me. They started me on such new tracks.[16]—

Yours Always
Josiah Royce.

To George Platt Brett, August 22, 1901[17]

103 Irving St.
Cambridge, Mass.
Aug 22, 1901

My Dear Mr. Brett:—

I send by express, this evening, the MS of my second course of Gifford Lectures, revised, and in very large part rewritten. It is now ready for the printer. The MS as sent is very variously gotten into shape—two or three different typewriting machines, and some pretty variable masses of my own hand-written sheets, making up the whole. But after going pretty carefully over the finished MS I feel sure that the resulting book will be decidedly shorter than the former series, since there is this time no supplementary essay. I estimate some 460 pp. of print for the ten lectures,—perhaps 480.

I shall send in an Index to both volumes when returning the last pages of this. The title is to be *The World and the Individual: Second Series. Nature, Man, and the Moral Order*. In every way this series is the continuation and completion of the former series, and should so appear on the title, and on the cover.

As to the time of publication, I have worked very hard to be prompt with this revision of the MS. By the contract with the

[16] This paragraph is printed in *TCWJ*, 2: 421, and also in James Harry Cotton, *Royce on the Human Self* (Cambridge: Harvard University Press, 1954), p. 217. Peirce's Cambridge lectures on "Reasoning and the Logic of Things" were given from February 10 through March 7, 1898, at the home of Mrs. Ole Bull, 168 Brattle Street. For a bibliographical description, see Arthur W. Burks, ed., *Collected Papers of Charles Sanders Peirce* (Cambridge: Harvard University Press, 1958), 8: 287–88. Considering the struggles between James and Peirce over the content of the lectures (James officially made the arrangements), Royce's word "devised," as a description of James's role, is not perhaps too strong a term. See *TCWJ*, 2: 418–21.

[17] ALS. Macmillan Papers. NYPL.

University of Aberdeen the finished volume *ought* to be published, at the latest, by Feb. 1, 1902. Is there a chance of that?

Since all details as to form of page, &c., were settled by the case of the former vol., I hope at all events that the printer may soon get to work. Except for Index & Preface & Contents the book goes to you now *entire.*

Yours Very Truly
Josiah Royce.

To Hugo Münsterberg, August 25, 1901[18]

103 Irving St
Aug. 25, 1901

Dear Münsterberg:—

Your letter reached me just as I was struggling with the last agony of my "Gifford Lectures" book. I had been confident of finishing sooner; but the job dragged. I waited before answering until I could get breath, and see, after finishing the job, whether I should have any leisure to accept your so good invitation. I have been looking over the ground of engagements, and I now can*not* see how to get away. I had planned to do so if possible, but there are the Phil 15 lecture tasks to be looked over; and I owe to various editors several different things. Before the end of the first week in September, I fear that I shall not be free at all; and then—well the proofs will begin to come; and I cannot venture away, unless I should find my health (which is now very good), absolutely demanding relaxation. I thank you very cordially for the invitation, and wish that I could come. Please give my cordial thanks to Mrs. Münsterberg.

The lectures are finished, and have been sent to the printer. They contain some fresh matter on the topic upon which you and I, by such different roads, have reached, as I understand our views, a substantial agreement, viz., as to the general relations of the "World of Descrip'n" & the "World of Apprec'n."—Only this time I have made some new cosmological speculations that have to do with the possible origin and ground of this very difference between these

[18] ALS. Münsterberg Papers. BPL.

two worlds, or points of view. I wonder what you will think of them.—Let me keep Radcliffe Phil 1b, & let Carson[19] take the other.

Yours Very Truly
J. Royce.

To Benjamin Ide Wheeler, September 28, 1901[20]

Cambridge, Mass.
103 Irving St.
Sept. 28, 1901

Dr. Benj. I. Wheeler,
President;

My Dear Dr. Wheeler:—

Your letter of September 23 contains a very attractive proposal; and I thank you heartily for the honor of the offer contained in it. Before I could venture to accept a task of the sort in question, namely a six weeks lectureship in the Summer School at Berkeley next year, I should have to consider a little carefully what extra work would be involved in preparing for the engagement. For the last three or four years my Gifford Lectures, delivered in 1899 & 1900 at Aberdeen, and since published or now on the road to publication, have absorbed my attention, in all the time at my disposal outside of my academic engagements at home. First the preparation, and then the rewriting of the lectures for print, have pretty well deprived me of vacations. While I am in reasonably robust condition, I have still felt that *next* year, I ought to have a decidedly longer and clearer summer rest than I have allowed myself for a long time. Now a California visit would have its very attractive side; but how much of a task would the whole involve? How many hours of lectures in the six weeks? How much needed preparation before I went out? How much work outside the lecture-room while I was there? I have to ask such questions, just because I feel, at the moment, that I shall have to be a little cautious, for a time, about all extra tasks.

I shall be glad to hear more on the subject. It is good to learn, as

[19] Lewis Clinton Carson took a Ph.D. in Philosophy at Harvard in 1901.
[20] ALS. President File. UCA.

I frequently do, about how prosperously you are guiding the ship on her voyage in California. Long may you be the Captain, and long and profitable the cruise!

Yours Very Truly
Josiah Royce.

To George Platt Brett, October 27, 1901[21]

103 Irving St.
Cambridge, Mass.
Oct. 27, 1901

My Dear Mr. Brett:—

I have been unable to write earlier in answer to yours of the 18th.

I accept your offer, and shall be prepared to revise the "Outlines of Psychology"[22] as desired, extending the book to some fifty thousand words, *provided* that you remember that the task is thus suddenly proposed, without my getting adequate notice beforehand, and provided that you accordingly give me until next August, 1902, in case I cannot finish the sketch earlier, to get the book ready. I have already many engagements for the year. To revise the book will be a hard job, brief as it looks; and I can only do my best to get things into shape. If I *can* hand it over to you in Spring, I will do so; but that you must not expect with too great confidence. I do not believe that I can do it *before* August.

The terms, $200 down at publication, as advance on the earnings of a ten percent copyright, the balance to be paid as earned by sales, and the rate of that copyright to be advanced to fifteen percent after the sale of five thousand copies, are satisfactory.

Yours Very Truly
Josiah Royce.

I have now no copy of the *Sickness & Health* Book. You seem to have one. Can you let me have it to use the pages of the article as a basis of my revision?

21 ALS. Macmillan Papers. NYPL.

22 Royce had contributed "Outlines of Psychology, or a Study of the Human Mind" to *In Sickness and in Health*, ed. James W. Roosevelt (New York: D. Appleton and Co., 1896), pp. 171–233. This chapter was expanded into the book, *Outlines of Psychology* (New York: Macmillan Co., 1903).

To Charles Sanders Peirce, January 6, 1902[23]

103 Irving St.
Cambridge, Mass.
Jan. 6, 1902.

Dear Mr. Peirce:—

Your letter came to me just on the eve of my setting out for Chicago, where, as President for the year of the Amer. Psychol. Assoc'n, I had to deliver an address.[24] I was too busy to answer until now. I returned at the close of last week.

My two volumes of the *World & Individual*, each as it came out, were sent to your address at my request. I am a poor correspondent, but am not an ungrateful student, and I wanted you to have the books as a token of my sense of indebtedness to you, even if they are a rather inadequate token. I ought to have thanked you long ago for your note in *Science, a propos* of the concept of the infinitesimal, and my passing remark about the latter.[25] I have long meant to return to that topic some time, and perhaps print a word about it; but it does not lie directly in my line, and I was quite content to have drawn from you so plain an expression of your own position, as to that matter.

Both the Supplementary Essay to Vol. I (despite its polemical relations to Bradley) and (still more) Vol. II, could be in large part understood, so far as the positive aspect of my own theses is concerned, by one who has not read Bradley, although of course such a reader could not fairly judge the merits of my criticisms of the latter, or the extent of my indebtedness to Bradley's books, and would probably skip the passages in which I refer at length to Bradley. But on the whole, my argument stands enough apart from Bradley to be quite intelligible, in the main points by itself. Please don't wait therefore for Bradley before reading my Vol. II, in case you want to read that at all.

I hear that you have an article on Symbolic Logic for Baldwin's

23 ALS. Peirce Papers. HL.

24 "Recent Logical Inquiries and Their Psychological Bearings," *Psychological Review* 9 (March 1902), 105–33; reprinted in *RLE*, pp. 3–34.

25 "Infinitesimals" [a letter to the editor], *Science*, n.s., 11 (March 16, 1900): 430–33; reprinted in *CPP*, vol. 3, secs. 563–70. See also Royce's "The Concept of the Infinite," *Hibbert Journal* 1 (1902): 21–45.

Dictionary.[26] I should be glad to pay the cost of the printing of say ten copies of that article as separate documents, if the publisher would consent. I should like such ten separate copies for use in my Seminary. When will ever your complete Logic appear? I want it.

With many wishes for a good New Year to you, I remain

Yours Very Truly
Josiah Royce.

To George Pierce Baker, January 30, 1902[27]

103 Irving St.
Cambridge, Mass.
Jan. 30, 1902.

My Dear Mr. Potter:—

I have your letter of Jan. 14. Of course you need not expect to find a treatise, by any prominent author, dealing at all exclusively with a "form of mania," to be called, as a special disease, "kleptomania." You might as well expect to find modern medical treatises on "backache," or on "cold feet." When I was a boy, I used to be troubled with a disorder known to me only under the name "earache." There was no doubt about the fact of the disorder; but if I suffered so now, I should expect the doctor to find out, by examination, *what made* my ear ache. At the time in question, I never learned and nobody knew. Well, just so, very various sorts of people may steal,—missionaries in Pekin during the late unpleasantness, bank officers, Legislators, pickpockets, hysterical women, cranks and degenerates of all sorts that could happen to tend that way, small boys looking for apples, professional bandits in Turkey, &c. &c. Some of these would steal from more or less obviously diseased or insane conditions, some from causes due to lack of mental or moral development, some from social custom or calling, some

[26] James Mark Baldwin, ed., *Dictionary of Philosophy and Psychology*, 3 vols. (New York: Macmillan Co., 1902), 2: 645–50. Peirce's many contributions to Baldwin's *Dictionary* are listed in the bibliography in *CPP*, 8: 290–93.

[27] ALS. Royce Papers. HUA. This letter to "My Dear Mr. Potter" was actually a reply to an inquiry from Royce's colleague, George Pierce Baker, but misreading Baker's signature, Royce took his correspondent to be a total stranger.

from causes indistinguishable from the deliberate desire of healthy people to be bad. The diseased or insane persons, whose thefts were incidents of their diseased condition, would again be of very various sorts:—some of them epileptics; some of them hysterical patients; some of them morphinists, some of them victims of chronic forms of weakness of mind or imbecility;—some of them cranks of greater vigor, but of deeply distorted habits. Thefts of a pathological sort are frequently, in the cranks last mentioned, incidents of some chronic sexual perversion, whose psychology is complex, and hard to work out, but whose cases have been a good deal studied. Stealing then, if a diseased act, would never be, *of itself*, the mark of any one form of disease, any more than stealing, in a healthy person, would be an act sufficient by itself to tell you all about that person's character. As the healthy thief might be missionary or bank-officer or small boy, and might also be of any degree of guilt or relative innocence according to circumstances, and social position, so the pathological or insane thief might be a chronic or a more acute sufferer from any one of a large number of mental ailments, and might be, according to circumstances, seriously or lightly disordered, in very various degrees. There is then no "theft-disease" any more than there is a disease of "cold feet" or of "backache" or of "earache."

As a *symptom*, impulsive theft occurs often enough, upon a diseased basis, to have been honored with a name,—a poor and deceptive one, viz. *kleptomania. Mania*, as thus used, must be taken in its inexact sense of "uncontrollable tendency towards,"—and not in its sense as a name for a distinct disease. The symptom in question is most frequently reported, I fancy, in the cases of the cranks or degenerates of various sorts, who get into trouble by stealing, but who are not obviously enough victims of any one form of disease to be easily classed; so that they get named by their salient symptom, as one might name a person a "pug-nose," or a "red-head." But with such persons the true question always is: *Why* do they steal? And only when this question has been answered can they be classified rationally or studied fruitfully, or treated rationally, or portrayed in literature intelligently.

As to literature,—what you need is the literature of "Degeneration" generally, and then the literature about Hysteria, Insistent Impulses, Sexual Anomalies, Epilepsy, &c,—in sum a vast mass of stuff, which you will have more or less to master if you are going to understand any symptom of this sort in its true relations. You simply *can't* take it alone without making nonsense of your study of it.—Of course all such knowledge would go into the background as soon as you returned again to literary portrayal. The concrete case would stand alone in your play. But your understanding would have to be based on comparative study.

A list of books would be too extensive a job here. Any good text-book of insanity will start you on the road—Maudsley, Krafft-Ebing, Kraepelin, Mercier, &c. For the rest, you had better let the whole business alone, or else trust wholly to your fancy, and picture a diseased thief as you please. Any sick person who steals will do.

Yours Truly
Josiah Royce.

To James McKeen Cattell, February 3, 1902[28]

Monday, Feb. 3, 1901 [1902]

Dear Cattell:—

I enclose herewith my Presidential address.[29] I read it over recently to a meeting of colleagues and students, and have been looking for the opinions of others about its general soundness. Hence the delay. I have stricken out some passages of the MS as first written. I hope that the paper will still be in time.

I write this on the train, on my way to Northampton, where I have to lecture.[30] The train's motion is responsible for my especially poor handwriting.

Yours Truly
Josiah Royce.

[28] ALS. Cattell Papers. LC. Though the letter gives the date as 1901, it is clear from the internal evidence of Royce's presidential address to the American Psychological Association (Chicago, January 1902) and his trip to Northampton to lecture at Smith College that the date should be 1902.

[29] See fn. 24 above.

[30] On February 3, 1902, Royce spoke to the Philosophical Society of Smith College on "Recent Discussions of the Concept of the Infinite."

To James McKeen Cattell, March 3, 1902[31]

March 3, 1902

I thank you for the offer of a chance to review Clifford's essays; but I can undertake no new engagements this year. I think of publishing a catalogue of my engagements now pending, and unfulfilled in 2 vols. quarto.—

Yours Truly
J Royce

To Edward Bradford Titchener, March 29, 1902[32]

103 Irving St.
Cambridge, Mass.
March 29, 1902.

Dear Professor Titchener:—

I enclose Stout's letter. I have at once written to Richardson, demanding full explanations.[33] I knew nothing of the complaints of Stout, or of Meumann, of Külpe, or of Sully, before. Of course positive action is necessary. I shall write Stout as soon as I have heard from Richardson in reply to my demand. I thank you for your letter.

So far as I have yet known, Richardson has seemed to me a somewhat dreamy, but high-minded and well intentioned man, who might delay an answer, or be careless as to a date, but who

[31] APS. Cattell Papers. LC.

[32] ALS. Titchener Papers. CUA.

[33] Frederick Albert Richardson was editor of *International Monthly* (later *International Quarterly*) during the five and a half years of its existence, 1900–1906. G. F. Stout wrote to E. B. Titchener on March 18, 1902 (Titchener Papers, CUA): "I don't know what the grievances of Sully, Külpe, & Meumann are, but I have a pretty bad one myself against the I. M. I sent them, about the time when the thing was started, a long paper which they had engaged me to write by an express arrangement. This paper has never appeared and I presume never will. . . . Is Royce aware of the way in which the paper is conducted? It was he who led me into the thing. Of course I don't in any way blame him, but he ought to be told about the way they treat their contributors . . . ."

would in the end meet all his obligations. His youth and inexperience as an editor I have hoped that he would soon outgrow. Ambition, means, ideals, and essential integrity of motives, I have believed him to possess, and have stood by him, so far, accordingly. But of course complaints such as these must be at once explained and satisfied if I am to retain any confidence in him.

Yours Very Truly
Josiah Royce.

To George Holmes Howison, April 8, 1902[34]

103 Irving St.
Cambridge, Mass.
April 8, 1902.

Dear Howison:—

I have been sorry to hear that you have been more or less out of health for so long. It is however a great satisfaction to learn that you are once more in reasonably good condition. I hope that you will long remain in the mood for vigorous work. I shall be glad to meet you at the Summer School. I am sorry that you are not to be there all the time. But I hope that the vacation rest, up to the middle of July, will precisely meet your wishes and your needs. After that I hope to see you, and to have some good talks.

I have now received the printed Statement of Courses, as well as your letter announcing your plans for the Summer School. Of course I am glad to know that you also are taking part. I am glad to have you take up and consider precisely whatever topic seems to you most suitable, and to set forth your own views as fully as possible.

I have, however, a decided complaint to make as to the form of announcement which you have chosen for the pamphlet of courses. The untrammelled freedom to choose one's topic, and to treat it in one's own way, belongs of course without the least doubt to anyone in your position. I do not for an instant call in question that freedom, or object to it. But the right to announce, as part of a scheme of instruction, what you yourself call in your letter to me a "scrimmage" with a colleague who comes as an

[34] ALS. Howison Papers. UCB.

official guest, is a right which can only rest upon previously consulting the person with whom you propose to have the "scrimmage." For a polemic announcement of this sort necessarily predetermines the plan, not only of your work, but, in some measure of mine, since it brings students to the class with a sort of interest which I may, or again may not choose to use for the purposes of this course.

As a fact, I did not and do not come to California for a "scrimmage." Once I did so.[35] That was by express invitation. That is past. This time I was invited by your President to repeat, as far as time would permit, one of my courses as given here. I was expressly assured of entire freedom from entanglements other than those of my two hours a day. I was expressly promised a quiet summer. I was expressly relieved of any such public responsibilities as an announced polemic exhibition before the general public may, in my opinion, very possibly and naturally involve. Had your announcement been shown to me in advance, I should simply have declined the call,—not because I am indifferent to your views, or am in the least unwilling to be criticized, or am unmindful of the value of polemic when wisely conducted, but because, this summer, I chance not to choose any such situation as that in which your announcement places my course. And, as I must repeat, this was a matter about which I had every right to choose.

As it now turns out, I shall of course go on with my announced course. I only expressly point out, once for all, that while I hope that you will do and say in your course whatever you please, I myself do not come to California to engage in any controversy with you, but solely to get my students to worm out of me whatever they can, in the time, in the way of help about thinking for themselves. I shall be glad that, from you, these students are hearing the exposition of views whose importance, and whose weighty presentation, I shall fully recognize. I am wholly accustomed to work side by side with colleagues who widely disagree. I can only gain by having my poor attempts criticized. But I repeat that to require a man to take part in a controversy, of a set public nature, is to do something for which his prior consent must be asked. As mine has not been asked, and, for just this form and instance of controversy, is not given, I hope that you will not expect more than a passive, and perfectly cheerful acquiescence, on my part, in your

[35] I.e., for his talk on "The Conception of God" in 1895.

right and duty to set forth to your students exactly what you think proper. For my part, I shall try to confine myself to telling my own story, without joining any public issue of any sort with you. As you know, owing to the incomplete statement that, even at the present time, your system has received in any form accessible to me, I should be at a loss to form any adequate view of the "Fifth Conception," and should have no right to criticize it.

Please understand my objection then to be, not to the proposed topic or content of your course, but to the form of announcement, which puts me in a false position.

—Yours Truly
Josiah Royce.

To George Platt Brett, June 18, 1902[36]

103 Irving St.
Cambridge, Mass.
June 18, 1902.

My Dear Mr. Brett:—

I write at the close of College work, to explain my delay as to the revision of my little "Psychology." When you first urged upon me the task, and I consented, I said that I should act as promptly as possible, but that it would be hard to be as prompt as you wished. I have since worked on the matter when I could. But the great mass of novelties in Psychology makes the task harder than I expected. I can now only hope that by September first, or thereabouts, I can get into your hands the revised copy. I shall do my best. But my time's much taken up with many unavoidable tasks.

Yours Very Truly
Josiah Royce.

[36] ALS. Macmillan Papers. NYPL.

To George Holmes Howison, June 18, 1902[37]

103 Irving St.
Cambridge, Mass.
June 18, 1902.

Dear Professor Howison:—

On the eve of setting out for California, I feel that I must still write you a word before I leave my own place, to express, not only my very sincere sorrow that your ill health should have interfered with your plans of work, but my very great regret that I should have so completely misunderstood your intentions as to the matter of my complaint. Of course I now entirely withdraw the complaint, as it was made, viz. with reference to your former plans for the discussions of the Summer School, because as your letter convinces me I entirely misapprehended your purpose. You will understand that, as I expressly said in writing, I had, and have, no sort of objection to having you criticize me in every way, and before any public. My sole objection related to what I supposed to be an understanding that our courses were so to be given as to constitute a sort of public discussion between us. I now see that my interpretation of the intended situation was wholly wrong, and I have no wish, at this time, to defend the grounds of that interpretation, as I then made it. Enough, if the interpretation was my blunder, the complaint founded thereon by me entirely falls to the ground. I am sorry indeed that my blunder caused you pain. The long and somewhat straining job of the past five or six years has left me perhaps too anxious to avoid for the time any unnecessary public discussion. I like to be criticized. But I don't like any longer the responsibilities of controversy, where I can escape them. Hence my undoubted over anxiety, and my blunder as to your really so kindly purpose.

As to you, my honored colleague, and if you still consent, my friend, I have only regret and sympathy when I learn that you are at all out of health. We all need you to have full strength. We need to read what you yet have to say. We prize what you have done

[37] ALS. Howison Papers. UCB. The last three sentences of this letter are printed in John Wright Buckham and George Malcolm Stratton, *George Holmes Howison: Philosopher and Teacher* (Berkeley: University of California Press, 1934), p. 102.

too much to believe that you will soon cease to be as powerful a teacher and as effective a producer as ever.

With best wishes
Yours Truly
Josiah Royce

To William James, June 20, 1902[38]

Chicago, Illinois.
June 20, 1902.

Dear James:—

It was heartrending to have all my arrangements made for leaving Cambridge yesterday, just in time for the California engagement, and then to learn that you were to arrive at almost precisely that moment. However, I came out on the train with one of your fellow passengers, and got a good account of you (he was a Glasgow School Inspector, I understood,—in any case a good young smooth-faced fellow, and fond of you). As to your book: I had it for *a day* or perhaps two or three days.[39] Harry gave me a copy. I looked at it a very little, as I had time. Thereupon, just before Faculty-meeting, Eliot eagerly inquired whether a copy was accessible yet, anywhere. I said that I had one, and as he seemed very eager, I went home, got my copy, brought it to him, laid it beside him as he sat in the Faculty,—and have never seen it since. I told him at the time that it was my own advance copy. But he must have forgotten. So much for Eliot's variety of religious experience. But to lose the book thus gave me still another "variety," from which I haven't recovered yet. The few hours spent over your book gave me great delight. It is a wonderful thing.

I return from Cal. sometime in August. If you want to write me address me at 2401 LeConte Avenue Berkeley.

Yours Always
Josiah Royce.

[38] ALS. James Papers. HL. Partly printed in *TCWJ*, 2: 336.

[39] *The Varieties of Religious Experience: A Study in Human Nature* (New York: Longmans, Green and Co., 1902).

To Charles Sanders Peirce, June 20, 1902[40]

Chicago, Illinois.
June 20, 1902.

Dear Mr. Peirce:—

Ever since your last letter reached me, I have been the slave of circumstances,—a trip West to be made for Phi Beta Kappa and Commencement Addresses,[41] my examinations at Cambridge to be attended to,—still a second trip West to be prepared for (—a trip which I have now begun), and all the other confusing responsibilities of the closing weeks of our Academic year. I seize almost the first free time, during my passage through Chicago, to do what I in vain tried to do before leaving Cambridge yesterday morning, —viz., to write you the letter that I have so long owed.

First then, as to your kind proposal about the cooperative study of Logic on my part, and of Hegel on yours, this summer.[42] The plan, which is in any case very attractive, is rendered extremely so by my wish to make some real progress before long as to some logical questions about which you, of all men, could best enlighten me. But, on the other hand, the project is rendered simply impossible by the fact that I am under engagement to teach this summer at the Summer School of the University of Cal., and am now on the way thither. I shall not return until too late to leave any time for your plan to be carried out. It is, as you see, a peculiarly busy time with me. This, as I said, is my second trip to the West within a few weeks, and this one is to be a long one.

Secondly, as to the general topic of your former letter to me,—a letter of which you must have thought me shamefully neglectful:— As a fact, I was not only very busy, but I was unwilling to write you mere good wishes in reply to your statement of your practical situation. I wanted, and still want, to do something more effective than merely to express sympathy. Poor and uninfluential as I myself

[40] ALS. Peirce Papers. HL. Partly printed in James Harry Cotton, *Royce on the Human Self* (Cambridge: Harvard University Press, 1954), pp. 301–2.

[41] Royce delivered the Phi Beta Kappa Address at the State University of Iowa on "Provincialism"; the essay was printed in the *Boston Evening Transcript* and later reprinted in *RQP*, pp. 57–108.

[42] Peirce, in a previous letter, had invited Royce to spend several months of the summer at Milford, Pa., working together as indicated.

am, I have been much perplexed to know how best to serve your interests, which, as I am sure, are the interests of advanced work in Logic in this country. So, although I did not write, in direct reply to you, at that time, I did act as I could to pave the way for further efforts in your behalf. I had a long personal interview with D. C. Gilman, during a visit at Baltimore, in the course of which I urged your case upon his attention.[43] In answer to a further request of his, I wrote (sometime, I think, in March), a very full semi-official letter to him, for him to use with the Carnegie trustees. In that letter I stated my view of the importance of your proposed work in Logic, as well as my appreciation of what you have already done. I said very plainly that, *if* I had money of my own to spend upon supporting your Logic work, I should unquestionably be ready to spend such money, & to make considerable sacrifices to get that done. And I said what else I could to urge upon the Carnegie Inst. trustees the importance of offering you such support as they felt to be consistent with their plans.

Gilman replied cordially, and said that he would represent the matter as strongly as possible to his trustees. But he made no other promise, and has not since notified me of the result.

You see then that despite my remissness, I am not as bad a rememberer of my obligations to you as my silence may have indicated. As a fact, I shall do what I can to further your interests as a Logician, and as an investigator. But my power to be of aid is indeed small.

I have also spoken to the Secretary of the American Academy of A. & S. as to the possibility of printing a paper for you. He seemed to think that, if the paper were ready, I could probably get the Academy to print it for you. But that is not quite certain.

If you see any way in which a word from me would be serviceable in getting you better chances for the Carnegie aid, or for some similar chance, please write me at 2401 LeConte Avenue, Berkeley, California, at any time until Aug. 1. After that I am not sure of my

[43] Gilman was the founding president of the Carnegie Institution of Washington, 1902–4. During 1902 Peirce planned and partly executed a book entitled, *Minute Logic;* see bibliography in *CPP*, 8: 293–94. Although Gilman envisioned that the Institution would seek to encourage "unusual talent" and "to secure the publication of very extended memoirs, for which there is at present no adequate provision" [see Fabian Franklin, *The Life of Daniel Coit Gilman* (New York: Dodd, Mead and Co., 1910)], the Institution did not offer Peirce a subvention and his book was never published.

precise address for some time. But a letter sent to 103 Irving St., Cambridge, would always be forwarded to me.

I thank you for your critical remarks about my own work.[44] I know that it still needs much improvement. If I ever come to a revised edition of my *World & Indiv.*, I will try to set right the matter as to your relation to Dedekind. I meant to be fair to you. But it is hard to get all details right.

Yours Very Truly
Josiah Royce.

To Hugo Münsterberg, July 14, 1902[45]

2401 LeConte Avenue
Berkeley, Cal.
July 14, 1902

Dear Münsterberg:—

I learn that they need here, at the University of California, an Instructor in Psychology, to work with Stratton, as the latter's subordinate. Wheeler, as President, asks me to get you to suggest one. I feel uncertain myself whom to propose. The place is a good one,—the salary probably in the neighborhood of $1000 to $1200. A laboratory man is needed,—not a Carson, or any such philosopher.

I lecture on Metaphysics here, at the Summer Session; see friends; hob-nob a little with Baldwin;[46] keep out of the way of the summer school women students, whose name is Legion; watch the sunsets; and revel in youthful memories. Howison is at Shasta Springs,—invalided. He has given up doing anything at the school. Baldwin's family occupy Bakewell's house. Montague is faithful, and has matured a good deal, showing signs of improvement.[47] California, as

[44] Peirce's abridged reviews of the two series of *WI* appeared in *Nation* 70 (April 5, 1900): 267, and in *Nation* 75 (July 31, 1902): 94–96. Fuller drafts of these are in *CPP*, 8: 75–102. In private letters to Royce (May 27, 1902, and May 28, 1902), Peirce offered further criticism of *WI;* the former contains Peirce's famous word of advice: "My entreaty is that you will study logic."

[45] ALS. Münsterberg Papers. BPL.

[46] James Mark Baldwin also taught in the Summer School of the University of California in 1902.

[47] William Pepperell Montague (1873–1953) received his Ph.D. from Harvard in 1898 and taught briefly at the University of California before moving permanently to Columbia in 1903.

a State, seems to me not to have progressed as it ought; but the University, at all events, is in a wholesome state of progress. Wheeler works like Hercules. Yet education here shows some signs of the approaching deluge of feminism that you predict, and against which Wendell,[48] as our Noah, preaches, and builds his ark. I begin to think that after all I too shall have to take to the ark.—

Yours Truly
Josiah Royce.

To Alice Gibbens James, September 9, 1902[49]

103 Irving St.
Cambridge
Sept. 9, 1902.

Dear Mrs. James:—

I reached home yesterday afternoon in good time, and found all well.[50] Mrs. Royce seems well over her cold, and is free from discomfort.

Two things stand out with special prominence in my mind as I look back upon my brief but very delightful visit at your beautiful home;—first, the satisfaction that I felt in finding my beloved colleague so strong and well again, so free of movement about the woods, and so heartily his old self; and secondly, my sympathy with you yourself as I saw you with all the family once more together about the same table. Such good things seemed so far off when I saw you at Rye.[51] And now I have seen the fulfilment of what you then so patiently were working to accomplish. I thought of you for so long after my visit at Rye with such sorrow for your divided household and your long waiting, that it was especially

[48] For Barrett Wendell's criticism of coeducation, see part 3, fn. 248 above.

[49] ALS. James Papers. HL.

[50] After returning from California, Royce evidently visited the Jameses at their summer home in Chocorua, N.H.

[51] Royce had presumably visited James early in January, 1900, at Lamb House, Rye, England, the home of William's brother, Henry, as Royce was on his way to Aberdeen for the second series of Gifford Lectures. Such a visit, however, is inconsistent with the dates given in Gay Wilson Allen, *William James: A Biography* (New York: Viking Press, 1967), p. 408.

joyous this time to witness the fruition of your labors. As for my visit with James, I hope that my cantankerousness didn't weary him too much. I dearly love to argue about some things, but I hope that he didn't find me unbearably disputatious. I thank him much for his good care of me.

I send warm regards to Mrs. Gregor, and love to the dear little girl. Please remember me warmly to the young gentlemen, and to Mr. and Mrs. Salter.[52] With many thanks for your kindness I remain

Yours Very Truly
Josiah Royce.

To Houghton Mifflin Co., September 11, 1902[53]

103 Irving St.
Cambridge, Mass.
Sept. 11, 1902.

Houghton, Mifflin & Co.,

Gentlemen:—

In answer to the inquiry of Mr. Perry, made in your name in his letter of the 9th, I have to reply that I shall make every effort to have a considerable body of the MS material for the *Cosmic Philosophy* edition in your hands by the 20th of this month.[54] In the original agreement, no especial requirement was made as to whether my editorial additions should take more the form of notes, or more the form of an introduction. As I at present find the material shaping itself, the introduction will be long, and will contain most of the explanatory and supplementary materials needed. The footnotes will be very brief, containing little more than references, either to the sections of the introduction that will be each time in question, or to some passage in Spencer, or in some one of Fiske's

[52] William Mackintyre Salter and his wife, Mary Gibbens Salter, Mrs. James's sister.

[53] ALS. Houghton Mifflin Papers. HL.

[54] John Fiske, *Outlines of Cosmic Philosophy: Based on the Doctrine of Evolution, with Criticism on the Positive Philosophy*, 4 vols. (Boston: Houghton Mifflin Co., 1903). Royce's introduction is in vol. 1: pp. xxi–cxlix.

later books, or to still other sources. This will tend to greater brevity of the whole material.

Yours Very Truly
Josiah Royce

To Richard Clarke Cabot, September 20, 1902[55]

103 Irving St.
Cambridge, Mass
Sept. 20, 1902.

Dear Cabot:—

I ought to have acknowledged earlier your list of concepts, which I read with interest. We shall use it. Please prepare a little speech telling the members of the Seminary how you view the work, and how you would like to see it done; and present this speech at the opening meeting, side by side with mine, so that we may be seen to be working jointly from the start.[56] I think that we are agreed as to all the practical points that you made.

The Sem'y will meet this year in the Psychol. Laboratory, unless Münsterberg objects, which I do not think likely. You will get further notice in case he does object. Otherwise, please come there Tuesday, the 30th Sept, at 7.30.

I leave town today for a few days. I return by Thursday morning.

Yours Very Truly
Josiah Royce.

To Richard Clarke Cabot, September 29, 1902[57]

103 Irving St.
Cambridge.
Sept 29, 1902.

Dear Cabot:—

Being, as you insist, my pupil, you surely won't object to pre-

[55] ALS. Cabot Papers. HUA.
[56] See fn. 60 below.
[57] ALS. Cabot Papers. HUA.

senting to the Seminary, Tuesday evening, your scheme of all possible concepts as the *first paper* of the year. *So* much, at least, you can't object to. I shall hope for that at least. Appear then as a sort of model of the former pupils, and show them,—the new ones of today—how we do it. If you are my pupil, at least you have learned to use your wings, and I want you to set the fledglings an example in flying. The Seminary promises to be rather too large. We shall see, and do our best.

The Psychological Laboratory is the place, next Tuesday.

Yours Truly
Josiah Royce.

To Hugo Münsterberg, December 15, 1902[58]

103 Irving St.
Dec. 15, 1902.

Dear Münsterberg:—

I learn from James that Perry is not to be reappointed. In that case, Phil 2, your second Psychology Course, goes next year begging. I shall be very glad to undertake that course if you want me to do so. My conscience will then be easier about making a full offer of work; and Psychology of that sort will come in very well with my Phil 15, so as to make me a pleasant year's work.

I am very sorry indeed that you are so much beset with cares, of late, as to your health. I wish that I could see any way to ensure for you a freer outlook upon work. The offer to take charge of Phil 2 next year if necessary, or if you desire, is my only present chance of showing my willingness to help. And that is, after all, rather a selfish suggestion, since I should enjoy the course. I fear that at the moment I can only offer to you sympathy, which I do most heartily. It is a great work that you have already accomplished amongst us; and sad indeed will be our lot if your working powers do not return to the desired measure,—the sooner the better. Meanwhile, you, even when out of condition, accomplish more than any of the rest of us when in condition. But we want the whole of you. And we are deeply sorry to see you feeling in any

[58] ALS. Münsterberg Papers. BPL.

way below your natural strength. But I hope that you will be better soon.—

Yours Very Truly
Josiah Royce

To Richard Clarke Cabot, January 31, 1903[59]

103 Irving St.
Cambridge, Mass.
Jan. 31, 1903.

Dear Cabot:—

The departure of my steamer has been delayed by the Company until Friday, Feb. 6.[60] We shall therefore have time to consult about the matters mentioned in your letter sometime next week. I should be glad to call on you either Monday or Tuesday, at such time as you may name, and should prefer that way of meeting just because I want to call on you before I go in any case, and have other duties also that call me into that part of town before I leave, and so shall be glad to combine the two matters in one.

I have had, early this week, a light attack of what my doctor viewed as grip—one night's decidedly high temperature, & some later vexations. But that is over now, and my doctor has no objection to my going where I please. I want to ask you, on my own account, about some matters in the text of my forthcoming *Outlines of Psychology*, which I am just about to leave in the publisher's hands as I set out on my journey.

Yours Truly
Josiah Royce

59 ALS. Cabot Papers. HUA.

60 Royce took a sabbatical leave during the spring term of 1903. He spent the time traveling and visiting friends in California with his son, Stephen. Anticipating this leave, the Harvard administration apponted Cabot to be co-instructor in Royce's seminar, Philosophy 20c.

To George Platt Brett, January 31, 1903[61]

103 Irving St.
Cambridge, Mass.
Jan. 31, 1903.

Mr. Geo. P. Brett,

Dear Mr. Brett:—

By a change in the plans of the Panama S. S. Co. my sailing from New York, which was to take place Tuesday, Feb. 3, is postponed to Friday, Feb. 6, when I sail on the steamer *Seguranca*, and am due at the Isthmus a week later, but in San Francisco (owing to the delayed connections) not until March 11. Otherwise, I shall be able, I think, to meet your wish as to the *Psychology*, which I now propose to deliver at your office by Thursday afternoon, the 5th, at about 4 P.M., as soon as possible after my arrival in the city. I shall intend to leave Boston by the 10 A. M. express on Thursday, due in N. Y. at 3 P.M.

Yours Very Truly
Josiah Royce.

To George Platt Brett, February 4, 1903.[62]

103 Irving St.
Cambridge, Mass.
Feb. 4, 1903.

Dear Mr. Brett:—

Finding my *Outlines of Psychology* now finished, I have concluded to send you the package today by the American Express Company. The finished result contains probably nearly 100,000 words; but I believe that the original practical quality of the book has not been sacrificed. I hope that, when printed, it may meet your wish.

61 ALS. Macmillan Papers. NYPL.
62 ALS. Macmillan Papers. NYPL.

My address during my absence in California will be
"Care Miss Ruth Royce
72 South 3d St.
San Jose, California."

I am due in S.F. by March 11. Proofs sent to me at the address mentioned will be read promptly. A preface and an index will be supplied at as quick a speed as possible. On my arrival, if page proofs are awaiting me, I shall give my whole attention to finishing the matter up as promptly as may be.

I may not be able, after all, to call on you in New York tomorrow afternoon. I shall try to do so Friday morning. My steamer leaves at 3 P. M. Friday for Panama.

Yours Truly
Josiah Royce.

To George Platt Brett, March 23, 1903[63]

March 23, 1903.

My Dear Mr. Brett:—

An apology and explanation are due to you regarding the delay of the proof-sheets of my *Psychology*. I am working on them as well as I can, and shall be able to send them in a few days. The delay, however, is due to the fact that instead of reaching San Francisco March 11th, as I expected to do, I was detained at the Isthmus of Panama nine days, by the failure of the Pacific Mail S. S. Co. to provide the connecting steamer that had been promised. In the end I reached San Francisco last Wednesday, the 18th. Since then, in the midst of a great mass of traveller's engagements, such as necessarily accumulate at the end of such a voyage, I have been devoting what time I could to the proofs, which need considerable care. I shall be able to send them back now in a very few days, and shall use every effort to make them prompt and well cared for, so far as the conditions permit.

Yours Very Truly
Josiah Royce.

63 ALS. Macmillan Papers. NYPL.

To Hugo Münsterberg, April 12, 1903[64]

Los Gatos, Cal.
April 12, 1903.

Dear Münsterberg:—

I write from an altogether temporary stopping place. My regular address, while I am in California, is "Care of Miss Ruth Royce, 72 South Third St., San Jose, Cal." I ought to have written to you sooner. I fear that I forgot to send you the announcements of Phil 15 and Phil 20c for next year. But the old announcements will do very well indeed; and no doubt you published those.

The immediate stimulus which sets me writing is the news, just published in the newspapers here, that Dr. Montague has resigned, in order to go to Columbia. I am impelled to express the hope that one of our men may be found to fill his place in the University of California. I have been only once at Berkeley since I reached California, and have not attempted to keep track of what goes on there; but I suppose the news to be authentic; and, if so, it will doubtless be already in your possession. But if I can do anything to further the matter of presenting the case of one of our candidates at Berkeley, please let me know.

I have been wandering a little, here in California, looking, in the woods and mountains, for the place best suited to relieve my boy's asthmatic breathing, and to please myself. The season proves to be rather a cold one for California; but there is much beautiful weather already. As you may well imagine, I am neither seeking nor finding any great intellectual experiences in these parts. I am much out of doors, and have considerable moderate exercise. I have been forced to spend some time over the proofs of my *Outlines of Psychology*, and have just finished my Index to that not very promising book. Otherwise I have little to report except the beauties of nature, which I have no time to describe at this moment.

Please let me know whether Faculty votes have led to any new arrangement of either the lecture hours or the ordering of groups for next year. I have as yet no information upon that point, and am anxious to plan my next year's programme with reference to what hours of the day are likely to be at my disposal.

My best regards to Mrs. Münsterberg. My love to my colleagues

[64] ALS. Münsterberg Papers. BPL.

of the Division of Philosophy. My hearty greetings to all my friends.

Yours Affectionately
Josiah Royce.

I do not plan to give any courses in Radcliffe next year.

To William James, April 29, 1903[65]

Avalon, Santa Catalina Is'd.
California.
April 29, 1903.

Dear James:—

After a number of experiments, in my search for a place where my boy might breathe freely, without any nightly wheezing, I have for the present hit upon this island, Santa Catalina by name. Here we now abide in a cheap little cottage by the shore, row occasionally in our rented boat, read our Latin or our Logic, according to our age and our business, loaf a good deal, wash dishes a little, eat also part of our meals at restaurants, and look out upon a very peaceful sea, in excellent weather. The place is the property of a corporation, who devote their island partly to sheep-raising, and partly to the entertainment of fishermen, hunters, and tourists. The fishing, done for sport, constitutes the chief basis for the local reputation of the island. At the height of the summer season, the place is crowded with six or eight thousand guests, who fish, camp, and tell lies about their fish, as well as live in hotels and do whatever else befits such places. The island itself is some twenty miles long, and three or four wide, has high hills, a few harbors, and, on the lee side, a very quiet water. The one town, where I am, is situated on one of the best of the harbors. We shall stay here, I suppose, some weeks.

I have been reading the proofs of my poor little *Psychology*. It is to appear before June 1. I have also done some quite pleasant reading in Logic, and in current literature. The boy breathes very well here. We exercise a good deal together. The climate is perfect. On the whole, I suppose that this is a very good way to pass my vacation, although it isn't quite equal to Italy. I am very well, and

65 ALS. James Papers. HL.

am in a fair way to become quite hungry for work before I get back. Logic, treated in the main as an empirical science of the morphology of the concepts in actual use in human thinking, and of the reasoning processes also in actual use, looms up before me more and more as the thing to be worked upon. I enjoy greatly what I have time to do with it. It is just as "pragmatic" a study as any of your work on the religious experiences; for all thinking is doing; and logic might be defined as the science of the forms of conduct, so far as they are not so confused by passion as to be unconscious forms of conduct.

I was very glad to hear through Mrs. Royce that you got a chance for Charles Peirce to lecture again in Cambridge.[66] I am only sorry that I miss what he this time says. Apart from hearing that, and one or two other scraps of official business, I have so far only family news from Cambridge. That, of course, is my own fault; since I have let my letter writing pretty well go by the board for awhile,—travel and the little events of each day (including occasional proofreading, Logic-reading, &c.) having filled up the moments pretty steadily. If there is anything of official interest that you know, I shall be glad to hear. Meanwhile, I wonder a great deal, of course, how you are feeling, and what you have been doing with your time and your plans since I saw you. I didn't write you about the Isthmus journey, because you said, before I left, that your mind would be made up as to your plans before I could have time to send you word as to the merits and demerits of that undertaking. As a fact, the Isthmus journey is not one to be recommended to anybody except the born lover of the sea and of ships, to whom it is enough to loaf on a deck, whatever the weather or the fare. The voyage is slow, is full of delays, and is without much incident. The food on the steamers is poor. The human interest is mild, and occasionally turns to a certain disgust, at Central American conditions, or at fellow-passengers. The Central American ports fester in a condition which combines a ragged and pompous officialism with a squalid degradation of the common folk rather tedious to witness. The coast is beautiful, the volcanoes, especially, loom up in beauty; but the weather, at the best is ener-

[66] Peirce gave a series of public lectures on pragmatism at Harvard, March–May, 1903; during November and December of 1903, he had a series of Lowell lectures on "Some Topics of Logic Bearing on Questions Now Vexed." Both series are bibliographically described in *CPP*, 8: 294–96.

vating. The treacherous coast is unlighted at night, is full of unpredictable currents, and is strewn with wrecks. The surf beats heavily on a burning strand. The waiting at each port grows tedious. It is a land where nothing decent appears to the passing stranger to be going on.—Yet I would not now miss having thus once taken the journey although I cannot recommend it to you.—Give my best love to my colleagues, and to your house—

Yrs. Affectionately
Josiah Royce.

To Hugo Münsterberg, May 17, 1903[67]

Avalon, Santa Catalina I'd.
May 17, 1903.

Dear Münsterberg:—

I am just leaving this island, where I have spent four weeks with my son, under conditions very favorable to his health, and to my own relief from cares of all sorts. I write this, not only to express thanks for your kind letter, but to say a single word that may put me on record, as an officer of the Department, in connection with the laying of the cornerstone of the new Emerson Hall, on May 25th.

Owing to my lack of ability in such matters, I have had very little part, as an individual, in the movement that has resulted in providing the means for the building of Emerson Hall. I can take, in view of my incapacity for such practical enterprises, no credit for the result. That result has been due to the enthusiasm, the skill, the energy, and the generosity of others, who as officers of the Department, or as benefactors of Harvard and of Philosophy, have accomplished this great task. But I have all along ardently desired this result, and I am able, as fully as anyone, to appreciate how great is the boon for our common study which the establishment of a building for the teaching of philosophy at Harvard implies. I also feel very deeply how great are the responsibilities which the new gift places upon the shoulders of each teacher of the Department which is thus endowed. I do not know how much I shall be able to do to live up to these new responsibilities. I only know that the

[67] ALS. Münsterberg Papers. BPL.

news of the success of the Emerson Hall endowment fills me with a desire not only to improve here and there, but quite to make over afresh, and to change throughout for the better, my methods of work as a teacher of philosophy; and with a determination to devote myself as never before to the task of offering to philosophy and to Harvard my best services. That the founding of this new building may mean the beginning of a new life for philosophical study in our country, and the dawning of a new day for the interests of higher thought in our national affairs, is the earnest wish of your absent colleague. I also heartily wish that I could be with you on this occasion.

Should this letter reach you, as I hope, in time for the meeting proposed for May 25, I hope also that you may be able to make use of at least the main point of it as my little contribution to the good wishes and hopes of the day. In any case I heartily thank our benefactors, and wish to assure them of my full appreciation of the seriousness, the dignity, and the beauty, of the task which their bounty sets before every officer of the Department of Philosophy at Harvard.

With hearty greetings to all colleagues and friends at Cambridge, I remain,

Yours Very Truly
Josiah Royce.

To George Platt Brett, July 13, 1903[68]

103 Irving St.
Cambridge, Mass.
July 13, 1903.

Mr. Geo. P. Brett:—

My Dear Mr. Brett,

I have now returned from California, and my address is henceforth as before my journey, namely my Cambridge address above. Please have this change noted by your mailing clerk.

I was sorry to find, on inquiry yesterday, that your agent had not

[68] ALS. Macmillan Papers. NYPL.

yet supplied any copy of my *Psychology* to the University Bookstore here (C. W. Sever & Co.). The Harvard Summer School is now in session. The Educational Association has brought many teachers here, many of them to stay hereabouts for some time. If copies of the book are under their noses, a few may be sold here. Two or three different people among my visiting colleagues at the N. E. A. meeting—well informed men as to current books,—have just been asking me when my *Psychology* would appear. They had not seen it anywhere, and had seen no notice of its appearance. Of course that is inevitable in such cases, with many people. I only suggest that Boston, and vicinity, during the next few weeks, will contain people who might take notice of the book if they see it on counters.—

Yours Very Truly
Josiah Royce.

To Frederick James Eugene Woodbridge, N. D. (July, 1903)[69]

103 Irving St.
Cambridge, Mass.

Dear Professor Woodbridge:—

I have just returned from a half-year's leave of absence, and have not yet very well mapped out my coming year's work. It is therefore not quite in my power, at the moment, to answer definitively your question of your letter of July 13. I thank you, however, for your very kind and flattering proposal, and I am grateful for the honor that your Department and the University confer in thinking of me as a possible lecturer in your proposed course. I will come, at once, as near as I can to a definitive reply.

Your series of lectures is to take place on Monday and Tuesday afternoons at 4.30. It would not be possible for me to lecture away from Cambridge on Tuesdays; but *probably* I could get a chance to take part in your work by lecturing on ten Mondays in the second half of the coming Academic year, that is, after Feb. 15, 1904. Whether that will prove possible I can tell you in a few days, after

[69] ALS. *Journal of Philosophy* Papers. CUB.

I have had time to get answers from one or two sources that I must first consult by letter. At the moment that has to remain doubtful, although, as I say, such a result is probable.

Should I be able to get this time free, and should the dates thus indicated meet your wish, then, indeed, so far as I can at the moment see, it would be possible, and to me very attractive, to undertake, as you request, ten lectures that would fall within the field of Metaphysics. I think, on the whole, that I should be disposed to choose topics connected with the relations between Logic and Metaphysics. The lectures would need to be specially prepared. I could not bring merely a fragment of my old classroom course on these topics. For the ten lectures would have to possess their own unity, and to be intelligible to an audience that might know little or nothing, beforehand, regarding any of my metaphysical positions. I think that I could find time for such special preparation.

As to compensation,—each lecture would demand not only its own preparation, but also an absence from Cambridge for a day and a night, and a night-journey. For I should have, each time, to go to New York probably by the ten o'clock A. M. train of Monday, and to return by the midnight train for my Tuesday work. I suppose that the ancient honorarium of "fifty dollars and the expenses" for each lecture, would be, under these circumstances, the fair thing. Of course if I could get time, and if you had the wish, to have the course given at one visit, in daily lectures for a fortnight, both the expense and the labor would be far less. But I suppose that impracticable. As your plan now goes, the care of adapting each lecture to an otherwise strange audience, of getting some substantial result in a series of only ten lectures, delivered at weekly intervals, and of travelling to and fro, each time, would be sufficient to make this compensation natural.

In a few days I can answer as to whether I can get the Mondays free. Meanwhile, please let me know whether my proposal otherwise meets your wish. If we find it worthwhile to consider matters further, we can then agree, no doubt, as to some further definition of the topics to be discussed. You do not say how far the lectures are intended to appeal to the general public, and how far they are meant to appeal to already initiated University students.

This is as much as I can say at the moment. In any case it is a pleasure to hear from you, and to know that you are well and prosperous in the new work at Columbia. With my best wishes for your success, I remain,

Yours Very Truly
Josiah Royce.

To George Platt Brett, July 15, 1903[70]

103 Irving St., Cambridge
July 15, 1903

Dear Mr. Brett:—

I shall be glad to read and advise about MSS in philosophy and psychology, in the way that you suggest in your letter of July 14, whenever I have time. This vacation I could find some time for such work easily; and with somewhat less promptness, could do such work from time to time during the term.

Yours Very Truly
Josiah Royce

To George Platt Brett, July 17, 1903[71]

103 Irving St.
Cambridge, Mass.
July 17, 1903.

Dear Mr. Brett:—

I have read Mr. E. P. Tenney's table of contents, and his letter to you.[72] I suppose that from a knowledge of his previous MS you are able to judge better than I can as to the prospects of the present work. But as to whether, from the papers sent me, I judge that the

[70] ALS. Macmillan Papers. NYPL.

[71] ALS. Macmillan Papers. NYPL.

[72] In this letter and in much of the succeeding correspondence with Brett, Royce is acting in the capacity of reader-consultant for Macmillan Co. The arrangement lasted until 1912 when Royce's apoplectic attack caused him to restrict his activities. Edward Payson Tenney was a New England minister and former president of Colorado College. Macmillan did not publish this book, but Tenney's *Contrasts in Social Progress* (New York: Longmans, Green and Co., 1907) may have been a revised version of the proposed work.

MS now offered ought to be read, I can only reply, (1) That the general idea of his proposed work seems to me a good one, *if only* the fashion of treatment should prove to be both scientific and judicial in spirit and in method; (2) That his title might be improved so as to render his book more available, say by calling the book "The Social Influence of the Great Religions," or by some other device to make the title more concrete; and (3) That the table of contents, as it now reads, suggests to me, nevertheless, a partisan and therefore not exactly an enlightening method of treatment on the part of the author. Of course we all can thank God that we are not as other men, such as the Chinese, the Hindoos, the Siamese, the Turks, and the other poor devils of misbelievers. And we can all say, on occasion, that we owe to Christianity a great deal of our exalted character. But it hardly seems worthwhile to bring together all the resources of science (if our author succeeds in doing so), *merely* to prove to us the truth of such gratifying presuppositions. A comparative and scientific study of the social influences of the great religions is not needed to make us think well of Christianity, or of our own civilization, but will help us most, if it helps us at all, by assuming, as far as possible, a highly judicial, an impartially appreciative attitude, and by telling not so much who has done best, but *what* each civilization in question has done to meet its own problems. Now if our author's book has actually done thus, the result may be very interesting. If the book is only one more glorification of our own civilization as against others, it may be sound, but seems to me needless, and not likely to attract much general attention. What modern readers need, I take it, is an objective and impartial understanding of alien civilizations. Any child can of course form an impression that such civilizations are not equal to our own.

Accordingly, I should say that if, despite this impression of partisanship which the author's table of contents produces, there is fair reason to suppose that nevertheless his mode of treatment is judicial, and that he handles well the instruments of the modern Science of Comparative Religious History,—*then* his MS ought to be read and carefully considered. But if there is good reason to suppose that he writes rather as a partisan, the MS need not be further considered.

Yours Very Truly
Josiah Royce.

To JAMES MCKEEN CATTELL, JULY 23, 1903[73]

103 Irving St.
Cambridge, Mass.
July 23, 1903

Dear Professor Cattell:—

I have hesitated about answering your proposal regarding the grading of the psychologists, because, in the first place, I am aware how ignorant I am about the details of the work and of the merits of many of my colleagues, and because, in the second place, I have always found it impossible to arrange men in any straight row as to their merits, even in a single profession. Of course Darwin is a greater man than David Starr Jordan. But with such judgments I have to be content. Thus, for instance, if in my mind I try to decide on the relative places of Titchener and Baldwin in such a row as you suggest, I should not know how to decide,—so different are their ideals and the types of their services to Psychology. They simply belong in different rows (excuse the ambiguity of the term as written). And when I think of myself as trying to decide on the relative places of yourself, Ladd, Hall, James,—I feel as if I were asked to decide how many quarts would exceed in value one acre, or how many stars are together more important to mankind than is one symphony, or whether a ton is bigger than a league. It isn't merely that one star differs from another star in glory, but that I don't see how to compare even intensive magnitudes that are graded according to different types of intensity. If you insist on my doing it, I shall be glad to accommodate you; but with the proviso that my results, although they would of course be reached as carefully as possible, would be certainly false. If you assent to such an effort, send on your list, and I will give you the most conscientious misstatement that I can produce as my return.

With best wishes
Yours Very Truly
Josiah Royce.

[73] ALS. Cattell Papers. LC.

To Frederick James Eugene Woodbridge, July 23, 1903[74]

103 Irving St.
Cambridge, Mass.
July 23, 1903.

Dear Professor Woodbridge:—

As it chances, Tuesday is my principal day of the week throughout the coming Academic year here, since both my Seminary and my Advanced Logic course fall on that day. In view of numerous indulgences that the Harvard Corporation has otherwise shown to me, I therefore could not think it right deliberately to arrange in advance to give away any Tuesday for an engagement conflicting with my Cambridge work. There remain, to be sure, *two* Tuesdays in the first half of February that would fall within our examination period. Those I could give; but those are the only ones that I could devote to your now defined engagement. Taking those Tuesdays together with the corresponding Mondays, one could get room for four (or at most, by adding on one following Monday) five consecutive lectures of the sort that your plan as your last letter suggests, would tend to find feasible. Of course, five lectures could doubtless be prepared; and I should find the idea attractive if you wished them. But they would contain decidedly less than half of what one could give in ten lectures, owing to the difficulty of presenting the introduction to such a course, since it takes so much time to get started, in metaphysics, on the lines of any particular discussion. So I am not sure whether it would serve your purpose for me to arrange for such a course. I mentioned ten lectures only because you suggested that as the advisable number. With best wishes for all your plans

Yours Very Truly
Josiah Royce

[74] ALS. *Journal of Philosophy* Papers. CUB.

To Frederick James Eugene Woodbridge, July 27, 1903[75]

103 Irving St.
Cambridge, Mass.
July 27, 1903.

Dear Professor Woodbridge:—

I will name, as the days for my lectures at Columbia:—

Monday, Feb. 1
Tuesday Feb. 2
Monday Feb. 8 } 1904.
Tuesday Feb. 9
Monday Feb. 15

I am obliged to set these dates without having the University Calendar for next year before me; but I feel sure that the computation will prove to be correct. I can only arrange for five lectures. The topics I will announce later.

I shall be very glad both to give the lectures, and to visit in this way my colleagues.

Yours Very Truly
Josiah Royce.

Are the lectures to be before a general academic audience? Or before a class of students only? What previous training can I assume in my hearers?

To George Platt Brett, August 14, 1903[76]

103 Irving St.
Cambridge, Mass.
Friday, Aug. 14, 1903.

Dear Mr. Brett:—

I have examined with care the MS sent me by the Macmillan Company, viz.: *Transitional Eras in Thought*, &c. by Professor A. C. Armstrong, of Wesleyan University.[77]

[75] ALS. *Journal of Philosophy* Papers. CUB.

[76] ALS. Macmillan Papers. NYPL.

[77] Andrew Campbell Armstrong, *Transitional Eras in Thought: With Special Reference to the Present Age* (New York: Macmillan Co., 1904).

The work, so far as its intrinsic merits are concerned, is a very scholarly and careful study,—the outcome of much acquaintance with the history of thought. The fashion of treatment is very judicial; the tone is of the mildest and gentlest, yet with a great indication of a good deal held in reserve. The author very carefully limits himself to his chosen topics, shows an almost disappointing unwillingness to let himself go in the expression of opinions not directly called for by the announced undertaking, and so arouses a good deal of expectation that he may have more to say about many serious problems, on other occasions. The reserve and the studious fairness of treatment are in themselves attractive. One wishes for more rather than for less; and the book has no errors of excess. The style is somewhat too slow and unadorned. The sentences are long; the paragraphs often too long. There is little picturesqueness about the fashion of expression. But the language used, if not precisely fascinating, is still on the whole clear, precise, and dignified. There is a grave cheerfulness about the book which will not indeed arouse the multitude, but which will also not make graver readers, such as are interested in the author's point of view, complain. The readers to whom Professor Armstrong most intends to appeal, will understand him, will find him instructive, and will prefer him, in all probability, to a less self-controlled and more extraordinary writer. In any case they will not find him obscure.

As to the audience likely to be reached by the book, that, I take it, will be first of all a clerical audience. His colleagues in his profession will also respect the book, and will want it in the libraries whose purchases they advise or control. Studious laymen there will also be to whom the book will appeal. Its tone, at once tolerant and conservative, will make it well spoken of by religious journals, and not unwelcome to philosophical reviewers. To judge by some successful books, such as have appeared in the past, I should think that, in view of its positive and comforting, although so modestly stated results, it might obtain a really quite respectable, although no doubt reasonably limited, public success. I am, to be sure, at a loss to see how it could be used for students, except as a volume for collateral reading in certain courses (theological courses, courses in history of philosophy, &c.). The chapter on "The Relation of Thought to Social Movements" will in some measure attract to the book a class of readers who are nowadays very good buyers. But it is true that this chapter does not offer to these distinctively sociological students anything very startling. The treatment of evolution-problems will also serve to win readers who need not be either clergymen or philosophers. And so the book is entitled to the advantage that anything dealing with "society" and with "evolution" nowadays has, although this advantage is here, once more, decidedly limited by the author's avoidance of all startling effects.

On the whole, I think well of the chances of the book for a moderate sale. It has not the advantages of a probable text-book. It has the advantages, such as they are, of appealing to a considerble number first of clergymen, then of professors, and finally of such people as those who subscribe to the *Outlook*, or to the *Independent*. How many readers especially of the latter class, the book could get, you may be aided in judging by the statement that I make of the sort of appeal which I conceive the book likely to make. Of course I am hardly in a position to know the state of the market for such wares, so far as concerns the numbers of the probable buyers. But I should judge, from what I see in print, and from what I hear, that this market must be good. Certainly whoever tells the people, in a calm and reasonable way, that our age is after all coming out right, despite the pessimists and the sceptics, seems of late to find a very respectful, and I should think, a very fairly book-buying audience.

Of course I need not say that Professor Armstrong stands high in his profession, and commands a respectful hearing from his philosophical colleagues, for whatever he may choose to say. I hope, then, that you can print the book, in view of the whole situation.

I shall send back the MS by express tomorrow.

Yours Very Truly
Josiah Royce.

To George Platt Brett, September 3, 1903[78]

103 Irving St.
Cambridge, Mass.
September 3, 1903.

Dear Mr. Brett:—

The book of Professor Arthur Kenyon Rogers, on *The Religious*

[78] ALS. Macmillan Papers. NYPL.

Conception of the World,[79]—the book whose MS you have sent to me, is one about which I must be regarded as a somewhat prejudiced judge, since one chapter of the book is devoted to criticizing my own views. The prejudice in question is however, such as to tend to make me favor the publication of the book, since the tone of the criticism in question is very courteous, and since philosophers live on the notices which they have the good fortune to get from other philosophers. I have to mention, however, my personal interest in the book as a preliminary to any further report.

The book, as a whole, seems to me to be a very fair-minded and judicially wrought piece of work, written with an essential clearness of style, although not in a way to make as easy as possible the work of the unlearned reader in holding his attention to the author's pages. For the discussion is minute and detailed, and the style, although, as I said, essentially lucid, is never brilliant. The book lacks, I think, any *very* notable originality. It is a very kindly survey of the field of controversy in question, a good, although elaborate, presentation of the case for the author's views, and, in sum, is a very gentle piece of work. The position defended is near to that of Howison; but the author lacks somewhat Howison's impressiveness. In part the position is also close to that of Dewey; but Professor Rogers lacks Dewey's incisiveness and ruggedness of style. Yet there is quite enough of the author's personal method in the book to make it worth printing, if only it can attract sufficient attention to float. I doubt whether the author has enough vigor of personal influence about him, or about his style, to attract such a degree of attention to so considerable a volume as this one is. The sale of his previous and smaller book on *Modern Philosophy* will enable you to judge that matter better than I now can. I can only say that, unless the sale of that book was decidedly encouraging, this book will hardly be startling enough to command, as a larger book, any very extensive hearing. But if you *can* print it, the book will be a creditable, although by no means a very striking addition to our academic philosophical literature. It would make decidedly good collateral reading for college students of sufficient advance in their studies. And its influence would make for sanity and good sense.

Yours Very Truly
Josiah Royce.

79 Arthur Kenyon Rogers, *The Religious Conception of the World: An Essay in Constructive Philosophy* (New York: Macmillan Co., 1907).

I acknowledge receipt of the cheque for $15 for my reading of the MS of Armstrong. I return the Rogers MS by express today.

JR.

To George Platt Brett, N.D. [September, 1903?][80]

103 Irving St.
Cambridge, Mass.

Dear Mr. Brett:—

I have received, and have carefully considered, so far as is needed for a decision, the MS entitled: *A Treatise on Cosmology*. Vol. I by Herbert Nichols.[81]

The book is the product of an immense industry, of no small erudition (of a certain sort), and of no little ingenuity. On the other hand, the whole plan of the MS shows that the author leaves out of account many matters belonging to the recent literature of his subject that are of essential importance for his inquiry. Side by side with the one-sided erudition, an ignorance is occasionally displayed such as renders the author unable to cope with his problems. The English is occasionally hopelessly involved; and errors amounting to positive illiteracy occur from time to time, side by side with a good deal of clear and accurate expression. Despite the aforesaid ingenuity, the author, at certain most critical points of his work, also commits blunders of the most elementary sort, relating to the simplest matters of mathematical expression and computation,—blunders, too, such as show not mere oversight, due to haste, but a fundamental confusion of mind about certain elementary mathematical conceptions.

The book is large, and its argument is complex. In order to gain a respectful hearing for his main theses, the author would have to purge his treatise of the elementary faults pointed out. I do not believe that he could do so by means of any brief revision.

In saying this, I am not pretending to judge of the value which the author's main philosophical theses would possess if, through careful revision, his book had been freed from its present elementary defects. As a fact, I should be disposed to think that the

80 ALS. Macmillan Papers. NYPL.

81 Though Macmillan did not publish this work, it was published by University Press of Cambridge, Mass., in 1904.

author's main theses, once accurately expounded, would have a good deal of interest and value, and would deserve a careful hearing. What I am sure of is, however, that, in its present form, the book is disfigured by obvious blunders *not* relating to the deeper problems of philosophy, but obvious to any careful reader capable of making or understanding precise statements. Accordingly, I am sure that, in its *present* shape, the book could be no credit to the firm that printed it, could do no justice to the author's true intentions, or to his real powers, and could win neither commercial nor scientific success. In future, if the author succeeds in ridding his text of its now far too heavy burden of blunders, one's judgment of the book might be altered. I try to judge this book apart from my previous knowledge of its author. I should however prefer to have my judgment of the book regarded as confidential in any of your possible further correspondence with the author. Dr. Nichols was formerly Instructor in Psychology at Harvard, for a time; and his failure with us was due to the same baffling inequality of mind and of expression here shown.

Yours Very Truly
Josiah Royce.

To George Platt Brett, October 8, 1903[82]

103 Irving St.
Cambridge, Mass.
Oct. 8, 1903.

Dear Mr. Brett:—

I have been delayed in my examination of the book: "Hume's Psychology of Knowledge,"[83] first by the absence from home that I reported to you, and, since my return, by the very numerous and extensive demands made on my time by the tasks of the opening of the College year—consultations with students, meetings, &c. I shall hope to do prompter work in case you send me MSS hereafter, since I shall seldom be so interrupted again.

This work, the "Hume" book, is a fine and scholarly philosophical essay. I fail however to see the crying need for its publication.

82 ALS. Macmillan Papers. NYPL.

83 Author unknown; not published by Macmillan.

As an exposition of Hume, it is hardly needed, either as text-book or as contribution to general philosophical literature. Hume is his own best expositor, and he has very often been expounded. As historical summary of Hume's relation to his predecessors, the book is good, but again hardly needed as the tale has often been told. As a criticism of Hume the book seems to me in many ways admirable, —but again hardly needed; because much the same point of view has often been taken. I respect the author's scholarship, admire his spirit, agree on the whole with his position, but cannot believe that the book, dealing as it does with so well-known a topic, could command much attention. Were it a book in a series of historical monographs, like Sneath's Philosophical Classics, it might be in place there, and sell well in its company. Alone, it would seem to me to occupy a doubtful place, and to be unlikely to pay its way.

I found on reading the end of the MS that a few pages (or, at least, as I judge from the context and the table of contents, not more than a few pages), are now lacking at the very end. I took good care of the MS, so far as I know, and I do not find any of these pages after a careful search in my library. Can it be that they were not sent to me? Or have I somehow mislaid them in handling the MS before I read it? I cannot tell. I report the loss (if indeed it is my fault) with regret; but I cannot see how the loss can have been mine. I have handled great numbers of MS before without any such mishap. In any case I am sure that the loss cannot involve more than a very few pages.

Yours Very Truly
Josiah Royce.

I return the MS by express today.

To Richard Clarke Cabot, October 9, 1903[84]

103 Irving St., Cambridge
Oct. 9, 1903

Dear Cabott:—

In accordance with our conversation, and your letter, I now propose a series of informal meetings at my Library, at this house in Cambridge (provided that the place seems not too remote to

[84] ALS. Cabot Papers. HUA.

you). You can best reach me by the Hampshire and Beacon St (Somerville) cars, which pass the corner of Marlborough St and Mass. Av. Boston, about 10 or 15 minutes past the hour, 30 or 35 min. past the hour, and 50 or 55 min. past the hour; you leave them at this end at the corner of Scott & Beacon Sts, on the Somerville line, about five or six minutes quick walk from my house. This I say in case you do not yet know that way to get here, which is as quick as was the way to Harvard Square and direct to Dane Hall.

I propose fortnightly meetings, subject of course to special changes as we find convenient, but for the present to occur, if that suits you and Mrs. Cabot, on Monday evenings, at 8 o'clock (or 7.30 *if* you prefer).

The topics to be on the lines that you suggested:—Practical applications of speculative problems and attitudes,—everybody to ride his or her own hobby, but with the intent to edify the rest.

I propose, at present, as sharers in the enterprise, yourself, Mrs. Cabot, Miss Rousmaniere (if she can come), Mrs. Evans (if she wishes), Hocking, Miss Sears, and such of my colleagues of the Dep't as can take part and choose to do so,—and finally one or two or three other students in case I can find them.[85] Miss Sears I am inviting in a note written tonight. I don't know Miss Rousmaniere's present address. Could you tell me what it is? I haven't yet appealed direct to Mrs. Evans, but shall do so if you think that she would wish to come. I am quite open to suggestions from you as to the persons to be asked to take part.

The first meeting I propose for Monday Oct 19, that is, one week from next Monday. I should hope to have Hocking lead off with an account of the new "Pragmatism" of Rickert and Windelband, of whose ideas he seems to be just now very full. He seems to have come back in a very inspired mood, and I hope for good results.

As to the spirit of the occasions, I intend neither a purely scholastic exercise, nor yet, in any sense, a social entertainment other than such as talking together of good things involves. We shall all be busy folk, with some things to say, and many things to think over. I believe that we might gain something from one another, at least during the course of one winter. I propose no organization, no

[85] The group known as the Philosophical Conference met with fair regularity at Royce's home during 1903–4. A few of Royce's contributions are preserved in the Royce Papers, HUA.

officers, no order of business except, each time, one or two short papers,—a general discussion of these,—additional voluntary notes if anybody has them to offer,—a planning just a little ahead as to our choice of topics,—a trusting to the general course of reason to give our work unity in case the enterprise proves worthwhile. I shall sit at my desk and perhaps call names if necessary to set the conversation going. Otherwise the affair shall manage itself. We shall simply talk as at a Seminary, but with less formality.

Your comments will be welcome. If the day appointed doesn't suit, please let me know.

Yours Truly
Josiah Royce

To Richard Clarke Cabot, October 15, 1903[86]

103 Irving St.
Cambridge, Mass.
Oct. 15, 1903.

Dear Cabot:—

I have written to ask Miss Calkins to come. I have also addressed a letter of invitation to Miss Rousmaniere, at 66 Chestnut St., Boston. Hocking will read a paper as I indicated. I shall say a few introductory words on our plans. I should be glad if you also could be ready to state, in a ten or fifteen minutes series of explanations, what you would like to have such a company discuss, what spirit of work promises to your mind most of profit, what *are* the more practical problems of philosophy, and what topics you are yourself most disposed to talk about, in later meetings. You can feel quite free to make your suggestions in your own way; and I am certain in advance of a general agreement with your suggestions. In any case, I do not intend to act as director, but only as a sort of moderator; and we shall gain by a variety of expressions about what we can hope to do, as well as by doing something at once.

I enclose a list of the invited. It turns out larger than I had meant. But all the people are mature in interest. None of them is likely to be helpless or wholly speechless. All of them are pretty busy folk; and seldom or never will they all come any one evening,—at least

86 ALS. Cabot Papers. HUA.

after the opening occasion. Hence we ought not to be at a loss to get these occasions to lead to a relatively free interchange of thoughts. We may have to meet in my parlor. The library is too small.

I shall hope to have people gather at my house between 7.30 and 8. We shall want to have a few minutes to become acquainted. At 8 o'clock we shall set to work. Don't come in evening dress. All is absolutely informal.

Yours Truly
Josiah Royce.

To Hugo Münsterberg, December 9, 1903[87]

103 Irving St.
Dec. 9, 1903.

Dear Münsterberg:—

As requested by James & Baldwin I left for you, today, the letters of Baldwin on the issue between Cattell and himself as to the proposed new publication of Cattell.[88] I hope that they may divide territory without bloodshed. I propose myself to have the matter referred to the Hague tribunal at once. Otherwise the peace of Europe may be endangered before they get through, even though the conflict so far seems to have been confined to this country. But since it is interacademic already, how soon might it not become international? Seriously, I want to cooperate with them both; I cannot see why there need be any rivalry at all, if only they can be induced to agree on distinct provinces without both arming all the earth.

What is to be the date of my proposed St. Louis address next summer?[89] Will it conflict with my Summer School dates? I saw

87 ALS. Münsterberg Papers. BPL.

88 *Journal of Philosophy, Psychology, and Scientific Methods* was founded at Columbia University in 1904. Though the journal was officially edited by Professor F. J. E. Woodbridge, Cattell was active in its founding and its operation. At this point, Cattell withdrew as co-editor of *Psychological Review*, leaving it in the hands of James Mark Baldwin.

89 Münsterberg was vice-president and principal organizer of the International Congress of Arts and Science at the St. Louis World's Fair, September 19–25, 1904. Royce read a paper on "The Sciences of the Ideal," *Congress of Arts and Sciences, Universal Exposition, St. Louis, 1904* (Boston: Houghton Mifflin Co., 1905), 1: 151–68.

Newcomb[90] the other day, and talked over plans, with the result that I felt new and still stronger interest in the plan. Many thanks to you for getting me into it.

Yours Truly
Josiah Royce.

To George Platt Brett, December 21, 1903[91]

103 Irving St.
Cambridge, Mass.
Dec. 21, 1903

My Dear Mr. Brett:—

I very greatly regret my delay in returning the MS of Mr. Alfred Lloyd, Professor at the University of Michigan, entitled "The Place of Doubt in Experience.[92] I owe him and you an apology for my tardiness. But the MS has reached me at the most absorbed and busy time of year, when my strength is not my own to dispose of as I choose. I perhaps ought on this account to have declined the MS altogether when it came to hand, and to have sent it back at once. But I have been hoping daily for leisure. At last I am able to report.

My present report is based upon such knowledge of the MS as I have been able to get in reading by snatches. There is now no doubt left in my mind that this is an important and in many parts inspiring book,—a very decided advance upon some previous publications of its author. The weakest part, as I believe, is Chapter IV: "The View of Science and its Contradictions," where the author, using the term "Science" as a sort of sectarian term, speaks as if there were some one set of views of things to be attributed to "science," and to be criticized as such; whereas there are only sciences; and whereas the various special sciences, and the countless conscientious workers in them ought not to be held responsible for the extravagances or the contradictions of certain more or less popular representatives who have assumed to speak for "science" as if it had, as such any one philosophical bias or any one teaching

[90] Simon Newcomb was president of the International Congress of Arts and Science.

[91] ALS. Macmillan Papers. NYPL.

[92] This work was not published. Another book by Lloyd on skepticism, *The Will to Doubt: An Essay in Philosophy for the General Thinker*, was recommended by Royce and published by Macmillan Co. in 1907.

about life and about the world. Apart from my objection to this form of polemic, I have no criticism to offer of the main trend of the argument. I think that the book, if printed, would find a serious, if not a very large audience, not only amongst academic circles, but amongst the general public; and would probably make its mark, not as a sensational, but as a very vital piece of work.

I may add that, after next Feb. 15, I shall be free, during the second half of the academic year, to examine such MSS as you may send me, in case you still wish me to do so, and to report, I hope, with promptness, as I have tried to do in former cases. I deeply regret the delay in this case.

Yours Very Truly
Josiah Royce.

I return the MS by express today.

To Frederick James Eugene Woodbridge, January 21, 1904[93]

103 Irving St.
Cambridge, Mass.
Jan. 21, 1904.

Dear Woodbridge,

In view of what you say as to the fixity of the programme, I shall try again to do my best to abate, in your favor, the conflict of engagements of which I spoke in my last, and shall try to arrange to deliver the expected Tuesday Feb. 2 lecture.

Yours Very Truly
Josiah Royce.

93 ALS. *Journal of Philosophy* Papers. CUB. This letter was sent with a "Programme of Lectures to be delivered at Columbia." The dates are the same as given in the letter to Woodbridge, July 27, 1903, and have the general title, "The Comparative Study of Scientific Concepts." Lecture I is to be an introduction. Lectures II and III will deal with specific concepts: (1) Classes and Classification, (2) Relations and their Types, (3) Ordinal Concepts and Ordered Series, (4) Concepts of Transformations, (5) Concepts of Levels. Lecture IV is to deal with "Applications of the foregoing survey to various Special Problems," and Lecture V will be on "Philosophical Considerations suggested by the foregoing survey." These unpublished lectures are preserved in Royce Papers, HUA.

To The Macmillan Company, January 23, 1904[94]

103 Irving St.
Cambridge, Mass.
January 23, 1904.

Macmillian Co.,

Gentlemen:—

There is no doubt of the great importance of the book entitled *A System of Metaphysics*, by Professor G. S. Fullerton, whose MS you have asked me to examine.[95] Few teachers of philosophy in this country have succeeded as well as he has done in producing careful and critical thinkers as a result of their teaching. His pupils form a distinct type of workers, some of whom have already won good places as teachers themselves. His influence is growing. His work is sure to demand and receive a wide and careful attention from his colleagues. I have gone over the MS, summarily, but quite enough to be sure that it is a work for which I have long been waiting, that it is very clear in statement and finished in form, and that it is likely to find use as a text-book. I differ strongly in many points from Professor Fullerton. Upon some topics he seems to me to lack the actual knowledge of recent logical researches (in the logic of mathematics), which he ought to show. If the book is printed, and I review it, I am therefore likely to attack it, at some points, pretty sharply.[96] But all this leaves me no doubt that the book is to be greatly respected, and will have a powerful influence. No *System of Metaphysics* can have a great sale. But this one will not be a bad example of its type as to sale. I recommend the printing of the work.

Yours Truly
Josiah Royce.

[94] ALS. Macmillan Papers. NYPL.

[95] Published by Macmillan in 1904.

[96] Royce, however, did not publish a review of Fullerton's *A System of Metaphysics*.

To James McKeen Cattell, February 20, 1904[97]

Feb. 20, 1904.

Dear Professor Cattell:—

In answer to your request, made some weeks since, I have had prepared, by the Harvard Library, regardless of expense (which latter I have to bear),—as complete a bibliography of my writings, "scientific," and otherwise, as that institution has found possible.[98] As a fact, a good many of my youthful articles are not included. I don't vouch for the accuracy of the type-writer, and cannot spend time now in revision.

As you see, the bibliographer finds evidence of 99 pieces, varying in length from scraps to 2 vols 8°.—These, in fact, are the "ninety and nine sheep" which I have "left in the wilderness." I am at present in quest of the hundredth sheep,—not yet published.

I cannot conceive why any bibliography of me should interest you, or your associates in any scientific society. Since you ask, —there you have it. I cannot undertake to draw the line between what is and what isn't "scientific" in the list. Much of it isn't scientific, of course.

Yours Truly
Josiah Royce.

To George Platt Brett, February 24, 1904[99]

103 Irving St.
Cambridge, Mass.
Feb. 24, 1904.

Dear Mr. Brett:—

It is my intention to state publicly, quite soon, the facts regarding my relation to the readers called "The Indiana State Series" on

[97] ALS. Cattell Papers. LC.

[98] Royce was elected to the National Academy of Sciences in 1906. The bibliography was evidently used by Cattell in presenting Royce's nomination.

[99] ALS. Macmillan Papers. NYPL.

whose title-page my name still appears in the revisions of 1903.[100] Had my attention been earlier called to this continued use of my name in these readers, I should have tried to set the matter right long since. I have been taking counsel of late of some of my friends regarding the best way to explain my position effectively. But as there may be still a little delay in getting a statement printed, I deem it right to say to you, in view of your own inquiries regarding the matter, that I have had no part in any revision of those readers since the first appearance of A. L. Bancroft's series of readers, in California, in 1882,—a series of which, as I understand, these "Indiana State" readers are successors.

In the beginning of the eighties, in California, A. L. Bancroft and Co. undertook a series of readers intended for local use. I was then a young instructor in English Composition in the University of California. As such an instructor I was asked to do, and did, some work as editor (one of three editors), towards the preparation of that series. I was then a little over twenty five years of age. I never had any pecuniary interest, in this or any other series of readers, after the publication of this series at that time, namely about 1882. I was paid for my share of the work before the publication of the books. I know only by hearsay that the copyright of the readers in question was transferred later by A. L. Bancroft & Co. to other persons. Until very recently I never heard who had possession of the copyright, or how my name was still used in connection with the later forms of the series.

I have never been consulted as to any later revision of the series, and have no responsibility whatever for its present form. I judge, from some examination,—which I have but recently had a chance to make—that the readers, in their present form, are very unlike the original California series. The changes may be, for all I know, for the better. My present profession, that of teacher and student of philosophy—a profession which I have followed since 1882, disqual-

[100] *Bancroft's First [-Fifth] Reader*, ed. Charles H. Allen, John Swett, and Josiah Royce (San Francisco: A. L. Bancroft [1884]). See Frank M. Oppenheim, S. J., "A Critical Annotated Bibliography of the Published Works of Josiah Royce," *Modern Schoolman* 41 (1964): 345, where this item is listed with the following note: "These readers were adopted at least by the Standard Education Series, St. Louis, and the Indiana State Series, and underwent repeated revisions. Royce's contributions to the first edition remains to be clarified as does his connection with subsequent editions of these readers."

ifies me to judge what constitutes a good school reader at the present day. I regard my judgment, as it was in 1882, as having been of no great importance in the original enterprise. I did my little share of work; my cöeditors were elder and wiser men. They largely overruled my opinions, and were doubtless right in so doing.

In any case, it seems to me something wholly unjustified to keep my name on the title page of the present series. It also would seem to me very misleading if anybody represented these books, in their present form, as standing for any mature judgment of mine; and it would be equally misleading if anybody represented the revision as at all my work.

You are at liberty to make use of this letter at your discretion. I give it to you solely because it concerns a matter of fact, which I have a right to have understood by anybody who may be interested in school-books. You will understand that I pretend in no way to pass upon the value of the "Indiana State Series," which may be, for all I know, of very high value. I only insist that it is wrong to use my name in connection with them as they now are.

I am

Yours Very Truly
Josiah Royce.

To Reginald Chauncey Robbins, May 1, 1904[101]

103 Irving St.
Cambridge, Mass.
May 1, 1904.

Dear Robbins:—

As far as the time has permitted, I have looked, from one moment to another, at various intervals, into your book.[102] I find many things that appeal to me strongly, and that seem both deep in insight, and of very genuine vigor as expressions of life. What my final view is to be, I cannot yet surely say; for your poems are strongly individual, and their world is one whose colors are newer

101 ALS. Robbins Papers. HL.

102 Either *Love Poems* (Cambridge: Riverside Press, 1903) or *Poems of Personality* (Cambridge: Riverside Press, 1904).

to me than are its laws, which latter, to be sure, seem deeply genuine, so far as I yet grasp them.

But of this another time. Tomorrow evening, at 7.30-8 we assemble, as usual, for our Conference here at my house. At 8, there are due papers by Hocking and perhaps by Dr. Southard. I hope that you can come. I welcome your safe return.

Yours Truly
Josiah Royce.

To George Bucknam Dorr, May 1, 1904[103]

103 Irving St.
Cambridge.
May 1, 1904.

Dear Dorr:—

My son, in sending out the cards for my next Conference, used a list of names to which, as I now find, I had neglected to add, as I had meant to do, yours. I am very sorry for the omission. If you are still in town, this note is to say that the "Philosophical Conference," of which I told you in a previous note, meets again at my house tomorrow, Monday evening, May 2, at 7.30 P. M. The papers are read at 8 o'clock. There are to be two of them,—both brief. Then a general discussion. Our topic is still:—"The Religious Consciousness." I hope that you can come.

Yours Very Truly
Josiah Royce.

I have been meaning to call since my delightful evening with you; but a lot of extra papers that I have been called, for various academic and other occasions, upon to write have been holding me back.

[103] ALS. Royce Papers. HUA.

To Florence Sparks Moore, May 3, 1904[104]

103 Irving St.
Cambridge
May 3, 1904

Dear Mrs. Moore:

I feel distinctly encouraged, as to your son's general prospects as a student and as a possible teacher of philosophy, in view of the account that I obtained from him this morning. His record and what I already know of his work were, as you know, favorably viewed by me before this talk. My favorable impression is rather strengthened by our discussion.

He has come to philosophy in a wholesome and natural way. He has made good use of his time so far. His present difficulty in making his thoughts intelligible to other people is due, not, I think, to any fundamental defect of clearness in his thinking, but to the way in which he has read himself into certain aspects of his subject, to the exclusion of certain other aspects which he will in time learn to emphasize. His mental development, so far as philosophy is concerned, has been a little too solitary and independent. He needs practice in teaching, in discussion, etc. But there seems to be no trait in him that forbids him to get such practice as time goes on. I looked (as we talked together) for the various more or less defective, or if you choose, morbid motives that sometimes are present in young men who are driven into philosophy by a false or unfortunate sort of reflectiveness. I could find no sign of such motives in him. His philosophizing seems so far to be a natural and sensible enough process, imperfect as is still his power to convey to other people what he means. His religious experience seems to have been of a normal enough type, whatever you may think of the outcome, —an outcome with which I myself do not agree, although I have learned to respect strongly the motives which I have several times seen leading young people in the direction that he has followed,

[104] TLC. Royce Papers. HUA. Printed in Daniel S. Robinson, *Royce and Hocking—American Idealists* (Boston: Christopher Publishing House, 1968), pp. 140–41. The letter is written to the mother of Jared Sparks Moore (Ph.D., Harvard, 1905; later Professor of Philosophy, Western Reserve University). A note at the top of the typescript identifies the addressee and adds: "The original was given to E. S. Brightman by Professor Moore's widow."

and that has led him into his present church connection. On that side he seems to me to be growing safely enough.

He has considerable independence and productiveness of thought, a pretty large power for work, a knowledge of what scholarship is, a high ideal, a healthy mind, and a good deal of learning. He ought to have paid more attention than he has done to natural science, and would have done well to study more mathematics, and also psychology. But there is time to make up for such incompletenesses.

I think that he ought to try to get a job of tutoring during the coming summer, so as to earn something. I should be glad to see him study here next year, and should think it justifiable to make considerable sacrifices to let him do so. Whether we could find a place for him as Assistant I cannot yet say. In any case he can make better use of his time here than elsewhere next year, so far as I can see.

It looks to me as if he would develope somewhat slowly, but very healthily, as a student and teacher of philosophy, and as if that were likely to be a good career for him.

His temperament,–cheerful on the whole, but not exactly sanguine,–unaggressive, but persistent,–seems to be favorable to a reasonable success. His health, as you all say, seems very good; but I should be glad to know that he exercised,–moderately, but regularly,–enough to ensure his always retaining, during his years of trial, his present soundness. He will have to study hard. He needs therefore all possible physical soundness.

My practical result is that you would do well, even at considerable cost to your patience, to let him go on developing in his present way, hoping, as I hope, that before too long a time he can be on his own feet as a professional man.

Yours Very Truly
Josiah Royce.

As I read over my letter, I feel of course how fallible my judgment has to be. I can only report what so far I seem to see. I have done my best with the imperfect data so far accessible to me.

To The Macmillan Company, May 21, 1904[105]

103 Irving Street
Cambridge
May 21, 1904.

The Macmillan Company,

Gentlemen:—

The book of Taylor: *Elements of Metaphysics*, is already known to me. [106] It strikes not only me, but my colleagues here, as a strong book, and a good text-book. If properly brought before the public in this country it ought to be decidedly well used (for a book of its size and topic), as a class text-book, and as a book for serious readers. It is well written, of high professional character, and of timely interest so far as current discussion goes. As the author mentions me freely, perhaps I am prejudiced in his favor. But James, as I know, fully agrees with my view of the book as a text-book, although his philosophical sympathies are not with the author's views nearly as often as mine are.

Yours Truly
Josiah Royce.

To George Bucknam Dorr, May 21, 1904[107]

103 Irving Street
Cambridge
May 21, 1904

My Dear Dorr:—

The Spinoza[108] has come, and I enjoy very greatly both its ap-

[105] ALS. Macmillan Papers. NYPL.

[106] Alfred Edward Taylor, *Elements of Metaphysics* (London: Methuen and Co., 1903). This highly popular textbook was reprinted by the New York office of Macmillan in 1904.

[107] ALS. Royce Papers. HUA.

[108] A typescript of this letter in the Royce Papers contains the following footnote, presumably written by Dorr: "An old edition of Spinoza, much annotated, which had come to me by gift from an old student and follower of Spinoza's philosophy."

pearance and the notes. I still more prize it as your gift, and as a reminder of old times, when first we met. Many are the gifts and good hours that I have owed to you and yours. This will add still more weight to my obligation, and to my satisfaction.

I enjoyed the evening with you very much. It has been sad to be unable to help practically in this matter of Emerson Hall. All the more do I appreciate the work of those who have both the will and the power to help.

Yours Very Truly
Josiah Royce.

Many good wishes for the summer.

To JOHN COTTON DANA, JULY 23, 1904[109]

103 Irving St.
Cambridge, Mass.
July 23, 1904.

Dear Mr. Dana:—

My paper on "Provincialism," concerning which you inquired in your letter of July 8, has never been reprinted since the *Transcript* printed it. I have been waiting until I should some day have a number of such papers for a volume upon some of the needs of our American life.[110] I thank you for your interest. Someday I hope to be able to meet your wish.

As to your views on "godishness," I doubt if you, after all, are so far away from idealism as you suppose. Some people veil their piety from themselves by a certain semblance of heresy, forgetting that the Absolute, if he exists, is the freest souled and most liberal and least petty or jealous minded or tyrannical of us all. One way to serve God is by doubting or even denying his existence, if only thereby you give your own faithfulness to ideal interests, and to truth, the clearest expression now possible to you. For faithful self-expression, with loyalty to ideal interests, is I take it, all that God means, for himself or for you; and so we don't disagree so much after all.

Yours Truly
Josiah Royce.

[109] ALS. Public Library of Newark, New Jersey.
[110] *RQP*, pp. 57–108.

To George Platt Brett, July 23, 1904[111]

103 Irving St.
Cambridge, Mass.
July 23, 1904.

Dear Mr. Brett,

I am very decidedly disposed, whenever I can get my lectures on "Introduction to Philosophy for Teachers" into a good shape, to offer them, for publication to you. But, after some waiting, and endeavor, I now see that, since I am still experimenting with my "Summer School" class at Harvard as to the best form in which to put the lectures, I cannot hope to get them into shape for publication this summer. As soon as they take on a more permanent form, I shall hope to let you know, and to send them to you. This in answer to yours of July 5.

Yours Very Truly,
Josiah Royce.

To George Platt Brett, September 15, 1904[112]

103 Irving St.
Cambridge.
Mass.
Sept 15, 1904

Dear Mr. Brett:—

I have just returned from a vacation visit of four weeks in Jamaica, whither I went on the conclusion of the Summer School. I have now had time to examine the MS of Mrs. Richard Cabot's book on "The Secret of Power."[113] I have known for some time

111 ALS. Macmillan Papers. NYPL. The lectures mentioned in this letter were never published, though a subsequent series of summer-school lectures for teachers prompted *PL*. See letter to Münsterberg, August 12, 1906.

112 ALS. Macmillan Papers. NYPL.

113 Ella Lyman Cabot was the wife of Dr. Richard Cabot, a close friend of the Royces, and a member of the Philosophical Conference. Though she wrote several books, she published nothing under this title, nor did Macmillan Co. handle any of her writings. This MS may be related to her *Everyday Ethics* (New York: H. Holt and Co., 1906).

about Mrs. Cabot's work, although I had not seen so complete a statement of her methods; still, the main drift of the book has become known to me from frequent conversations with Mrs. Cabot.

I unhesitatingly commend the contents and the general method of the book. I should think that it ought to appeal to a fair number of teachers, pupils, and general readers. Its style is good; its points are well made; it is wholesome, sensible, progressive, and interesting, as well as philosophically deep; it is, in mode of presentation, clear and popular. I recommend its publication. I should myself prefer to see its title changed. I should think that the title: "Conduct and Power" would be more indicative of its contents and purpose, and perhaps a little less pretentious in seeming. The book itself is very free from pretentiousness, and is well worthy of attention.

Yours Very Truly
Josiah Royce

To The Macmillan Company, October 23, 1904[114]

103 Irving St.
Cambridge, Mass.
Oct. 23, 1904.

The Macmillan Company,

Gentlemen:—

I return by express the MS of Professor Hyslop's work on *The Problems of Philosophy*.[115] The fact that the MS reached me for review just at the outset of the work of the College year, has much delayed my examination of the MS,—an examination not very easy to make.

Hyslop is a man of a good deal of strength, although certainly *not* of a very high grade of originality. His MS contains a good many things which would interest serious students of philosophy,

[114] ALS. Macmillan Papers. NYPL.

[115] James Hervey Hyslop, *The Problems of Philosophy: Or, Principles of Epistemology and Metaphysics* (New York: Macmillan Co., 1905). Reviewed by Royce in *International Journal of Ethics* 16 (January 1906): 236–41.

and also *some* things which would interest a certain portion of the general public. The great size of the proposed book, its rather difficult method of presentation, the fact that it could hardly be used as a text-book, the fact that it is not of any especially marked originality,—these facts together lead me to regard the book as probably not a safe venture for publication, unless the author will pay a large share of the expense, or assume the risk. Hyslop's former work, and his reputation, which (despite his quasi-spiritualistic adventures) is fairly solid, would secure the book *some* sale. I fear not enough to float so big a book.

I say this with regret. I wish that Hyslop could have more hearing. A small book on the same topic from him might go very well.

Yours Very Truly
Josiah Royce.

To George Platt Brett, January 28, 1905[116]

103 Irving St.
Cambridge, Mass.
January 28, 1905.

Dear Mr. Brett:—

I send by express today Rev. J. Macbride Sterrett's MS on the *Freedom of Authority*, concerning which my opinion was asked.[117] The book, like other philosophical books, is formidably long. On the other hand, it seems to me a strong book. The author has now won, by his previous books, a good place in professional literature. He will get a considerable attention, from theological quarters; the philosophers will also find him useful. Some body of general readers will also give him attention, outside of professional circles.

My disposition is to think that the book would command a fair sale, although its size and probable price are of course against it. I venture to recommend its publication.

Yours Very Truly
Josiah Royce.

[116] ALS. Macmillan Papers. NYPL.

[117] James Macbride Sterrett, *The Freedom of Authority: Essays in Apologetics* (New York: Macmillan Co., 1905).

To Charles William Eliot, May 11, 1905[118]

103 Irving St.
May 11, 1905.

Dear Dr. Eliot:—

I ought not to let the opportunity pass without adding my very unauthoritative note to those which you have asked officers to send in, regarding the question as to the way in which funds can be most effectively used for the bettering of the profession of the college teacher.

I am with those who hold that one of the weakest portions of the present system is the position in which the Assistant Professor is placed during his first term. The Instructor needs, I suppose, to be held to a pretty narrow material advantage until, by scholarship and service, he has shown his right to a permanent place in the academic world. The Assistant Professor should be chosen as a man who has already proved that he has such a right. He should then be put into a position wherein he is, not indulged, or pampered, but distinctly encouraged to meet the problems of young married life without undue anxieties, and without such distracting cares as tend to destroy his ambition for the more ideal aspects of service and of scholarship. His brain is worth cultivating for its own sake. That fact he has already shown, if he has proved his right to his Assistant Professorship. His interest in good work is not mercenary. That he has already proved by enduring the toil so far required of him. The question is whether he shall now, in the best years of mental expansion, be helped to give himself over, devotedly, to the best service, of his science, and of his art as a teacher, whereof he is capable. Fill his head, just then, with too many painful distractions, keep him where his duty to his family forces him to repress his ambitions, drive him to wear out his energies in extra tasks for the sake of bread,—and the result is that a possibly good man is often lost, not to the college (for he often stays and works), but to higher service (for he often is worn or discouraged into an industrious but inefficient routine). Of course I do not mean that the salaries at this stage should be very large, but that a little chance of surplus, rather than an inevitable deficit, should encourage a man

118 ALS. Eliot Papers. HUA.

to keep his joy in his profession. The present disparity between the salary of the Assistant Professor in his first term, and the later salaries, seems to me too great. A few hundred dollars could be wisely and fruitfully used, at this stage, I think, as an addition to almost any salary that is now given to such men.

Later, as well as earlier, the use of money for salaries ought, in my view, to be further guided by this consideration also, viz.:— The interference between the administrative and the more directly academic duties of officers is one of the principal evils of the modern university. I speak of the interference of two very important tasks. I fully believe in the importance of administration. I very greatly depend on administrative officers. I need them, and admire their powers, and am fond of following them as my leaders. They, then, should be well paid. But scholars also are needed. I regret such disposition of our funds as makes it necessary for so many, especially of my younger colleagues, to give themselves over, unwillingly, to administrative tasks which hamper their scholarship, and which take up their time, when they are capable of other than administrative work, and can do better service as productive scholars, or as devoted teachers, than as administrators.

I plead then that salaries should be so adjusted to powers and services that the career of the productive scholar, and of the effective teacher, when chosen by the proper person, should be viewed by all as having the same prospects of support as has the career of the administratively busied teacher. In other words, give Mary as good a chance (I do not say as high wages) as Martha. This is now often, but not always done. I want to see, not fewer Marthas, but more Marys.

Yours Very Truly
Josiah Royce

To James Brander Matthews, May 22, 1905[119]

103 Irving St.
Cambridge,
Mass.
May 22, 1905.

My Dear Mr. Matthews:—

I return unsigned the promise, regarding spelling.[120] A general agreement upon a reformed English orthography is obviously impossible, in any systematic way. By introducing varieties of habit, while still attempting to make these varieties matters of rule, of promises, of authority, and of system, one can only complicate further the situation. The proposal of your committee is in substance this, viz., that, because the present memorizing of rules for English spelling is a burden, you propose to alleviate the burden by adding one more rule, and by asking people to commit to memory one more list,—this time a list of twelve "simplifications." I decline to cooperate. If the committee proposed, as a general rule: "Spell as you please, but as phonetically as you can find it in your heart to do," that would at least be a plan to simplify, although hardly indeed to beautify, the situation. For my part, I have no protest to make if people like to learn the new twelve word list. For my part also, I have too many serious issues to attend to as it is, without burdening my soul with a promise regarding one further complication of life. This reply is made with every feeling of personal respect for the members of your committee.

Yrs. Truly
Josiah Royce

119 ALS. Matthews Papers. CUB.

120 Matthews was chairman of the Simplified Spelling Board, which, with the financial support of Andrew Carnegie, sought to eliminate some of the vestiges of English orthography. The board had a distinguished list of members, including William James. They compiled and distributed a list of three hundred words with two or more accepted spellings, asking writers to use the shortest form. See Brander Matthews, *These Many Years: Recollections of a New Yorker* (New York: Charles Scribner's Sons, 1919).

To Frederick James Eugene Woodbridge, June 28, 1905[121]

103 Irving St.
June 29, 1905.

Dear Professor Woodbridge:—

In reply to your very kind invitation of the 25th, asking me to take part in the work of the summer session at Columbia, in 1906, I am now able to reply that, since receiving your letter, I have had a consultation with the Chairman of our own Summer School. He urges me to continue the work that for two years past I have been doing here, at the Harvard Summer School. And I therefore feel that if I decide to do any summer work whatever, it ought to be done at home.

Your call is none the less kind, and I thank you for it. I should greatly enjoy a visit of the sort to Columbia.

I have been trying to get to a place in my work where I could promise to undertake the review of the Russian mathematical-philosophical treatise of which you speak. But I see that I am now simply unable to wedge in another job at any point. So I shall have to decline.

I hope to see you at Christmas time, for the meeting at Emerson Hall.[122] We shall be glad to see you in Cambridge.

Yours Very Truly
Josiah Royce.

121 ALS. *Journal of Philosophy* Papers. CUB.

122 The American Psychological Association and the American Philosophical Association held a joint meeting at Harvard, December 27–29, honoring the opening of Emerson Hall.

To George Platt Brett, July 13, 1905[123]

103 Irving St.
Cambridge, Mass.
July 13, 1905.

Mr. George P. Brett,

My Dear Mr. Brett:—

The book on "Spinoza and Religion"[124] was returned to you today by express (American Express Co.). The book shows a great deal of scholarship, and of serious work. The thesis of the author, viz., that Spinoza was an atheist, with no religious doctrine, is an old one, and, as I believe, an incorrect one. It is here defended with no little acumen, but hardly with any startling originality of argument. The mode of treatment is temperate and careful. The author's case is worthy of consideration, in view of the detail and of the care shown. Some scholars would take interest. It would find a place in some libraries.

I do *not* believe, however, that the volume will fill a sufficiently important place in Spinoza literature to make it a standard book. I doubt whether it would interest a very wide circle of readers. Unless it chanced to arouse sufficient controversy to draw a pretty artificial attention, it could hardly get a large sale. As a teacher, I do not think that this way of treating a philosopher is a very profitable one. A good *genetic* account of Spinoza's thought would be a good thing in our literature. A *judgment* of him, as an atheist, or as not an atheist, doesn't help much to make one see where he stands in the growth of thought. Hence, for the purpose of a student, this book helps little.

On the whole then, I could not much recommend the book for class use, or for students' reading. I doubt whether it could sell much. I do not believe that you had better publish it.

Yours Truly
Josiah Royce.

My work in the Summer School has delayed this reply.

[123] ALS. Macmillan Papers. NYPL.
[124] Author unknown; not published by Macmillan.

To Frederick James Eugene Woodbridge, August 8, 1905[125]

9 University Hall
Harvard University, Cambridge
8 August 1905

Dear Professor Woodbridge:—

I have learned from Professor James that you are looking for a man to fill a position at Columbia in Logic and Psychology. I suppose from the way in which Professor James stated your request that you lay more stress upon the Logic. It is especially in view of that fact that I recommend most heartily Mr. Harold Chapman Brown,[126] whose present address is C/o M. A. L. Brunham, Highland Lake, Bridgton, Maine. Brown is a Ph.D. of the present year at this place. Partly in consequence of my influence, he devoted himself, throughout his Graduate work, to modern Logic—especially to symbolic Logic and Logic of Mathematics, with considerable attention paid to the history of Logic as set forth by Prantl. He prepared a thesis on a "Problem of the Kantian Mathematical Antimonies"—a thesis, as I believe, which will lead to a good deal of further research on his part, in the same direction. He is already acquainted with Russell's book, and with the rest of the recent literature of the subject.[127] As to his quality, he is a progressive and ingenious man, with a great deal of interest in these problems, and with a very real prospect of success.

He took his degree of course in Philosophy in general, and the Laboratory speaks well of his Psychological work, although Psy-

[125] TLS. *Journal of Philosophy* Papers. CUB.

[126] Brown received his Ph.D. from Harvard in 1905 and taught at Columbia before moving permanently to Stanford in 1914. He described his relationship to Royce and his early teaching at Columbia in "A Philosophic Mind in the Making," *Contemporary American Philosophy*, ed. George P. Adams and William Pepperell Montague, 2 vols. (New York: Russell & Russell, Inc., 1962), 1: 174–79.

[127] Ibid., p. 175: "Royce—and I think this grieved him a little—sent me out from Harvard well started on the road to pragmatism. This resulted from trying to clear up for myself the problems of the new mathematics of number theory and the problems of Russell's Principles of Mathematics which had just appeared. A year of my work, taken in Germany just after my marriage, and prior to my Ph.D., did little but get me acquainted with another type of life, give me some mastery over German, introduce me to a few philosophers of a different sort, and let me read Prantl's *Geschichte der Logik* and Schroeder's *Algebra der Logic, in toto*."

chology is not his specialty. He ought to prove a good Instructor in general courses in that subject.

Brown is still a young man, and full of eagerness to get a position where he can do some research work. He is a companionable fellow, and would make a congenial member of the Department. I am therefore recommending him highly.

The only drawback that is to be considered is the fact that during the last year in consequence of a good deal of strain, and some family cares, he became nervously somewhat tired, and was for a time a good deal out of condition. Yet he was able to finish his thesis, even when he felt the worst. He has been taking a good summer's rest, and I believe that his future health will prove, if he is properly careful, decidedly controllable. He is married, and has one child.

Brown has been an Assistant here in our elementary courses and so is not without experience in class-room work. He has made a devoted and successful Assistant. I cannot of course certainly know how well he would succeed in organizing independently courses for which he alone was responsible, but I should expect him to do well in this respect.

James compared Brown in his reply to you, as I understand, with two or three other men. I do not think any other of our men is as well adapted, to a position in which Logic would be prominent, as Brown is. Arthur Dewing, also a Doctor of the present year, whose thesis was entitled "Negation and Intuition in the Philosophy of Schelling," is a very strong scholar and a very promising man. The history of Philosophy is most prominent in his work. He has already published a volume on the history of modern Philosophy. Ewer, of whom James spoke to you, is already I think placed for the coming year. He is a good man, but has not given the attention to Logic in the modnern sense that Brown has given. Buck I do not believe to be available at present.

I hope to be able to send you within a few days a logical research of my own that has just been published in the *Transactions of the American Mathematical Society*.[128]

Yours very truly,
Josiah Royce

Professor F. J. E. Woodbridge.

[128] "The Relation of the Principles of Logic to the Foundations of Geometry," *Transactions of the American Mathematical Society* 24 (July 1905): 353–415; reprinted in *RLE*, pp. 379–441.

To Charles Sanders Peirce, September 21, 1905[129]

103 Irving St.
Sept. 21, 1905

Dear Mr. Peirce:—

In my letter mailed this morning[130] I believe that, in one passage, in rendering my own definition of non-equivalence, I made a slip in expression, through haste in writing. To assert that, in my system Σ, as my Principle IV requires it to be constituted, there exists a pair (x, y), such that $x \neq y$, is to assert, as my text states, that there exists at least one O-collection of elements whereof one of these elements (say x) is a member, while the other element (say y)

[129] ALS. Peirce Papers. HL. This and the succeeding two letters consist of Royce's part in a flurry of correspondence which extended through August and September of 1905. The corpus of this exchange was Royce's "The Relation of the Principles of Logic to the Foundations of Geometry." Here Royce advanced his System Σ, considered by C. I. Lewis, J. H. Cotton, and others to be among his most significant contributions to logic. Though the three letters by Royce included in this edition are all that survives of his part in the correspondence, Peirce's letters to Royce for this period, drafts of letters, fragments, notes, etc. exist in profusion, both in the Royce Papers and in the Peirce Papers. On August 19, Peirce opened the exchange (Royce Papers): "I received today your highly important Memoir, and although I have not yet had time to read far into Chapter II, I will venture on a few remarks which may for aught I know be contained in the Memoir itself." He then proceeded to introduce criticisms of Royce's §§19–24. Peirce advanced other criticisms on later parts of Royce's paper in drafts of letters, dated August 21 (Peirce Papers), and in a postcard of August 22 (Royce Papers). Peirce's annotated copy of Royce's paper is in the Robbins Library, Harvard University.

[130] This letter, probably a long one, is not contained in either the Royce Papers or the Peirce Papers. In a second postcard, postmarked September 21, 1905 (Royce Papers), Peirce writes: "Yours rec'd. I shall not read it at once because I should be sure to lose time owing to being too interested in it. I see I blundered as to finite systems. My study of your paper had to be done in walking, and so I was led to assume that (ϛ) in your principle VI might be thought of as a collection of 3 elements. I have put my interpretation of the O relation into strictly demonstrative form. Your notion that a disquiparance can be composed exclusively from equiparences & for which you argue by a weaker variation of Kempe's argument, *Math. Form.* §69 is *absurd* & the fallacy is a strange one to come from *you,* trained as you are. Also you say nothing that weakens the distinction between dyadic & triadic relations. Look at my original definition of a disquiparence & my noticing that a cousin of a friend is such (because *cousin* & *friend* are composed of *disquiparances*). Also consider my existential graphs."

cannot *be substituted for x* (if x was the one in question) in that collection *without rendering the collection an E-collection.*

I believe that I hastily wrote something like this: "That there exists an O-collection into which one element enters while the other does not." *If* I thus hastily expressed myself, I beg you to be sure that I recognize the difference between the two modes of expression.

Yours Truly
Josiah Royce.

To Charles Sanders Peirce, September 22, [1905?][131]

Cambridge
103 Irving St.
Sept. 22.

Dear Mr. Peirce:—

Doubtless I bore you beyond measure; yet regarding your interpretation of my O-system in terms of the "respects," there is still this to say, which you may consider at your leisure, or not at all, as you will.

Your interpretation in terms of "respects," as you state it, is founded on my Laws I and II. The other laws are existential. What you say, if true, must apply to *any* system which obeys my Laws I and II, whether or no the other laws are satisfied. For what you say about the respects is supposed to result from Laws I & II together, apart from the others; at least so your letter states the case.

Well, consider a new system N, possessed of the following characters: It consists of any objects whatever in suitable multitude. By an O-collection in N, I now (for the moment) propose to mean *any collection of the elements of N which is a collection infinite in multitude.* The O-collections thus defined are subject to the following laws:—

I. If O (α), then O $(\alpha\gamma)$, whatever collection γ may be.

II. If, whatever element b_n of β be considered, $O(\delta b_n)$, then $O(\delta)$ (whatever collection β may be, whether an O-collection or not).

131 ALS. Royce Papers. HUA. At the top of p. 1, Royce wrote: "Rewritten & sent in other form."

The first of these laws is identical with my Law I. The second includes my Law II as an obvious, although here pretty trivial special case. For of course, if $O(\beta)$ is true, $O(\delta)$ is, under the conditions also true.

What are the "essential respects," in none of which do all the members of *such* an O-collection as this agree?

Now this system N is *not* my system Σ; nor are these my O-collections. But the system does obey the first pair of the laws of the system Σ. It breaks laws IV, V, VI. But your criticism, so far as concerns the "respects," is not founded, as I understand you, upon those later laws.

I conclude then, that your interpretation in terms of "respects," although important as a possible view of my system, is in any case *not* made inevitable merely by my Laws I and II.

Forgive me my importunity. I simply want, if ever you find time for me, to have my case in your hands.

Yours Truly
Josiah Royce.

To Charles Sanders Peirce, September 24, 1905[132]

103 Irving St.
Cambridge.
Sept. 24, 1905.

Dear Mr. Peirce:—

Whenever you *do* read my letters,[133] please note that, after reading your kind note of Sept 23, I very much doubt whether we differ at all (except in mode of expression), as to the one funda-

[132] ALS. Peirce Papers. HL.

[133] Peirce's final letter in this exchange, dated September 23, 1905 (Royce Papers), begins:

My dear Prof Royce,

At present I have to think of earning money & cannot think of your letters. I thought any hints would suffice to show you your fallacy, but I will interrupt my work to point it out more distinctly.

What you say is that you show how to build up an asymmetrical relation out of symmetrical elements *exclusively*. Symmetry is the equality of certain parts. Asymmetry an inequality among them. So what you say is that inequality can result from equality and nothing else. You cannot be surprised if I say that this is too Hegelian.

mental matter of the true nature of what you define as disquiparance and equiparance. Our difference is as to the interpretation of what I have said in my paper.

I beg you to note that I have *nowhere* said that "inequality can result from equality and nothing else," as you suppose me to say. My postulate IV *distinctly* shows that I had *no* such idea, since I there assert a certain existence of certain defined inequalities as one explicit basis of my system Σ. You are attacking, then, a position which I have nowhere taken.

What I *have* said is that my asymmetries can and do result from "asserting that certain elements do while certain *do not* stand to one another in a perfectly symmetrical relation." In other words, I show how fruitful a certain difference (viz. the difference between *do* and *do not* stand, &c), or what you call "disquiparance," is. But I do state my asymmetries "*in terms of* a certain symmetrical relation." How? By showing what follows from saying that certain elements *do*, while certain *do not* stand in that relation. In other words I get certain differences out of an explicitly asserted fundamental difference. Your example of the "pretty near" case is not in the least analogous to my very explicitly asserted view. I repudiate entirely such an interpretation, which is without basis in my text.

I have also asserted that the *contrast* of symmetrical and asymmetrical relations is "superficial." *Your* analysis, in your latest letter, asserts that all relations are of the *one* kind, viz., "disquiparance." So far we appear to differ mainly in mode of expression. Your Hegelian thesis:—"*Alles ist unterschieden*," is doubtless (in substance) correct. I nowhere have denied that in my paper, and have taught it for years. That thesis however is *not* at issue in my paper.

What I have undertaken to show, in my paper, is that *certain* differences are reducible to a certain fundamental difference, viz. to this that some element, say x *does*, while some element y *does not*, stand to the elements of a certain collection in a relation which, *so far as concerns that collection* is symmetrical for all the elements of that collection.

As to what I mean by symmetrical, I agree in usage with the now current usage, which as you are aware, seems to you defective. But whatever you think of my vocabulary, you have no right to charge me with a doctrine nowhere asserted in my paper.

Again I thank you for your kindness. I shall of course never trouble you further with letters so long as these cannot be read. I send this merely as a last deposit so to speak, against the day when you may have time to find out what it is that I *have* said.

Yours Truly
Josiah Royce.

To Charles William Eliot, December 3, 1905[134]

103 Irving St.
Cambridge
Mass.
Dec. 3, 1905.

Dear President Eliot:—

I thank you for your letter of information regarding my salary for the present year. I am glad to find that there is no doubt as to the intentions of the Corporation. That there may be no misunderstanding of my own position, I add this further statement:—

As a fact, I am now giving one half of Phil 1a in Radcliffe; also I am giving there what I was led to attempt only at the request of a small company of advanced Radcliffe students,—viz., a repetition of my course in Kant for their benefit. I did not at first intend, or wish, to undertake so much Radcliffe work this year. But the special request for a whole course in Kant was made, and I consented, so that the course was duly announced and taken in Radcliffe, as well as in Harvard. Thus I have 1½ Radcliffe courses.

On the other hand, I did not mean that the Corporation, or anybody else, at the time when we were planning this year's work, last year, should get the impression that I was to sacrifice any Radcliffe work in the present year in order to take the extra Kant course in Harvard College. I am sorry if any impression of the sort affected any act of the Corporation. I did what I thought would avoid any false impression by repeatedly saying, in our department meeting, and to our Chairman, that I took the Kant course, Phil 8, in Harvard College, this year, simply to fill up a gap, and without any wish or request on my part that I should receive any extra pay for the work. I regarded it, and regard it, as a serious extra task beyond

[134] ALS. Eliot Papers. HUA. The second sheet of this letter is marked "(3)" but this seems to be Royce's error in pagination, for the transition is smooth and the letter appears to be complete.

the customary one. Its principal effect, however, is to keep me from doing as much studious work and research, this year, as I should like to do, for my own scholarly welfare. In the long run it would be indeed unwise to give myself over to teaching quite so much. But a year more or less of a little over-absorption in teaching, and comparative neglect of studious acquisition or production, is no great loss. For the sake of what little usefulness I may have to Harvard, I ought not to teach every year quite so much as I this year do. That is all. This year, I can get on well enough, so long as I escape any mishap as to health. And in this latter respect, of late years, I have had fairly good fortune,—in fact, very good fortune most of the time.

I viewed my taking the Kant course, then, as a willing, but temporary, extra task. I do not think that the Corporation does well to pay $500 extra for so small a course. I did not ask them to do so. Next year I shall be very unlikely to do so much extra teaching, either in Harvard or in Radcliffe; and shall plan to take only the usual amount.

These then, are the facts, so far as I know them, regarding my Harvard and Radcliffe work. Like other people hereabouts, I am always doing a good many kinds of things. The Corporation have always treated me with great consideration and liberality. They must judge what my work is worth to Harvard. If they voted me the extra $500 for this year with any misapprehension of my intentions, they will seem to me no less considerate and no less liberal than I have always found them, in case they even now revise their vote. I am,

Yours Very Truly
Josiah Royce

To The Macmillan Company, December 15, 1905[135]

103 Irving St.
Cambridge
Mass.
Dec. 15, 1905

The Macmillan Company,

Gentlemen:—

I report herewith upon the two book MSS lately put in my hands, by you, for my estimate.

1. As to the MS of Miss Calkins:—*The Persistent Problems of Philosophy*, I have a decidedly high opinion to express.[136] It is true that I am very favorably inclined to the work by my personal friendship for the author, who was for a time a pupil of my colleagues and of myself here at Harvard. Apart from any prejudice of mine, however, I should believe that the fine scholarship of the book, its novelty of method, and the author's previous work, would combine to attract attention to the book; and that the author's standing as the most notable of the women who teach philosophy in this country, would also help to attract public attention. The book is worthy of the one who is, as you know, the President, for the present year, of the American Philosophical Association,—a place to which Miss Calkins was called because of her previous work.

I believe that the volume, although big, would have a fair chance in the market. It would be useful in libraries, would have a place as collateral reading for students, and might be used to some extent, as a class text-book. It is clearly written, well-planned, and readable. General readers of philosophy would find it, in a good many cases, welcome. It would probably attract a fair share of discussion. It would be aided by the attention attracted by the fact that it would be the first so considerable American philosophical treatise written by a woman.

135 ALS. Macmillan Papers. NYPL.

136 Mary Whiton Calkins, *The Persistent Problems of Philosophy: An Introduction to Metaphysics Through the Study of Modern Systems* (New York: Macmillan Co., 1907).

2. Professor J. E. Russell's *Elementary Logic*[137] is not a notably original book, but a sensible and carefully prepared, rather commonplace, text-book, following well-known, and, as I believe, antiquated methods. It is somewhat better, objectively speaking, than Jevons's *Elementary Lessons*. It is the product of good teaching experience. It is pedagogically a reasonable and sane piece of work, once granting that one has to teach this sort of logic. Teachers of Logic still seem to like to "change the place and keep the pain," by trying some new text-book from time to time, however persistently such a book clings to the essentially worn-out procedure of the traditional logic. Russell's is a better attempt than most to make a new text-book to meet such tendencies on the part of teachers. The book might have, therefore, a fair sale for a time, until somebody else added his own variations on the old song. I do not strongly commend the book; but it is not a bad horse *if* you like that kind of a horse.

Yours Very Truly
Josiah Royce.

To Charles William Eliot, December 25, 1905[138]

Cambridge.
103 Irving St.
Dec. 25, 1905.

Dear Dr. Eliot:—

In answering the question which Mr. Greene's[139] letter of yesterday, regarding the marks in Philosophy 1, transmits to me, it is proper for me to say that I do not myself assign the mark for the *whole* year's work in Philosophy 1a, and am responsible only for one half year's work in that course viz., the first half, including the Mid Year Examination. The Assistants mark examinations, &c., under general instructions for which, so far as my half of the course is concerned, I am of course responsible. Professor Münsterberg has charge of the second half year, and of the Final Examination.

137 John Edward Russell, *An Elementary Logic* (New York: Macmillan Co., 1906).

138 ALS. Eliot Papers. HUA.

139 Jerome D. Greene was an administrative assistant to President Eliot.

Moreover, I have this year, with the consent of the department, changed the method of using the time of the assistants somewhat. Instead of conferences, which as I fear, have tended to be a little perfunctory, I have called upon the students, up to the present stage of the course, for written papers on assigned topics. These papers the Assistants have so far read and marked. The time thus taken up by the Assistants has been not less than, but also not much more than that which was formerly needed for the conferences. I now propose to have one conference for each small group of students between the holidays and the Mid Year Examination. Each Assistant will then meet his own group in such conference. This method of written papers, handed in and marked, has not previously been tried in Phil 1a, and is an experiment,—I believe a fairly successful one. In due combination with conferences, I believe it a method that is likely to prove permanently useful.

In former years, when the conference method was used largely,—as well as in the present year, when written papers are substituted for several of the conferences,—it has been my own opinion that nobody should be able to pass in the course solely by virtue of a pass mark on the examination, in case he failed on the conference or other work. Still more is it true that, in the present year, when several pieces of written work are an essential part of my half year's instruction, nobody is to pass who fails in this written work, unless his examination record is so high, and his explanation of his failure in written work is so satisfactory, that this failure may be viewed as otherwise made good (e.g., where absence from College, illness, &c., are part of the explanation of temporary failure in written work).

You may wonder what written work we can require in Philosophy 1a. I answer: (1) Certain exercises in Logic, such as call for some independence of judgment in the student; (2) Some questions about topics which have been explained in the lectures, and which are discussed in Paulsen's *Introduction to Philosophy*. In such cases a student hears the lecturer's statement, reads the chapter of Paulsen, and then responds to some such question as: "What do you think about this problem,—issue,—opinion,—so far as the matter has yet been presented to you?"

Work written in small classes, or otherwise, in presence of the instructor, I have demanded only in case of hour & Mid Year examinations. The so-called "written recitation" I have not regarded as a good device for my part of the course. A written recitation of course enables one to control somewhat the tendency of students to get tutors, or others, to prepare their written work for them. But I have not believed that this advantage justifies that use of time. When a student is asked to think over a question in Logic, or in Philosophy generally, he ought to have ample time to think it over, and to write out his result. Of course he may cheat. I do not regard that evil as one to be contended with by written work in the instructor's presence, unless such written work is otherwise of sufficient value, for the purposes of the course, to justify this use of time. I am of course ready to employ such a method should the department deem that advisable.

The change in method of tests in Phil 1a, as thus indicated, has been due to my own effort to meet the one need which our discussions in the Faculty have brought out. This need seems to be, not so much for more formal tests, but for more call upon our students for work in their courses which shall be at once interesting, responsible, and personally engrossing. I propose setting the elementary students *as early as possible* at the task of expressing their own opinions, or their own problems, questions, doubts, comments, regarding the subject matter of the course. This method seems applicable in philosophy. Hence my present experiment. My Summer School work, in which I last summer first tried just this form of experiment with entirely elementary students, helped me to see that I could call for written reports from students at an earlier stage in their elementary philosophical work than I had previously supposed suitable for that purpose. I have of course always employed thesis-work in all more advanced courses. I am now trying it at the very outset of philosophy.

I shall be sorry if our very instructive recent discussions in the Faculty lead merely, or mainly, to votes about how many courses, formal tests, or other numerically definable tasks we permit or require. Our problems are to be solved only by the efforts of individual instructors to get responsible work done by the students. Whatever legislation encourages instructors to require serious work, is useful. The votes so far before the Faculty have too frequently concerned mere mechanism,—as if five poorly done courses were better than six!

Yours Very Truly
Josiah Royce.

To George Platt Brett, March 2, 1906[140]

103 Irving St.
Cambridge,
Mass.
March 2, 1906.

Mr. George P. Brett,
President of Macmillan Company.

My Dear Mr. Brett:—

I return today, by express, the MS of Professor Aaron Schuyler's "Critical History of Philosophy."[141] My delay in reporting upon the book is due to the fact that it first came to hand just as I was leaving Cambridge for a fortnight of lecture-work at the Johns Hopkins University,[142] where all my time was occupied by various affairs incident to my task. Since I returned to Cambridge, many arrears of work have been on hand.

I am now, somewhat regretfully obliged to report that this book, although written with great care, tolerance, and good will by its patient and (I may add) somewhat venerable author, is laborious rather than really scholarly, and is *not* on a level with the fair requirements of present scholarship. I have tested it enough to see that it would make a distinctly unsatisfactory text-book, and a very inadequate guide for readers. If printed at all, it should be published only as a personal tribute to the very devoted life-work of its author. Otherwise it has, to my mind, no standing at the present day, in view of modern demands upon such books.—

Yours Very Truly
Josiah Royce

140 ALS. Macmillan Papers. NYPL.

141 Not published by Macmillan, but see Schuyler's *A Critical History of Philosophical Theories* (Boston: R. G. Badger [c. 1913]).

142 Posthumously published: Josiah Royce, *Lectures on Modern Idealism*, ed. J. Loewenberg (New Haven: Yale University Press, 1919).

To The Macmillan Company, April 6, 1906[143]

103 Irving St. Cambridge, Mass.
April 6, 1906

The Macmillan Company,

Gentlemen:—

I advise in favor of printing Professor Fullerton's book, *Introduction to Philosophy*.[144] It is not a great book; but it is modestly and judiciously wrought out, is the work of a very able teacher, is a book that ought to be useful in the classroom, and is likely, in my opinion, to have as fair a sale, for class-room purposes, as any other "Introduction" to Philosophy which you are likely soon to have in your hands. There seems to be nothing in it to add notably to its author's reputation; but, on the other hand, there is nothing in it to detract from that reputation; and the reputation will do much to give this unpretentious but wholesome text-book a good place in the esteem of teachers of philosophy.

Yours Very Truly
Josiah Royce.

I return the MS by express today.

To Charles William Eliot, May 7, 1906[145]

103 Irving St.
May 7, 1906.

Dear President Eliot:—

I have held back a little from addressing you about the desire of our Philosophical Department that, if possible, Dr. Yerkes should be promoted to an Assistant Professorship.[146] I have been thus

[143] ALS. Macmillan Papers. NYPL.

[144] George Stuart Fullerton, *An Introduction to Philosophy* (New York: Macmillan Co., 1906).

[145] ALS. Eliot Papers. HUA.

[146] Robert Mearns Yerkes finally became Assistant Professor of Comparative Psychology in 1908.

tardy in speaking, first because I had hoped that our official expression upon the subject would find the Corporation in a position to accede to our wish at an early date, secondly because you were away until so recently, and thirdly because I doubted whether my judgment could add anything to what the Psychologists would, of themselves, be able to tell you.

But now, as I understand the matter, while the Corporation finds some difficulties standing in the way of any such increase in the financial budget as the new appointment might seem to involve, there is still some reason to suppose that the proposed promotion can be made before long, and that the Corporation might wish to know how far the various officers of the Department think the matter, from our point of view, important. Hence I venture to offer my word.

As a student of the problems of current philosophical discussion, I feel that the new Comparative Psychology is no "frill," no ornament, no merely external affair to be added to our department work, but is a very central and significant branch of investigation. I confess that, to me personally, the results reached along a good many lines of research in experimental psychology have proved to be disappointing; but *this* branch of comparative observation and experiment is surely on lines that must grow increasingly valuable, and that have already proved their worth. It is not "animal" psychology merely that is in question. Comparative human psychology, race psychology, social psychology, educational psychology, must all make use of the means that the work followed by Dr. Yerkes is now developing. If we want to keep in the modern movement at all, we need this work to go on, and to grow. I heartily beg that the Corporation may take account of the great importance of the new comparative researches before taking any step that would seriously impair our prospects with regard to the future of that work.

As for the man, Dr. Yerkes, I have followed him from his student days. I have recently had various occasions to rely upon, and to use his judgment and skill regarding the application of his own profession to practical problems of teaching. I trust him implicitly. I believe in him thoroughly. He is the only born naturalist, the only man who is *by temperament* an observer of nature,—and a close and loving one,—in the department. The rest of us in the philosophical group observe where we can and must observe. Yerkes has the quality of the true lover of nature and of the phenomena of life. I believe thoroughly in the work of the philosopher; but it is well for the philosophers to have the naturalist among them. Yerkes is a great prize for us to possess. I hope that we shall be able not only to keep him, but to ensure for him his natural, and, as I firmly believe, his well earned place amongst us. I fear for some of the most important aspects of our future reputation as a department if his work cannot get its normal recognition.

I have, as you know, no wish to intervene in affairs that are not mine. I do not often write letters on our practical official questions. But I feel that this matter does concern me as much as other members of the department. I heartily hope that Dr. Yerkes may be, as soon as it is practicable, promoted to an Assistant Professorship, and that his work may be viewed as a permanent and necessary branch of our undertakings.

Yours Very Truly
Josiah Royce.

To Charles Eliot Norton, May 24, 1906[147]

103 Irving St.
May 24, 1906.

Dear Professor Norton:—

Your very good and kind letter, with its enclosure, is at hand. Our sister, Miss Anna Head, of Berkeley, is now a centre of a considerable range and variety of relief work. Families of her pupils, young teachers who have lost their jobs, and various others, come to her for refuge, advice, and other aid, at her large school house in Berkeley, which seems to be at present a sort of Noah's ark. I am sure, then, that the best which I can do to meet the letter and the spirit of your deed of gift, is to enclose your letter to her, changing the cheque into a P. O. order as I do so, and leaving her free to apply the sum, at her discretion, in the spirit of your letter,

147 ALS. Norton Papers. HL.

to her sufferers.[148] She herself has come through fortunately enough. Hence she is all the more called upon for her aid. I thank you most heartily for your gift.

Yours Very Truly
Josiah Royce.

I have not forgotten your so kind offer to me, earlier in the stages of this relief work. I have so far been able to do by my own relatives what they need. But I thank you again for your forethought.

To The Macmillan Company, June 7, 1906[149]

103 Irving Street
Cambridge
June 7, 1906.

The Macmillan Company,

Gentlemen:—

When you sent me, over a month since, Professor Ormond's *Concepts of Philosophy*,[150] I fully intended to deal with the volume of MS promptly, and adequately. But I have since then been extraordinarily beset by fortune, so far as my power to finish tasks is concerned. Not only ordinary and extra teaching work, but illness in my family,[151] as well as concern regarding relatives in California, for whom (since the disaster),[152] I have had to do various things, have preoccupied me.

I am therefore only now able to form and express the distinct judgment, which I herewith render, viz., that Professor Ormond's new book *ought to be printed*. His prominent position as a scholar and teacher is an important guarantee in any case. His new work, although reviewing matters which he has already in part treated, is

148 Norton's gift was presumably an act of charity to the victims of the San Francisco "Fire."

149 ALS. Macmillan Papers. NYPL.

150 Alexander Thomas Ormond, *Concepts of Philosophy* (New York: Macmillan Co., 1906).

151 Possibly a reference to Christopher Royce, whose mental illness became severe at about this time.

152 The San Francisco "Fire."

a large synthesis, and is certain to attract attention. The principal objection to the book lies in the difficulty of regarding it as a wholly new treatment of its topics. For the ground has been partly covered by the author before. But the book is *sufficiently new to be well worth printing*, and ought to have a good, if not a very large sale.

Yours Truly
Josiah Royce

To Hugo Münsterberg, August 12, 1906[153]

103 Irving St.
Cambridge, Mass.
August 12, 1906.

Dear Münsterberg:—

Your letter of August 10, with the quite unexpected enclosure, came to hand yesterday afternoon. I should have supposed that Miss Rousmaniere's fifty dollars ought indeed to be divided amongst the Committee who took charge of her examination. But since it is true that I had main charge of her work for some time (although, since I am no laboratory man, I took no such exclusive charge as you, by the nature of the work, took of Miss Rowland), it may well be that the larger part of the fee falls to me. As a fact, I directed the choice, and followed the writing, of Miss Rousmaniere's thesis-investigation; and she was in large part my pupil. Subject, then, to any review of your judgment in the matter which may be desired by other members of the Dep't, I am willing to keep the fee for the time. I thank you heartily for the kind thought that prompted the remittance.

Summer School nearly over. My only accomplishment during this period is a partial working out of a somewhat systematic view of ethics, in my Course B. I am to repeat that course in our afternoon lectures to teachers next autumn & winter.[154] Kallen, my assistant, proves to be a very remarkable fellow indeed, barring his rather doubtful health, which is of the too familiar and pathetic

[153] ALS. Münsterberg Papers. BPL.
[154] Revisions of these lectures led to *PL*.

variety.[155] But he has held out to do his work for me very effectively, despite his delicate constitution. J. S. Moore should be pushed for the place as well as possible. He can do the work, and he strongly needs the chance.

Yours Truly
Josiah Royce.

Best regards and good wishes to all your family.

To George Platt Brett, October 24, 1906[156]

103 Irving St.
Cambridge, Mass.
Oct. 24, 1906.

Dear Mr. Brett:—

You ask in yours of the 23d, concerning Bakewell's standing. He is a rising man, from whom we expect much. Our principal disappointment with him is that he has not yet produced enough. A book from him would be welcome; and his position is such as would ensure to the book wide and careful attention.[157]

As to his position itself,—he was called to Yale (rather against their precedents, for they usually call Yale men), as a result of a very careful examination of their needs, after Ladd's retirement. The situation at Yale was delicate. An able, discreet, progressive, but also not too radical a man was needed,—one able to win

[155] Horace Meyer Kallen received his Ph.D. from Harvard in 1908. See his important memoir, "Remarks on Royce's Philosophy," *Journal of Philosophy* 53 (February 2, 1956), 131–39—particularly, in this connection, p. 132: "Royce's courses held no such allure as did Santayana's and James's. But, although I disagreed with him from the very beginning, my studies with him, even through the dissent they aroused, nourished and on occasion enhanced the feelings of release and adventure that came from my studies with his colleagues. As compared with theirs, his philosophy was, of course, a closed system; nevertheless he communicated a similar spirit of intellectual sportsmanship, a similar ethic of openmindedness, free communication, a generosity of intellect which could lead him to appoint me his assistant when he gave a summer course, regardless of my philosophic dissidence, perhaps even because of it, and because he knew that I needed the money."

[156] ALS. Macmillan Papers. NYPL.

[157] The work in question was probably *Source Book in Ancient Philosophy*, but this was published by Charles Scribner's Sons in 1907. Bakewell published nothing with Macmillan Co. at this time.

attention, to reconcile opposing interests, and to disarm prejudices. A committee of Yale professors, themselves not philosophers, but men able to view matters intelligently, considered the whole situation, and asked the advice, as I believe, of nearly all the established and competent philosophical teachers who were accessible. We who were asked said what we could, in answer, to help the committee. As a result of the inquiry, Bakewell was appointed as the best available man. It was, I think, a good choice. You are probably safe in offering what you like to Bakewell for his book.

Yours Truly
Josiah Royce

To Hugo Münsterberg, October 25, 1906[158]

Emerson Hall
October 25, 1906.

Dear Professor Münsterberg:

At the special request of Professor Davis,[159] and also in my own name, I cordially invite you to take part, as a guest, in the coming meeting of the National Academy of Sciences, either by presenting a paper on some scientific topic of research, or by authorizing one of our teaching staff to present the summary of a research that you know to be important enough for such an occasion, or by having some Exhibit of scientific interest prepared, under your direction, to be exhibited to the "Conversazione" of the Academy, by anybody whom you may appoint for the purpose.

The meeting of the Academy is announced in the enclosed circular. I am a new member, and have never previously attended a meeting. I want to do my part to make the meeting a success. It seems to me a specially good opportunity to bring forward the Psychological Laboratory work as an important part of our Harvard, and in particular our philosophical contribution to knowledge. I shall be glad to consult you as to anything that can be done. This is merely a general statement of my hope that we can do something. And your own region of work is the one best adapted, in all

158 ALS. Münsterberg Papers. BPL.

159 Probably William Morris Davis, Sturgis-Hooper Professor of Geology at Harvard and a member of the National Academy of Sciences.

the philosophical department's undertakings, to provide a topic for a paper, or for an exhibit.

It is supposed that the Academy desires to hear a variety of papers, all special enough in character to seem like deep and important new work, and all summarized so that everybody present will understand. This second desire, as I am told, is seldom fulfilled at the meetings. Usually nobody but the reader knows what his paper is about.

The question is whether we can meet this last desire. I do not know anybody more likely than you are to meet both desires.

Yours Very Truly
Josiah Royce.

To Mary Coale Redwood, December 17, 1906[160]

103 Irving St.
Dec. 17, 1906.

My Dear Mrs. Redwood:—

I have hesitated about writing to you, at this time of your so great grief, for fear of burdening you with one more bit of paper to attend to. I have not been without very frequent thoughts of sympathy and I have merely felt how powerless I must be to give you any help.

I have waited, then, until I could see your son, on his return, and learn a little how things stand with you, and with him.[161] I was very busy all this past fortnight; but yesterday I found time to call at your son's room, and to talk over matters with him. He is a very dear and brave youth, and I deeply admired, as I talked with him, his calm and courage, and the serious and yet fully self-controlled way in which he views his situation and yours, and the spirit in which he takes up again his work,—so sadly interrupted. I believe that he fully realizes how much he is now needed to be a man and a mainstay for his mother; and he seems to me to give very real promise that he will live up to the demands of the future, so far as he can.

160 ALS. Redwood Collection. JHU.

161 Mrs. Redwood's husband, Francis T. Redwood, died on November 29, 1906.

My first word then, to you, takes the form of offering whatever I can, for the future, in the way of personal encouragement to him. Is there *any*thing, then, that as your friend and his, I can do for your son, to make him feel more at home here in Cambridge, or to make you, who have now so much loneliness to face, feel any the less lonely to have him away from you? Your son is, as you know, not at all forward in seeking company. I fear to push attentions upon him. I also feel as if I had, in my own preoccupation, neglected him. I do not want to do so. I wish that he could be often at my house, in whatever way would most please him. I wish that he could feel himself always free to come to us. I know that Mrs. Royce feels much pleased with what she has seen of him, and wants to see more of him. I know that his classmate, my own boy Stephen, would welcome more acquaintance with him. And so, while I do not want to seem to intrude upon your son,—(least of all to undertake any supervision of him,—he seems quite to stand on his own feet),—I wish that he would think of me not as a professor, but as a friend. I owe very much to your house, of old, for happy hours and for great kindness. I wish that I could repay however little of that debt, to your son. And while he is at home at Christmas time, I should be glad if you would tell him so, so that he may let us see him often after the holidays.

This I say at once, because it is the best I can do to express what I feel by way of sympathy, and because I mean it, and Mrs. Royce means it with me. For the rest,—I was one of the many who prized your husband. I am one of the many who grieve with you in this sudden loss. You know as well as I do that all these great blows tell us that this poor little world that we now live in, or seem to live in, is not the whole real world that we believe in, and really belong to. The *true* world, near as it is to us, is not the one that we see with our ordinary eyes. To that larger world our dead belong,—and we with them. It is hard to be lonely. It is good that, after all, we are not really left alone, even by death, but really belong to that better and unseen world. I know that you know how to find comfort there.—Meanwhile, be sure that if, in any way, I can do anything to serve you, I shall feel it an honor and a privilege to do so, in memory of all that your dear father and mother did of kindness to me, and in memory of the hearty hospitality that I have so often received from you, and from your husband, whenever I have passed through Baltimore of late years.

Mrs. Royce joins me in the most earnest expression of her sympathy. We both hope that your health and strength will be equal to the great call that fortune has made upon you.

I remain, most heartily

Very Truly Yours
Josiah Royce.

To The Macmillan Company, April 28, 1907[162]

103 Irving St.
Cambridge, Mass.
April 28, 1907.

The Macmillan Company,

Gentlemen:—

The book of Professor J. A. Leighton: "Reality and Personality," belongs to a type of treatises which is now very well represented in the literature of the subject.[163] The view maintained by the author is one in line with the general sort of philosophy with which I myself agree:—Taylor's, or Miss Calkins's book, amongst the more recent works, may also stand for the sort of general philosophical view that is in question; Ormond's *Concepts* would suggest the sort of standing to which the book would naturally aspire.

Of its sort this book is very clear and wholesome;—diffuse, as you see, and containing much matter that has been stated, in very nearly the same general form, time after time in recent discussion. But the closing chapters are the most original, and would attract the most attention, I think, from students. Scattered all through the book there also appear good comments, sometimes fairly original. The author has taken good account of recent discussion. In general (apart from this book) he stands well amongst his fellow students; although he has thus far produced nothing that has made any great disturbance in literature; and I somewhat doubt whether this book would stir current discussion very vigorously.

On the whole, however, it is a book that is worthy of respect.

162 ALS. Macmillan Papers. NYPL.

163 Nothing published under this title, though Macmillan Co. did publish Joseph Alexander Leighton's *Jesus Christ and the Civilization of To-Day: The Ethical Teaching of Jesus Considered in its Bearings on the Moral Foundations of Modern Culture* (1907).

It is as readable as most such books are. If not very original, it is decidedly scholarly; and the author makes free acknowledgement of his indebtedness. It should, if published, find a fair, although not, I think, a very prominent place, in the now large literature of Idealism. It would be good collateral reading for students.

I think that a good bibliographical appendix, with notes to indicate better how the author estimates the principal current and classic works that he cites, would much increase the value of the work. I should also prefer a longer preface, or introduction, in which the author should state, more fully than he now does, what he regards as *distinctive* of his own method and results. While the present preface does this to some extent, the author is not full enough to let the reader see just what this treatise, in this now so well-represented literature, stands for. Since the best originality appears in the *last* chapters of this large volume, an opening indication of what is to be done, is especially needed; and so the present preface is not full enough. On the other hand, the book might well be shortened by an omission of some of the earlier discussions, without impairing the originality.

My opinion is that the book would, in the present state of public hospitality to Idealism, probably sell fairly well for its size and its weight, and has a fair, although not a great chance, of justifying, from the publisher's point of view, its existence.

Yours Very Truly
Josiah Royce

MS returned by express today.

To The Macmillan Company, May 6, 1907[164]

103 Irving St.
Cambridge, Mass.
May 6, 1907.

Macmillan & Co.,

Gentlemen:—

The translation of the *Einleitung in Die Philosophie* of Professor Dr. Wilhelm Jerusalem,—a translation which you have asked me to look over in MS would need at least in some parts a good deal of

[164] ALS. Macmillan Papers. NYPL.

very careful proof-reading in order to make the English version acceptable, were the MS to go to print as it is.[165] The English runs smoothly for long stretches, and then occasionally lapses into a painfully foreign idiom or phraseology, and in such cases fails sometimes to give in intelligible English the accurate sense of the original. Such is what I gather from the comparisons of specimen passages with the original, so far as I have had time to make them. I also gather, however, that apart from these lapses, the translation is done in a scholarly fashion. The use of the German habits of transliterating or spelling the names of authors: "Aristoteles," &c., is troublesome, and would have, I think, to be corrected.

The author of the original, Jerusalem, is especially known, in Germany, by his theory of the psychology of judgement,—a theory which constitutes one of the central thoughts of this *Einleitung*. I cannot say that this theory seems to me very highly original or important. And I do not think Jerusalem a man of great mark or originality. This *Einleitung* however, has had its good success in Germany. It is superficial, facile, intelligent, but not momentous. If the English were corrected so that the book read smoothly throughout, the book might sell very fairly. It would in that case be a fair, although not a very important addition, to the books that can be used in elementary courses.

I am not enthusiastic about seeing the book printed in English; but I have no positive objections to the work, if taken as a sketch of philosophy.

Yours Truly
Josiah Royce.

To Edwin Francis Edgett, July 4, 1907[166]

103 Irving St.
Cambridge, Mass.
July 4, 1907.

My Dear Sir:—

I have just returned, for my Summer School work, from a sea

[165] *Introduction to Philosophy*, trans. Charles F. Sanders (New York: Macmillan Co., 1910).

[166] ALS. Berg Collection. NYPL.

voyage. Hence my delay in responding to yours of June 21, asking me to review James's *Pragmatism.* As I shall have to discuss that work in other connections and places, and am very busy now, I shall have, with many thanks, to decline to undertake the review that you propose.

Yours Very Truly
Josiah Royce

Mr. E. F. Edgett
Boston Evening Transcript.

To William James, N. D. [1907?][167]

[. . .]good will. I thank you very deeply for that, and for all that you have done.

I hope that my criticism, in answer to your question, did not seem austere or too blind, this afternoon. A man's personal tone is his own. Yours is a most effective one. I have no wish to urge any subjective attitude of mine regarding your method in your *Pragmatism* book. And all that I have said in an appreciative tone about the book is sincere,—heartily so. As to the one criticism,—I can only say: Consider your own manner & method in the "Dilemma of Determinism"[168] as well as in the *Varieties of Rel. Exp.* & the rest. It *does* seem to me that then there was no danger of having the people regard the discussion just as some of them now do regard the *Pragmatism,*—viz., as in large part a splendid joke,—a brilliant *reductio ad absurdum* of all attempts at serious grappling with any philosophical issue. This was in no sense your intent; but, as a fact, the externals,—the mere setting & style of the *Pragmatism,* tend to produce on the man in the street this impression,—an impression that those earlier papers would not make, and that you in no sense mean these to make.

Meanwhile, no criticism of mine is hostile.—Life is a sad long road, sometimes. Every friendly touch and word must be pre-

167 ALS. James Papers. HL. Partly printed in *TCWJ*, 1: 820–21. A single sheet marked "(2)" is all that remains. The date "[1907?]" is given in another hand. James's *Pragmatism* was published in May, 1907, which suggests that this letter was written two or three months after this date.

168 *Unitarian Review* 20 (1884): 193–224.

ciously guarded. I prize everything that you say or do, whether I criticize or not.

Yours Affectionately
Josiah Royce.

To George Platt Brett, October 6, 1907[169]

103 Irving St.
October 6, 1907.

Mr. George P. Brett,
President of the Macmillan Co.,
New York City.

My Dear Mr. Brett:—

My eldest son, Mr. Christopher Royce, the bearer of this letter, will present the letter in consequence of a suggestion of mine; and I shall esteem it a great personal favor if you can give him a little of your time, and, if possible, a little advice.

My son is twenty five years of age, was an A. B. of Harvard in 1900, and an A. M. in 1903. As an undergraduate and graduate student he devoted himself to Chemistry, Mathematics, Astronomy, Music (but not to my own philosophical studies); and he looked forward, for some years, to a life as a teacher. He may yet succeed in that profession; but of late years he has made some acquaintance with Real Estate business, and with financial business. It now looks to me as if he would do well to find employment with some business house. He has a *little* capital, and is a young man of steady habits. He is, as a man of long training as a student, no man of the world. In the business world he is so far unpractical. Yet he has in him the making of a useful servant of a serious enterprise, if he finds and pursues a steady practical employment. His wide range of information about scientific and mathematical topics might be of service in various enterprises.

My question is, 'Do you think that, in connection with a publishing house, a young man of his equipment might find a place?' I should not object to his accepting any plain business employment that offered him any chance to earn his own way in touch with a

169 ALS. Macmillan Papers. NYPL.

good business. As clerk, as salesman, as proof-reader, as agent, as in any other definite place, he might make a beginning, if the publishing business has any openings for him.

You will see, from this note, that I do not now expect my son to make a permanent profession of teaching; although there is indeed some reason to suppose that he may actually follow that calling for some time in the near future. I do see, however, that there have now developed in him interests that might lead him to his best success in contact with the business world. Hence, since twenty five is not too late an age for a change, I venture to ask your kind advice. Anything that you can suggest to my son will be very welcome to me. I ask only for your personal judgement, whatever it is.

I hope to have ready for you, pretty soon, a new book,—and, as I hope, one that is likely to be fairly popular in its appeal,—namely my coming course of Lowell Lectures,[170] which I am to deliver next November and December. Will you wish to consider such a book?—

Yours Very Truly
Josiah Royce.

To George Platt Brett, October 8, 1907[171]

103 Irving St.
Cambridge, Mass.
Oct. 8, 1907.

My Dear Mr. Brett:—

I wish to thank you very heartily for the attention that you have given to my son, and to his inquiries.[172] I appreciate the seriousness of calling on so busy a man as you are for such a use of his time. I shall be glad if, hereafter, I can at any time do you a service by a similar amount of my time expended in some way that may be of service to you.

170 *PL.*

171 ALS. Macmillan Papers. NYPL.

172 Brett to Royce, October 7, 1907, reports that he has met Christopher and that an evening engagement has been arranged; Brett to Royce, October 8, 1907, regrets that Christopher "was unable to keep the engagement to call upon me yesterday evening."

As to my proposed book,—it is to appear, if possible, simply as a course of Lowell Lectures. The general title, and the special titles of the lectures, are as follows:—

The Philosophy of Loyalty.

1. The General Nature and the Need of Loyalty.
2. Individualism.
3. Loyalty to Loyalty.
4. Conscience.
5. Training for Loyalty.
6. Some Present American Problems in Relation to Loyalty.
7. Loyalty, Truth and Reality.
8. Loyalty and Religion.

These titles are subject to possible slighter changes.[173] They indicate the scope and plan. The lectures begin at the Lowell Inst. Nov. 18 next, and occur twice weekly until finished,—the last one being, I suppose, Dec. 12. I now expect to have the MS ready by the conclusion of the lectures, and should be glad to get the book out as soon as possible thereafter.

My summer ethics course for teachers has suggested the topics and the treatment. But this Lowell Lecture statement is prepared for a general audience. The plan of the book is a sketch of an ethical philosophy, with Loyalty as the central concept, and with practical applications to various current issues. The time seems to be ripe for such appeals to the public.

I should be glad to propose to you putting the book into your hands. Would terms like those of my Gifford Lectures be proper? The book would not exceed, I suppose, some 60,000 words.

Yours Very Truly
Josiah Royce.

[173] The lecture topics, as published, were unchanged, but the order of lectures V and VI was reversed.

To The Macmillan Company, November 3, 1907[174]

103 Irving St.
Cambridge, Mass.
November 3, 1907.

The Macmillan Company,

Gentlemen:—

At your request I have examined the two books:—

1. Professor Alfred H. Lloyd: *The Will to Doubt.*[175]

2. Typewritten MS. "History of Philosophy."[176]

I report herewith upon both, in order.

1. Professor Lloyd holds the Harvard Ph.D., and was once a pupil of my own. His previous works have given to him a reasonably good, although not a very prominent position as a philosophical writer. There is a pretty stubborn complexity and intricacy about his way of stating his views, which are themselves views of a good deal of value and originality. I still wish that he would strike fire more vigorously, sometimes; but this book seems to me a very distinct advance upon his earlier work so far as effectiveness in stating his case is concerned. Despite some of his characteristic defects of presentation, the work impresses me very favorably, and I advise the publication of it in this country, where it ought to have reasonable sale. I regret the parallel to James's famous title: *The Will to Believe*, and I wish that Lloyd had found, instead, some title as original as Palmer's: *Glory of the Imperfect.* Nevertheless the title, as it stands, appeals to a decided present public interest, and should bring to the book enough readers, in and out of college circles, to warrant the publication. The book could, however, hardly serve as a text-book; and this fact should be considered in the decision. As to the matter of the book, I am in essential agreement with Lloyd's main view as to the function of "doubt"; and I think that his position is well worthy of the attention of his colleagues, and of the "general thinkers" to whom he appeals.

174 ALS. Macmillan Papers. NYPL.

175 Alfred Henry Lloyd, *The Will to Doubt: An Essay in Philosophy for the General Thinker* (London: Swan Sonnenschein and Co., Ltd., 1907; New York: Macmillan Co., 1907).

176 Author unknown; not published by Macmillan Co.

2. The MS text-book of the "History of Philosophy" is, as it stands, almost wholly worthless. The English is impossible in many passages; the accounts of the principal philosophers (e.g., Kant, Hegel, Aristotle) are unintelligible; the general summaries and sketches of schools and movements are both loosely and far too summarily stated. Whoever knows anything about the subject would have to read into the text whatever would give it meaning. Whoever looked to it for first impressions would be left utterly in the dark as to what most of the philosophers were trying to do, and as to why they are remembered at all. I cannot imagine why the book was written. I cannot advise the printing of it by anybody.

Yours Very Truly
Josiah Royce.

To James McKeen Cattell, November 11, 1907[177]

103 Irving St.
Cambridge, Mass.
Nov. 11, 1907.

Dear Professor Cattell:—

I shall not be able to attend the meeting of the Academy in New York, and consequently shall be quite unable to accept your kind invitation to dine with you on the Wednesday evening in question.

I deeply regret not being able to come. You at Columbia are always most hospitable and kindly to your association-visitors. It is a pleasure when one can come. But I confess that I greatly wonder how my colleagues can so frequently get away from home to attend such meetings, pleasant as they are. For my part, I work day by day. I go once a week to Yale this year; but that visit is a part of regular business, arranged in the year's schedule by interacademic agreement. Otherwise, in term time, I simply have no control over my engagements, except when examinations intervene. My employers, of course, lay down no rules, more than the usual ones; but there is the day's work, and I must do it or run away from it. I cannot do the latter. I say this not to criticize others who can travel

177 ALS. Cattell Papers. LC.

in home lecture time—God forbid that I should; still less to criticize the goodness of those who entertain the travellers; but in sheer wonder that so many can fling a free foot away from home.

Yours Very Truly
Josiah Royce.

To The Macmillan Company, December 23, 1907[178]

103 Irving St.
Dec. 23, 1907.

The Macmillan Company,

Gentlemen:—

I have examined the MS of the book by March, on *The Theory of Mind*,[179] which was sent to me for inspection and report; and I have returned the MS by express, today, to you.

So far as its own merits are concerned, this book seems to me to deserve publication. It has originality, especially in its later comparative studies of individual and social types. It is a serious piece of work. It is worth reading, and deserves to take a good place in current literature.

On the other hand, it can hardly attract much *popular* attention, and is not in line with any one of the now prevailing academic movements in psychology; so that it *might* get respect rather than sale.

Hence I venture to suggest that this *might* be a case for the author to pay for his plates, or for some such arrangement to diminish the risk as to the sale. Granting commercial possibilities for sale, the book would, I think, be well deserving of attention.

The work is somewhat in line with [Charles Augustus] Strong's *Why the Mind has a Body*, and with the "Mind-Stuff" literature generally. It is also very interesting in its *social* analyses; and might get attention as a contribution to social theories. A *right choice of title* might serve to bring out some such fact, and so might decide

178 ALS. Macmillan Papers. NYPL.

179 John Lewis March, *A Theory of Mind* (New York: Charles Scribner's Sons, 1908).

favorably the commercial aspect of the book. Why not suggest this to the author?—

Respectfully,
Josiah Royce

To William James, January 12, 1908[180]

103 Irving St.
Jan. 12, 1908.

Dear James:—

What I have done with your exquisitely beautiful offering is this:—I have endorsed it over to "Prescott F. Hall, Trustee," and have instructed him that if, in his opinion, such a course is wise, he should at once deposit it in a trustee-account opened for the benefit of C. R.,[181] of whom, as soon as the court can act, he is to be, in any case, appointed special guardian. All future expenditures on behalf of the patient, so long as he remains under guardianship, are, in any case, to be subject to the approval of Hall, since this arrangement will free the patient from the irritation of feeling himself subject, as to his comfort and as to his business chances, to the discretion of his father. A third person, and, in such matters, a lawyer, is the right person to use. Regarding your so good and generous offer as one to C. R., and not to me directly, I thus propose to Hall to accept it, and to put it in his charge, to be used, like the rest of the patient's property (now about $1000 in amount, apart from your gift), for the patient's future benefit. The probate court will of course have power to direct Hall's discretion, and my death, should it chance soon to intervene, would thus leave the patient not wholly to the cold world, and not merely a burden on his mother, *resp.* his brothers,—even if the case continues a good while.—It would be best, I suppose, thus to reserve the use of this your gift for the time. In this way, however, it is at once and now a sustaining power to me; for it increases the height of that barrier between a possibly helpless man,—the patient—, and pauperism, which I of course regard with peculiar horror. Or again, if I fail, through illness, at any time,

180 ALS. James Papers. HL.

181 I.e., Christopher Royce, who was committed to Danvers State Hospital, January 9, 1908.

to provide necessary current expenses, the guardian would have so much the more reserve.

Should the patient soon recover enough to begin anew a fight with the world, his guardian could use the sum to help start him afresh. Should cure prove hopeless, the sum would sometime be used up in care and keep. Should recovery be followed (vain hope!) by any chance worldly success, then the patient could himself return the sum to you or to your heirs.

Is not this, in view of your so eager desire to aid, and in view of my natural unwillingness to miss any of my responsibilities, the right compromise? Thus the sum goes at once to the patient's estate.

In any case I have sent your letter and the cheque to Hall, have asked him to make acknowledgement to you, and shall never use the money except through the guardian, and in this way.

From Aug. 1, 1906, to Aug. 1, 1907 I spent $1850 net on the case alone, apart from some incidentals & from all other family expenses. I earned that, & was glad to do so. But the money might have been thrown into the sea for all the good it did to the poor boy.—

Yours Most Affectionately
Josiah.

Mrs. Royce approves my course, and deeply feels your goodness and your expression of sympathy.

To The Macmillan Company, February 17, 1908[182]

103 Irving St.
Cambridge,
Mass.
Feb. 17, 1908.

The Macmillan Company,

Gentlemen:—

I have had considerable doubt about the proper decision to give you, as my personal opinion, about the book of Professor H. Heath

182 ALS. Macmillan Papers. NYPL.

Bawden on *The Principles of Pragmatism*, whose MS you have sent me.[183]

In itself the book is good,—a scholarly presentation of Pragmatism by one of the followers of the movement, and by an academic teacher and writer of reasonably good position and reputation for his age. But Bawden is not a very original man. His book does not flash much new fire. It is a good synthesis of known opinions. It is reasonably individual in its way of putting together the materials; and it does its work with dignity, with fairness in polemic, and without any notable defects of any elementary sort. What I miss is any commanding quality,—any originality sufficient to compel attention, or to ensure a deep impression.

Pragmatism is, however, so popular at present, and so much in need of synthesis and of connected presentation, that there is a good chance that this book could find its way to a fair sale. On the whole, then, I recommend its publication,—not as a great book, but as "a good horse if you like that kind of horse." The public seems just now to like the kind of horse called Pragmatism. Hence, I say, the book may be a good success.

Yours Truly
J. Royce.

To Thomas Henry Briggs, February 23, 1908[184]

103 Irving St.
Cambridge, Mass.
Feb. 23, 1908.

Mr. T. H. Briggs,

My Dear Sir:—

The literature of Pragmatism is vast. I do not want to urge my own treatment of the subject upon you; but since you ask as you do in your letter of Feb. 18, I may venture to reply that in a forthcoming book entitled *The Philosophy of Loyalty*, which the Macmillan Co. will probably publish within a month or six weeks from

[183] Henry Heath Bawden, *The Principles of Pragmatism: A Philosophical Interpretation of Experience* (Boston: Houghton Mifflin Co., 1910).

[184] ALS. HL.

now, I have a chapter, entitled "Loyalty, Truth, and Reality," in which I especially discuss Professor James's conception of Truth, as set forth in his book.

Yours Very Truly
Josiah Royce

To Alfred Deakin, April 18, 1908[185]

103 Irving St,
Cambridge, Mass.
April 18, 1908.

My Dear Mr. Deakin:—

About a week since, a little book of mine, entitled *The Philosophy of Loyalty*, was published by the Macmillan Company of New York City. I asked the publisher to send you a presentation copy at the earliest opportunity. I hope that that copy will have reached you in advance of this letter.

As to the letter itself, it is an effort to fulfil a long neglected duty. I have always been a poor letter writer,—how poor you know, if you ever bear me in mind at all. I deserve to have been forgotten by you long since. Perhaps I have been forgotten. But now that I have passed my fifty-second birthday, and the shadows begin to lengthen, conscience reproaches me often for having neglected so long to send you in writing the good words of friendly greeting that often arise in my heart when I think of you. Having not written to you for so long, I have grown ashamed to write at all. Now, however, my little book, written upon what (for me) is an uncommonly practical theme, and for a very human sort of purpose, may serve to make my excuses for me. It deals with qualities and interests that you love and know better than I can.

Few memories stand out more clearly and encouragingly, and more pleasingly in my life, than our meeting in 1888, our days together in the wonderland of your mountains, our talks, and your kindness, and the gracious cheer of all your hospitality. What a place the meeting, and your presence and personality, have since occupied in my life, I can hardly tell you. It is partly the inability to make my feeling clear that has kept me from much writing. For,

[185] ALS. Deakin Papers. NLA.

being a lonely and abstract student, I have no sort of return to offer you, who are an empire-builder, and a man of affairs. I hear of your long career of service with delight and admiration;–not indeed with envy, for I am a student, and love the life apart from affairs;–but I can fully appreciate the world's work, if I cannot do such work; and I reverence the power that has made you so long a leader in your country's affairs. I wish that we in America had a system in which public men could *last* as you, with your system have been able to do. With us, a powerful personality such as Roosevelt simply wears out his great power by the storms and the contests of his second administration. I doubt whether he could be elected again were he nominated. The greatness of the American type of executive power, in hands like his, arouses reactions. Popularity, even as great as his has been, cannot endure the strain of the manifold hostilities that he has, even through his best services, awakened. But with your system (whether because the constant presence of direct parliamentary responsibility moderates, in the long run, the isolation that great power so often, with us, brings,–or for some other reason), a man can have, if he possesses the strength of personality for the task,–a long lease of political power, or a return, after retirement, to renewed power,–as has been the case with you.

In any case, I congratulate your country upon having you, and you upon your career. And I am glad to let you know that faithless as I may have seemed, I remember you still with a hearty gratitude, and a personal affection, of which I still hope to be able to talk with you afresh, someday,–if not in this world,–then in some convenient place on the boundary of whatever Elysian fields you make your future home, as I myself wander about from one place to another in the unknown worlds.

As for me, I am now an oldish professor, who stoops a little, and carries too many books about, and plans many books that I do not write. I am already supposed by younger colleagues to be an old fogey. The "Pragmatists" wag their heads and mock when I pass by. My colleague James, who although so much my senior, is eternally young, has all the interest on his side,–even although he is now an *emeritus* professor. I am rapidly passing into an early but a well earned obscurity of professorial old age.–Meanwhile, as a sort of last expression of ideals, I put forth my book on *Loyalty*. Our fleet is going to see you soon,–as I hear, next August. I venture to send in advance of the fleet,—vast and noisy as it is,—my very tiny and silent book, as the word of just one obscure American,—a word of greeting about our common ideals. If you have time to look at it some day,—for an hour or two,—remember that its author still loves you.—

Yours Affectionately
Josiah Royce.

If you ever are to visit America, let me know.—It is hardly possible that I shall ever see Australia again.—But it would be a pleasure to do something for you if you visited this country.

To George Platt Brett, July 14, 1908[186]

Cambridge, Mass.
103 Irving St.
July 14, 1908.

My Dear Mr. Brett:—

The *Athenaeum* notice of my book on *Loyalty* was welcome. I am glad to hear well of the work.

My plan for the volume of essays has been delayed by the need that I have felt to do some revising work upon some of the papers.[187] Mrs. Royce has now undertaken to do for me a part of what is needed. I feel sure that with her help I can have the various papers ready to send to you soon. The plan of the book is substantially as follows:—

I propose to give to it the title: "Some American Problems," or else "Some Problems of American Life" (or "of American Culture"). The precise form of the title could be agreed upon after further consultation between us.

The essays to be included are all now completed (except for the minor revisions that Mrs. Royce has now undertaken to superintend). Some of them are MS lectures that I have at various times delivered. Some have been printed already. The needed revisions concern mainly the omission of references to the special occasions

186 ALS. Macmillan Papers. NYPL.

187 Royce, in a letter to Brett, March 20, 1908, had briefly proposed that Macmillan might wish to publish *RQP;* Brett seemed hesitant and in a letter to Royce, May 6, 1908, had requested a full description.

upon which the lectures have been delivered, or else the explanation or clarification of such references, the correction of the English here and there, and similar minor details.

The essays are:—

I. "Race-Questions and Prejudices"

⟨Published in the *International Journal of Ethics* in 1906,—cited with approval, in a book of the topics in question, by Gov. Ollivier of Jamaica,—variously discussed at the time of its publication.⟩

II. "Some Limitations of the Thoughtful Public in America"

⟨A lecture originally delivered in 1899, as a "Founder's Day" Address, at Vassar, since frequently read to various audiences East & West. MS not yet printed.⟩

III. "Provincialism"

⟨A Phi Beta Kappa address at the University of Iowa in 1902. Since much read to various audiences. Printed in the *Boston Transcript* at the time, but never put in more permanent form. The topic is mentioned in the *Loyalty* book, which this lecture supplements.⟩

IV. "On the Relations of Climate to Civilization in California"

⟨An essay originally prepared for the National Geographical Society at Washington. Later published in F. A. Richardson's *International Review*. The only thing of mine which President D. S. Jordan of Stanford ever spoke well of (so far as I know). —A study of provincial psychology from the point of view of a former Californian.⟩

V. "An Address to Graduate Students"

⟨MS, prepared for our Graduates one year, at Harvard, for our meeting of "welcome" at the opening of the year. I have sometimes called this paper: "How to be cultivated *although* a Graduate."—Often read to various companies,—never printed.⟩

VI. "Some Relations of Physical Training to the Problem of Moral Education"

⟨An address before the Boston Physical Education Society in the spring of 1907. Since printed as a pamphlet by the Boston Normal School of Gymnastics. The address sketched my views on "Loyalty." It applied them to the problems of the physical trainer. While the book on *Loyalty* was written months later, this lecture independently sketches my ethical position, & would help out the *Loyalty* book in a way. The pamphlet printed by the Boston Norm. Sch. of Gymn. has been circulated only in physical training circles, & is not likely to hurt the more formal publication.⟩

This then is the proposed book.[188] It may contain some 50,000 or 60,000 words. It ought to have a moderate sale, & to help to keep the *Loyalty* book warm. It is conceived in the general spirit of that book,—most of the essays having been studies preparatory to my ethical generalization.

If your offer for the book can be agreed upon between us, I think that you could have the book by about Aug. 1.

Yours Truly
Josiah Royce

To George Platt Brett, July 21, 1908[189]

103 Irving St.
Cambridge,
Mass.
July 21, 1908.

My Dear Mr. Brett:—

I have been too busy to reply earlier to your last letter. Mrs. Royce, however, is engaged in looking over the essays for special corrections. The book will soon be in shape.

As to your proposal, and suggestions, I reply as follows:—[190]

1. I agree that a volume of essays has a somewhat doubtful chance of any large sale.

2. I suggest, however, that 10%, while a sufficient royalty in case the sale is as a fact small, is not sufficient, or would not be, in case the sale actually exceeded what we now both think probable.

[188] These, with the exception of the fifth essay, are the contents of *RQP;* the order of the second and third essays was reversed, and in some cases the titles were altered slightly.

[189] ALS. Macmillan Papers. NYPL.

[190] In a letter to Royce, July 16, 1908, Brett was still hesitant about publishing *RQP*. He feared a lack of unity and resulting poor sales. Nevertheless, as Royce's regular publisher, Brett agreed to proceed with publication, but offered a straight 10% royalty. He concluded by hoping for considerable revision, so that the language of the lectures might conform to standards of the essay.

I should propose then, in this contract, as in others, a *contingent* increase of royalty in case the sales exceed a certain amount. 15% instead of 10% in case the sales exceed ____ copies (the number in question to be reasonably adjusted), would satisfy me.

3. The character of being partly "addresses" is inherent in the papers. I have too often succeeded with books in lecture form, and know of too many successful books of addresses, to think that the otherwise moderate expectations that I have about this book are likely to be much affected by this aspect of the matter. I shall not unduly emphasize this aspect. But I cannot remove it.

4. The book has a genuine unity. It has to do with a set of important American questions viewed from the point of view of my ethical and philosophical tendencies. This could be indicated in the preface,—perhaps in the title.

5. The title: "Provincialism, Race-Questions, and other American Problems" is possible if you approve.

6. I think that you will now find it easy to make out a contract that I will gladly sign.—[191]

Yours Truly,
J. Royce

To James McKeen Cattell, October 15, 1908[192]

103 Irving St., Cambridge.
October 15, 1908.

Dear Professor Cattell:—

At the International Congress of Philosophy, in September, at Heidelberg,[193] I discussed with some of the Germans and Italians present the desirability of getting a mutual interest in the translation of philosophical literature, of decided and general importance, from one of our various languages into another. I have some prospects of seeing soon one book of mine published in an Italian edi-

[191] Brett sent the contract to Royce on July 22, 1908, agreeing to all of Royce's proposals.

[192] ALS. Cattell Papers. LC.

[193] Royce participated in the Congress by reading "The Problem of Truth in the Light of Recent Discussion," reprinted in *WJ*, pp. 187–254, and in *RLE*, pp. 63–97.

tion,—another in a German edition.[194] I made some offers to do what little I could to get translations published of two or three foreign books of mark, which, as I believe, our public ought to know. All this involves a certain reciprocity, such as congresses ought to promote.

Prominent amongst the books that I thought of was the one entitled *Problemi della Scienza,* by F. Enriques, of Bologna, who will be the President of the next Intern. Congr. of Phil., when it meets at Bologna.[195] Enriques is mathematician, logician, and philosophical worker in comparative science. His reputation will be known to you,—perhaps also his book (published in 1906), which covers in a different way the sort of field that Poincaré has dealt with. It has the advantage over Poincaré of going deeper into the modern logical problems. But I believe that the book would prove clear, and, despite its depth, generally readable to our scientific-philosophical public. I believe too, that, as the book of a modern geometer, and a notable representative of the great Italian school of logic, it would occupy a novel place in the literature. It is a volume of some 580 pages, of rather less than 300 words to the page. Its range is wide. It is genuinely philosophical and comparative.

I got the direct authorization of Enriques to do whatever I may find possible, and think best, to get his book translated, to find him an American (or English) publisher, and to make arrangements. Mrs. Royce and myself together, with a possible occasional assistance from a colleague as to technical matters, can translate the book,—the main work on the Italian side being done, of course, by Mrs. Royce, whose work as translator you already know. If advisable, I could write an introduction. I feel strongly interested in getting some such books as this before our public. One would want an arrangement securing a division of royalties between author and translator, or some such plan. Of course the sale of such a book is not big. But I should hope for a reasonable sale, such as would float the book, and furnish a little royalty.

I write thus first to you, to know whether you, as editor and as one interested in such enterprises, think well of such a plan, and

[194] See André A. Devaux, "Bibliographie des traductions d'ouvrages de Royce . . . ," *Revue Internationale de Philosophie,* nos. 79–80 (1967), pp. 159–61.

[195] Royce contributed an introduction to Federigo Enriques, *Problems of Science,* trans. Katharine Royce (Chicago: Open Court Publishing Co., 1914); reprinted in *RLE,* pp. 254–59.

whether you have a suggestion as to where I had better turn for my publisher. Brett of course might accept a proposal at once for the Macmillians; but I suppose that he would lay much stress on your approval.[196] If he hesitated, I might appeal to Carus, or to Longmans, or to Scribner's. But you may be able to make some other suggestion. I venture to trouble you, just because you have now become a sort of general counsellor as to such various scientific enterprises, and are so open to new ideas.

Yours Very Truly
Josiah Royce.

I have, as you see, other translation plans in mind. But this is enough for one letter.

To James McKeen Cattell, October 23, 1908[197]

103 Irving St.
Cambridge, Mass.
October 23, 1908.

Dear Cattell,

I should be very glad to know what "editorial and financial arrangements" (to use the wording of your kind letter of October 20), would be possible in case you were willing to undertake the publishing of the book of Enriques in the series that contains the Poincaré volumes. I should think that Enriques' work would be an admirable companion to the treatises of Poincaré.[198]

Yours Truly
Josiah Royce.

I thank you for your letter, and your interest.

[196] The fact that Mrs. Royce was to be the translator may help to explain Royce's reluctance to write directly to Brett. In December, 1907, she had proposed that Macmillan Co. publish her translation of Giovanni Papini's *Pragmatism;* after a cool exchange of correspondence with Brett, the negotiations ended. Again, in January, 1909, Brett rejected Royce's proposal that Macmillan Co. publish Mrs. Royce's translation of Eugen Kühnemann's *Schiller*. This work was later published with Royce's introduction by Ginn and Co., in 1912.

[197] ALS. Cattell Papers. LC.

[198] Royce wrote the introduction to H. Poincaré, *The Foundations of Science,* trans. G. B. Halsted (Lancaster, Pa.: Science Press, 1913).

To Charles William Eliot, October 29, 1908[199]

103 Irving St. Cambridge.
Oct. 29, 1908

Dear Dr. Eliot:—

In accordance with the request of Mr. Greene, I write to you this statement of the facts regarding my invitation to Dr. E. Katzenellenbogen to be present at meetings of my Seminary, Philosophy 20c; and I submit to your judgment the question as to the official aspect of my action in the matter.

My Seminary in question is concerned with an investigation in Logic, and in particular, with certain problems of what is called Methodology.[200] In various sciences, differing very widely in their objects of inquiry, and in their special methods, certain common conceptions, modes of description, and general methods of inquiry, are, as everybody knows, present. Thus any science may use "numerical" conceptions; any inductive science uses some form of "the inductive method"; any theoretical science uses "deduction"; and other common features make up the form of "scientific method." It is the business of Logic to inquire into the nature of these common features of scientific method. The inquiry is an old one. Some of its results are in every text-book. It is also, so far, a very incomplete inquiry. It is in need of passing on to new results. Such results can only be reached by the aid of an empirical comparison of the actual methods and conceptions which are in use by workers, engaged in various branches of scientific work, at the present time.

But it is usually hard to get the actual investigators, absorbed in special researches, to discuss their methods with people who are not of their own province. A student of the logic of scientific methods and conceptions is therefore hindered at every turn when he tires to get at the facts which he needs to know. He does not care for chemistry, perhaps; but he does want to find out what "chemical thinking" is,—what its characteristic modes and fashions

[199] ALS. Eliot Papers. HUA.

[200] For a detailed study of this celebrated seminar, as it was conducted in later years, see *Josiah Royce's Seminar, 1913–1914*. ed. Grover Smith (New Brunswick, N. J.: Rutgers University Press, 1963).

of conception are. And the chemists are usually too busy, or too unreflective, to tell him. So too it usually is with medical men, and with all other specialists.

Now my Seminary, Phil 20c, is a very small effort to advance a little in the study of the common methods and conceptions of various sciences. I have this year had the good fortune to get the help of a few patient and kindly colleagues to assist me in the discussions. My regular students (Graduates, and usually candidates for Ph.D.) are attempting such logical studies as these as parts of their own work. My visiting colleagues are aiding by reporting or discussing such modes of conception and investigation as are familiar to them, and as fall within the scope of our inquiry. We especially need, for this purpose, *a variety of investigators*, whose special tasks lie rather far apart, and whose contributions to our logical interests are so much the more striking for this their variety.

Amongst the visiting colleagues whom I have induced to consent to some cöoperation, Dr. Katzenellenbogen, Psychopathologist, of Danvers, is not connected with Harvard. He is, as I understand, an official regularly employed by the State. Dr. Southard knows him well, and it is through Dr. Southard that I have come to know him. Dr. Ellenbogen (this abbreviation of his name he, as I understand, permits to his friends), is a pupil of Wundt, as well as a doctor of medicine, and is a fully equipped member of his profession.

I have supposed it right, for the sake of my regular students of the Seminary, and for the sake of the research in which we are engaged, to ask Dr. Ellenbogen to be present, when he can be present, at our conferences, and occasionally to contribute to our discussions. He represents certain psychological methods which we cannot otherwise get so well expounded to us. I shall gain more from his presence than he can gain from me. He is in no proper sense my pupil or student. He helps me. I do not see how such a research as that of my Seminary can be carried on without my having a certain reasonable freedom to ask for such outside cöoperation, due care being taken, of course, that no abuse shall result.

I hope that there will be no reason to raise the question of this letter in any conversation or other dealing with Dr. Ellenbogen himself. I alone am responsible for the irregularity of his presence, so far as that irregularity exists.

I have stated the case at length, simply because an important principle of the conduct of academic research is involved. I ask for your ruling.

Yours Very Truly
Josiah Royce.

President C. W. Eliot.

To Sara Norton, November 1, 1908[201]

103 Irving Street
Cambridge
November 1, 1908

My Dear Miss Norton:—

When, two or three days since, it fell to my lot to be going over a list of those to whom I wanted to send copies of a very fragmentary little book of essays that I have just got through the press,[202] one of my saddest reflections was that I could not this time have on my list your father's name. For years past, whenever I vented my restlessness by publishing one or another of my too many books, it has been a very dear privilege, first to send him a copy, and then to receive his always so kindly, so careful, so considerate, so judicious word of acknowledgement,—the best, always, amongst the replies that came to me. He never expressed a merely formal acquiescence in the fact that I thus once more troubled him. His word, always kindly, was also always discriminating, effective, enlightening,—no matter how little time he might have to spare for me. He was not only thus unwearied, but also guided me by his comments.

I have ventured, this time, simply to ask my publisher to send to *you* a copy,—not that I ask you to give it a second look for its own sake, or to write a word in response, but merely in order to be able to say to you that I send my poor pages as just one least proof that I remember my year long counsellor, whose friendship I prized far more than I was ever able to express, and whose word and greeting I shall now always miss,—and shall also always recall with thankfulness.

Your father, and all your household, have been from our first

201 ALS. Norton Papers. HL.
202 *RQP.*

coming as strangers to this place, amongst our kindest and dearest friends. When sorrow comes to you, it clouds the sky for all of us. When we must part from your father whom we have so enjoyed and venerated, the parting is as sad as his life was inspiring. But the inspiration is still ours to look forward to. It will always be with us.

We have been near you all in sympathy during these days, just as we have felt and prized your own beautifully expressed words and acts of sympathy in the past,—and in the flowers that you sent the other day.

I want to send all of you my affectionate greeting, and to confess how much I have owed, in more ways than I can tell, to your father's whole personal influence,—an influence that, as you well know, he could embody afresh, at any moment, in a word, a phrase, a tone of voice,—and also could expand into a lifetime of noble work.—

Yours Truly,—
Josiah Royce.

To Frank Thilly, November 17, 1908[203]

104 Irving St.
Cambridge, Mass.
Nov. 17, 1908.

Dear Professor Thilly:—

Ever since I got home from Europe, Oct. 2, I have been trotting along, trying to catch up with my correspondence, and other business, which are running some distance ahead of me, like a trolley car that will not stop.

I owe you two letters, and several apologies apiece for the delay in each of them.

First, I will take part in a discussion of Realism, Idealism, Pragmatism, Anarchism, or (if you prefer) Eddyism and Psychotherapy, or whatever else you will, at the meeting of the Philos. Ass'n at Baltimore, Dec. 29 to 31.[204] Please notify me as soon as possible

[203] ALS. Thilly Papers. CUA.

[204] Royce took part in a discussion on "Realism and Idealism" at the meeting of the American Philosophical Association at Johns Hopkins in 1908. Others reading papers in this symposium were John Dewey, Frederick J. E. Woodbridge, Charles Montague Bakewell, and Norman Kemp Smith.

when, and how long, I am to talk. I don't think that anything I can say will be of much use, but I am willing to try.

Secondly, I want to thank you most heartily for your kind reviews of me, in the *Rev. d. Met. & Mor.* and in the *Philos. Rev.*[205] The latter review,—that of the *Philos. of Loyalty* was especially careful and kindly. I don't agree with you that "justice to justice" or any analogous generalization, could stand anywhere nearly on a logical level with my own "loyalty to loyalty." The ground of that generalization of loyalty which I undertake lies in the intimate relation of loyalty to the very essence of self-consciousness, so that it is only when loyalty takes on the "reflective" form, as an essentially self-sustaining process, that it becomes at once truly universal, and truly individual. Justice and other fragments of loyalty cannot receive any such reflective form in any adequate way.—But your review is very kind.

Yours Truly,
Josiah Royce.

To Richard Clarke Cabot, March 9, 1909[206]

103 Irving St.
Cambridge.
March 9, 1909.

Dear Cabot:—

Having just looked over your interesting Report of the Social Service Dep't[207] (a sort of Purgatorio and occasionally Inferno,

[205] Thilly contributed "La Philosophie Américaine Contemporaine" to an issue of the *Revue de Métaphysique et de Morale*, 16 (September 1908): 607–34, devoted to "Études sur le mouvement philosophique contemporain à l'étranger." He reviewed *PL* in *Philosophical Review* 18 (1908): 541–48, where he wrote (pp. 546–47): "The reason why Professor Royce is able to deduce from the concept of loyalty all the fundamental virtues and duties is that he reads them into it: he simply succeeds in getting out of his notion exactly what he has put in. He cannot therefore be said to have reached 'the roots' of human conduct. . . . All this appeals to us, and there is no particular harm in bringing all these excellent precepts under the term 'loyalty,'—other terms would do equally well,—but that does not make loyalty the ground of our moral standards."

[206] ALS. Cabot Papers. HUA.

[207] Cabot was one of the leaders of the social-welfare movement; his *First Annual Report of Social Service Permitted at Massachusetts General Hospital* (1909) had a considerable impact on the movement.

wherein the visits of you and of your workers seem to appear more useful than was Dante's, since, if I am right, he got nobody out of either place except himself),—I am moved to enclose a cheque. It is little. I should have sent one before, and a larger one now, were it not that I have had, and still have, other investments to make in the problem of evil,—investments some of which are sad enough.

I am glad to hear of you and your work at all times. As for me, I lecture more constantly than ever, and am more devoted to logic than ever. And thus I live,—in good health, but without much leisure. I have to give a Lowell Evening Class course, at the moment, in your luxurious medical school,—a marvelous marble wilderness, which serves as a fine frame to set off the winter stars when one approaches it from Longwood avenue in the evening, as I now do twice a week. You must have a hard time to live up to your buildings, you medical men!

My hearty best wishes to yourself and Mrs. Cabot.

Yours Affectionately
Josiah Royce

To Edward Bradford Titchener, October 21, 1909[208]

Cambridge, Mass.
103 Irving St.
October 21, 1909

Dear Professor Titchener:—

The small Committee, representing a part only of the interests of the academic bodies,—the committee of which I was at first appointed chairman—was merged into a larger committee, wherein the Arts and Sciences, & the Law and Medical Faculties, were all at once represented, for the purpose of conferring together upon the honorary degree recommendations to the Corporation.[209] This merger took place, through a change of official plan, before my own committee had time to act. I was a member of the larger committee itself. My own committee never acted separately. It was as such a member, and acting only in that capacity, and not as a Chairman of anything, that I had the pleasure of presenting your name as

[208] ALS. Titchenor Papers. CUA.

[209] Titchenor received an honorary D.Sc. from Harvard in 1909.

that of one to whom an honorary Doctorate was due. In so acting, I stood for my own opinion indeed, but also for the views of our Philosophical Department, whose committee (of which I am *not* chairman) went over the names proposed before instructing me how to represent philosophy on the general committee.

And so, while I do not want you to attribute any decisive action in the matter to me alone, or to conceive of the recommendation of your name for the Degree as to be *more* attributed to me than to several other people, I can assure you that I was glad of my part in the recommendation, while your name got on the final list because a number of very critical judges,—men more competent than I am,—agreed with me that it ought to be there. My part was that of proposer and seconder. Others decided.

In fact, our Honorary Degrees, especially in so far as they were not given to College Presidents (the choice of whom we mainly left to the Corporation), were the result of a very extended consideration, in which many experienced men took part. The large Committee, of which I was a member, included, as I have said, the Law and the Medical representatives, as well as men interested in one part or another of the whole range of the work of the Arts and Sciences. E. C. Pickering, Agassiz, and such men were present. The competition of various branches of learning was keen. Each department had to look out well for its chance to get a hearing. And so you may be sure that you were finally recommended for the degree for reasons much more important than any personal or official opinion or recommendation of mine was or could be. I may add that Professor Münsterberg is quite as responsible as I am for what was done, although he was not on the Committee.

In any case, however, in proposing your name, I did what I could, and am rejoiced that I could do it. Why you received the degree the President in part expressed in the words that he used when your name was announced. And I am free to confess that I had *some* part in suggesting the phraseology in question, although others also considered the wording, which was weighed, like the choice, carefully. I suppose that what we wanted, and still want to honor, was your steady, earnest, and so largely successful search for solid and new truth, relating to such vital topics, and involving both methods and results which are of growing importance. I do not know that in these days Experimental Psychology itself stands much in need of recognition as a department of work. Its position is secure among the scientific tasks of the present and the future. Everybody recognizes it. But the leader in Experimental Psychology, who has done in his own field as long and as fruitful a work as you have done, ought, upon such an occasion, to find himself receiving the honor that, in turn, it is an honor to offer to him.

Such relations, when they come, are very pleasant. I am sorry that, in the hurry of the Inauguration days, I missed seeing you, except for just a momentary greeting. I hope that I may be able to see you at the Christmas meeting here, although I am to be at New Haven, I fear, for a part of the time of the meeting that occurs here.[210] With hearty good wishes for you and your work I remain

Very Truly Yours
Josiah Royce.

To Agnes Boyle O'Reilly Hocking, December 2, 1909[211]

103 Irving St.
Cambridge,
Mass.
Dec. 2, 1909.

Dear Mrs. Hocking:—

I am at the mercy of my various tasks and duties, and must use next Sunday in various efforts to keep up with various enterprises that are running past me. So I ought not to, and cannot, accept your very kind invitation to stay over the coming Sunday, and to meet the Cabots. I send to all my love and greetings. I wish that I could be with you.

The "work of God" in the world not only "joins onto," but is *identical with, consists in,* the work of all rational beings whoever they are, men or not men, who so work that the devine ideal is genuinely, even if not abstractly, present to their minds. These beings, taken at any one time (say today) are finite beings. Nobody not a finite being can exist today in the world. No one of the finite

[210] The American Philosophical Association met at Yale on December 27–29, 1909, and the American Psychological Association met at Harvard on December 29–31.

[211] ALS. Hocking Library, Madison, N.H.

beings is God,—viz. the *whole* and real God *as* God. Everyone of them, however, in so far as he is rational and a worker, is an incarnation of God, looking Godwards. I mean by "looking Godwards" viewing the fragmentary life as an expression of the one whole purpose (the divine ideal as one conceives it),—that is, viewing the temporal in the light of the eternal, and seeking "the city that is out of sight." The "work" of each finite God-representative is, more or less consciously, blindly, instinctively, or explicitly, a practical expression of the prayer: "Thy will be done on earth" (that is in this realm of these individual temporal crises, hesitancies, wanderings and deeds) "as it is in heaven" (that is in the eternal totality of the divine life). In no other sense than as thus incorporated in and through the personal deeds of finite beings, can God just now "work." He "joins" us in so far as we join him. The deed is ours, and is his through us. "Our wills are ours to make them thine."—As for our fortunes (apart from those that our finite fellows make),—these mere fortunes are determined by the whole nature of the finite world but are not specifically guided by special deeds of God except so far as he is incarnate in our fellows. Our fortunes are the material for our duty, our opportunity to win for ourselves union with God,—not themselves providentially determined.

This mere indication of a view that both you and the Cabots have often heard me expound, is all that I can now contribute to your discussion.

Yours Affectionately
Josiah Royce

To Douglas Clyde Macintosh, December 14, 1909[212]

103 Irving St.
Cambridge,
Massachusetts.
Dec. 14, 1909.

Dear Mr. Macintosh:—

I will lecture March 11 as you request. My topic might as well

[212] ALS. Royce Papers. HUA.

be this:—"The Sources of Religious Insight:—What are they? How can they be tested?"[213]

I propose briefly to sketch these following supposed sources of the insight in question, and to consider which ones of them, if any, can be regarded as adequate to found or to prove a religion:—

1. Tradition and Historical Revelation: What value have such sources?
2. Mystical Insight.
3. Practical Religious Life, and the Pragmatic Test.
4. Reason.
5. The Loyal Life.

This is a mere suggestion of my plan. I may change the detail later. I might call the topic: "The Possibility of a Revelation"; or, "Is any Revealed Religion possible?" But I do not want my title to be sensational. Do you think my topic is suitable?

Yours Sincerely
Josiah Royce.

To WILLIAM JAMES, N. D. [JANUARY, 1910?][214]

103 Irving St.
Cambridge,
Mass.

Dear James:—

I enclose herewith the Lady Stanley letter, which ought to have been returned long ago. Many thanks for the sight of it.[215]

Typewriter copies of my fragmentary tribute to you are to be prepared and sent to those directly interested—the guests at your

[213] Also presented at Smith College, April 18, 1910, as a conclusion to a series of lectures on the "Modern Philosophy of Life." Presumably this lecture was expanded into *SRI,* the Bross Lectures, delivered at Lake Forest College, November 13–19, 1911.

[214] ALS. James Papers. HL.

[215] Probably a letter from the wife of Henry Morton Stanley, the explorer, to Royce, October, 1909, expressing admiration for *WI,* both volumes of which she had read after her husband died. The letter is reproduced in Ronald Albert Wells, "A Portrait of Josiah Royce" (Ph.D diss., Boston University, 1967), p. 152.

dinner.[216] You will get one of the copies. It is the one written record of our meeting at your house. Hence it may be worth preserving from envious time's jaws so far as the type-writer can preserve. We had a very good evening with you, and the portrait is surely good in all that it gets of you,—especially eyes, brow, pose, and pleasing impression. I see in you more Titanic features, *beside* those that the portrait gets. I am glad of what has been got.

Yours Always
J. Royce.

To William James, February 10, 1910[217]

103 Irving St.
Feb. 10, 1910.

Dear James:—

I return the letters, with thanks for the information. In justice to Baldwin the matter certainly ought to be cleared up.[218] If his present statement of his mishap is true, then not only is Münsterberg's letter perfectly correct and fair, but we ought to stand together to see that Baldwin gets fair play in future from his fellow workers, however inevitable may be his momentary eclipse.

But *if* the now common report of the facts is true, *then*, of course, the matter would stand quite otherwise. For it would then be no question of our playing the Pharisee, or the prude, as against an unfortunate victim of some temptation that we have no concern to judge. *If* his statement is false, and *if*, as apparently authentic report has it, he admitted, at the time, that frequent and habitual practices of his own, deliberately pursued, had led to the final scene; if, in the eyes of his University, he had long carried on a mode of

[216] A dinner to celebrate the unveiling of a portrait of James by Ellen Emmet Rand was held at the James home on January 18, 1910. Royce's remarks were published as "A Word of Greeting to William James," *Harvard Graduates' Magazine* 18 (1910): 630–33.

[217] ALS. James Papers. HL.

[218] James Mark Baldwin had been forced to resign from the faculty of Johns Hopkins after being accused of visiting a house of prostitution. Baldwin denies this charge in a letter to Hugo Münsterberg, February 16, 1910, Münsterberg Papers, BPL.

life that violated his trust as an officer, and if he had been dismissed for *this* turpitude,—well then, it wouldn't do to have him trying, by further false statements, to hold himself in the position of a man worthy of the moral support of the general body of his fellow workers in this country. In so far as he wants us to stand by him as friends, he wants what surely involves more or less public approval on our part, now or hereafter.—I have been his friend; I want to be so in future. I shall be so if he is now telling the substantial truth.

So the question now is: Is he telling the truth? If so he is a wronged man, who deserves the help of his friends. If he is lying, then one can't help him, and ought to know it.

I have written to Griffin in this spirit, as Münsterberg has written to Remsen.[219] Really they have no right at Baltimore to stand on mere silence any more. To talk mystery, as Griffin did to me not long since, becomes now intolerable. I have now said so to Griffin.—

Yours Truly
Josiah Royce

To Bertrand Russell, June 29, 1910[220]

103 Irving St.
Cambridge,
Mass.
June 29, 1910.

My Dear Mr. Russell:—

Although it is now a long time since I met you at Wm. James's house,[221] and we have not met since, I hope that you will allow me, both as an officer of Harvard, and as an admirer of yours, to introduce to you my friend, and my late Assistant, Henry M. Sheffer, Ph.D.,— and now holder of a Sheldon Travelling Fellowship from Harvard.[222]

[219] Edward Herrick Griffin was Dean of the College Faculty at Johns Hopkins; Ira Remsen was President.

[220] ALS. Russell Archives. Continuum 1 Limited (London).

[221] Russell had visited Boston in the fall of 1896; it was, presumably, at this time that he and Royce first met.

[222] Sheffer received his Ph.D. in 1908 with a dissertation on "A Programme of Philosophy, Based on Modern Logic."

Mr. Sheffer is a good philosopher, and especially a devout student of Logic in general, with most especial reference to Mathematics, and with a great fondness for your own work, of which he is a serious student. I think that I may call him a disciple of yours. I think also that we have, in America, no more promising research student of the new logic than Sheffer is. His Fellowship is to be devoted to work upon that topic. I expect important results from him.

Mr. Sheffer is desirous of getting some advice from you as to how he may best pass his year of work.

Any suggestion that you can make to him as to this or any other topic will I believe, help on a very good cause, namely that of your own most important region of research, for which, in my own way and measure, I too, as teacher, try to win students.

I am, with great respect,

Yours Sincerely
Josiah Royce

The Hon. Bertrand Russell.

To Hugo Münsterberg, August 12, 1910[223]

103 Irving St.
Cambridge,
Mass.
August 12, 1910

Dear Münsterberg:—

Your very kind letter of farewell reached me after I returned from a little sea-voyage to Costa Rica about a month since.[224] I have been busy over various things about Cambridge since then. I am now just going off on another voyage,—this time to Paramaribo, Dutch Guiana. I expect to return about the middle of next month. You know about my little voyages. I find them a great refreshment, and feel as if only one who sees the wonderful tropical ocean, and the lofty cumulus clouds of the trade winds, from time to time, really comes in touch with the larger aspects of natural beauty.

[223] ALS. Münsterberg Papers. BPL.

[224] Münsterberg was the Harvard Exchange Professor at Berlin, 1910–11.

The sea is to me what Switzerland is to many;—only, not the North Atlantic of high latitudes,—the tropical sea is my joy.

I believe that it will be a great and good year with you. Surely "the harvest is plenteous," where you are going. And surely you are the man to go. I shall miss you much, even if our deeper philosophical sympathies, which I feel more and more, have seldom been talked out between us during the past year,—busy as we both have been.

My own work has not seemed fruitful of late, although some of my logical researches are reaching a point where I hope to be soon able to publish good things. Your work is aboundingly fruitful, and I rejoice in it. What I shall miss however is just what there is time for when you are near by,—the occasional greeting, the personal word, the kindly touch that your presence gives. Now that I move about, and am henceforth always to move about under a shadow of sorrow that can never be lifted, these little personal meetings mean much more to me than I can express. You always cheer me. And I shall miss you.—Meanwhile I give you my most hearty good wishes for the year. May you be heard as heartily as the truth that you have with you to tell is a hearty and much needed, and indeed eternal truth.—We are all doing as well, here at home, as is possible under the conditions. I am sorry that Palmer is to go.[225] I am sure that, as you say, Riley is a good man.[226] My warm greetings to your family, in which Mrs. Royce joins.

Yours Truly,
Josiah Royce.

[225] In 1912–13, Palmer became Exchange Professor at Colorado, Grinnell, Knox, and Beloit Colleges.

[226] This may have reference to the fact that I. Woodbridge Riley was the Acting Chairman of the Committee on Early American Philosophers (American Philosophical Association). Royce, together with H. N. Gardiner, was a member of the Committee.

To Robert Underwood Johnson, September 16, 1910[227]

103 Irving St.
Cambridge,
Mass.
Sept. 16, 1910.

Dear Mr. Johnson:—

I am sorry to have been slow in responding to yours of Sept. 9. When it came here, I was at sea, far to the southwards, on a boat that carried no wireless. Of James's death I heard on my return, an hour before I read your letter.[228] His death was in fact the first bit of home news that reached me when I got to Boston, and was an entire surprise to me.

James was, as a friend, very near to me. To return and find five or six different editorial requests on my table to write about my next friend, of whose death I learned only upon reaching home, is baffling. I hardly know what request to consider the prior one; still less can I compose myself at the moment to think how best at once to be just to my feeling for him, and to meet the need of the reader, whether the "average reader" of your request or the technical reader whom others of my editorial correspondents have in mind.

After hesitating over the conflicting calls, I simply find that, at the moment, my friend is too dear, the shock of his death is too sudden, the event is too near, for me to choose the right word. Later I shall hope to write about him,—lengthily I suppose—and I hope in a way that may be just to the task so far as I can be just.[229] But for the moment I must simply wait.—I thank you for your request, kindly and honorable as it is. I wish that I could meet it. I am sorry to have to decline.—

Yours Truly
J. Royce.

[227] ALS. Century Collection. NYPL.

[228] James died on August 26, 1910, at his home in Chocorua, N. H.

[229] See "James as a Philosopher," a Phi Beta Kappa Oration delivered at Harvard, June 29, 1911; printed on that day in the *Boston Evening Transcript* and reprinted in *Science,* n.s., 34 (1911): 33–45; in *Harvard Graduates' Magazine,* 20 (1911–12): 1–18; and in *WJ.*

To Charles Rockwell Lanman, September 24, 1910[230]

103 Irving St.
Saturday Evening.

Dear Lanman:—

If I did not suppose that you are very weary with all your good deeds, I should come over to thank you and dear Tom for what you have done, and I should do so tonight before I go to bed. As it is, I must not come. But I do most heartily thank you both. The worst thing about many sorrows is their lonesomeness. James said, when he observed the fortitude of the earthquake sufferers in California, in 1906,[231] that he was impressed with the fact that, because they all suffered together, and because nobody was lonesome in his grief, they all could be relatively cheerful.

Well, we do not want earthquakes to relieve our lonesomeness. And I most earnestly hope that all the friends who were with us today, may be rewarded by fortune for their goodness, and may often join with their dear ones in rejoicings that are not lonesome, and in occasions, at home and elsewhere, that draw souls together in love and delight. But it was their part today, and it has been your part for several days, to make grief for us more what it is whenever the sufferers know that they are not left alone with their dead and their lost hopes. You helped to surround us with whatever makes sorrow bearable. You did this freely, lovingly, gently, with the kindest touch, with the closet devotion. And Tom has nobly done his part too. We thank you heartily, lovingly, and with the hope that we may repay you, not in moments of affliction, so much as in the prosperity that as we hope may be yours.—

Always Your Friend
Josiah Royce.

I don't write on the black-bordered paper, simply because the "trappings and the suits of woe" are not needed when I speak to one who understands me. And when they are not needed, I do not myself find them fitting.

230 ALS. Lanman Papers. HUA. The letter was written just after the funeral of Christopher Royce who died on September 21.

231 James had been lecturing at Stanford at that time.

To George Platt Brett, September 26, 1910[232]

103 Irving St.
Cambridge,
Mass.
Sept. 26, 1910.

My Dear Mr. Brett:—

Upon my return from my sea journey I found your letter regarding my various literary plans, and regarding our conversation of August as to future publications of mine.

I thank you for your interest, and shall later try to get something ready for print on the lines that we talked over. And then we can see what the prospects are, and can probably agree as to terms without difficulty.

Since my return here, on Sept. 13, I have been very much absorbed in cares. My eldest son, Christopher Royce, has just died,—after a protracted period of invalidism indeed,—but in direct consequence of a very malignant attack of typhoid fever, which came to a fatal termination in its second week on September 21. He was buried Saturday.

In consequence of this event, and of the very numerous resulting expenses, I find myself forced to ask you whether it would not be possible for the Macmillan Company to send me now at once (with due deduction, of course, of the discount for the advance), the amount of my next copyright payment which, by contract, is due at the end of November next, but which, I believe, you are usually ready to pay earlier with a discount. The payment is the one for which the statement of Aug. 1 last gave account. I hope that this request will not seem troublesome.

I am, with regards,

Very Truly Yours
Josiah Royce

232 ALS. Macmillan Papers. NYPL.

To William Bennett Munro, October 1, 1910[233]

103 Irving Street,
Cambridge, Mass.,
Oct. 1, 1910.

Prof. W. B. Munro,
Division of History and Political Science,
Harvard University,
Cambridge, Mass.

My dear Professor Munro:

In answer to yours of Sept. 29th, I can only say that, ever since I have returned, I have been refusing requests of editors to write about James. There were a good many reasons for these refusals, especially: the importance of the task; my expectations that I shall in time write something very serious and possibly lengthy about him; and the fact that, in the June number of the *Harvard Graduates' Magazine*, I have already published the words that I spoke at the dinner which occurred at the time of the presentation of his portrait. All this gives some grounds why I had better not try to undertake any article relating to him at just this time. I have, in fact, agreed with Mrs. James, that the best I can do about the matter, from her point of view as well as mine, would involve postponing any further expression about him in public beyond what my little address at the dinner contained.

Your letter reached me just as I was leaving for my regular Yale engagement at the end of the week. Please forgive delay in answer. It is not from neglect nor unwillingness that I have to decline your request.

Sincerely yours,
Josiah Royce

[233] TLS. HHL.

To George Herbert Palmer, October 28, 1910[234]

103 Irving St.
Oct. 28, 1910.

Dear Palmer:—

I have your letter, and thank you for it. I have just been looking up afresh Paul on the subject of spiritual gifts,—for the sake of my Yale Philos of Religion class. I wish to remark, and my language is plain,—that you have *all* of the said gifts, except possibly that of speaking with tongues,—which perhaps you also possess and keep dark, as the blessed Paul recommends. You know that, in Second Corinthians, Paul lays some stress upon knowing rightly to whom to apply for subscriptions in support of good causes.

I am now off to Yale.

Yours Always,
Josiah Royce

To Elizabeth Randolph, November 16, 1910[235]

November 16, 1910.

Dear Elizabeth:—

Your letter of the 13th reached me on Monday. Ever since then, I have been too busy to find any time to write. Lectures, conferences, committee meetings, have claimed me. I write now at my first opportunity.

Your questions are those that everybody has a right to ask. In the book that I sent you, I have tried to answer some of them. But the book is lengthy, and your time is much taken up. I wish that I could effectively condense it all into a word. Perhaps what I now suggest may help to tell you, not so much what I chance to think, but what, as I believe, your own heart has been teaching you for a good while. I can only try to bring the truth as to such things to

[234] ALS. WCL.

[235] ALS. Private collection of James Royce. Miss Randolph married Edward Royce on December 29, 1910, in Germantown, Pa. The book under discussion in this letter is *PL*.

your notice, now that you already have that truth within you. Life teaches pretty much the same lesson to everybody. The chief question is whether or no you get your eyes open to what that lesson is.

You ask: "Why *must* we live?" You wonder whether there is some "definite purpose" in life. And you also wonder whether we have to "take all this for granted," without proof, and whether "faith or fear is the stronger" as a guide to life.

My answers to such questions you find at length in the book on Loyalty. But if you will accept a mere condensation of an answer into a few phrases, I may state the case thus:—"Why must I live?"— Well, first, take me just as I *happen* to be,—a mere creature who happens to have been born, and to want happiness, and who happens to breathe and to eat and to long vaguely for I know not what, —take me merely thus, as a creature of nature,—and the question has no particular answer. Any other creature might,—so far as the mere natural fact of existence goes,—any other creature might as well be living in my place. I shall die after a while,—and what will it all have meant? That, I say, is all that can be answered to your question, Why must we live? *so long as* you consider us merely as accidental creatures of nature.

But let me look at my life otherwise. Suppose I come to see, or even just to imagine, that there is some good to be done in the world that nobody but myself can do. Suppose I learn that there is something or somebody who needs just me to give aid for worthy ends of some sort. Suppose that this world of people, all so needy, *needs my help*. Well then the question, Why must I live? begins to get its answer. *I must live because my help is needed*. There is something that I can do which nobody else can do. That is: I can be friend of my friends, faithful to my own cause, servant of my own chosen task, worker among my needy brethren. I can thus join with the world's work of trying to make the whole situation better and not worse. And because I can live thus, I am more than a chance creature of nature. My life has sense and meaning.—That is the first and simplest answer to the question: Why must I live? But of course that *first* answer does not of itself tell you *what* it is which you are needed to do to help the other people. And a great many good people who want to be helpful do indeed pass much of their life in a more or less amiable ineffectiveness, because they have not yet quite defined the "purpose" which gives life its true sense. It is just that purpose which I have tried, in my book, to define by the word "Loyalty." *The* help which my friends really most want of me, is help in living "in the unity of the spirit," as lovers and faithful friends, and patriots, and all those who together are devoted to art, to humanity, to their religion, or to whatever *binds the souls of men in the common ties of the spirit*,—as all such, I say, are, in their various ways, trying to live. Whenever and however I can steadily and faithfully live in this way, I am really helping,—helping not only my own nearer friends, but, by my example and my indirect influence, I am helping everybody who is even remotely related to me or influenced by me, to give sense to his life. Now thus to live,—to live for the sake of the "unity of the spirit," to live for some "cause that binds many lives in one,"—to live thus is to possess what I call Loyalty. Very various "causes," such as the service of a country or a church or a fraternity or a family, or a friendship or a love,—or a science or a profession or an art,—very various causes, I say, can for various people form part of their personal "cause," or be selected as the principal means of living in the loyal spirit. But the great principle of the art of giving sense to life, is the principle:—Have a cause, choose it, and having chosen it, be fearlessly and steadily faithful to it.

In my book I have stated this view of the business of life partly, also, in the following way:—

"By nature," that is, apart from some choice of a cause to which to be loyal, each one of us is a mass of capricious and conflicting longings, passions, impulses, motives. We want happiness, but do not naturally know how to get it. We want "independence," and yet are always dependent upon other people's company, good will, or admiration, or other help. We want "power," but grow weary with our struggles to get power. We are fond of our fellow mortals, yet constantly tend to one or another sort of conflict with them. And in countless other ways we find that the first thing to note about our merely natural desires is that they endlessly fight one another, and that every one of us is, "by nature," a mass of contradictions.

Now is there any one way of escaping from this sort of conflict of desires? There is. This way is suggested whenever we come to feel that there is in the world something that not only, as I just said, *needs our help*, but that is, in its own importance, so vast, so dignified, so worthy or so precious, that, no matter how we happen to feel at any one moment, and no matter what the present state of our natural desires is, that something is always *worth helping*.

Now that is exactly what we come to know whenever we fall in love with what, in my lectures on Loyalty, I have called a "Cause." What a "cause" is, my book has tried to tell and I have just suggested to you. There are countless special "causes." And you always have to find out what your own special cause is, and to find that out for yourself. Only with regard to choosing a "cause" there are two things to remember:—*First* that, however various the special "causes" are which the people whom I call "the Loyal" serve, there is a sense in which all devoted people serve the same great "cause," the cause of helping mankind, by example and by service, to get out of the confusions and conflicts of our natural impulses, to stop fighting and rivalry, and hatred, and "selfishness," and to live in unity and the spirit of faithfulness. And *Second*, that *nothing* in life can be better than to find some cause to which, through your own resolute will, you *can* be devoted for life. For devotion, faith, giving ourselves to our chosen cause, isn't bondage. It is the only possible freedom. It is the only way, if not wholly to calm, then at least to control, to centralize, to unify, our naturally so varying and capricious selves. It is so, because, when I find what is *outside* of me, and *greater* than I am, and more precious than is my private happiness, that very finding of my cause begins at once to hold me together,—to give me sense and unity, to make me indifferent to my own moods and caprices. It is then no longer what I get, but what I give to my cause that I find valuable about my life. And so long as I have strength, I can give, whatever my luck. And so long as I can do something for my cause, life is worthwhile, and has sense, whatever my private fortunes. If I then ask: "Why must I live?" the answer is always ready: "Because my cause needs my help."—If I still ask: Why choose a cause?,—the answer is,—"Only thus can my life get sense, only thus can I help my fellows to give sense to their own lives."

As to "fear," there is nothing so much to be feared as aimlessness and chaos. As to "faith," there can be no faith more rational than the faith in the value of spiritual unity and faithfulness.

It is this sort of doctrine that I have long been preaching, and trying in my poor way to live out. I am sure at least that I haven't been inventing this doctrine to suit just your questions. I taught it long ago to Ned so far as I could teach him anything. I hope and believe that he has found his "cause," and is living for that cause as best he can. I believe heartily that this is also *your* doctrine.

Katharine sends love. We are glad to hear of Dec. 24 as the probable date. That would be a very good date from our point of view as well. And whatever you tell us is most prized, and whatever we can do to help you our dearest desire.–

Yours Lovingly
Josiah.

To Harry Norman Gardiner, November 20, 1910[236]

103 Irving St.
Cambridge, Mass.
Nov. 20, 1910.

Dear Professor Gardiner:—

The hours that you propose are precisely correspondent to those that I chose, by Miss Rousmaniere's request, last year, for the last three of four lectures of the couse that I then gave. The train was always on very fair time. I had no difficulty in making the connections that you now set down on your programme, although I had forgotten the precise schedule again, until your last letter refreshed my memory.

I propose then, if you accept the arrangement, to give six lectures to your class on Fridays, Feb. 10, 17, 24, March 3, 10, and 17, 1911, from 3.10 to 4 P. M.;–leaving Boston at 12, being due at Northampton at 3.02; leaving Northampton on return either by 4.35 or by the 5.10 train, according as the state of my New Haven engagements may permit or require.[237] My lectures will be upon: "The Nature, Use and Accessibility of Absolute Truth." Special topics;–The Definition and Uses of Absolute Truth; Theoretical

[236] ALS. SCA.

[237] The President's Report for 1911 (SCA) confirms that Royce lectured at Smith on these dates and also on March 18. The Report lists the lectures as follows: February 10, "The Nature, Use and Accessibility of Absolute Truth"; February 17, "The Case of Absolute Truth Against Pragmatism"; February 24, "Comparison of the Absolutist and the Pragmatist Accounts of Truth"; March 3, "The Relation of Truth to Time"; March 10 and 17, "Accessibility of Absolute Truth"; March 18, "Immortality."

and Practical Truth; The Ideal and the Accessible; Applications to Metaphysical, Ethical and Religious Questions.–

The programme seems large; but I am only going to sketch. I understand this to be the desired number of lectures; payment $50 per lecture. Is this right?

Spaulding's papers are conscientious.[238] Like Herbart (as Schopenhauer described him), Spaulding "*ist einer der seinen Verstand verkehrt angezogen hat.*" Otherwise he is all well enough.

Yours Heartily
Josiah Royce.

To George Platt Brett, January 2, 1911[239]

Cambridge, Mass
103 Irving St.
Jan 2, 1911

Dear Mr. Brett:–

Professor Boodin is a rising man, with a good record and standing as a philosopher,–as strong a man as any of his age in the West. I have advised him to get himself into book form as soon as possible. His essays, so far, are predominantly although not extremely technical. But he is clear and wholesome, and ought to win a good hearing. I should certainly advise your taking up the question of his proposed book.[240] And I commend him to your earnest consideration.

I talked with him last summer about the general plan of his book. I do not undertake to advise further about it in the shape in which he now intends to submit it to you; for I have not seen it in that form. But I think that you will find it worthy of attention.

Yours Very Truly
Josiah Royce.

[238] Edward Gleason Spaulding was one of the original "Six Realists." Preceding the actual formation of the movement, his papers–"The Postulates of a Self-critical Epistemology," *Philosophical Review*, 18 (1909): 615–41; "The Logical Structure of Self-Refuting Systems," *Philosophical Review*, 19 (1910): 276–310, 610–31–were critical of Royce's absolutism.

[239] ALS. Macmillan Papers. NYPL.

[240] The Macmillan Company became John Elof Boodin's regular publisher. The book in question was presumably *Truth and Reality: An Introduction to the Theory of Knowledge* (New York: Macmillan Co., 1911).

I re-enclose the documents sent. Holiday absence on my part must excuse my delay.—

To Abbott Lawrence Lowell, February 1, 1911[241]

103 Irving St.
Cambridge,
Mass.
Feb. 1, 1911.

Dear President Lowell:—

I have just returned from one Mid Year lecture visit, and am soon to set out upon another. I have found time, after careful consideration, to reply to President Wheeler's letter inviting me to accept the Mills Professorship at California. My reply told him that I had laid my case before you, as well as before others, and that, after your reply, I can henceforth feel sure that it is my duty to continue to work for Harvard as long as my work remains useful here. And so, with thanks, I entirely declined his offer. The matter is thus closed.

In a certain sense, as I suppose, I may henceforth regard myself as here by your appointment. At all events I wished you to have every chance to choose as to my decision; and if you had thought best, I should have done what I could for Harvard by going, as I shall now try to do by staying. Whatever other fortunes life brings, there is no doubt that to teach here is the best of all the academic opportunities for one in my calling and with my interests.—I thank you for your kind interest in the matter.

Yours Truly
Josiah Royce

241 ALS. Lowell Papers. HUA. Lowell wrote to Royce on February 6, 1911: "The University is built not of bricks, but of men; and you have long been one of the cornerstones. A dozen such men would alone make a great University."

To Charles Sedgwick Minot, March 26, 1911[242]

103 Irving St.
Cambridge,
Mass.
March 26, 1911.

Dear Dr. Minot:—

Southard tells me that there is some chance that you might be so good as to come to my Seminary on "Methods" sometime soon,—perhaps next Tuesday evening,—and let my students ask you some questions about your recent Address on Scientific Method.[243] If you have time, and if you are most kindly willing to do so, nothing could be more useful or welcome to the Seminary than that you should come; and, with every sense that I am asking a great favor of you, and that it is a pity to intrude thus upon your time, I cordially invite you to come to some meeting,—either next Tuesday or later, at your pleasure,—and take any part that the occasion may suggest. No sort of preparation or formality would be asked of you,—only conversation.

My Seminary on "Methods" meets Tuesday, at 7.30, in Emerson Hall, Cambridge, on the lower floor, on the north side of the building, and on the east side of the centre, in the "Seminary Room." About a dozen graduates and sometimes two or three colleagues are present (including often Southard and Dr. Woods).[244] The Seminary stands for no theories of my own. It is meant to help philosophical students to think about methods. It is no formal school of Logic. Anybody who has a rational method of doing

[242] ALS. Minot Papers. Countway Library, Harvard Medical School.

[243] Minot, "The Method of Science," *Science*, n.s., 33 (January 27, 1911): 119–31—a vice-presidential address to the section of Physiology and Experimental Medicine of the American Association for the Advancement of Science, Minneapolis, December 29, 1910. Royce acknowledged his debt to Minot's theories of scientific method in "The World of Interpretation," chap. 13 of *PC*, pp. 321–42.

[244] Elmer Ernest Southard was professor of neuropathology at Harvard Medical School. Frederick Adams Woods, M. D., was curator of Portuguese history at Harvard University and special lecturer in theoretical biology at Massachusetts Institute of Technology. Both were frequent visitors of Royce's Philosophy 20c, Seminary in Logic: A Comparative Study of Various Types of Scientific Method.

anything,—especially a scientific method,—is invited to tell us about it. Recently I furnished the Seminary with copies of your recent Address, and also with copies of Davis on "Geography" as set forth in the Jan. or Feb. *Pop. Sci. Monthly*.[245] The latter was, as you know, a general discussion on scientific method,—an interesting companion to yours. I asked my students to write notes on both papers.—It would be a great treat to talk over matters with you.—

Yours Truly
Josiah Royce

To Edwin Francis Edgett, June 27, 1911[246]

103 Irving St., Cambridge.
Tuesday, June 27, 1911

To the Editor of the Transcript,

Dear Sir:—

In consequence of our conversation over the telephone this morning, I send you a corrected type-written copy of my proposed Phi Beta Kappa address which is to be delivered on Thursday next, at 12 o'clock in Sanders Theatre.[247] I understand that you will print the address as an article Thursday afternoon, or not before that time, and that you offer me $50 for this use of the address. I hope that you can get a proof into my hands by tomorrow, Wednesday evening, at my house. If other newspapers ask me for advance reports of any kind, I shall simply refer them to you. And you, on the other hand, may be expected, I suppose, to give the other papers reasonable chance in whatever way you think best. Of course *if* any paper sends a stenographer to the Phi Beta Kappa meeting, I cannot control what he does; but I know how unlikely any stenographic report of such an address is.

Yours Sincerely
Josiah Royce.

[245] William Morris Davis, "The Disciplinary Value of Geography," *Popular Science Monthly* 78 (February 1911): 105–19.

[246] ALS. Berg Collection. NYPL.

[247] "William James as a Philosopher." See fn. 229 above.

To WARNER FITE, JULY 11, 1911[248]

103 Irving St.
Cambridge,
Mass.
July 11, 1911.

Dear Professor Fite:—

I am just going to sea for one of my favorite plunges into the trade winds, by a United Fruit Co. boat. I shall be away a little over three weeks. I shall return, I hope, more disposed to philosophical details. I write now only to say that your plans, outlined in your letter of July 6, are of course perfectly satisfactory to me.[249] You shall have complete freedom as to your whole undertaking. I do not think that we shall anywhere interfere or duplicate. To be sure I shall mention, incidentally, the syllogism. But I shall make nothing in my part of the course of its "three forms." For me all syllogisms are variations on one theme, the transitivity of the illative relation (as Peano states the case) or, in other words, the "triadic inconsistency" which Mrs. Ladd Franklin so prettily stated in her Johns Hopkins contribution to the *Studies in Logic*.[250] —The topic of my half of the course is: "The Logical Genesis of the Categories"; or otherwise "The Theory of Order."—"Symbolic Logic" I use, not as an end in itself, but merely as a means to state some exact relations so that one sees them for what they are, and gets clear of all this desolating pragmatistic psychologizing tendency which now undertakes to save us from the trouble of having any thoughts at all.

I shall be delighted to know you and to be near you. A lovely book, your *Individualism*![251]—

Yours Truly
Josiah Royce.

[248] ALS. Royce Papers. HUA.

[249] Fite was temporary lecturer in Philosophy at Harvard during the first term of 1911/12. Here Royce and Fite are making arrangements for Philosophy 8, Advanced Logic, which they taught jointly.

[250] Christine Ladd-Franklin, "On the Algebra of Logic," *Studies in Logic by Members of the Johns Hopkins University*, ed. Charles S. Peirce (Boston: Little, Brown and Co., 1883). This paper, as Royce makes clear in *RLE*, p. 384, was important in his development of the O-relation.

[251] *Individualism: Four Lectures on the Significance of Consciousness for Social Relations* (New York: Longmans, Green and Co., 1911).

To Edmund Janes James, July 12, 1911[252]

103 Irving St.
Cambridge,
Mass.
July 12, 1911.

Dear President James,

I thank you heartily for your kind telegram of notification regarding my son's appointment as Instructor in Music at the University of Illinois. My importunity was due to the fact that, even while the definitive action of your Trustees was still pending, my son received a definite offer of an appointment elsewhere, with a request for an immediate reply. He was puzzled with the situation. He was, of course, already committed to you in case your Trustees confirmed. You did confirm. You kindly notified us. He has accepted your appointment; and I hope that he will make you a good servant. I am glad to have him near you, and to renew in this way my relations with the U. of I.,—relations that I so pleasantly remember for my visit to you in 1907.

Yours Truly
Josiah Royce

To Charles Lewis Slattery, August 8, 1911[253]

103 Irving St.
Cambridge,
Mass.
Aug. 8, 1911

My Dear Mr. Slattery:—

On my return from a vacation sea voyage I find your letter of July 18 awaiting me. I am sorry for the delay in my reply.

I could upon *no* account authorize the printing of my casual, very unguarded, and careless remark in my letter of 1889, ad-

[252] ALS. Faculty Appointments File. University of Illinois Archives.
[253] ALS. HL.

dressed to Dr. A. V. G. Allen about Adler's enterprise.[254] I can easily remember why I amused myself with writing the sentences at the moment. When one is called to an extra task, and to a journey, one sometimes sputters a little to a friend about having the thing in question to do. Allen would have understood the remark, and smiled, and dropped the matter. But to print such words,—years afterwards,—how they might wound or seem unfair!—Adler is a near friend of mine. I am very near in interest to him, and value him. The enterprise in question was, as a fact, never brought to success. And my careless characterization of that enterprise was not just to the real plan, although, at the moment, I remember using the same expression to Adler, in jest. The jest seems bad enough now.

Moreover, the quotation from my note throws no light whatever upon Dr. Allen, or upon his own work or interests.

So please cancel the quotation from me.

Yours Truly
Josiah Royce.

To George Platt Brett, N. D. [August, 1911?][255]

103 Irving St.
Cambridge,
Mass.

Mr. Geo. P. Brett,
The Macmillan Co.

My Dear Mr. Brett:—

Some literary plans, including a proposed book on "The Vital features (or elements) of Christianity," and a further book on "The Art of Loyalty," as well as a more technical treatise on "Logical Theory," were discussed with you by me, as I passed through New

[254] Slattery evidently intended to include this remark in his *Alexander Viets Griswold Allen, 1841–1908* (New York: Longmans, Green and Co., 1911). Royce's letter to Allen has not been located, but it doubtlessly had reference to Felix Adler's plans for a meeting in Philadelphia, on January 25, 1889, to establish a "School of Philosophy and Applied Ethics."

[255] ALS. Macmillan Papers. NYPL.

York, about a year ago.[256] The past academic year proved too busy a time for me to make further books; but I have progressed as to all the topics in question, and still retain, in outline, the same plan for three different books that I hope to be able, in two or three years, to have ready for you.

Meanwhile the Harvard Corporation has seen fit to grant me, for three years from Sept. 1, 1911, the "Walter Cabot Fellowship," an honorary grant especially intended to give me extra time and opportunities for research and publication. Hence I am likely to be able to do more in preparing for publication than I otherwise should do.

At the present moment, however, I have in mind to offer to you for publication a brief volume of rather closely related essays that, if you published them,—may well serve as an introduction to the expected future volumes. The volume would consist of these essays:—

1. "William James and the Philosophy of Life"
2. "Loyalty and Insight"
3. "What is Vital in Christianity?"
4. "Recent Discussions of the Theory of Truth"
5. "Immortality" ⟨See *Hibbert Journal*, July 1907⟩.

I should propose, as a general title for the book:—*William James and Other Essays on the Philosophy of Life*.[257] All these essays have been printed in magazines; and I enclose all but one of them for inspection. The "James" essay was a Phi Beta Kappa Oration delivered at Harvard last June, at this last commencement. The essay on "Christianity" is a sort of programme for the volume that I talked over with you last year; but this essay will not be repeated in, and will not stand in the way of that more formal volume. The latter volume, viz. on "Christianity," I have now agreed with President Lowell to prepare as a series of Lowell Lectures, to be delivered sometime during the academic year 1912–13; and then to be published at once,—with you if you then still wish it.—The essay on "Immortality" I have not by me at the moment in a convenient copy. It was published in the *Hibbert Journal* for 1907, in July, & is easily accessible.

256 The first of these proposed books was published as *PC;* the latter two were not published.

257 Except for a minor revision of the title of the fourth essay, these are the contents of *WJ*. In a letter to Royce, August 10, 1911, Brett officially accepted this book for publication by Macmillan Co.

I should be content with substantially the same copyright agreement, as to this proposed volume of essays, as the agreement that we made in the case of the "Race Prejudices" &c.

I am going over to Scotland to be present as Harvard delegate at the St. Andrews 500th Anniversary. I leave Aug. 19, and return about Sept. 25. If you can reply to me as to the proposed volume of essays before Thursday or Friday of next week, I shall be glad. You know, by this time, how my books go, and what you want of me. If you want to print, I can easily get a copy of the essay on "Immortality."

Yours Truly
Josiah Royce.

To Frederick James Eugene Woodbridge, January 5, 1912[258]

103 Irving St.
Cambridge,
Mass.
Jan. 5, 1912.

Dear Woodbridge:—

I enclose my proposed criticism of the committee's definitions.[259] If it is unwise, or too austere, or seems unkindly, suppress it—by burning it if you want. Otherwise print it if you will. If you think better to use it simply as a document for the records of the committee, do that.

In any case, I have no personal, i.e. private, interest to push in

[258] ALS. *Journal of Philosophy* Papers. CUB.

[259] "On Definitions and Debates," *Journal of Philosophy, Psychology, and Scientific Methods* 9 (1912): 85–100; reprinted in *RLE*, pp. 232–53. At the 1911 meeting of the American Philosophical Association, a general discussion was held on "The Relation of Consciousness and Object in Sense Perception." A committee, composed of the formal participants, also set limitations on the discussion by asking certain specific questions and by defining the critical terms. Royce, together with many members of the Association at the meeting, objected to this procedure and to these definitions on grounds that they were sometimes arbitrary, sometimes confused, and did not lead to fruitful paths of investigation. See H. A. Overstreet, "Eleventh Annual Meeting of the American Philosophical Association," *Journal of Philosophy, Psychology, and Scientific Methods* 9 (1912): 103–9.

the matter, and simply offer the paper for what it is worth, to be used or not, as you please.

Yours Truly
Josiah Royce

To George Platt Brett, January 7, 1912[260]

103 Irving St.
Cambridge,
Mass.
Jan. 7, 1912

Dear Mr. Brett:—

I have been too busy to write as I should have done in answer to your kind letter. The state of the case about the discussion of Christianity, proposed for my coming volume, is this:—

I am to take a Sabbatical year in 1912–13. This year of leave of absence, the next academic year,—so far as my powers permit, is to be devoted to study and writing. I have a special grant from the University,—the Cabot Fellowship,—to help in making the period of study free for production. I have a special arrangement with President Lowell to have me deliver one course of Lowell lectures, —on the Vital Features of Christianity ⟨the precise title to be arranged in due time⟩,—the lectures to come probably in Jan. or Feb. 1913. These lectures will be put into your hands as soon as delivered, and will constitute the book in question. Since no other work of an academic or otherwise engrossing sort, except my proposed studies, can interfere during the year in question, the lectures are likely to be ready in time.—So much, then, I can assure you. The proposed volume is in full prospect of being completed.

But, as in case of my Gifford Lectures, it is not possible to announce in detail what the book will be, until I am more nearly ready with it. Its plan you know. Its general character you can judge from my essay in the book just published by you.—I think that no further than a very general announcement,—say that Royce is preparing a book on the lines indicated in his recent volume of

260 ALS. Macmillan Papers. NYPL.

essays on *Wm. James* &c (see preface, & essay on Xianity) and that the book is to be expected in 1913—is yet in order.

I had recently to deliver in Lake Forest College a course of lectures on the so-called "Bross Foundation." The trustees of that foundation buy the copyright with the lectures and give the lecturer a lump sum. So there I had no control over the publication. But in that book, which is to be on *The Sources of Religious Insight*, I definitely say that I *omit* any study of Christianity therein, just because I propose, erelong, to write *another* book, intended to *apply* my philosophy to the special case of Christianity.

So the Bross Lectures, which the trustees of that foundation will soon publish in their own way, will not in the least forestall the book that I proposed to have you undertake if you will, but will, I hope, whet the curiosity of the reader for that book,—since my Bross book simply declines to discuss Christianity.

Yours Always
Josiah Royce.

To Frederick James Eugene Woodbridge, January 20, 1912[261]

103 Irving St.
Cambridge,
Mass.
Jan. 20, 1912.

Dear Professor Woodbridge:—

I see no way to shorten my article on "Definitions and Debates."[262] I am perfectly willing, however, to have it printed piecemeal,—say in two or three successive numbers. That I leave wholly to you.

Verbal discussions, such as my paper in this case is, are always unwelcome to me, and have to be minute,—if adequate at all,—in a case of this sort. But it is not my fault that the committee's definitions furnished what I have thus to treat as a verbal problem. I should like to deal with the matter more fruitfully. But since we are now committed to this sort of programme, it is well at this time

261 ALS. *Journal of Philosophy* Papers. CUB.
262 See fn. 259 above.

to discuss the committee's methods, despite the irksomeness of all such discussions. That is my sole reason for writing the paper. And I shortened it as much as I could.

Yours Truly
Josiah Royce.

To Frederick James Eugene Woodbridge, March 15, 1912[263]

103 Irving St.
Cambridge, Mass.
March 15, 1912.

Dear Professor Woodbridge:–

A word from me as to my state of health, and about my plans, may be of interest to you.

As you doubtless heard, I had, about February first, an apoplectic attack. The attack proved to be,–of its type,–a very light one; –as light, in fact, as any attack of the sort could be. What happened was a very minute cerebral haemorrhage, somewhere in the optic region, on the right side,–with the result of a left sided hemianopsia. Except for the defect of the field of vision (which I could only find out, myself, indirectly, since there was no immediate sense of the existence of any blank in the field), there were almost no objective symptoms. For a day or two after the attack there was some somnolence and confusion. Then there followed, of course, a good deal of depression and moodiness, with a general emotional flabbiness. And there were naturally plenty of headaches. But there was never any motor paralysis, or serious interference with mental processes of any level. I soon took to my usual interests and plans, with a considerable sense of relief from responsibilities; since the Harvard Corporation at once relieved me of my academic duties for the time, with a vote of full pay till September next. The field of vision rapidly cleared, and now only a moderate amount of fatigue symptoms remain. My medical advisors encourage me to keep all my usual interests alive; and I philosophize as cheerfully as ever, and plan essays, books &c., as if all were as before.–My heart,

263 ALS. *Journal of Philosophy* Papers. CUB. See Woodbridge TLC answer to this letter, March 18, 1912, CUB.

arteries, kidneys, &c., turn out, on examination, to be sound and in good order. My general nervous condition is better than it was before I thus took to loafing.

In brief, I have won a very fine vacation, which I could not have got in any other way. So nobody need shed any tears for me *at present.*

The prospects of a return of the seizure are, for the present,—according to my advisers,—small. Of course, *all* such attacks are serious, as far as they go. The cause was, I suppose, partly congenital. Several years of very severe strain, care, and contest with fortune, gave the occasion. A long walk in the cold and in the snow, Feb. 1, immediately preceded the definite attack.

So much I say, merely to give you the facts so far as I can. I am doing very well, then, as to my condition. I cannot return to *full* work for some time. But there is no ground for concern as to my prospects. I bid fair to live a bit longer, and to do a bit. I find myself fonder of my friends than ever; and I hope that you will call to see me whenever you are hereabouts; and that others also will come when they can.

Now as to one or two matters relating to my work as contributor, author, &c:—

First: *If* anybody wants to reply to anything in my paper on "Definitions & Debates," please don't suppress or hold back or discourage comments on that paper,—or on anything else of mine,—out of consideration for my health or for my feelings. I am all game enough for controversy, *if* anybody wants it; although my illness has left me a little disposed to the tender mood, and to a peaceful disposition, so that I shall not *provoke* any quarrels or any polemical disquisitions for some time to come. But should there be discussions, they will find me a willing and a cheerful reader.

Secondly: Your current number of the *Journal*, in the Notes, mentions my illness, and says that I have been "obliged to give up the Bross Lectures on the Sources of Religious Insight."[264] This note is inaccurate, although the mistake is not at all surprising. Here is the actual state of the facts:—

(a). The Bross Lectures in question, on "The Sources of Religious Insight" were finished last autumn, and were actually delivered in full, in accordance with my contract, at Lake Forest Col-

[264] *Journal of Philosophy, Psychology, and Scientific Methods* 9 (1912): 168.

lege, Illinois, last November. They were therefore *not* "given up." I received my full pay for them after delivery; and I handed over the complete MS to the Bross Trustees.

(b). The lectures in question are *now in press* (in page proofs). They will be published by Scribner's Sons very soon. No obstacle lies in the way of their publication. They should be out by May. My illness will delay their publication not an hour, after this.

(c). The only sense in which there had to be any "giving up" of matters relating to those lectures was this:—I had promised to *repeat* the reading of the MS of the lectures here at Harvard. The repetition was to be *gratis* and intended simply for my friends and students on the spot, as an advance reading of the forthcoming book. When, on Feb. 1, my little crack of a blood vessel occurred, it was necessary to give up *this* part of my plan. The Bross Lectures themselves, are safe, are in type, and will soon be in your hands.

—If you care to say anything further, about me, or about my dilapidated head piece, or about my lectures, &c.,—perhaps the foregoing may make it easier to correct whatever needs correcting. But really, I do not care to have any corrections made, unless you desire. What I want is, to send most affectionate greeting to my friends, to give hearty thanks to them for the numerous expressions of sympathy that have come to me, and to have them know (when they inquire), that I am doing well, am cheerful and hopeful, and mean to write more in due time.

"In the days of my youth," his father replied,
"I thought it might injure the brain,"
"But now I am perfectly sure I have none,
"I do it again and again."[265]

Yours With High Regard, and Hearty
Good Will,
Josiah Royce.

[265] An adaptation of Lewis Carroll, "Advice from a Caterpillar," *Alice's Adventures in Wonderland.*

To George Platt Brett, March 29, 1912[266]

103 Irving St.
Cambridge, Mass.
March 29, 1912.

My Dear Mr. Brett:—

I have been intending, for some time, to write to you as to the present state of my proposed book on the vital elements of Christianity. Illness has delayed my plans. I am now nearly recovered, but I have not found time to write my intended letter until now.

As to the illness itself,—you may have seen or heard the statement that, about Feb. 1, last, I had a slight attack of apoplexy. This statement is correct, although the attack in question was indeed *extremely* light. A very small haemorrhage in some blood vessel in the optic region of the brain, injured temporarily the left side of the field of vision. The attack occurred Feb. 1. The field of vision rapidly cleared up, and is now, for all practical purposes, in perfectly good condition. There was at no time any motor paralysis. There was temporarily a little confusedness from the shock; but there was no suspension of any important mental function, except for this purely temporary vexation. Memory, speech, coordinations of all sorts, &c., remained undisturbed. The net result is no discoverable impairment whatever. After careful examination, my medical advisers tell me to go on with study, reading, &c., as if nothing had happened; and simply advise that I should avoid the heavier cares and responsibilities of my profession,—such as lectures to classes, administration, &c. Harvard has accordingly granted me a leave of absence for the rest of the year. I am enjoying a good vacation; and have been reading more philosophy during the sixty days since my attack than I had read in any similar period for years before. My literary plans are prospering. I am in excellent spirits.

The result, however, makes it proper for me to plan a good and extended further vacation. I shall probably not travel much; and shall write a good deal. But my book will *not* be ready for publication next autumn. By agreement with President Lowell, I now propose to prepare my volume on Christianity as a course of Lowell lectures, to be delivered, if all goes well, in the spring of 1913, and

266 ALS. Macmillan Papers. NYPL.

to be ready for publication probably by the autumn of 1913. As I am also likely to deliver a course of "Hibbert Lectures" at Oxford in the summer or autumn of 1913, and shall probably arrange to use the same material (in part) for both the Lowell and the Hibbert course, it *may* prove best to publish the volume on Christianity as a volume of "Hibbert Lectures," rather than as a volume of Lowell lectures. This last matter concerns only the name and title,—not the topic or contents of the volume. But since the changes of the place and time of the delivery of the lectures (changes which will thus indirectly result from my present illness and my leave of absence), make any precise announcement of the precise title and the time of publication of my book at present impossible, I must beg you not to expect any announcement for publication from me this season. You are of course free to say in print, if you wish, that I propose to expand my recent essay on "What is Vital in Christianity" into a volume of lectures on the same topic; and that the volume is expected to be ready for publication in 1913. But I am not free to announce, as yet, whether the volume will be one of Lowell lectures or of Hibbert lectures. And my Oxford engagement is not yet quite officially settled, and cannot be mentioned in print for the present. I merely tell you the foregoing facts to show you that my plans for the book are prospering as well as could possibly be expected under the circumstances. Of course you do not wish me to hasten things unduly. If I am able to work over the material for an Oxford audience, the result will certainly be advantageous both for the volume, and for its sale. So the enforced delay will probably prove to be a very good thing for the plan.

Please do not make any other public announcement then, for the present, except a general statement that a volume on "What is Vital in Christianity" is in preparation by me, and is expected by sometime in 1913. You may call it a volume of lectures if you wish. But please do not mention either "Lowell" or "Hibbert" or "Oxford" lectures, or say anything about such matters, unless I notify you further.

My leisure for reading on the topic of the book is giving me daily new materials. And I am sure that the delay thus foced upon me will make the book better, and will result in making it more notable than it could otherwise be. In any case, the public interest of the topic will not decline before 1913!

I shall be glad to look over MSS for the firm from time to time if you send them; and I wish to be considered as in good shape for any current matter that you desire to call to my attentions. I write as I do because I am anxious to keep in touch with you, and to have you know how I am doing. I am certainly not neglecting the Christianity plan.

Yours Sincerely
Josiah Royce.

How does the volume of essays, *William James* &c., prosper?

To BERTRAND RUSSELL, APRIL 8, 1912[267]

103 Irving St.
Cambridge, Mass.
April 8, 1912.

Dear Mr. Russell:—

Before you receive this letter, you will doubtless have heard, from one or another of my colleagues, of the mishap which makes it inadvisable for me to attempt to accept the extremely kind and flattering invitation contained in your letter of the 16th of March. In fact, I have been recovering, with excellent success, but of course rather slowly, from a slight haemorrhage of the brain, which attacked me February first, last. The attack itself was the very *least* (so my medical advisers assure me) which is possible of its type. There was no motor paralysis, no interference with any notable mental process (apart from the immediate shock of the attack, and apart from the temporary depression and emotional flabbiness that attended the little incident). There was a slight damage to the field of vision on one side. This damage rapidly passed away, except for a slight remainder. In fact the whole was a mere "pinpoint" injury. But it has left some fatigue behind it. I work on my logic-studies much as usual; and greatly enjoy the leisure to read, and to work over some of the materials that, until this illness, my ordinary academic duties had prevented me from mastering as I had intended. I have secured a leave of absence from Harvard, and intend to make use of my enforced leisure to become a better student of logic. I shall not teach again for a year; and shall try to get some writing done.

In view of these facts, your kind proposal, of March 16, inviting

[267] ALS. Russell Archives. Continuum 1 Limited (London).

me to attend and to take part in the mathematical congress next August, is especially welcome and interesting. And were I *sure* of being in full condition for work and for travel as soon as my very good recovery, up to this date, has thus far indicated that I shall be, I should joyously accept your invitation, despite my little apoplexy and its consequences.

However, I find, upon consulting my medical advisers, that they do not think it best for me to promise to meet a public gathering so soon as August. They think that my vacation should be leisurely, and without new responsibilities of so serious a character as a Congress meeting within a few months. They require me to make haste slowly.

With very many thanks, then, for your kind invitation, I must most regretfully decline to attend the Congress, or to take part. I am sorry to have delayed this answer for a few days, until I could get this advice. I now have to abandon the hope of taking part in the Congress

While I write these words, the second volume of your *Principia* reaches me, forwarded, from you, through our Smithsonian Institution. I thank you deeply for the gift. I hope soon to finish some long planned work that I have yet to do on the first volume, and to spend part of my vacation on the second volume.

May I yet be able to get some logical work of my own done such as may serve to justify, in a measure, your kind words about the little that I have so far done.

With regret that I cannot be present, or take part in the Congress, I remain,

Heartily Yours
Josiah Royce.

To Alfred Deakin, April 17, 1912[268]

103 Irving St.
Cambridge,
Massachusetts, U.S.
April 17, 1912.

My Dear Mr. Deakin:—

Your two recent letters,—both so good,—and the second one

268 ALS. Deakin Papers. NLA.

so undeservedly kindly in its appreciation of my book of essays entitled *William James* &c.,—have found me at a time when I am especially able to prize such a friendly greeting.

On February first, last, I had a very slight stroke of apoplexy. It only very slightly injured my field of vision on one side. There was no disturbance of movement or speech. No motor paralysis has resulted. My mind is in as good shape as ever (so my advisers assure me after careful examination). But the attack produced some temporary depression, considerable fatigue and temporary weakness, and a good deal of sentimental longing for sympathy. Your letters, both of them, came as a boon and a blessing to both these moods. I thank you for your kind words a thousand times. I am now very much better; and your letters aided in the recovery.

I hope soon to be working as briskly as ever upon philosophy. Meanwhile I have one more book (just published) to send you.[269] It is one of the easiest of my books to read,—so I fancy. And it contains the whole sense of me in a brief compass. So sometime you may be pleased to show me still one more kindness and to read that also. It should reach you along with or shortly after this letter.

The shadows grow longer for both of us. But I want you to know what a comfort to me both the memory of our former meeting is, and the coming of any new letter from you always afresh brings.— May you prosper and live long to do your country good, and to cheer your friends.—

Yours Always,
Josiah Royce.

To George Platt Brett, June 5, 1912[270]

103 Irving St.
Cambridge, Mass.
June 5, 1912.

My Dear Mr. Brett:—

I have now in my hands the MS of a proposed textbook in Logic, which has come to me from the Macmillan Company for my opinion regarding its publication. The book is

[269] Presumably, *SRI*.
[270] ALS. Macmillan Papers. NYPL.

"Textbook in Logic
"Translated from the Italian work
"by G. Morando, by Rev. J. A. Dewe
"Duquesne University, Pittsburg, Pa."[271]

The MS attracts me in some respects. I am still in doubt how to estimate its relation to the present need in this country for new text-books in Logic. As the book is a Catholic text book with some notable modern coloring, it occupies a peculiar position, and is a little hard to estimate.

In order to reply properly to your request for an opinion, I need to know more than I do about the "Duquesne University," and its constituency, and the relation of the author to what is the probable view of Roman Catholic teachers, reviews, &c., as to the sort of tendency that this book represents. This is a "borderland" sort of book. It *might* appeal to non-Catholic teachers of Logic more or less. It might displease some Catholics (e.g. the Jesuits, who like "straight" scholastic logic). Judgment involves a delicate problem. I think the matter worth a little care.

If you think the matter worthwhile, please let me know what your information is about the Rev. J. A. Dewe, his institution, plans for publication, &c. I can then reply giving you my opinion of this text-book. I think the extra trouble to be possibly worthwhile for your purpose.

I seem to be in very good health now. I am busy on the "Christianity" book. The present plan is to deliver the book both as a course of Lowell Lectures, and as a longer course of (say 16) Hibbert Lectures in Oxford. The present proposed title is *The Problem of Christianity*. The MS ought to be in the main ready for you by April, 1913. I am not ready to make *public* announcement as yet; but the plan grows, and absorbs my main interests.

Yrs. Truly
Josiah Royce

[271] Macmillan Co. did not publish this work.

To George Platt Brett, June 12, 1912[272]

103 Irving St.
Cambridge,
Mass.
June 12, 1912.

My Dear Mr. Brett:—

My colleague and friend L. J. Henderson, M. D., Assistant Professor of Biological Chemistry in Harvard University, and one of the most original and active of the younger scientific men of the medical side of our institution, has been led, in connection with his special researches, to work out a discussion which seems to me to have very great philosophical, as well as scientific interest. I have advised him to make a book of it. The plan of this book is fully worked out; and three chapters of the little treatise lie, in finished form, on my own desk as I write. I have heard Henderson read these chapters to me. They are well and clearly written, are the work of a master, and include some of the most original views that I have heard for a long time. Quite spontaneously, and without any request to me from Henderson, I have offered to support, by my opinion and advice, any plan that he makes for the publication of his book when it is finished,—as it is likely to be finished within the coming year.

Henderson's topic is *The Fitness of the Environment*.[273] Approaching the subject as a physiological chemist, he has been led to certain generalizations as to the way in which the properties (and the probable evolution) of the existent chemical elements and substances, have been such as to be adapted, in advance of the appearance of life, for the production and preservation of living organisms. The result of these generalizations is to show a new way in which the physical world possesses a so-called "teleological constitution." Henderson treats the topic as a scientific man, and not as a speculative philosopher, and is very cautious as to the conclusions that he draws beyond the range of experimental science. But the philosophical side of these results will be obvious to any reader of the

[272] ALS. Macmillan Papers. NYPL.

[273] Lawrence Joseph Henderson, *The Fitness of the Environment: An Inquiry into the Biological Significance of the Properties of Matter* (New York: Macmillan Co., 1913).

book, and is extremely beautiful and novel. "Teleology" is, in these days of Bergson, Driesch, &c., once more in the forefront of public interest; and I should be surprised if Henderson's statement, crystal-clear, self-restrained, far reaching, and original, as it is, did not make, when it is finished, a very marked impression, and get a wide reading from his colleagues, and from the public interested in the larger problems of science and philosophy.

Henderson is no pupil or disciple of mine.[274] His chemical work is very remote from my range of studies. He is no enthusiast as to speculative interests. All the more, his ideas come to me as a free gift, that I prize much, and that I expect to find others prizing.

The proposed book on *The Fitness of the Environment* will contain somewhere between 100,000 and 150,000 words,—so Henderson tells me,—the smaller rather than the larger figure being the probable one. He does not write diffusely.

I have told Henderson that I should write to you telling you of his plan. I think that you might find it an advantageous plan to write him saying something to make him disposed to offer his MS to you whenever he gets it done. His position and record here make it quite safe to regard his enterprise as commercially feasible. At least that is my opinion. The matter has no connection, beyond what I have told you, with any of my own plans and interests; and I mention it to you for your own advantage, in case you take interest in it.

Henderson is not connected with the Philos'l Dep't here in any official way; but he has now been conducting, for two years past, an undergraduate course on the "History of Science" (using Merz's *History of European Thought in the 19th Century* as a text-book). This seems to me to be a very important course. Henderson is likely, in future, to develope in the direction of the history and philosophy of science; and I venture to suggest that, if you get into touch with him, he may be led to do various things that, in the future, you might find it important to publish. He seems to be a man with a future worth following. He is not yet in *Who's Who.* His address is 67 Sparks St., Cambridge.

My plans for my lectures on Christianity are progressing well. I write on them steadily.

Yours Truly
Josiah Royce

[274] Henderson did, however, participate frequently in Royce's seminar in logic.

To Richard Clarke Cabot, June 19, 1912[275]

103 Irving St.
Cambridge,
Mass.
June 19, 1912.

Dear Cabot:—

My son Edward, just after finishing a professionally successful year at the University of Illinois, as instructor in music, and after having accepted a new and somewhat more advantageous appointment which had been offered to him at a musical Institute in Westminster, Pennsylvania, set out, a fortnight or so since, to return here with his wife for the summer. Their baby boy is still with us, and is in that splendidly prosperous shape in which Dr. Ladd's care has put him.—But Edward and Elizabeth, visiting on the way their mother at Germantown, Penn., first telegraphed a few days ago that Elizabeth had a sudden "bronchial" attack (although a week before they had reported all well with the health of both of them), and then sent the news contained in the enclosed letter of Ned to his mother, received here yesterday. To you as an old friend I venture simply thus to enclose Ned's own words, because they help to indicate what the situation is, and in what spirit the poor kids take it so far. I know nothing else; but am prepared of course to do whatever I can for them when duly advised.

Now I hate to add to your cares, and to my many appeals for a kindliness that I can no longer hope ever to return to my good friends in any really effective way,—old hulk that I am. But *if* you could tell me how to see you for a short time within two or three days, perhaps you could make me one or two practical suggestions as to how we might advise our babes to proceed, both in the rest of their summer plans, & otherwise. I do not know who are their medical advisers in Germantown, and can speak now only for my own guidance.

When fortune lets me, I work a little on my lectures. The hope of getting a little done that may prove worth doing is, after all, my principal means of keeping up the sensible amount of pluck.

—Yours Always Affectionately
Josiah Royce.

275 ALS. Cabot Papers. HUA.

To Richard Clarke Cabot, June 24, 1912[276]

103 Irving St.
Cambridge, Mass.
June 24, 1912.

My Dear Cabot:—

I have no right to take an hour of your time on behalf of Ned. But your very kind suggestion about undertaking, under certain conditions, to go to see him and the "situation," is one of which I can only say, with a deep sense of my indebtedness, that whatever you think best to do about the matter has of course, in advance, the certainty of my full approval, so far as I have any right to deal with the matter at all. Ned is entirely ignorant of what to do. I know nothing of the medical adviser whose name you will have found in the letter of Ned that I yesterday forwarded to you. The family of dear Elizabeth have for years held as a pious article of faith the view that she is a great and beautiful treasure who *must* be regarded as in some mysterious way an invalid, to be repeatedly assured of the fact, and to be carefully protected from any sort of toil or care—with the exception of such toils as social frivolity or artistic interest might involve, and with the exception of such cares as their own solicitude, and their insistence upon her helplessness to judge for herself or to do for herself, might entail and of course have entailed. Physicians who have seen her have frequently thought or seemed to think, reasonably well of her constitution. Her own household have always held that she needed petting and scolding solely as a person with deeply invalid tendencies. She has been for years trained accordingly, with success.

This I say with regret, and of course in confidence, and solely because whatever the situation is, it is certainly dominated by that motive which I thus am compelled to characterize. So long as Elizabeth remains where she at the moment is, she will unquestionably be *as* helpless and *as* tuberculous as the most unreasonable solicitude can make her; and no reasonably courageous or vigorous policy or procedure will be either permitted or even considered.

I hope that I speak with no unjust motive. Of course I ought not to judge anything connected with the case. What I say is of no

[276] ALS. Cabot Papers. HUA.

importance as a guide. I can only say what I have good reason to suppose true, so far as my poor wits guide me.

Elizabeth herself seems to me in many ways a very sensible girl, and is certainly a very faithful and devoted one. She is intelligent, well-read, cultivated, and at heart religious in a real sense. She has never been permitted to become a capable woman. I do not know why she might not become one. If ineffectiveness *can* be made fatal to her, it will be made so in case the advisers who intend to keep her ineffective remain in touch with her daily doings, and influence the conduct of her case. Her present visit at home was intended to be a very brief one on her way to be with her baby here. You see the result so far. The baby is with us, as you know.

So unquestionably Ned,—who knows and sees much of all this, but who is absorbed in his art in the way that his last letter shows,—needs positive and sensible personal advice and direction. For various reasons I cannot write to him as effectively as I could wish, in the present situation. I am obliged, by motives of discretion, to confine what I just now say to him in my letters, to general expressions of paternal sympathy, and to assurances that I propose to stand by him until my end. He is a heartily good boy, and deserves a better fate. His professional work seems to have been successful since he got to work as a teacher. His teaching, guidance of chorus work &c. have shown apparently fine qualities. He has done well in academic sorts of public concerts &c., and in his own calling promises to get a decent standing, unless he is overdriven. But he has no skill in coping with such a conspiracy of fortunes and of other conditions as now seems to confront him. Nor can I do anything myself but sit by while these conditions aim to wreck both of these young lives.

Approached discreetly, Ned would probably take good advice easily and kindly. He is amiable, and very square and trustworthy, and a worshipper of his wife. She is immensely devoted to him. Both of them are, as you see, in many ways, babes.—As I feel myself also a babe—the more so the older I grow,—I cannot complain of the young people.

Don't spend time or care on us beyond absolute necessity. I deeply regret causing care to my friends in this or in any other way.

Your words about my book are very dear and heart warming,

and are also full of real instruction and guidance. I will answer them soon,—especially as to the point about "beauty."

—Yours Always Affectionately,
Josiah Royce.

On Friday next, the 28th, I have my passage engaged on the United Fruit banana boat for Port Limón, Costa Rica, for the round trip only,—due on return by July 15;—I do not like to desert my post, but need the chance to work as steadily as possible at sea, in good conditions, on my lectures. There is no way of foreseeing that I could be of use by abandoning the trip. I must do the best I can to get the job done. In my absence, I of course fully authorize any act of yours on my behalf as your please.

To RICHARD CLARKE CABOT, JUNE 25, 1912[277]

103 Irving St.
Cambridge,
June 25, 1912.

Dear Cabot:

Your letter received this morning gives me great comfort, and once more I thank you from the whole heart. You are doing all that can be done to help us all.

Your words about my book have been carefully pondered as my time and momentary preoccupation permit. What is needed at the moment is a word of reply to you as to "beauty."—Yes, beauty is a "source" that my list ought to have contained, and that you, I am sure, will rightly emphasize in your coming book, and that I want you to emphasize and interpret.[278] My omission of that source is a defect, and needs a simple confession as such, although I believe that I have never heretofore told you what I suppose to be the nature and source of this defect in my view of such things. Personally, I have *some* access to beauty especially in *two* realms, viz.; music, and nature-beauty; together with a fairly warm, but, as you know, limited access to poetry. As to music and nature-beauty, I am, and must remain, naïve, ignorant,—at best childlike. My own childhood was passed in a mining town, and later in S. F. I never

277 ALS. Cabot Papers. HUA.

278 Royce does not include "beauty" as one of the "sources" in *SRI*.

saw any beautiful object that man had made until after I was twenty years of age, I left California for Germany.—I do know enough about such beauty as it is given me to love, to feel deeply the vanity of my saying anything abstract about it when I am so ignorant. I never was, in my youth, a person "cultivated" in any aesthetic sense; and I remain more barbarous as to such matters than you can easily suspect. Of beauty, therefore, I must not prophesy. The less I say about beauty, the more sincere will be, and sound, the little that I have any right on occasion to stammer. That is very little. So when I get my moment or days of enjoyment of beauty,—alone with the sea, or with the hills,—or when my soul gets free again to listen a little to what (before so much tragic association came to cloud my appreciation), *was* one great source of strength to me,—namely music,—well, when such times now come to me, I try to remain a little child as to beauty, and to say nothing. For if I preached of what I know in such matters, some would be repelled by my real ignorance, and others would justly think me engaged in filling up my columns with more "copy," or would regard me as playing the professor simply with a view to saying something more than I had yet crammed into print.

So here is the defect. It is subjective and insignificant. I do best not to mention it. What beauty I *have* known has meant to me some things that I long to be able to say, if so I might, and that have brightened the world for me with a light that I deeply wish to be able to characterize. But it all remains for me, in *this* life, either unutterable, or tragic, or sacred. And I must not and will not preach about it; for such preaching, *for me*, would prove to be prating. Read me then, always subject to this defect, which you, or anybody, must condemn, without my being able to defend myself.

I leave, as I told you, next Friday, for my little sea voyage. May all be well with you and yours.

Yours Always Affectionately,
J. Royce.

To George Herbert Palmer, August 15, 1912[279]

103 Irving St.
Cambridge,
Mass.
Aug. 15,1912.

Dear Palmer:—

Many thanks for the letter of Santayana, which I return.[280] As you say, he speaks for the moment with a very human, and, as I suppose, a very sincere and hearty voice. Yet, as I finish the letter, I find him, after all, passing away to his own region in his own heavens, where he discourses with the seraphs of his own order and choir; and I find myself sad to be left behind. I cannot follow, although I would fain do so. In any case he promises to be both happy and increasingly valuable. I hope that his books will come soon.

I have been most of the time on the sea, and shall go again to-morrow. Four lectures of my eight Lowell lectures on the "Problem of Christianity" are now, after much reading of literature and much planning, and much rewriting, finished in type written form. The next four will go more rapidly. The task gives me a better hold on whatever powers I have than any other plan could do. I seem to be doing very well as to health.

—Yours Most Affectionately
Josiah Royce

Mrs. Royce sends love.

Loewenberg's outcome is indeed good.[281] I am glad of him,—very glad.

279 ALS. WCL.

280 Santayana formally submitted his resignation from the Harvard faculty on June 6, 1912.

281 Professor Loewenberg has informed the editor that this might be a reference to his being appointed to the faculty of Wellesley College.

To Warner Fite, September 5, 1912[282]

103 Irving St.
Cambridge,
Mass.
Sept. 5, 1912.

My Dear Professor Fite:—

Yours of August 11 came to me just as I was getting ready to take my MSS with me for one more voyage; and I had no time to answer then. I hope that this is in time to find you before you leave your Maine summer place. I fully agree with you "that to ascribe to Jesus the last word in ethical insight," implies a position inconsistent with that of the really representative "modern man." My own position is that the recorded parables and sayings (to say nothing of the fragmentary view that we have of his person and life), actually cry out for a further interpretation, beyond what the records contain. Here is no "last word in ethical insight" expressed. The master intended (if I judge the reports rightly,—so far as they are authentic at all)—he intended, I say, to have the "grain of mustard seed" *grow*. The seed is the beginning of an ethical insight, and not the last word (if I may mix the metaphors). You are surely right, also that our modern ethical ideals are "an essential advance upon the ideals of Jesus."

My lectures on "The Problem of Christianity," planned for delivery partly at the Lowell Institute in Boston late in November, partly at Oxford between Jan 12 and the middle of March next, will be a definite effort to interpret the essence of Christianity in the light of some of its leading ideas, as these gradually developed in the apostolic and post apostolic churches, and as these same ideas are with us (as developing, and not as finished ideas), today, not only in the Church but in the world. There will be some new things in the lectures, I think,—despite the age of the subject.— Certainly, I am neither an apologist for traditional Christianity, nor one who can see in modern Liberal Christianity anything but an effort to lose the best in Christianity, by attempting to get back to its "primitive state."

282 ALS. Royce Papers. HUA.

I hope to see you soon again, as you pass through.

Yours Always
J. Royce.

To George Platt Brett, September 6, 1912[283]

103 Irving St.
Cambridge, Mass.
Sept. 6, 1912

Mr. Geo. P. Brett:—

My Dear Mr. Brett:—

My proposed work on *The Problem of Christianity* (that being, as you will remember, the altered title which I now propose for the book), has progressed to a stage where I wish to give you more definite expectations than I could last June.

I have definitely arranged to deliver a course of *sixteen* lectures on "The Hibbert Foundation" at Manchester College Oxford, in January, February, March, next. The title of that course will be "The Problem of Christianity." *Eight* of these lectures, under the same title, will be delivered before the Lowell Institute in Boston in November and December next. I have permission to use the material for both courses.

The result of thus combining a Lowell Institute course with an Oxford course,—the Lowell course of eight lectures, and some additional lectures for Oxford—is that, as I write out the lectures, they naturally fall into two parts, of eight lectures each. The lectures run fairly uniformly a little over 9000 words each, but usually not over 10,000. Each part would make a book, about the size of my *Philosophy of Loyalty*. Each could be printed separately. The first part is so nearly an independent book, that it could be published & sold without any need of waiting for the second part. Of the Lowell lectures,—the first part of the whole,—*seven* are now completed in MS. The eighth will be ready within three or four weeks. The second part ought to be finished before I set out for Oxford in December,—say by Christmas.

283 ALS. Macmillan Papers. NYPL.

This being the present state of affairs, I am ready to get your view of the following questions:—

(1). In your opinion, is it best to publish the sixteen lectures all together as one large volume, or to publish the book in two parts, of eight lectures each, selling the first part separately to people who may not want to buy the second (as you do in case of my *World & Individual*)?

(2). If you elect to publish in two parts, shall I send on the eight lectures of the first part as soon as I have a typewritten copy ready? And would you then begin at once getting that part through the press, without waiting for the second?

(3). If you prefer this plan, is it well to amend our present copyright agreement, or to make a new one, in order to cover the case of the second volume? What royalty &c., would you offer for the second part?

(4). I suppose that at least the first part could be published by April 1, next. Could proofs be sent me at Oxford, during my stay there, so as to push on the second part as well as possible? And if the second part were completed in time, could the publication of the two parts be nearly contemporaneous? I may have the second part ready before I set out for England.

In order that you may know how the present plan stands in my mind, I enclose a sketch of the contents of the two-part book as now planned.

The Problem of Christianity ⟨General Title for the two volumes⟩
Part I. The Christian Doctrine of Life. ⟨Say 75,000 words or with notes &c. 90,000 words at most.⟩

Lecture I. The Problem and the Method
" II. The Idea of the Universal Community
" III. The Moral Burden of the Individual
" IV. The Realm of Grace
" V. Time and Guilt
" VI. Atonement
" VII. The Christian Doctrine of Life
" VIII. The Modern Mind and the Christian Ideas

Part II. The Christian Ideas and the Real World.

Lectures IX to XVI. ⟨Nothing yet written on this part. Plans fairly worked out.⟩[284]

[284] In the margin Royce writes: "Lectures I–VII now ready in MS."

If you elect to have the first part sent to you as soon as I get it typewritten, it would be possible for you to make announcement soon. I should need to see proofs of the announcements, to avoid mistakes due to the mixing of my Lowell Inst., and of my Oxford plan. I suppose that the announcement should run thus, whenever the lectures have been delivered:—

The Probl. of Chr. ⟨as above⟩
⟨appointed to be⟩
"Lectures delivered on the Hibbert Foundation,
Manchester College, Oxford, in Jan–March, 1913;
and before the Lowell Institute in Boston, Nov.
Dec., 1912."

Since I may not be able to deliver the lectures,—if health prevents,—the announcement should be, in advance of delivery, worded accordingly,—that is cautiously.

One thing more:—I may be able to arrange with one or two editors for an advance publication of some of the lectures in magazines either here or in England.[285] So long as such publication were in advance of yours, I suppose that you see *no* objection to such a plan. If so, please notify me.

I am fairly well now, and, as you see, am writing pretty busily. Please excuse my long letter.—

Yours Sincerely
Josiah Royce.

To Arthur Oncken Lovejoy, November 8, 1912[286]

103 Irving St.
Cambridge,
Mass.
November 8, 1912.

Dear Lovejoy:—

I have long prized your work; and am especially instructed by

[285] Three parts of *PC*, 1, were published separately: "The Second Death" and "Atonement" were printed in the *Atlantic Monthly* 111 (1913): 242–54, 406–19; "The Christian Doctrine of Life," *The Hibbert Journal* 11 (1912–13), 473–96.

[286] ALS. Lovejoy Papers. JHU.

your recent studies of "Time" problems.[287] I await the remaining papers on "Time" with interest.

I believe that I have always treated you with respect, as well as friendship.

On p. 634 of the current number of Woodbridge's *Journal* I find words of yours which seem to me to need a little explanation.[288] They stand in a context in which the same thoughts as the ones which I have to ask you to explain are two or three times repeated. As I understand the matter, you accuse some friend of yours of deliberate and willful "imposture."[289] You repeat and vary the charge with use of the form of innuendo, in such wise as to make reply impossible. You thereby shield your attack. You in substance also appear to make Perry responsible for the same attack. I believe that Perry himself has avoided such responsibility, and is very scrupulous about fair play in polemic.

Now I suppose that you do *not* wish to use the privileges of Roosevelt. I suppose also that you do *not* mean wantonly to insult an old friend. But a repeated accusation of "imposture" constitutes an insult. An accusation so shielded as to be quite secure against any reply that one would print, does *not* constitute fair play. Such has to be my impression of the matter, despite the supposition that I have just mentioned.

I have long tried,—vainly it seems, to promote mutual and kindly understanding in philosophy. Do we gain by this talk about "im-

[287] Lovejoy wrote much on this topic; Royce probably has direct reference to "The Problem of Time in Recent French Philosophy," *Philosophical Review* 21 (1912): 11–31, 322–43, 527–45.

[288] " 'Present Philosophical Tendencies'," *Journal of Philosophy, Psychology, and Scientific Methods* 9 (1912): 627–40, 673–84. A review of Ralph Barton Perry, *Present Philosophical Tendencies: A Critical Survey of Naturalism, Idealism, Pragmatism and Realism* . . . (New York: Longmans, Green and Co., 1912). On p. 634, Lovejoy writes: "One of the most admirable chapters in the book, that entitled 'Absolute Idealism and Religion,' exposes with merciless lucidity the confusions and equivocations through which alone many neo-Kantian or eternalistic idealisms of the last half-century have acquired a speciously edifying sound:—for example, the confusion, characteristic of much of Eucken's writing, between the notion of 'the primacy of spirit' in a purely epistemological and practically barren sense, and the notion of man's practical dominance over his environment and of his power over it and over himself. Especially telling is Perry's 'showing-up' of the imposture in the pseudo-voluntarism of the neo-Fichteans."

[289] Presumably Royce himself (though Lovejoy seems to have denied this intent) and possibly also Hugo Münsterberg, who was most open in tracing his heritage to Fichte.

posture"? Do you help your friend, or yourself by insulting words? —But no doubt you can easily set me right.

Yours Truly
J. Royce.

To Ralph Barton Perry, November 11, 1912[290]

103 Irving St., Cambridge.
Nov. 11, 1912.

Dear Perry:—

I mentioned to you the other evening my letter to Lovejoy, to which the enclosed is a reply. I pointed out to him, in that letter, three matters:—(1) That he accused some friend of his of "imposture"; (2) That he shielded himself, quite unjustifiably, I believe, behind you in making this charge; (3) That he repeatedly, in the form of innuendo, so returned to the charge in various ways that, while no initiated reader was likely to mistake his meaning, a printed reply was impossible. All this, I said was not fair play in controversy. I added that I myself have long tried to promote mutual understanding and good will in philosophy, and have prized his own work highly.

Of course I have no temptation to reply to Lovejoy's letter, or to the article in Woodbridge's *Journal.* Nor do I ask you to take the least trouble about the matter. I believe that you and I understand each other, as to all our personal and controversial interests, very well, and disagree only with the heartiest good will and the most genuine friendship. I am sorry to call to your attention any such matter. But Lovejoy remains a fact that we have to consider. I will not characterize his letter further, at present. "Imposture" is not an "equivocal word."—

Yours Apologetically
J. Royce.

[290] ALS. Perry Papers. HUA.

To Arthur Oncken Lovejoy, December 30, 1912[291]

103 Irving St.
Cambridge, Mass.
Dec. 30, 1912.

Dear Professor Lovejoy:—

I beg to thank you for your very kind and friendly letter printed in Woodbridge's *Journal*.[292] Objectively, of course, it quite covers all the ground that was suggested, as well as the ground that was directly mentioned, in my letter to you, and completely removes every cause for complaint. So far as my own mind is concerned, I assure you that I am wholly content with your attitude and position, in respect of all the personal regrets that my former letter expressed about your original statement as I then understood it. I regret, on my own behalf, any unnecessary asperity and any unkindness, of my own letter to you. I hope that I may have the opportunity in future to treat you as generously as you have now treated me.

As to the ethical question itself:—I personally believe entirely in the sincerety of the neo-Fichtean, of Eucken, and of the rest, whom you had in mind in your criticism. In dealing with the words and phrases that already are supposed to have had their range of meaning established by popular religious usage, I have always acted under the influence of what Socrates says, in the *Phaedrus*, as he prepares to begin his "palinode" about Love. Socrates found the word "love" misused. He proposed a new account of its meaning. "God," "salvation," "the good," "evil," "love," "grace," and a hundred other terms of popular religion, are simply *not* terms whose relation to a technical definition of the problems at issue either has been or can be settled in advance of philosophical reflection, by the popular consciousness of any one or any dozen ages of religious opinion. The popular mind is deep, and means a thousand times more than it explicitly knows. The philosopher's endless task is to

[291] ALS. Lovejoy Papers. JHU.

[292] See "Letter from Professor Lovejoy," *Journal of Philosophy, Psychology, and Scientific Methods* 9 (1912), 720–21, where Lovejoy withdraws the word "imposture" and restates his criticism.

find out what this deep mind means, and to tell what it means. He ought to be as careful as he can to make clear what he means. He has a right to interpret as best he can the popular mind while he does his own work. His interpretation is always open to criticism. But it seems to me useless to tell him that the popular mind has settled for him in advance the meaning of the very terms which it is his main business to subject to a process of reflection such as the popular mind has not yet reached.—

Yours Most Cordially,
J. Royce.

To Ralph Barton Perry, January 6, 1913[293]

On Board the
Cunard
R. M. S. "Campania."
Monday noon
Jan. 6, 1913

Dear Perry:—

We are nearing the Irish coast, after a very fair sort of a winter-voyage. I write to acknowledge your kind note of farewell, which I received at the dock in New York. I am in apparently good health, after finding the sea as good to me as it usually is; and I expect to be in good shape for my lecture job. The lectures are safely stowed in my bag; and I begin them Jan. 13 if all goes well. I shall do whatever I can about Russell and Hoernlé[294]; and also about Hobhouse (whom I am only to "observe," as I understand).—If there is anything to report, I shall do so as soon as I get facts or fancies worth reporting.

Please remember me to all the department, and in particular to Bakewell. My best wishes and hearty New Year's greetings to

[293] ALS. Perry Papers. HUA.

[294] In addition to delivering the Hibbert Lectures at Oxford, Royce was appointed to attempt to rebuild the Harvard Philosophy Department. As subsequent letters describe, his efforts to get Bertrand Russell permanently to Harvard failed. R. F. Alfred Hoernlé joined the Harvard faculty in September, 1913.

your family, and my especially good wishes for the new home that you are soon to build.—When do you begin building?[295]

Yours Truly
Josiah Royce.

To Ralph Barton Perry, January 29, 1913[296]

Manchester College
Oxford Jan 29 1913

Dear Perry:—

Jacks has been obliged to decline the offer of Peabody's chair.[297] But Jacks will be able at once to give me great aid in finding out about Hobhouse, who is just at the moment in Italy. Without Jacks I could not be able to find where Hobhouse is during his absence; and should not be able to get in touch with him. But while I failed to get Jacks himself for Peabody's place, the failure itself puts into my hands the aid of a most competent adviser about men, and a controller of the means of getting further information about them. For the editor of the *Hibbert Journal* is a good bureau of information in himself, and will act confidentially as well as in a most friendly mood. Jacks told me of his own decision about Peabody's place last night. I then at once laid before him the Hobhouse problem, of which he had had no previous hint; and Jacks took a warm, but now, of course, quite unprejudiced interest in this matter. Jacks believes Hobhouse to be a very good teacher, as well as writer, and also is strongly hopeful that we can get him, and thinks that the Department has been right in its estimate of his various values as man & philosopher. I appreciate the need of promptness, and the gravity of our Harvard situation in philosophy. I shall let you hear further as soon as I can get the information about Hobhouse. I have so written to President Lowell. I send regards and greetings to all the Department.

Yours Always
Josiah Royce.

[295] In 1913 Perry built a house on the east side of Irving Street.

[296] ALS. Perry Papers. HUA.

[297] Francis Greenwood Peabody retired as Plummer Professor of Christian Morals in 1913; Lawrence Pearsall Jacks, editor of the *Hibbert Journal*, became principal of Manchester College, Oxford, in 1915.

Jacks supposes Russell to be wholly inaccessible to us.—For Russell is the only man of scientific genius whom his ancient family has produced. The family will hold him fast.

To Jacob Loewenberg, January 31, 1913[298]

Manchester College
Oxford Jan. 31 1913

Dear Loewenberg:—

I lecture here to an audience which, as they tell me is as good,—on the whole—as the Oxford conditions make possible for lectures of this kind. Some very good people are present each time. I am doing well as to my health. I live with the same routine as at home, have an early morning walk in the beautiful park here, whatever the weather, and am trying to lead a discreet sort of a life.

I have sent today, to the Macmillan Co., the corrected galley proofs of Vol. I, entire. The page-proofs of that volume should be soon in Mrs. Royce's hands. Will you, for fifty dollars, make an index, from the page proofs? I propose soon to send, through Mrs. Royce, a few instructions as to how the index is to be devised. You are the only person besides myself who could properly make the index. The offer of compensation is small; but the book is much smaller than was the Kühnemann.[299]—They treat me very kindly here, and the climate is reasonably decent. I do not now see why I shouldn't get through the whole affair in reasonable shape, and without making any international scandals. After all, this isn't Berlin, and I am no diplomat! ! A suffrage outbreak seems imminent; but I shall try to avoid feminine wiles & stone-throwing.

Mrs Royce tells me good things of you. I am glad to hear of your good health and spirits, and of your work.

Yours Always
Josiah Royce

[298] ALS. Printed in facsimile in *The Letters of Western Authors: A Series of Letters, Reproduced in Facsimile of Twelve Distinguished Pacific Coast Authors of the Past . . .*, no. 8 (San Francisco: The Book Club of California, 1935). Professor Loewenberg has informed the editor that the original for this letter and all of his other letters from Royce have been lost.

[299] Eugen Kühnemann, *Schiller*, 2 vols. (Boston: Ginn and Co., 1912), translated by Katharine Royce with an introduction by Josiah Royce.

To Bertrand Russell, February 2, 1913[300]

Manchester College
Oxford Feb. 2, 1913

Dear Mr. Russell:—

I thank you very much for your kind invitation to lunch with you at Cambridge, at Trinity College, on Tuesday the 4th, when I shall leave Oxford, as you advise, by the 10.50 train, arriving 1.20.

I have, as you know, to return the same afternoon. But you need not think about my diet, or about any other invalid provision for the care of me. I am really quite well now, except that it is well for me not to be away from my usual surroundings over night, unless I make special arrangements for such a journey. The night is the only time when I have to be careful.

It will be a satisfaction to talk over your coming Harvard work with you. I need not say that we are all expecting a great many good times as a part and as a result of your visit to America. With pleasant anticipations of our meeting I remain,

Sincerely Yours
Josiah Royce.

To Ralph Barton Perry, February 11, 1913[301]

Manchester College
Feb. 11, 1913.

Dear Perry:—

I feel like an unwilling but doomed bachelor who is always proposing to somebody. It is useless to duplicate what I have written to Lowell; I refer you to my letter to him of this date, which he will probably let you see.[302] I shall probably consult James Ward before long as to possible younger men. There seems to be one young man in Scotland, as Assistant of Jones, about whom I may be able to say

[300] ALS. Russell Archives. Continuum 1 Limited (London).

[301] ALS. Perry Papers. HUA.

[302] In a twelve page letter to President Lowell, also dated February 11, 1913, Royce reported on his unsuccessful efforts in recruitment. The contents of the two letters are nearly identical.

something soon. I am impressed with what I learn both about young Moberly and about Alexander Lindsay.[303] Joachim,[304] and several of the other younger philosophers here are *very* strong men, but too technical in their bearing and interest for our sort of job. J. A. Smith is really *great*, but not only too old, but as inaccessible for our purpose as an archangel, and as critically dialectical as Mephistopheles,—although otherwise a beautiful personality.

Russell, with whom I have had a very long talk, is utterly immovable for any permanent foreign appointment. In his larger "theory of knowledge" course at Harvard, he would like to find men already more or less trained in Hume. He thinks of using Poincaré as an elementary text-book in this larger course, also Couturat in French if possible. He would also like the men to be trained beforehand (in your first half year of work with them), in James's *Pragmatism* so as to face those issues readily. He plainly thinks well of your own Introduction to Philosophy[305] as part of the preparation for this general course in Theory of Knowl.

Russell would like to enlarge the income furnished by his own Harvard course. He seems to be not exactly over wealthy in worldly goods, although not poor. It seems that you have already informally mentioned to him in a letter the possibility that there might be a Lowell Institute Course. He seems now to be so awake to the ethical and religious attitudes that have already been suggested in his *Philosophical Essays*, and in his (really wonderful) recent *Hibbert Journal* article (of last autumn, I think)[306] that I believe it to be decidedly possible that he could if Lowell consents prepare a Lowell Institute Course of great originality, and power, on some of the general life-problems. The course would be "radical" but inspiring. There is a wonderful frosty atmosphere about Russell's mind just now,—an infinitely pathetic and manly and calm resoluteness: His last *Hibbert Journal* essay on "religion" was to me like a landscape of moonlight on the snow, when a cold wave has just died out and become still. This sounds sentimental, but is not in his case, such. He has seen deeply into the dark.

For the rest, Russell wants to know whether an academic extra

[303] Walter Hamilton Moberly was a Fellow of Lincoln College, Oxford; Alexander Dunlop Lindsay was a Fellow of Balliol College, Oxford.

[304] Harold Henry Joachim was a Fellow and Tutor of Merton College, Oxford.

[305] *The Approach to Philosophy* (New York: Charles Scribner's Sons, 1905).

[306] "The Essence of Religion," *Hibbert Journal* 11 (October, 1912): 46–62.

course could be arranged for him at Columbia,—once a week, perhaps,—on spare days. I do not know what his topic would be,—perhaps Logic. Write him about it when you can. His advanced logic course with us will certainly need a good assistant, able to take care of technical matters and papers. Otherwise that course will easily take care of itself.

There is no doubt that Russell is a great man; and we must make the best of our half year with him.—I have not been idle as to our interests.—All are very kind to me here. I seem to be well.—

Yours Always
Josiah Royce.

Show this to Lowell or to colleagues as you think best.

To Lawrence Joseph Henderson, March 22, 1913[307]

On Board the
Cunard
R. M. S. "Ivernia."
March 22, 1913

Dear Henderson:—

I had no time to tell you, during the last busy days of my Oxford visit, about my little efforts to call the attention of my friends to your book, in advance of the reviewers who will no doubt soon find their way to it.[308]

Your proofs went with me in a bag. I did not know when I left home when the book would be published. My first effort at Oxford to call attention to its coming was in a conversation with F. C. S. Schiller,—who, as you know, is the double dyed pragmatist who would have packed up & carried off James's mantle if there had ever been one to fall from the chariot. But James disliked being called a prophet, & left no mantle. Schiller has lost some of his old polemic aggressiveness, but has not thereby gained in ideas. He still plays "jesting Pilate," never stays for an answer, and never takes any more new ideas. On hearing of the topic of your book, he at once replied to me that all such ideas must be old stuff. You couldn't prove teleology that way. He had heard about the be-

[307] ALS. Henderson Papers. HUA.

[308] *The Fitness of the Environment* (New York: Macmillan Co., 1913).

havior of water near the freezing point when he was a child. He didn't want to hear any more. Besides,—a designer "would have to be a finite being." He was a "teleologist" himself in a pragmatic way. But philosophy had nothing in particular to learn from chemists.—This pragmatistic point of view (as thus expressed by Schiller to me) was important merely because Schiller is, just now, president of the "Philosophical Society,"—a very interesting group of mostly younger Oxford philosophers. Of course if he decided *a priori* (being himself an empiricist) that he didn't want to know anything new about "fitness," then the "fit" way to call attention to your book would not easily become mine; and so far I should be unable to help the new book onwards at Oxford so early. I didn't suppose my poor efforts to be useful in any really needed way. But Jacks and I wanted to get a little further if we could. For a good start helps a book.

So next I told some bits of your story to Jacks's seminary,—a company of young theologues, who are mostly deep in social questions, and who know much more about suffragettes than about either chemistry or theology; but they are "plastic youth" in the Socratic sense, and have had some very valuable philosophical training from Jacks, in his own lines of problems.

So I told them about your book one day, and showed them the proofs. The ablest man of the lot was deeply impressed: "Just fancy," he said, "that the world should go and give away to one man *such* a part of its secret as *that*." So I saw that even the babes and sucklings were able to have these things revealed to them. And since I myself am as innocent of chemistry as are these theologues, I could only attempt to prophesy to the philosophers a little, using simply your own words.

By this time my social obligations in Oxford were accumulating. For everybody had been, as is their nature there, *very* kind. I was staying in lodgings at Manchester College. Jacks and Carpenter, who had already done much for me otherwise, now, at my request, generously granted me the privilege of using the dining room and the household staff of the College at my own expense to get up a bit of an entertainment to pay off my Oxford debts, or some of them. So then I next conspired with the Secretary of the "Philosophical Society"—one J. L. Stocks,—to call an "extra meeting" of the Society,—despite Schiller's indifference,—wherein I should expound something of your "fitness." I invited, in return, the "Committee" of this society, and some other philosophers, to come, in advance of this "extra meeting," on the evening of March 1, to dine with me in hall at Manchester College,—at 7 o'clock,—the general meeting of the Society coming at 9 P. M. (—while a larger company than I could hope to dine, would take part in this more general meeting). Jacks and Carpenter I invited also to be my guests at the dinner.

Accordingly, about a fortnight in advance of March 1, I found an amiable secretary-lady to prepare my invitations; and appealed to the steward of Manchester College,—a high and mighty official of the place, and an amiable person also, to devise a "contrapshun," —to be called a dinner.

The steward in question is no genius as a caterer; but he did his best, by March 1, to make the "environment" a little bit "fit." We had some carbonic acid, and a little water, and various compounds of the "three elements." There was also one alcohol in the environment,—and of course we tried to have it exceed the water in quantity. If I may judge by flavors, names, and some other indications, I think that there were *more* alcohols than one scattered about, here & there. We got as near to Harvard colors in decoration as we could; but that was hard to compass owing to the state of the market. Oxford dark-blue we mingled in with the rest; and *that* part could be made more certainly authentic.

The evening came, and the philosophers assembled. Grippe (then epidemic in Oxford), and various romantic entanglements of the Secretary of the Society, and of other of the younger philosophers, together led to the loss of some of our guests;—26 or 27 had accepted. But at last we sat down 20 at table, including myself.[309] The dinner company was very varied in studies, opinions, and academic seniority however; and I felt very content with them. —After dinner, at 9 P. M., we went to the general Society "extra meeting," which was much better still as a company; for to my special guests a good many good men were added. So your introduction, poor as I had to make it, was made to a strong company.

309 Royce kept a guest list for this dinner in one of his logic notebooks (Royce Papers, HUA); it includes Vernon Bartlett, Estlin Carpenter, F. Rudolph Hoernlé, L. P. Jacks, A. D. Lindsay, W. McDougall, W. H. Moberly, R. R. Merrett, Gilbert Murray, J. E. Odgers, John Powell, W. B. Selbie, D. C. Simpson, J. A. Smith, J. A. Stewart, H. Sturt, H. H. Turner, G. E. Underhill, Albert Way, and Royce. Those who declined were F. C. S. Schiller, Sidney Ball, R. Alfred Hoernlé, Sir William Osler, Canon Rashdall, and J. L. Stocks.

I delivered an exordium on the conception of "fitness" in general, —much in the taste of my old seminary talks on conceptions. Then I told some of your story, in your own terms. Then followed a discussion.—The best contribution to this discussion in the whole evening was a pretty point made by Turner the astronomer, who with characteristic skill aimed at the heart of things, seeing your main idea at once, although it was wholly new to him. He remarked that, until recently, the evidence for the *wide* cosmical distribution of oxygen had seemed,—to him personally,—very small. Only β (of something or other which I forget) had shown direct stellar evidence of oxygen until a few years ago. Since then O, in combination with Titanium (I speak doubtfully from memory) had as you incidentally say turned up in the sun. Your evidence from O in the meteorites still left the very *frequent* or *massive* presence of O, throughout the cosmos at large, disappointingly (to his mind) incomplete. His remark was, he insisted, wholly tentative, and not at all hostile. But Turner thinks with instinctive skill in terms of statistical probabilities. And what he had in his mind was the thought (which to me seems a deep one, although of course not very formidable for your position), that *in case*, in the long run, O should turn out to be only very sparsely distributed in the cosmos, *then* the vast odds which you emphasize *against* the occurrence of a chance "fitness" of the sort that you describe would be really, although perhaps not very greatly, diminished. For then your "fitness" would occur *only* in those places where by chance the O happens to be massed in large quantities. In such a place we ourselves chance to be, together with all the organisms that we know to exist (even with your enlarged definition of the essential conditions of life).—The wonder would thus become less a *cosmic* wonder in its extent. Your marvel that all the properties of your "environment" *do* thus conspire would indeed quite remain as you make it. But the "environment" itself would become a less highly marvelous occurrence. For it would be "life" that would be exceptional. Surely this suggests a possible although not a great modification in the estimate of the significance of your facts. I wonder what you will think of the matter. I hope that I make Turner's point clear.

There were other remarks, & some good ones. Several of the philosophers commented very neatly;—Schiller commented only inanely, although kindly. The only biologist present thought the hour too late for further speech.—Your book had begun to be sold in Oxford only two days before my meeting.—The meeting broke up at 11.30.—I heard later that some then present have bought the book, & are working upon it.—Such was my little effort in the matter. I shall hope to find you well when I get home. My regards to Mrs. Henderson—

Yours Always
Josiah Royce.

To James Jackson Putnam, March 24, 1913[310]

On Board the
Cunard
R. M. S. "Ivernia."
March 24, 1913

Dear Dr. Putnam:—

Your most grateful patient ought to have written a farewell letter, and another letter from Oxford. If these things were not duly done, because of my manifold tasks, let me write now to say that the whole job at Oxford passed off without any mishap whatever,—not even a cold. There were some late evening affairs of course. In fact an Oxford term is a busy one; and dinners, as you know, are the very centre, not only of English life in general, but of academic life in particular.

But I have had perfectly good health, and no scares, and I also seemed to find easily my routine. I had an hour's walk in the Oxford park daily,—sometimes more than that,—without regard to the weather. The news from home was good. Everybody was most kind. I slept well. Sir Wm. Osler looked me up of his own accord,—as an act of pure friendship. When I showed a wish to learn how the Regius Professor would view me, he (who had previously, by chance, heard nothing about the nature of my last year's illness, and had only known that I had been somewhat out of health) very kindly gave me his general view of my case, together with a careful examination (of heart, blood pressure, &c.); and in addition even went to one of my lectures!—and then of course told me that I was perfectly right to have undertaken the Oxford task, and to go on

310 ALS. Putnam Papers. Countway Library, Harvard Medical School.

working as any healthy man of my age would work.—All this advice was, no doubt, unnecessary; but it was of course a pleasing added comment. Sir Wm. approved all my regimen, and had no new suggestions. I of course had no desire for more than such a result.

The voyage home, with some decidedly lively weather, is very restful and cheerful,—fresh air, exercise on deck, and good sleep. So you see that your very good and kind and patiently spent labor and care have not been in vain. That, in fact, is the result of your "kindness to dumb animals."—May we soon have a good talk again on philosophy,—whenever you will, and about whatever you choose, so long as I do not bore you.

With heartiest thanks,—

Yours Always,
Josiah Royce

The Letters

Part V

1913–1916

Part V

1913-1916

Royce spent the last three years of his life working on his logic and exploring further the novelties of his theory of interpretation. As his letter to Warner Fite, July 20, [1913?], indicates, he felt that the most specialized principles of logic are intimately related to the deepest problems of humanity. Consequently, he viewed the war, when it came, as a dramatization of the central features of his latest philosophy—the problems of conflicting loyalties and of dyadic human relationships. This last section of Royce's correspondence finally and most clearly illustrates the coherence of his thought in all facets of intellectual endeavor.

TO EDGAR SHEFFIELD BRIGHTMAN, JULY 16, 1913?[1]

103 Irving St.
Cambridge, Mass.
July 16, 1913.

Dear Professor Brightman,

I thank you for your kind letter of July 13, and, in particular, for your reference to Deissmann's two monographs, which I have not seen.[2] I am, of course, no theologian, in any technical sense, and I make no attempt to keep up with New Testament literature. But both your references help me; and I shall hope to use them in future.

[1] ALC. Royce Papers. HUA. The letter is copied in an unknown hand. The following note, in the same hand, accompanies the letter: "On July 13, 1916 [*sic*], Professor Edgar S. Brightman, then teaching at Nebraska Wesleyan University, University Place, Nebraska, wrote to Royce a letter occasioned by the reading of *The Problem of Christianity*. It contained two points: a reference to the relation of Royce's view to Deissmann's interpretation of the New Testament formula, *In Christo*, and a question about Royce's estimate of Borden Parker Bowne."

[2] The reference is probably to Gustav Adolf Deissmann, *Licht vom Osten: Das Neue Testament und die Neuentdeckten Texte der Hellenistisch-römischen Welt* (Tübingen: J. C. B. Mohr, 1909) and Deissmann's *Paulus: Eine Kultur- und Religionsgeschichtliche Skizze* (Tübingen: J. C. B. Mohr, 1911).

I wish that somebody would tell me what my precise relation to Bowne is. I suppose that our arguments were rather on the increase towards the end of his work. I always prized him much; but each of us had many irons in the fire. I ought to have come closer to him before he left us.[3]

Yours Sincerely,
Josiah Royce

To WARNER FITE, JULY 20, [1913?][4]

103 Irving St.
Cambridge,
Mass.
July 20.

Dear Professor Fite:—

Your extremely kind letter of June 19 is one of the best which I have received from readers of my book.[5] It ought to have been answered long ago. But petty details of many sorts have interrupted my vacation; and now I am just about to go off on one of my favorite sea voyages into the tradewinds. My health is fair, if a little fussy sometimes. I hope that you are well, and it is plain that whether the temperature is 100° where you are or not, your thought is cool and calm and clear.

Yet I am not quite sure that you see precisely what the *most* elementary logical problem involved in my theory of the "community" really is. Of this elementary problem, in my book, I said nothing explicit, because my audience was popular. Being a logical problem, this one is, in its simplest form, quite formal. And the formal aspect of the case seems at first remote enough from the moral, the pathetic, the religious issues about salvation, atonement & the rest. But *you* take interest in such formalities; for you know that they throw, or may throw, light on life. So I say to you what I could not say in my book.

[3] Bowne died in 1910; he had been, since 1876, a member of the faculty of Boston University.

[4] ALS. Royce Papers. HUA. Partly printed in James Harry Cotton, *Royce on the Human Self* (Cambridge: Harvard University Press, 1954), p. 248. The date, 1913, is supplied in another hand.

[5] *PC*.

The relation of an individual entity to a "collection" or "assemblage" to which it "belongs," is the relation to which Frege and Peano (independently of each other),[6] first called due logical attention,—although the facts in question are of course of the most familiar possible type, since we cannot talk of any set of objects in heaven or on earth, real or fancied, without mentioning such facts. But these most familiar facts are logically the hardest to grasp. It was the effort to clear up the logical foundations of arithmetic & geometry which first brought to light the real sense of the relation in question. Peano dubbed it the "ϵ-relation." In his vocabulary "xϵa" means "The individual entity x belongs to the collection or assemblage a."—Now some properties of the ϵ-relation are very general, and can be illustrated with the most varied sorts of material. Of these properties the first is that the ϵ-relation is *intransitive*. This fact Peano noticed.[7] Thus "Socrates is an Athenian" can be put in shorthand thus: "sϵa," where s is the individual called Socrates, and a is the set or assemblage of the beings called Athenians. Keeping the same meaning for a, namely "The set or assemblage of the Athenians," we can hereupon form the definition of a new object h, where h means "the assemblage whose units or individual members are the classes or assemblages or 'sorts' of Greeks which anybody, for any purpose may distinguish." The proposition "xϵh" would mean "x is one of the 'sorts' or 'sets' or 'collections' of Greeks." With this definition of the terms used, the two propositions: "sϵa" and "aϵh" have the perfectly definite meanings: "Socrates is an Athenian" (that is: "Socrates belongs to the set of Greeks called Athenians"); and: "The set called 'the Athenians' is one of the sets or classes of Greeks."

[6] Gottlob Frege, *Grundgesetze der Arithmetik* (Jena: H. Pohle, 1893–1903); Giuseppe Peano, *Formulario Mathematico* (Rome: Edizione Cremonese, 1960). Royce adopts Peano's notation and, in general, his analysis.

[7] *Formulario*, §2. Note that Royce does not observe the distinction between those relations which are *not transitive* and those which are *intransitive*. Relations of the former type simply lack the property such that xRy and yRz always imply xRz; relations of the latter type always exclude that implication. Peano maintains that the ϵ-relation is *not transitive*. Royce's illustration of this point is misleading. Though it is true that sϵa and aϵh do not imply sϵh, his reading of these statements—Socrates is an Athenian; Athenians are Greeks; Socrates is a Greek—does not clearly illustrate the point. The *non-transitivity* of the ϵ-relation might better be illustrated in the following way: if xϵy (California is a member of the United States) and if yϵz (the United States is a member of the United Nations) it does not follow that xϵz (California is a member of the United Nations).

But from "sϵa" and "aϵh" does *not* follow sϵh. For Socrates is *not* one of the classes or assemblages of Greeks. This *non* transivity of the ϵ-relation is obvious, but neglected. It is the *first* property to which I now call attention.

The *second* notable fact about the ϵ-relation is that, in general, *no entity is* ϵ *of itself*. That is, in general, the ϵ-relation is "non-reflexive." A few cases have attracted attention to the fact that the ϵ-relation may in those cases be viewed as reflexive. But Russell has shown that if sufficiently generalised, the attribution of reflexiveness to the ϵ-relation leads to contradictions.[8] It is now fairly well agreed that a rational theory of assemblages can be formed only by defining the ϵ-relation as non-reflexive, and by proceeding upon that basis.

Closely related is the *third* principle, that ϵ is an asymmetrical relation. If "xϵa" then "aϵx" is false.

A secondary result and accompaniment of this elementary third fact in my list, is that, in general if xϵm, where x is an individual chosen as you please, and m is a collection to which x belongs,—then all the other, and especially all the most notable, significant, relevant, interesting relations in which x stands to m are,—whether in pure mathematics or in daily life,—in geometry or in the Kingdom of Heaven,—in love or in war or in practice or in theory, *non-symmetrical* if not wholly *asymmetrical* relations. That is, if "xϵm," then "mϵx" is, in general, false, while whatever interesting other relation R you may mention in which x stands to m, you find that, in general m does *not* stand in this relation R to x. Thus, if I am ϵ of a given club, or gang, or pair, or crowd, that club or gang or pair or crowd is not ϵ of me; and so, in general, in whatever relation I stand to that assemblage, the relation of that assemblage to me is *not* the same as is my relation to it. Use points on a line, planets in a solar system, numbers in a set of numbers, digits in such an assemblage of digits as, 654321,—use such formal examples as an introduction to your study of the ϵ-relation; and then you will be ready to appreciate better, I think, the formal logic of my own doctrine of the "two levels" in my book on the community. You

[8] Russell's famous antinomy [see *The Principles of Mathematics* (Cambridge, England: University Press, 1903), §100] shows a special case of non-reflexiveness in the ϵ-relation: a *class of all classes* is clearly a member of itself, but a *class of all classes not members of themselves* is and is not a member of itself.

will be prepared to see that if I am ϵ of a given community, and if I love that community, and if that community also loves me, still our loves are *different* loves and lie on different levels, the relation of lover and beloved being, in the two cases, quite distinct relations.[9]

Of course, if a member belongs to a club, the club may also rightly be said to "belong" to the member (as one says: "my club"). But the *belongings* in the two cases are quite sharply distinct relations. The member is ϵ of the club; and all his other relations to the club are secondary to this ϵ-relation, and result from it and from its context. But the club is *not* ϵ of the member. And all its other relations to the member are colored by the *asymmetry of the ϵ-relation.* If "$x \epsilon a$" and if "x also loves a," then the love of x for a is a love of one who is ϵ of a; while if, meantime "a loves x," the love of a for x is the love of a for that of which a is *not* an ϵ. The two loves are thus profoundly different, both formally and materially.

Look at any constellation,—say the Big Dipper or Orion—; look at three stakes in a row, or at the trees in an orchard, or at the oarsmen in a boat, or at any other interesting set of visible objects; and then see whether you can find in such objects any case of an interesting and important ϵ-relation without an obvious asymmetry, —not only in that ϵ-relation itself, but in all its accompaniments, results and context.

The *final* property of the ϵ-relation which here concerns us is the fact that whenever "$x \epsilon a$," the ϵ-relation in which the individual x stands to the assemblage a is profoundly different from *any* relation in which x stands to any one of its own fellow-members in the collection a, or to any partial set of these fellow-members in case x is not ϵ of that partial set.

Consider, as a simple instance of what I mean, a "linear triad" of points in space. A linear triad of points in space, is a triad such as (p, q, r), when p, q, r lie on one right line. In our ordinary "descriptive" space, *one* of the members of such a linear triad lies

[9] Royce gave attention to this application of logical theory as late as the spring of 1916. Victor Lenzen, who was a member of Royce's seminar and its official secretary in 1915–16, wrote on April 25, 1916: "At the meeting of the seminary for April 18, Professor Royce discussed the asymmetry of the epsilon relation with reference to the argument of Fite that the individual and the social environment are in reciprocal relationship. Professor Royce pointed out that the individual and the social order are not on a level. The community doesn't depend upon me in the way that I depend upon it." See Lenzen Papers, UCB.

between the two others. Now let T be used, for the moment, to name this linear triad as an assemblage or set of points. We can then say: pϵT," "qϵT," and also "rϵT." Notice how different is the relation of q to T from the relation of q to p and to r or to the pair (p, r). q is *a member of T*. q is *between* p and r. The distinction is fundamental for the whole of geometry.

This case is typical of all ϵ-relations. If I am a member of a community, *all* my relations to that community depend upon my ϵ-relation and upon its context. But I am *not* ϵ to any one of my fellow-members. And *all* of my relations to my individual fellow members differ down to their very roots and into their very core from my relations to my community, just because I am not ϵ of any of my fellow members.

Now these elementary logical facts seem to be wholly ignored in your comparison of the relations of which I speak "to the relation of the lover and the beloved" where (in your example) both lover and beloved are individuals. An "individualist" ought to be the first to see that just because I am *not* ϵ of my individual beloved, nor she of me, *all* of my relations as lover to my individual beloved must have values, interpretations, meanings, which cannot be the same as the corresponding values and meanings of my relations as lover of that to which I *am* ϵ, viz. my community. If you want to find out the properties of *triads* of points, you must study them *as* triads,—linear or non-linear, &c.—If you want to find out the relations which a point may have to another point, or to a pair of points, when they are all members of the same triad,—then you in vain study the relation of one point to another individual point *without* considering any triad *as* a triad.

Now that is in brief why the whole lore of "salvation," "atonement" &c.,—in brief the whole lore of community relations, can never be rightly approached by one who simply proceeds as if such problems could be solved by considering "one individual" and "another individual," &c., without ever explicitly facing the ϵ-relation. The ϵ-relation is one of the most elementary and elemental of logical relations. But it is *never* any relation of any individual to any other individual. It is the relation of a member to a set. My book deals with a special case of the ϵ-relation.

But all this goes with great & deep thanks for your kindness, & with hopes for more from you.

Yours Sincerely
J. Royce.

That the ϵ-relation although itself so abstract & formal is a presupposition of relations that may be rich & concrete, any *ordered* assemblage shows. The moral relations simply exemplify all this on an especially high level. You may see the application of the foregoing to your various objections to me if you take the latter up in detail. My view is that the ϵ-relation is a necessary basis and presupposition of all our deeper social relations. That is why my "consciousness" of another individual, or of countless other individuals can never do for me what my consciousness of my community can do. That is why I can never save myself,–simply because I am not ϵ of myself.

TO FREDERICK JAMES EUGENE WOODBRIDGE, AUGUST 18, 1913[10]

103 Irving St.
Cambridge, Mass.
Aug. 18, 1913.

Dear Professor Woodbridge,

I enclose herewith an article which explains itself. It is, as you will see, neither controversial nor directly representative of any general philosophical position.[11] It concerns the pure algebra of logic, and contains a note which is as much mathematical as logical. My colleague E. V. Huntington, to whom I showed an outline of the investigation last June, thought that your *Journal* could deal with it more promptly than any existing mathematical journal, and therefore recommended me to offer it to you rather than to the mathematicians, although he believed it to be of a certain mathematical interest. I have just finished it in the present shape. If you can print it, I do not greatly care whether or how you divide it into parts; although of course an algebraic "continued story" is not a very pretty form. But be that as you please. I hope to send you some other papers on closely related lines later on, unless you discourage that sort of thing. On whatever terms you think proper, I should like to get as many as two hundred separate copies, since I want to send the contribution to various logicians abroad. All this

[10] ALS. *Journal of Philosophy* Papers. CUB.

[11] "An Extension of the Algebra of Logic," *Journal of Philosophy, Psychology, and Scientific Methods* 10 (November 6, 1913): 617–33; reprinted in *RLE*, pp. 293–309.

is of course, subject to your willingness to print my paper at all.
I hope that you are prosperous. I myself get on well.

Yours Very Cordially,
Josiah Royce.

To Frederick James Eugene Woodbridge, September 16, 1913[12]

103 Irving St.
Cambridge, Mass.
September 16, 1913.

Dear Professor Woodbridge:—

My answer to yours of September 9 has been delayed by various family affairs incident to this time of year. I am now ready for further work on logic.

I propose, if you feel kindly inclined towards my little enterprise, to send you, within the next three or four months, six more articles,—making seven articles in all,—each of about the length of the article now in your hands. If the enterprise appears to you hopelessly diffuse in its plan as outlined, or too abstruse or narrow in its appeal, do not hesitate to discourage my presenting these articles to the *Journal*. They are possibly not worthy to be printed in that way; but are intended to form part of a forthcoming book on the relations between logic and geometry, and on some general philosophical issues connected therewith.

The list of seven articles, as proposed, would be:—

1. "An Extension of the Alg. of Logic" (now in your hands).
2. "Kempe's theory of the analogies between the logical and the geometrical relations" (a summary of the still neglected theory that I worked out at length in 1905, in the *Transactions of the Amer. Math. Society*).
3. "The Logical Continuum."
4. "A New Type of Logical Entities" (this I suppose to be both a novel and an important contribution).
5. "The Transformations of the logical continuum, and the invertible pair-operation."
6. "The Philosophical Significance of the Logical Continuum."

12 ALS. *Journal of Philosophy* Papers. CUB.

7. "What is Vital in Logic?" (Summary & Controversial appendix to the whole series).[13]

You will understand that, of these seven articles, only the first is now written out. But all are nearly ready to be penned, since the researches concerned have busied me for a long time. The second and third will contain some repetitions of what I have otherwise published. But these repetitions are necessary, owing to the extremely technical and neglected character of the theory in question, —a theory which I now want to bring in this way within the reach of a wider range of philosophical students. Articles 6 and 7 will draw out and state some of the moral of my story. Only article 7, however, will be distinctly controversial.—I can send you article 2, if you wish it, within the next three or four weeks, if you send me the proof of article 1 within that time. The other articles, I hope, will follow at pretty regular intervals, until Christmas, or thereabouts.—

Yours Faithfully
Josiah Royce.

To George Arthur Plimpton, December 6, 1913[14]

103 Irving St.
Cambridge, Mass.
December 6, 1913

Mr. George A. Plimpton,

My Dear Mr. Plimpton:

I have received with great pleasure the kind invitation to be one of those who will unite on Thursday Evening, December eleventh, in the Testimonial Dinner in recognition of the Public Services of Mr. Robert Underwood Johnson.

[13] Articles 2–7 were never published. Woodbridge had written to Royce on September 9, 1913: "Let me thank you for your article. I shall be very glad to publish it, but may I inquire how extended will be its continuation in future articles, and how frequently you would like the instalments to appear? I do this in the interest of the proper arrangement of the material which we have on hand." Woodbridge's reply to this letter by Royce does not appear in the *Journal of Philosophy* Papers.

[14] ALS. Johnson Papers. UCB.

I very greatly regret that my academic and personal duties make it quite impossible for me to be present at this testimonial dinner. In the guest of the evening I see not only the long-honored citizen, editor, and poet to whom all who join in this testimonial once again express their homage; but also the personal friend whom I remember with affection and with gratitude for the hours which, as editor, he long ago kindly gave, on various occasions, to literary plans and interests of my own. I remember Mr. Robert Underwood Johnson also for other courtesies that he showed me then, and since then; for his unfailing patience; for his clear insight and for his far reaching tolerance; for his sympathy and for his wise counsel; for his love of the ideal, and for his inspiring example.

At a moment when you all acknowledge the public services of the guest of the evening, this word of hearty personal appreciation of the poet, the literary guide, and the man, may not be out of place.

I cannot be one of your number next Thursday evening. I am and shall remain while I live an admirer and grateful friend of the man whom you meet to honor.

Sincerely Yours
Josiah Royce

To Frederick James Eugene Woodbridge, [1913? or 1914?][15]

103 Irving St.
Cambridge, Mass.

Dear Professor Woodbridge,

Perry tells me that there is some chance of your having a place as lecturer, next year, in Logic or in general philosophy, for Costello. If so, I certainly ought to put on record, as I now do, the fact that Costello is a man whose power as a logician, as a critic, and as an increasingly constructive student of the methods and of the philosophy of science, grows upon me yearly. This year he has taken part in my logical seminary, criticizing the work of each

[15] ALS. *Journal of Philosophy* Papers. CUB. The letter is catalogued as having been written in 1913. Harry T. Costello acted as secretary of Royce's seminar during 1913–14; the letter, therefore, must have been written in late 1913 or early 1914.

meeting in a report made at the next meeting. Costello's reports, which he spontaneously offered to prepare to help me, are often veritably classical in their skill and their finish. Use him as lecturer or instructor if you can. He will soon be ready for much more advanced academic tasks. He is modestly sententious, humorously obstinate, very original, and very telling.

Yours Truly
Josiah Royce

To George Platt Brett, January 27, 1914[16]

103 Irving St.
Cambridge, Mass.
January 27, 1914.

Mr. Geo. P. Brett, The Macmillan Co.

My Dear Mr. Brett,

Shortly after the death of Herbert Spencer, (or about the time when his *Autobiography* appeared), the editor of the then flourishing *International Review* asked me to write for his magazine an article on Spencer,—summary and criticism.[17] I wrote the article. After printing it, the editor asked me, as a personal favor, to let him publish the article as a little volume with the firm Fox Duffield & Company. I consented; for the editor was an old friend of mine.

After years, the little book—on *Spencer*—which had the fortune natural to such a monographic sketch, thus put into hopelessly inefficient hands,—comes back upon my hands with the offer which I now enclose to you.

I have lately printed in magazines quite a number of essays on matters of scientific history and methodology. You know that I plan various future studies on Logic, and on related topics. You know that I know that books and essays of that kind have a very limited sale; but, poor a "seller" though I am, you have so far

[16] ALS. Macmillan Papers. NYPL.

[17] Frederick A. Richardson was editor of the *International Monthly*, later the *International Quarterly*. Royce's "Herbert Spencer and His Contribution to the Concept of Evolution," *International Quarterly* 9 (1904): 335–65, was reprinted in *Herbert Spencer: An Estimate and a Review* (New York: Fox, Duffield and Co., 1904).

encouraged me to send you my various things as they come to hand.

Would it be worth your while to consider taking over this *Herbert Spencer* book, in any form which pleases you? I leave the whole matter to you; and if you choose to communicate with these Duffields about the topic of their enclosed letter to me, I should be glad to have you do so in my name.[18]

Yours Truly
Josiah Royce.

To Charles Sanders Peirce, March 4, 1914[19]

103 Irving St.
Cambridge, Mass.
March 4, 1914.

Dear Mr. Peirce:—

It is long since I have had time to write to you. I hope that your health is good.[20] I venture to enclose to you a recent paper of my own, about which I want to say a word, since you are mentioned in the paper, and the topic may interest you, although it will not be new to you.[21]

A company of my colleagues, younger and older, including several medical men, recently proposed to form a society for the general discussion of various scientific questions, including "Vitalism." They asked me to take some part; so, at the opening meeting, I read them a comparative review of various methods that interest different sciences. The paper is of course very general and elementary. Of course I used, for my purpose, your papers and ideas,

[18] Brett replied to Royce on January 27, 1914, outlining plans to reissue *Herbert Spencer* with the Macmillan imprint. These plans were never carried out.

[19] ALS. Peirce Papers. HL. First three sentences of the second paragraph are printed in Cotton, *Royce on the Human Self*, p. 302.

[20] Peirce died on April 14, 1914.

[21] The paper appears to have been "The Mechanical, the Historical and the Statistical," subsequently published in *Science*, n.s., 39 (1914): 551–66, and reprinted in *RLE*, pp. 35–62. On March 3, 1914, the night before writing this letter, Royce read this paper to his seminar. See *Josiah Royce's Seminar, 1913–1914*, ed. Grover Smith (New Brunswick, N. J.: Rutgers University Press, 1963): pp. 128–30.

as well as others. I hope that my acknowledgement of my indebtedness to you is sufficient for the occasion, which was a semi-private one, with seventeen persons present.

I may print the paper. It otherwise explains itself. You are mentioned on pp. 25 and 32 of the mimeographed copy which I send you herewith. Please excuse mistakes of copyist. I often talk of you in my seminary to my students of logic.—

Yours Truly
Josiah Royce

Professor E. C. Pickering was present at the meeting and spoke with warm appreciation of your early photometric contributions to the Observatory Annals.[22]

To Benjamin Ide Wheeler, August 20, 1914[23]

15 Cañon Road
Berkeley,
Aug. 20, 1914

Benjamin Ide Wheeler, L. L. D, President

My Dear President Wheeler:—

I thank you very much for your kind invitation to take lunch with you and Mrs. Wheeler on Friday, August twenty-eighth, after the University Meeting, and for your further invitation to me to address the University Assembly.

So far as the University Assembly is concerned, I am very sorry to have to say that I shall be quite unable to accept the honor of delivering the address which you ask me to give to your University family. My reasons for thus declining a request which it would surely be my duty to accept if I were able, are these:—

1. Thursday evening, the 27th, I am, as you know, to deliver an Address before the Philosophical Union. I have been forced, because of the importance of that task, and because of the very grave problems which the war brings before every philosophical student's

[22] Charles Sanders Peirce, *Photometric Researches, Annals of the Astronomical Observatory of Harvard College* 9 (1878).

[23] ALS. President File. UCA.

mind, to change that address very largely.[24] I had spent a good many weeks preparing for this one occasion. At the last moment I have felt required to lay aside all my MSS and notes intended for the address to the Union. I am now rewriting the address. It will still be a philosophical (and certainly not a political or a contentious) discussion. But it will deal with problems about which I have had to think in new ways since August the first. The preparation of this address for the 27th is inconsistent with my attempting a serious task on Friday morning the 28th.

2. I have been working here at Berkeley somewhat unsparingly, before Aug. 1, on my fortnight of Summer Session lectures. I have, therefore, somewhat less energy to spend, at this moment, upon extra tasks, than I otherwise should have.

3. On Feb. 1, 1912, I had a slight, but somewhat impressive cerebral hemorrhage, and have ever since been working,—not indolently, I hope,—but with a certain limitation of freedom as to the adjustment of morning to evening engagements. I can sometimes lecture late. I can sometimes lecture early. My medical advisers (who happen to be both of them not only doctors of medicine but philosophers), have carefully observed what I can and cannot wisely undertake; and have certainly encouraged me to do all reasonable tasks that come my way. But they have also given me warnings which I know to be not whimsical. I am sure, not only that they, if they were now here, would forbid me to accept your very kindly and flattering offer, but also that Mrs. Royce, who has carefully watched my recovery, and has learned to estimate my various forms and fits of fatigue, since my illness, would wholly forbid me to undertake any such tasks two days running. Such warning she specially gave me when I left home.

4. Finally, I have to say that I had in advance no indication whatever that you might wish me to meet your University family in this way. Since the dates of the Address and of the Assembly were known here long since, and since my need of caution as to great strains was also known, to some at least of my friends,—we could long since have arranged some plan for giving these two proposed addresses, if you had thought best to propose such an arrangement.

I must therefore regretfully, but positively decline the great, and

[24] Royce's previously announced topic was "The Spirit of the Community"; his revised address was "War and Insurance."

—but for my infirmity—the most welcome honor that your letter offers me. I cannot burn *this* candle at both ends.

Yours Sincerely
Josiah Royce

To Abbott Lawrence Lowell, October 18, 1914[25]

Cambridge, October 18, 1914
103 Irving Street.

A. Lawrence Lowell, Ll. D. President.

Dear President Lowell:—

Your kindly and prompt acknowledgement of my *War and Insurance* gives me the opportunity to say what I had not time, I believe, to express to you, the other day, when you so kindly gave me the copy of your book on *Popular Government*.[26] My *War and Insurance* was written in California partly in the woods, and all at places and times when I had no opportunity effectively to refer to any book, or to verify any memory. I clearly remembered our conversation of 1907 or 1908 when you gave me the word about the broker and his civilization. But I have learned to mistrust so much my memory of details, that I resolved to postpone a definite mention of your name until by a direct appeal to you I could verify both the name and the passage, in case the passage should prove to be already in print. When I reached home in September, it seemed unfair to intrude my insurance plan on your vacation. So the war and the printer went on until the book appeared with you named only as a "noted publicist." If my book reaches any later edition, you shall be more precisely and duly brought before the reader's eye in a brief word, whether of preface or of note.

I take this opportunity to say that *War and Insurance* was written in the closing weeks of my Cabot Fellowship which expired September first. Since the theses of my discussion are applications of the philosophy which was developed in my *Problem of Christianity*, you will see, I hope, that, in my poor efforts at research

[25] TLS. Lowell Papers. HUA.

[26] *Public Opinion and Popular Government* (New York: Longmans, Green and Co., 1913).

during my Cabot fellowship, I, like the Barrister in the Hunting of the Snark "went bellowing on to the last."

Very truly yours,
Josiah Royce

To Reginald Chauncey Robbins, November 8, 1914[27]

103 Irving St.
Cambridge, Mass.
November 8, 1914.

Dear Robbins:—

Your very kind reply to my last (wherein I accepted your dedication) puts me deeper and deeper in your debt.[28]

You are one of the few independent thinkers, writers, and friends of the truest and the best, whom the community has. I prize all the times when I can be with you, and am sorry that the cares of life, and my own constantly besetting narrowness of range in desultory work,—work such as correspondence, evenings out, general conversation, the reading of current books & MSS—all serves to make my return of your many courtesies and gifts so inadequate, and my seeming ingratitude so great. I hardly hope to get together any comprehensive summary and survey of my philosophical contributions before my little span of working day ends; but, as a fact, my philosophical contributions, both "pure" and "applied," hang pretty closely together. I am disposed to believe that you are one of the few men who understand, or much care, what the real connection of these various contributions is. But I thank you for caring; and I prize your judgment in the matter because I believe that you know.—Most of course I prize at present my latest theory, that of the Peircean "interpretation," with its peculiar "triads." But in germ I had it (not yet on any Peircean, nor yet on any Hegelian basis), in my Chapter on "The Possibility of Error" in the *Religious Aspect*. Here, in its latest form (as in my book on *War and Insurance*) is a theory that allows for endless variety of individual "interpretation," and for endless change,

27 ALS. Robbins Papers. HL.

28 Robbins published several volumes of verse, but none of them is dedicated to Royce.

growth and fluency, while "absoluteness" is nevertheless "chrono-synoptic" and universal, above all and in all the flow and the tragedy of this world whose unity means that it "contains its own interpreter."—I thank you for your cooperation and for your friendship.

Yours Always,
Josiah Royce.

To Hugo Münsterberg, December 17, 1914[29]

103 Irving Street
Cambridge
December 17, 1914

Dear Münsterberg:—

I am very sorry to be unable to accept your very kind invitation to luncheon on Sunday, January the 10th, at half past one, to meet Colonel Roosevelt.[30]

I thank you deeply and warmly for the invitation. I have enjoyed many good hours in your house. I remember them frequently and gratefully. That you honor me with this invitation to meet Colonel Roosevelt is something that I greatly prize, and that I both view with affectionate regard, and wish that I could accept.

But, as a fact, deeply as I desire to be one of the company whom you are so kindly and thoughtfully bringing together, I feel that, at present my own personal duty as a lover and teacher of philosophy requires me to be absorbed in ideas and in the service of

[29] ALS. Münsterberg Papers. BPL.

[30] See Margaret Münsterberg, *Hugo Münsterberg: His Life and Work* (New York: D. Appleton and Company, 1922), pp. 265–66. A passionate advocate of American neutrality, Münsterberg sought to advance his cause through a renewal of his long-standing friendship with Theodore Roosevelt, who, because of his noted admiration of the German people, was thought at that time to share Münsterberg's views. Roosevelt, however, published his *America and the World War* in January, 1915, in which he condemned Germany and argued that America should be prepared to enter the war on the side of the Allies. As this letter clarifies, Royce's friendship with Münsterberg had faded during the early months of the war, but their social relationship had not yet been completely severed, nor had Royce yet taken a clearly partisan position. That developed later, after the sinking of the *Lusitania* on May 7, 1915.

interests which unfit me to take part in such a discussion of European politics as you propose. I should indeed delight to listen to such a discussion. I should especially listen to your own part in that discussion with close attention and interest. I should learn much that I indeed very much need to learn from you and from your company, and I should greatly profit by the union of minds that you are sure to secure on this occasion. But I should be simply powerless to take part. The few and powerless ideas that I have to offer, as you know, as my petty contribution to the problems of this moment, I have already expressed. They are non-political ideas. But, now that I have expressed them, they form my little all. Therewith, as a contributor to the discussion, I must at present be content.

I very deeply sympathize with all devoted and loyal men who, at this moment, serve their cause, as you serve your own cause, with earnestness, with charity, and with an enlightened humanity of spirit. May more light, and may peace come soon to us all.

I hope that you will understand the happy memories, and the warm present affection for you and for all of yours, which are in my mind as I regretfully decline this very kind invitation.

—Yours Cordially
J. Royce.

To Hugo Münsterberg, December 21, 1914[31]

103 Irving Street
Cambridge
December 21, 1914

Dear Münsterberg:—

No, I did not misunderstand you, when I read your most kind note; nor had I any expectations that I personally, or anybody else, was to be called on to make a speech, nor that you intended any but a social luncheon, such as the one that we had with Riehl in your company. And all that I said about my past satisfactions in my attendance at many delightful occasions in your house, and about my present friendship for you, and for all your house, I earnestly beg to repeat and warmly to confirm by this letter.

But I knew when I replied that Roosevelt has been a sovereign,

[31] ALS. Münsterberg Papers. BPL.

that he still feels "every inch a king,"[32] and that, in his presence, no one directs the course of conversation but himself. All this your kind letter of Dec. 19 only confirms; and herein our views agree.

Since this is true, my acceptance of Roosevelt's direction of his own and of other people's topics and modes of conversation about the political situation in Europe would demand, if I were present on this occasion, my liability to take a part in the discussion which I could not beforehand predict, or control. I should not indeed, be expected to make a speech. And your part of the conduct of the occasion would be, as your conduct of similar occasions always is, kindness and discretion that would be ideal in their spirit. But Roosevelt,—although I doubt whether he even remembers my existence,—would be, if I were present, the arbiter of how far and how much I should have to commit myself to and in a possible discussion of European politics. I am indeed a wholly ignorant person about all such topics. But, all the more, I have interpreted my little duty as I told you in my last letter. Therefore,—deeply as I thank you both for the kindness and for the honor of this invitation,—I find, with hearty regret, that I have to decline. Please forgive me.

Always Cordially Yours,
Josiah Royce.

To Wendell T. Bush, January 13, 1915[33]

Cambridge, January 13, 1915.
103 Irving Street.

Professor Wendell T. Bush.
Journal of Philosophy, Psychology, and Scientific Methods.

Dear Professor Bush:—

I shall be glad to take part in the proposed discussion of the work of Charles Peirce.[34] How many words do you want me to contribute? As to other contributors, you will of course have thought

[32] Shakespeare *King Lear*, act 4, sc. 6, line 109.

[33] TLS. *Journal of Philosophy* Papers. CUB.

[34] "Charles Sanders Peirce" (with Fergus Kernan), *Journal of Philosophy, Psychology, and Scientific Methods* 13 (December 21, 1916): 701–9. The entire issue was devoted to Peirce; this article appeared with articles by John Dewey, Christine Ladd-Franklin, Joseph Jastrow, and Morris R. Cohen.

of Mrs. Ladd-Franklin, who, if accessible, should be indispensable. I have heard nothing of her since the war began. Another contributor to the *Studies in Logic by Members of the Johns Hopkins University*, survives, and is in good health. I had the good fortune to meet him about a fortnight since. He is Benjamin Ives Gilman, one of the curators of the Boston Museum of Fine Arts. You may address him at that institution, although I do not know what the present title of his special department at the Museum is. While logic is now mainly a reminiscence to Gilman, he used to follow Peirce's work closely, and is both a good judge and a good writer. Jastrow you no doubt already have in mind.

We have just received at the Harvard Library the extant logical manuscripts of Charles Peirce,—a gift from his widow, and, as I hope, a real prize. I look forward to some arrangement for editing them. They are certainly fragmentary, but almost certainly inclusive of some valuable monuments of his unique and capricious genius.

Yours very truly,
Josiah Royce

To Edward Royce, January 30, 1915[35]

Cambridge, January 30th, 1915.

Dear Ned:—

I am sorry that I have been neglectful until today about consulting Miss Macready about your plans and prospects. The closing of the first half year's work kept me very busy until Wednesday. Thursday I had an examination to look out for. Friday was my first day of relaxation, and I walked a good deal, also napped. Today I had a pretty full talk with Miss Macready. This evening Kitty kindly undertakes to type this letter for me.

I find that Miss Macready has been thinking a good deal about you, and has been talking over your affairs, in a very friendly spirit with Davison, who, in view of the fact that Spaulding is just now not in a very good condition, is taking temporary charge for the department, of plans and appointments.[36] I have not seen Davison

[35] TLS. Private collection of James Royce.

[36] Archibald Thompson Davison and Walter Raymond Spalding were members of the music faculty at Harvard.

myself, but shall be free to do so next week, especially if you request me to do so.

First, regarding school supervisorships of music in Boston, Miss Macready has, at the moment no adequate information, but promises to lay that matter before Davison at once, as I shall also try to do at my first opportunity. You know, I suppose, that Davison's official address is Mr. Archibald Thompson Davison, George Smith Hall A 21 (one of the new freshman dormitories). But his father's family are very near by,—Francis Avenue neighbors of ours, in fact. I shall make a special effort to arrange a meeting with Davison some time early in the week.

Miss Macready, I find, understands that all school affairs in Boston are at present in a very unstable condition. She believes not, I suppose, without reason, that supervisorships are inevitably made unstable by the political conditions. This, as she supposes, would be true in any of the cities, and that without regard to the way in which the supervisor in question might have acquired his position, and without regard to his merits. If he stood in the way of some favorite, or were either personally or politically unwelcome to some superior official, or if the School Board were notably changed in constitution at an election, the School Supervisor of music might find his place suddenly vacant. His qualifications might be what you please. But such incidents would not make his career more prosperous, and might have an unpropitious effect. This is Miss M's present impression, not founded upon any memory of special instances of supervisors of music, but founded rather upon a general acquaintance with the uncertainty of tenure which seems to belong especially to the more attractive grades of appointment in our modern municipal school organization. I shall ask Davison about just this matter when I see him. But it would be of course well not to risk or invest much in the search for such appointments, until we know something more positive about their stability.

According to Miss M., Davison is now especially hoping for some college place for you, where teaching powers will secure a fairly permanent appointment, and where requirements extraneous to teaching, or out of harmony with its spirit will not be likely to interfere in any way that you would find detrimental. Davison has some hopes that there may prove to be some sort of good vacancy at Smith College this year. Miss M. thinks that there is more hope of such a vacancy at Vassar. Neither of them definitely knows of any such vacancy, or of any teaching vacancy for the coming year. But both Davison and Miss M. seem to think that you have won your spurs in the profession, that you deserve a solid teaching place, and that we may hope to get you one without your having to wander too far in search of it.

This reports my present state of progress regarding your prospects. Before the coming week is over I hope to find out something more about what the prospects are. I hear nothing further from Middlebury College at present. But Miss Macready says that she has heard President John Thomas speak very highly and favorably of you. So that there is reason to suppose that if Middlebury College gets the resources to pay for music next year, you will get a fair chance there.

This latter part of this letter is dictated Sunday P.M. We were interrupted last night by a telegram from Stephen beginning "Baby dead. Acute indigestion. Ill only fourteen hours." We have not yet heard what Marion and Stephen will do about the funeral. I leave further comments to Katharine who will finish this letter. Please let me know of anything that I can do for you and the family. There seems to be no doubt that Randolph is progressing, and that Katharine is doing the best for him that can be done, with good results for herself.[37]

Lovingly,
Josiah.

To Alden March, April 2, 1915[38]

Cambridge April 2nd, 1915.
103 Irving Street

Mr. Alden March,
Sunday Editor of the *New York Times*,

My dear Mr. March:—

I enclose herewith my proposed article for the Sunday edition

[37] Edward's son, Randolph, was born in 1912; he remained in the care of his grandmother. Mrs. Royce's postscript expresses sorrow concerning the death of Stephen Royce's baby, adds news of Randolph, and concludes with hopes that Edward will find a good academic post.

[38] TLC. Royce Papers. HUA.

of the *New York Times* on "The Possibility of International Insurance."[39] I also enclose a very kind letter which I have received from my colleague Mr. W. B. Medlicott, Lecturer on Insurance in the Graduate School of Business Administration at Harvard University.[40] Mr. Medlicott is a prominent fire insurance underwriter, a man very deeply and constantly engaged in the affairs of his business, as well as in the work of his insurance lectureship. Because of his manifold engagements, he has been obliged to delay somewhat his answer to my own appeal for guidance, and to the statement of my plan which I submitted to him. I value very greatly the general approval which, as you see, he actually gives me. He permits, as you will also see, the use of his authority as an expert which I have made at the close of my article. I have also submitted my general plan to Mr. H. B. Dow, lecturer on Life Insurance in the Harvard School of Business Administration. Mr. Dow is Actuary of a prominent Boston Life Insurance Company. When I stated my plan to him, he replied that to begin the undertaking of international insurance in this way, namely with some international conduct of the business of reinsurance, seemed to him "probably the most practicable fashion of beginning the undertaking as an international enterprise." You will understand that the idea of thus beginning with international reinsurance is my own; but that I have wished to be very careful in getting the advice of experts before printing this version of my proposal, and that the delay of my article has resulted from this precaution.

I hope that, especially after reading Mr. Medlicott's letter, you will find that my contribution is not altogether too long. As you will see, the article is nearer 3600 words than to 2500 words although you assigned 2500 words as the desired length. On the other hand, the article as it stands proposes a definite plan for

[39] "Wants International Insurance: Professor Josiah Royce of Harvard Advocates Insurance by the Nations of the World," *New York Times Magazine*, July 25, 1915, pp. 2–3; reprinted as "The Possibility of International Insurance" in *HGC*, pp. 71–92.

[40] See ALS. William B. Medlicott to Royce, April 1, 1915 (Royce Papers, HUA): "The article is surely deserving of publication through the medium you have told me of. While to the practical busy underwriter it will doubtless appear visionary, it will set men thinking & afterall where would progress be if it were not that some men can see visions that to the man constantly striving up the dusk of business ventures are completely hidden. I shall be greatly interested to see what comment is brought out when the article is published."

making international insurance, in this limited form, something practicable at once, at the close of the present war, or at any time thereafter. It also states reasons why such a beginning of international insurance would be likely to lead in the future to important results, which would go far beyond the mere beginning of international insurance here outlined. Furthermore, while the ideas stated in *War and Insurance* were, as I believe, novel, the present statement of my plan involves another entirely new idea, that regarding reinsurance as the type of insurance business with which to begin the international undertaking. In view of this fact, and of the somewhat unexpectedly cordial approval of my expert colleagues, who are actually engaged in practical business, I venture to hope that my present paper will not seem too much to have exceeded your limits.

You will notice that I have followed Mr. Medlicott's recommendation in regard to one of my sentences which I have struck out of the MS for fear of giving offence by the suggestion of financial weakness which he justly points out as present in the sentence as I wrote it.

I have somewhat carefully considered whether I have been right in explicitly mentioning the name of my book on *War and Insurance* and that of my publisher. I of course leave wholly to you the decision as to whether I ought to make such an explicit mention. My own feeling is that my book is so bound up with the new plan set forth in my article, that it would be vain to ask the reader to take interest in my article, without telling him what book is in question. If my article did not name the book, I should receive a good many letters asking me for the title and publisher. But of course you both will decide and ought to decide what is right in this matter.

I do not know whether you would have any use for my photograph. I have one, all prepared for duplication, in case you have any use for it. I myself have no great desire to see my picture in print. But I am perfectly neutral regarding the subject, and am ready to do whatever you desire.

With thanks for your kind encouragement,

I remain,
Very Truly Yours,
[Josiah Royce]

To Lawrence Pearsall Jacks, N. D. [June, 1915?][41]

In my last letter I believe that I laid some stress to you upon the necessity, both patriotic and academic, of my trying to preserve a formally strict neutrality of expression, not merely because the community of mankind as a total community is my highest interest, as it is yours, but because our President's advice to the nation, and our manifold relations to foreigners, both in academic life and in the world at large, limit our right, or have limited our right, to express ourselves regarding matters of the war and of current controversy. It is now a relief to be able to say with heartiness, that one result at least of the *Lusitania* atrocity has been and will be to make it both necessary and advisable to speak out plainly many things which an American professor in my position has long felt a desire to say upon occasions when he still supposed it to be his duty not to say them. Thus, for instance, immediately after the *Lusitania* incident, and before Wilson's first letter, addressed to Berlin, I quite deliberately told my own principal class in metaphysics that, and why, I should no longer endeavour to assume a neutral attitude about the moral questions which the *Lusitania* incident brought to the minds of all of us. That friends of mine, and that former pupils of mine, near to me as the students whom I was addressing are near to me, were on the *Lusitania*—this, as I said to my class, made it right for me to say, "Among these dead of the *Lusitania* are my own dead." And so, I went on to say, "I cannot longer leave you to suppose it possible that I have any agreement with the views which a German colleague of mine, a teacher at Harvard, recently maintained, when he predicted what he called 'the spiritual triumph of Germany.'[42] It makes very little difference to anybody else what I happen to

[41] Printed letter. "An American Thinker on the War," *Hibbert Journal* 14 (1915), 37-42. Reference to the sinking of the *Lusitania* (May 7) and to Wilson's first two notes (May 13 and June 9) makes it clear that the letter was written during the latter part of June, 1915. The original and complete letter has not survived. The editor has been informed by S. L. Short that neither Manchester College nor the *Hibbert Journal* has any of Royce's letters. The editor has also been informed by Mr. S. B. L. Jacks, son of L. P. Jacks, that his father destroyed nearly all of his correspondence and that no letters from Royce are to be found in his personal papers.

[42] Hugo Münsterberg.

think, but to you, as my pupils, it is my duty to say that henceforth, whatever the fortunes of war may be, 'the spiritual triumph of Germany' is quite impossible, so far as this conflict is concerned. I freely admit that Germany may triumph in the visible conflict, although my judgment about such matters is quite worthless. But to my German friends and colleagues, if they chance to want to know what I think, I can and do henceforth only say this: 'You may triumph in the visible world, but at the banquet where you celebrate your triumph there will be present the ghosts of my dead slain on the *Lusitania*.' "

I insisted to my class that just now the especially significant side of this matter is contained simply in the deliberately chosen facts which the enemy of mankind has chosen to bring into being in these newest expressions of the infamies of Prussian warfare. I should be a poor professor of philosophy, and in particular of moral philosophy, if I left my class in the least doubt as to how to view such things. And that, then, was my immediate reaction on the *Lusitania* situation.

Of course, one still has to live with his German colleagues in the midst of this situation. I am glad to know at least one such German colleague—and, I believe, a thoroughly good patriot—who views the *Lusitania* atrocity precisely as any honest and humane man must view it, unless wholly blinded by the present personal and social atmosphere of ferocity and confusion in which so many Germans live. I do not endeavour to have unnecessary controversy with these colleagues, or with anybody else, and have spoken of the matter both to colleagues and to students precisely as much and as little as the situation seemed to me to permit and require. But it might interest you to know that, in my opinion, the *Lusitania* incident has affected and will affect our national sentiment—and what has been our desire for a genuine neutrality—in a very profound and practical way.

Of the political consequences of the incident up to this date, you will have, I hope, a sufficiently definite ground for judgment. Fortune is fickle; and war is a sadly chaotic series of changes. But this I warmly hope: henceforth may the genuine consciousness of brotherhood between your people and mine become more and more clearly warm, and conscious, and practically effective upon the course of events. The *Lusitania* affair makes us here, all of us, clearer. A deeply unified and national indignation, coupled with a strong sense of our duty towards all humanity, has already resulted from this new experiment upon human nature, which has been 'made in Germany,' and then applied to the task of testing what American sentiment really is. I do not know how often the changing fortunes of war, or the difficulties about neutral commerce, will bring to light causes of friction or of tension between our two peoples. But I cordially hope that we shall find ourselves, henceforth, nearer and nearer together in conscious sentiment and in the sort of sympathy which can find effective expression. It is a great thing to feel that Wilson, in his last two notes to Germany, has been speaking the word both for his nation and for all humanity. I am sure that he has spoken the word for a new sort of unification of our own national consciousness. Unless Germany substantially meets these demands, I am sure that she will find all our foreign populations more united than ever through their common resentment in the presence of international outrages, and through their common consciousness that our unity and active co-operation must have an important bearing upon the future of all that makes human life precious to any of us. In so far as our German-American fellow citizens fail to appreciate the call of humanity in respect of such matters as this, they have further lessons to learn which America will teach them,—peaceably if we can, but authoritatively if we must, whenever an effort is made to carry dissensions into our national life for the sake of any German purpose. As a fact, I believe that unless Germany meets the essential demands of President Wilson, our German-American population will be wholly united with us, as never before, in the interests of humanity and of freedom. In brief, the *Lusitania* affair, and its consequences, give one further tiny example of that utter ignorance of human nature and of its workings which the German propaganda, the German diplomacy, and the German policy have shown from the outset of the war. Submarines these people may understand, certainly not souls.

I do not love the words of hate, even now, or even when uttered over the bodies of those who were slain on the *Lusitania*. It is not hate, but longing and sorrow for stricken humanity, which is with me, as I am sure it is with you, the ruling sentiment. I have no fondness for useless publicity. Nevertheless, it is fair to say that the words which I have just written down may not only have a little friendly interest to you as expressing a certain change in my own attitude towards these problems about neutrality which I mentioned to you before, but may conceivably suggest to you some way in which a more public expression of mine might be of real service to some cause which you, or which other of my English friends, hold dear. The controversial literature of the war is, as you know, and as you yourself have said, a cup which seems to be overfull. Yet I now no longer feel that any duty or desire makes me hesitant concerning the expression of whatever plain speech and worthily strong sentiment might be able to contribute to a good cause. You will see from the way in which I spoke to my class, after long dutifully preserving a deliberate reticence in the classroom regarding the war,—you will see that my mouth is now open enough, if only any words that could be of use for the cause of true peace, or against the deeds and the motives of the declared enemies of mankind, could be uttered by me. It is a relief to have in such matters not only a free soul, but a perfectly free right of speech, so long as one's speech promises to contribute anything, however little, to the cause of mankind which such bitter and cruel enemies are now assailing in the sight of us all. So do with this letter, or with any part of it, precisely as you think best,—not indeed making it seem as if I were at all fond of notoriety, but merely using the right which I give you as my friend to let anybody know where I stand. I am no longer neutral, even in form. The German Prince is now the declared and proclaimed enemy of mankind, declared to be such not by any "lies" of his enemies, or by any "envious" comments of other people, but by his own quite deliberate choice to carry on war by the merciless destruction of innocent, non-combatant passengers. The single deed is indeed only a comparatively petty event when compared with the stupendous crimes which fill this war. But the sinking of the *Lusitania* has the advantage of being a deed which not only cannot be denied, but which has been proudly proclaimed as expressing the appeal that Germany now makes to all humanity. About that appeal I am not neutral. I know that that appeal expresses utter contempt for everything which makes the common life of humanity tolerable or possible. I know that if the principle of that appeal is accepted, whatever makes home or country or family or friends, or any form of loyalty, worthily dear, is made an object of a perfectly deliberate and merciless assault. About such policies and their principles, about such appeals, and about the Prince who makes them, and about his underlings who serve him, I have no longer any neutrality to keep. And without the faintest authority in any political matter, without the faintest wish for any sort of notoriety, I am perfectly willing to let this utterance receive any sort of publicity that, in its utter unworthiness to express adequately or effectively the nature of the crimes and of the infamy which it attempts to characterise, it may by chance get, should you or anybody else wish to make use of it. Of course, I need not tell you that a Harvard professor speaks only for himself, and commits none of his colleagues to anything that chances to be in his mind or on his tongue.

Josiah Royce.

Harvard University.

To Albert Perley Brogan, July 6, 1915[43]

103 Irving Street,
Cambridge, Mass.,
July 6, 1915.

My dear Professor Brogan:

I am very glad to get such good news about you, your reappointment, and your prospects.[44] I am especially glad that you can give, under the existing conditions, advanced courses in both Logic and Ethics. So far as I know, there is no text book for advanced Logic which meets the purpose which you mention,—that is, no really compendious work, which, while dealing with the problems of advanced Logic, is in a genuine sense sufficiently elementary to furnish a text with which to accompany a course of lectures. In my own effort this year to give advanced Logic, I very naturally made use of my own article in Ruge's Encyclopedia of Philosophy.[45] Since there are several other articles in that volume, such, for instance, as that of Couturat, and since one can expand any one of these little treatises, more easily than one can secure without any text the attention of a class, it seems not impossible to use any one of

[43] TLC. Royce Papers. HUA.

[44] After receiving his Ph.D. from Harvard in 1914, Brogan joined the faculty of the University of Texas where he remained throughout his teaching and administrative career.

[45] "The Principles of Logic," *Encyclopedia of the Philosophical Sciences*, ed. Wilhelm Windelband and Arnold Ruge (London: Macmillan and Co., Ltd., 1913), 1: 67–135; reprinted in *RLE*, pp. 310–78.

the articles in question as a basis for your course. A better plan would be to write a text book of your own, as you go. It would not cost you very much to have a few copies made of your MS, for the use of the class. Perhaps you might get some sort of aid, from the Department, or from some official source, in defraying such expenses. The text book thus produced might furnish you, by the end of the year, with some very good book to bring before a publisher.

I shall not forget that on the return of Professor Keen, you may be free for a new appointment a year from now. I shall then be glad to cooperate if I can, although I have no very high idea of my ability to get anything for anybody, whether it be wisdom or an appointment.

With best wishes,
Yours truly,
[Josiah Royce]

To Edward Bagnall Poulton, July 6, 1915[46]

103 Irving Street
Cambridge, Mass.
July 6, 1915.

To Professor E. B. Poulton of Oxford

My dear Professor Poulton:

I must again apologize for my delay in writing this second letter, in answer to your inquiry which reached me last summer in California. When I wrote in California, I think that I already apologized for some delay which had then occurred. Now my delays, as I fear, have passed beyond the reasonable limits of apology. My own excuse, such as it is, lies in the fact that my powers to keep up with obligations, both personal and official,—with obligations both of correspondence, and of other modes of expression,—have been very greatly hindered, and at times almost wholly inhibited, by the war, and by its chaos of sorrows and of crimes,—a chaos from which, as I well know, and often sadly remember, my dear Oxford friends suffer in a vastly more manifold and intimate way than is possible to me.

[46] TLC. Royce Papers. HUA.

What poor sympathy I, in my helplessness, am at the time able to show, I wrote down not long since in a personal letter to Professor Jacks,—a letter which I asked him to show to friends, or, if he pleased, to print, or in any way whatever to make public, however he might choose. I do not think much of that letter as an adequate expression of my views, or of anybody's right views of a situation which now concerns humanity as a whole, more and more as the time goes on. My letter, however, contains some few words that might possibly interest Oxford friends. If you were to find any interest or relief in listening to a voice from a distance, you might at some time remind Jacks of my letter, and of my willingness to have him show it to anybody, at his own choice. And in that way my words might, by chance, be of momentary interest to you.

And now to return to your memory and to your question regarding William James's words about Wallace, and about the séance.[47] My present memory is that James and I were coming home after the séance, which had taken place at a private house in the South End of Boston. On this occasion, we had together seen, several of the supposed "materialization-forms." These forms had moved about among us, very much in the way which I suppose Wallace himself to have described in his various later statements. I myself had not been very strongly impressed, with the materialized forms in question. I had no theory as to how they came to appear when and how they did. By chance, they did not arouse my curiosity in any memorable fashion. Like a number of other persons present, I had expressed scepticism, and had not proposed any method, or tried any device of my own, for investigating the phenomena.

My memory of James's words, during our return to Cambridge together, was substantially this, that he said in effect: "I suppose that it must seem strange to Wallace to watch us standing thus together on the shore of the water of this whole spiritualistic business, dipping in one foot and then another, and then shaking our feet, while he has taken the plunge, and is wet all over with the flood of spiritualism."

I do not know whether, either in writing, or in speech to you, I have ever reported my memory of these words of James otherwise than as I now do. Such memories are seldom trustworthy as to

[47] Alfred Russel Wallace, the great naturalist, was also a convinced spiritualist. During a lecture tour in America, 1886–87, he attended materialization séances in Boston. He and Poulton were close friends.

detail. In my own mind I lay stress only on the spirit of James's comment, which would have been expressed with the use of some of those inimitable phrases of William James, which came so easily from him, but which were often so hard to remember, just because they were so perfectly adapted and uniquely characteristic, in view of the speaker and of the situation.

My memory as a witness about what followed that particular séance was fallible enough last summer, and is still more so now. But as the matter now lies in my mind, there was a determined effort, somewhat later than the time when James and I visited the séance, —an effort to seize and hold the materialized form. So far my memory appears to agree with that of Wallace, as you report Wallace's account in your letter of February 7th. But my own memory continues by making me believe that the report generally current in Boston and in Cambridge about that time amongst those interested in the séances in question, declared that, at least on one occasion, the seizure of the "materialized forms," and the "exposure" both of the medium and of the confederates, was successfully accomplished. But then this current report, if I am now correctly remembering what was then reported in my hearing was, at best, a more or less untrustworthy report. In sum, there remains of the entire incident, in my own mind, James's characteristically apt comparison between Wallace, who had plunged in and was wet all over in the water, and ourselves, the supposedly critical inquirers, who stood on the shore shaking our feet, and so

> "Letting 'I dare not' wait upon 'I would'
> Like the poor cat in the adage."[48]

I do not remember that James used this quotation or mentioned "the cat in the adage." James, as I remember, seemed merely to be referring to the timid or uneasily curious experimenters in sea bathing, at the moment when they find the water chilly and a little unwelcome, and so splash a little and shake their feet.

So much, I hope, meets your wish, after this long delay,—a delay for which I once more humbly beg your pardon.

With every good wish for you, for all my dear Oxford friends, for Oxford, and for England, I remain

Yours very truly,
J. R.

[48] Shakespeare *Macbeth*, act 1, sc. 7.

To Ferdinand Canning Scott Schiller, August 24, 1915[49]

103 Irving Street,
Cambridge, Mass.,
August 24, 1915.

My dear Schiller,

I enclose the letter supporting your candidacy, and hope that it will meet your purpose, and that you will get the professorship. As a fact, the troubles of the war haunt me a great deal, and are a very heavy burden to me as onlooker, unable to counsel and unable to help, but longing for the triumph of the true Humanism, whenever this horror is over, and whenever the Devil has got so much of his due as I hope that he will soon get. Meanwhile, I do what I can with my not wholly inhuman form of Absolutism. May you prosper. I often think how sad this would make James, if he had been forced to witness it. The brevity of life has its conveniences.

Yours most cordially,
[Josiah Royce]

To the Lords and Gentlemen of the University of Oxford, August 24, 1915[50]

Harvard University
August 24, 1915.

My Lords and Gentlemen:

I beg leave to recommend Mr. F. C. S. Schiller for the vacancy in the chair of Logic, of which he informs me, and for which I understand he is a candidate.[51]

49 TLC. Royce Papers. HUA.

50 TLC. Royce Papers. HUA. The index to this collection, prepared by Victoria Hernandez, *et al.*, lists the addressee as "The Lords and Gentlemen of Harvard," but as the contents obviously indicate, the letter was sent to the University of Oxford.

51 A tutorial fellow of Corpus Christi College, Oxford, Schiller was never elected to a professorship. Reuben Abel, *The Pragmatic Humanism of F. C. S. Schiller* (New York: King's Crown Press, 1955), p. 5, suggests that F. H. Bradley might have prevented Schiller's election.

My principal ground for venturing to feel sure that this recommendation is fully warranted by the situation, depends upon two facts. First, that movement in thought to whose whole modern development Mr. Schiller has contributed for quite a number of years, and with which his name will very long be associated, namely, the very justly so-called Humanistic movement, is one which is purely destined to play a very important part in the coming decade of philosophical thought. Secondly, Mr. Schiller has increasingly shown in his recent work his power as a productive student of Logic, and has contributed to that ancient branch of learning distinctly new and significant ideas and theories. And if anything is at the present time more needed in philosophy than another contribution to fundamental thought, such need especially exists for new contributions to Logic.

I have for a good many years followed the thoughts of Mr. Schiller, sometimes with more [or] less explicit polemic, but always with stimulation and aid in my efforts to do my own philosophical work. I certainly feel that the time has come to give his position as philosopher, as productive scholar, as a leader in his time, and as a teacher who is an ornament to his college and to his university, that sort of recognition which a professorship will express. I lay special stress upon the fact, already mentioned, that this is especially the moment when the growing significance of what Mr. Schiller himself has called the Humanistic movement, is impressed upon the mind of every serious student of philosophy, by the great events of the moment, and by the great prospects for the future of philosophy at Oxford, which the present situation, despite all its grave cares and dangers, brings before the mind of all who love Oxford and philosophy. By Humanism I mean, as Mr. Schiller means, no one set of unchangeable theses, but a spirit, a method of philosophical enquiry, which my dear colleague at Harvard, and Mr. Schiller's friend, William James, so unweariedly encouraged, exemplified, and, as Mr. Schiller has also done, applied. Such a spirit in philosophy is much wider and deeper than any one of the special doctrines that, in the course of the philosophical controversies of recent years has been associated with it. I believe that Mr. Schiller, throughout all his varied philosophical investigations, has stood rather for the spirit of humanism, than for any one of the more or less polemical assertions which have been associated with the name. It is because I recognize that Mr. Schiller has now come to be the principal representative of the philosophical tendencies in question,—the tendencies to which William James's later years were devoted,—it is because I also believe that these tendencies will play a great part in the next generation of philosophical thought, that I feel how important it would be for Oxford were Mr. Schiller's position as fully recognized as an election to this Professorship in Logic would cause it to be recognized. It is, furthermore, because I so much value the study and teaching of Logic, and feel grateful to Mr. Schiller for his original and independent contributions to a reform of Logic, that I regard precisely this Professorship as peculiarly adapted to meet the requirement of recognizing the region where Mr. Schiller has done that portion of his work which is most likely to play a part in future discussions of this fundamental region of philosophical enquiry.

That I myself stand in a good many ways in a certain contrast to the positions most frequently emphasized by Mr. Schiller, makes this tribute to the significance of what he has done, the more hearty and sincere, and the more the result, not of today's nor of yesterday's acquaintance with his work, but of my own long and gradually acquired knowledge of his modes of thinking, and of what seems to me their significance.

The opinion of an American who has every reason to be, both a grateful friend of Oxford, and a friend deeply concerned for the best possible future, both of philosophy in general and of Logic in particular at Oxford, may be not wholly out of place in case the Electors are kind enough to consider what I have said. In any case, I venture to lay my words before you, with sympathy for the present cares which beset my friends at Oxford, and with the confident hope that all may be well with them, with learning, and with the University, as well as with humanity, in the future for which I earnestly hope.

Believe me, with great respect,

Your obedient servant,
[Josiah Royce]

To Douglas Clyde Macintosh, November 7, 1915[52]

103 Irving St.
Cambridge, Mass.
November 7, 1915

My Dear Professor Macintosh:—

I learn with interest and gratitude of the kind intention of the Theological Society to discuss some opinions of mine, relating to the interpretation of Christianity at the meeting which is to be held on December 18 in New York City.[53]

Mrs. Royce, I believe, has already written to you, notifying you of my acceptance of your invitation, and of that of the Theological Society. I shall be very glad to hear the criticisms which your members have to pass upon my opinions. I can hardly venture to "hope," as you so kindly do, that I shall be able to offer any effective "reply to the criticisms that may be offered"; for your society contains, as I learn from you, "thirty or more professors of systematic theology," while, apart from my metaphysical and other philosophical interests, I am neither a "theologican," nor "systematic" ("*bin weder Fräulein, weder schön*"), and consequently shall come to the meeting of your society with no hope whatever of being able to reply to my expert and authoritative critics. In fact, if I were coming to your meeting in anything resembling a controversial spirit, I should look forward to the occasion as to a sort of *Dies Irae*,[54] and should fervently ask:

> Quid sum miser tunc dicturus
> quem patronum rogaturus
> dum vix justus sit securus?

—You may translate *justus* by the word pragmatist, realist, hyper-pragmatist, mystic, conservative, or otherwise, as you please.

[52] ALS. Royce Papers. HUA.

[53] The exact arrangements of this meeting remain unclear, but at least two of the articles in the special issue of the *Philosophical Review*, (May 1916) seem to have been prepared for this theological meeting: William Adams Brown, "The Problem of Christianity," pp. 305–14, and B. W. Bacon, "Royce's Interpretation of Christianity," pp. 315–35.

[54] A thirteenth century Latin poem, ascribed to Thomas of Celano. The verses quoted below constitute one stanza from this poem.

But since I do not look for controversial good fortunes, nor shrink from the doom of a heretic, but do feel very thankful that so kindly and authoritative a company of my colleagues have been pleased to give me an evening of their time, I shall do my poor little best to make the evening that you have named one of welcome experience for myself, and of whatever service I can offer to your Society and to yourself. I await your further instructions and shall be glad to do whatever I can to assist in making your plan successful from the point of view of my most generous hosts.

Yours Very Truly
Josiah Royce

To Wilbur Lucius Cross, November 8, 1915[55]

Cambridge November 8th, 1915.
103 Irving Street.

Professor Wilbur L. Cross
Yale Review;

My dear Professor Cross:

I enclose herewith the manuscript of the article which you requested me to prepare for the December number of the *Yale Review*.[56]

The article has been a good deal revised and condensed. I hope that, in its present form, it is not too long. You did not assign any precise limits to its length. In your letter of October 7th you named the tenth of November as the date when you wished to have the manuscript in your hands.

With thanks for your kind request, I remain

Yours very truly,
Josiah Royce

55 TLS. *Yale Review* Papers. YUB.

56 "The Hope of the Great Community" *Yale Review* 5 (January 1916): 269–91; reprinted in *HGC*, pp. 25–70.

To Douglas Clyde Macintosh, December 4, 1915[57]

103 Irving Street,
Cambridge, Mass.,
December 4, 1915.

Professor D. C. Macintosh,
1113 Yale Station,
New Haven, Conn.

My dear Macintosh,

I certainly ought to have responded more promptly to yours of November 22. But there have been numerous interruptions since then. This is my first opportunity to answer with assurance your questions.

First, regarding your proposal with regard to an informal meeting, and a dinner which you kindly propose, and at which you ask me to meet a group of my colleagues, "either at the Faculty Club, Columbia, or elsewhere";–I thank you very heartily for [the] proposal about the dinner, and accept with thanks the invitation. I should of course be glad to meet the group of colleagues in question wherever you wish, and at whatever hour. If you wish me to dress for this dinner, I can come prepared, and can dress at the hotel.

As to the hotel which I prefer, I am, like a good many old-fashioned professors who occasionally visit New York City, an old customer of the Manhattan Hotel. I used to be well known there, and then my preferences as to some quiet outside room, well up above the noise of the street, were known and remembered. But nowadays the flight of time has changed the clerks at the counters, and when I visit the Manhattan Hotel, although I still like the place, and still find it a quiet region where professional men frequently go, nobody knows any longer who I am. If you see no objection to the Manhattan Hotel, that would therefore be quite welcome to me as a place to stay Saturday night. So long as it is quite in accordance with your plans, and those of your Society, that I should go to New York by the ten o'clock Limited Saturday morning, the time of my return from New York on Sunday remains wholly undecided. I should be glad to come back by any train that gets me to Boston in the afternoon or early evening. This

[57] TLS. Royce Papers. HUA.

fact might have some relation to your own wishes. For instance, it would be perfectly possible for me to go to church on Sunday, in case the presence of such a heretic was in no danger of disturbing the congregation. A member of your Society, who was himself preaching on Sunday, and who desired to use the opportunity to confound, and overawe an impious philosopher, might arrange with me, if he chose, to bring to naught my false doctrines, in a sermon, and I could then promise him, on that one occasion, to listen, to make no reply, and to go away a wiser man, even if not a convert. Thus the truth would hereby win the last word in a discussion. Of course, I lay no stress upon this suggestion, except that, if somebody wants to bring the matter to a duly triumphant conclusion, the way proposed constitutes one possible one.

I think that this will sufficiently indicate to you my plans. I thank you warmly, as before, for your invitation, for that of your Society, and for the opportunity which the proposed meeting on Saturday afternoon, the eighteenth of December, offers to me.

Very sincerely yours,
Josiah Royce

To the Members of the American Philosophical Association, January 11, 1916[58]

To the Members
of the
American Philosophical Association

Since I am unable adequately to express, by means of separate letters, how deeply I am moved by what was said and done for me at the meeting of the Association held at the University of Pennsylvania on Tuesday and Wednesday, December 28 and 29, 1915, I beg my friends to accept this word of thanks, and of greeting for the coming year.[59]

[58] Engraved letter. Royce Papers. HUA. The signature, place of origin, and date are written in Royce's hand. The editor has seen several copies of this letter in other manuscript collections; some of these bear the date, January 10, 1916.

[59] The papers read at this meeting, together with others, were printed in a special festschrift issue of *Philosophical Review* 25 (May 1916).

The love of my students and of my guides, helpers, and fellow servants in the search for truth, is very precious. I shall never forget (while memory remains mine), the thoughtful care which devised and the patient labor which carried into effect the plan followed by the Association in its Philadelphia meeting. That plan was wisely considerate of the philosophical interests of your guest, and was also well adapted to remind me of that union of minds and of hearts which underlies and justifies all our differences of opinion and inspires our common labors in the task of philosophical research.

Affectionately Yours,
Josiah Royce
Cambridge, Massachusetts
January 11, 1916.

To Wendell T. Bush, February 7, 1916[60]

103 Irving St.
Cambridge, Mass.
Feb. 7, 1916.

Dear Professor Bush:—

One of my Assistants, in two of my Philosophy Courses, is a man of considerable promise,—Mr. W. F. Kernan (whose address is 2 Holyoke St., Cambridge). Kernan proposes to prepare his Ph. D. thesis (due about a year from now), on some topic connected with C. S. Peirce's philosophy. Kernan has also become quite familiar with a large body of the Peirce papers (kept at present in my study in Emerson Hall), and is quite competent to prepare,—in cooperation with me,—the needed introduction and close to my proposed sketch of Peirce's philosophy. Your letter of Jan. 28 explains what you want done about the Peirce paper which I prepared a year since, and have since sent for your Peirce number. Since I myself am so beset with cares of one sort or another, I can see no better way of meeting your wish about my MS on Peirce than to ask you to send it to Mr. Kernan, at the above address, with a word explaining that you send it at my request, and that you are willing to have him collaborate with me in finishing up the MS for publication.

60 ALS. *Journal of Philosophy* Papers. CUB.

Then Kernan & I will do the work together.[61] Meanwhile, Kernan is, I believe, also planning some other Peirce article (based on Kernan's use of the Peirce papers) on a topic of his own choosing; and whenever he offers you a MS of his own devising, I think that both you and the *Journal* will be interested in giving his offer some attention. I ask, therefore, for Kernan your kindly interest whenever he sends you MSS.

Yours Very Truly
Josiah Royce

To James Hastings, March 14, 1916[62]

103 Irving Street,
Cambridge, Mass.,
March 14, 1916.

Dear Dr. Hastings:

I enclose herewith the long promised article: "*Order*."[63] Let the chaos of the time in which both you and I have to try to live,—not indeed excuse,—but, if you will kindly permit,—do something to explain the delays to which this article has been, against my best will, subject. No doubt the article is much too long. I fear that it comes much too late, even to be useful, as something to be cut down, and hewn into shape for your pages. Do with it what you will. If it is useless, throw it away. I have retained a copy of it, so that you need not send it back to me, unless you can find space to put it into print. You mentioned a while since a possible article of mine on "Philosophy." Do you still want one? If so, what shall I do, and when?—in case I get any time.

I am doing my regular academic work, and a good deal of extra work also. But the distractions and disorders of the times render it very hard for me to finish things on time, especially when the

[61] "Charles Sanders Peirce," *Journal of Philosophy, Psychology, and Scientific Methods* 13 (1916): 701–9, is signed by both Royce and Fergus Kernan.

[62] TLC. Royce Papers. HUA.

[63] "Order," *Encyclopaedia of Religion and Ethics*, ed. James Hastings, 13 vols. (New York: Charles Scribner's Sons, 1928), 9: 533–40. Royce also contributed articles on "Axiom," "Error and Truth," "Mind," and "Negation"; all reprinted in *RLE*, pp. 125–38, 146–231.

things in question lie at all aside from the track of my Harvard daily work.

May somebody find for us the long-sought way to light, to order, to peace. It will seem strange, and strangely, almost weirdly delightful, if ever the time comes when you and your country, and your allies, and humanity, have won, if we ever win, the way to genuine and rational peace. For my part, I wait, in anxiety, but not without hope, for the dawn light. Forgive my uselessness as a contributor. As for my diffuseness, and intolerable long-windedness, you may cure that, if you will, so far as this contribution is concerned, with the aid of your waste basket.

Yours sincerely,
[Josiah Royce]

Dr. James Hastings,
11 King's Gate,
Aberdeen, Scotland.

To Mary Whiton Calkins, March 20, 1916[64]

Cambridge March 20th, 1916.
103 Irving Street.

Dear Miss Calkins:

Professor Hocking has sent to me the paper which you have so kindly contributed to the forthcoming discussion of my philosophical teaching.

Let me say at once that I hope that you will print the paper precisely in accordance with your own wishes, with your own views regarding the relation between my philosophy and Christian theism, and in accordance with your own views regarding the sense in which my most recent book on *The Problem of Christianity*, is or is not in accordance with the spirit and the letter of my earlier works. Your paper about me, and about my relation to Christian theism is too valuable to be tampered with, too kindly to be used as an opportunity for a further discussion from me. You are an expert on all the questions at issue. The account which you kindly give of

[64] TLS. WCL. Partly printed in Miss Calkins's "The Foundation in Royce's Philosophy for Christian Theism," *Philosophical Review* 25 (1916): 293–6.

the position taken in my earlier books,—that is in all the books that precede *The Problem of Christianity*,—is as accurate and scholarly as it is friendly. I am not conscious of having taken in my recent work a position inconsistent, in its genuine meaning, with the positions which you recognize, and have so frequently and ably expounded. Therefore, precisely in so far, I have and can have only thanks for your interpretation and for your aid. But the two central ideas upon which my *Problem of Christianity* turns, the idea of the community, and the idea of what the historical theology of the Christian church early learned to call "the holy spirit" are ideas which are as living, and growing, as they are ancient. They grew when the prophets of Israel began to formulate their doctrine of Jerusalem, which, in the beginning, was a city, of somewhat questionable architecture, and morals, in the hill districts of Judea; but which, in the end, became the heavenly realm of which the mystic author of the well known medieval hymn wrote, and which the world is still trying to understand. These two ideas, the Community, and the Spirit have been growing ever since. They are growing today. They certainly have assumed, in my own mind, a new vitality, and a very much deeper significance than, for me, they ever had before I wrote my *Problem of Christianity*. My book on the *Problem of Christianity* records the experience and the reflections which both led over to that book, and have been working in my mind daily more and more, ever since I wrote that book. The reflections in question constitute, for me, not something inconsistent with my former position, but a distinct addition to my former position, a new attainment,—I believe a new growth. I do not believe that you change, in a way involving inconsistency, when you re-interpret former ideas, as I have surely known you frequently to do, and have rejoiced to find you doing.

To borrow a figure from a remote field, I do not believe that Lincoln acted in a manner essentially inconsistent with his earlier political ideas when he wrote the Emancipation Proclamation and freed the slaves. To be sure, before he wrote that proclamation, he had seen a new light. My poor little book on *The Problem of Christianity* is certainly no Emancipation Proclamation, and is certainly no document of any considerable importance. But it certainly is the product of what for me is a new light, of a new experience, of ideas which are as new to me as the original form of my idealism was new to me when I first defined it.

As to whether these new views are consistent with my foregoing views, I can best express my position by saying that if, tomorrow, or at any later time, you are to re-interpret the very thoughts which you have expressed in your so kind review of my Theism, in such a way as to set forth in your own words the doctrine of the Spirit and of the Community which I have tried, very imperfectly to formulate, I should not think that you were saying anything inconsistent with what is now in your paper, but were only formulating a perfectly rational enrichment and development of your present opinions.

As for what my present position means, there is here space to say only this:—For me, at present, a genuinely and loyally united community, which lives a coherent life, is, in a perfectly [literal][65] sense, a person. Such a person, for Paul, the Church of Christ was. On the other hand, any human individual person, in a perfectly literal sense, is a community. The coherent life which includes past present and future, and holds them reasonably together, is the life of what I have also called, both in *The Problem of Christianity* and elsewhere a Community of Interpretation, in which the present, with an endless fecundity of invention, interprets the past to the future, precisely as, in the Pauline-Johannine type of theology, Christ, or the Spirit, interprets the united individuals, who constitute the human aspect of the Church, to the divine being in whom these members seek, at once their fulfilment, their unity, their diversity, and the goal of their loyalty. All this is a scrap of theology, which serves as a hint of what I have been trying to formulate in this recent phase, not merely of my thinking but of my experience. I do not know any reason why this phase of my thinking should attract any other interest than what may be due to its actual relations to a process which has been going on, in human thought, ever since Heraclitus remarked that the Logos is fluent, and ever since Israel began to idealize the life of a little hill town in Judea.

I stand for the importance of this process, which has led Christianity to regard a community, not merely as an aggregate but as a Person, and at the same time, to enrich its ideal memory of a person, until he became transformed into a Community.

The process in question, is not merely theological, and is not merely mystical, still less merely mythical. Nor is it a process invented merely by abstract metaphysicians. It is the process which

[65] This emendation is made on the MS, but it is not in Royce's hand.

Victor Hugo expressed in *Les Miserables,* when he put into the mouth of Enjolras the words: "*Ma mère, c'est la république.*" As I write you these words, Frenchmen are writing the meaning of these words in their blood, about Verdun. The mother which is a republic, is a community, which is also a person,—and not merely an aggregate, and not merely by metaphor a person. Precisely so the individual patriot who leaves his home behind, and, steadfastly serving, presses on in ardent quest of the moment when his life can be fulfilled by his death for his country, is all the more richly and deeply an individual, that he is also a community of interpretation, whose life has its unity in its restless search for death on behalf of the great good cause,—its ever living Logos in its fluent quest for the goal.

Now this view is at present an essential part of my idealism. In essential meaning I suppose that it always was such an essential part. But I do not believe that I ever told my tale as fully, or with the same approach to the far off goal of saying sometime something that might prove helpful to students of idealism, as in the *Problem of Christianity.*

Subject to this comment, which is intended altogether as a self-criticism, your article,—kindly, minute, scholarly, thorough, and accurate as it is, in all the expository notes which it includes, relating to all that I published, before my *Problem of Christianity* is a paper for which I thank you most heartily, and which I hope that you will publish precisely as it stands. Whether it would be at all worthwhile to add any mention of or quotation from this reply of mine to you, is a matter that I leave herewith entirely in your hands and in those of Professor Hocking, as well as of the editor of the *Philosophical Review.* My dear friends did so much for me at Philadelphia. Your own contribution was so gracious, so fair spirited, so generous, and so kindly, that you have already done a great deal too much for me. I am sorry to give you an hour's further trouble of any sort. I shall always be grateful for your encouragement, for your counsel, for your clear understanding of me, and for your cooperation. My debt to you is of very long standing, my gratitude is very deep. That your name appears among the contributors to this piece of common work constitutes and will constitute one of the principal features that makes this collection of papers a delight that will last as long as I live.

As I understand Professor Hocking, he asks me to hand him your manuscript at once, and I shall do so today. You may show him this letter or not just as you wish. I should sign,

Gratefully and affectionately yours,
Josiah Royce

To Richard Clarke Cabot, April 21, 1916[66]

Cambridge, April 21st, 1916.
103 Irving Street.

My dear Dr. Cabot:—

It is known to you, and to the citizens' committee for America and the allies, that I have not only agreed to deliver an address on May 7th next at the Lusitania Memorial Meeting in Boston, but have also been invited to do what neither my time nor my powers will permit, namely to be present in New York, at Carnegie Hall, at 8-30 P. M. on that same Sunday, to take part in the proposed *Lusitania* Memorial Meeting of the American Rights Committee.[67]

The American Rights Committee in New York fully understand, I think, that they are not to expect my presence on that occasion at Carnegie Hall. But it has occurred to me that I might cooperate in their enterprise to some extent, if I were to send to them in advance a copy of the Lusitania Memorial Address which I propose to deliver in Boston. If the New York committee should think well of this plan, they might then have, if your own Committee here in Boston consent, so much material for publication in connection with the report of their meeting. Perhaps they might get somebody in New York to read some part of my address to such portion of their audience as chose to listen. The mere offer of such a use of an advance copy of my address might not seem to the New York Committee intrusive, and would not be ill meant on my part.

My question is: Would your Committee, at its meeting tomor-

[66] TLS. Cabot Papers. HUA.

[67] Royce delivered an address at the Tremont Temple on "The First Anniversary of the Sinking of the Lusitania, May 7, 1916," *Boston Evening Transcript*, May 8, 1916; reprinted in *HGC*, pp. 93–121. The Carnegie Hall Meeting was postponed until May 19, at the request of Mayor Mitchel, who objected to a resolution which was to be introduced. Both Cabot and Royce were honorary vice-presidents of the American Rights Committee.

row, be willing to consider this proposal of mine, to approve or disapprove it, as you may collectively think best, and to advise me what to do?

I am still looking for advice about my own *Lusitania* address before the meeting which your committee proposes to hold on the 7th of May. Mrs. Cabot, as well as Dr. J. J. Putnam and others, have already given me very kindly and welcome counsel, which I shall try to use as I can. I am now disposed to lay strong emphasis upon the thought that the best memorial of the victims of the *Lusitania* consists in the unity of spirit which their unjust fate has aroused, and rendered effective in the minds of their brethren who mourn them, and of all who love mankind the better because of these who were thus sacrificed. Christianity was much aided towards its triumph by the indignation which the unjust death of an innocent man aroused. But the indignation which the memory of the crucified founder, and the treason of Judas kept alive, was a less potent factor in the spirit of Christianity, than was the loving memory that it had been needful for this death to take place, in order that humanity might be awakened, unified, strengthened in spirit, brought together in brotherhood. At the present moment, the memory of the *Lusitania* is acting in a more potent fashion as an awakener and unifier of the spirit of brotherly endeavor, than as an unique instance of "frightfulness." In my former address at Tremont Temple I spoke of Cain, and of his mark. In my *Lusitania* Memorial address, I should like to say something, in no merely traditional spirit, of what I may venture symbolically to call, in traditional terms, the memory of our Lord, and the hope of those "who love his appearing."

I write this on Good Friday. Hence my momentary choice of phraseology. I hope to find some way of putting some such idea into fitting language.

You know why I cannot come to the meetings of the Committee. I am always with you in spirit.

Affectionately yours,
Josiah Royce

To Richard Clarke Cabot, June 14, 1916[68]

103 Irving Street
Cambridge
June 14, 1916.

Dear Cabot:—

The first copy of the number of the *Philosophical Review*, with my anniversary papers in it, which has just reached me, came to hand this morning; and I have now passed two hours over it, with constantly increasing joy in this new evidence of the kindness of you, of Hocking, and of all the friends who planned and carried out this really wonderful expression of faithful and thoughtful care. I can only dare to enjoy so undeserved and welcome a token of goodness, by keeping in mind that after all it is rather our common cause,—that of philosophy and of mankind,—than my particular interest, that is in question.

Last Sunday, when Mrs. Royce told me, on my return from a long afternoon walk, of the added kindness which you and Hocking have devised—namely that of preparing for me, as a gift, a few special bound copies to be used as I please, Mrs. Royce fully agreed with me that, (—despite your kind willingness to provide somewhere about a dozen of these special copies, in case I was clear in *my* plans about the use of so many extra copies as this),—I must carefully limit my request to a very small list of those who have been nearest to my work, and especially to the later and latest phases of that work.

After several changes of plans we now agree that the following list completes all that we ought to think of as recipients of this special gift of yours. The names are:

My two sisters, Mrs. H. E. Barney and Miss Ruth Royce.

My two sons, Edward Royce and Stephen Royce.

Mrs. Royce and myself for directly personal use here at home.

Dr. J. Loewenberg who helped me so much in 1912 to pull together for the *Problem of Christianity*, and made that book possible.

Professor L. P. Jacks, who got me the Hibbert Lectures of 1913, and whose guest I was in Oxford in 1913.

[68] ALS. Cabot Papers. HUA.

This would make in all eight special copies to supply in full the most kindly offer which Mrs. Royce conveyed to me on Sunday as you wish and as the wish of Hocking.

How much I thank you both I cannot rightly say. Please forgive my imperfect expression of my deep gratitude and convey my loving greetings to Mrs. Cabot.

Yours Most Affectionately
Josiah Royce

Appendix A

Biographical Notes on Addressees

The following is an alphabetical listing of notes concerning those persons to whom Royce sent the letters printed in this edition.

ABBOT, FRANCIS ELLINGWOOD (1836–1903), entered the Unitarian clergy after receiving his A.B. from Harvard University in 1859. A leader of the "free religion" movement, he became minister of the Independent Church in Toledo, Ohio, where he edited the *Index*, a weekly journal of free religion. Returning to Cambridge, he received the second Ph.D. in philosophy granted at Harvard (1881) and established the Home School for Boys. During the second term, 1887–88, he was appointed instructor in philosophy at Harvard. JR vigorously attacked *The Way Out of Agnosticism* (1890) in *The International Journal of Ethics*—thus initiating a notorious controversy.

BADGER, CHARLES W., was secretary of the Berkeley Club.

BAKER, GEORGE PIERCE (1866–1935), taught English and drama at Harvard University (1887–1925) and at Yale University (1925–33). In 1888–89, he was JR's assistant in Forensics. He is best known for the "47 Workshop" attended by Eugene O'Neill, Sidney Howard, and others. He was author of *The Development of Shakespeare as a Dramatist* (1907) and *Dramatic Technique* (1919).

BALDWIN, JAMES MARK (1861–1934), a founding editor of *Psychological Review*, held professorships at Lake Forest College (1887), University of Toronto (1887–93), Princeton University (1893–1903), Johns Hopkins University (1903–8), and at the National University, Mexico (1908). In 1901, Royce contributed articles to Baldwin's *Dictionary of Philosophy and Psychology*. Though he had been a student of Wundt in Leipzig, Baldwin abandoned experimental psychology in favor of genetic studies and social psychology. These interests are apparent in *Mental Development in the Child and Race* (1895) and *Social and Ethical Interpretations in Mental Development* (1897).

BARNEY, CHARLES ROYCE, was JR's nephew, the son of Harriette Royce Barney. Despite his uncle's offer of assistance, "Roy" never attended eastern schools.

BRETT, GEORGE PLATT (1858–1936), was president of Macmillan Co. and JR's principal publisher from 1897 to 1916. Brett is often noted for having achieved depth and diversity in American publishing, and for encouraging new developments in scholarship and poetry.

BRIGGS, THOMAS HENRY (b. 1877), wrote several books on public education, including *Pragmatism and Pedagogy* (1940).

BRIGHTMAN, EDGAR SHEFFIELD (1884–1953), a disciple of Borden Parker Bowne, held professorships at Nebraska Wesleyan University (1912–15), Wesleyan University (1915–19), Boston University (1919–53).

BROGAN, ALBERT PERLEY (b. 1889), was educated at Harvard University: A.B. (1911), A.M. (1912), Ph.D. (1914). He has been on the faculty of the University of Texas since 1914.

BUSH, WENDELL T. (1866–1941), was an editor of the *Journal of Philosophy*. He received an A.M. at Harvard University (1898) and a Ph.D. at Columbia University (1905) where he spent his professional career.

CABOT, RICHARD CLARKE (1869–1939), a physician at Massachusetts General Hospital (1898–1921), taught in the Harvard University Medical School (1899–1933) and also held the chair of Social Ethics (1920–34). He was a close personal friend of JR and a frequent participant in his seminars as well as in informal gatherings. A leader in the development of social work, Cabot published, in 1906, an important *Annual Report of Social Service Permitted at the Massachusetts General Hospital.*

CALKINS, MARY WHITON (1863–1930), was one of the first American women to attain eminence in philosophy and psychology. After receiving A.B. and A.M. degrees at Smith College, she completed all requirements for the Ph.D. at Harvard University (1890–96), but was declared ineligible because of sex. A professor at Wellesley College (1890–1926), she was author of *Association: An Essay Analytic and Experimental* (1896), *The Persistent Problems of Philosophy* (1907), and other works.

Cattell, James McKeen (1860–1944), a psychologist with a Ph.D. from Leipzig (1886), taught at the University of Pennsylvania (1888–91) and Columbia University (1891–1917). He was extremely active as an editor, working on *Psychological Review, Science, Scientific Monthly, American Naturalist,* etc. He was also president of the Science Press Printing Co.

Coale, Caroline Dorsey, was the wife of George Buchanan Coale.

Coale, George Buchanan (ca. 1819–87), was a prominent Baltimore businessman and cultural leader. He was founder of the insurance firm, George B. Coale & Son, and president of the Merchant's Mutual Marine Insurance Co. In 1870, he founded and became director of the Maryland Academy of Fine Arts; he was also active in the Wednesday Club, an amateur group devoted to music and drama. JR became attached to Coale and his family in 1876–78; *RAP* is dedicated to him.

Cross, Wilbur Lucius (1862–1948), was a member of the Yale University faculty (1894–1930) and editor of the *Yale Review.*

Dana, John Cotton (1856–1929), a graduate of Dartmouth College, was head librarian at the Free Public Library, Newark, N.J.

Davidson, Thomas (1840–1900), founded and supervised the Summer School of the Culture Sciences at Glenmore, N.Y., in the Adirondacks.

Deakin, Alfred (1857–1919), was prime minister of Australia (1903–4, 1905–8, 1909–10). Deakin and JR became fast friends during the latter's trip to the antipodes in 1888. Though they never met again, they kept their friendship alive through correspondence.

Dorr, George Bucknam (1853–1944), was the son of Mary Ward Dorr and a close friend of JR. A member of the Visiting Committee, Dorr played an important role in the building of Harvard's Emerson Hall.

Dorr, Mary Ward, was a leader of Boston-Cambridge Society. JR was closely attached to her for many years and expressed his gratitude through the dedication of *SMP.*

Edgett, Edwin Francis (1867–1946), a Harvard University graduate, was on the editorial staff of the *Boston Transcript* (1894–1938).

Eliot, Charles William (1834–1926), was president of Harvard University (1869–1909). He is widely praised for his leadership during a critical period of Harvard's growth.

FITE, WARNER (1867–1955), is noted for his works in ethical theory: *Individualism* (1911) and *Moral Philosophy* (1925). With a Ph.D. from the University of Pennsylvania (1894), he held positions at Williams College (1895–97), University of Chicago (1897–1903), University of Texas (1903–6), Indiana University (1906–15), Stanford University (1913), and Princeton University (1915–35). In 1911–12, Fite was Lecturer in Philosophy at Harvard University.

FRÉMONT, JESSIE BENTON (1824–1902), was the daughter of Senator Thomas Hart Benton of Missouri and wife of John Charles Frémont.

GARDINER, HARRY NORMAN (1855–1927), taught philosophy at Smith College (1884–1924).

GILDER, RICHARD WATSON (1844–1909), became editor of *Century Magazine* in 1881.

GILMAN, DANIEL COIT (1831–1908), was president of the University of California (1872–75) and of Johns Hopkins University (1875–1901). Thus he had a profound impact on JR's professional development. After retiring from Hopkins he became president of the Carnegie Institution, Washington, D.C. (1901–4).

GILMAN, NICHOLAS PAINE (1849–1912), a Unitarian clergyman, taught at Meadville Theological School (1895–1912) and edited *Literary World* (1888–95) and *The New World* (1892–1900). JR published several pieces in these periodicals.

HALL, GRANVILLE STANLEY (1844–1924), studied experimental psychology under Wundt in Leipzig and received the first Harvard University Ph.D. in philosophy (1878). In 1882 he joined the faculty of Johns Hopkins University; in 1888 he became the first president of Clark University.

HANUS, PAUL HENRY (1855–1941), was the first professor of education at Harvard University (1891–1921).

HARRIS, WILLIAM TORREY (1835–1909), was a leading spokesman for the so-called St. Louis Hegelians. He was editor of the *Journal of Speculative Philosophy* (1867–93), and U. S. Commissioner of Education (1889–1906).

HASTINGS, JAMES (1852–1922), was a Scottish clergyman who edited the *Encyclopaedia of Religion and Ethics* (12 vols., 1908–21).

HENDERSON, LAWRENCE JOSEPH (1878–1942), a biological chemist at Harvard University who became professor in 1919, was a frequent visitor of JR's seminar. JR was a strong supporter of the teleological argument of *The Fitness of the Environment* (1913) and *The Order of Nature* (1917).

HITCHCOCK, JAMES RIPLEY WELLMAN (1857–1918), was editor and literary advisor for D. Appleton and Company (1890–1902). He handled the publication of *SGE*.

HOCKING, AGNES BOYLE O'REILLY was the wife of the philosopher William Ernest Hocking who received a Ph.D. from Harvard University in 1904. Between 1908 and 1914 the Hockings lived in New Haven, Connecticut. In 1914 Hocking became professor of philosophy at Harvard University.

HOWISON, GEORGE HOLMES (1834–1916), was Mills Professor of Philosophy at the University of California and founder of the Philosophical Union. He was educated at Marietta College, Lane Theological Seminary, and the University of Berlin. Before moving to California he taught at Washington University, St. Louis (1866–69), Massachusetts Institute of Technology (1871–79), Harvard University (1879–80), and the University of Michigan (1883–84). His philosophy is fragmentarily presented in *The Limits of Evolution* (1901). He was a participant in *CG* which he also edited.

JACKS, LAWRENCE PEARSALL (1860–1955), was the first editor of the *Hibbert Journal* (1902–43). He was professor of philosophy, Manchester College, Oxford from 1903, principal from 1915 until his retirement from both posts in 1931.

JAMES, ALICE GIBBENS (1849–1922), was the wife of William James.

JAMES, EDMUND JANES (1855–1925), was president of the University of Illinois (1904–20).

JAMES, WILLIAM (1842–1910), was JR's closet friend. During the thirty-five years of their association, they had profound effects on one another's thought. James's major works are *Principles of Psychology* (1890), *The Will to Believe* (1897), *Varieties of Religious Experience* (1902), *Pragmatism* (1907), and *A Pluralistic Universe* (1909).

JOHNSON, ROBERT UNDERWOOD (1853–1937), was on the editorial staff of *Century Magazine* (1873–1913).

JONES, WILLIAM CAREY (1854–1923), was one of JR's college friends; both received B.A. degrees from the University of California in 1875. But as a nephew of John Charles Frémont, Jones found his friendship with JR cooled after the publication of *California* (1886). He had a long tenure on the faculty of the University of California (1877–1923).

JORDAN, DAVID STARR (1851–1931), was the first president of Stanford University (1891–1913). Previously he had taught zoology at Butler University (1875–79) and Indiana University (1879–85); he was president of Indiana University from 1885 to 1891.

KNIGHT, WILLIAM ANGUS (1836–1916), was professor of moral philosophy at University of St. Andrews (1876–1902).

LANMAN, CHARLES ROCKWELL (1850–1941), a Sanskritist at Johns Hopkins University (1876–80) and Harvard University (1880–1941), was a close and loyal friend of JR for forty years.

LOEWENBERG, JACOB (b. 1882) was JR's most trusted assistant. He edited *FE* and *Lectures on Modern Idealism*. Loewenberg is professor emeritus at the University of California.

LOVEJOY, ARTHUR ONCKEN (1873–1962), was one of the most distinguished American philosophers and intellectual historians of the twentieth century. He received his A.B. from the University of California in 1895 and his A.M. from Harvard University in 1897. Abandoning graduate study without the Ph.D., Lovejoy held positions at Stanford University (1899–1901), Washington University (1901–8), University of Missouri (1908–10), and Johns Hopkins University (1910–38). He is best known for *The Revolt Against Dualism* (1903) and *The Great Chain of Being* (1936).

LOWELL, ABBOTT LAWRENCE (1856–1943), practiced law in Boston (1880–97), taught government at Harvard University (1897–1909), and was president of Harvard (1909–33). He was author of *Public Opinion and Popular Government* (1913).

MCCHESNEY, JOSEPH BURWELL, was secretary of the Berkeley Club.

MACINTOSH, DOUGLAS CLYDE (1877–1948), received a Ph.D. from the University of Chicago (1909) and became professor of theology at Yale University (1916). Several of his many books are concerned with philosophical foundations of theology: *Reaction Against Metaphysics in Theology* (1911), *The Problem of Knowledge* (1915), etc.

MARCH, ALDEN (1869–1942), was Sunday editor of the *New York Times* (1910–17).

MARKHAM, EDWIN (1852–1940), the poet, is best remembered for *The Man with the Hoe and Other Poems* (1899).

MARSHALL, HENRY RUTGERS (1852–1927), followed two professions, architecture and philosophy. Though he never held a regular academic post, he lectured on esthetics at Columbia University (1894–95), Yale University (1906–7), and Princeton University (1915–17). He was author of *Pain, Pleasure, and Aesthetics* (1894) and several other works on related subjects.

MATTHEWS, JAMES BRANDER (1852–1929), taught English literature and drama at Columbia University (1891–1924).

MAY, ABIGAIL WILLIAMS (1829–88), was a reformer and a life member of the Massachusetts Society for the University Education of Women.

MINOT, CHARLES SEDGWICK (1852–1914), anatomist, received a B.S. from Massachusetts Institute of Technology (1872); studied at Leipzig, Paris, and Würzburg; received a S.D. from Harvard University (1878). In 1880 he joined the faculty of the Harvard Medical School where he remained for the remainder of his professional career. He and JR were first associated in the 1880s as prominent members of the American Society for Psychical Research. In later years JR was greatly interested in Minot's theories of scientific method.

MOORE, FLORENCE SPARKS, was the mother of Jared Sparks Moore, philosopher and student of JR.

MOSES, BERNARD (1846–1930), was professor of history at the University of California (1876–1930). One of JR's early colleagues, Moses also edited the *Berkeley Quarterly* which printed four of JR's essays (1880–81).

MUNRO, WILLIAM BENNETT (1875–1957), taught history and government at Harvard University (1904–45) and was an editorial writer for the *Boston Herald* (1907–21).

MÜNSTERBERG, HUGO (1863–1916), a student of Wundt, was brought from Germany to be professor of psychology at Harvard University (1892–1916). He was on close terms with JR until after the sinking of the *Lusitania* when their attitudes toward the German government brought their friendship to an end.

NORTON, CHARLES ELIOT (1827–1908), was professor of fine arts at Harvard University (1874–98).

NORTON, Sara, was one of the daughters of Charles Eliot Norton.

OAK, HENRY LEBBEUS (1844–1905), was librarian and superintendent of the H. H. Bancroft Library and claimed, apparently with justification, that he was the sole author of many of "Bancroft's *Works*."

PALMER, GEORGE HERBERT (1842–1933), taught philosophy at Harvard University (1872–1913) and for many years was department chairman.

PEIRCE, CHARLES SANDERS (1839–1914), was a founder of pragmatism, logician, and eccentric genius who was unable to hold a permanent academic post or publish a completed philosophical treatise. JR regarded Peirce with profound respect.

PERRY, RALPH BARTON (1876–1957), was one of the "Six Realists." After teaching briefly at Williams College (1899–1900) and Smith College (1902–5), he joined the Harvard University faculty (1905–46) where he had received his Ph.D. in 1899. Although their philosophies were in direct conflict, Perry and JR remained personally on excellent terms. Perry's early work includes *The Approach to Philosophy* (1905) and *Present Philosophical Tendencies* (1912). He is best remembered for *The Thought and Character of William James* (1935). His article on JR in *Dictionary of American Biography* is a classic of its kind. See also his essay on Royce and James in *In the Spirit of William James* (1938).

PLIMPTON, GEORGE ARTHUR (1855–1936), was in the publishing business in New York City.

POULTON, EDWARD BAGNALL (1856–1943), was Hope Professor of Zoology, Oxford University (1893–1933).

PUTNAM, JAMES JACKSON (1846–1918) was educated at Harvard University—A.B. (1866), M.D. (1870)—taught at Harvard Medical School (1872–1912), and was neurologist at Massachusetts General Hospital (1874–1909).

RANDOLPH, ELIZABETH, a sculptress, became JR's daughter-in-law—married to Edward Royce on December 29, 1910.

REDWOOD, MARY COALE (d. 1940), was the daughter of George Buchanan Coale and wife of Francis T. Redwood.

Reid, William Thomas (1843– ?), became president of the University of California in 1881 following six years as principal of San Francisco Boy's High School. After his resignation in 1885 he established and supervised a preparatory school in Belmont, California.

Robbins, Reginald Chauncey (1871–1955), was a poet, composer, and amateur philosopher. Educated at Harvard University, he became a disciple of JR and a patron to the philosophy department. For many years he served on the Harvard Visiting Committee, and in 1905, founded the Robbins Library of Philosophy and Psychology. He was twice delegate to the International Congress of Philosophy (1908, 1921), and author of *Love Poems* (1903–12) and *Poems of Personality* (1904–19).

Rowell, Joseph Cummings (1853–1938), received a B.A. from the University of California in 1874 and remained permanently as librarian after 1875. Rowell and JR were good friends as undergraduates and as colleagues.

Royce, Edward (1886–1963), second son of JR, was a composer and professor at the Eastman School of Music, University of Rochester.

Russell, third earl, Bertrand Arthur William (b. 1872), Fellow of Trinity College, Cambridge (1895–1916), was visiting professor at Harvard University during the second term, 1914. One of the greatest logicians of all time, Russell came to JR's attention in 1903 with *Principles of Mathematics* and in 1910–13 with *Principia Mathematica* (A. N. Whitehead, co-author).

Schiller, Ferdinand Canning Scott (1864–1937), was a British pragmatist, and tutor at Corpus Christi College, Oxford.

Schurman, Jacob Gould (1854–1942), was Sage Professor of Philosophy at Cornell University (1880–86), and president (1892–1920). He was founder and editor of the *Philosophical Review.*

Scudder, Horace Elisha (1838–1902), was a reader for the Houghton Mifflin Company and editor of *Atlantic Monthly* (1890–98). He directed the publication of five of JR's books: *RAP*, *Feud*, *California*, *SMP*, and *CI*.

Shinn, Milicent Washburn (1858–1940), edited the *Californian* (1882), and the *Overland Monthly* (1883–94). She was a close friend of the Royces and published works by both Josiah and Katharine.

SLATTERY, CHARLES LEWIS (1867–1930), was educated at Harvard (A.B., 1891) and Episcopal Theological School (D.B., 1894). He entered the clergy and, in 1927, became Bishop of Massachusetts. His many writings in addition to *Alexander Viets Griswold Allen* (1911) included works on religion and biography.

STEIN, GERTRUDE (1874–1946), was educated at Radcliffe College where she was a student of JR, James, and Münsterberg. Later she settled in Paris where she became an important writer and leading spirit in the arts. Her main works are *Three Lives* (1908), *The Making of Americans* (1925), and *The Autobiography of Alice B. Toklas* (1933).

STILLMAN, JOHN MAXON (1852–1923), received a Ph.B. (1874) and Ph.D. (1885) from the University of California where he was an assistant (1873–75) and instructor (1876–82). From 1882 to 1891 he was a chemist for the Boston and American Sugar Refining Co. He completed his career as professor of chemistry at Stanford University (1891–1917).

THAYER, WILLIAM ROSCOE (1859–1923), was an alumnus of Harvard University, editor of the *Harvard Graduates' Magazine*, and member of the Board of Overseers. He was author of many books of poetry, literary history, and biography.

THILLY, FRANK (1865–1934), taught philosophy at Cornell University (1891–3, 1906–21), University of Missouri (1893–1904), and Princeton University (1904–6). He was a follower of Paulsen, translator of his works, editor of *Philosophical Review* and *International Journal of Ethics* (1909–14).

TITCHENER, EDWARD BRADFORD (1867–1927), an experimental psychologist, born and educated in England, was professor of psychology at Cornell University. Among his major works are *Psychology of Feeling and Attention* (1908) and *Experimental Psychology of the Thought Processes* (1909).

WARNER, JOSEPH BANGS (1848–1923), was educated at Harvard University: A.B. (1869), A.M. (1872), LL.B. (1873). He was a member of the law firm of Warner, Warner and Stackpole (1873–1916).

WHEELER, BENJAMIN IDE (1881–1927), taught at Harvard University (1885–86) and at Cornell University (1886–99) before becoming president of the University of California (1899–1919).

WHITNEY, ANNE (1821–1915), sculptress and reformer, was a resident of Boston.

WOODBRIDGE, FREDERICK JAMES EUGENE (1867–1940), editor of the *Journal of Philosophy*, taught at the University of Minnesota (1894–1902) and at Columbia University (1902–29).

Appendix B

Textual Note and List of Substantive Emendations

Whenever possible and practicable the text of the letters in this edition follows Royce's actual form of expression. Original letters, to the extent that these have been available, are the basis of the text. Copies have been used whenever originals have not been available. Only in those cases when neither originals nor copies have been available have printed versions been used. A footnote to the title of each letter identifies the source for the text. Extraneous marks and notes on the manuscripts are ignored; pertinent additions are cited in footnotes.

The text has been emended only when Royce's language appears ambiguous and when the problem can be corrected simply and indisputably. Emendations of sentence mechanics—spelling, punctuation, and type face—are made *silently* in keeping with modern American usage. Certain mechanical emendations are regularly employed regardless of the source text:

1. Spelling errors are corrected.
2. Unclear abbreviations are spelled out.
3. Titles of articles, lectures, unpublished manuscripts, and proposed but unpublished books are set in quotation marks; actual titles of published books and periodicals are set in italics.
4. Closing quotation marks are set outside accompanying commas and periods; otherwise the position of closing quotation marks relative to other punctuation depends upon whether that punctuation is or is not a part of the quotation.
5. Royce's brackets are indicated by angle brackets: ⟨. . .⟩; the editor's interpolations are set inside the usual brackets: [. . .].

Emendations of sentence structure—grammar and diction—are considered substantive and are listed below.

PAGE. LINE	SOURCE READING	EMENDED READING
92.34	some time passed	some time past
99.19	have seemed so	having seemed so
115.24	will indeed by welcome	will indeed be welcome
125.5	remember my to all	remember me to all
131.36	at total of	a total of
140.14	shall here from	shall hear from
141.16–17	that in accepting	that accepting
268.8–9	has been very cordially	has been very cordial
288.27	although your are	although you are
290.23	any more are than	any more than are
313.8	you know what your	you know what you're
324.1	person, who know	person, who knows
340.3	philosophically and studious	philosophically studious
343.33	none of us know	none of us knows
345.2	for "man," "man," and sees	for "man," and sees
360.2	yours and Tarde's is	yours and Tarde's are
361.7	as his even	as he is even
365.26	to the understood	to be understood
399.8	"Conception on . . ."	"Conception of . . ."
419.12	even although	even though
465.34	are likely	is likely
467.23	believe, as Chapter IV	believe, is Chapter IV
499.11–12	in you hands	in your hands
502.18	finish task	finish tasks
522.8	system whose public	system in which public
522.31–32	professor, who stoop . . . carry . . . and plan	professor, who stoops . . . carries . . . and plans
548.11–13	creature who happen . . . and who happen	creature who happens . . . and who happens
551.24	. . . 17, 1910	. . . 17, 1911
565.6	in they way	in the way
568.24	apart the	apart from the
573.28	*History of Thought*	*History of European Thought*
587.6–7	which it his	which it is his
589.13	and any trying	and am trying
590.14	satisfaction thing to	satisfaction to
609.21	F. V. Huntington	E. V. Huntington
634.21	In some,	In sum,

638.22	to you	to your
638.27	quum vix justus	dum vix justus
640.24	quite outside room	quiet outside room
647.38	one of the principal features that make	one of the principal features that makes
649.5	Committee propose	Committee proposes
650.7	has yet reached	has just reached
650.10	planned an carried	planned and carried

Appendix C

Supplementary List of Letters

The following is a list of those letters seen by the editor but not included in this edition. Items are listed alphabetically by depository, and chronologically within collections. Undated items are placed at the end of the appropriate listings.

In addition to the items listed here, there are several letters of Royce in the Hocking Library, Madison, N. H., which the editor has not seen: five letters written to William Ernest Hocking (1901–16) and eighteen letters written to Daniel Gregory Mason and other members of his family (1900–1904).

THE AMERICAN ACADEMY OF ARTS AND LETTERS

ALS. JR to Hamilton W. Mabie. May 13, 1899, 2 pp.
[Accepts invitation to join AAAL.]
ALS. JR to HWM. April 22, 1902. 2 pp.
[Submits vote on proposed member.]
ALS. JR to ——— Johnson. April 15, 1904. 2 pp.
[Encloses $2; intends to attend dinner April 23.]
ALS. JR to HWM. n.d. 1 p.
[Encloses $5 annual dues for 1905.]

AMERICAN PHILOSOPHICAL SOCIETY

ALS. JR to Edgar F. Smith, December 23, 1903. 2 pp.
[Concerns confusion of names, American Philosophical Society and American Philosophical Association.]
ALS. JR to I. Minis Hays, n.d. 3 pp.
[Accepts membership in American Philosophical Society.]

BOSTON PUBLIC LIBRARY

Authors' Club Scrapbook

ALS. JR to T. W. Higginson. May 7, 1887. 4 pp.
[Accepts membership in Authors' Club.]

Hugo Münsterberg Papers

ALS. JR to HM. June 18, 1892. 16 pp.
[Living arrangements in Cambridge.]
ALS. JR to HM. August 26, 1892. 19 pp.
[Living arrangements in Cambridge.]
ALS. JR to HM. December 15, 1892. 1 p.
[Returns an essay on hypnotism.]
ALS. JR to HM. March 1, 1893. 6 pp.
[Get-well greeting, signed also by students in psych. lab.]
ALS. JR to HM. December 13, 1893. 2 pp.
[Declines dinner invitation.]
ALS. JR to HM. January 18, 1894. 8 pp.
[Attempts to settle an argument between HM and a student.]
ALS. JR to HM. January 23, 1901. 2 pp.
[Encourages HM to write note on philosophy dept. for *Harvard Graduates' Magazine.*]
ALS. JR to HM. March 11, 1901. 3 pp.
[Recommends that the Corporation reappoint Miller.]
ALS. JR to HM. April 28, 1901. 4 pp.
[Invitation to dine at Colonial Club to meet William A. Knight.]
ALS. JR to HM. February 25, 1902. 1 p.
[Accepts invitation to meet Prince Henry of Prussia.]
ALS. JR to HM. April 11, 1902. 4 pp.
[Report on Bowdoin Prize competition.]
ALS. JR to HM. February 17, 1904. 4 pp.
[Variety of university business.]
ALS. JR to HM. October 23, [?]. 2 pp.
[Encloses newspaper clipping on psychology.]

CALIFORNIA HISTORICAL SOCIETY

ALS. JR to Milicent W. Shinn. August 12, 1914. 4 pp.
[Attempts to arrange meeting.]

CALIFORNIA STATE LIBRARY

ALS. JR to Bernard Moses. May 30, 1886. 1 p.
[Accepts invitation to become corresponding member of California Historical Society.]

COLORADO COLLEGE, TUTT LIBRARY

ALS. JR to G. B. Turnbull. December 14, 1895. 3 pp.
[Declines invitation to lecture in Colorado during Summer, 1896.]

COLUMBIA UNIVERSITY, BUTLER LIBRARY

Journal of Philosophy Papers

ALS. JR to Frederick J. E. Woodbridge. February 17, 1904 3 pp.
[Encloses statement of expenses of Columbia lectures.]
ALS. JR to FJEW. November 9, 1913. 4 pp.
[Encloses corrections for "An Extension of the Algebra of Logic."]

CORNELL UNIVERSITY ARCHIVES

Frank Thilly Papers

ALS. JR to FT. December 28, 1905. 2 pp.
[Dinner invitation.]

Andrew Dickson White Papers

ALS. JR to ADW. March 13, 1883. 3 pp.
[JR sends Schiller article.]

HARVARD MEDICAL SCHOOL, COUNTWAY LIBRARY

Charles Sedgwick Minot Papers

ALS. JR to CSM. January 17, 1896. 4 pp.
[Recommendation for George B. Dorr.]

HARVARD UNIVERSITY ARCHIVES

Francis Ellingwood Abbot Papers

ALS. JR to FEA. November 7, 1885. 3 pp.
[Informs FEA of his appointment to Committee on Apparitions and Haunted Houses, American Society for Psychical Research.]

Richard Clarke Cabot Papers

ALS. JR to RCC. October 6, 1899. 4 pp.
[Thanks RCC for medical assistance.]
APS. JR to RCC. January 2, 1904.
[Invitation to Philosophy Conference; JR to read "The Eternal and the Practical."]
ALS. JR to RCC. June 23, 1912. 2 pp.
[Re Edward Royce; see letter for June 24, 1912.]

Charles William Eliot Papers

Includes correspondence with President Eliot [CWE], and his assistant, Jerome D. Green [JDG].

ALS. JR to CWE. July 5, 1886. 10 pp.
[Report on Harvard entrance exams.]
ALS. JR to CWE. April 7, 1891. 7 pp.
[Progress report, committee on instruction in pedagogy.]

ALS. JR to CWE. May 1, 1891. 4 pp.
[Further report from same committee.]
ALS. JR to CWE. September 4, 1891. 4 pp.
[Requests permission to teach psychology at Boston Normal School.]
ALS. JR to CWE. June 18, 1892. 8 pp.
[Supports candidacy of H. C. Bierwirth for Harvard German dept.]
ALS. JR to CWE. September 5, 1892. 8 pp.
[More on title of JR's professorship (see letters for September 2, 1892, and September 11, 1892); report on getting the Münsterbergs settled.]
ALS. JR to CWE. September 20, 1892. 7 pp.
[Requests additional asst. for psych. lab.]
ALS. JR to CWE. February 18, 1893. 4 pp.
[Report on Münsterberg's illness.]
ALS. JR to CWE. July 18, 1893. 4 pp.
[Faculty dispute involving P. H. Hanus.]
ALS. JR to CWE. March 18, 1894. 7 pp.
[Arrangements for new course in German metaphysics.]
ALS. JR to CWE. December 1, 1895. 7 pp.
[Corrects records re JR's salary.]
ALS. JR to CWE. September 17, 1896. 8 pp.
[Bakewell's illness; proposes MacDougall as replacement.]
ALS. JR to CWE. April 4, 1897. 7 pp.
[Instructional budget for next year.]
ALS. JR to CWE. April 6, 1897. 1 p.
[Seeks clarification of Lough's salary.]
ALS. JR to CWE. June 9, 1897. 2 pp.
[Recommends Rand's promotion to instructor.]
ALS. JR to CWE. June 11, 1897. 1 p.
[Recommends Lough's appointment; urges appointment of new asst. in psych. lab.]
ALS. JR to CWE. June 16, 1897. 4 pp.
[Settles administrative details before leaving town.]
ALS. JR to CWE. June 19, 1897. 3 pp.
[Appointment of asst. in psych. lab.]
ALS. JR to CWE. January 27, 1898. 3 pp.
[Recommends Santayana be promoted.]
ALS. JR to CWE. January 27, 1898. 1 p.
[Re Santayana, signed by JR, Palmer, Münsterberg, Everett, James.]
ALS. JR to CWE. May 10, 1898. 2 pp.

[Recommendations for annual appointments.]
ALS. JR to CWE. April 19, 1899. 4 pp.
[Report on W. B. Waterman, Ph.D. candidate.]
ALS. JR to CWE. July 6, 1900. 6 pp.
[Report on Arthur MacDonald as proposed director of research project.]
ALS. JR to CWE. November 15, 1900. 2 pp.
[Accepts appointment as Dudelian Lecturer, 1901–2.]
ALS. JR to CWE. May 2, 1902. 4 pp.
[Explains delay in depositing Dudelian lecture.]
ALS. JR to CWE. n.d. [May 28, 1905?]. 2 pp.
[Suggests inscription for Emerson Hall.]
ALS. JR to JDG. April 26, 1906. 1 p.
[Encloses information re JR's election to National Academy of Sciences.]
ALS. JR to CWE. October 25, 1906. 14 pp.
[Objects to proposal for budget committee.]
ALS. JR to CWE. November 27, 1907. 2 pp.
[Wishes to add Dr. A. S. Dewing to JR's seminar.]
ALS. JR to CWE. December 6, 1907. 7 pp.
[Recommends that William Salter lecture at Harvard.]
ALS. JR to CWE. June 7 [?]. 1 p.
[Encloses copy of Lord Gifford's will.]
ALS. JR to CWE. n.d. 15 pp.
[Recommends that William A. Knight lecture at Harvard.]

Paul Henry Hanus Papers

ALS. JR to PHH. May 16, 1891. 4 pp.
[Encloses next year's announcements; gives itinerary, June 22–July 16.]
ALS. JR to PHH. August 5, 1894. 3 pp.
[Arranges meeting re professional matter.]
ALS. JR to PHH. n.d. [August 11, 1894?]. 3 pp.
[Continues above.]
APS. JR to PHH. February 22, 1895.
[Announces meeting of Philosophy Dept.]
ALS. JR to PHH. April 8, 1895. 1 p.
[Announces meeting of Philosophy Dept.]
ALS. JR to PHH. June 4, 1895. 1 p.
[PHH to sign enclosed document.]
ALS. JR to PHH. November 4, 1895. 2 pp.
[Invites PHH to conference.]
ALS. JR to PHH. May 14, 1897. 1 p.
[Announces meeting of Philosophy Committee.]

ALS. JR to PHH. May 16, 1897. 2 pp.
[Schedule of meetings and examinations.]
ALS. JR to PHH. April 28, 1901. 4 pp.
[Invites PHH to dine at Colonial Club; to meet William A. Knight.]
ALS. JR to PHH. July 23, 1905. 4 pp.
[Arranges for PHH to use Colonial Club.]
ALS. JR to PHH. June 6, 1906. 1 p.
[Announces delay in meeting.]
APS. JR to PHH. March 7 [?].
[Announces meeting of Philosophy Dept.]

Lawrence Joseph Henderson Papers

ALS. JR to LJH. October 7, 1915. 2 pp.
[Invites LJH to dinner at Colonial Club for Estlin Carpenter.]
TLC. JR to LJH. April 4, 1915. 1 p.
[Announces meeting of New Club, May 9.]

Charles Rockwell Lanman Papers

APS. JR to CRL. July 7, 1878.
[Announces that JR will accept University of California offer.]
ALS. JR to CRL. December 26, 1886. 1 p.
[Acknowledges Christmas gift; announces birth of Edward.]
ALS. JR to CRL. October 7, 1915. 2 pp.
[Invitation to meet Estlin Carpenter.]

Abbott Lawrence Lowell Papers

Includes correspondence with A. Lawrence Lowell [ALL] and Charles Francis Adams, 2d [CFA].

ALS. JR to ALL. February 22, 1911. 4 pp.
[Discusses intercollegiate publications between Harvard and Yale.]
ALS. JR to ALL. August 16, 1911. 4 pp.
[JR about to leave for St. Andrews; return might be delayed.]
ALS. JR to CFA. December 2, 1911. 3 pp.
[Acknowledges first payment for Cabot Fellowship.]
ALS. JR to ALL. January 26, 1913. 4 pp.
[Recruitment report from Oxford, re Hobhouse.]
ALS. JR to ALL. January 29, 1913. 4 pp.
[Recruitment report from Oxford, re Hobhouse and Jacks.]
ALS. JR to ALL. February 10, 1913. 12 pp.
[Recruitment report from Oxford, re Hobhouse, Jacks, Russell, Moberly, and Lindsay.]
ALS. JR to ALL. May 29, 1913. 4 pp.
[Acknowledges ALL's thank-you note for copy of *PC*.]

ALS. JR to CFA. July 6, 1914. 3 pp.
[Acknowledges receipt of final payment for Cabot Fellowship.]
ALS. JR to ALL. March 1, 1915. 3 pp.
[Plans for giving extension course next year.]

Ralph Barton Perry Papers

ALS. JR to RBP. January 30, 1902. 2 pp.
[Social note; arrangements for trip to Springfield and Northampton.]
ALS. JR to RBP. June 3, 1907. 2 pp.
[Encloses $20 for contribution to James's portrait.]
ALS. JR to RBP. August 10, 1910. 1 p.
[Urges RBP to get Bergson for 1912–13.]
ALS. JR to RBP. February 26, 1911. 2 pp.
[Encloses $25 for contribution to Palmer dinner.]
ALS. JR to RBP. December 16, 1912. 4 pp.
[Congratulates RBP for appointment to professional office.]
ALS. JR to RBP. January 10, 1913. 4 pp.
[Announces arrival in Oxford; recruitment.]

Josiah Royce Papers

Includes correspondence with Charles Day [CD], Mary Ward Dorr [MWD], George B. Dorr [GBD], J. S. Cushing & Co. [CCo], Bejamin Ide Wheeler [BIW], W. E. Hocking [WEH], Mrs. W. E. Hocking [Mrs. H], and Miss —— Ruggli [Miss R].

TLC. JR to MWD. August 27, 1890. 2 pp.
[Thanks MWD for hospitality at Bar Harbor.]
TLC. JR to MWD. January 8, 1892. 1 p.
[Thanks MWD for gift.]
TLC. JR to MWD. September 12, 1892. 2 pp.
[Arranges a visit.]
TLC. JR to MWD. September 21, 1892. 2 pp.
[Thanks for hospitality during three-day visit.]
ALS. JR to GBD. January 6, 1893. 4 pp.
[Invitation to attend philosophy conference.]
TLC. JR to MWD. September 20, 1896. 1 p.
[Thanks for hospitality during three-day visit.]
TLI. JR to MWD. November 8, 1896. 2 pp.
[Arranges trip with LeContes to MWD.]
TLC. JR to MWD. December 19, 1897. 1 p.
[Accepts invitation.]
TLC. JR to MWD. February 28, 1898. 1 p.
[Arranges visit.]

TLC. JR to MWD. July 11, 1899. 1 p.
[Arranges visit.]
TLC. JR to MWD. August 30, 1899. 2 pp.
[Thanks for hospitality.]
ALS. JR to CCo. October 16, 1901. 4 pp.
[Directions to printers of *WI*, 2.]
ALS. JR to CD. June 13, 1904. 4 pp.
[JR's honorarium for lecture at Andover Theological Seminary.]
ALS. JR to BIW. July 31, 1904. 3 pp.
[Introduces GBD.]
ALS. JR to GBD. December 17, 1905. 3 pp.
[Invitation to dinner.]
ALS. JR to GBD. April 28, 1910. 2 pp.
[Arranges meeting.]
TLS. JR to WEH. July 6, 1915. 1 p.
[Requests new asst. for next year.]
TLS. JR to Mrs. H. July 6, 1915. 1 p.
[Courtesy note.]
ALS. JR to Miss R. n.d. 4 pp.
[Academic advisement.]

HARVARD UNIVERSITY, HOUGHTON LIBRARY
ALS. JR to Benjamin Apthorp Gould Fuller. March 14, 1915. 1 p.
[Invitation to Colonial Club to discuss C. S. Peirce papers.]
Houghton Mifflin Papers
Includes correspondence with the Houghton Mifflin Company [HMC] and Horace E. Scudder [HES].
ALS. JR to HMC. January 5, 1884. 1 p.
[Cover letter for prospectus of *RAP*.]
ALS. JR to HES. January 4, 1885. 13 pp.
[Reports on reading MS on Schopenhauer.]
ALS. JR to HMC. January 31, 1885. 3 pp.
[Requests that copies of *RAP* be sent to F. H. Hedge, Joseph LeConte, Anna Lazarus, Anna Head, A. P. Peabody.]
ALS. JR to HMC. February 3, 1885. 3 pp.
[Orders additional copies *RAP*, to be sent to libraries, journals; also to Francis Peabody, Wendell Jackson, Theodore Vetter.]
ALS. JR to HMC. February 7, 1885. 1 p.
[Orders another copy *RAP* for Rev. Tiffany of West Newton.]
ALS. JR to HMC. February 8, 1887. 2 pp.

[Orders *RAP* for Charles Renouvier and Karl Stumpf.]
ALS. JR to HES. February 10, 1895. 3 pp.
[Assists HES in locating passage in Fichte.]
Norton Papers
ALS. JR to Charles Eliot Norton. January 19, 1906. 4 pp.
[Declines invitation.]
ALS. JR to CEN. n.d. 3 pp.
[Declines invitation.]

JOHNS HOPKINS UNIVERSITY, EISENHOWER LIBRARY
Basil Gildersleeve Papers
ALS. JR to BG. February 16, 1902. 4 pp.
[Accepts invitation.]
Daniel Coit Gilman Collection
Includes correspondence with Daniel Coit Gilman [DCG], John M. Cross [JMC], T. R. Ball [TRB], and Edward Griffin [EG].
ALS. JR to JMC. July 9, 1876. 1 p.
[Accepts Hopkins fellowship.]
ALS. JR to DCG. June 24. 1877. 1 p.
[Accepts Hopkins fellowship for second year.]
ALS. JR to DCG. January 11, 1877. 3 pp.
[Reports on use of libraries in Boston and Cambridge, summer, 1877.]
ALS. JR to TRB. November 1, 1886. 1 p.
[Orders copy of diploma.]
ALS. JR to EG. April 22, 1902. 4 pp.
[Revisions of ceremony re JR's honorary LL.D. at Johns Hopkins.]
Johns Hopkins University Collection
Includes correspondence with David R. Dewey.
ALS. JR to DRD. January 9, 1901. 2 pp.
[Accepts invitation.]
ALS. JR to DRD. January 27, 1901. 3 pp.
[Encloses proposed address to Board of Trustees.]
Arthur Onken Lovejoy Papers
ALI. JR to AOL. June 11, 1907. 3 pp.
[Recommends C. E. Cory for academic appointment.]
The Mary B. Redwood Collection
Includes correspondence with George Buchanan Coale [GBC] and Mary Coale Redwood [MCR].
ALS. JR to GBC. December 11, 1878. 3 pp.
[Expresses sympathy, death of GBC's child.]
ALS. JR to MCR. January 30, 1906. 4 pp.

[Accepts invitation to dinner.]
ALS. JR to MCR. February 21, 1906. 4 pp.
[Confirms acceptance of invitation.]

LIBRARY OF CONGRESS
Josiah Royce Collection
[All addressed to Miss ——— Herrick [H].
ALS. JR to H. November 20, 1894.
[Expresses interest in firm's proposal that JR write "Outlines of Psychology" for *In Sickness and in Health.*]
ALS. JR to H. November 22, 1894.
[Questions language of contract.]
ALS. JR to H. December 2, 1894.
[Accepts arrangement; submits prospectus.]
ALS. JR to H. January 22, 1895.
[Progress report.]
ALS. JR to H. March 11, 1895.
[Discussion of title.]
ALS. JR to H. March 17, 1895.
[Biog. details.]
ALS. JR to H. April 6, 1895.
[Encloses synopsis.]
ALS. JR to H. April 24, 1895.
[Encloses corrected proof.]
ALS. JR to H. November 26, 1895.
[Declines to revise article.]
ALS. JR to H. November 30, 1895.
[Repeat refusal to revise.]
James McKeen Cattell Papers
APS. JR to JMcKC. November 5, 1900.
[Admires *Popular Science Monthly*.]
ALS. JR to JMcKC. October 5, 1904. 4 pp.
[Introduces F. A. Richardson.]
ALS. JR to JMcKC. June 3, 1906. 4 pp.
[Arranges for JMcKC to stay at Colonial Club.]

PIERPONT MORGAN LIBRARY
ALS. JR to William A. Knight. January 23, 1900. 3 pp.
[Arrangements for lecture at St. Andrews.]
ALS. JR to WAK. January 30, 1900. 4 pp.
[Thanks for hospitality at St. Andrews.]

NEW YORK PUBLIC LIBRARY
Berg Collection
ALS. JR to E. F. Edgett. July 20, 1901. 2 pp.
[Acknowledges receipt of $100 for Fiske paper.]

The Century Collection

ALS. JR to Robert Underwood Johnson. October 7, 1891. 3 pp.

[Explains delay in returning MS.]

Macmillan Papers

Includes correspondence with Macmillan Co. [MCo] and George Platt Brett [GPB].

ALS. JR to GPB. July 1, 1897. 4 pp.

[Arranges for publication of Caroline LeConte's *The Statue in Air*.]

ALS. JR to GPB. August 27, 1897. 3 pp.

[Introduces K. Nakamura for Japanese trans. of *CG*.]

ALS. JR to MCo. October 6, 1897. 2 pp.

[Requests copy of *CG* (1897).]

ALS. JR to GPB. November 17, 1898. 1 p.

[Encloses signed contract for *WI*.]

ALS. JR to GPB. November 27, 1898. 3 pp.

[Introduces F. A. Richardson.]

ALS. JR to MCo. August 30, 1899. 4 pp.

[Encloses corrected page proofs, *WI*, 1; editorial details.]

ALS. JR to MCo. September 10, 1899. 2 pp.

[Concludes agreement to print Suppl. Essay in *WI*, 1.]

ALS. JR to GPB. November 3, 1899. 4 pp.

[Editorial details, *WI*, 1.]

ALS. JR to GPB. November 7, 1899. 4 pp.

[Editorial details, *WI*, 1.]

ALS. JR to GPB. December 3, 1899. 3 pp.

[Copyright to "Outlines of Psychology," *In Sickness and in Health* (NY: Appleton, 1896).]

ALS. JR to GPB. December 6, 1899. 4 pp.

[Acknowledges receipt of advance copies, *WI*, 1.]

ALS. JR to GPB. December 12, 1899. 4 pp.

[Orders presentation copy, *WI*, 1.]

ALS. JR to MCo. April 25, 1901. 4 pp.

[Rejects offer that he be reader-consultant for MCo; busy with *WI*, 2; requests information re sales of *WI*, 1.]

ALS. JR to GPB. May 5, 1903. 4 pp.

[Completes corrections of *OP* proofs.]

ALS. JR to GPB. June 9, 1903. 1 p.

[Acknowledges receipt of $200 advance for *OP*.]

ALS. JR to GPB. September 19, 1903. 4 pp.

[Explains delay in returning MSS; spending last of summer in Canada.]

ALS. JR to GPB. n.d. [1904]. 1 p.

[Continuation of JR to GPB, see letter for February 24, 1904.]
ALS. JR to GPB. November 20, 1905. 2 pp.
[Expresses willingness to evaluate Mary W. Calkins MS.]
ALS. JR to MCo. April 22, 1907. 2 pp.
[Explains delay in reporting on MS.]
ALS. JR to MCo. May 18, 1907. 2 pp.
[Favorable evaluation of F. C. S. Schiller's (?) *Humanism.*]
ALS. JR to GPB. October 11, 1907. 1 p.
[Encloses signed contract for *PL.*]
ALS. JR to GPB. March 20, 1908. 4 pp.
[Requests copies of *PL* as textbook for Yale; proposes *RQP.*]
ALS. JR to MCo. April 10, 1908. 3 pp.
[Pays for copies of *PL;* requests advance payment.]
ALS. JR to MCo. April 12, 1908. 4 pp.
[Acknowledges receipt of $250 advance for *PL.*]
ALS. JR to GPB. January 8, 1909. 4 pp.
[Proposes publication of Mrs. Royce's trans. of Eugen Kühnemann's *Schiller.*]

HISTORICAL SOCIETY OF PENNSYLVANIA
ALS. JR to "My Dear Madam." May 16, 1898. 4 pp.
[Declines invitation to lecture.]

PHILLIPS EXETER ACADEMY
ALS. JR to "Dear Sir." April 30, 1885. 1 p.
[Biographical data.]

PRINCETON UNIVERSITY LIBRARY
Hyatt and Mayer Correspondence
Includes correspondence with Alpheus Hyatt [AH] and A. G. Mayer [AGM].
ALS. JR to AH. January 7, 1896. 2 pp.
[Invitation to meet C. Lloyd Morgan.]
ALS. JR to AGM. January 8, 1896. 2 pp.
[Invitation to meet C. Lloyd Morgan.]
ALS. JR to AH. n.d. 1 p.
[Declines invitation.]
ALS. JR to AH. n.d. 1 p.
[Declines invitation.]
ALS. JR to AH. n.d. 3 pp.
[Declines invitation.]

PRIVATE COLLECTION, IGNAS SKRUPSKELIS
ALS. JR to James H. Woods. May 18, 1899. 3 pp.
[Concerns JHW's application to teach as docent in philos. of religion.]

ALS. JR to JHW. April 27, 1914. 3 pp.
[Accepts invitation to dine with JHW and Bertrand Russell.]

REDWOOD LIBRARY AND ATHENAEUM, NEWPORT, R. I.
ALS. JR to Nicholas Paine Gilman. July 17, 1892. 2 pp.
[Acknowledges payment for article.]

SOUTHERN ILLINOIS UNIVERSITY ARCHIVES
Open Court Papers
Includes correspondence with Paul Carus [PC].
ALS. JR to PC. November 4, 1908. 4 pp.
[Proposal that PC publish translation of Enriques's *Problemi della Scienza.*]
ALS. JR to PC. November 15, 1908. 8 pp.
[Continued negotiations for same.]
ALS. JR to PC. January 17, 1909. 8 pp.
[Same continued; proposal that PC publish translation of Kühnemann's *Schiller.*]
ALS. JR to PC. n.d. [June 1909?] 16 pp.
[Progress report on Enriques project.]

STANFORD UNIVERSITY ARCHIVES
The American Authors and Literature Collection
ALS. JR to Miss —— Hecht. December 27, 1891. 2 pp.
[Thank-you note for Christmas gift.]
David Starr Jordan Papers
ALS. JR to DSJ. May 7, 1891. 6 pp.
[Declines call to Stanford.]
ALS. JR to DSJ. August 29, 1895. 4 pp.
[Responds to invitation to lecture at Stanford.]
Telegram. JR to DSJ. September 3, 1895.
[Seeks clarification re his lecture at Stanford.]
Telegram. JR to DSJ. September 3, 1895.
[Confirms speaking engagement.]
ALS. JR to DSJ. September 6, 1895. 4 pp.
[Clarifies arrangements for lecture.]

UNIVERSITY OF CALIFORNIA ARCHIVES, BANCROFT LIBRARY
Includes correspondence with Benjamin Ide Wheeler [BIW] and Victor Hendricks Henderson [VHH].
ALS. JR to VHH. May 12, 1902. 8 pp.
[Arrangements for JR's teaching in University of California summer school.]
TLS. JR to VHH. June 6, 1902. 1 p.
[Further arrangements for same.]
Telegram. JR to BIW. October 19, 1904.

[Declines invitation to represent University of California at inauguration of President Huntington of Boston University.]
ALS. JR to BIW. August 24, 1914. 4 pp.
[Arrangements for luncheon.]
Telegram. JR to BIW. March 4, 1916.
[Declines call to University of California.]
Telegram. JR to BIW. March 7, 1916.
[Repeats refusal to join University of California.]

UNIVERSITY OF CALIFORNIA, BANCROFT LIBRARY
Berkeley Club Papers
ALS. JR to Charles W. Badger. November 26, 1882. 4 pp.
[Resigns from Berkeley Club.]
George Holmes Howison Papers
ALS. JR to GHH. September 21, 1896. 1 p.
[Agrees to GHH plan for Suppl. Essay in *CG* (1897).]
ALS. JR to GHH. April 18, 1907. 4 pp.
[Recommends Miss A. Barnett for University of California fellowship.]
ALS. JR to GHH. August 14, 1914. 3 pp.
[Response to invitation.]
Robert Underwood Johnson Papers
ALS. JR to RUJ. n.d. 1 p.
[Inquiry re California section, *Century Magazine*.]

UNIVERSITY OF SOUTHERN CALIFORNIA,
HOOSE LIBRARY OF PHILOSOPHY
ALS. JR to H. Wildon Carr. April 26, 1913. 3 pp.
[Accepts corresponding membership in Aristotelian Society.]
William Torrey Harris Papers
APS. JR to WTH. October 23, 1878.
[Asks for correction in his Schiller article.]
ALS. JR to WTH. December 28, 1881. 3 pp.
[Acknowledges receipt of page proof; offers to write review.]
ALS. JR to WTH. February 3, 1882. 1 p.
[Sends $5 for copies of the journal.]

VASSAR COLLEGE LIBRARY
ALS. JR to James M. Taylor. April 26, 1899. 4 pp.
[Arrangements for Vassar lecture, April 28: "On Certain Limitations of the Thoughtful Public in America."]

WELLESLEY COLLEGE LIBRARY
ALS. JR to Caroline Hazard. May 12, 1900.
[Expresses thanks for opportunity to lecture at Wellesley.]

YALE UNIVERSITY, BEINEKE LIBRARY

ALS. JR to John Christopher Schwab. February 10, 1910. 2 pp.
[Arrangements for professional meeting.]
ALS. JR to William Lyon Phelps. March 3, 1910. 2 pp.
[Accepts invitation to dinner.]
ALS. JR to WLP. n.d. 2 pp.
[Accepts lecture engagement.]

YALE UNIVERSITY, STERLING LIBRARY

Thomas Davidson Papers

ALS. JR to TD. June 6, 1884. 2 pp.
[Declines invitation.]
ALS. JR to TD. June 23, 1898. 3 pp.
[Declines invitation to lecture at Glenmore.]

Gilman Family Papers

ALS. JR to E. S. Bristol. May 14, 1911. 4 pp.
[Acknowledges gift from "New Haven ladies."]
ALS. JR to E. S. Bristol. November 6, 1911. 4 pp.
[Offers advance reading of *SRI*.]
ALS. JR to E. S. Bristol. December 3, 1911. 4 pp.
[More on *SRI*.]

Index